Religion and the Working Class in Antebellum America

Jama Lazerow

Religion and the Working Class
in Antebellum America

Smithsonian Institution Press
Washington and London

Portions of this book originally appeared in "Religion and Labor Reform in Antebellum America: The World of William Field Young," *American Quarterly* 38 (summer 1986): 265–86, and "Religion and the New England Mill Girl: A New Perspective on an Old Theme," *New England Quarterly* 60 (Sept. 1987): 429–53. Parts of the introduction appeared in "Rethinking Religion and the Working Class in Antebellum America," *Mid-America* 75 (Jan. 1993): 85–104. Parts of chapter 7 appeared in "Spokesmen for the Working Class: Protestant Clergy and the Labor Movement in Antebellum New England," *Journal of the Early Republic* 13 (fall 1993): 323–54.

Editor: Joanne Reams
Designer: Alan Carter
Typesetter: Agnew's Electronic Manuscript Processing Service

Library of Congress Cataloging-in-Publication Data
Lazerow, Jama.
    Religion and the working class in antebellum America / by Jama Lazerow.
      p. cm.
    Includes bibliographical references and index.
    ISBN 1-56098-544-5 (alk. paper)
    1. Church and labor—United States—History—19th century.
    2. Labor movement—United States—Religious aspects—Protestant churches—History—19th century.   3. Working class—Religious life—United States—History—19th century.   I. TItle.
HD6338.2.U5L39   1995
261.8'34562'097309034—dc20   95-8600

British Library Cataloguing-in-Publication Data is available

Manufactured in the United States of America
02 01 00 99 98 97 96 95   5 4 3 2 1

⊗ The paper used in this publication meets the minimum requirements of the American National Standard for Permanence of Paper for Printed Library Materials Z39.48–1984.

Cover image: Drawing titled "A View of Fitchburg," courtesy American Antiquarian Society.

This book is dedicated to
Stokely Carmichael, who
inspired me to read, and
William Appleman Williams,
who inspired me to read
history.

Contents

List of Tables

Preface

When I became interested in the relationship between religion and radicalism many years ago, I had no idea just how big—and perplexing—a subject I had chosen. I was interested in American working-class consciousness, and my question, I thought, was a simple one: What role did religion play in free-labor protest during the pre–Civil War years, when wage earners became a majority of the work force in the nonslave states of America and citywide, regional, and national working-class movements emerged for the first time? Did it promote or hinder the development of class consciousness?[1] I knew that antebellum America was a society consumed by concerns about God, spirituality, and church life, and that religion—particularly evangelical Protestantism—had profoundly influenced all of the major forms of dissent in this era of reform ferment. What about labor dissent, as expressed in both individual and collective forms of resistance to the conditions of work and the attendant social changes that marked the early Industrial Revolution?[2]

The project seemed straightforward enough. But I had not counted on the fugitive nature of the sources I had to work with. There were several possible avenues of investigation: churches, unions, or, perhaps, reform movements—like abolitionism or temperance or utopian socialism—that attracted, among others, the religious and the labor activist. Now, every historian, especially the social historian, knows all too well the blind alley, the apparently fruitful path turned barren by lack of evidence. But, in this case, finding the precise connection between religion and labor reform was sometimes like looking for a needle in a haystack. Church records and the documents of antebellum reformers were often silent on labor protest per se, while the prolabor press was often silent—sometimes, I discovered, deliberately so—on specific church issues.

Fortunately, there would be major finds that at least cracked open a window onto the world of religion and labor protest, a world virtually lost to historians. Sometimes, that is, the needle turned up. Take Fitchburg, Massachusetts, a community that plays a part in the story I tell in this book. My first foray into the sources was in Fall River, Massachusetts, a place I knew to be an important center of nineteenth-century labor agitation. While reading the *Mechanic,* a

labor paper published there in the 1840s, I came across a reprint of a circular
from something called the Fitchburg Workingmen's Association (FWA), an
organization that existed for less than a year and is barely known in the history
of American labor. The document contained some striking religious language,
so, curious, I traveled to that small town in the Nashua River Valley northwest
of Boston and began reading in its local history.

The one modern history of Fitchburg, Doris Kirkpatrick's *The City and the
River*, had a small section on the FWA, the only known labor protest in the
town during the antebellum period. Much of her evidence came from a talk
given at the Fitchburg Historical Society in 1893 by an elderly resident of the
town who had once been an FWA member. In that talk, published in the
proceedings of the society, Ebenezer Bailey made reference to a record book,
with names and meeting minutes.[3] Now, this is the kind of thing that makes a
historian's heart beat fast. Names, with a good collection of church records,
would allow me to trace the religious associations of not just a few leaders
whose names might appear in the labor press, but the entire membership.
Moreover, with a town directory or two and local tax lists, I could begin to
penetrate that world where class and religion intersected. And, finally, the FWA
meeting minutes would allow a glimpse into the public concerns of these
people as no other available source could. It was the next best thing to what all
historians dream of—being there.

The problem was that, though Bailey indicated that the society had the
record book, it did not appear in any of the society's catalogs. I asked the
director if there had been a fire in the intervening time, but there had been
none. So, I asked for permission to search the society's safe, which might
contain some uncataloged materials. Sure enough, buried under an old, black
top hat on one of the upper shelves in the vault of the Fitchburg Historical
Society was the "Record Book of the Fitchburg Workingmen's Association,"
containing its constitution, minutes of all its meetings, and the names of its 131
members, including all officers.[4] There is no other document like it for the
antebellum period.

Fitchburg told me a lot, but I never again found anything else like that
record book. Moreover, it provided only a snapshot, a mere glimpse, of the
spiritual dimension of labor protest at one moment in time. And, though I
discovered that there was plenty of evidence of a labor–religion link in antebellum America—across time, space, and individual characteristic—the material was scattered and fragmentary: the discussions of religion in short-lived
labor newspapers, the expressions of religious doctrine and imagery in press
accounts of labor protest, the presence of known labor activists on church
membership lists and in reform organizations that met in churches. In the
end, the story buried in this evidence could not be adequately told by chronic-
ling one labor organization, religious denomination, occupation, community,
or even one region—both because none yielded quite enough for a com-

prehensive narrative and because the whole was simply greater than any of these parts.

Thus pieced together as a composite picture drawn from disparate sources, the portrait that emerges here may frustrate some readers, for while the main lines are clear enough, some of the finer features are less distinct than one might wish. But this story is too important to rush to judgment. In the course of my research, I learned just how dangerous it is to draw quick conclusions from fragmentary material on a subject about which we know so little. Take as one small example Charles Douglas, an individual who plays a part in the story I tell here. A Connecticut physician who became a prominent labor leader in New England in the labor upsurge of the early 1830s, Douglas insisted that labor's foremost goal was the diffusion of rational knowledge, he sang the praises of self-reliance, and when he invoked divine authority he spoke of "nature and nature's God," "the author of our existence," "the great governor of the universe," or "the Deity." Much of the time, as president of the New England Association of Farmers, Mechanics and Other Working Men, founder of the Boston Trades' Union, and editor of the labor oracles *New England Artisan* and Boston *Reformer,* Douglas sounded like a deist.[5] By the 1840s, in letters to the labor press, he sounded quite different, speaking of the "good work" of "missionaries of reform" who "preach[ed] political righteousness" and tended to "them who obtain their bread by the sweat of their brows." Perhaps this was an example, as much current historiography would have it, of the rationalist urban laborite of the 1830s turning to revivalist radicalism in the wake of the Panic of 1837.[6]

Then I happened across a letter Douglas wrote in 1836 on behalf of Orestes Brownson, one of Douglas's successors at the *Reformer.* Defending this pro-labor minister against attacks that he was not sufficiently friendly to labor— largely because of his attempts to bring the allegedly atheistic workers of Boston into his Society for Christian Union and Progress—Douglas aligned himself with Brownson on explicitly Christian grounds. Praising the "pure and undefiled religion" for which "Jesus labored in season and out of season," Douglas expressed his hope that Brownson would win many converts to his new church, "until the knowledge of the Lord shall cover the whole earth." Here was a very different religious tradition indeed, and its expression ante-dates the urban revivals that attended the depression of the late 1830s.[7]

What I have done in this book, then, is to piece together a story from a wide range of antebellum communities, labor organizations, and labor activists, paying close attention to the context of working-class behavior and thought by developing evidence on specific individuals that could be culled from news-papers and magazines, church documents, government records, and personal materials. The result is a rich array of empirical data on working people and religion. Together with the voices recorded in meeting minutes, editorials, speeches, songs, poetry, sermons, letters, diaries, memoirs, autobiographies, and fiction, these materials reveal a borning class every bit as engaged in the religious discourse of this age of religious revival as the classes arrayed against it. About these latter groups and their religion, historians have long known a great deal. About the early American working class and their religion, historians know almost nothing.

One word of caution on what this book is not. Mainly focusing on free white workers in the Northeast, glimpsed in labor movements often dominated by native-born Protestants, it encompasses neither the entire working class, the entire nation, nor the entire range of labor protest. Partly, this narrowness results from the myopia of the historian: in the late 1970s, for example, when the project was undertaken, it was still possible to conceive of the early American working class without close attention to black workers, slave and free, and to the role of race generally—despite the insights of W. E. B. Du Bois and the work of historians like Philip Foner.[8] But, more than that, the subject of religion and the making of the American working class is too new and too big to be fully treated in all its complexity in a single volume. In this book, I have addressed only the most obvious manifestations of the phenomenon, with the hope that its other aspects will soon receive sustained treatment. The story told here merely broaches the subject, opening a door that cannot be safely shut until more communities, groups, and individuals have been studied than are discussed here.

Even from the vantage of this study, the precise role religion played in the lives of antebellum working people defies easy characterization, as the reader will quickly see. One thing is certain, however: we cannot understand the emergence of an American working class before the Civil War—indeed, class relations generally in antebellum America—without first coming to grips with the powerful influence of religion on those who "obtained their bread by the sweat of their brows."

Acknowledgments

The research for this kind of book could not have been done without the scores of librarians, curators, ministers, parishioners, and local historians, who found me often obscure materials and secured me access to others. The most important were Florence Brigham of the Fall River Historical Society, Albert Canedy of Fall River, Elenora West of the Fitchburg Historical Society, Laura Husted of Lowell, Barbara Benson of the Delaware Historical Society, the Reverend Kenneth Dean of Rochester, Karl Kabelack of the Rush Rhees Library at the University of Rochester, and Rochester City Historian Ruth Rosenberg-Naparsteck. Sue Kaler of the Wheelock Library has been indispensible. Finally, in a class by himself, Charles Longley of the Boston Public Library shared with me his wealth of knowledge about nineteenth-century newspapers.

For their careful readings of all or parts of the manuscript, I thank Ken Fones-Wolf, Jonathan Prude, David Zonderman, Mark Schantz, Carol Hoffecker, H. Larry Ingle, Ron Formisano, Ruth Rosenberg-Naparsteck, and Blake McKelvey (who also allowed me access to his voluminous notes on Rochester). For their encouragement and example, I thank my teachers Ken Grief, Louis Ruchames, Stanley Remsberg, Paul Faler, Jim Green, and Alex Keyssar. For their keeping me stimulated, informed, and honest all these years, I thank my two dear friends from graduate school, Ellen Fitzpatrick and Mitchell Snay. For their extraordinary hospitality during countless research trips, I thank Abe and Sandy Scharf. And, for their crucial financial support at several stages of this project, I thank Wheelock College, the University of Puget Sound, and, especially, the National Endowment for the Humanities.

There are others whose contributions cannot be measured precisely. My editor Mark Hirsch rescued the project when it was headed for the basement boxes. He helped me envision the structure and argument of the book, read every draft, and was absolutely unswerving in his commitment to the work. In a very real sense, this is his book, too. During the last five years, my colleague Marcia Folsom has insisted that I keep at it when I did not want to. That insistence, rooted in her belief in me, is something for which I will be forever in her debt. My greatest debt, though, is to my father and mother, Sam and Sylvia

Lazerow, who gave me my political sensibilities and my love for the life of the mind.

Finally, there is my family, Irene "Buddy" Scharf, Max Scharf, and Dylan Irie Scharf-Lazerow, whose sacrifices have been the greatest of all. Buddy has read and criticized more drafts than she probably cares to remember; more than that, it was her intellectual companionship that allowed me to figure out much of what appears here. For their part, Max and Dylan have been patient beyond any reasonable expectation. They know, I hope, that *they* are the most important thing.

Abbreviations

AI	Association of Industry
AV	Authorized (King James) Version
AWPNCC	Association of Working People of New Castle County
B1OB	Barton's First Obituary Book
B2OB	Barton's Second Obituary Book
BC	Biographical Catalogue
BMSS	Brandywine Manufacturers Sunday School
BPL	Boston Public Library
BPU	Boston Printers' Union
BTU	Boston Trades' Union
DC	*Democrat and Chronicle*
DD	*Daily Democrat*
DFP	*Delaware Free Press*
DHS	Delaware Historical Society
DSA	Delaware State Archives
ES	East Society
FHS	Fitchburg Historical Society
FLRA	Female Labor Reform Association
FMMA	*Farmers', Manufacturers' and Mechanics' Advocate*
FRHS	Fall River Historical Society
FRPL	Fall River Public Library
FWA	Fitchburg Workingmen's Association
GT	*Germantown Telegraph*
IC	Industrial Congress
ICR	*Independent Chronicle and Reformer*

JCJS	Journeyman Carpenters' and Joiners' Society
JTS	Journeymen Tailors' Society
LA	*Liberal Advocate*
MA	Mechanics' Association
MBSL	Massachusetts Bureau of Statistics of Labor
MFP	*Mechanics' Free Press*
MLA	Mechanics' Literary Association
MM	*Mechanics Mirror*
MMPA	Mechanics' Mutual Protection Association
MP	*Mechanics' Press*
MUTA	Mechanics' Union of Trade Associations
NEA	New England Association of Farmers, Mechanics and Other Working Men
NEA	*New England Artisan*
NELRL	New England Labor Reform League
NEPU	New England Protective Union
NEWA	New England Workingmen's Association
NL	*National Laborer*
NR	(Rochester) *National Reformer*
NRA	National Reform Association
NTU	*National Trades' Union*
OCL	Old Citzen's Letters
PHS	Presbyterian Historical Society
PP	*People's Paper*
PT	*Plain Truth*
PU	*Protective Union*
QC	*Quaker City*
RDA	*Rochester Daily Advertiser*
RDAT	*Rochester Daily Advertiser and Telegraph*
RDD	*Rochester Daily Democrat*
RDU	*Rochester Daily Union*
RGLA	*Rochester Gem and Literary Advocate*
RH	*Rochester History*
RHSP	*Rochester Historical Society Publications*
RO	*Rochester Observer*
RPL	Rochester Public Library

RR	*Rochester Republican*
RT	*Rochester Telegraph*
RTA	Rochester Typographical Association
SN	Samson Notebooks
UA	*Union and Advertiser*
UR	University of Rochester
URL	University of Rochester Library
WI	*Wachusett Independant*
WMA	(New York) *Working Man's Advocate*
	(Rochester) *Working-Man's Advocate*
WMBERS	Workingmen's Benevolent and Equal Rights Society
WMC	Workingmen's Club, "The Democratic Working Men's Equal Rights Anti-Duebill Club"
WMP	Working Men's Party
WMPU	Workingmen's Protective Union
WMRC	Working Men's Reading Club
WRA	Workingmen's Reform Association
YA	*Young America*
YMA	Young Men's Association

Introduction.
Religion, the Working Class, and American Historians

In March 1847, the New England Labor Reform League met in Lowell, Massachusetts, to advocate, among other things, the ten-hour day, workers' cooperatives, and land reform.[1] A decidedly unsympathetic Dr. Tewkesbury, recently the editor of the *Temperance Review* (Concord, Massachusetts), was there to defend the status quo, including long workdays, low wages, and inequality of condition.[2] Pronouncing factory operatives the happiest class in the world, he denounced the assembled activists for what he said was their betrayal of Christianity in contesting the conditions under which they lived and worked. Quoting St. Paul's injunctions to the masses to be content with their God-given lot in life, the editor recommended that they follow Christ's peaceful example, chastising the group for unnecessarily promoting strife between workers and their employers.

The labor delegates responded in kind. First to speak was a "mill girl" (as female textile workers at the time were called) who insisted that she and her sisters were happy not because they were shut up in a factory, but "because they are blessed with a happy and hopeful vision which can pierce those thick walls, and [look] beyond to that coveted, but slow-coming hour, that shall place them beyond the influence of factory bolts, and locks, and factory oppression." In her statement, read to the convention and then "accepted to be placed upon file," the operative acknowledged that it was

> strange that in this land of freemen the voice of a female should be needed in a cause like this; and it might seem strange that in this, or in any cause, a female should be found willing to address a public meeting. But, my friends, it would be *more* strange, if, in the present state of things—if, when *her own sex* was subject to all the evils of poverty, and to the degraded servitude which is the consequence of that poverty . . . if united women should not, as with one voice, stand forth for the vindication of her rights.[3]

Another operative, perhaps a woman also, mounted a scriptural defense of labor's actions, casting Paul and Jesus in an entirely different light than that offered by Tewkesbury, claiming them as progenitors of the workers' cause.[4]

1

"As a Reformer, St. Paul was second to none, except indeed, it was that Master whom he professed to serve." Countering the editor's interpretation of Scripture, this worker suggested that Paul himself had not been content with his position in life.

> If he was, himself, so very content, why did he so agitate the world to remove those evils to which according to the gentleman's interpretation of the Great Apostle, he should have quietly submitted? If he was content with his own condition as a preacher, why the exhortation to give more liberally for the support of preachers?

The Apostle had not appealed for support of the clergy out of self-interest, but rather on behalf of the poor and oppressed. "Will not the gentleman, then," the operative asked, "allow us, also, to make an appeal in behalf of our oppressed and suffering brethren and sisters, everywhere, since we have so high an example?"

Then, responding to the doctor's use of Christ's example, this antebellum labor advocate offered biblical evidence of her own that Jesus too had been on the side of the poor and oppressed and had in fact encouraged resistance to oppression. Here, her religious defense of labor activism turned into a blistering attack on those Christians who opposed her movement: "If he was content with the state of things, as he found it in the world, why did he speak so frequently, and so earnestly, against those classes whom he designated as scribes and pharisees?" Indeed, he had quite harshly condemned the oppressors of his day, she noted.

> What else did he call them? Hypocrites, did he not? Hard names it is true, but we cannot doubt that he who applied it considered it as just as the others, and indeed, he proceeds to give his reasons for so considering it: "for ye pay tithes of mint, anise, and commin, and omit the *weightier* matters of the law as judgment, *mercy,* &c;" "ye make clean the outside of the cup and the platter, but within they are full of *exhortation and excess; ye devour widows'* houses, and for a *pretense make long prayers.*"

For the same reasons, the labor delegate continued, good Christians should condemn the great factory owners of the age. "It seems to me," she declared, "if our savior were here to-day, he would not fail to include the class to which our Abbott Lawrences and Nathan Appletons belong, although *their titles* may be of another sort."[5] "Christ had said, 'sell what thou hast and give to the poor,'" yet "many of our *professed* christians have their thousands and millions of dollars hoarded by them, while thousands are compelled to sell their very lives for bread." These contemporary defilers of the faith, then, were not true Christians at all. "Our savior has said 'if ye love me ye will keep my commandments,'" the operative reminded the doctor. "Who will pretend to say that the injunction

. . . is not equally binding upon all who wish, or profess to be, followers of Christ?"

No modern student of American history will be surprised to find opponents of labor reform like Dr. Tewkesbury employing the Bible to discourage social and political activism among working people in the early Industrial Revolution, for religion has long been recognized as a principal tool by which the few have sought to control the many. It is quite arresting, though, given our current historical understanding, to find labor activists—in this case, even female labor activists in an age when women were often attacked as "unladylike" for daring to speak in public—using Christianity to defend themselves, to attack their opponents, and to fashion a biting critique of prevailing social conditions. Yet the debate at the Lowell convention makes clear that in this period, as throughout most of its history to the present day, Protestantism was used to advance opposing points of view. For, as a powerful—perhaps the most powerful—tool of legitimation of the age, this religion articulated a system of belief that purported to explain the way the world ought to work, for defender and challenger alike. It was used by some to justify and applaud an emerging set of economic and social relationships, while it was used by others—even those who were supposed to be silent on such issues—to question and criticize changes they perceived as threatening to their interests. In the hands of factory operatives, Scripture became the authoritative text for advocating labor's rights, and biblical figures the authoritative examples for questioning and criticizing social conditions on behalf of a growing, and increasingly aggrieved, population of wage workers.[6]

Religion and the Historians

This book explores the role of Protestantism as the handmaiden, rather than the saboteur, of labor protest. It thus seeks to illuminate the long-neglected relationship between religion, radicalism, and class consciousness in antebellum America. In this, it challenges the dominant trend in recent labor historiography to portray the republican heritage of the American Revolution as the principal language of early American labor radicalism, to the exclusion of other, equally powerful traditions.[7] Indeed, for the most part, the religious conflict glimpsed in this debate between the temperance editor and the factory operatives was simply not part of the story, as scholars have either passed over the issue entirely or avoided its most significant implications, operating as they do entirely within prevailing assumptions about religion and labor radicalism.[8] A perfect reflection of this problem can be found in Katherine Paterson's *Lyddie*, a marvelous fictional rendition of a young mill girl's experience in Lowell during the 1840s. Paterson's portrait is remarkably true to the secondary literature, including that regarding religion: the only characters in the book who exhibit any religious concerns are the mill owners, who insist (apparently unsuccessfully) that the girls attend church on the Sabbath; Lyddie's mother, who lands in a mental hospital; and a mill girl who invokes religious strictures against reading Charles Dickens and signing petitions for the ten-hour workday.[9]

The problem of neglect can be seen in the classic texts of American labor history. Consider an example from what is still one of the most influential labor histories of this period, Norman Ware's *Industrial Worker*, published in 1924. In his chapter on the ten-hour movement of the 1850s, Ware discusses one of the era's key documents, the "Hours of Labor Address" issued by the Boston Ten-Hour Convention in 1852. Explaining that the group sought ten hours as potentially only a first step in a progressive reduction in the length of the workday, he quotes them as saying, "If it be God's will to abridge man's daily labor to eight, six, or even a less number of hours, we ought cheerfully to submit." But Ware omitted the end of the sentence in which this phrase appeared, where the authors quote directly from Scripture for their authority: "'Thy will be done.'" Moreover, he did not provide the context of the passage. For the writers began their address declaring their belief that "it is the intention of the Great Creator to shorten the time of man's toil, and to extend his opportunities for moral, social and intellectual improvement," and then expressed their skepticism that God's intention was ten hours as a minimum workday. They also insisted that if the ten-hour standard should at some point exceed "the measures of the Great Ruler's intentions," they would consider it unwise to set "its authority in possible opposition to His designs." Clearly, their interpretation of God's law was the very basis of their argument. Stripped of the explicitly biblical language as well as the context, Ware's account makes the invocation of God appear as a mere flourish, perhaps even a cover.[10]

In another classic study of this era appearing some forty years after Ware's, Hannah Josephson also overlooks the powerful religious influence on early labor protest, in this case among the New England mill women of the 1840s. When the author seeks to illustrate the optimism of the Lowell Female Labor Reform Association (FLRA) in early 1846 by quoting from one of their reports in which they discuss their support for a reduction in the hours of labor, Josephson cites the mill girls' declaration that they regarded this measure not "as an end, but only as one step towards the great end to be attained." With an ellipsis, she then skips to their closing: "'Onward,' is their watchword, and 'We'll try again' their motto." What Josephson omitted was the FLRA's explanation of just what that "great end" was. "They deeply feel," the group explained, "that their work will never be accomplished, until slavery and oppression, mental, physical and religious shall be done away, and Christianity in its original simplicity and pristine beauty, shall be reestablished and practised among men."[11]

More recently, when historians have broached the subject of religion and labor, the focus has consistently been on Protestantism's role in inhibiting, or at least severely limiting, working-class protest, emphasizing the way it has been used by other classes to ensure workers' acquiescence.[12] Thus, much of the recent historiography of both the middle and working classes of antebellum America casts evangelical Christianity as a mechanism for the establishment of bourgeois hegemony. Bosses, we are told, used religion to rationalize the exploitation of their workers while assuring that exploitation through the imposition of a new industrial morality. Meanwhile, workers were divided along Protestant/Catholic and evangelical/non-evangelical lines, thus fragmenting the class as a political force. Even when "radical," revivalist workers were too individualistic, socially ambitious, and reverent of authority to make good allies for their "rationalist" brethren in the labor movement. And, of course, given the familiar religious strictures, Christian workers were quiescent rather than militant. In this portrait, antebellum Protestantism allowed—indeed, promoted—interclass, religion-based alliances, while inhibiting the creation of a self-conscious working class. Here is religion as the "opium of the people."

Hence, forty years after Josephson, Bruce Laurie quotes the Lowell FLRA's remarks, this time in full, but to demonstrate that the religious orientation of these women explains the group's nonconfrontational stance! Unlike the Lowell mill women of the 1830s, Laurie points out, these activists generally rejected strikes as a method of winning their demands. But it was a proposed general strike of textile operatives for the ten-hour day—a "Declaration of Independence" to begin on July 4, 1846—that provided the occasion for the association's report. Thus, while these activists' voices are finally rendered accurately, their religion is portrayed as a measure of their accommodation rather than their resistance.[13]

During the last twenty years, this religion-as-opium interpretation has generally proceeded along two separate tracks—one focusing on employers, the other on labor—though there has been some cross-fertilization. On the one hand, historians of the emerging middle class of this era have developed a sophisticated variant of the old "social control" thesis, in which they locate the meaning of evangelicalism and antebellum reform in the matrix of a rising class's struggle to establish dominance over American society, economy, politics, and culture. The principal work here is the oft-cited *Shopkeeper's Millennium*, Paul Johnson's pathbreaking work on the Finney revivals in Rochester, New York, in the early 1830s. Johnson argues here that the "Christian self-control" at the heart of evangelical Protestantism was the "moral imperative around which the northern middle class became a class." In his view, religion, and the reform crusade that flowed from it, in essence rationalized employers' exploitation of their workers, while offering a convenient (and potent) tool for taming those same workers through their "conversion" (often cajoled) to desirable patterns of thought and behavior.[14]

Though his study focuses on the middle rather than the working class and derives from the field of the "new social history," Johnson draws on the labor historiography running back to John R. Commons. His suggestion that what "independent working class Protestantism" there was in the antebellum period was linked to "political helplessness," especially in the wake of the 1837 Panic and ensuing depression, is an old theme in labor history.[15] Moreover, in his notion that "the crucial first generation of industrial conflict . . . was fought largely along religious lines," he is indebted to Paul Faler's more recent loyalist-traditionalist-rebel typology.[16] Thus, when masters and manufacturers in the 1820s and 1830s sought to impose a new industrial morality on workers fresh from the farm or small artisan shop, they turned to religion and, in Johnson's view, converted some (loyalists) while generating resistance to change among others (traditionalists). In this rendition of the story, the rebels were those who rejected religion and protested their conditions as workers. Here, of course, Johnson has ignored the possibility that workers could have internalized their own version of the religion being employed to control them and used it to impose their own form of control.[17]

Another important study concentrating on middle-class manufacturers—textile owners and their families in Rockdale, Pennsylvania—suggests that the only radical tradition of protest and resistance available to early factory operatives was the Enlightenment, which the author counterposes to the evangelical Protestantism adopted and promoted by the mill owners. Even in this story, though, Anthony F. C. Wallace discovered a significant number of Rockdale strike leaders in the local evangelical church in 1843. But, typically, he concludes that these workers had simply strayed from the fold. Apparently rejecting the possibility that these were pious Christians using the gospel to denounce exploitation and oppression, Wallace implies that they became activists in spite of their religion. In the end, according to Wallace, the owners won out and converted their workers into foot soldiers of an army of "Christian capitalists."[18]

In a similar fashion, most historians of antebellum labor offer a picture of evangelical Protestantism as a source of working-class division. The most influential of these studies focus on eastern metropolitan centers; much of the work operates within the framework established by David Montgomery in his seminal article on religion, politics, and class conflict in 1840s Philadelphia. Here, using the case study of the Philadelphia nativist riots of 1844, Montgomery seeks to explain why American workers have been noted for their militancy in the economic arena but not for their class consciousness. He suggests that the divisions and political weakness among Philadelphia workers in the 1840s—in contrast to the unity and relative strength of labor in the city during the 1830s—can be traced not only to the uneven development of capitalism and shifting patterns of immigration, but also to the intervening depression, which generated an enormous burst of evangelical fervor and consequent political battles over religious and cultural issues. He concludes that the political demands of evangelical Protestantism profoundly shaped the responses of working people, ultimately fragmenting the Philadelphia working class as a potent political force.[19]

Bruce Laurie's 1980 monograph on the working people of Philadelphia, the first modern study to examine closely working-class religion, dramatically extends and refines Montgomery's argument. Like Montgomery, Laurie sees a great divide between the 1830s and the 1840s, with the evangelical revivals of the depression years imparting an inherently limited social vision and ultimately creating debilitating divisions within the fledgling labor movement. Here, though, in his portrait of revivalist shorter-hours advocates in the textile mills and what he calls the "revivalist radicals" in the shops during the 1840s, Laurie offers us the first extended discussion of the various ways certain groups of workers used religion (particularly evangelical Protestant language, imagery, and argument) to advance certain labor demands. Yet, again, the total effect of the story he tells highlights religion-as-opium while downplaying its stimulating functions. Consonant with Johnson's view, he insists that the revivalist workers of the 1830s were part of a distinct culture that "ruled out . . . radical politics." Only out of depression was evangelical radicalism born. And that radicalism, Laurie's account suggests, was deeply flawed. For whatever other countervailing tendencies it might sometimes have exhibited, essential to evangelical culture was reverence for individualism, social mobility, and authority, and, perhaps most important, a susceptibility to nativism.[20] Finally, in contrast to all this, like Wallace, Laurie celebrates the rationalist and republican radicalism of some journeymen leaders in the 1830s, which then becomes the standard against which all other radicalism is measured.[21]

In several respects, the foregoing historiography is quite surprising. To begin with, the literature—either silent on the question of religion and the American working class or stressing the negative—stands in marked contrast to English labor historiography, which has inspired so much of recent labor history on this side of the Atlantic. In England, historians have carried on a long and vigorous debate about the precise relationship between Christianity, particularly Methodism, and early working-class radicalism. That debate is many sided and complex, but it has generated a lot of evidence of evangelical Protestantism's institutional and rhetorical contribution to labor protest.[22] Moreover, it has now been over a quarter century since Herbert Gutman suggested that the roots of the evangelical language permeating late-nineteenth-century labor radicalism could be found in the pre–Civil War era.[23] And in fact, historians have known for over fifty years that, from the beginning, key voices of American labor spoke in a religious idiom. In an early essay on Seth Luther, the great labor firebrand of the 1830s and 1840s, Louis Hartz remarked, "Here was a time when, contrary to Marxian theory, preoccupation with religious imperatives strengthened rather than vitiated the campaign of labor."[24] And yet, most historians have assumed precisely the reverse, treating the relationship between religion and the early American working class without careful enough consideration to historical context.

How can we explain this treatment?[25] If we consider Hartz's remarks on Luther, perhaps we can attribute the problem here in some measure to the enduring influence of Marxism, among Marxists and even non-Marxist social and labor historians.[26] Though Marx (and particularly Engels) understood the powerful strain of protest embedded in Christian theology and tradition, most American historians seem to have implicitly adopted a simplistic reading of Marx's "opium of the people" dictum. And this, despite the available literature in anthropology and sociology that has in the last generation developed a far more positive picture of religion's historical role in radicalism and rebellion than this famous quotation might suggest.[27] Perhaps it took someone like Hartz, influenced by Marxism yet apart from it, to recognize what might have been assumed.

It is also possible that the lens labor historians have used in their work is yet too narrow to encompass the religious labor radical. Take Norman Ware, for example. A recent review of his work points out that he approached this period on its own terms as experienced by contemporaries, took words seriously and sought to resurrect the moral vision of the labor reformers, and "permitted voices of protest to be heard."[28] Why then are the voices of religious protest so muted even in his account? Because, I would suggest, of an old and enduring legacy in labor historiography: the search for the pragmatic, typically militant, "true" worker, whose "real" (or "rational") interests (in shorter hours, lower wages, better working conditions) are seen as too often betrayed by the imposed idealism and visionary schemes of middle-class, utopian reformer-intellectuals.[29] In this rendition of American labor history, "outsiders" are forever infiltrating and dominating preexisting groups of laborites or even establishing their own associations and appropriating the labels and language of the "genuine" workers' movement, all with the intent of advancing their own interests rather than labor's. Until very recently, this worker–reformer dichotomy has dominated historical writing on the early American working class.[30]

The debate over the "true" workingman has roots in the period itself—partly due to the elasticity of the term during the early Industrial Revolution—but the concept as used by historians has obscured more than it has illuminated. Early American labor movements were decidedly mixed affairs, socially and ideologically; moreover, the real-life "insiders" differed markedly from later historians' assumptions about them. The notion, for example, that literacy, standing in the community, involvement in non-"economic" reform activity, or spirituality disqualified an early-nineteenth-century American from the appellation "real" workingman simply misreads history—on the contrary, all of these characteristics typified antebellum labor reformers.[31]

Still, because the reformers of this age exhibited a strong religious orientation—indeed that, in great measure, explains the visionary and idealistic nature of these people that so many historians have noted—such expressions among labor reformers could naturally be taken by the same historians as evidence of "middle-class" influence, either in personnel or ideology. If labor radicalism expressed itself in a religious idiom, it must, by definition, be something that was imposed from outside the working class. The problem is that what has been ascribed to middle-class reformers in antebellum America cannot be confined to them. Religion was used by a rising middle class to establish a new economic and social system and thus their dominance over society; it was also used by workers who sought to resist changes they perceived as threatening to their lives and the life of the Republic.

Religion and the Working Class

The society that produced the first American labor movement was a deeply pious one—and likely the most Christian anywhere in the world at the time. Evangelical Protestantism was central to the creation of American national culture in the period before the Civil War; it was crucial in the development of mass democratic politics, party identification, and the formation of national identity.[32] Moreover, certain specific strains in American Protestantism were conducive to radical causes, most important of which were the pietistic and perfectionist traditions of the Reformation.[33] The key elements of this religious heritage in early-nineteenth-century America were the elevation of the individual over intermediaries, such as the church and clergy, and faith in an imminent second coming of Christ. Temporal authority was questioned and individual conscience exalted in the emphasis on the individual's direct relationship to God, the priesthood of all believers, and the plain testimony of Scripture as the ultimate source of truth. Fascination with the biblical prophecy of Christ's kingdom on earth provided a vision of a heavenly world of harmony and brotherhood that would supplant the miseries and chaos of earthly existence. If the first doctrine could legitimate rebellion, the second could buoy hopes for ultimate triumph.[34]

In the early nineteenth century, American Protestantism was an increasingly optimistic and egalitarian—indeed, militantly democratic—faith, a fervent popular religion that emphasized "works," free will, and the duty (and destiny) of the faithful to Christianize their world.[35] Unsurprisingly, evangelicalism was the language of antebellum resistance, reform, and radicalism in an era of enormous social and political ferment: witness the rhetoric and doctrine of those calling for temperance, peace, women's rights, health reform, utopian communities, an end to capital punishment, and the abolition of slavery.[36] It was also the language of defiance of the great dispossessed of the age, the slaves themselves and their free black allies.[37] The crusades of the antebellum activists, Ernest Tuveson tells us, answered Joseph Bellamy's eighteenth-century call for true Christians to "promote the cause of truth and righteousness in the world, and so be workers together with God."[38] Labor reformers of the age cannot be abstracted from this historical context, though that is precisely what has happened. Thus, relying on the available secondary literature in the late 1970s, a study of modern evangelical Protestantism declared that "evangelical-ism was a driving force in virtually all of the major reform movements of the eighteenth and nineteenth centuries in America (*with the exception of the labor movement*)."[39]

But workers also imbibed the spiritual currents of their age; the movements of protest they created also exhibited religious visions and idealism. Indeed, as a small body of scholarship has now demonstrated, antebellum labor activists were often church members, even church leaders; they sometimes enjoyed important support from local congregations and clergymen; and, most impor-tant, they regularly employed Christian ritual, rhetoric, and doctrine to ad-vance the cause of labor reform. There is evidence of this pattern of religious influence throughout the period, among the rank-and-file as well as the leader-ship, in unions, Working Men's parties, and labor reform associations, along the religious spectrum from deists to evangelicals and Arminians to Calvinists, in New England, New York, and the Mid-Atlantic states, in big cities and village hamlets.[40] There was, in other words, an ongoing, widespread, national con-nection between religion and labor dissent that was deeply rooted in ante-bellum American culture.[41]

In antebellum America, evangelical religion furnished certain workers with crucial tools of resistance that helped them make sense of their rapidly chang-ing lives.[42] It offered a powerful language of protest out of which workers fashioned a critique of the exploitative and oppressive conditions of work and life in which they increasingly found themselves enmeshed, while it allowed those same workers to attack their employers as fallen Christians. In building a labor movement, activists took Jesus (the carpenter and carpenter's son) and his artisan disciples as models for emulation; they adopted for their own uses the contemporary evangelical style, language, and ritual (including the use of religious tracts, hymns, and grove meetings); they adopted biblical names when they wrote letters and articles in the labor press. They also fashioned from religious materials a transcendent vision of an alternative future. In this way, too, they gained inspiration and confidence in mounting the struggle, boosted morale during difficult times, and provided ready exhortation to workers and legitimate appeals for support from the broader community—all in the fur-therance of what they called a "holy cause." Ultimately, religion provided the focus, unity, and legitimacy desperately needed by a fledgling labor move-ment.[43] Far from being mere window dressing, the religious language of labor constituted the voice of a self-consciously Christian working class.

To be absolutely clear here: the argument being advanced is not that religion *caused* labor protest—undoubtedly, changing social relations of production did that. Still, labor activists responded not solely as Christians nor as workers, but as self-consciously Christian workers. Hence, the argument: religion decisively affected the nature of antebellum labor protest.[44] Hence, too, the obvious question that follows: what ultimately was religion's role, beyond those effects outlined above? Answering that question is especially difficult because of the fundamental ambiguity embedded in labor's religious critique of industrial America—a critique rooted in a religion that workers shared with their employers.[45] For example, antebellum activists could articulate a fierce Christian condemnation of long workdays, the degradation of labor, and inequality, at the same time that they sang the praises of individual morality, community, and harmony—a song their employers, too, were singing. One side of the consequent ambivalence led to labor organization, conflict, even violence. The other led to a preference for testimony over concrete action, a principled rejection of antagonism, and a rather mystical idea of exactly what foes the activists were fighting.[46]

Now, there was nothing specific to these workers' religion that predetermined a particular program, strategy, or tactic.[47] But there were two related tendencies that did distinguish Christian labor activism in this period. First, these radicals—often identifying themselves as conservatives—saw history as something to be transcended, or reinvented, rather than confronted, because they perceived history as a drama of Eden and descent, good and evil, fall and regeneration. For many, it appears, history was prophecy, and progress meant a return to pristine beginnings.[48] More important, though they often railed against an abstract "class of men" and attacked the sinful "bad boss," they could not connect the two, because they identified employers as Christians and their religion taught them to hate the sin but love the sinner. Ultimately, these radicals saw only degenerated individuals, not classes. Both tendencies put labor activists in the odd position of engaging in class conflict while denying what they were doing.[49] And that clearly made a difference in how this new working class conceived of itself and the historic project in which it was engaged.[50]

The foregoing must not be seen as a restatement of the religion-as-opium argument, for, in stark contrast to the traditional story, the evidence reveals that Christianity helped bring a self-conscious American working class to life. If working-class religion cannot be ignored, neither can it be explained away.[51] Working-class consciousness in the antebellum era was not "poisoned"—and thus nullified—by religion; it was "leavened" with religion, rendering the product sui generis.[52] Here, religion (God and spirituality, as well as the language and doctrine of Christianity) was a path to protest and resistance, even radicalism. These Christians did not see poverty as a punishment for sin, they did not stress the afterlife over this life, nor did they encourage obedience to rulers. To the contrary, their religion legitimated rebellion by elevating the individual over intermediaries in church and theology; it even assured eventual triumph by envisioning the long-predicted Second Coming. The "meekness" of these Christians was clearly double edged.[53] The issue here is thus not the measure of these activists' militancy or their radicalism. What historians need to do is to document the religious nature of their activism and, in that context, to identify and trace their evident ambivalence about certain aspects of that activism, in order to better understand the complex meaning of religion in their lives and the life of their movement.

This book is an extended exploration into the nature and impact of this two-sided character of religion among working people in antebellum America—one side promoted class consciousness, the other, in the context of labor activism, diluted it. The story here is told topically rather than chronologically, for two reasons. First, given the current paucity of scholarship on the subject and the fugitive and fragmentary nature of the evidence, judgments about change over time—particularly this short a span of time—are dangerous.[54] Second, and more important, regarding the principal characteristics of the religion–labor relationship in antebellum America, I have been more impressed by continuity than by change.[55] To be sure, the religious language of labor did not emerge full blown with the labor activism of the late 1820s and early 1830s, but religious traditions and terms of dissent were already available when the changes wrought by the early Industrial Revolution created the conditions for such a movement; they did not have to be invented.[56] Still, specific strategies and tactics did have to be invented for confronting Christian employers and their allies who had a different perspective on the Industrial Revolution, and I discuss here how certain approaches emerged and evolved over time, how traditions of dissent were fashioned in the course of struggle. And yet, linearity is not the dominant thread in this story; those who insist on such a progression may be imposing, rather than uncovering, one.[57]

I have also been more impressed by the common ground many workers and their allies found in religiously informed radicalism—and the similarity in the way they expressed that radicalism—than by the undeniable variations of region, type of community, occupation, gender, and so on. Hence, while discussing certain peculiarities, this study tells the story of labor's spiritual stance, its relationship to the church, and especially its religious language of protest as a specifically antebellum American story.[58] What happened here cannot be confined to New England, the 1840s, women, or skilled artisans—to any one place, time, or group. Therein, I believe, lies its broader significance.

The book is organized in three parts. In part 1, examples from a wide range of individuals and groups throughout the nation demonstrate the fundamentally religious character of early American labor struggles. Chapter 1 describes the religious world in which most early labor activists were born and matured, surveys the massive social and economic changes they encountered in the early

Industrial Revolution, and hints at the logical response to these conditions for many: labor reform as a Christian enterprise. Chapters 2 and 3 suggest some of the problems and ambiguities labor reformers faced in a militantly Christian society in spite of—and sometimes because of—their own piety, all of which generally helped to promote and deepen that piety. Here, the discussion focuses, first, on the various ways early activists handled the charge that their activism was perforce evidence of their "infidelity" to Christianity. Then, attention shifts to their ambivalent, though fundamentally committed, stance toward institutional Christianity; specifically, church attendance and the clergy.

Because only close up community studies that ground individuals and groups in an ongoing religious life can make sense of what these activists said about religion and how they used religious language, part 2 inquires into the relationship between antebellum labor and the church at the local level. Thus, chapters 4, 5, and 6 probe the extent and nature of church involvement among labor activists in a range of communities in New England (Fall River, Fitchburg, and Boston, Massachusetts), the Mid-Atlantic region (Wilmington, Delaware), and upstate New York (Rochester). These community studies reveal that however complex and variable, religion's influence on antebellum labor protest was a national phenomenon. Chapter 7 explains how labor's institutional connections with the church were expressed in the use of church buildings, the introduction of religious ritual into labor protest, and the involvement at certain times of certain ministers in support of labor reform.

The general discussion of labor's religiosity (part 1) and the specific labor and religious history of these several communities (part 2) provide the necessary foundation for part 3, which examines the way religion informed the language of labor protest in antebellum America. It focuses on the way religion leavened working-class consciousness as it took shape during this period, as seen mainly in the way labor thought was expressed. Chapters 8–11 discuss labor's appeal for support among workers and in the broader community, its critique of prevailing social conditions and its vision of an alternative future, and the means—sometimes sharply debated—that it was willing to sanction for advancing its goals. The sum total of this articulated belief might be called this era's "social gospel of labor reform." The epilogue then considers some of the changes, and continuities, in the religious language of labor in the wake of shifts in the composition of the work force at midcentury; that story suggests an ongoing class struggle over the meaning of America's religious heritage.

Which brings us back to the Lowell convention of 1847, the good doctor Tewkesbury, and the mill girl who challenged his religious condemnation of labor reform. When Tewkesbury used the Bible to condemn the assembled labor reformers for unchristian behavior, one of the operatives in attendance proclaimed that were the Savior living in America in the 1840s, he would condemn precisely those Christians "who seem to be quite as much devoted to fashion, ease and popularity, as to the establishing [of] those principles of humility, self-denial and universal love for our race, which is among the first principles of *christianity*." And clearly, in these workers' view, Christ would be on the side of labor reform, because it sought to promote those very "first principles of christianity." Thus, one operative assured the assembled delegates of their eventual triumph over the forces that Tewkesbury represented, using the Bible to make her point.

> No great question of reform of any kind has *ever* triumphed but by the greatest exertions of its supporters and though our numbers are at present small, in this part of the country, it is no just cause for discouragement, and should only arouse us to more energetic action. A little leaven, (the good book tells us,) leaveneth the whole lump. And we may feel assured that the leavener of just and benevolent principles which are now operating through the labor, and land, reform movements will yet extend its influence throughout the entire nation.[59]

As students of history, we cannot understand these operatives until we understand the religious leaven that lay at the heart of their vision. Nor can we grasp the complex process of class formation in antebellum America until we uncover this struggle between those who used religion to justify the prevailing conditions of life and those who used religion to articulate what the mill girl called "a happy and hopeful vision" of a world "beyond the influence of factory bolts, and locks, and factory oppression."[60]

Part 1.
Religion and Antebellum
Labor: Overview

Chapter 1. The Inheritance:
The World They Encountered,
the World They Made

The labor activists of antebellum America—strikers, unionists, "labor reformers," disgruntled workers who wrote letters to newspapers—were a heterogeneous lot. They were often journeymen artisans, but also mill hands, common laborers, and outworkers laboring in their homes. Among their ranks could also be found farmers, shopkeepers, and a smattering of small manufacturers; editors, poets, students, reformers, and even some lawyers, doctors, and local politicians; longtime residents, recent migrants, and transients; rural folk, countryside townspeople, and denizens of big cities like Boston, New York, and Philadelphia or "western" boom towns like Rochester, Pittsburgh, and Cincinnati; New Englanders, New Yorkers, and the polyglot peoples of the Mid-Atlantic states. They can be distinguished still further by nativity, sex, race, age, political and religious affiliation, and more. But this diversity should not obscure the common ground that united many of these people and eased, rather than hindered, their entry into the first real expressions of an American labor movement—namely, the cultural heritage of Protestant Christianity. It is that heritage, in great measure derived from the fertile religious soil of late-eighteenth- and early-nineteenth-century America, that explains much about both the style and substance of antebellum labor protest, which sometimes took on the character of a religious—indeed, explicitly Christian—crusade.

Religion and Education in the Early Republic:
Home, School, Church

Like the mill girls who took on Dr. Tewkesbury, most antebellum labor activists were born in rural and small-town America during the early years of the Republic, into a world in which religion was a central fact of life.[1] Here, much of what was ancient and established was religious, while, increasingly during the nineteenth century, religious awakening became the order of the day. In this world, they formed many of their basic beliefs and values; from this world came their basic education.[2] Reformation Protestantism, of course, had a powerful influence over colonial America. And, despite the disruptions of the Revolution, the Enlightenment rationalism, deism, and skepticism of many of the founders, and the veneer of secularism in much of late-eighteenth-century public life, it appears that the common people remained on the whole deeply pious.[3] And, with the rise and spread of a genuinely popular evangelical Christianity beginning at the turn of the century—the quickening of the faith historians call the "Second Great Awakening"—the culture became more devout still.[4]

To be sure, with the flowering of the Enlightenment, sectors of late-eighteenth-century America did witness something of a retreat from militant Protestantism. But Enlightenment thought was diverse, the religious concerns of important Enlightenment thinkers evinced deep religious concerns, and, most important, the American Enlightenment had a pervasive religious character.[5] Moreover, Enlightenment thought never reached the American majority, who lived in the countryside; for them, Protestantism remained the principal source of values and beliefs.[6] The element of Enlightenment thought that did filter down through the social structure and survive into the nineteenth century was in fact heavily laden with Christianity. Meanwhile, the public discourse of late-eighteenth-century America, often dominated by learned, apparently rationalistic men of the Enlightenment, was also steeped in the language of millennial expectation, as America's birth seemed to many—at least, so they said—the heralding of the long-predicted Second Coming.[7] Here, more than anywhere else in the Western world at the time, Protestant millennialism was yoked to the idea of progress, as ancient biblical prophecy dovetailed with the much more recent belief in the possibility of human improvement toward perfection.[8]

Most important, perhaps, virtually everyone, liberal and orthodox alike, agreed that religion was an essential bulwark for a healthy social order—a crucial matter for future labor reform. Indeed, whatever the actual inheritance from the Puritans a century and a half later—and, to be sure, part of that inheritance was a healthy disrespect for Puritan intolerance—there was a broad consensus in the early Republic that religion was necessary to society. Even those at the "liberal" end of the religious spectrum—like Benjamin Franklin, George Washington, and Thomas Jefferson—insisted on it. The proponents of the separation of church and state in this age often sought to thereby magnify, not lessen, the impact of religion on American society.[9]

As for the vaunted deism of some prominent Revolutionary era Americans, their main project was the refutation of Scripture as the revealed word of God, not the rejection of the Deity.[10] "Unbelief" was simply not an intellectual alternative in America during this period; the existence of the Supreme Being was, quite simply, assumed. Thus, for example, supernatural references justified the assertions in the Declaration of Independence about the inalienable rights of man; here, God may have been the removed "Creator" or "Nature's God," but a "Father" nonetheless, who bestowed legitimacy on both the individual and the nation.[11] In fact, the "natural religion" of most late-eighteenth-century deists was a form of theism that arose in great measure from their fear that the intolerance of orthodoxy would lead to the widespread rejection of Christianity. What appears to have united them was an embrace of a kind of "stripped-down" Christianity, without "mystery" or "superstition." After all, godlessness violated the moral realm they expected to find in nature (thus their belief in future "rewards and punishments"). God required worship, primarily through a moral life.[12] Here then, at the outer edge of the spiritual world of early America, even these spokesmen for the new nation proclaimed the need for religion, and their views existed alongside, even blended with, Protestant thought.[13]

Briefly, at the turn of the century, there was an organized deist presence in America, which elicited condemnations of a rising infidelity from prominent figures like Samuel Morse and Timothy Dwight, refutations of deism and atheism in early-nineteenth-century schoolbooks, and clergy-led revivals.[14] But, the threat was greatly exaggerated by defenders of the status quo as a way of ensuring their continued hegemony over the national culture. What Martin Marty has said about the Christian–infidel battles of nineteenth-century America accurately characterizes this earlier period as well: "the deep approbation of the faith that existed at the very core of the society and the disproportionate power of the warring parties had made it possible for the churches to have the luxury of employing the image of the infidel to their own ends."[15] And with much success, apparently: "a heretical voice in an orthodox wilderness," as its principal historian describes the movement of the 1790s, the forces of organized infidelity were largely vanquished during the opening years of the new century.[16]

Hence, among ordinary Americans in the early Republic—at home, in school, and at church—the essence of education, the inculcation of basic moral and social values, derived to a large extent from religion.[17] This process of socialization was, in a fundamental sense, an apprenticeship education, with children learning from adults both work and thought.[18] The training began in the home—what antebellum Americans called the "domestic altar"—which helps explain the deep attachment of first-generation industrial workers for what one Lowell mill girl called "this sacred, this enchanted spot."[19] Here, intense indoctrination began early and could amount to a kind of religious conditioning, in a world that acknowledged the Bible, the ministry, and the church as the authorities on childrearing.[20] In many families, this was simply a continuation of tradition. Joseph Packard's father spoke often of his parents' instructing their children in a "pious and prayerful" life. Joseph, raised in a Maine seaport town in the 1810s, remembered vividly the morning and evening family prayers of *his* youth, during which even the smallest of the children read aloud from the Bible. The hand of God was everywhere in that home, he recalled, a constant presence. And how was that accomplished, exactly? "It must have been the force of example and the religious atmosphere that filled the house," he said, "*unconsciously affecting us, as does the earthly atmosphere.*"[21]

But there was also something quite tangible that imparted such intense spirituality to so many homes in the early Republic: the Word. For Protestantism was a profoundly Bible-based religion; in America, Scripture became the bedrock of the national faith, forming one of the crucial ingredients in a child's early development. The deist Paine knew enough about the nature of Revolutionary America to appeal to the authority of the Holy Bible in *Common Sense.* Some states—in parts of New England, for example—actually required every home to keep a Bible; but required or not, the practice appears to have been widespread, and reading from Scripture was a common means of learning to read.[22] Indeed, in an age when reading became a "material necessity of life" for the rural peoples of the northeastern United States, creating the first literate rural generations in the Western world, "Bible reading was the most common reading experience."[23]

This was especially so for children between 1776 and 1835, when American publishers began producing editions of the Bible aimed at a young audience. In these volumes and the more standard versions, young people learned their first lessons.[24] Austin Bryant, for example, who grew up on a farm in western Massachusetts during the 1790s, was an uncommon child whose thirst for knowledge was evident at the precocious age of two. He tried his young hand at the Bible just six weeks after he began mastering the art of reading. Before he turned three, he had finished the Book of Genesis and by the age of four had completed both the Old and New Testaments.[25] Lucy Larcom, who grew up in the New Hampshire countryside and worked in the Lowell mills as a young adult, recalled fondly how in her childhood she and her siblings gathered around their father for family worship, as he read to them from the family Bible.[26] When it was her turn, she learned to read by reciting aloud from the New Testament.[27] Bryant and Larcom were uncommon individuals, but their experiences in learning to read were common for the age: the family was the center of reading in the early Republic, and the family Bible—usually a huge volume, often called the "sacred encyclopedia" by contemporaries, which included not just the Old and New Testaments but Christian history, principles, admonitions, guidelines, and aids as well—occupied center stage.[28]

The result was a culture steeped in biblical language and imagery. One antebellum American recorded having read biblical passages aloud so many times in his childhood home and then as a young domestic servant that "I have no doubt that I read the Bible through *in course* at least a dozen times before I was sixteen years old."[29] Another, the publisher and writer Samuel Goodrich, had been so early and so thoroughly immersed in the Scriptures that later in life, as a publisher and author, he found he could not write without affecting a biblical style.[30] Thus, too, the *Lowell Offering,* a literary mill-girls' magazine for which Larcom wrote during the early 1840s, revealed a heavy biblical influence, clearly derived from early childhood indoctrination.

And so it was with antebellum activists as diverse as Thomas Wentworth Higginson, Elihu Burritt, and Orestes Brownson, who would make good use of the Bible in their several crusades. Higginson, a prominent abolitionist raised in the home of a Unitarian divine during the 1820s, escaped the rigors of New England Calvinist theology but was nonetheless expected to vigilantly study the New Testament. Burritt, the "learned Blacksmith" of Connecticut who became America's leading antebellum peace activist, was an evangelical reformer who did his first reading, under the tutelage of his Calvinist mother, in the family Bible. Brownson was a preacher and radical labor advocate in Boston during the 1830s before his conversion to Catholicism (and conservatism) the following decade. In his childhood home, God's Word held the same exalted position that it did in Higginson's and Burritt's. Although he was one of the most unusual of all antebellum Americans, his religious upbringing was not, for he received his spiritual training at the hands of an elderly Vermont couple who adhered strictly to the tenets of old-fashioned New England Congregationalism. And since his guardians were too old to travel the several miles from their country home to the nearest meetinghouse on the Sabbath, Brownson's indoctrination into the Christian faith centered on the family Bible and the daily regimen of saying grace before all meals, daily Scripture readings, and morning and evening prayers.[31]

The school system, which underwent significant expansion during this period, constituted a second locus of education for antebellum activists. Here, teachers were enjoined to "(teach) Christian principles to a Christian community."[32] As in the home, Holy Scripture was key. Copying and memorizing passages from Scripture, America's "scholars"—from common schools to academies—learned the Ten Commandments, the Lord's Prayer, the Apostles' Creed, and the catechism, pretty much as they had during the colonial period.[33] School materials also taught national history by biblical analogy: the first settlers as Hebrews coming to the Promised Land (and, later, western migrants as Hebrews in the Egyptian diaspora), the young Revolutionary America as David, the Constitution as a Mosaic Code, and George Washington as America's Moses.[34] And, even for those deprived of formal schooling, as for example many girls were, familiarity with Scripture was generally considered the essential ingredient in everyone's education. Thus, in a short story that appeared in the *Lowell Offering* in 1841, one character ("Squire E"), "believing women needed to know nothing of books, never suffered his daughter to attend school *after she could read her Bible*."[35] For, it seems, in the world of early-nineteenth-century America, everyone needed to read the Bible.

The key underlying assumption of early school curriculum was the "moral character of the universe," with religion itself "more a matter of morals than theology." The basic message was that God was the creator of the world, a benevolent presence in that world, and the commander of human action. Men and women were to obey divine laws, as revealed in Scripture.[36] Since virtue here was identified with Christianity and with humanitarianism, the message—given the right circumstances and the right hearer, of course—was reform, which could translate later into a militant activism.

Such was not, of course, the goal of America's early educators, whose stated purpose was to sustain the nation as a republic and to ensure individual salvation and the "Biblical Commonwealth" by inculcating its future citizens with Christian values, moral fiber, and civic virtue—to create, in short, a nation of "Christian republicans." But, though "conservative" in intent, the creation of a literate populace had unintended consequences. For when the sacred was fused to the secular, when personal salvation was linked to the fate of the nation, when children mastered literacy while also learning to accept and relish the God who had created them and their world, and to develop a grasp of moral and religious knowledge for use in their everyday lives, to develop a conscience, all in the context of a rapidly changing social and political landscape—then, the stage was set for an explosive combination of religious and political fervor.[37]

Beyond the hearth and the district schoolhouse, there was a third, if some-what more problematical, locus of education for these children of the early Republic: the church, or "meetinghouse" as it was generally known during these years.[38] In some ways, it was an extension of home, as families generally attended together, with children going to Sabbath services at an early age, parents often carrying their youngest in their arms. In fact, Sunday worship sometimes formed the earliest childhood memory outside the home. Typically, it was an all-day affair, with morning and afternoon sermons that sometimes lasted several hours. Moreover, until well into the nineteenth century, these were not terribly comfortable places, at least in the countryside. Not only did attenders sometimes stand or kneel through prayers of up to a half-hour in duration, but they also had to endure the cold and wind that penetrated broken windows and porous facades in the winter, the chickens and turkeys that came in through the open doors in the summer, and the refuse of the food their brethren brought with them throughout the year to sustain them through the long services.[39]

Especially in the towns, this institution was typically the community's vital core. In some states, the law sought to ensure church attendance. Article 3 of the Massachusetts Constitution of 1780, for example, noting the prevailing view that "the happiness of a people, and the good order and preservation of Civil government, essentially depend upon piety, religion and morality," autho-rized the legislature to ensure for worship at the local level, and even to require church attendance.[40] But, required or not, observance of the Christian Sab-bath, and churchgoing in particular, was a formative experience for many, perhaps most, early Americans. The frequent nostalgic references to the "old town meetinghouse" in the writings of the mill girls, for example—"the Meeting House, as in most country villages, is conspicuous, as the greatest ornament," wrote a Lowell operative of her New Hampshire home—provide ample testimony to the prominent place it played in these early American communities.[41]

We also learn of its importance from those who complained about its absence. Lydia and Erastus Brigham, ordinary folk trying to make it in the West in the early 1830s, wrote home to Connecticut from Ohio that they no longer lived where they could enjoy "every religious privilege." Nearly thirty years later, now in Missouri, they still complained to correspondents back East "that want of Church privileges is our greatest cross."[42] In fact, churchgoing was apparently quite common among the vast majority of late-eighteenth-century American families and expanded rapidly in the next century.[43] Many of those who came of age in the antebellum period, especially those who came off the farms and out of the small towns of the northeastern countryside, were born into a churchgoing world.[44]

More important for the education of young Americans in the early Republic—and for future movements of American labor—church teachings in many Protestant denominations at the turn of the nineteenth century became increasingly democratic. This theological revolution helped lay the groundwork for social activism the likes of which America would not see again until the 1960s.[45] Critical in this was the Second Great Awakening, a national quest for salvation that signaled the maturation of the most distinctive mode of thought in nineteenth-century America: evangelicalism.[46] Literally "the bringing of good news," evangelicalism in this period was characterized by belief in the necessity of a spiritual change of heart (or new birth) and a consequent crusading fervor to change the world. Perhaps the greatest renewal of piety since the Reformation, the revivals that embodied this evangelical fervor began in the 1790s and gathered strength in the early 1800s, sweeping through the countryside, towns, and cities of the nation.[47]

Though the fires of a general awakening were dying out in many rural areas by the 1840s, grove revivals and protracted meetings had become familiar features of life in what was by then a militantly Protestant society.[48] So much so, in fact, that a foreign visitor like Frances Trollope believed that, at least in the smaller cities and towns of antebellum America, prayer meetings had taken the place of all other amusements.[49] Sometimes, as we shall see, they literally brought the business of the community to a standstill; after all, the point of these revivals was not just to harvest souls but to redeem the community.[50]

In these revivals, "populist" preachers welled up from the ranks of the common people and, armed with what Nathan Hatch has called "the transforming power of the word, spoken, written, and sung," led a democratic religious revolution that dwarfed all others in this age of democratic revolutions.[51] The revivals thus posed a threat to the religious Standing Order, even where leading clerics had a hand in beginning the work. This spiritual outpouring both reflected and deepened the democratic, popular, and reformist features of early American Puritanism: the simplicity of the meetinghouse, lay participation in congregational activities, the priesthood of believers, and the acceptance of the plain testimony of Scripture as the ultimate authority in religious matters. For the revivals often meant abandonment of pomp and ceremony, encouraged, at least theoretically, the direct involvement in spiritual affairs of all men and women as the common children of one God, and taught adherence to the Bible without the imposition creeds or clergy.

The tendencies of the age also conspired, from a number of different directions, to erode the Calvinist theology of the colonial past. In New England, for example, the reign of strict Calvinism began to crumble with the rise of the New Divinity Congregationalists, Arminian Methodists, Freewill Baptists, and the new "Christian" movement. From another side came the Unitarian challenge to Congregational orthodoxy; from still another, the Universalist. Finally, with the progressive lifting of legal sanctions against non-Congregational "sects," a variety of denominations quickly proliferated in the region. To be sure, the pace and nature of religious change differed in other regions (and, indeed, within New England as well), but everywhere during these years, young Americans faced a world in which challenges to orthodoxy and calls for "revival" constituted the order of the day. Increasingly, the rigidity and determinism of a life framed around conditional election, total human depravity, and an inscrutable, arbitrary, and sometimes malevolent Deity gave way to a more malleable and open world, offering the possibility of universal salvation through the free moral agency of children capable of doing good under a benevolent, loving God.[52] By thus suggesting that all God's children were equal in the Maker's eyes, and by raising the possibility of unlimited improvement, the new theology articulated a more optimistic, and democratic, view of human destiny.

All these democratic tendencies, signaling a general revolt against authority within American Protestantism, spilled over into the secular realm, as American Protestants of the early nineteenth century took it upon themselves to remake their society, typically in accordance with the spirit and doctrines of their religion.[53] Just how society should be "remade" was a matter of some debate among antebellum Americans, of course. But the basic thrust in American Protestantism during this period was toward saving the society as well as the individual. Partly, this social Christianity was rooted in certain key changes in Protestant theology, most importantly a renewed emphasis on works as a test of faith and the notion that true virtue consisted of "disinterested benevolence." As already noted, the penchant for saving society was also embedded in the nature of the founding of the nation. For although the founders had taken pains to separate church and state in law, they yoked the nation's fate to the coming Kingdom by linking America's moral purity (rooted in Protestantism) to God's favoring the American Republic as the world's savior, thus conjoining church and society.[54]

Proclaiming America a "Christian Republic" that had a distinct mission in the world, the regenerate of this culture anxiously anticipated the establishment of Christ's kingdom on earth. They were living, they believed, in the "last days." This anticipation often bred action, for theology increasingly stressed human efforts to bring about the long-predicted "new heaven and new earth." Increasingly, they came to believe that Christ would return *after* the thousand years of holiness predicted in Revelation and other parts of the Bible. This postmillennialist vision of an earthly utopia ruled by Christian principles— what Ernest Tuveson has called "Progressivist Millennialism"—implied that institutions could be perfected by human efforts, though the transition would not be smooth. These Christians doing the work of God on earth were "revolutionaries" of sorts, whose historical vision necessitated the clashing of adversaries, the overturning of obstacles, and general apocalyptic warfare. This view of the world offered not just the possibility but also the promise of radical transformation.[55]

To be sure, the promise could be construed in many different ways when it came to deciding how to respond to such vexing issues of the day as slavery, alcohol, women's rights, education, capital punishment—and the rights and prerogatives of workers and their employers.[56] But the injunction to enforce divine law, however understood, along with the democratic exaltation of free will over determinism, did animate the spirit of antebellum Protestantism, pressing Americans increasingly toward public action.[57] Thus, the language of American reform during these years was not the anticlerical rationalism of some contemporary European radicals, who often expressed their critique of society as a critique of religion, but rather revivalist Protestantism and Christian perfectionism. In America, it was evangelicals, not atheistic philosophes, who led the struggle for church disestablishment, while the clergy's general support for the American Revolution rendered them potential allies of those who sought social change in its aftermath.

Most important, the evangelical style so permeated the age that even those who rejected many of the practices and doctrines of the revivalists exhibited much of this same righteous and crusading spirit of moral reformation.[58] And, given its democratic implications, evangelicalism lent itself to broad-based movements for radical social change, with the potential to turn these movements into religious crusades. With this religious inheritance, it should not surprise us that the men and women who mounted the labor protest of early-nineteenth-century America adapted evangelical Protestantism to their own purposes, that in fact the labor movement was also a religious movement. Indeed, at times, labor activists, just like other activists of the age, turned their movement into a religious crusade.

Capitalism and Christianity:
Labor Activism in a Religious Culture

The occasion for this labor evangelicalism was a series of dramatic alterations in the American social order. In the massive transformation unleashed by the capitalist revolution that swept across portions of the northeastern United States in the second quarter of the nineteenth century—a worldwide process Karl Polanyi called "The Great Transformation"—antebellum labor activists perceived a challenge to a whole way of life.[59] Given the pious world in which they were born and matured, religion was a natural means of defense against unwanted, or at least tremendously threatening, change. Their refashioning and use of that faith rendered them religious—as well as labor—radicals.

Antebellum Americans confronted a rapidly expanding world: explosive population growth and rapid movement westward, a revolution in transportation and communications, the mushrooming of inland cities and the burgeoning of old ports, increased production for the market on the land, the spread of commercial and cash transactions, the expansion of handicraft manufacturing and the appearance of a mechanized factory system, dramatically broadened citizen participation in public life, national self-assertion abroad. Though unevenly felt and often modulated by persistent if reshaped tradition, these changes ultimately transformed life in the northeastern part of the nation. Collectively, they offered enormous opportunity; they also entailed enormous cost. Traditional farmers and artisans were forced to compete in ever-widening markets; by 1850, perhaps half the labor force, on and off the land, worked for wages, a dramatic increase over the previous generation. The population of towns and cities became more heterogeneous and anonymous, as the pace of life—indeed, the pace of change itself—quickened. Mill and shop workers now found themselves working in larger and more diverse groups, sometimes far from home, producing only part of the product, often under noisy, dirty, and dangerous conditions, and working by the clock for long hours at low wages under significantly tighter supervision than they had experienced in the past. Families came under increased pressure, forced to devote more time—and more of their members—to procuring the cash necessary to survive in a competitive commercial environment. Meanwhile, large-scale, impersonal institutions like banks and corporations now threatened to rule where local communities once held sway. And, as rapid economic growth was accompanied by bouts of inflation and unemployment and cycles of speculative boom and bust, demands on government mounted. With the aspiring seeking support for enterprise and the weak seeking protection from the strong, a raucous democratic polity emerged, managed by professional politicians who spoke in the name of the people but sought to advance the needs of particular constituencies.

Above all else, these changes were radically fragmenting and were experienced as such by many. Migration to fresh lands westward or to find work in towns and cities divided families and disrupted rural communities. At work, in the shops and factories, tasks were divided and subdivided, the workers set apart by discrete skills, separate rooms, noisy machinery, competitive pressures. Meanwhile, work itself became increasingly divorced from life, the division between sex roles sharpened, communities fractured along class lines, new extremes of wealth and poverty emerged, older forms of mutualism and interdependence were replaced by individual striving and egoism. In the rough-and-tumble of antebellum America, contention and strife seemed the order of the day.

Everywhere, hope mixed with fear, desire with disquiet, as prosperity and individual social mobility expanded alongside poverty, exploitation, dependency, frustration, insecurity, uncertainty. Out of this matrix of aspiration and anxiety, of course, came the greatest outpouring of reform activity in American history, an often religiously informed agitation in which an enormously diverse cross section of the citizenry sought in different and often conflicting ways to remake American society. But labor protest, too, can be understood only as part of this larger ferment.

Typifying labor's response to the capitalist revolution, for example, were the editors of the *Wachusett Independant*, a Fitchburg labor newspaper that appeared for a short time in 1845. In an editorial entitled "Oppression of Caste," these activists declaimed against the "unrighteous distinctions" of their day, telling the story of a "young mechanic" they knew who had suffered an all-too-familiar "insult and injury" after having failed to establish his own shop. Most important to the editors was the fact that this craftsman's family shared his burden, his children feeling the invidious distinctions of being poor, while his wife was excluded from the "social festivities" of their more wealthy neighbors, "though both may be members of the same professedly christian church, and occasionally sit down together at that solemn feast where we are taught to love one another, as he who suffered on the cross, loves the erring sons of men." Ultimately, the young mechanic lost his home and furniture, and then his entire family to disease—a not uncommon occurrence, the editors reminded their readers—and all this while a member of an evangelical church![60]

Beginning in the 1820s, a range of disgruntled workers and their allies—strikers in countryside mills and urban workshops, members of journeyman craft societies and citywide and national trades' union federations, activists in "workingmen's" parties and associations, editors and correspondents of labor newspapers—began developing the Christian social critique and vision that we can glimpse in the *Wachusett Independant*. They used religious appeals, reasoning, and doctrine; they adopted Christian imagery, symbols, and ritual. The worldview that emerged from this effort bore the imprint of their religious heritage, which venerated home devotion, Bible reading, and church involvement.

A wide range of antebellum activists, reformers, and independent spirits associated with early American labor protest paid regular homage to this heritage, some even claiming to be engaged in an explicitly religious project.[61] During the 1840s, a writer in the prolabor *People's Paper* of Cincinnati could be found preaching that the "Creator holds the family ties in his hand" and that society should not "loosen what God has bound." At about the same time, the editors of the Fall River *Mechanic,* the voice of striking building tradesmen in that mill town, reminded their subscribers that "no one that loves his family" could neglect "worship at home." Even more important than home devotion, though, was Bible reading. In 1829, a correspondent for the Philadelphia *Mechanics' Free Press* (*MFP*), the first labor paper in America, submitted an article that the editor titled, "Frequent Reading of the Old and New Testaments Recommended." In Boston, four years later, a booster for the region's principal labor organ, the *New England Artisan,* advised "the Farmers and Mechanics to read [the paper] with as much reverence as they do the Bible."[62]

Given what we know about these activists' religious culture, it should hardly surprise us that their principal authority was the Bible. For, alongside the Second Great Awakening, the first half of the nineteenth century marked the rise and maturation of a movement in American religion whose slogan was "no creed but the Bible," a radical extension of the Reformation doctrine *sola scriptura.* Although Protestants from the Reformation through the First Great Awakening of the eighteenth century had advanced that doctrine, it was not until the Second Great Awakening that the Bible, without any mediation of the clergy, was turned against theology and tradition and became a weapon in the hands of the common people mounting a revolution against established authority. By the 1840s, some contemporaries believed, this scriptural Christianity—a kind of "populist hermeneutics"—had in fact become the dominant characteristic of American religion, with the King James Version the apparent authority for all thought and action.[63]

Antebellum labor activists were heir to this tradition. One such rebel, who grew up in what she described as a recently settled part of the country where there was little means of formal education, was typical of other Americans in that the Bible had been the main source of her early instruction. That education was moral and social as well as intellectual, for, she said, Scripture had taught her duty to God, neighbors, and self, and, too, "that justice and mercy are attributes of his character, and that there is no respect of persons with him." All this would come back to her later in life when, as a domestic servant, this future labor advocate would be exposed to the invidious distinctions of wealth and power both at work and at church.[64] Here, in other words, was a moral and ethical yardstick by which to judge contemporary events, in both the material and spiritual realms, a fund of bedrock values on which to draw when antebellum Americans confronted a rapidly changing world.[65]

Although church attendance was more problematical for labor activists, for reasons discussed in coming chapters, it was not uncommon for workers to also claim the mantle of loyal practitioners of the faith. Sometimes, this could take the form of individual resistance to the dictates of an employer, as it was for a young and defiant domestic servant named Mary Adams in 1832. The product of Scottish-Irish and English ancestry and life on a New Hampshire farm, Adams quietly protested to a prospective master who suggested that she help his wife on Sundays should she come to work for his family. "I should rather think it my duty to attend public meeting," she admonished him.[66] Claims of faithful churchgoing could also offer legitimacy for groups of resistant workers. Two years after Adams made her case, a Boston workingman insisted in the labor press that there were very few "unbelievers" in the Boston Trades' Union, asserting that the overwhelming majority were in fact churchgoing Christians. The editor agreed, praising these "respectable" men "who number among them a large proportion of church members and pew holders."[67] A generation later, a Boston shipyard worker told the Massachusetts Bureau of Statistics of Labor that in the 1850s the demand for increased wages among working people came "almost exclusively" from those who attended religious services.[68]

But the religiosity of antebellum labor dissent went beyond even this commitment to home devotion, biblical authority, and church attendance. In some instances, labor protest literally manifested itself as a religious enterprise—in keeping with the democratic theological revolution of the age—blurring the lines between secular and spiritual reform, between demands of the flesh and needs of the spirit, as activists sought to make whole again what capitalism had torn asunder. The movement's style was, in fact, often decidedly evangelical. This was so despite the fact that many were not members of evangelical churches and that the overwhelming majority abhorred the efforts of certain evangelical societies (the "Benevolent Empire") to enforce "proper" behavior on the community, upholding instead the right of private conscience.[69] They were crusaders nonetheless. Perfectly attuned to the spirit of the age, antebellum labor activism often took on the characteristics of a religious crusade, its style and methods of organizing reflecting the evangelicalism that permeated the broader culture.

How else can one explain the nature of the labor upsurge of the mid-1840s, when workers and their allies came together in the New England Workingmen's Association (NEWA)?[70] In 1846, the editorial committee at the *Voice of Industry*, organ of the association and the leading labor newspaper of the day, exhorted its readers to circulate copies of the newspaper in language redolent of contemporary religious proselytizers: "God said, 'let there be light!' We say so too—and when the light shall become universal, the present system of unmitigated toil and servitude shall flee away before its glorious brightness." The path to this great future was the wide dissemination of truth, in the tradition of all great evangelical movements, including those of the antebellum era. "What has not been performed by tracts and papers?" the editors asked. "Where would not have been the so-called orthodox societies, if it had not been for the circulation of tracts?" They then called on their minions to emulate the evangelicals' success, declaring, "Let *us* profit by their example." Here were Christian soldiers ready to spread the Word—only theirs was the gospel message of labor.[71]

In the same spirit, Fall River workers, who had issued the call to establish the NEWA, used evangelical hymns during their local struggle for the ten-hour day. Appropriating the style and melody of the "Gospel Banner," they fashioned their own "Ten-Hour Banner" to advance the central demand of their movement. Their numbers included church members from a range of Fall River churches; on one occasion they met at the local Universalist chapel, and there the choir of the Mechanics' Association struck up this chorus:

> Now be the 'ten hour' banner,
> In every land unfurl'd;
> And be the shout hosana,
> Re-echoed thru the world.
> Till ev'ry isle and nation,
> Till ev'ry tribe and tongue,
> Receive the great salvation,
> And join the happy throng.

The tune came from a religious hymn, the site was a church, the singers were congregants—but it was to the glorious mission of labor reform that those in attendance were pledging themselves.[72]

The appropriation of evangelical language, frame of reference, and practice can be seen as well among the mill girls. So, a poet in the Lowell FLRA, a constituent group of the NEWA, exhorted her sisters in 1846 to "chide the sinful, turn the erring," while another cajoled the uninitiated, "Come! join ye this worthy band / And drive oppression from the land."[73] Another reminded her compatriots in a sister association in Manchester, New Hampshire, that they would probably meet many "faithless and indifferent ones," who must be shown "the error of their ways."[74] Meanwhile, the Manchester FLRA itself vowed not to suffer factory evils "without our testimony against them."[75] At "social gatherings" and "fairs" in Lowell, Manchester, and elsewhere during this upsurge, female operatives joined with male workers in "nigh fancying ourselves in a 'better land' where sin and oppression were unknown."[76] The language and imagery fit a movement whose votaries believed it had been brought into being by an irresistible religious impulse. In its quarterly report to the NEWA in April 1846, the Lowell group talked of a "spirit abroad in the world" that would not be stilled until justice, right, and brotherhood were established throughout the land. "Let no one disregard the holy, benevolent promptings of this heaven-driven spirit in the soul," the association cautioned, "but rather heed its kind warnings, and obey faithfully its imperative commands!"[77] Here was nothing less than the adoption—absorption, really—of the evangelical style by labor activists.

Though most fully and dramatically rendered in this moment of labor upsurge, the adoption of an evangelical style was unique to neither New England nor the 1840s. In the fall of 1833, for example, the Baltimore labor newspaper the *Mechanics' Banner and Working Men's Shield* noted "a spirit of holy enthusiasm" among local striking journeymen hatters. They have proclaimed "to those who would question their heaven-born and blood-bought privilege to think and act for themselves," the editors of the *Shield* wrote, " 'so far shalt thou come and no farther.' "[78] Three years later, the editor of the *National Trades' Union (NTU)* in New York castigated the master tailors of that city for their "combination against the journeymen," imploring them to "forsake their evil ways and sin no more."[79] In Philadelphia nearly twenty years after this, the Association of Working Women and Men, who called themselves the "Pioneers of the Second Coming of the Savior," published the *Jubilee,* in which they spoke of a coming "new birth," "the great change" that would inaugurate "Heaven on earth." To that end, they met on Sundays during the early and mid-1850s at their "Jubilee Grove" in what they themselves described as "a great revival."[80]

What all these various activists evinced was not merely the trappings of religious zeal. When an *MFP* correspondent took his pseudonym from the Old Testament ("Genesis"), he also wrote that a successful assault on the "American Nobility" required, most of all, "piety toward our Creator."[81] Moreover, the rhetoric of antebellum labor was often explicitly committed to Christian reasoning as well as to Christian forms. Living in a society where Christianity was the arbiter of value, they turned to basic Christian doctrine, *as a matter of course,* for arguments against an emerging economic and social system that they had come to believe degraded both workers and the community at large. Weaned on the Bible, they measured contemporary conditions by the light of Scripture and found society wanting, a situation made all the more painful since that society professed vociferously a Christian foundation. In their view, this "so-called Christian civilization" cried out for redemption. And they were to be its redeemers.

In a fundamental sense, then, the early American labor movement was something of a Christian movement, too, and it is a mistake to try to entirely separate the two. In effect, these activists were both social reformers and religious reformers. Indeed, they drew no distinction between the religious and social reform they advocated. In their worldview, the material and the spiritual were inexorably linked: humanity could not prosper without Christianity, and Christianity could not flourish in a world of degradation and misery. Thus rendered, the quest for salvation became at once social and individual, a religion of works as well as of faith.

Reflecting this basic orientation, activists frequently testified that their goal was the establishment of "practical Christianity," a kind of early version of the Social Gospel—only here welling up from the grassroots, rather than brought to workers from an estranged clergy—which called for the application of the tenets and spirit of the gospel to everyday life.[82] Tirelessly criticizing "professed Christians" who attended church while violating God's law by oppressing their fellow men, *Voice* editor William Young dreamed of the day when "justice shall dwell among men and the pure principles of christianity be made *practical*," when Christians would practice "deeds of justice to man and *practical* devotion to the laws of God."[83] A dedicated Christian who adhered to no particular creed and apparently eschewed church membership until relatively late in life, Young even went so far as to proclaim, in this land of the Puritan, "works must be the test of our faith."[84] "True religion manifests itself in outward expressions," he told his readers, "'by their fruits ye shall know them.'"[85]

Nearly twenty years earlier, "Paul," another *MFP* correspondent taking a biblical pseudonym, had made the same point in the first installment of his column, "Practical Christianity." After a long biblical exegesis of the doctrine of works as contrasted to the "falsity of profession," he proclaimed, "show me thy faith without thy works, and I will show thee my faith by my works."[86] But, perhaps the quintessential statement of this view among antebellum labor activists was uttered by Young's collaborator at the *Voice*, D. H. Jaques, when he asked working men and women, "Is our christianity only a name?" The choice was clear, Jaques insisted, for those "who believing in Jesus of Nazareth, believe also in the practicability of obedience to his precepts"—namely, establish the Christian religion in the community through labor reform, or live in a world that betrayed God and religion.[87] Here, then, was a standard neither secular nor religious but both, and the only appropriate one by which to judge contemporary society for many labor activists.[88]

It was within this framework that they denounced contemporary society— an economic system of exploitation, oppression, and poverty and a social system of selfishness, corruption, and strife, they said—as a betrayal of Christianity. Hence, as labor reformers, their demand was for spiritual sustenance as well as for daily bread. "Modern society," the editorial page of the *Voice* proclaimed in 1846, was "infidel to God and to man." Though contemporary civilization professed Christianity, its organization prevented human beings from living a practical Christian life. Drawing on their cherished Bible, and citing two of labor's favorite injunctions, they continued:

> Christianity says, 'thou shalt love they neighbor as thyself.' 'All things whatsoever ye would that men should do unto you, do ye even so unto them.' Is not the lesson which society instills into the minds of every one on entering its atmosphere of selfishness exactly the reverse of this?[89]

This predicament formed a major theme in the labor expression of the period. As Young asked, "Can men become christians and moralists while mammon overrules the laws of God?"[90] The great labor orator Seth Luther had answered the question in biblical language a decade earlier, quoting Jesus: "YE CANNOT SERVE GOD AND MAMMON," he told the workingmen of Charlestown.[91] Plainly, for such activists, true religion could only thrive in a world actually operating on Christian principles.[92]

Here then was labor activism as a religious endeavor. Typically, Young captured the essence of the creed in an editorial in which he sought to explain the broad-based goals of the New England Workingmen's Association. "We wish to make people christians," he stated simply, "by placing them in christian relations." Others claimed as much, if in somewhat different language, concerning more mundane matters. Thus, Robert McFarlane, founder and leading light of the Mechanics' Mutual Protection Association (MMPA), an artisan fraternal order that spread through the northeast during the 1840s: "It is our Christian duty that our mechanics should be better paid for their labor."[93] But if labor needed a mandate for a long list of other demands—and McFarlane advocated working-class mutuality and self-respect through "small but universal ownership" of property, public education, the shorter workday, an end to seasonal as well as long-term unemployment, and workers' cooperatives—one was readily available in Scripture. The Ten Commandments, McFarlane told the readers of the MMPA newspaper, the *Mechanics' Mirror*, constituted the "working-man's charter of rights."[94]

We glimpse the same conflation of the demand for radical religion and radical social action in the Lowell mill girls' endorsement of the ten-hour day as a step toward the reestablishment of primitive Christianity.[95] For the Lowell mill women, as for Young and McFarlane, shorter hours, decent wages, and fair treatment at the workplace were basic Christian demands. And, therefore, only by eradicating poverty and dependency, and all that came in their wake—the fruits of the capitalist revolution—could humanity achieve the lofty goal of "improv[ing] the moral and religious condition of the world"—which, in a word, is precisely what many antebellum labor activists believed they were trying to do.[96]

Chapter 2. The Problems
They Faced: Labor and Infidelity

America might be "infidel to God and to man," as the *Voice of Industry* claimed, but labor's opponents insisted on precisely the opposite: that labor activism itself heralded the rise of religious infidelity. Try as they might, activists could not reject this charge out of hand, and it portended difficulties for their fledgling labor movement. Not all Americans of the era embraced the Protestant heritage described in the last chapter; many disagreed on exactly what that heritage was.[1] And among early labor activists, as we shall see, the orthodox rubbed shoulders with the heterodox, the churched with the unchurched, the "professing Christian" with the "Free Enquirer." Moreover, while many of the more traditional Christians in this movement had come to social reform out of an adherence to religious principles and imperatives, the "heretics" among them had often come to social reform out of a rejection of orthodox manifestations of religion. If Protestantism was a common heritage that could unify workers and provide the basis for resistance and protest, religious differences within the movement invited attack and could promote division and impotence. Infidelity, whether real or imagined, was thus a problem for every labor activist, regardless of religious orientation.

One solution was to eschew theological disputation—or indeed any hint of religious contentiousness at all—in the belief that such discussions would only weaken an always tenuous unity within the young movement. But, despite many early efforts at this, activists achieved little success in avoiding the subject. Ultimately, forced to confront the charge of infidelity in a world where religion mattered deeply, they returned to the subject again and again. In the process, they revealed a bewildering variety of working-class religious expression in early American labor movements that coexisted—if sometimes uneasily—alongside a basic commitment to a laborite version of the "true" Christian faith. Over time, it was the voice of religion, not irreligion, that captured the public persona of early working-class protest.

Confronting the Infidelity Charge

The infidelity issue arose from the very beginning, though its genesis is complex. The emergence of an organized and vocal Freethought movement in the late 1820s was in part a response to the rise of an organized and vocal orthodox movement that sought to purge America of sin and remake the nation in its own image.[2] Facilitated on the national level by the revolutions in transportation and communication and the waxing of nationalist sentiment after the War of 1812, this Benevolent Empire, in gestation since the 1780s, established itself through the creation of several interdenominational voluntary associations between 1815 and 1826. Then, coincident with some of the most intense revivalism of the Second Great Awakening, these elements mounted a high-profile national campaign to ban the delivery of the mails on the Sabbath.[3] For many, the danger of this crusading orthodoxy crystallized in the call during the 1828 presidential campaign for a "Christian party in politics," which seemed to portend a re-union of church and state.[4] In fact, many "believers," including many evangelicals, were alarmed by this—such political religion was unchristian and anti-American, they said—but it was positively mortifying to freethinkers of all sorts, labor activists among them. Typically, these activists portrayed the danger emanating from among affluent orthodox churchmen as the threat of "aristocracy."[5]

At the same time, with the emergence of widespread and sustained working-class protest, opponents of labor reform, as self-styled defenders of the faith, railed against what they claimed were the harbingers of irreligion. Though clearly here again the orthodox availed themselves of what Martin Marty has called the "useful image" of the infidel, it is not difficult to imagine how they might have perceived widespread and sustained working-class protest and the situation generally. After all, they were witnessing the emergence of local, regional, and, by the mid-1830s, even national labor associations and political parties, whose ranks included advocates of redistributing property, and whose tactics sometimes embraced strikes, which occasionally led to violence. They also noted a proliferation, particularly in large urban centers, of public celebrations of Paine's birthday, societies of Free Enquirers, and Freethought newspapers, all of which were characterized by a general questioning of authority, sometimes including the church, the clergy, the Bible, Christ, Christianity, religion, and even—though in rare cases—the very existence of God.[6] The connections between these two movements were not lost on the business, political, and clerical elements they often targeted. After all, the Freethought movement seemed to flourish, especially in urban centers like New York City, among the emerging working class. Their leaders included the British immigrant artisan George Henry Evans, editor of the *Working Man's Advocate,* and the communitarians Robert Dale Owen and Frances Wright, editors of the notorious Freethought paper, the *Free Enquirer.*[7]

The alarm against rising infidelity among the working classes was sounded by a wide variety of groups, including both orthodox and liberal churchmen, entrepreneurs and politicians, reformers and intellectuals. In 1834, sure that all his readers would agree that religion was the foundation of order and morality in all communities, the wealthy Boston reformer and philanthropist Samuel Gridley Howe warned that tens of thousands now filled the anti-Christian ranks—with several large societies of Free Enquirers in New York City, organized Freethought groups in Boston, Providence, Wilmington, and Philadelphia, reports of hundreds of heretics as yet unorganized in places like Lowell, and numerous papers providing them an open forum for their "atheism." Howe prodded the well-to-do to respond to these infidels who, he said, were turning the poor against the rich.[8] A few years after the appearance of Howe's essay, clergyman Hubbard Winslow warned that the "reckless and revolutionary" spirit of infidelity was rendering some workers "dangerous men to the Republic," and a few years after that, Whig publicist and Episcopal bishop Alonzo Potter suggested that the cure for the baleful influence of the infidel labor unions was the promotion of "a pure and undefiled religion."[9] Like Christian labor activists, these defenders of the faith insisted that secular and religious protest went hand-in-hand, the difference here being that they sought to put an end to both.

Now, the truth of such claims about the extent of infidelity among antebellum America's poor and working population is difficult to gauge.[10] By the early 1830s, churchmen and self-proclaimed Free Enquirers alike were alternately decrying and hailing the erosion of orthodoxy, but both sides, for their own obvious reasons, were clearly exaggerating the extent of Freethought's popularity within the broader culture. In his exhaustive study of the letters and diaries of ordinary Americans during this period, Lewis Saum found little irreligion among commoners, concluding that this was "a supremely religious society working feverishly to become more so."[11] Most labor activists at the time would surely have agreed. Typical was the *MFP* correspondent "Yorick," who in 1829 lamented the numbers of poor driven to madness and suicide "in a Christian country, where almost all profess to be followers of him whose commands were 'Do unto others as ye would have others to do unto you, and love your neighbors as yourselves.'"[12] And, indeed, much of the railing at the time against the alleged rising infidelity was often more about "professors" who had defiled the Sabbath with work and play, and abandoned their Bible reading and family prayer, than it was about the unchurched masses.[13]

Moreover, whatever its actual size, antebellum Freethought no more represented a single religious point of view than did evangelical Protestantism. Many Freethinkers, for example, rejected the infidel label, and, in their own defense, were careful to point out the hyperbole of their opponents.[14] Also, the strength of organized Free Enquiry varied considerably by region and community structure; its presence was noticeably weaker (or nonexistent) in large parts of New

England and in small towns and villages throughout the country. And finally, both the class character of infidelity and the infidel character of labor, as we shall see later in this chapter, existed more in the minds of those sounding the alarm than in the reality of those movements themselves. In hindsight, the problem was not nearly as great as the feverish discussions of the day would suggest.

Still, in this self-consciously Christian society, laborites were concerned to counter any public perception that their movement—and, more broadly, the rise of the working class—signaled the collapse of the Christian Republic. Take the Working Men's movement, which articulated a program of broad-based labor reform during the late 1820s and early 1830s.[15] In Woodstock, Vermont, the Working Men complained in the summer of 1830, "we are charged with being Deists and Infidels."[16] Just days later, the editor of the establishment Boston *Courier* insisted that the Working Men's party in his city had been formed "under the patronage of Fanny Wright," who had been touring the northeastern United States advocating women's rights, labor reform, and deism, acquiring along the way the sobriquet, "the Red Harlot of Infidelity."[17] Similar charges were made against the movement in Philadelphia and New York, with the desired effect.[18] Indeed, in the latter city, from the beginning the local press referred to Working Men candidates for political office as the "Infidel Ticket" and the movement generally as the "poor and deluded followers of a crazy atheistical woman." And, in fact, the key factional division here was rooted at least in part in a religious controversy between the Owenites ("communist infidels") and the Cookites ("Church and State men"), each blaming the other for raising the issue.[19]

Laborites thus had no choice but to respond in some way. The range of responses reveals a complex religious terrain, but the nature of those responses reveals just how profoundly Christian this movement actually was. One common tack was to simply announce—in labor papers, in speeches, and most directly in resolutions of workers' gatherings—that labor was bound to no religious creed or party and that it would brook no discussion of the subject within its ranks. Some among the Working Men tried this approach.[20] The analogue to this distaste for theological disputation was a similarly vehement distaste for political contention; both underscore the fear of division that permeated this movement. Thus, the *Working Man's Friend* of Cincinnati in 1836: "Bound to no *political, religious,* or anti-religious party, we design to dedicate our labor to the elucidation and defence of the rights and privileges of the producing classes."[21] The disapprobation here was of "party," or particularism, which was to be avoided because it pitted one against another when the true destiny of humanity was to live in harmony.[22] True, for many nineteenth-century Americans, politics was something dirty at its roots, while Christianity was rarely so reviled, but in both cases the objection was to the spirit of antagonism engendered by the corruptions of basic human needs and desires, which should remain "pure and undefiled." In this way, the opposition to party—religious or political—was a call for unity and purity.[23]

Thoroughly typical of this stance was the religious position taken by the *National Trades' Union (NTU)*, organ of the short-lived group of the same name in the mid-1830s, the first such national union in the United States. Responding to an article in the *Long Island Farmer*, which not too subtly suggested that advertisements for "atheistical works" in the labor paper rendered the constituent unions of the National Trades' Union "disciples and missionaries of infidelity," the editors denounced the charge as "altogether erroneous." Admitting that there may have been some allied to the movement who "both surreptitiously and openly" advocated their individual religious views (a right protected by the Constitution, they reminded the *Long Island Farmer*), they insisted that "the inculcation of any religious or irreligious creeds, constitutes no part of the objects of the Trades Unions, nor of those properly devoted to their advancement." To make the point absolutely clear, the editors declared, "*we* have nothing to do, in our public capacity, with the religious opinions of any," advocating only "the physical—the moral—the intellectual powers of society," and leaving religion a matter "between man and his Creator."[24]

Obviously a way of avoiding internal divisions, as well as muting the charges of infidelity, this strategy nevertheless demonstrated the overweaning power of religion in the prevailing culture.[25] Indeed, it reflected a broad religious tradition that swept across the spectrum of Christian labor activists, from liberal to orthodox.[26] To be sure, as is evident in the *NTU*'s protestations, the argument was always grounded in the sanctity of individual liberties—"we oppose no man's private feelings," was the way the editors of the Utica, New York, *Mechanics' Press* put it in 1830—which was, in great measure, a reaction to attempts at enforcing a common standard of public behavior by political means.[27] But this civil liberties position was regularly advanced on religious grounds, with the New York *WMA*, for example, insisting that if the Bible were "candidly consulted," men would understand their religious rights.[28]

It is important to note that, although officially tolerant of all views, labor sought to silence discussion of theological matters more from fear of the heretics offending the orthodox than the reverse, and in virtually all instances, as we shall see, when a dispute arose the latter's voice drowned out the former's. In this respect, labor's attitude toward religion was fundamentally different from its attitude toward politics—because "true" religion was recognized by virtually everyone as an essential (and beneficial) force in a decent society, while politics was, at best, a necessary evil. And, though the "Manifesto of the Principles of the Working Men of New York" might insist in the summer of 1832 that religion was not a public but a strictly private concern, the drafters' primary purpose, once again, was to oppose sectarian religious legislation (i.e., political religion), not to deny the importance of religious principles and spirituality in ordering society.[29] To the contrary, particularly in New England

and areas heavily populated by New Englanders, labor activists insisted on reinfusing religion into a world increasingly dominated by the laws of supply and demand over the laws of God. Moreover, that sentiment would deepen as time passed.

And, in fact, all of the best efforts of these activists to the contrary, they could not answer the infidelity charge—potent as it was—simply by declaring neutrality and attempting to suppress debate. The charge "infidel!" in that day was something akin to what "communist!" would become a hundred years later.[30] Thus, a second tack was to point out the indiscriminate and therefore false application of the accusation. As the prolabor New York *Man* noted, in reprinting a piece in the Providence *Herald:* the orthodox called the Unitarians "infidels," both used it to denounce the Universalists, all three similarly accused the deists, and then *they* joined in stigmatizing Owen and Wright in the same manner![31] And yet, this strategy, too, failed to respond adequately to the crux of the charge—namely, that labor actually opposed religion in general and Christianity in particular. Consequently, labor's most common response was a third tack: simple, forthright, and sometimes righteous denial. Hence, for example, an editorial in the *WMA* had this to say about Frances Wright: "Miss Wright has boldly and strenuously advocated the cause of irreligion. If this is 'Wrightism,' we *do not* wish to build up the superstition of 'Wright.'"[32]

In all this, it appears there was a mixture of calculation and genuine senti-ment. Certainly this was the case with Massachusetts labor advocate George Dickinson. When he asked the popular Jacksonian orator George Bancroft to speak before a gathering of workingmen in 1835, Dickinson made specific reference to the infidel charge, expressing his hope that the speaker could set the record straight. Dickinson found the label particularly ironic, as he indi-cated in a private letter to Bancroft. "It would be highly satisfactory," he wrote, "if the opportunity should be embraced to vindicate the party from some of the calumny with which they have been assailed and particularly the charge that the party is principally composed of unbelievers in the christian system. This is a singular charge when the great object of the workingmen is to place the business of society on the basis of the moral righteousness of Christianity."[33] Dickinson sought help for his movement, but there is no reason to doubt his sincerity. Here again was the claim, this time in private correspondence, that labor reform was in fact a form of religious mission.

In some cases, to be sure, this stance meant a softening of labor radicalism, at least in the movement's public posture. Because their opponents so often linked their denunciations of irreligion to attacks on radicalism, activists some-times found it desirable to simultaneously repudiate "agrarianism," or social leveling.[34] Thus, while proclaiming its support for the movement of the "pro-ducing classes," the *Mechanics' Press* at once rejected "an equal division of property" and "the name of Infidel." On the latter subject, the editors declared that on behalf of "the mechanics . . . few would wish that body to bear the title of Infidel," for "Religion is the school of morality, without which the condition of man is little above that of the wild beast."[35] In this, of course, they echoed the popular belief in religion as the essential bulwark of a healthy social order that even eighteenth-century rationalists had insisted on. But, in denying not only infidelity but radicalism as well, some labor activists tacitly accepted the link between the two.

Not all, though. A decade after Dickinson's letter, labor activists in New England were still fighting the same accusations. Far from being harbingers of infidelity, they said, as labor reformers, they were Christianity's true defenders. Instead, they castigated their opponents, defenders of prevailing social arrangements, as the true infidels. Here, labor sought to redefine the terms of the debate, turning the accusers into the accused. "The cry of *Infidelity* . . . salutes the ear," a mill girl leader in Lowell lamented in the 1840s. But, she went on, "if it is infidelity to plead for justice and right—in God's name we are willing to be branded with the title—we fear little the *name* and much less the influence which such unchristian epithets will have over the minds of a thinking community."[36] At one point, this stance actually became the official position of the New England labor movement as a whole. "Infidelity," an NEWA resolution proclaimed in 1845, "is the denial, either by practice or precept, of the great fundamental law of 'doing unto others, as you would that they should do unto you,' upon which all genuine religion is based, and that those who oppose and denounce the workingmen's reform as being 'irreligious' and those who openly and willfully violate this righteous principle . . . have 'denied the faith,' and are more guilty than those they so unjustly represent." Those who fought on behalf of labor, on the other hand, were "true" Christians, these workingmen insisted, for it was this movement that sought to convert society, as Dickinson had said a decade earlier, to "practical Christianity."[37] The infidel label, then, was merely a smear, a way of denigrating the movement without confronting its true character. It was, in short, the enemies of labor "employing the image of the infidel to their own ends."[38]

Confronting the Infidel Within

It was not as simple as this, of course. For there was an enormous diversity of religious opinion within this fledgling movement. And, despite labor's frequent denials, there was in fact an organized heretical presence in their ranks, who usually went by the name "Free Enquirers."[39] Moreover, although there was tremendous diversity within this element as well—including, for example, those who rejected and those who embraced the name "infidel"—these Freethinkers constituted a force to be reckoned with for both the broader movement and its enemies. And yet, in the end, the salient characteristic of antebellum infidelity was its relative isolation, being restricted to major urban centers, to areas outside New England, and largely to the late 1820s and early 1830s. Indeed, the size, nature, and ephemerality of antebellum Freethought underscores the general point: a product of a militantly Christian world, the basic character of the early American labor movement reflected much of that militant Christianity.[40]

Consider the fate of attacks on orthodox Christianity from within the movement in urban New England. A significant Freethought movement— with a press and an organizational life—did arise in Boston during the 1830s, if not generally in the region's countryside. Even in this major urban center, though, the more traditional religious elements among the working class rendered such apostasy relatively insignificant. The city's Freethinkers never approached, either in political strength or in numbers, those of New York City or Philadelphia. When Abner Kneeland, probably the most famous heretic of the age, came to Boston in 1831, he found a working class and labor movement quite different from the one he had left behind in New York. As noted, in New York, where he had formulated most of his ideas on social and political questions, important sections of organized labor were closely associated with a small circle of Freethinking British immigrants. In Boston, however, where Kneeland started his Freethought paper, the *Investigator,* and promoted lectures and social gatherings to spread the gospel of skepticism, he found not only a generally unreceptive audience among most workers, but an organized opposition within the labor movement itself. Moreover, this resistance to heretical ideas would grow with time.[41]

By the 1840s, Kneeland's successors sometimes found it difficult to even gain a hearing for their position. Though the *Investigator* remained a mouthpiece for Freethought prolabor sentiment within the labor movement proper, its voice was weak and often silenced by the preponderantly Christian working-class element in the city. In fact, in 1844 the first NEWA meeting excluded Horace Seaver, Kneeland's editorial successor at the *Investigator.*[42] Disregarding his newspaper's support for their movement, the delegates apparently believed that allowing a well-known infidel to sit in a workingmen's convention would damage their image among other workers and the general public. Similarly, the NEWA's organ, the *Voice of Industry,* censored the views of a prominent Freethinking Boston trade unionist named J. J. Mitchell, who wrote frequently in the *Investigator,* when he sought to counter a mill girl's argument that the Bible was the sole source of truth in the world. Though Mitchell was a regular contributor to the *Voice* as well, editor William Young refused to print his letter.[43] The case is a revealing one.

Clearly, Young's editorial policy reflected the prevalent fear among antebellum labor leaders of sectarian division within the movement. In refusing Mitchell's letter, he expressed his apprehension that "a discussion of this subject would be unsatisfactory to both parties and in some respects unprofitable," as it would encourage bigotry and dissension in the ranks. But there was more to it than that. After all, the article to which Mitchell objected had pronounced the sacred texts the only means for understanding "the real character and condition of the Deity, his eternal destiny, the way in which he may be delivered from the effects of evil and the whorship and services he owed to his almighty Creator." The author had further contended that humanity was destined for "eternal progression," that the present world was only a "transitory scene," and that the "Bible is a revelation from God to man" whose truths must be embraced. This paean to Scripture, representing the orthodox Christian view within the labor movement and reflective of powerful devotional currents in the broader culture, was printed in the *Voice* without comment.[44] Moreover, in explaining his decisions about what to print and what not to print, editor Young informed his readership that he adhered to "the fundamental principles of Christianity promulgated in the Bible," while Mitchell had sought to prove the Bible "an absurdity and the religion founded upon it, erroneous and superstitious."[45] And that was simply too much for the oracle of New England labor in the 1840s.

In fact, even Young—though a devout Christian—was not sufficiently orthodox for many of his readers, some of whom seem to have successfully pressured him to temper his own freethinking. A year before the Mitchell incident, for example, Young was attacked for an alleged lack of vigilance regarding another *Voice* article about Scripture. The essay in question had suggested that the Bible was internally contradictory and therefore not a proper guide to social and political arrangements. Significantly, Young printed this one, but not without editorial comment, as he would the mill woman's piece a year later. Here, he felt constrained to point out that the author, drawing largely on the Old Testament, had confused what Young called "old Jewish notions" with the religion of Jesus, whose doctrine was " 'love' or 'whatsoever ye would that men should do unto you, do ye even so unto them.' "[46] In the effort, the editor sought to defend the New Testament gospel as an inspiration and guide, distinguishing his religion from the harsher spirit of the Old Testament. This caveat alone did not satisfy some of his readers, though. A month later, Young lamented that some who were "friendly to the cause" had heaped censure upon him and the newspaper for printing the article at all, several even canceling their subscriptions. Vehement in their condemnation of any kind of freethought, a few of the complainants unceremoniously reminded the editor of the state's blasphemy laws![47]

Outside New England, the nature of working-class infidelity was not significantly different. In New York State, the *Mechanics' Press* insisted in 1830 that "if infidelity can be charged to the Workingmen, it must be done in the city of New York alone; for, out of it, there is not the *least* appearance of truth in the assertion."[48] There is an element of truth in the paper's statement, for Freethought was more significant in the city than in the countryside. But it obscures both the existence of Freethought in certain (usually urban) centers

outside New York City and, more important, the significant Christian composition of the labor movement (and, indeed, even of the Freethought movement)
both inside and outside that city. In Rochester, for example, there was a significant dissenting, sometimes Freethinking, press during the late 1820s and 1830s,
which influenced the development of labor activism there; the range of expression, though, encompassed everything from atheism to what might be called
"anticlerical primitive Christianity."[49] Moreover, the thrust of heterodoxy here,
as in antebellum America generally, was unorthodox Christianity rather than
opposition to Christianity. And again, as in New England, in Rochester an
organized movement of religious dissent outside church walls was fading by the
1840s. As for New York City, probably the center of antebellum Freethought,
there too, a Christian voice could be heard from the earliest stirrings of the
labor movement, a voice that grew louder and more sophisticated over time.[50]
The voice of Freethought, in any case, seems to have been confined to the
leadership, and mostly among the British immigrants in that leadership.[51]

In other important centers of labor activity, like Philadelphia and
Wilmington, Freethought sentiment did gain a hearing in the labor movement,
but here too it took many forms and abated somewhat over time, its heyday
being the late 1820s and early 1830s. In Philadelphia, Freethought was mixed
with Universalism, and in Wilmington, with Hicksite Quakerism. The salient
fact about both places was the enormous diversity of religious opinion in the
labor movement, running the gamut from atheist to orthodox evangelical,
including materialists, various kinds of skeptics, defenders and detractors of
Jesus (as either divine or human), deists, numerous Protestant denominations,
and "come-outers."[52] There were, as well, those who touted universal salvation,
a benevolent, loving God, and the gentle invocations to fairness and mercy of
the New Testament, alongside those who clung to distinctly more orthodox
renderings of the faith: conditional election, a judging and sometimes angry
Lord, and the prescriptions and meted justice of the Old Testament. All this, as
we shall see, was enlisted in the service of labor protest. And, in fact, the story
was much more complex than even this list of religious identifications suggests,
for few fell neatly into any one of these categories alone, generally agreeing on
only a part rather than the whole. As one self-confessed "believer" aptly put it
in addressing his compatriots in the pages of the *Mechanics' Free Press*, "some
of you may be believers, some sceptics," and within these "many
subdivisions—the gradations between the most approved orthodoxy, and the
greatest extent of doubting, are numerous."[53]

This activist knew his audience. For the letters to the editor in the *MFP*, the
mouthpiece of America's first working-class movement, dramatically reveal a
wide and forever-shifting spectrum of religious perspectives—a by-product of
the proliferaton of "dissenting" churches and creeds from the late eighteenth
century onward, which in great measure allowed for the development of a
Freethought movement in the first place.[54] Here we find—in addition to what

appear to be orthodox Christian writers—Quakers and Universalists alongside avowed infidels, vehement disagreements about the infamous Fanny Wright, denials of biblical revelation and paeans to "the authority of revealed religion," including copious quoting from both the Old and New Testaments.[55] And all this, despite the ritual avowals—by editor and correspondent alike—to avoid the subject of religion! As elsewhere, try though they might, Philadelphia labor activists simply could not suppress the issue.

More important, even in a major center of Freethought like Philadelphia during the 1830s, where much of the labor leadership may have been Freethinkers, the *MFP* allowed the voice of Christian labor activism to generally drown out the voice of infidelity.[56] Indeed, Philadelphia verifies what we have already seen: the futile attempts to remain silent on the subject of religion because of the religious fires burning in the breasts of labor activists, the resulting conflicts, and the triumph of the religious over the irreligious. All this can glimpsed in dramatic form in the fierce battles waged for the hearts and minds of the city's working class in the columns of the *Free Press*.

In August 1829, a correspondent calling himself "Silas Simple, Jr.," warned his compatriots, "*Let the subject of Religion alone.*" He then went on to discuss the issue. The "foul charge" that "we oppose the Christian religion, and want it put down," he declared, "must be refuted, and that soon and publickly." Typically, he affirmed his and his movement's faithfulness ("we profess to be favorable to the Christian religion"), while rejecting either legal protection for religion or interference with any individual's creed. But his fire was directed primarily at the infidel: "I earnestly entreat all those who have but this object in view (i.e. the prostration of the Christian faith,) to *let us alone.*" Moreover, he insisted that these were indeed the minority within his movement: "I believe . . . there are few, if any of this description among us; and those who denounce us as infidels, &c. do it to weaken the power they fear, rather than a belief in the slanders to which they give currency."[57]

But, as elsewhere, the problem did not lend itself to simple statements or easy solutions. Three months later, the publishing committee of the Mechanics' Library Company, which made editorial decisions for the paper, announced the rejection of numerous articles that treated "matters not within our range"—that is, religion. Exasperated by the deluge of letters that "relate rather to religious than temporal matters," they declared that they had done their best "to hold the balance as fairly as possible between our orthodox and heterodox correspondents." In fact, the scales appear to have consistently tipped in favor of the former. The editors' reason for refusing to print an attack on "Predestination and Sabbath Schools," for example, was the prospect of being "overw. .ned with replies." Conversely, while also rejecting an attack on Frances Wright, they reminded the author of that piece that they had declined defenses of her as well, and, "so far from showing a partiality to anti-religious essays, we have *suppressed hundreds.*"[58] In other words, there were significant

Freethought elements within the movement, but the leadership seems to have generally silenced them. The subsequent history of the newspaper suggests that this early statement continued to reflect basic editorial policy: as in New England, when there was conflict, it was Freethought sentiment that was excluded rather than Christianity.[59]

And, as at the *Voice, MFP* editorial policy was not the product of an orthodox leadership making decisions contrary to the preponderant interest of the rank-and-file. The editors' position was clearly stated on numerous occasions, most pointedly in their recommending to "all journals devoted to the working men's cause" a Virginia newspaper's warning to the deist editor of the *WMA* for his attack on the American Tract Society. George Henry Evans should remember, the Wheeling, Virginia, *Eclectic Observer* had written, "that the prejudices of men are not to be trifled with, and if once excited, they are never to be removed." Insisting on the absolute importance of steering clear of unnecessary rifts, the *MFP* editors favorably reprinted the *Observer*'s conclusion, which used the terms *secular* and *religious* in the narrowest possible sense: "The interests of our party are of a secular nature; but if we make them religious, we shall certainly fail; for in pecuniary matters we can unite, but in religion we never can. Religion is a subject of practice, rather than newspaper disputation. For it every man is accountable to his own heart and his God."[60] Here, though, it was not Christian language and doctrine that was being banished from the pages of the *Free Press* but, as the context of the *Observer*'s comments makes clear, Freethought attacks on Christianity. The reason is not hard to find: the editors were responding to their constituency.[61]

Even in Philadelphia, then, activists did not—could not—ignore the subject of religion. Moreover, in the pages of the *MFP*, far more common than the occasional antireligious diatribe were communications like the letter from "Investigator" in the summer of 1830. Hardly one of the orthodox (note his pseudonym), he was also probably a freethinker with a small *f*. He was also very definitely a patriot and a Christian. Reminding his readers that the principal causes of the overthrow of republics in the past had been "ignorance, immorality, and irreligion," he promoted the idea of Sabbath school education (a principal subject of contention in the pages of the paper, as in the nation at large), which he argued was a nonsectarian form of intellectual, moral, and spiritual instruction. Choosing a label commonly used by the Freethinkers— and thus revealing the incredible elasticity of language in this age—he suggested that encouragement of Sabbath schools was appropriate "in this age of free enquiry"! America's youth must understand, he cautioned, the "relation which they sustain to God, and to their fellow-men, and the duties which result from this religion."[62] And, significantly, even those who opposed such schools (or at least the American Sabbath School Union) typically proclaimed their commitment to religious training in childhood, insisting, as one put it, that there was no necessary equation of the Sunday school movement and "the calling of children to '*come unto him*' by Christ."[63] Such was the nature of discourse in the pages of Philadelphia's principal labor paper in the Age of Jackson.

The early American labor movement, even in the heyday of organized Freethought, in one of the principal centers of Freethinking, was predominantly Christian, and the activists' most characteristic response to the "infidel within"—even while eschewing any religious contention—was repudiation. Thus, at the founding meeting of the Working Men of Upper Delaware Ward (Philadelphia) in November 1829, the gathering invoked biblical precept ("the labourer is worthy of his hire") to explain their reason for organizing. At the same time, the group found it necessary to resolve, "we disclaim all interference with religious matters, or adherence to Miss Wright's principles, and hold them entirely foreign to our views." What they really meant, then, was that they disavowed any connection to irreligious matters. Accordingly, in their secretary's address that evening, the problem was spelled out in no uncertain terms: Let not the world be deluded, he declared, "that we have some immorality or opposition to religion connected with us. I presume you are as well aware as myself that the moment we introduce a matter of this kind into our contention, we strike at once the death-blow of our cause."

Again, this was not merely the calculation of leaders about the movement's censure by a Christian community, though such considerations obviously played a role. More important was their fundamentally God-centered worldview. Indeed, even their insistence on the right of private judgment was based on fundamentally religious grounds. Thus, this secretary's stated rationale for avoiding the subject in the first place: "Any interference of ours in religious matters would amount to an invasion of the conscience of men, *which the Almighty has created.*"[64]

Chapter 3. The Problems They Faced: Labor and the Infidel Church

Labor's opponents accused them of infidelity not just because of their radicalism and the infidels in their midst. More important perhaps was the blistering attack activists mounted against the hypocrisy, sectarianism, and clergy of a church that they claimed had become infidel to itself. For neither veneration for the Christian deity, Bible, and tradition nor even imitation of evangelical methods required love and respect for what antebellum Americans sometimes referred to derisively as "churchianity." Indeed, quite the opposite in this case: labor activists were among the most vocal of the era's many critics of institutional Christianity as it had emerged in the contemporary world—sometimes even when, as we shall see, they were themselves church members.

Too often, both their contemporaries and their chroniclers have mistaken such "anticlericalism" for hostility to religion. But critics of the church and clergy in the early American labor movement were, generally, pious heirs to the traditional suspicion of church institutions, dogma, and "priests" smoldering in American Protestantism from its inception, with infusions from the English Civil War and the First Great Awakening. The fiery revivalist James Davenport—a product of Puritan New England—had put the matter simply when he demanded, in his harangues against "unconverted" ministers in the 1740s, "don't tell me what creed, only Christianity." In its extreme forms, this critical stance did lead some early-nineteenth-century workers to abandon the established churches altogether.[1] It also, however, tapped a long tradition within Christianity that has been called *chrétiens sans église* ("Christians without a church"), which accepts a perpetual antagonism between Christian values and church institutions and rejects organized religious life as being part of the corrupt world.[2]

Indeed, whenever they spoke harshly of the church, labor activists were careful to distinguish between what they called "true" Christian faith and the contemporary institutions of Christianity.[3] They insisted that worship involved "not a change of garments but a change of hearts," advocating a "practical Christianity" over "unmeaning phrases, forms and ceremonies."[4] Some even argued that there was an inverse relationship between commitment to the faith and fidelity to the present-day church. "Honest attachment" to religion grows, wrote "An Orthodox Seeker" in a prolabor reform journal, at the "same rapid pace that dislike of the church and priestcraft" increases. True to his chosen name, this activist contended that criticism of contemporary religion actually enhanced Christianity's prospects, insisting that his goal was reform of the church rather than its destruction. The idea was to make society more, not less, religious.[5]

But the matter was not quite as simple as "An Orthodox Seeker" implied. As already noted, in antebellum America, church worship was considered an important—if not necessarily required—component of proper Christian devotion.[6] And so, like the charge of infidelity generally, labor's proper relation to the church itself was a problem that could not be ignored. In fact, the issues were not entirely separate. Church attendance was especially poignant for these men and women, in part because business, political, and religious leaders so persistently charged that they and their working-class constituency had abandoned the church and were therefore the primary cause of the alleged rise of infidelity in America. Since many workers had indeed left the church— something activists believed made a certain amount of sense, given the current state of the institution—this particular accusation presented a serious problem for the movement: could activists countenance—indeed encourage— working-class abandonment of the church and still maintain their identity as a Christian movement?

Certainly, activists rejected attempts by employers, like some mill owners, to force workers to go to church.[7] Still, how could men and women fulfill their obligations as "true" Christians outside the bounds of organized religion? Was home worship—Bible study and prayer—enough to cultivate the individual soul and maintain the moral character of the community? Most labor activists thought not, accepting the popular notion that an institutional church was essential to the progress of Christianity, and therefore of the Good Society. After all, even the rabidly anticlerical "Orthodox Seeker" argued for rectification of the church. There was another problem, though: How was this rectification to be brought about? Was it the duty of all Christians to work for reformation from within, or should Christians withdraw and build a purified church outside the contemporary institutions of organized religion?

Not surprisingly, labor activists followed a variety of paths in their quest for a "true" Christian church. There was no typical antebellum labor activist in this regard. Some left the church entirely and worshiped on their own, like the mill girl who urged her sisters "to go out upon the hills, where she might worship in the great temple of the universe, without a priest, as proxy, to stand between her and her Maker."[8] Others withdrew from the mainstream denominations and founded new churches.[9] Some joined prolabor congregations or churches headed by sympathetic ministers. And still others, already members (or, at least, adherents) by the time of their involvement in labor activity—perhaps the largest group—pressured for reform from within. Among the major labor advocates of this period, most remained committed to some kind of organized religious devotion, despite their awareness of the problems within contemporary Christianity.

In the end, antebellum labor activists responded to the charge that they were unfaithful to the church in ambiguous ways, once again reflecting their dual identities as social and religious reformers. Deeply conflicted about their own participation, they sometimes explained labor's negligence as a natural outcome of prevailing conditions, while at other times they condemned it as a dangerous abandonment of the faith. Indeed, Christian labor activists never quite resolved the problem of being Christian in a world that they believed had defiled Christian principles. They were, in a word, ambivalent. Once again, though, their predicament—and how they handled it—serve to underscore the deep religious commitment that underlay their labor activism and, ultimately, their consciousness of themselves as a class.

Labor's Critique of the Church

The Problem of the Sabbath

For workers, the issue of church attendance was inextricably bound up with what might be called the problem of the Sabbath. Sunday, the Christian Sabbath, was observed as the Lord's Day in most parts of America in the early nineteenth century. By the 1830s, rural New England was probably the most traditional sector of the society in this regard, reflecting the customs of the seventeenth and eighteenth centuries: the general practice was only a bare minimum of work on that day, with Bible reading and prayer beginning on Saturday evening.[10] Sunday was devoted to rest and devotion. Elsewhere—in the West, in the new commercial and industrial towns, in the port cities— standards were often more lax and habits less uniform. In general, some erosion of strict adherence to the Sabbath was inevitable, given the centripetal forces of immigration and migration, the revolution in commodity production, commerce, and transportation, and the spread of secular "amusements" like organized sports and games, gambling, circuses, and the theater, voluntary associations like fire companies, fraternal organizations, and unions, and alternative meetingplaces like taverns and public rooms. For workers especially, Sunday was often occupied by things other than devotion: rest (and, perhaps, recreation), marketing (they were sometimes paid on Saturday evening), and even Sabbath labor required by the boss.[11] Wage labor in antebellum America ran up against traditional notions of the Christian Sabbath. Nevertheless, there was a broad consensus that there was something sacred about that day.[12]

However, a fierce debate raged during this period over just how to keep it so. In 1846, the New York *Mechanics' Mirror* printed a story entitled, "The Mechanic Who Would Not Work on the Sabbath."[13] This little tale, set in the late 1830s, a morality play with themes that would resonate in the fiction of the American labor press throughout the nineteenth century, aptly captures what many perceived as a glaring contradiction between capitalist enterprise and Christian piety.[14] Explaining that since his earliest days he had been taught to revere the Sabbath, millwright James Robertson of Fall River reminds his boss, Mr. Thompson, that Scripture prohibited his helping to build a millwheel for him on Sunday: "'Six days shalt thou labor and do all thy work, but the seventh day is the Sabbath, in it thou shalt do no work,' saith the Lord." This was "the greatest boon that ever was granted to poor working men," Robertson says; it was his duty to his Creator, his person, and his fellow workers to protect its sanctity. The perfect foil for this adherent to Christian piety and morality, Mr. Thompson contends that working on that day constituted an act of necessity and mercy, since not working meant that the worker lost wages and the employer lost money. To which Robertson responds: money is not the beginning and end of life for either the rich or the poor. Better liberty with bread and water than the "crown of a pampered monarch," he says; better independence with pudding and milk than wealth, if that wealth means sacrificing freedom of conscience.

Once engaged in this debate, Robertson is the very model of Christian probity. He explains that he is willing to work on Monday, reminding his employer that he has always worked hard and has always sought to be honest. Don't consider me ungrateful, he pleads; only understand that I cannot work on the Sabbath. Typically, the narrator remarks that the words did in fact touch the other man. "Had they been spoke ten minutes before, what happened would not have occurred." For the millwright is fired, even though the boss's daughter, with whom he is much taken, supports his principled Christian position.

And so, Robertson leaves Fall River the following Monday in search of work, choosing the path of righteousness rather than pecuniary reward. The following year (1836)—a "blighting year to commerce, mercantile and land speculation" marked by a "democratic revolution in wealth" in which the rich became poor—boss Thompson's business is destroyed. He manages to pay his debts and purchase some farmland in Michigan. Again, typical of this kind of drama, with its emphasis on mercy, forgiveness, and the basic goodness of humanity, the narrator remarks that few in Fall River were happy to see Thompson go, "for although a haughty man, and could ill brook opposition in opinion, yet he had a kind heart, and many a good act he performed." In any case, in the fall of 1838, the now-itinerant mechanic Robertson happens by Thompson's place after hearing that the owner (he doesn't know it is his old boss) plans to build a sawmill on his stream and needs help erecting the machinery. Despite his having been fired three years earlier, the millwright is glad to see his former employer and grasps his hand warmly. Apparently, Thompson has changed his ways, because Robertson works for him again and marries his daughter, and they raise a family. Their subsequent lives form the very picture of piety and virtue: living in a modest cottage (a "nest"), the children of the mechanic (this "nature's nobleman") play in the yard during the day and sit on their grandfather's knee at night. As for the grandfather, once so much in love with wealth that he defiled the Lord's Day, "in his democratic rural simplicity of life, he experiences a happiness which all the riches of his early life failed to confer."

Among the many revealing aspects of this story is the complaint here, common among antebellum labor activists, that with the rise of wage labor, increased competition, and the scramble for ever-greater profits, employers often demanded that employees work on the Sabbath, preventing them from discharging their duties as good Christians.[15] At the same time, as noted in the last chapter, such activists rejected legally enforced Sabbath observance, or Sabbatarianism, condemning it as anti-Christian and hailing their opposition to it as a defense of religion.[16] They also denounced the requirement of many textile mill owners and others that their employees attend church as a condition of employment. Observance must be voluntary. But, there was more to it than that—even if they were not compelled to work on the Sabbath, the long and arduous hours of labor during the rest of the week left them too tired or too busy with domestic chores to go to church.[17] "Can it be reasonably supposed," asked Sarah Bagley, a labor leader in Lowell who had worked as a mill operative in that city during the late 1830s and early 1840s, "that those who are called to their task every morning at half past five, and kept until seven at night, will have sufficient energy to be constant in their attendance at church on the Sabbath?[18] And, there was still more: the employers and their allies had gained control of the meetinghouse, and church life had become corrupted as a result. As "Lynn Bard, Jr.," put it in the *Voice of Industry,* an "unholy alliance" of church and aristocracy had desecrated the Sabbath. "Purse-proud nabobs," he declaimed, hold a "Bible in one hand and gold in the other" in a devilish copartnership between God and Mammon.[19] Here, the problem of laboring for the capitalist and the problem of attending public services dovetailed. Class distinctions had invaded the church.

The Problem of Wealth

In fact, precisely because the churches were filled with those very employers who, among other things, "compel their help to labor on the Sabbath day or lose their situations," activists insisted that Sabbath worship had become nothing more than a "pastime," signaling a general corruption of institutional Christianity.[20] Such was the emphasis of Sarah Bagley's many commentaries on the church in her capacity as editor of the *Voice* in 1846. The leading female labor activist of her day, as founder and president of the Lowell FLRA, officer of the NEWA, and delegate to national reform conventions, this product of a pious home and New Hampshire common schools repeatedly expressed her concerns about the operatives' difficulties in taking advantage of Lowell's many churches.[21] Her principal focus was the social distinctions within the various congregations, which, she insisted, violated not only American republicanism but the egalitarian traditions in Protestant Christianity. "Our Agents and the aristocratic class to which they belong," she wrote, "have ordained fashion in dress and equipage, which the operative is unable to follow, and they must at any rate *ape them,* or they will be wanting in self-respect." As for the operative who went to meeting in her "plain country dress" because she simply could find neither the time nor the money to keep her "wardrobe in church-going order," she is "almost stared out of countenance."[22] Moreover, the employers enjoyed the same dominant position in the meetinghouse that they held in the workplace. "Is it strange," Bagley asked, "that the operatives should stay away from the churches where they see the men filling the 'chief seats,' who are taking every means to grind them into the very dust?"[23] As women and as workers, she insisted, the operatives found in the local meetinghouse in Lowell a distinctly inhospitable environment.

Most antebellum labor activists located the principal source of working-class antipathy to the church in this patent hypocrisy of the institution, which in turn mirrored the inequities and distortions of an unjust social system. Seth Luther spent the 1820s as an itinerant carpenter, mill worker, and laborer.[24] In his many travels, he experienced firsthand the contradictions of capitalism in this Christian Republic, particularly the conspicuous display of wealth and comfort amidst the poverty and misery in mill towns and commercial centers. Hence his cry: "While debtors sleep on the damp floor of Boston's jails, how can I sit easy, and look on splendid pulpits, and crimson damask curtains, pews lined with costly stuffs, luxuriously carpeted and cushioned, for the seat of the opulent?"[25] Philadelphia's "Peter Single," who very likely read Luther's sentiments when they were published in pamphlet form, would have recognized an affinity with his New England compatriot in this regard. A few years earlier, writing in the *Mechanics' Free Press,* he complained of the developing distinctions in the contemporary church. Today, he lamented, "the old fashioned churches are too common for members of 'good society'; hence the splendor of our modern churches, and the downfall of the old."[26] For this activist, though, the problem penetrated virtually every aspect of church life, even singing. "When I went to church (which implies, gentle reader, that I do not go now)," he began one column, the clerk read out the hymn or psalm and everyone sang. But now, he said, the music was the province of a few, who were tutored and drilled in this now-fine art, who have made of it a "property" of theirs.[27]

Workers who had imbibed the biblical precept that the Lord is "no respecter of persons"—one of the favored scriptural slogans of the age—angrily pointed out that God's house was defiled by these social distinctions. In this vein, a Fall

River working man described his view of a typical laborer's Sabbath in a letter to a local labor paper in 1844. On Saturday evening, he began, "the christian laborer . . . rejoices that a day is coming, that he can read his bible, pray with his family and go to the house of prayer." But churchgoing was an arduous, demeaning, even torturous affair for many workers. The writer pictured "a poor laborer . . . as if he had a ton of leather on his shoe sole," then "another with every part of himself deformed and bent," and finally "a female, with consumptive countenance and cough." The employer, on the other hand, arrived "in a carriage of beautiful workmanship, glittering with silver, and drawn by a span of horses. With all the 'pomp and circumstances,' he steps out of his vehicle with his family."[28]

And, inside the church itself, such dissenters pointed out, religious meetings were "governed . . . by wealthy persons," the employers and the rich in the pew seats, the poor and laboring classes in the gallery or "pauper seats," all for a gospel that was supposed to be dispensed "without money and without price."[29] Here, tensions generated by a new social order spilled over into the spiritual world. When the editors of the *United States Gazette* advanced the notion that pews were "private property," and therefore conferred certain rights on owners to control what went on inside the church, *MFP*'s "No Sectarian" denounced the argument as "blasphemy," the "orthodoxy of certain professing Christian characters" who "have yet to learn the first principles of the doctrines of the Redeemer's plan for regeneration, for the salvation of mankind." Without actually rejecting the idea of purchasing seats—but rather the "selfish, and anti-christian principle, that actuates many who hold the right of freehold title"—this writer condemned "private property churches" where parishioners actually locked pews, suggesting that if they could, these Christians would "bar the gates of the kingdom of heaven, against the admission of a soul, that did not possess their congenial temperature." And then he warned, in "the admonitory language of the Redeemer": "MAKE NOT MY FATHER'S HOUSE AN HOUSE OF MERCHANDISE."[30]

Despite his critical stance, "No Sectarian" apparently remained a churchgoer. He claimed to be a lifelong member of Christ's Church (Episcopalian) in Philadelphia while preferring the free seating of the Methodists and Quakers (which, he said, had a more suitably "primitive appearance"). Still, the distinctions he criticized were humiliating and unjust and were likely unbearable for many workers. Complaint about such distinctions formed a consistent theme in labor rhetoric from one end of the era to the other. "Common Sense" set the tone for the age in 1829 when he announced, again in the pages of the *MFP*, "godliness must [now] come in silver slippers."[31] A year later, the New York *Working Man's Advocate*, insisting upon the spiritual equality of all, complained of the difficulties young mechanics experienced in trying to worship in that city because its churches had created "invidious distinctions, which should not exist in a republican government like ours." "Is the Lordly Christian of the city of New York too good to worship his maker in the presence of one who earns his bread by the sweat of his brow?" the editors asked.[32]

Nearly twenty years later, the same complaint could be heard from laborites, only perhaps with even more disgust. "View [the employer] on the Sabbath at Church occupying the best seat," a Fall River worker bristled in 1847, "while the poor laboring man and his family has to sit back at a remote distance from the speaker, where they can with difficulty hear what is said."[33] Another activist of that decade recalled being forced to go to church by a wealthy family while a servant in their home. They sent her off to church at the back door, she recalled bitterly, and told her not to sit in "the wrong *pew*," providing her with her first glimpse of the "chief seats of the synagogue." This worker, whose main education, she said, was from the Bible, knew enough to recognize that these "professing" Christians "made void of the law of God . . . which requires man to deal with his fellow man as he would be dealt by."[34] And in the following decade, the editor of the Philadelphia *Jubilee* remarked angrily, in language strikingly reminiscent of Seth Luther's, that in a new Baptist church in Philadelphia "every seat is stuffed, covered and cushioned with damasks; and here the rich men will loll at ease, in purple and fine linen, while the poor will be refused the crumbs that fall from their tables."[35]

Finally, much of the working-class distaste for the contemporary church, particularly in the major urban centers and especially during the late 1820s and early 1830s, stemmed from the prominence of wealthy "professors" (or "*nominal* Christians," as the *MFP*'s "Opifex" called them) in church-sponsored benevolent activities. These included participation in various societies that sought to regulate community behavior, but also involvement in the various charities of the age, which were seen as a diversion from the real problem, caused by these very philanthropists.[36] These "charity-mongers," in "Opifex's" term, only gave to have their names printed in the donation book, hypocrisy that hardly advanced the cause of Christianity.[37] "Never," said "A Working Man," "was there such trumpeting of religion, and so little to be found."[38] Indeed, "A. G.," calling on his readers to be good "after the manner of Jesus Christ," contended that the ostensible patrons of religion in his day were "utterly sceptical, respecting all religion," wealthy men attaching themselves to the church only to gain its help in hoodwinking the masses." "Orthodoxy," he had concluded, was "but the hand maid of aristocracy."[39] Some, in fact, held that the force behind this kind of religion was not God but Satan. Thus, "Brutus" began with, "Ye *working men* I address myself to you," and ended by declaring, "think not that I would condemn all religion—God forbid!":

> [A]rise in the majesty of your strength and hurl the despotic monster down to the confines of the lowest hell. . . . Beware, or he may deceive you—he cometh not as an enemy armed and battle-proof, that you may know him;

not so:—but he comes as a pretended friend—he has stolen the garb of your *holy* religion, and approacheth you with deceit.[40]

Little wonder, then, from this point of view, that some workers had a strained relationship with the church.

The Problem of Sectarianism

Labor also railed against sectarianism in the churchgoing community. Part of its general opposition to "party" and the danger of division it posed—"rather the same under another name," one activist said—the religious critique here mirrored the activists' critique of contemporary society.[41] Like Sabbath labor, the long workday, the splendor of the meetinghouse, social distinctions within the congregation, and the use of religion to hoodwink the masses, religious strife seemed to reflect a society that rewarded the selfish, self-interested, and intolerant aspects of human nature while neglecting the warm, humanitarian Christian spirit that most activists embraced. So, when "Opifex" condemned the "charity-mongers," it was also for their intolerance, as they defamed those who had "different rules of faith."[42] Here was another by-product of a world that was "infidel to God and to man."

But, again, there was more to it than this. For bigotry afflicted many Christians in the labor movement as well as those in the larger community, and labor leaders were deeply concerned about it. "Of all employments, quarreling about religion is the worst," the *Voice* advised its readers. "He that quarrels about religion has no religion worth quarreling for."[43] Once again, an unsavory aspect of "churchianity"—the hypocrisy of sectarianism—hindered the progress of Christianity. Far from representing opposition to religion, labor's antisectarianism stemmed in great measure from their religious zealotry.[44]

For, first of all, religious creeds violated the individual's right to practice religion free of the dictates of others, a right considered sacred by post-Revolutionary Americans. Part of a religious culture that insisted on "no creed but the Bible," "the sacred secret between man and his God," and the inviolability of the "dictates of conscience," these workers condemned churches that peddled religious dogma.[45] Aaron H. Wood lamented that Americans enjoyed only a nominal religious freedom, "notwithstanding our Protest-ant religion." Maintaining that his countrymen valued sects and creeds more than Christianity, this collaborator of Seth Luther's in the Boston Trades' Union insisted that it was "solemn mockery" to brag of "Christian liberty." In Wood's view, sectarianism had stymied true religion. "We as a religious people have many lessons yet to learn," he contended, "before we can boast loudly of the liberty wherewith Christ maketh free."[46]

Sarah Bagley also rejected religious intolerance and sectarianism in favor of free and open discussion because, like Wood, she believed this freedom would promote rather than harm Christianity; she flatly denied the argument that it posed a danger of infidelity or "fanaticism." "He who would shut up the free soul by creed," she wrote, "has to learn that the mind is of greater parchment." Reared in the New Hampshire countryside, with its Puritan legacy stressing the direct relationship of the individual to God and personal interpretation over creed, she vowed "not to be driven into dark caverns by any theology save that written by the Great Architect, on the blue arch of heaven."[47]

In this rejection of dogma and the sectarianism that they perceived flowing from it, many labor activists embraced the tolerant gospel of the New Testament. Once again, their religion here was intertwined with their social theory. One of the reasons for "No Sectarian's" opposition to "private property churches," for example, was his abhorrence of the treatment of some churchgoers as "strangers" rather than as neighbors. Christ had established a "perfect equality," he reminded his brethren: "'for all have sinned, and come short of the glory of God.'" Christians must respect this fundamental law, he warned: "LOVE THY NEIGHBOR AS THYSELF."[48] Likewise with differing religious views among advocates of labor's cause. When several irate readers of the *Voice* censured William Young for printing that letter critical of the Bible, the editor defended the act by proclaiming his commitment to the Christian spirit of "tolerance and indulgence." He did not fear, he insisted, that the "sophistry" of those in error could overturn the "eternal truths of God." "True Christianity never shrinks before error and infidelity," he reminded his more orthodox constituents, "but rather loves to grapple with them."[49] Whether advocating open seating in Christian churches in 1830 or open religious discussion in labor newspapers in 1846—from the letter to the editor in Philadelphia to the editorial in Lowell a decade later—antebellum labor advocated an inclusive Christianity, even as they criticized exclusive versions of it.

Indeed, even labor activists who regularly attended church condemned the sectarianism they perceived within American Protestantism. William S. Wilder, a leader of the Fitchburg Workingmen's Association in the 1840s and an active participant in the local Baptist church, advocated "equal rights" in religion as well as politics and the unity of all Christians. Following the town's first inter-denominational Sabbath school celebration, he rejoiced that the affair had been conducted "in a manner becoming a Christian people, as children of one common Father and as grateful citizens of a Christian republic."[50] While Wilder believed that denominational choice was an important individual right, he recognized the community's need for all Christians to unite in a spirit of brotherhood.[51] He inveighed against "ultraists" like the Mormons, but precisely because they were an exclusivist sect; moreover, he insisted upon treating "such errors" not by prosecution but with the "calmness and stability of a pure faith and christian forbearance, a faith which works by love, and a forbearance that suffers rather than does wrong."[52] Here, even from those within the church itself, was the ecumenical voice of antebellum Christian labor reform.[53]

To be sure, this very voice sought to heal the spiritual rifts within the movement, both potential and actual, as already noted. And yet, the spirit it reveals characterized the Christian nature of that movement throughout this period, and that appears to have been the main source of this opposition to sectarianism. Thus, one "believing" activist in Philadelphia in 1830, crediting his faith with whatever contentment he had had in life, nevertheless warned, "this is no warrant for intolerance." To "believer" and "sceptic" alike, he pleaded, oppose "inveterate orthodoxy" of whatever stripe.[54] The plea for tolerance, common throughout the period, typically came in the garb of "true" religion, even from those who at once criticized and embraced the institutions of organized religion.

The Problem of the Clergy

The last, and perhaps the greatest, problem of the contemporary church for antebellum labor activists was the clergy. Tapping into the well of anticlerical sentiment at the core of Protestantism (and, for that matter, Christianity itself), the indictment did not arraign every Christian preacher, but rather the "priestly" class that stood apart from the masses. Boston labor advocate Orestes Brownson, recently the minister of his own church aimed at working people, articulated the essence of the idea when he proclaimed Christianity "the sublimest protest against priesthood ever uttered," reminding his brethren that Christ's mission had been "a solemn summons of every priesthood on earth to judgment."[55] As for the Boston clergy of the 1830s, "not a prouder nor more avaricious race of beings, are to be found on earth," said Aaron Wood.[56] From this perspective, the clergy were more often the enemies of religion and of the people than its friends. And that fact, more than perhaps any other, helped precipitate for some a total break from institutional Christianity.

The specifics of labor's critique of the clergy is instructive in that it echoes the themes of their critique of the contemporary church in general, and indeed of contemporary society as a whole. As Wood's comment hints, activists blasted ministers for the hypocrisy of their station in life, Wood himself denouncing preachers who warned their flocks to shun pomp and vanity but lived like princes themselves. "We have no faith in the clergyman who cannot live as cheaply as a Carpenter, Blacksmith, or Tailor," he maintained,[57] in a deliberate attempt to contrast ministers both with the working class they preached to and with the early ("primitive") Christians whose example they were supposed to emulate.[58] In their profligacy, these activists argued, ministers oppressed the people. It was with this in mind that a Fall River "Mechanic" sat down in 1844 and penned a letter condemning organized religion in his town as "an engine of tyranny over the less privileged classes of society," because, he wrote, it had betrayed "the preaching of the gospel of Christ in its truth and simplicity." Listing the valuation of each church and the annual salaries of its ministers, he concluded that the bill for religious activity in Fall River was well over $100,000 a year. In his view, these clergymen had denied the very foundations of their religion. "Whoever heard or read of *Rev.* Paul or *Bishop* Peter," he railed, "being stationed and receiving a stipulated sum from the people?"[59] Moreover, in this, these putative representatives of God had made common cause with those "avaricious professing Christian(s)," the wealthy.[60] How could they be trusted, "M. J." asked, when they "mountebank-like, whirl about in the vortex of self-interest with the sons of mammon?"[61]

Labor denounced clerical teachings as well, in as much as ministers generally preached forbearance in this life and directed the materially and socially disadvantaged to look for salvation only in the next. As Bagley's collaborator Huldah Stone put it in a spirited defense of "true" Christianity, "unholy 'ministeries' and *infallible* clergy have kept the *laboring classes* too long in awe, compelling them to pay for preaching which instead of raising and ennobling their views and conceptions of God, served only to give them false and pernicious ideas of his government, character, and attributes—of their own relation to that best of Beings and to the whole brotherhood of man." For Stone, officer of both the FLRA and NEWA, traveling lecturer and organizer, correspondent for the *Voice,* and another product of the New England countryside, the place to express the "deepest reverence and love toward the Great and Mighty Architect" was not at the home of the mainstream American ministry.[62]

Activists also denounced clerical activities in the secular realm, picturing ministers in league with the "aristocracy," plotting to reunite church and state for the sake of money and power. Here, the critique was articulated in explicitly Christian terms, typically condemning the clergy's work as a betrayal of Christ's example. Thus, in 1830 a group of artisans in New York City condemned clergy who solicited money from the ordinary to fund their Bible societies. This kind of activity, they declared in one of their resolutions, was "in direct contrariety with the example of our Savior, whom they adopt as their pattern, and by whose precepts they affect to be governed."[63] And any attempts to unite church and state—through laws governing morality—threatened liberty of conscience, which Christianity, alike with the constitution of the United States, guaranteed equally to all men.[64] Here, while true religion was the defender of freedom, current-day religion was the embodiment of tyranny.

Thus allied with the rich, the clergy failed to speak out against contemporary injustices and even opposed efforts to remedy them—the principal issue for labor activists. The editor of the *Gleaner,* a radical newspaper that appeared briefly in Manchester, New Hampshire, during the mid-1840s, cautioned the labor movement about such "opposition of Priests, for they as a body are opposed, and ever have been to all wholesome reforms." Insisting that all reformers had to therefore discard "the shackles of priestcraft" before becoming true advocates for their cause, he called on the members of the New England Workingmen's Association to leave the church. "Look at the reformers of the present as well as those of bygone ages, and what do you see?" he asked.

"Why, you see those who have left the church, and taken a decided stand against the priests."[65] In a word, since ministers were the enemies of the labor movement, and ever had been, their institutions were unworthy of labor's support.

Again, as with the critique of the wealthy in the church, some even held the ministry to be an agency not of the Lord, but of the devil. Lamenting that ministers of the gospel are "*foremost* in the work of despotism over the working classes," "M.J." insisted that they were "not priests of God, but ministers of Satan." For this, he maintained, they "should be shunned, and their churches forsaken," leaving Sabbath observance to the guardians and parents of youth.[66] "M.J.'s" was a prescription for religious fidelity, but in this case outside the walls of the contemporary church. The same was true for the "Sabbath labor Christians," a group of discontented workers who held religious meetings in the streets, groves, and canals of Lowell in the mid-1840s and published sermons that denounced the local ministry's very existence as a betrayal of Christianity.

> While those around you have risen at dawn, you have slept to seven or eight o'clock [one sermon roared]. While they toil until dark, you have managed to live at your ease. While they have lived on the coarsest poorest food, you have been loaded with luxuries. While they have worked for their daily bread, you have PRAYED for yours. . . . You have enjoyed all the privileges and luxuries of the world without making a just return.[67]

And, in fact, some laborites claimed to have abandoned the church in response to precisely this perception of class division. One Lowell mill girl in the late 1840s publicly renounced the religious institutions of her day, because she believed the clergy had become servants of the corporation owners rather than the Lord. Censuring ministers with biblical admonitions, she reminded her audience of an oft-cited passage from the Book of Revelation: "God spoke by his prophets, saying 'the priests teach for hire, they have violated my laws, etc.' The Savior taught of all nations 'my house shall be called a house of prayer; but ye have made it a den of thieves.'" "These churches which are so mightily exalted," she announced, "have become the hold of every foul spirit, and a cage of every unclean and hateful bird." For this radical operative, as for the editor of the *Gleaner* and the Sabbath Labor Christians, church attendance was impossible.[68]

And yet the thrust of labor's critique—that the ministry had defiled the faith by setting a poor example for the people, that it had failed to speak out against injustice—suggests that activists recognized these church representatives as crucial role models in the community, just as they recognized the church itself as an important institution in the community. Thus, the heading of one "Sabbath Labor Christian" sermon read, "As is the priest, so are the people."[69] Indeed, these labor advocates were part of a broader religious culture that suspected clerical establishments while venerating preachers of the gospel. As a result, their anticlericalism was often tempered by a countervailing respect for their targets.

Take the Fall River "Mechanic," whose letter denounced the local ministry as "an engine of tyranny" and boldly attacked "the present system of priestcraft." He also disavowed any intention to besmirch preaching in general, and actually defended the church as a valuable institution that had deteriorated under corrupt conditions. Moreover, he denied that he was a radical in either politics or religion, painting himself as an ordinary laborer deeply concerned about his community. "We are no communitist or comeoutist but a plain Mechanic." And, in a final testament to his ambivalence, he added a short paragraph after his signature, perhaps as an afterthought, assuring his audience that he "highly respect[ed]" the town's clergy as worthy members of the community. His only purpose, he said, had been to pose a simple question: "what do they return to the people for their money?" Here, the Fall River "Mechanic" exposed one of antebellum labor's central conflicts: how to criticize an institution they and the rest of the community venerated as a crucial support for a decent society.

Sarah Bagley offers a particularly poignant example of the ambivalence that the foregoing suggests. When she discoursed on the working-class neglect of churchgoing she observed in Lowell in the spring of 1846, she registered her amazement that Lowell operatives attended Sabbath services at all. Indeed, if they did not it "would be quite excusable," she said, recognizing that some would call her an infidel for offering "an apology for a neglect to attend worship." But, in fact, Bagley was not willing to accept an unchurched community. In the same editorial, she assured her readers that she addressed the entire subject only "with painful emotions" and "regret," while she made clear that her remarks were a plea for church and labor reform—the Christian laborite's two-pronged aim—not a justification of current conditions. A month later, at the end of a blistering attack on the church-attendance requirement in Lowell, she pleaded that she "not be understood . . . to lend our influence on the side of neglect of religion." For, she concluded, "we would thank God most devoutly if there could be found a house of worship in Lowell, where the Gospel, as preached by ancient disciples, could be heard by every operative."[70]

This was no mere posturing by a leader trying to legitimate her movement in the eyes of a pious community, though that, of course, could never have been far from her mind. Rather, this was a woman who had joined a Lowell Universalist church in 1840 and may have still been a member in 1846; in any case, her writings and speeches throughout the period reveal a deep reverence for organized religion.[71] Her remarks on the matter reflected her apparently sincere hope for genuine devotion among her fellow workers—indeed, her recognition of the necessity of such devotion for a healthy community.

The Varieties of Labor's Religious Expression

Most labor activists in this period shared Bagley's critique of the contemporary church and her commitment to a devout, churchgoing populace. Even the most forthright labor anticlericalism did not necessarily mean rejection of the church, as regular churchgoers in labor's ranks often complained about the clergy in harsh terms while leaving open the door to reformation. MMPA founder Robert McFarlane, a lifelong and consistent member of the Presbyterian Church—a Sabbath school teacher!—condemned the ministry's failure to speak out against social injustice. "The holy doctrine 'the laborer is worthy of his hire'" had been "audaciously violated" in antebellum America, he intoned, warning especially "those who preach the gospel to the poor" that their failure to do anything about that crime would put them under the sentence, "'extortioners of God will judge.'"[72] Similarly, the Fall River *Mechanic* harshly castigated ministers who opposed labor reform while praising "our ministers friends" and consistently encouraging clerical support.[73] Alternatively, an FWA resolution announced "That no obstacle whether of *church* or *state* shall prevent us from doing our whole duty"; the sponsors of the motion had been communicants of a local Congregational church for nearly twenty years.[74]

Activists' animadversions against organized religion, then, represented an attempt to explain nonattendance, even to justify it, while simultaneously focusing attention on the importance of church worship. In this way, they mirrored the devotion of many churchgoing workers, as well as the frustration of those workers who embraced Christianity but rejected its contemporary institutional forms. Ultimately, too, the anger and force of labor's critique of these institutions reflected a surprisingly strong attachment to traditional forms of Christian worship. Despite the charges of infidelity that they incurred in the process of articulating their critique of an infidel church, the argument itself actually placed them in the mainstream of American religious history: theirs was a critique born of a desire for purification, not for destruction.

Still, the problem of churchgoing for labor activists who claimed to be saviors of the community, in an age when such devotion was cherished, posed a dilemma that the movement never quite resolved. While they stressed that "true" Christianity dwelt in the heart and not in a building, they also recognized the importance of organized religion. Thus, the anticlerical "Orthodox Seeker" called for the dissolution of "all institutional orders" to set religion free as a "spiritual element," while insisting that his goal was church reform.[75] Moreover, as noted, many of these activists themselves were deeply concerned about the danger of infidelity in the community, taking every opportunity to separate themselves from critics of the church who had abandoned the faith entirely. "Those who call themselves doubters of the word of God, instead of judging of its truths by the falsities and errors of its professors," warned the

Lowell mill girl who had herself denounced the church as a nest of priests and employers, "had better examine and know for themselves that there is not a curse or a blessing predicted, within the sacred volume, but what will be fully verified." While this operative insisted that those who prayed by themselves were "as near the kingdom of God" as those who "worship where the useless show of vanity characterizes the appearance of a playhouse," even she recognized that failure to go to meeting was "trifling with holy time."[76] Unable to embrace the church wholeheartedly, but also unwilling to let it go entirely, the labor rebels of the age sought as best they could to stake out Christian ground for their nascent movement, as they tried to define themselves and their class.

So they expressed their piety in a variety of ways: no one expression was typical. For some, labor protest was compatible with churchgoing. Indeed, virtually every sustained expression of activism during the period revealed the presence of loyal churchgoers. The extent of their involvement was probably more significant in the 1840s than earlier, more in New England than elsewhere, more in the industrial towns and villages than in the large urban centers. But, despite these variations, and despite the widespread and often strident anticlericalism within the movement, churchgoing Christian labor activists could be found in all ranks throughout the period. Consider the following fragments.

Detroit, Sunday, New Year's Day, 1832. Journeyman carpenter William C. King attends "divine service" at a local Baptist meetinghouse, where he listens to sermons in the morning, afternoon, and evening.[77] A regular churchgoer during the early part of 1832, King is actively engaged in the life of this young community: when he can, he attends the services of other local churches, he participates in local temperance society meetings—with his minister offering prayer before the proceedings—and he joins a fire company, whose celebration of Washington's birthday offers the opportunity, he says, for both patriotism *and* food. During the city election that spring, though, he refuses to vote, proclaiming in his diary in typical antebellum Christian fashion, "I'll none of sin." As for the "Great Revival about these days" that King records for the same period, he is hopeful but realistic about the current state of affairs among men: "Christians say Christ is paying us a visit and note it as a memorable epoch. Maybe so, hope it is, he will find us a hard lot of beings."[78]

May 1832. Perhaps in response to the general condition to which King refers, a meeting of local mechanics resolves to work only ten hours a day. And, though King acknowledges his dislike for the "motives of the originators," he declares "the cause a just one and therefore for the sake of some few honest fellows will go it in." Two days later, on the Sabbath, King attends the Methodist church in the morning, the Baptist in the afternoon, the Methodist again in the evening, and participates in family prayer at his boardinghouse.[79] Eventually, he is discharged, along with all the hands in his shop, "for adhering to ten hour system."[80] Throughout the struggle, which lasts well into the summer and ends in a settlement with his employer, King is a regular worshiper in the churches of Detroit.

Allegheny City, Pennsylvania, 1849. The scene: the trial of more than a dozen local citizens for an attack on a local factory during a strike for the ten-hour day the previous year. The charge: treason against the state. The defense calls a deputy policeman, Joseph Scott, as a character witness for one of the strike leaders, George W. Gungle. Do you know if Gungle is a member of any church? the attorney asks Scott. Though the prosecution objected, and the judge sustained the objection, all involved understood the import of the question: Gungle was a churchgoer.[81]

Lynn, Massachusetts, 1860. Year of the Great Shoe Strike, the largest strike in American history to that date. One of the prominent leaders of the struggle is a young Canadian named Napolean Wood. A shoeworker living in the city since 1851, Wood insisted that his involvement was designed to maintain decent living standards, as those of the Lynn workers were now in conflict with his religious beliefs. For he was not only a strike leader, but also a leader in the local Methodist Church.[82]

We do not know just what these particular church congregants thought about the state of the institutions of religion in their day. Presbyterian Robert McFarlane left a record of his views on the matter, however. He believed that in his church, the "professors" had forgotten the "precepts of Christ," who had preached a universal religion of brotherly love and "pure liberty." The evidence was everywhere, he said, in the emphasis on forms and ceremonies, in the profession of religion as "a fashionable thing," and most of all in "Mechanics [being] ground to the dust by deceiving capitalists" in a putatively Christian country. And yet, despite these criticisms of contemporary Christianity—at one point even insisting that there was "something rotten at [the] very heart's core" of the American church—McFarlane enjoined his audience to embrace the Christian faith as he did and to observe the Sabbath.[83] Here was an activist who, though critical, remained a dedicated churchgoer. There were many others.

But these stories represent only one part of the spectrum. There were at least four other general patterns of working-class spiritual expression. Some leaders, like William Young, for example, eschewed church membership while maintaining a deep reverence for organized devotion. Born in the rural hamlet of Burrillville, Rhode Island, his childhood and early adolescence spent in the farmlands of western and southern New Hampshire, he imbibed deep respect for religious institutions that was common in rural New England homes in the early nineteenth century. Although he denounced sectarianism and the general failure of the ministry to adhere to the original principles of Jesus, he also emphasized the positive aspects of contemporary religion and energetically supported the efforts of sympathetic clergymen. A proponent of church reform, he believed it his Christian duty to encourage the good and discourage the bad. But he was clear on the state of Christianity in his day: it was mired in "a dark deep pit of selfishness, falsehood and corruption," with sectarian doctrines, bigotry, and intolerance masquerading in the name of religion. That kind of Christianity, he maintained, "stifles pure and undefiled religion, and [makes] inroads upon the Gospel of Christ." Searching for a place in the church as a young labor activist in Fitchburg and Lowell, he apparently did not join a religious organization during the 1840s.[84]

There were prominent laborites of this era, particularly urban artisans, who evinced a much more profound aversion to organized devotion than Young's. Seth Luther, for example, though raised in a Rhode Island Baptist home and admitted to his mother's congregation at the age of twenty, thoroughly rejected the antebellum church.[85] Urban American religion of the early 1830s, with its ostentatious church buildings and ministers who preached resignation to the poor, "is not Christianity as I understand it," he insisted. Moreover, since the church necessarily reflected conditions in the community as a whole, social injustice had to be rectified before true religion could flourish.

> I, for one, cannot enter the temples of the living God, and ask pardon for my errors, with expectations of mercy, while these things . . . exist, unless I lift my voice against them. . . . Every man who attempts to pray to God in the language of supplication for pardon, is guilty of sin, if he use not his exertions to obey the precepts of Him, who came to open prison doors, and let the prisoners go free. We are guilty of hypocrisy, religiously and politically, while we pursue such a course.

Though Luther implied here that true church worship was possible if one spoke out against prevailing inequities, he rejected contemporary religious institutions as reflections of a profane society. "Believing in the Christian faith as I do," he announced, "I deny any community deserves the name Christian Community when such evils exist."[86] Consequently, though he continued to loudly profess his religious faith during his career as a labor advocate in the 1830s and 1840s, Luther refused to participate in church life.[87]

Other activists resolved the conflict between their dislike for contemporary Christianity and their commitment to religious institutions by adherence to what they called "primitive Christianity."[88] Conjuring up the world of Jesus and his disciples, they spoke of a "truly Christian commonwealth (that) did not long exist," of "those primitive days of simplicity" when "men of simple habits preached 'the words of truth and soberness,'" in open fields and groves."[89] To make this lost world a reality, some formed their own congregations, however small and ephemeral. After all, noted one Philadelphia activist, the charter for such devotion had come from the Messiah himself: "'where two or three are gathered together in his name,'" there is a church.[90] The evidence of such extra-institutional Christian churches in or around the early American labor movement is fragmentary, but this kind of worship involved hundreds, perhaps thousands, of antebellum workers. Their piety was rooted in both early Christian and Reformation traditions, nourished by experiments in Europe and America in the seventeenth and eighteenth centuries; in a sense, their activities were a radical extension of the early American emphasis of faith over forms and ceremonies.

These were the *come-outers,* a term usually associated with the abolitionists, but the practice went well beyond that movement. Among the Associationists in the 1840s, American disciples of the French utopian socialist Charles Fourier, whose ranks included a preponderance of poor and working people and a number of prominent labor activists, there was a particular affection for such Christians. In 1848, an Associationist in Abington, Massachusetts, bemoaned the pain of having his movement labeled "agrarian" and "infidel" in the face of the hypocrisy of "professed Christian Churches" that looked to a "far-off Heaven" but never that "the Kingdom of Heaven is to *come,* and God's will be done on *earth* as it is in Heaven." He felt cheered, however, by the presence of come-outers who held frequent reform meetings at the local town hall.[91] And, there were come-outers in the labor movement itself. Listen to William D. Leavitt, a labor leader from Woburn, Massachusetts, as he implored his brethren to cease patronizing a "lazy, idle priesthood" and to do their own preaching in "Free Meetings": "Let them assemble together and talk for the edification of each other," he advised, "by discussion on different subjects which have a tendency to the weal or woe of the great brotherhood of man."[92] A correspondent to the *Voice* agreed that the people should begin taking over the functions of overpaid clergymen who opposed essential reforms. Noting that the minister's inflated salary "does not grow on every bark," he reported that some Christians had "an idea of doing their own preaching."[93]

Some antebellum workers did precisely that, finding devotion and spiritual sustenance in their own organizations. In late 1845, a Lowell newspaper reported that "fashion" had rendered church attendance "so expensive" that many operatives now held Sabbath meetings at the Mechanics' Reading Room, where they read from Scripture, sang hymns, and discussed "topics affecting the rights and interests of the laborer."[94] About the same time, the Lowell FLRA held its initial meetings on the Sabbath "to discuss the great principles which pertain to human rights and human duties." Sarah Bagley, organizer and leader of the association, conceived these gatherings as a possible alternative to the contemporary church, since they brought workers together to worship and advanced the righteous cause of social reform without the "creedalism" that polluted present-day religion.[95]

The "Sabbath Labor Christians," the religious mill operatives who rejected the local ministry as allies of the mill owners, became so numerous in 1846 that at least three separate societies were established in Lowell. Anticipating charges of infidelity from their opponents, these workers exalted the "practical Christianity" at the core of labor's religion. "If we take the Christian Bible as a guide," one of their sermons maintained, "we are justified in judging men by their works."[96] Like Bagley's group and those who met in the Mechanics' Reading Room, the "Sabbath Labor Christians" offered Lowell workers who were disillusioned with local churches an opportunity to express their piety collectively with other believing Christians.

Moreover, Lowell was hardly unique in this. In New York City, in the 1830s, a group calling themselves "friends of pure Christianity [and] 'Peace on Earth and good will amongst men'" took up the issue of labor reform in several "private conferences." Claiming to be Christians without connection to party, society, or sect, but holding to the teachings of Jesus, they drafted an "Address to All Mankind," in which they announced that they would follow biblical injunction to perfect the world in preparation for Christ's second coming ("'tarry not until I come'").[97] A decade later, in Pittsburgh, local activist Samuel Fleming reported to the *Voice* that a "flourishing association" called the "Practical Religionists" was disseminating "useful knowledge" to the "producing portions" of the community, while the "Christian Union" sought a revival of "practical Christianity."[98]

Two years later, Philadelphia labor reformer Fanny Lee Townsend reported the efforts of a Reverend Mr. Stockton, who had been condemned years before, she said, as a "mad-dog infidel" after proclaiming the church of his day unchristian for neglecting its duty to apply Christianity to the "social relations of man." Stockton had recently organized the "Christian Society of Brotherly Love," Townsend wrote, the object of which was to supply the natural and social as well as spiritual needs of its members. Consonant with the return to "pure and undefiled religion" championed by antebellum labor, the criteria for membership in this group were good moral character, christian discipleship, and faith in the Bible as the word of God.[99]

Townsend pronounced them good people, but the movement somewhat superficial—even though, as an advocate of women's rights, she was clearly enamored with their insistence on the equality of females and males in the group's fellowship—because it did not go far enough in revolutionizing American society. Several years later, in the 1850s, she would help organize the "Sunday Institute" in Philadelphia, grove gatherings ("woods meetings") of labor reformers and others that attracted upwards of a thousand working people. This working-class "church" had a fiercely democratic character: the "preachers" who delivered sermons on Christianity and reform were elected by open vote at the outset of the service. Townsend herself preached here frequently, telling her flock on one occasion, in the tradition of laborite come-outerism, to "come out from the old schools [and] throw off your old cocoon of false religion and false politics . . . [make] for yourselves a Heaven on earth."[100]

Finally, workers were also exposed to Christianity through the preaching of itinerants in the labor movement, who were in a very real sense evangelists for labor. During the late 1850s, for example, John C. Cluer, a Scottish immigrant who had been a prominent NEWA figure in the previous decade, established a type of open-air church in Boston. Preaching from atop a crate in the Common or on a nearby street corner, this ex-Methodist minister reached thousands of the city's workers. So alarmed were the municipal authorities at his popularity that they moved to stop this "street preaching" by passing a special ordinance against such activity, resulting in physical confrontations and his arrest on several occasions.[101]

The extent to which this particular kind of popular evangelism took the place of attachment to an established church is hard to determine, but there is no doubt about the influence such a dynamic personality could have over antebellum working people. Take the fascinating case of the Allegheny City riot of 1848, in which striking mill girls attacked a cotton factory in order to shut it down, precipitating the trial noted above. The principal leader of the women, the local press reported at the time, was a beautiful young Kentuckian who was not an operative herself and whose motives were "obscure," a striking figure described as pale and dark eyed, well built, and intelligent. She was present at all of the strike meetings and, directing the strikers but without committing any illegal acts herself, she was said to have had a strange control over them. Adding to the mystery, no one seemed to know anything about her—or, perhaps, they just would not say—even her name. Among the female strikers of Allegheny City, she was called simply, "the unknown."[102]

All of these various alternative sources of popular authority and unconventional forms of religious devotion, outside the mainstream Protestant denominations of antebellum America, underscore labor's marked disaffection with the contemporary church and its representatives. But the movement—as indeed its working-class constituency generally—would always be somewhat uneasy remaining outside the fold, especially where, as was often the case, those who protested prevailing conditions claimed to be Christians, seeking the redemption of communities whose dominant institution was organized Christianity. Here, in the emerging industrial towns and villages of the northeastern countryside, a significant minority of activists were members of local congregations. Together with those who attended but were not members, this attachment to the institutions of Christianity probably represented the dominant element in antebellum working-class activism outside of the major urban centers.

In any case, the preeminent—if suspect—role of the church and clergy throughout antebellum America in effect forced any movement for social change to confront the question of organized religion. The precise relationship between labor and the church, of course, depended in great measure upon a variety of local factors. Sometimes, in fact, even where significant numbers of activists were churchgoers, labor and the church, as institutions, faced each other across a great ideological divide. Here, religion often played a crucial role in determining the nature and course of labor protest, but the development of that role occurred outside the confines of institutional religion.

At other times, matters were essentially reversed. While activists might articulate some of the same criticisms of contemporary Christianity as their compatriots who eschewed attendance, churchgoing activists claimed the mantle "citizen and Christian" and advocated the cause of "labor's sacred rights" from inside the institutions of organized religion. In many local struggles, in fact, a sympathetic minister or mobilized congregation rendered at least a portion of organized religion an ally of labor. At these moments, labor's ambivalence about the church was resolved in favor of attachment. Here, activists rejoiced that at least one part of a professedly Christian community—in its public manifestation—had been true to the original spirit of the religion it claimed as its own, offering hope that perhaps America would live up to its billing, in Tocqueville's words, as a republic and democracy "peopled by men professing a democratic and republican Christianity."

Part 2.
Labor and the Church

Chapter 4. Labor Activists in the Church: New England

At the local level, antebellum labor agitation and church life were intimately linked. From the late 1820s, activists could be found among area congregants, meetinghouses often providing space for organizing efforts. The Working Men's movement of the late 1820s and early 1830s—the institutional beginnings of the modern American labor movement—established a pattern that characterized the entire period. Appearing in scores of towns and cities in the northeastern United States, such groups produced the nation's first labor parties.[1] In September 1830, the Working Men of Woodstock, Vermont, organized to fight what they perceived as growing dependence and inequality in their small, northern New England community; fully two-thirds of their number were church members, a higher percentage than in any other insurgent movement in the area during the period.[2] The representation of church members among labor activists was similar in early American strikes and unions. In Manayunk, an industrial suburb of Philadelphia, the textile turn-outs of the early 1830s followed immediately on the heels of a religious revival among Baptists and Presbyterians; at least six strike leaders were recent converts.[3] In the New England shoe industry, the first known protests of female outworkers also made good use of local churches: in 1833, in response to a cut in their wages, shoebinders in Lynn, Massachusetts, organized a society at the local Friends' meetinghouse; their sisters in nearby Saugus followed suit in a Methodist church.[4]

Several caveats are in order before addressing the nature and scope of this relationship between labor and the church in antebellum America, however. Measurements of church involvement at the local level for this period must be approached with a good deal of caution. First, as can be seen in Tables 4.1–4.9 (pp. 319–30), the documentary record is fragmentary, often inexact, and uneven—both within and among communities. The same computations cannot be made for each church, labor group, or community. Second, the reader should note that figures here denoting church-affiliated labor activists likely understate significantly the number who were actual churchgoers. The principal quantitative measure of church involvement, of course, is church membership, which can be calculated by analyzing extant membership lists. But, whereas today there are generally many more nominal members of congregations than there are faithful churchgoers, in the early nineteenth century it was just the reverse: membership requirements were quite rigorous and yielded few church members relative to those who attended regularly.[5]

Finally, evidence regarding denominational affiliation must be read with caution, because the typically mobile Americans of this era often attended—and even joined—whatever church was the most convenient. An excellent example is one Henry Clark, who hosted at his inn a meeting of the Association of Working People of New Castle County, Delaware, in the summer of 1831. Clark and his wife were Presbyterians who were admitted to full communion in the Red Clay Creek Presbyterian Church the following fall. In their application for admission, they testified that two years earlier, as members of the Presbyterian Church in Frankfurt, Delaware, they had moved to a neighborhood without a Presbyterian church, and therefore they had taken communion with local Methodists.[6]

Indeed, denominational affiliation often had more to do with local circumstances than with adherence to a specific creed. As historians of the contemporaneous abolitionist and Antimasonic movements have discovered, though the theology and structure of various churches might create conditions conducive to political or social reform activity among their congregations, no one denomination possessed the soul of either movement, nor did one particular church produce most of the clerical supporters for the cause. Local conditions and other factors were determinative during this period.[7] The same was true of labor reform. Across a wide spectrum of church belief and practice—from Presbyterians to Hicksite Quakers—those involved in the early American labor movement drew upon shared Protestant traditions and, in the process, forged a kind of laborite religion, a social gospel of labor, that would serve the cause of labor radicalism for the rest of the century. As we shall see when we turn to religion's impact on the language of antebellum labor in part 3, certain themes emerge repeatedly, in some measure because of the enormous geographical mobility during this period.

There was, in fact, no single relationship between labor and the church in antebellum America. The church affiliation of labor activists and the direct involvement of the church and clergy in their movements reveal an enormous diversity of experience. But, throughout the Northeast, throughout the era—in various towns and cities in Massachusetts, in Rochester, New York, in Wilmington, Delaware—the church decisively shaped the nature of labor protest. Everywhere, activists whose concerns were both material and spiritual could not escape the realities of contemporary religious life. As religious as well as social reformers, they were anxious to confront those realities.

Perhaps it is best to think of each of the stories that follow as different streams or currents that flowed into one river—the unfolding relationship between religion and working-class formation. For, from one perspective at least, this was the working out of a collective identity in a world where identity was in great measure defined, or at least profoundly influenced, by the institutions of religion. The variations in the early labor activists' relationship to the church were no doubt a source of weakness for a nascent movement seeking to challenge the direction in which they saw their society moving. Hence labor's early attempt to avoid the topic of religion. At the same time, though, such diversity was also a source of strength. For it revealed a movement seeking to forge a Christian tradition of resistance, across denominational boundaries and in varying local circumstances. Only in this way could labor gain spiritual legitimacy as the "bone and sinew" of a society that regarded fidelity to religion as all important, a society that they themselves helped to create.

"If you persist in driving your machines on the Lord's day, your course is a short one," one labor activist warned Lowell's mill owners in 1847. Though they might accumulate riches, he told the architects of antebellum New England's factory showcase, they would surely lose their souls, for God demanded Sabbath observance. More important, their transgressions would "afford a license and precedent for others to do the same." "Demons will rejoice, while angels will weep over the obduracy of your hearts; the church will lament your loss and pity you; the sceptic will laugh and the Infidel will say ha, ha—so would we have it." Ultimately, organized religion would dissipate and God's wrath would descend upon the entire community. "A volume might be written to show how the Deity has, in divers manners, scourged nations, expressly for their disregard of his Sabbath." "Therefore," preached this activist, "it is a duty you owe to the city, to those by whom you are surrounded, to the church, and to God; to renounce at once this nefarious practice."[8]

The demand here was typical of labor radicalism in New England before the Civil War: secular reform in the name of religious devotion. Activists might criticize the contemporary state of the church, but most held proper Sabbath observance in high regard. From the first stirrings of a regional movement for labor reform—the formation of the New England Association of Farmers, Mechanics and Other Working Men (NEA) in 1832—the leadership included a prominent number of churchmen; at the local level, labor activists were often deeply involved in their communities' churches.[9] The scope and nature of these ties, of course, varied both among and within New England communities. The number of church members seems to have been higher in the smaller industrial towns and villages of the region than in Boston; local peculiarities directly influenced congregational preference; and there were sometimes significant denominational divisions between leadership and rank-and-file. Everywhere in the region, though, antebellum labor reform was bound up with the life of the church.

Fall River

If Lowell was the premier factory center of antebellum New England, Fall River was a close second. With thousands of mill operatives and hundreds of wage-earning craftsmen, this rapidly growing textile town in the southeastern corner of Massachusetts along the Rhode Island border also produced one of the region's strongest labor movements. Before the onset of massive foreign immigration in the late 1840s, the townspeople involved in these movements—artisans and factory workers, supported by shopkeepers, petty professionals, and small farmers—lived and worked in a Protestant community whose churches were an essential aspect of social and cultural life. Typically, they criticized those churches for, among other things, failing to condemn injustice in the community; they emphasized the Bible and "practical Christianity" over mere attendance. But, Fall River's early labor activists were also churchgoers. They advocated workers' rights within the moral-religious framework of a Christian community, as churchgoing members of that community.[10]

Here, the Great Transformation was compressed into a single generation, as small-scale craft production and family farming, based largely on a barter system and mostly for local consumption, gave way to a radical division of labor and mechanization in manufacturing and to commercial agriculture. In 1820, Fall River was a "struggling hamlet" of fewer than sixteen hundred residents with a largely maritime-farming economy. Though local residents had begun to tap the enormous waterpower potential of the Quequechan River as early as 1811 by building textile mills, only two survived by the end of the decade; in 1820, the town had neither a bank nor a newspaper. Then, during the 1820s, population and industry exploded: six new factories were built, and the number of inhabitants increased to more than four thousand. By 1845, Fall River was the manufacturing center of Taunton Valley, a bustling factory town of more than ten thousand, with eleven mills producing cotton and woolens, printed cloth, iron, and textile machinery. Well over two thousand factory operatives toiled away in those establishments, and hundreds of artisans—stonemasons and carpenters, blacksmiths and machinists—worked for wages, many of them in the service of the mills.[11]

Confronted with the divisions, dependencies, and perceived disorder that marked this transformation in Fall River, the new commercial and industrial elite and many wage earners embraced self-interest and individual upward mobility as the proper direction for a new economic and social order. Others, though, rejected these changes in work and life as antithetical to cherished traditions of mutuality and independence. They began publicly agitating for labor reform in the early 1830s, when local mule spinners, machinists, and housewrights helped organize the NEA. Sometimes described as America's first attempt at industrial unionism, between 1832 and 1834 this association tried to

For statistics on Fall River, refer to tables 4.1–4.3.

organize disaffected farmers, factory workers, journeymen artisans, and common laborers against "the oppression of the idle, avaricious, and aristocratic." Though it advocated a range of social reforms—including universal education, the abolition of child labor and imprisonment for debt, and consumer cooperatives—its principal focus was the ten-hour workday, through strikes and then political action. In Fall River, some carpenters apparently succeeded in winning shorter hours during these years, but the town's factory workers were not so fortunate. Their agitation led to the spinners' dismissal, while the owners of one factory actually raised the number of hours in their employees' workday. In late 1832 and 1833, local activists continued to meet under the auspices of the Association of Mechanics and Workingmen, but the movement soon petered out.[12]

The town's workers were quiet for the remainder of the decade. Indeed, the labor movement in New England all but disappeared in the industrial depression that followed the Panic of 1837. But Fall River would again play a leading role when another regional labor movement arose during the 1840s. In late 1840, organized labor agitation resurfaced here with a series of ten-hour meetings under the banner of the "Association of Industry."[13] After three years of shorter-hours agitation, local housewrights took the lead in founding the Fall River Mechanics' Association, which pressed for shorter hours and general labor reform.[14] Shortly thereafter, in the spring of 1844, the overwhelming majority of the town's carpenters, masons, and painters—their numbers swollen by the rebuilding effort that followed a devastating fire the year before—announced their refusal to work any longer than ten hours a day.[15] Their advocate was the newly formed association; their voice was the its weekly newspaper, the *Mechanic,* which quickly became the voice of labor reform in the southern Massachusetts-Rhode Island area. As the movement caught fire around New England during the late spring and early summer of 1844, it was Fall River that issued the call for a regional organization. The result was the New England Workingmen's Association, a kind of "recurrence" of the NEA of the early 1830s.[16]

Nearly all of these activists were native-born Protestants with roots in the town and the surrounding area.[17] They lived in a militantly Protestant community whose residents cherished the Bible and went to church. In 1846, a citizens' committee found that more than 85 percent of the town's families kept the Bible in their homes; a survey of church membership five years earlier claimed that nearly every family in the town considered themselves "nominally connected with some congregation."[18] The number of communicants in Fall River's churches at the time approached two thousand, representing a significant proportion of the adult population in a town of sixty-five hundred.[19]

Memorialists and contemporary observers asserted that the workers also participated in this religious life. Alice Brayton remembered that the mill workers, "boys and girls from nearby farms," had been devoted Christians:

"they all kept holy the Lord's Day . . . even though they worshipped in many meetinghouses, in many different fashions and sometimes fought bitterly for they felt deeply."[20] A correspondent for the *Monitor* claimed much the same at the time. Deploring the physical conditions in the factories, he insisted that the spiritual state of the workers remained intact: "it has always been so that among the laboring, and industrious and the poor, the Christian Religion has taken the deepest root—produced the greatest results—and there has been found its most zealous advocates and brightest ornaments."[21]

Among those who championed the rights of "the laboring, and industrious and the poor" in Fall River, Christianity had indeed taken deep root. The town's leading labor activists, mostly skilled artisans, were members of local congregations. In fact, nearly two-thirds of the period's labor leaders were church members, many of them respected and longtime members of their congregations. Moreover, substantial numbers of the movement's rank-and-file and supporters—factory workers, artisans, laborers, shopkeepers, professionals, farmers—were also church members.[22] Fully 40 percent of the 603 townspeople who signed ten-hour petitions during the 1840s were communicants of Fall River congregations. Although a significant minority had entered the church during the revivals of the early 1840s, most had joined earlier. Like the churchgoing labor leadership, the Christian rank-and-file had deep roots in the religious community.

The same could be said even for some immigrants in this movement. Robert Adams, for example, who signed the 1845 ten-hour petition, was born in Scotland but came to Rhode Island in 1828 at the age of twelve. A year later, he was sent into one of the Slater mills in Pawtucket, Rhode Island, probably to work with his father, who was a weaver and spinner. After a short time, he left the factory for a local bookshop where he worked as a clerk during most of the 1830s. Adams's father became "very much interested" in the antislavery movement when it arose in the Providence area, and he took his son to meetings of the local antislavery society. By the mid-1830s, Robert counted himself among the movement's advocates. In 1842, he moved to Fall River where he opened a book and stationery store. Remembered as a "public spirited" resident of the town, who served on the school committee, the common council, and on the boards of several local charitable institutions, Adams was also known as a staunch abolitionist and a "consistent friend of the operative." He regularly attended the Unitarian church.[23]

The Unitarians and Congregationalists accounted for a number of prolabor shopkeepers like Adams, but the majority of the mill workers, laborers, and artisans in the movement were Baptists, Christians, and Methodists.[24] Fall River's religious history explains this denominational pattern.[25] Though most of the town's early settlers were descendants of the Pilgrims, they failed to establish a solid foundation of Congregationalism in the area. It was the Baptists who exercised the most powerful influence on Fall River's early religious development, claiming more adherents than any other Protestant church before 1850. Although the Christians and Methodists did not establish congregations in the town until the late 1820s, both claimed more adherents than the Congregationalists by the mid-1840s.[26] Together, the three denominations accounted for more than two-thirds of Fall River's Protestants by 1840; they accounted for approximately the same proportion of churchgoing laborites in the town.[27]

These churches carried their religious fervor into the streets of Fall River, holding mass public conversion rites. During one revival in the spring of 1836, which actually brought town business to a standstill for a time, three thousand people watched as the pastor of the Christian church baptized seventy-five converts in the Taunton River. During another enthusiasm in 1840, the Baptist minister publicly baptized fifty-five townspeople, while an estimated two to three thousand spectators assembled on wharves, beaches, and boats to witness the scene.[28] These spiritual outpourings—1826–27, 1831–32, 1836, 1838–39, 1840, and 1842—pushed religion to the center of town life. Although Congregationalists participated in these revivals, it was the Baptists, Christians, and Methodists who went into the streets. They led the movement, bringing hundreds of Fall River workers into the church, among them men and women who would later join the labor movement.

The Baptists made up the largest group of these churchgoing laborites, not simply because they constituted the town's most numerous denomination but also because they uniquely combined an interest in workers and a strong reform tradition with a respectability derived from their long history in Fall River. During the 1830s and 1840s, their minister was the Reverend Asa Bronson, a descendant of the same Connecticut family as Orestes Brownson. Under Bronson's leadership, the Baptists held special middle-of-the-night prayer meetings for mill operatives and raised money for the poor of the church and the community. Meanwhile, Bronson became a prominent local reformer. He was an officer of the town antislavery society from its founding in 1834, president of the temperance society in 1836, and, from the first stirrings of labor agitation in 1841, one of the area's most popular labor advocates. At the same time, though, Bronson maintained an important and respected position in the community. In 1835, he was elected chairman of the town's school committee; he coordinated his antislavery and temperance activities with the First Congregational Church. Most important, he led the oldest and largest congregation in Fall River, with a following among local shopkeepers and skilled artisans as well as mill operatives and the town's poor. Bronson's church, then, could claim both the community's respect and a strong commitment to working people and to social justice.[29]

As it turned out, Bronson's labor activism prompted his removal at the height of the ten-hour agitation in 1844. But such tensions within congregations merely reflected just how intertwined labor activism and religious devotion were in Fall River. In 1846, 149 members of the congregation formed the Second Baptist Church and brought Bronson back to town.[30] Among the membership were a number of labor leaders; among the church leadership were a number of labor advocates.[31] And the Baptists were not unusual in this regard. Indeed, during the early and mid-1840s, over 40 percent of the churchgoing labor leadership were officers in their respective congregations: vestrymen, treasurers, deacons, class leaders. At the same time, some of the town's most prominent and active congregants, although not movement leaders, were labor advocates or supporters. As we shall see, this connection to the local church formed the basis of the movement's claim that it spoke not in the interest of one segment of the community but on behalf of all Christians.

Among churchgoing labor leaders, unsurprisingly, Baptists were the most numerous. Philip Smith, a machinist who joined the First Baptist Church during the 1826–27 revival, was active in labor circles and town affairs throughout the period. President of the local auxiliary of the NEA in 1833, president of the Association of Industry in 1841, and an officer of a local workingmen's cooperative during the late 1840s, Smith also chaired a meeting of local Democrats in 1837 and was elected to the town's street committee in 1841. An activist in the antislavery and temperance struggles as well as labor reform, he was a leader of the local Liberty and Free Soil parties and a member of a citizens' committee to prosecute violations of the town's liquor license law. He was an active Baptist: elected a trustee in 1836, and a deacon ten years later, he remained a church officer until his death in 1870.[32] The labor activists who organized the Second Baptist Church were also devoted churchmen. One of the new congregation's deacons was Mechanics' Association officer Charles Borden, who had been a Baptist since the summer of 1833. The church treasurer, Joseph Borden, joined during a massive revival in 1840, participating in a wage strike at a local print works barely a month after he was baptized.[33] The church clerk was lifelong Baptist John C. Milne, the typesetter for the *Mechanic*.[34]

The other popular revivalist churches in the community also contributed solid church members to Fall River's early labor leadership. John Hull, a housewright who served as a Fall River delegate to several regional workingmen's conventions, was a committeeman in the First Methodist Church. Samuel Gardner, a Mechanics' Association officer, joined the same congregation in 1829 and was active in church committees from the 1830s.[35] Wilbur Reed, Mechanics' Association president in 1844 and 1845, had been a member of the First Christian Church since 1830. Edmund Davis, another officer of the association, joined the Christians in 1834 and was an active participant in church activities throughout the period.[36]

If some of the labor movement's most active participants were solid church members, some of the town's leading communicants were supporters of that movement. Three of the six charter members of the Presbyterian Church, organized by English and Scottish operatives in 1846, were ten-hour men.[37]

Similarly, several of the leading congregants in the Episcopal Church, also popular with immigrant Protestant workers, were labor supporters and activists. In fact, the worker who gave the church its first Bible at its founding ceremonies in 1836 was a ten-hour operative and congregation vestryman during the early 1840s. At least three other vestrymen in the church were local activists.[38] Leading Methodists and Christians were also supporters of the movement. Among the Methodists who signed ten-hour petitions were four class leaders, two Sabbath school assistants, and several church committeemen. Mill operative William Winter served as a Methodist steward throughout the 1830s and 1840s. Shoemaker Leonard Garfield had been an early officer of the First Christian Church. When the North Christian Church was founded in 1842, the moderator of its first meeting was a ten-hour advocate.[39]

Early labor activists in Fall River were integrated into the churchgoing community. When they claimed the mantle of that community, it was much more than an attempt to gain legitimacy and support. It reflected their institutional connection to the churches in their town and the powerful strain of Christian piety that was at the core of their movement.

Fitchburg

In February 1845, the Fall River *Mechanic* reprinted a circular that had been recently issued by the "Workingmen's Association of Fitchburg," in that small mill village some seventy miles northwest of Fall River in northern Worcester County near the New Hampshire-Massachusetts border.[40] The language in the broadside, addressed to their fellow "Mechanics and Workingmen," suggested that the powerful strain of Christian piety so evident in Fall River coursed through this hamlet as well. It lamented what it called the destruction of humanity's "gifts of God" and its capacities for happiness that had been designed to be cultivated "for His glory alone," and announced that they had come together out of the "duty we owe God" on the basis of the "spirit and doctrines of Christ."

The words could as easily have been the *Mechanic*'s: like Fall River, Fitchburg produced a labor movement of churchgoers in a churchgoing community. Once again, the leadership and a portion of the membership were longtime and established members of the community and could be found in an array of local congregations. One aspect of this movement differed from Fall River, however: a significant number of the rank-and-file, as distinct from the leadership, were recent converts to one particular church, the one church in town that had an overwhelmingly working-class clientele—the Methodists. In Fitchburg, then, unlike in Fall River, two distinct kinds of churchgoing activists coexisted in the same movement for labor reform.

For statistics on Fitchburg, refer to tables 4.4–4.8.

In November 1844, a couple of months before the circular appeared in the *Mechanic,* disaffected workers and their supporters in Fitchburg had organized a local workingmen's association, the FWA.[41] The society's secretary, a shoe-maker named E. R. Wilkins who had recently come to Fitchburg from nearby Lowell, duly recorded its first meeting:[42] "A respectable number of *Labours* and mechanics of Fitchburg met at Town Hall on Wednesday Evening November 13th, 1844 To take into consideration the present depressed and grevious condition of the Laboring population of *Americans* and to form themselves into an association for their amelioration and *mutual welfare.*" The keynote speaker that night was another recently arrived shoe worker, an E. Birch of Lynn. His address on the "evils of society which oppress poor and laboring classes" was a fitting opening salvo for this movement. Establishing a workers' association, he told his audience, was "necessary to protect their rights and secure the blessings bequeathed to them by *nature's God.*"[43] Others in the association used more specifically religious language: they demanded a redress of their grievances as "Christians and philanthropists."[44]

The FWA founding was a direct response to Fall River's call for a regional workingmen's association; it was made possible by the social and economic changes in the town during the previous decade—the expansion of factory production, rapid population growth, and the perception of a growing chasm between rich and poor. Situated along the Nashua River, Fitchburg boasted several paper, scythe, and textile mills by the early nineteenth century.[45] But it was not until the mid-1840s that these factories employed the majority of those engaged in manufacturing.[46] During the 1830s and 1840s, the proportion of mill workers and general laborers in the work force increased steadily, while the percentage of farmers declined.[47] Meanwhile, Fitchburg's small population swelled, as industry and opportunity drew young men and women from nearby farms and communities.[48] From 1840 to 1845, the town's population grew nearly 50 percent, the most dramatic increase before midcentury.

If the Great Transformation in Fall River was compressed into a single generation, in Fitchburg the shock of change seemed ruder still. Until recently a village of farms, small shops, and a few simple mills, in the 1840s the town seemed to be losing its simplicity and moral order all of a sudden. "Oh! what a maddening cadence floats / Around the factory bell," one resident wrote, expressing the deep resentment many felt at the intrusion of the mills (and mill time) into their lives.[49] The first sentence of the preamble to the FWA constitu-tion articulated the same sense of disorientation, warning that violations of God's laws, such as "unjust toil or servitude," brought "consequent penalties—*pain confusion strife* and *misery.*"[50] For such townspeople, peace and quiet came to symbolize the community they believed had been disrupted by forces that were strange and beyond their control.

At the same time, Fitchburg retained much of its villagelike quality. In contrast to larger factory centers like Lowell or Fall River, in Fitchburg the work force in its eleven mills averaged just twenty hands, and none of its other manufacturing establishments employed more than ten.[51] Moreover, the townspeople clung stubbornly to the customs and values of a passing age. When a group of Fitchburg businessmen proposed building a rail link with the Boston and Worcester Railroad in 1841, for example, they encountered fierce citizen opposition. At a raucous town meeting, one resident warned of the "dangerous tendencies of increasing wealth and power of privileged corporations." A farmer objected that the railroad would bring cheaper produce from distant places, thereby driving down the price of local goods, while an innkeeper feared he would lose the stagecoach trade. But the most poignant remark came from the citizen who declared, "It's sinful to travel at a speed of fifteen miles per hour—the Lord provided men and animals with legs!"[52]

Amidst these changes and resistance to change, residents formed the FWA to advocate the rights of the "laboring classes." Generally native New Englanders, most FWA members were born in Massachusetts or New Hampshire.[53] Journeymen artisans with little or no property formed the largest occupational group in the association, supplying most of its leadership as well.[54] Representing a typical array of small-town craftsmen, they included carpenters, masons, shoemakers, harnessmakers, a bookbinder, a gunsmith, a chairmaker, and a carriagemaker. Shopkeepers and professionals, though few, were also involved: two young law students and a bookseller provided essential debating, writing, and publicity skills, while a Congregationalist minister lent church space and an important measure of legitimacy to the movement. A third of the membership worked in the mills or were common day laborers.[55]

As in Fall River, many in the movement were active and respected members of the Fitchburg community: associates of the Fitchburg Lyceum, officers of the town militia, lesser officials of the town government—and members of local churches. John Caldwell, a local sash and blind maker, had been chosen "measurer of wood and bark" by his fellow townspeople as early as 1831. Before joining the FWA, he had served as selectman, firewarden, and captain of the local militia. An early temperance advocate, he was a member of the executive committee of the local Washingtonian Total Abstinence Society. In 1844 he owned his own house, barn, and lot of land. He was also a churchgoer—indeed a longtime member and leader of the First Parish Church (Unitarian). Active in the political, economic, and social life of Fitchburg, he participated in the town's cultural and spiritual life as well.[56] As a member of a local church, he perceived no conflict between his advocacy of labor's rights and his religious faith. To the contrary, activists like Caldwell insisted that membership in the Christian community decreed their involvement. As one early FWA resolution declared, "The Workingman's caus is one of philanthropy and Christianity and as christians and as citizens we are bound to sustain it."[57]

Congregationalist FWA members Ebenezer and Goldsmith Bailey had grown up in Fitchburg, coming to town with their mother in 1826 shortly after their father died. When they first arrived, the small family stayed with Benjamin Snow, a prominent local manufacturer. Most likely, the two young brothers played with Snow's son Benjamin, Jr., who would become one of the town's leading reformers and a compatriot in the FWA. They also had early contact with factory workers, for their mother quickly secured a "tenement" for her family, paying for it by taking in boarders who worked in a nearby mill. As young boys, Ebenezer and Goldsmith became acquainted with male overseers and female operatives drawn to Fitchburg from surrounding Massachusetts and southern New Hampshire communities.[58]

The Baileys' early religious training was typical of the era. One of Ebenezer's childhood pastimes was reading aloud from the "Old Family Bible," which he recalled was prominently displayed on the living room desk. He also remembered attending religious services at the First Parish Church, sitting in the Snows' pew for the first few Sundays the family lived in Fitchburg. When his mother joined the Calvinistic Congregational Church shortly after their arrival, he worshiped there with her and attended its Sabbath school. Both he and his brother became lifelong members of this congregation.[59]

They also took a leading interest in FWA affairs. In its early stages, they offered an important set of resolutions outlining the group's basic beliefs, demands, and vision, and they helped draft a critical address to the inhabitants of Fitchburg. Ebenezer served on a number of association committees and was for a while the group's secretary. Further, both brothers regularly participated in FWA debates, one of the organization's principal activities.[60] Since both were highly literate—Ebenezer a bookbinder and stationer and his brother a printer and law student—participation in these debates must have come naturally to them. Indeed, they regularly discussed matters of public concern at the Fitchburg Young Men's Lyceum, whose first president was their childhood friend, Benjamin Snow, Jr.[61]

Jeremiah Kinsman, Jr., one of the FWA's three directors, was the grandson of Jeremiah Kinsman, Jr., of Ipswich, who had settled in Fitchburg after the American Revolution. A war hero and skilled cooper, he and his son, the second Jeremiah, helped found the Calvinistic Congregational Church in 1805. The third Jeremiah, in his midthirties in 1844, became a cooper as well, with a house and shop on Main Street. During the 1830s and 1840s, he served as "culler of hoops and staves," "hogreeve," and school committee member. Following the course set by his father and grandfather, he joined the Calvinists in 1826. Here, he helped lead the fight for a strong declaration against slavery, which led to the formation of another Congregational church, known as the Trinitarian, in 1842. Kinsman became one of the new congregation's early officers.[62]

FWA vice president William S. Wilder was also a prominent citizen, churchgoer, and reformer. A bookbinder and printer, he was editor of the town newspaper during the early 1840s. Arriving in 1834 with a letter from the

Baptist Church of neighboring Ashburnham, he became a leader of the Fitchburg Baptists. In 1846 he left for New York City, where he spent the rest of his life working as a minister among the city's poor.[63] Another FWA Baptist, Hosea Proctor, a carpenter who presided at meetings and helped draft the association's constitution, was a longtime resident of Fitchburg. Captain of the local militia, he served as the town's tithingman in 1830 and as its surveyor of lumber in 1831. A stable member of the artisan community, in 1844 Proctor owned half a house, half a barn, and a small piece of land.[64]

Again, as in Fall River, it was not just the FWA leadership who attended local churches: the percentage of communicants in the association as a whole approximated the proportion of churchgoers in the broader community.[65] The percentage of those belonging to the Calvinistic Congregational, First Parish (Unitarian), and Baptist churches reflected their numerical strength in the community. Fitchburg Congregationalists, who dominated the town's early religious life, divided into Calvinist and Unitarian camps in the early nineteenth century.[66] By the 1840s, the Calvinists ranked first in membership, while the Unitarians ranked third. The Baptists, who had worshiped in private homes or schoolhouses from Fitchburg's formation in 1764, were unable to organize a society and build their own church until the 1830s. In the revivals of this decade they won enough converts to constitute the town's second largest congregation by 1844.[67]

While the numbers of Calvinists, Unitarians, and Baptists in the association can be explained by their predominance in the community, the Trinitarians (Third Congregational Society) and the Methodists accounted for a disproportionately high percentage of FWA churchgoers. With 13 percent of the association's communicants but less than 5 percent of the town's total church membership, the Trinitarians had seceded from the Calvinist Congregationalists during the early 1840s after several years of unsuccessful agitation for a firm church declaration against slavery. Their covenant of 1843 proclaimed their opposition to liquor, slavery, and all social distinctions. Rejecting discrimination based on nationality or race, they pledged themselves to "regard all persons according to their moral and religious worth."[68] Born of the antislavery struggle and explicitly dedicating itself to equal rights, this church contained many of Fitchburg's leading reformers. Indeed, its minister, the Reverend Philo Columbus Pettibone, was one of the FWA founders, and many of its meetings were held in his vestry.[69] Hence the disproportionate number of labor activists found in Pettibone's church.

The number of FWA Methodists is more difficult to explain. Having only 15 percent of the town's communicants but 40 percent of the FWA churchgoers,[70] this congregation did not have a strong reform tradition in Fitchburg, nor did its minister lend support to the movement.[71] The key to understanding their disproportionate presence in the FWA is their marginal status in the town—this made them a distinctive labor consituency. Though they organized a society in 1833, one year before the Baptists, they remained without a meeting-house during the 1830s, worshiping in one of the town's old public buildings. Their grove revivals reportedly drew more than a thousand people on occasion, but their apparent popularity was not reflected in their membership. Even in 1836, a revival year, they could claim no more than seventy-five congregants. Moreover, during the late 1830s, church membership declined in the face of open persecution by local townspeople. When the Methodists attempted to build a church near the local common, the town tried to block their purchase of the proposed site. Failing in that, the chairman of the board of selectmen then denied their request to use the common for their wood and supplies during the church construction. Only after several raucous town meetings was permission finally granted.[72]

The explanation for the Methodists' difficulties here no doubt lay at least partly in their constituency: the town's less stable laboring population. Though manufacturers, farmers, merchants, professionals, clerks, and public officials made up roughly 60 percent of the Unitarians, Calvinists, and Trinitarians, and 45 percent of the Baptists and Universalists, these occupations accounted for less than 20 percent of the Methodists; most Fitchburg Methodists were ar-tisans, factory workers, and laborers. Although the Baptists also claimed a number of mill workers and the Universalists a number of laborers, only the Methodists were so clearly overrepresented in the manual labor occupations. The extent of the working-class predominance in this church is strikingly revealed in the congregation's leadership in 1845: among its ten officers were five skilled artisans, two mill workers, a common laborer, and a farmer.[73]

Significantly, the real growth of the congregation occurred during the dra-matic revival of 1842–43, which immediately preceded the labor agitation of the FWA. Accompanying a wave of spiritual rebirth that swept New England during these years, this awakening in Fitchburg brought the business of the town to a standstill as townspeople attended meetings in local churches and groves. The editor of the local newspaper reported that God was "pouring out His Holy Spirit on the town of Fitchburg."[74] Though the Baptists and Calvinis-tic Congregationalists were drawn into this enthusiasm, it began among the Methodists, and they were its principal beneficiaries.[75] At its outset, this con-gregation was significantly smaller than the other two, numbering no more than fifty communicants. By late 1843, the Methodists had more than tripled in size, receiving 127 new members during the course of the revival.[76]

Most of the FWA Methodists (nearly three-quarters) were swept up in this 1842–43 revival; only two were longtime members of their congregation. By contrast, only a third of the Calvinists and none of the Trinitarians or Uni-tarians were recent converts. Although three of the seven Baptists in the organi-zation joined during the enthusiasm, two had first gone on "trial" in the Methodist Church. Furthermore, like the Fitchburg Methodists in general, the FWA Methodists were mostly mill workers and laborers. Artisans in the association were fairly evenly distributed among all of the churches, shopkeepers, clerks, professionals, and farmers were mostly Congregationalists and Unitarians, and nearly all the mill workers and laborers were Methodists.[77] Most of these FWA members had been converted in the 1842–43 revival.[78]

And, unlike the other churchgoers in the association, the Methodists were less established in the community. Only four of the FWA Methodists owned their own homes in 1844.[79] Although six had been in Fitchburg since the 1830s, residence did not always provide stability and security. Simeon Shattuck, a laborer who joined the Methodists in 1834, moved frequently during the late 1830s and 1840s. In late December 1843, the house he and his family rented burned to the ground, leaving the Shattucks "in a desperate condition." They survived through the aid of friends, eventually reestablishing themselves as renters.[80] Denis and Clarissa Blood, mill hands who were swept up in the revival, had lived and worked in Fitchburg since the late 1830s. Though they owned an ox in 1844, the following year they were propertyless.[81] The other FWA Methodists, unskilled and poor, were recent arrivals. Eliza Kimball, a twenty-two-year-old domestic from New Hampshire, lived with a local clergyman and his wife. Mary J. Wright, a young Maine native, left Fitchburg in 1845 for New Harwich, New Hampshire. William L. Davis, also from Maine, soon moved to New Bedford, Massachusetts. Scottish mill operative William Romans and laborer Francis Williams, like Kimball, Wright, and Davis, owned nothing but their labor.[82]

The historical record reveals little about life within the Fitchburg Methodist Church, the message its ministers preached, or its proselytizing activities among workers; it is difficult to know precisely why it appealed to the less established among the labor activists here, though what we know of this denomination allows some guesses. The methods and message of Methodism did attract society's poor and outcast in the early Industrial Revolution and had potentially radical social implications. Its ministers, though appointed, were often itinerant and uneducated, and they went directly to the people, with an unadorned biblical message. Theirs was a living rather than a learned clergy, whose very existence privileged emotional commitment over intellection, orality over literacy, equality over hierarchy. Meanwhile, Methodism's style was egalitarian and down-to-earth, with its insistence on the republican simplicity of the sparse and simple, even crude, meetinghouse, and its preference for the emotion-filled, mass spectacle of the protracted open-air revival. Finally, its close-knit structure—its local societies and their subdivision into "bands" and "classes" keeping the converted on the right path—offered a surrogate community amidst the fragmentation of the capitalist revolution. Stressing experience over doctrine, the ability of the individual to exercise free will in accepting or rejecting divine grace, and Christian perfection through a regenerated heart, Methodism offered the poor and oppressed a straightforward path to righteousness that took account of human actions. To be sure, Methodist doctrine ran in several directions at once, as with the simultaneous emphasis on both spiritual equality and restrained human behavior, but its potential for radicalism is clear. For the unskilled and itinerant in the FWA, Methodism offered the style and substance of total and sudden change, an eradication of human sin through the activity of ordinary individuals instilled with the spirit of Christ.[83]

Whatever attracted these activists to Methodism, the denominational spectrum within the Fitchburg Workingmen's Association suggests two quite different types of churchgoing laborites. Here, the Fitchburg experience appears to have departed from that in Fall River. Some churchgoers, particularly among the leaders and the most active, were established citizens in the community who had long been connected to its institutions of religion, just as was often the case in Fall River. But, a sizeable minority of FWA communicants were mill workers and laborers who were recent converts to Methodism. These Methodists were poorer and less rooted in the Fitchburg community; in the association, they neither held leadership positions, participated in debates at meetings, nor helped formulate the group's principles. While the Calvinists, Trinitarians, Unitarians, Baptists, and even one Universalist took leading roles in the association, the FWA Methodists were exclusively rank-and-file.[84]

Men like Ebenezer Bailey, Jeremiah Kinsman, and William S. Wilder, longstanding members of established churches in their community, probably chose their particular church because of family tradition or the progressive orientation of the congregation. Integrated into the social and cultural life of their town, they participated in the institution that constituted the social and cultural core of the town: the local meetinghouse. When they perceived that the conditions of life violated the spirit of that institution, they helped lead a movement for a redress of grievances in the name of the community and its professed religion.

But activists like Denis and Clarissa Blood, Eliza Kimball, William Davis, and Francis Williams were recent converts to the pariah Methodists, apparently attracted by a faith that preached directly to the outcast and oppressed, the unskilled poor, with few ties to the broader community. Their religion represented more of a protest against that community than an identification with it. As churchgoing citizens of a self-consciously Christian community, they enlisted in a movement that condemned the prevailing labor system and its social consequences as a betrayal of Christianity. But as they were soldiers of the movement rather than its generals, their activism provided less a way of expressing their longstanding interest in community affairs than a way for them to speak out in a community that allowed them no other voice.

Typically enough, none of this forestalled the inevitable accusations of infidelity, which surely provided a basis for unity. When he helped launch the *Wachusett Independant* as a mouthpiece for labor reform in early 1845, FWA member and Baptist communicant William Wilder noted that the charge was frequently leveled against both the paper and the association. "'First hear, then judge,'" he and his co-editor, E. R. Wilkins, advised their townsmen in the language of the Bible, warning them to "bear not false witness against thy neighbor." Disclaiming anything in their movement that was "unreasonable or unscriptural," like good Christians they set their course on the rocks of "truth and righteousness." No doubt the Methodists in the FWA would have said something similar, had they but had the voice.[85]

Boston

Though labor agitation in this era often began in factory centers like Fall River and spread to smaller industrializing towns and villages like Fitchburg, the movement's organizational center of gravity was in Boston. Here too, where early labor activism was dominated by native-born skilled artisans in the traditional crafts, laborites could be heard insisting that their constituents were churchgoing Christians.[86] When twenty-two religious societies refused to host the Boston Trades' Union's (BTU) Independence Day celebration in 1834, for example, BTU leader Seth Luther denounced the lockout as a "denial of the liberty to enter the house of God" to a body of mechanics that contained "large numbers of members of churches."[87] But, in this big and diverse city, which already numbered more than sixty thousand inhabitants by 1830, the Protestant meetinghouse was not the unchallenged center of community life that it was in smaller, more homogeneous towns and villages. While several prominent Boston labor leaders were faithful churchgoing Christians—and while many others accused their opponents of promoting infidelity by their pious hypocrisy and insisted that only labor represented the interests of "true" Christianity—comparatively few labor activists appear to have been members of the city's Protestant churches. In contrast to the churchgoing labor activist in Fall River and Fitchburg, the typical Christian laborite in Boston—at least among the leadership—was an adherent who worshiped outside the mainstream church life of the city.[88]

It is impossible to determine church participation in Boston with any real precision, but the percentage of labor activists who were church members here appears to have been significantly less than in Fall River and Fitchburg.[89] In the 1830s, there were some longtime members of local congregations in the Boston movement. Ebenezer Seaver, a Roxbury delegate to the NEA, and William G. Spear, chairman of a local NEA meeting in 1833, both had owned pews in the Hollis Street Unitarian Church since 1811.[90] Heman Holmes, a committeeman of the South Boston Shipwrights and Other Mechanics in 1834, had joined the Congregationalists in 1826.[91] And several of the most prominent leaders in the movement were churchgoing Christians. George W. Light, secretary of both the Boston Mechanics and Other Working Men and the NEA, attended the Salem

For statistics on Boston labor leaders, refer to table 4.9.

Street (Trinitarian Congregationalist) Church.[92] Aaron Clarke, secretary of the Charlestown Mechanics and Other Working Men and a longtime activist in the city's ten-hour movement, was a leading Methodist.[93]

But these laborites appear to have been in the minority in Boston. More typical was *New England Artisan* editor and BTU founder Charles Douglas, who professed faith in Christianity while maintaining his distance from the city's regular church life. His response to Boston's Freethought movement illustrates the pattern. Unlike the smaller towns and villages of the region, where Freethinkers were few and rarely organized, Boston had its own Society of Free Enquirers and a professedly infidel newspaper, the *Investigator*.[94] In early 1832, the *Investigator* boasted a readership of one thousand, and hundreds reportedly attended weekly lectures by its editor, Abner Kneeland.[95] Two years later, nearly five hundred followers had to be turned away from one of Knee-land's Sunday evening services, while the society's Wednesday night socials drew as many as two thousand. By 1836, the *Investigator* claimed more than three thousand subscribers.[96] Though little is known about the Bostonians who came to hear Kneeland, read his newspaper, and danced at his Wednesday evening affairs, it seems that Freethought did gain a following among the city's working population.[97]

In response to this movement, Douglas announced his concern about the dangers of infidelity, while taking care to blame orthodox clergymen as well as infidels like Kneeland for the problem. Condemning the Freethinker who sought to make everyone "atheists," Douglas equally condemned the "christian theologian (who) reckons it reform to evangelize the world," while "dividing themselves into a hundred parties," seeking only converts to his own sect.[98] He was more receptive to the efforts of Unitarian clergy like George Ripley and William Ellery Channing, who sought to stem the advance of Freethought by inviting their colleague Orestes Brownson to town in 1836. Once a skeptic himself and a former colleague of the Freethinkers in the New York labor movement, Brownson, they reasoned, would be the ideal candidate to win over those workers who had fallen under Kneeland's influence. In May and June 1836, Brownson delivered a series of lectures at Lyceum Hall, proclaiming Jesus "the prophet of the workingmen" and calling for the establishment of "true" Christianity through social reform. Shortly thereafter, he founded his own society, aimed at Boston's working people, calling it the "Church of the Future, the Society for Christian Union Progress."[99] At about the same time, Brownson took over the editorship of the Boston *Reformer,* successor to Douglas's *New England Artisan.*

When some local activists questioned Brownson's fidelity to the working-men's cause, Douglas came to his defense, praising the Unitarian minister's new religious society and his dedication to labor reform. Once again seeking to steer between the mainstream contemporary church on the one side and the infidels on the other, Douglas declared Brownson's effort in accord with "nature's principles, the rights of humanity and the precepts of Jesus." He predicted that the enterprise would rescue Christianity "from the grasp of selfish and designing priests and aristocrats," who had turned his religion of "charity, benevolence and kindness" into a system of "superstition and bigotry, hatred, revenge and cruelty." "Pure and undefiled religion," he insisted, echoing Paul, "does not consist in unmeaning phrases, forms and ceremonies but in the constant practice of charity, benevolence and kindness of every human being."[100] Here in Brownson's independent congregation, Douglas seemed to say, was a home for the Christian labor activist estranged from the contemporary church.

Like Douglas, most labor leaders in Boston during the 1830s professed Christianity but did not appear on the city's church membership lists. Among the three artisans who wrote the famous "Ten Hour Circular," for example, only one was a member of a Boston church. The product of a local building trades' strike, the circular sparked national agitation for shorter hours in 1835, including the first general strike in American history (in Philadelphia). It was written in the voice of the angry Christian. Labeling their movement a "holy enterprise," Seth Luther, Aaron Wood, and Levi Abell announced that the tenhour men had "taken a firm and decided stand, to obtain the acknowledgement of those rights to enable us to perform those duties we owe to God, our country and ourselves." They ended the pronouncement with this charge:

> The God of the Universe has given us time, health and strength. We utterly deny the right of any man to dictate to us how much of it we shall sell. Brethren in the City, Towns and Country, our cause is yours, the cause of Liberty, the cause of God.[101]

But, as far as we know, only Abell belonged to a local congregation, having joined the Church of the New Jerusalem (Swedenborgian) in 1823.[102] Wood often professed his faith, but denying that America had followed the path of "true" Christianity, he rejected contemporary religious institutions.[103] Luther, as we have seen, found the churches of his day too impure to warrant his devotion; indeed, he blamed them for the rise of infidelity. "Under the guise of that pure religion which proclaims 'peace on earth good will to men,'" he railed, after the BTU had been denied access to the city's churches, "they are impugning that religion, and compelling men to believe it is all deception."[104]

The pattern continued during the labor reform upsurge of the 1840s. Once again, some active members of local congregations could be found in labor's ranks. Albert J. Wright, head of a Boston branch of the New England Workingmen's Association, president of its first convention, and a founder of the local cooperative movement (Workingmen's Protective Union), had been a prominent member of South Boston's Phillips Church (Trinitarian Congregationalist) since 1838.[105] A printer, Wright started his own newspaper in 1847, the *South Boston Gazette,* in which he advocated not only shorter hours and higher wages, but antislavery, temperance, land reform, cooperation, strict observance of the Sabbath, domestic missions, and Christian morality. Meanwhile, his church, like some of those in the industrial towns, was a popular gathering place for activists in South Boston's young and growing community, including abolitionists, temperance advocates, and other reformers. Wright regularly expressed his dismay at lax church attendance, and though he blamed poverty for this sad state of affairs, he did not excuse it, appealing instead to the poor to seek salvation:

> We may be too poor to have much influence in the world, too poor to be ranked among the great of the earth, too poor even to receive the contempt of our fellow mortals;—but we are not too poor to listen to the offers of pardon which God makes to his repenting children.[106]

The commitment Wright expressed to organized religion here was not typical of his compatriots in the Boston labor movement, however. Fewer than 20 percent of the city's leading labor reformers in the NEWA and the Workingmen's Protective Union (WMPU) belonged to local churches. The editor of the *Laborer*, organ of the Boston Mechanics' Association in 1844, was more representative. In a piece entitled, "How to be Happy," Leonard Cox enjoined his readers to "honor the Sabbath, serve God, and be devoted to truth and religion." But apparently he was not himself a church member.[107] Similarly, the cooperative movement, a direct outgrowth of the struggle for the ten-hour day and general labor reform, exhibited a strong Christian spirit while its adherents maintained few ties to local congregations. Reviewing the original aims of the Boston WMPU, several of its founders remembered that "with faith in God and the right, we commenced our work by the purchase of a box of soap and one-half box of tea."[108] Among the five activists who penned these words, only one is known to have belonged to a local church. Indeed, just eight of the city's thirty-nine leading cooperationists during the late 1840s and early 1850s appeared on the city's church membership rolls.

The Boston editors of the *Voice of Industry* in the late 1840s do not appear on those lists, either; they told their readers that present-day Christianity was a sham, for "Mammonism" was the real religion of America. "Men serve the money God six days in the week and then seek an atonement by giving to their Creator a part of the Seventh," John Orvis and D. H. Jaques lamented. Businessmen, not Christians, held sway in the workshop, behind the counter, and in the marketplace; only a total restructuring of social arrangements along cooperative lines could promote "true" religion. "When Industry, Commerce, and Social Life, shall have been truly organized," they said, "we shall not only profess and preach as Christians, but shall work, trade, and live as Christians." Until then, however, "true" Christianity could flourish in neither competitive society nor in the contemporary church.

> Not by outward show,
> The church attendance and the loud voiced prayer

> Nor by the lengthened visage men shall know
> Him who the signet of the Master bears.
>> In the good time coming
>>> Not he who proudly stalks
> Into the flame, with grace and solemn face;
>> Who high of truth and justice talks,
>> And cheats his neighbor in his marketplace,
>> Shall be deemed great in the Kingdom of Heaven,
>>> but he who
>> Serves God by blessing humanity.[109]

In Boston, as in Fall River and Fitchburg, labor activists proclaimed their fidelity to Christianity. But, in this large and diverse city where the church did not enjoy the relatively unchallenged position it did in Fitchburg and Fall River, where labor leaders had to find their way between an organized Freethought movement and a generally unsympathetic clergy, where, as the BTU discovered in 1834, it was generally fruitless to look to the "religious societies" for aid and encouragement—here, apparently, relatively few labor activists were members of local churches.[110] Still, in this, Boston seems to have been the exception. Elsewhere, labor's proclaimed religious devotion did reflect a strong commitment to the mainstream church life of the community.

Was this commitment unique to pious New England, land of the Puritans? What about other areas of early labor protest, like the Mid-Atlantic region and upstate New York? Here, too, the church played a critical role in working-class formation, though the story is not a simple one, with Freethinkers of various stripes and members of a wide range of churches, from radical Quakers to outcast Methodists to mainstream Presbyterians. To determine more precisely the nature of the labor-church relationship nationally, we turn to two communities whose stories were both similar to and different from those we have seen in New England: Wilmington, Delaware, and Rochester, New York.

Chapter 5. Labor Activists in the Church: The Working Men of Wilmington, Delaware

In October 1824, Wilmington welcomed back to the United States the French general and politician, the Marquis de Lafayette, at the start of his long-awaited return visit to the nation whose independence he had helped secure. The residents of Delaware's principal town spared no effort in their preparations for the event. At the Pennsylvania state line, about seven miles away, this hero of the American Revolution was greeted by the cavalry and a contingent of some two hundred mounted civilians festooned in blue and white coats, blue stocks, and white pantaloons, after whom came the local band and a long train of equipages carrying many of the local citizenry. Clogging the road all the way back to Wilmington were the people of upper Delaware—on horseback, in carriages, on foot. As the retinue approached the town, to ringing bells and exploding cannons, this sea of humanity crossed over the Brandywine River— where Lafayette had been wounded, now the principal source of the area's industrial potential—and into Wilmington proper. Here, an enormous crowd numbering ten to twelve thousand—nearly twice the size of the local populace—awaited the general's arrival, in anticipation of the standard fare for such antebellum public celebrations: the parade through the streets, the speeches by local luminaries, and the inevitable "collation" at Town Hall.[1]

Six of those whose participation in these festivities has been recorded— William Chandler, John Clark, and Isaac Gibbs (members of various commit- tees on arrangements), Daniel Corbit (who helped draft an address to the general), Thomas Robinson (a parade marshal), and James Brobson (promi- nent guest at the dinner following the parade)—were well integrated into the Wilmington community. All were church members, several of them longtime and leading members of their congregations: Robinson, Brobson, Chandler, and Corbit were Quakers, the first two having been active in the Wilmington Monthly Meeting of Friends for the better part of twenty years at least; Gibbs was an Episcopalian, Clark a Presbyterian.[2] They also became involved in the Working Men's movement that would shortly emerge in the Wilmington area.

For statistics on the Wilmington Working Men, refer to tables 5.1–5.2.

Gibbs was a committeeman of the Association of Working People of New Castle County (AWPNCC) in 1830; the others were candidates on Working Men's tickets that emerged out of the association's activities during the early 1830s.

They were not unusual among early labor reform leaders in Wilmington, who were often churchgoers and active members of their community. Among the leaders of the AWPNCC—to take but three of many more examples—were Jacob Alrichs, a leading Quaker and town officer from the opening years of the nineteenth century; Benjamin Webb, another prominent Quaker and town officer from 1816; and James Siddal, a longtime and active Episcopalian. Indeed, as a mill worker in 1815, Siddal helped organize what may have been the first Sabbath school in America, and he was one of the citizens who offered a public toast at Wilmington's Fourth of July celebration in 1829.[3]

Much has been written about this early chapter in American labor history—known traditionally as the era of the Working Men's party (WMP)—though the movement encompassed much more than independent electoral activity. Precious little has been written about the importance of religion (and accusations of irreligion) in its life (and death). The Wilmington story—outside of New England, New York City, and Philadelphia, the Working Men had their greatest impact here—opens a window onto this neglected aspect of the movement, as it reveals an intimate connection between its religious zealotry and the charges of religious infidelity against it, between its twin goals of labor reform and religious reform, between class conflict and religious conflict. Here once again were activists who were openly critical of the church, while themselves church members. And, though accused of opposing religion, they crafted an ideology of labor reform explicitly based on their version of "primitive Christianity." They envisioned a secular utopia but spoke the language of Christian millennialism. Like their compatriots in many parts of New England, these were labor activists *and* churchgoers. Here, though, it was not the Baptists, Methodists, Christians, or Congregationalists who formed the dynamic core of the movement's church adherents, but a group of radical Quakers. The result was something both similar to and different from what we have seen in New England.

The Working Men

First "discovered" (though not settled) in 1609 by Dutch sailors in search of a western route to the East Indies, the land that became Delaware passed successively to Swedish soldiers and farmers, Dutch traders, and finally English settlers.[4] Wilmington, the hub and county seat of upper Delaware owed much of its character—in a sense, its very existence—to its northern neighbor, Pennsylvania.[5] For though there had been settlements on the site since the 1630s, it was largely wilderness until the 1730s, when the growing agricultural

surplus of nearby Lancaster and Chester Counties gave impetus to the establishment of "Wilmingtown," a transshipment point for the marketing of flour
in Philadelphia, only twenty-seven miles upriver along the Delaware.[6] Many of
the town's first settlers migrated from that city, the model for Wilmingtown's
original street plan.[7] In a kind of re-creation of the Quaker City in miniature—
a process that would both spur and frustrate early-nineteenth-century residents of Wilmington—the town was settled largely by Quaker artisans, millers,
and merchants, producing a world of small artisan shops, mills, and
countinghouses.

It grew rapidly in the early nineteenth century. Built between the banks of
the Brandywine and Christiana Rivers, astride the Delaware River as it empties
into Delaware Bay and the Atlantic Ocean, Wilmington was ideally located to
process and market the grain of New Castle County and southeastern Pennsylvania. Flour milling, moreover, gave rise to the ancillary production of barrels
and a brisk coopers' trade. And, too, given the plentiful waterpower in the area
(from the Brandywine, but also from the two tributaries of the Christiana, Red
Clay and White Clay Creeks), Wilmington and its environs in the first third of
the nineteenth century quickly became a manufacturing center as well as a port
and market town, producing textiles, paper, gunpowder, machinery, and ships.

But, in only the first three of these industries did owners employ more than
a handful of workers. Indeed, with few exceptions, certainly before the 1840s
and generally until the Civil War, industrial production in Wilmington was
financed by local capital, sometimes by skilled workers, and was carried on in
small groups of craftsmen in unmechanized shops. Throughout the early nineteenth century, small artisan shops proliferated in the production of, for example, consumer goods, notably in leather, clocks and watches, and carriages.[8]
There was, too, much interaction among these local industries as, for example,
tanners sold to carriage builders and small iron foundries turned out frames for
carriages and parts for machinery. Meanwhile, retail shops, taverns, and hotels
sprang up in response to the growth in population and income. Out of this
changing artisan world of wage earners and self-employed, working in small
groups or alone, would emerge a major center of labor reform.[9]

Organized activity began with the national upsurge of Working Men's parties during the late 1820s, a crucial moment in the history of the American
working class and a subject of much controversy among historians. Its genesis,
nationally and in Wilmington, merits some discussion.[10] The WMP first appeared in 1828 in Philadelphia, where the Mechanics' Union of Trade Associations (MUTA) decided to enter politics to advance "the interests and enlightenment of the working classes." The idea was quickly taken up in New York City;
here, a Working Men's party entered the fray in the elections of 1829, and in the
next few years similar groups appeared in scores of communities throughout
the nation, in small towns and rural areas as well as major metropolitan
centers, in the South as well as the Northeast. The movement peaked in most

areas in 1830 with several dramatic electoral successes and then rapidly dissipated, though there was a resurgence of labor politics in New England with the
founding of the NEA in late 1831.[11] The first labor parties in the world, the
Working Men put the United States, in this respect at least, in the forefront of
modern working-class agitation.

Close to Philadelphia, industrializing Wilmington caught the fever early on.
Local residents were well aware of the shorter-hours dispute in Philadelphia
that had led to the formation of the Working Men's party there, and they read
the *Mechanics' Free Press*.[12] In June 1829, a local editorial noted the activities of
the "mechanics" of nearby Lancaster and Carlisle, Pennsylvania; even before
this, there had been talk of establishing an organization of "citizen mechanics"
with aims similar to those of the MUTA in Philadelphia.[13] Though there may
have been secret meetings among local residents prior to this, the first public
notices, addressed to the "Mechanics and Operatives Generally," appeared in
late July.[14] More meetings took place in August, when a constitution was
written, and in September the group issued an address to the "Mechanics,
Manufacturers and Producers" under the name of the "Association of Working
People of New Castle County."[15]

The connection between this group and the subsequent emergence of a
WMP in the county is a bit murky, but it appears that the latter was the
former's political arm, just as the Philadelphia WMP was the political embodiment of the MUTA.[16] Unlike in Philadelphia, though, where months of organizing paid off in spectacular if ephemeral successes at the polls, in Wilmington
lack of preparation and experience resulted in a poor showing in most of the
"hundreds" in the fall of 1829.[17] Not so the following April: on the eve of the
municipal elections in the borough of Wilmington, the association passed a
series of resolutions that revealed a distinct political orientation. Announcing
that they had "associated together for the purpose of exercising for ourselves,
the right of choosing law makers and law enforcers, free from all party spirit,
party feeling and party interference,—and to exercise the privilege we possess
as freemen, of advocating such measures as are best calculated to promote and
perpetuate Freedom, Equality, and the Public Good," the group endorsed a
series of demands obtainable through political action. They called for a "Republican System of Education," a mechanics' lien law, abolition of public
lotteries and imprisonment for debt, less burdensome taxes, a simplified and
inexpensive legal system, and a more open and democratic electoral process.
On this platform—the basic platform of most WMPs throughout the nation—
a Working Men's ticket swept the town elections ten days later.[18]

In turn, the WMP spawned an independent ticket of delegates to the
Delaware constitutional convention of 1832. Indeed, the very idea for the
convention, the first in the state since 1792, was spearheaded by Wilmington-
area Working Men. In September 1831, after nearly a year and a half of debate
within the movement on the merits of democratization through constitutional

reform, an initial meeting was held in Christiana Hundred chaired by John Reynolds, successful candidate for town treasurer on the Working Men's ticket of spring 1830.[19] The assembly then called for a countywide meeting of the friends of Convention and Reform at Sawdon's Corner, where the WMP had met earlier in the year. Of the ten delegates chosen for an independent voters ticket by that body, half had previously been WMP candidates.[20] The movement for constitutional reform was not synonymous with the Working Men's movement, but many of the participants and the thrust of many of the proposed changes identify this episode, too, as part of a broader "moment" in the history of Wilmington labor protest.

In personnel, identity, program, and analysis, this movement—the Working People's Association, the Working Men's tickets of 1830–31, the subsequent independent delegation ticket of 1832—was a workers' movement with a workers' agenda, though others were involved. The principal leaders of the association were artisans (at least a third of the total, and nearly half of those whose occupations could be identified), mostly small masters who either worked alone or with a few journeymen and apprentices.[21] Typically, they worked in metal, leather, clocks and watches, wood, and printing. Few worked in the mills, though a couple were skilled mill workers; among them were a handful of professionals and shopkeepers.[22] Though the men on the various Working Men's tickets of 1830 and 1831 were clearly more affluent as a group than were the leaders of the association, they too were mostly artisans, with perhaps more farmers. Both groups were stable by early-nineteenth-century standards. In their ranks were longtime residents of the Wilmington area; indeed, a number could trace their Delaware ancestors back into the seventeenth century.[23] Many, particularly among the WMP candidates, had served on local civic committees and as town and state officers. The Working Men's movement in Wilmington was led by a mixed group of modest to prosperous Wilmingtonians, predominantly artisan and self-made and well integrated into the economic, social, and political life of the community in which they and their families had resided for a long time.[24]

As for the movement's self-identity, typical of labor movements throughout the nineteenth century, the Wilmington activists used many labels to describe themselves and their constituency. Claiming to be part of a movement of "the Working Classes" and seeking correspondence with their "fellow workmen" elsewhere, they chose the title "Working People"—"the 'bone and sinew' of the body politic"—for their association.[25] They spoke most often of the interests of the "Farmers, Mechanics and other Working Men," though they included in their constituency the unskilled mill worker (the "operative") and even the "manufacturer." Sometimes, they simply used the all-inclusive term, the *productive class*. And sometimes, their identity was broader still. Disdaining "speculators and designing men" of all stripes—"mere drones in the hive"—they pictured themselves as "the People" battling for the community against its enemies.26 Again typical of nineteenth-century labor reformers, they used terms like *republican* and *aristocrat* to refer to themselves and their enemies, and *freeman* and *slave* to refer to their present or future condition, respectively. Yet, *labor* was the common root of their analysis, the fulcrum of their worldview.

Thus, their principal activities—lectures and a Working Men's reading room, a debating society and a savings fund society, political lobbying and electoral campaigning—were geared to advancing the interests of workers, broadly defined. Thus, too, their demands, though broad and inclusive, were couched in class terms.27 Declaiming that "one class of men are sunk so far below the rest" in a nation that had been created upon the principle of freedom and equality, the association insisted that "though we are nominally a 'governing and self governed people,'" the "poor have no laws,—the laws are made by the rich, and of course for the rich." The solution: "*union among the working people.*"28 So, for example, they sought a lien law in order to secure "to the Mechanic and Working Man his just wages," while they sought the exemption from execution of "certain property, necessary to the Farmer, Mechanic and Working Man."29 The entire panoply of their demands—state-supported education; the abolition of debt imprisonment, chartered monopolies, and lotteries; law, tax, and militia reform; a prohibition on religious legislation—were seen as ways of freeing working people from the chains of ignorance and economic and political oppression and allowing their full participation in the life of the community and nation.30

Finally, they had a class analysis, locating present evils in systemic problems. Jonas Pusey, a leading officer of the AWPNCC, the Working Men's Reading Club, and the WMP, acknowledged that machinery was a boon to the community, but insisted that the "benefits are monopolized by the capitalist." His objection lay "not so much against their introduction [machines] as against the system—the circumstances of things under which they are brought into operation."31 And, focusing on enacting "good and wholesome" laws, the Working Men clearly connected political with class privilege. AWPNCC secretary George McFarlane reminded his compatriots that labor-saving machinery would inevitably "make the rich richer, and the poor poorer . . . so long as the benefits are all reaped by the employer, or by legislative enactment secured to chartered monopolies."32

Infidelity and the Church

Like labor reformers elsewhere, the Working Men of Wilmington were accused of being infidels; indeed, that charge may have contributed heavily to the movement's ultimate demise.33 In January 1830, George Reynolds, committeeman and business agent of the AWPNCC and an editor and general agent of the

Delaware Free Press, noted the cries of "combinations," "heresy," and "infidelity" against his movement; three months later Henry Wilson, association committeeman, librarian of the Working Men's Reading Room, and publisher and sometime-editor of the *DFP,* lamented that the Working Men were called "Rabble Mechanics" and their organizations, "Infidel Clubs."[34] The activists vehemently rejected the accusation. George McFarlane claimed that the "cry is getting rather stale," and challenged local editors to "bring forward some proof to substantiate this charge," while Reynolds condemned "malignant aspersions of slander" on the association, which was being "branded with the *unmeaning name of infidel.*"[35] For the Working Men, however, the fact that they were so labeled was itself evidence of their "authenticity," of the threat that they posed to their class enemy. So, Reynolds: "The charge of infidelity made against the voters [for the WMP], is proof of their being indeed *Working* Men—not that I would wish to insinuate the truth of the assertion of a worthy person of this place that 'all Working Men are infidels,' but that it shows them to be opposed to the interests of those classes who are always ready to raise the hue and cry of heresy and infidelity, when they have reason to think their craft is in danger."[36] In essence, when the "aristocrats" screamed "infidel!" the offending party must be the advocates of labor reform. Here, religion and class were joined.

In fact, there were heretical religious voices among the Wilmington Working Men. McFarlane, for example, was a deist from Philadelphia who later founded that city's Society of Free Enquirers.[37] Like his hero Tom Paine, he doubted Christ's divinity, rejected the Bible as the revelation of God, condemned the church and clergy as violent persecutors of the masses ("wily intolerants" and "priestly intermeddlers" who filled "the blood stained pages of religious history"), and repudiated any religion that threatened hell and promised heaven to ensure right thought and behavior.[38] But, again like Paine, McFarlane was no atheist. He believed in God and spoke of the "Creator," the "God of Reason," and the "spirit of nature."[39] He also had a religion—a "religion unsullied by crime," an "orthodoxy enough to be the creed of any rational human being"—which, based on fundamental principles of morality, could be found in Paine's *Age of Reason.*[40] Most important for his labor advocacy, though, he believed in Divine Providence, speaking not just vaguely of "that Power," but also of an "over-ruling Providence," which presided over the affairs of the nation and guided events.[41] And his writings and speeches were filled with religious rhetoric and imagery, as he could make effective use of the Old and New Testaments.[42] Indeed, when McFarlane quoted Shakespeare and Jefferson, the passages were often those that contained religious language![43]

Much of the "heresy" of other Wilmington Working Men was opposition to state-sanctioned religion, not to religion per se. Thus, amidst calls for the constitutional convention, the AWPNCC registered its objection to the first article of the current constitution—which declared it the duty of all "frequently to associate together, for the public worship of the Author of the

Universe"—arguing that while the idea "*may or may not be sound*" the entire matter was one of individual "concernment" rather than the business of government.[44] As we have seen, this would hardly have distinguished the Wilmington Working Men from labor activists elsewhere in antebellum America, including self-proclaimed Christian labor activists. Nor is it surprising to find that the Working Men railed against the depredations of a "designing priesthood," the threat of tyranny posed by the "union of church and state," and the "liars, hypocrites, and deceived" who filled the church—all these were complaints of Christian labor reformers everywhere.[45]

More important, though, the Working Men's "moment" in Wilmington was a "churched" affair.[46] Prominent among the churchgoing laborites were Quakers, but Working Men could be found among the Methodists, Presbyterians, and Episcopalians as well. Indeed, of the nearly one hundred association leaders and Working Men's candidates named in the local press, at least 40 percent were church members.[47] Quakers accounted for at least one-quarter of this movement's spokesmen and representatives, and better than two-fifths of its church members, the rest divided among the other three principal denominations, with, it seems, a preponderance of Methodists.

The denominational preference of early Wilmington labor reformers is explained in some measure by the simple fact that when the movement first surfaced here in the late 1820s, the principal denominations among the populace were the Quakers, Methodists, Presbyterians, and Episcopalians.[48] Wilmington Episcopalianism had emerged from the late-eighteenth-century anglicization of Delaware's first congregation, a Swedish Lutheran church known in the nineteenth century as "Old Swede's" or "Holy Trinity." More important in the nineteenth century, though, were the Presbyterians, who began meeting in New Castle in 1685, building their first church in 1707; by 1829, there were three such congregations in Wilmington itself.[49] More important still were the Methodists, who had emerged dramatically in the area at the time of the American Revolution, only to face severe persecution in its aftermath, no doubt in part because they were popular among the poor. By the 1820s, Methodism was the town's fastest-growing denomination.[50]

It was not the Methodists, however, but the Quakers who proved the most important Christian denomination in the emergence of labor reform in Wilmington. They had organized a congregation (New Wark Friend's Meeting) in Brandywine Hundred as early as the 1680s; they founded Wilmington in the 1730s, establishing a meeting in 1737 and a meetinghouse, the first in the borough, a year later; they controlled essential activities in the town at least until the 1830s.[51] Quaker simplicity set the tone for the community: their meeting was its most potent private institutional force, their school (established 1748) its first permanent school, their philanthropies its dominant benevolent institutions.[52]

Moreover, though very different in theology and organization from the

Methodists, this group also possessed a style and message that was potentially radical in its social implications: founder George Fox's emphasis on the "Inner Light" as the essential guide to both salvation and human behavior, the rejection of social distinctions, opposition to any controls on the human conscience, and, correspondingly, the general tolerance for differing views. With William Penn's early control over New Castle County, the Wilmington area became, in a sense, part of that Quaker's Holy Experiment of those fleeing religious persecution.[53] Wilmington Quakerism, moreover, was fiercely egalitarian: in the graveyard, there were no family plots, and no head or foot stones; in the meetinghouse, as with the Asbury Methodists, all seats were free; in the meetings, the proceedings began with the biblical injunction to "love one another" and carried on in a plain style.[54] From among these radical religionists came the most prominent churchgoers among the Working Men, the first labor activists in Wilmington.

Religion and the *Delaware Free Press*

At the same time, these Quakers were also the source of heretical religious ideas among the Wilmington Working Men. Their voice was the *Delaware Free Press,* which was similar in origin, focus, and style to the *Mechanics' Free Press* of Philadelphia. Not devoted entirely to "labor" issues, and not controlled by the AWPNCC, the *DFP* nevertheless deserves the label of "labor newspaper."[55] Arising out of the perceived need within the movement for its own press—it was to be "dedicated to Truth, and espousing and advocating the rights of even the Mechanic and Working Man," as Reynolds put it in the first issue—the paper listed as a principal objective, "to awaken the attention of the Working People to the importance of co-operation in order to attain that rank and station in society to which they are justly entitled by their virtues and industry, but from which they have been excluded."[56] Moreover, its founders were AWPNCC leaders, as were most of its half-dozen editors during its three-and-a-half-year lifespan.[57] As for content, its columns carried notices of strikes in the Wilmington area, descriptions of workers' celebrations in Philadelphia, excerpts of labor addresses in Massachusetts, and reprints from labor papers in New York. Correspondents identified themselves as "A Working Man" or "A Laborer" or "A Mechanic"; many discoursed on the virtues of the shorter workday. The *DFP* was the Working Men's only outlet in the Wilmington area, and it was popular among area workers.[58]

In the pages of this paper, activists articulated a religious and class perspective within the dissenting Protestant tradition we have seen in New England. First and foremost, it was devoted to "free discussion"—that is, free of "orthodoxy" of any sort.[59] However, though some of its correspondents were Freethinkers who rejected religion, the editors rejected much heterodoxy as well.

For, as "sincere and honest inquirers after truth," they insisted that liberalism inhered in disposition rather than content, that "true and general liberality is not the necessary consequence of sceptical opinions."[60] Indeed, the discourses on religion in its pages, by editors and correspondents alike, reveal a movement dedicated more to "pure" religion—even "primitive Christianity"—than to what is usually associated with Freethought. Hence, they reprinted letters from Cornelius Blatchley, the Quaker physician whose writings in the 1820s helped establish the framework for the trenchant critique of inequality, competition, and property relations that developed among New York City artisans in this period. Blatchley, an associate of Owen and Wright who was nominated for office by the New York WMP in 1829 and who ritually denounced "priestcraft or churchcraft" and the "Christian party in politics," was regularly labeled an infidel, but he consistently affirmed his belief in revealed Christianity. A habitual quoter of Scripture whose "perfectionist millenarianism" drew on the traditions of the seventeenth-century English sectarian radicals, Blatchley blended Christian ethics, republican politics, and the labor theory of value.[61]

Blatchley's fellow Quakers associated with the *DFP* were cut from the same cloth. Listen, for example, to their response to the infidelity charge in their first issue: quoting from Sewell's *Sir Walter Raleigh*, the editors reminded their readers, "when prejudice and strong aversions work / All whose opinion we dislike are Atheists," noting that often those who were called "atheists" were in fact those with "pure" religion in their souls. Meanwhile, in a spirited defense of Voltaire's religion, "W" declared that "protestants are all infidels, in the mother church of Rome." Indeed, said "G.P.," all followers of "the meek and quiet spirit promulgated by Jesus Christ" had been charged with heresy and had been called "infidel," "deist," and "atheist"; working people should expect to be unjustly slandered in this manner by these "followers of the 'meek and lowly Jesus.'"[62]

Partly for this reason, the *DFP*—like its counterparts elsewhere—sought to avoid the subject of religion, rejecting both religious sectarianism and "sceptical speculation."[63] And yet these Working Men—again like their compatriots elsewhere—were strikingly unsuccessful in keeping religion off the agenda. By the end of the first month of publication, the editors had received more than one hundred articles on religious topics. This outpouring marked the Working Men's movement unmistakably as an unorthodox but predominantly Christian movement, though typically there was enormous diversity in the ranks. The columns of the paper provide a window onto that world.

On the far end of the spectrum were deists like "Amen," who professed belief in a God of Nature as the motive of the universe, and relegated Moses, Jesus, and Muhammad to the status of men who provided good examples and moral precepts. There were also materialists like "Observer," who denied the truth of creation entirely.[64] Beyond even these elements was "Cato," who condemned the American Sunday School Union as an "engine of superstition and priestcraft," the tool of "ambitious religionists."[65] In registering this fear of organized religion, his views were unexceptional—he merely tapped a deep-seated suspiciousness in the culture of an unholy alliance of church and state. But "Cato" went further, rejecting what he called the modern definition of religion, namely that "Christianity is the only true religion." The "bible" was "in some respects" "a good book of morals" but not a revelation of God to humanity.[66] Jesus, who "taught nothing but morality," was employed to attack the churchgoers of the day: "he was no sectarian, but was an enemy to priests, and all preaching for money." This writer even assailed, as "a position too weak and absurd for even a lawyer to assume," the widely held belief that the prosperity of nations depended on religion. Infidelity, in fact, suggested merely a want of faith, which proved only that the bearer was too honest and independent to pretend to believe what no one could comprehend.

But such heretics represented only one extreme in a diverse movement. At the other end of the spectrum were the more traditional religionists found in and around the labor movement everywhere during these years. "Mosheim" may have feared that *DFP* correspondents "disbelieved the sacred truths of the scriptures," but "Common Sense" looked forward to the Millennium ("'peace on earth and goodwill towards men'"), while "An Unprejudiced Observer" pronounced Jesus "the high priest and ruler," whose divinity must be acknowledged ("surely there is but one true God, and Jesus Christ is his son, and mediator between him and man").[67] Similarly, there were many who accepted the Bible as revelation, even if they insisted that the disbeliever be tolerated.[68]

Actually, most of the writers in the *DFP* were neither heterodox nor orthodox; like their counterparts in New England—and, as we will see, upstate New York—they were critics within the Christian tradition. Typically, they championed "true," sometimes "primitive," Christianity by distinguishing, in Voltaire's words, "religion and its abuses" and "christianity and its corruptions."[69] Thus, "Justitia" had a rather different perspective than "Cato" on the question of Sunday mail: "this religion of the *law* and the *state* is the very reverse of things pure and excellent," but "religion is emphatically a good thing."[70] Generally, this majority position rejected deism and materialism because of the sectarianism and intolerance of their purveyors—and rejected contemporary Christianity for the same reason. At the same time, however, many were too much wedded to the Christian Bible and tradition to embrace an openly infidel position.

When *DFP* writers rejected revivals, for example, they did so on moral-religious grounds. In the spring of 1831, amidst a series of protracted meetings, "Truth" warned in "Night Meetings" that such events drew sons, daughters, and apprentices out of the house and into all kinds of mischief in the community, leading the females to corruption and the males to drunkenness and crime. His advice to parents? Keep your children at home and have them read the Bible.[71] The following summer, one of the editors warned that an ongoing revival would inevitably lead to injury to both the community and the individual. Why? Because it represented a rejection of Christian humility in usurping the power to bestow grace from God to man through prayer.[72] Wouldn't it be better, the editor asked, quoting Jesus, to seek first the kingdom of heaven that is "'within you,'" and trust that all things will be added, leaving the disposal of the future "to that power which has regulated and governed the past"?[73]

The most telling evidence of the Christian, if unorthodox, character of the movement, is that most of the editors, notably Benjamin Webb and his assistant George Reynolds, were members of the Wilmington Monthly Meeting of Friends.[74] They fit the mold—so common in labor circles of these years—of the deeply pious Christian alarmed at developments in religion and society, determined to set both right through Christian labor reform. Reynolds, a printer who had been born into a Quaker family in Brandywine Village at the turn of the century, opposed "the present system of Christianity" (even in his own faith) for its "rules, disciplines, creeds, and dogmas" and its corrupt clergy ("who have ever discovered enemies of God in the friends of mankind, and haters of religion in 'lovers of truth'"). In its stead, he advocated "true" religion based on the Quaker "Light within," works over faith, and especially the traditional Jesus, who had "exposed the church and priesthood."[75]

Webb, a key committeeman in the AWPNCC, left the greatest mark on the *DFP;* the sheer volume of his writings in the paper mark him as a figure worthy of some attention. He was a Quaker, but the religion he articulated on behalf of labor reform was remarkably similar to that of other labor reformers who were Baptists, Congregationalists, or Universalists, and even of those who adhered to no particular church at all. Webb's obituary in 1851 summed up his life in explicitly religious terms. Few had passed away "with a conscience clearer toward God and man" than this abolitionist, temperance advocate, education reformer, and champion of the Working Man, his eulogizer wrote. A prominent and active member of the Wilmington community for nearly half a century—as a trustee of the African School Society in 1816, director of the local Temperance Society at its founding in 1827, organizer of the Free Produce movement in 1825 and the Delaware Abolition Society in 1827, and member of the Wilmington town council in 1816 and 1829—Webb was a model Christian.[76] A Quaker "from youth up," he sought "the essential secret of goodness," "Truth as the highest good of life." His idea of religion came from the apostle Paul: "Pure religion and undefiled before God and the Father, is this: to visit the widows and fatherless in their affliction, and to keep himself unspotted from the world."[77] Ever the pious Quaker, on his deathbed he advised minding the Light, and finding its saving power. "It is," he said at the end, "the Savior of the World."[78]

At times, Webb's religious framework was explicitly Christian, even evangelical, as he spoke of the "universal savior of the Holy Spirit Jesus said was in the Kingdom of Heaven and within you."[79] At other times, the message seemed fiercely rationalistic: the "Light within" was "nothing more than the internal sense of right and wrong that every rational creature possesses."[80] But, though Webb exalted human reason, he was thoroughly a Quaker in crediting feeling rather than ratiocination in coming to "know" God.[81] Ultimately, he embraced a thoroughgoing spiritual individualism that categorically rejected any set language to describe what was ultimately an intimate relationship between individual and Maker. As he once pointed out, language was a contrivance of human beings, and words could no more explain "the Power that pervades nature" than one's name could delineate one's physical or moral character.[82] Indeed, he rejected all intermediaries and creeds, insisting that Jesus had in fact established no particular religion.[83] This reasoning took him about as far as he could go in the Protestant tradition while remaining a Christian.

But Christian he was, and he summed up his religion in the same phrase used by other antebellum labor advocates: "practical Christianity." For Webb, as for Fitchburg's William Young, this theology was predicated first and foremost on a religion of "works": "not by their faith, but by their works are they known."[84] Proclaiming no fear of a future hell or anticipation of a future heaven, he spoke of living in the "eternal now," in conformity with "'thy will, not mine be done.'" The only preparation for this—contrary to the proscriptions of most "professors" and "priests" who tormented congregations with the threat of future punishments—was the "faithful discharge of our social duties through life," since "no life can be pleasing to God, but that which is useful to man." This was the way to heaven, he insisted, "a *state* of existence, not a *place* of abode." Webb's reform activity was thus rooted in a kind of "primitive Christianity," based on the teachings and example of Jesus: "that religion which leads us to do good, and to love all men, 'even our enemies,' must in itself be good, and so proceed from God."[85] The rule and law of his life had always been, he said in 1831, to make his life useful to others, and to do as done by: "if christianity means righteousness, or the practice of those moral virtues which relieve the widow and the orphan, gives comfort to the disconsolate and afflicted, and in short makes man better and happier in his present condition, then I am a christian."[86]

The Hicksite Schism

As an advocate of religious and labor reform, Webb also did battle with some of his fellow Quakers. Along with several other Working Men, he was at the center of a controversy in the Wilmington Friends community whose origins lay in the momentous division in American Quakerism known as the "Hicksite schism" (1827–28).[87] In the end, Webb would have to defend both his religious views and his social activism before his Quaker brethren, though to no avail.

He was expelled from the Wilmington Monthly Meeting in the summer of 1831; presently, several of his Quaker compatriots in the Working Men's movement suffered the same fate. Revealing the emergence of a thoroughgoing individualism and the consequent fragmenting tendency within contemporary religious and social movements, the episode also reveals just how intertwined were religion and working-class radicalism in this era.

In the late 1820s, American Quakerism was racked by disrupted meetings, physical confrontations, even near riots, which divided families, neighborhoods, and, for well over a century, the faith itself.[88] Building for the better part of the decade, with roots that stretched back well into the eighteenth century, the schism involved the expulsion of rural, small town, and recent urban migrant followers of the New York farmer-preacher Elias Hicks by a socially prominent urban minority. The struggle pitted the Hicksites, who championed local autonomy and the mystical, inward religion of Quakerism's seventeenth-century founders, against the orthodox, who insisted on some centralized control and the more recent evangelical emphasis on the formal and outward, such as prescribed behavior, the Bible as absolute authority, and benevolent associations.[89]

The epicenter of the controversy was Philadelphia, the cradle of American Quakerism. But Wilmington, the second largest city in the Philadelphia Yearly Meeting, was the site of the movement's most radical manifestations. It was here, free of the limiting influence of the Philadelphia elders but without the stifling provincialism of rural life, that liberty of conscience enjoyed its greatest play. Indeed, after the Hicksites had triumphed in Wilmington, there was a second division—a schism within the schism—as a handful of Quakers, several of whom became deeply involved in the Working Men's movement, came to champion free inquiry and radical tolerance. Such advocacy proved too much for most Hicksites, though not for labor activists, and, in some measure, this second religious rift among the Quakers paralleled the class rift signified by the Working Men's movement.

In Wilmington, the proper beginning of the story is 1824, when local Friends William Gibbons and Benjamin Ferris founded the world's first Quaker periodical, the *Berean*. This journal quickly became the house organ for the Hicksites, contributing mightily to the initial schism. Its pages also adumbrated arguments and language that would surface later in the Wilmington Working Men's movement. Gibbons and Ferris announced that their goal was to make Christianity simple, rational, and practical, specifically distinguishing between orthodox "professors" of religion, who were concerned with books and creeds, and "possessors" of religion, who placed actions over opinions. The *Berean* went beyond Hicks in unequivocally claiming the importance of individualism over unity, even announcing that, as friends of "pure and undefiled Religion," they would usher in an age marked by the "spirit of free enquiry."[90] And yet,

Gibbons and Ferris were, in turn, confronted by men like Benjamin Webb, general agent and editor of the *Berean*, who insisted on pressing liberty of conscience and freedom of the press further still.

The precise origins of this second rift—giving rise to what Webb would later condemn as "Hicksite orthodoxy"—are obscure.[91] The dispute apparently began when Gibbons tried to force a reluctant Webb to use the *Berean* to attack Robert Dale Owen, soon to be Francis Wright's collaborator.[92] The rift was greatly exacerbated in 1828 by the involvement of Webb and later *DFP* editor William Baker in a short-lived Bible discussion group called the "Lovers of Truth," in which, Gibbons claimed, Webb and Baker spoke against Scripture.[93] For that crime, Gibbons and Ferris would speak against the two in the Wilmington Monthly Meeting, using the very kinds of disciplinary measures they had opposed earlier while editors of the *Berean*.[94] In 1829, with Wright's lectures in Wilmington followed by the founding of the AWPNCC, Gibbons publicly attacked Webb and several other local Quakers in an open letter to Owen entitled, *Exposition of Modern Scepticism*. Here, Gibbons accused his Wilmington opponents of being among the followers of the "Red Harlot of Infidelity."[95] The failure to discipline "disorderly" members who had participated in the Bible group had emboldened the "skeptics," Gibbons said, leading directly to the invitation to Wright. Three months later, just as the Working Men's star rose on the Wilmington horizon, the first number of the *Delaware Free Press* appeared.[96]

For Gibbons, that paper—and the movement for which it was a mouthpiece—was nothing less than an attempt to overthrow Christianity, to eradicate religious sentiment, and to disseminate infidelity, "*even to the disbelief of a God!*"[97] But for men like Webb, the *DFP* merely sought to apply the principles of tolerance and freethought upon which the Hicksite movement had been founded in the first place. Indeed, they had little trouble hoisting their accusers with their own petard. Having fought a revolution for liberty of conscience with his erstwhile allies, Webb claimed to be now cheated out of its fruits by a new set of masters. The irony of it! Gibbons, said Webb, was the "founder of heresy in Wilmington," who with his friend Ferris now carried on a "crusade of persecution" against fellow laborers in the work they themselves had originated, and had now "passed sentence upon us for their own sins."[98] Gibbons and his compatriots, Webb exclaimed, were "time serving religionists, who yet have all their former heresies dangling at their heels." In the pages of the *Berean*, Webb continually reminded his antagonists, the Bible was not only questioned but all those who opposed such questioning were called "enemies to truth." It was Gibbons and Ferris, after all, who had written, "belief is no merit nor unbelief a crime."[99] Yet now, it appeared, their object all along had been to "dispose of orthodoxy of authority, in order to exercise it themselves."[100]

Echoing precisely the argument advanced by other Christian laborites from an array of Protestant denominations, Webb and his associates insisted that the problem was creed itself, regardless of the belief. If systematized, all creeds—Quakerism or Catholicism, deism or atheism—were deleterious to the cause of truth.[101] Moreover, his erstwhile allies now tried to enforce a set of beliefs on the members of the society through disciplinary action. Just as the Working Men had done in their battle against their political, business, and clerical opponents, this struggle within the Wilmington Friends community was cast by these radical Quakers as a struggle between liberty of conscience and despotism of opinion. But, more important—and not at all surprising, given the generally pious character of the Working Men's movement of which several of these Quakers were adherents—the battle here was joined as one of religious purity versus religious profession: "we believe more stumbling blocks are thrown in the way of the principles of the Friends by its professors, than by all the sceptics on earth."[102]

Thus, the *DFP* took religious ground in a war of words with the "Hicksite orthodoxy."[103] As Webb's son James put it, the "true" church in the New Testament had the spirit of Christ, not the spirit of persecution; men like William Gibbons were "the Scribes, Pharisees, and rulers, of the present day."[104] Here, the concerns of religious rebels dovetailed with the religious concerns of this early "moment" of labor reform. For among these radical Friends—in a split within a split—was the virulent strain of antichurch sentiment so evident among Christian labor activists virtually everywhere in this era, but particularly in the late 1820s and early 1830s: they did battle against the "heretofore meek and unoffending Quakers," contrasting the "true" Christianity of the "founder of the Christian religion" with the "professed" Christianity and "clerical imposters" of the "present distracted state of religious society."[105] Along these lines, Webb inflicted what was perhaps the deepest cut of all: "we're becoming like Presbyterians!"[106] As one Webb defender asked, quoting the Book of John on following Jesus' example: should one reject the Light within, just because "degenerate Quakers of the present day" expel those who champion it? In the spirit of the come-outerism taking hold in other denominatons of the era, this Quaker advocated upholding the faith by leaving the society: if we cannot make some men sincere—like Jesus—"can we do otherwise than come out from among them, and be separated from them?"[107]

In the event, the ruling elders of their congregation decided for them. After nearly eight years of skirmishing, three in public, Webb was dismissed from the Wilmington Meeting. Not before he had his day in court, however; he was "charged" in late 1830, and in a series of gatherings the following year, his case was "tried" within the Meeting.[108] With the focus of attention on what Webb (and others) had written in the *DFP*, at the Wilmington Quarterly Meeting in February 1831 the prosecution committee read aloud from the paper for some seven hours.[109] Webb and his supporters followed with a weekly pounding of their opponents in the pages of the same journal, usually under the heading, "Persecution." Although still officially a member in good standing of the Society of Friends, he was forcibly prevented from attending the Philadelphia Yearly Meeting in April 1831.[110] Finally, the following June, after more than a year of meetings, interviews, public attacks, and defenses, Webb was disowned. The Hicksites in Wilmington then underwent a kind of purge, in which those who sought to extend the Liberal reformation were driven from the fold.[111]

Not all of these new rebels were part of the Working Men's movement, but their expulsion from the Wilmington Friends accompanied the folding of the *Free Press* in 1832 and paralleled the simultaneous demise of the Working Men's movement. Moreover, the coincidence of both personnel and program in the two movements is unmistakable. Ten—nearly one-quarter—of Webb's forty-two defenders in the Wilmington Meeting were involved in the AWPNCC and/or the WMP.[112] Indeed, one of his most outspoken advocates within the Monthly Meeting was AWPNCC president and WMP candidate Jacob Al-richs.[113] More important, the groups shared the same mouthpiece, the *DFP*, both were castigated by their opponents as infidels, and both claimed— sincerely, it would appear—to be acting as defenders of the faith concerned with renewing the covenant of their Protestant forbears. Finally, much of the Working Men's rhetoric—their opposition to state-sponsored public worship as an intrusion on individual "concernment," for example—echoed Quaker language.[114]

Webb and his associates defined "true" religion much as labor reformers of other denominational traditions did. For the Quaker radicals among the Wilmington Working Men, as for other Protestants in the labor movement elsewhere in this period, religion was a way of life, not a body of rules. And that way of life—in the context of the birth pangs of the Industrial Revolution— provided the foundation for what was essentially a social gospel of labor reform. Their religion may not have caused their labor advocacy, but the fit of their Quaker-based social philosophy and the labor movement's "religion" is too striking to ignore. In a very real sense, as in Fitchburg and Fall River, Massachusetts, part of the Working Men's movement welled up from inside the Quaker Meeting in Wilmington, just as that movement expressed pent-up desires for religious as well as secular reform. Here, as elsewhere in antebellum America, religion and politics, the spiritual and the secular, were so intertwined as to make any history of that era that accounts for one without the other a deficient history indeed.

From the beginning, throughout the nation, the church was intertwined with the emergence of an American labor movement. In Wilmington, the Working Men were well integrated into local church life. They were affiliated with a range of local congregations but, not surprisingly given their role as dissenters who braved the prevailing social currents, they were religious rebels as well. Many of them were Methodists, a group long persecuted in the town, but the most significant religious presence in the movement were the Quakers, and here too the Working Men were dissenters. For whereas the Quakers were well established in the community, the Working Men Friends were the dissidents of the flock. At the same time, like early labor reformers elsewhere, they claimed to be traditionalists, upholders of the faith who sought only to champion "true" Christianity.

As elsewhere, though, they were stigmatized by their opponents as infidels—to them a galling charge, given their institutional affiliations and religious orientation. In their defense, as they advanced the cause of labor, they fashioned a critique of contemporary religion and, in the process, labor reform became intertwined with religious reform. Though in Wilmington the movement did not actually organize within the church, as it would in some other communities, it did, in the light of the second Hicksite schism, come from it. In Wilmington, radical Quakerism was the handmaiden of early labor protest.

The story of the churches and labor in this period is thus clearly not the story of any one denomination. Indeed, what the Wilmington Working Men— Quakers, Methodists, and others—fashioned in the early 1830s was an embryonic tradition of labor religion that crossed denominational boundaries, appearing among a wide range of Protestants in communities throughout America that were swept up in labor agitation during the antebellum years and beyond. In Rochester, New York, working-class formation was also bound up with religion. There, Presbyterians played an important part in the story, but, as in Wilmington, so did Freethought and "primitive Christianity," as well as Methodists and other local congregations; most especially, so did the battle between labor and its opponents over who were the real infidels and who represented the "true" interests of American Christianity.

Chapter 6. Labor Activists in the Church: Rochester, New York

"The town had sprung up like a mushroom," Nathaniel Hawthorne wrote of Rochester, New York, after a visit in the mid-1830s. "Its attributes of youth are the activity and eager life with which it is redundant."[1] In a few words, Hawthorne captured the essence of the place. Founded in 1812, Rochester was the nation's premier inland boom town, the Erie Canal in 1825 rendering it a pivot in the flow of population and trade between New England and the rising West.[2] Community life was so fast paced that the local directory of 1828 omitted residents' names for fear of inaccuracy.[3] By 1830 a major marketing and manufacturing center of some ten thousand souls, Rochester was tumultuous and noisy, with farmers hawking produce, shopkeepers and peddlers selling wares, journeymen mechanics and laborers toiling in workshops and mills, porters and lawyers, horses and ox teams, stages and wagons scurrying back and forth, prostitutes, pickpockets, and gamblers plying their own specialized trades— "all hurrying, trotting, rattling, and tumbling, in a throng that passed continually, but never passed away." Rochester was a world in flux.[4]

It was also a world that was especially prone to conflict—the people of Rochester, one resident said, tended to high "excitability."[5] Though rooted in economy and society, this excitability had a sharply religious character, pitting a variety of religious (and antireligious) perspectives against one another.[6] Embedded in these battles were two intimately related dialectics: in the world of the flesh, there were attempts by a new middle class of entrepreneurs to tame a rapidly expanding and seemingly uncontrollable working class, while, in the face of an emerging social order of exploitation, domination, and dependency, there were the first stirrings of organized labor unrest; in the spiritual world, Evangelical religious fervor vied with a kaleidoscope of religious dissent often called "Freethought."[7]

In this world, we might expect to find the elite embracing religion, with the working class hostile to it. The story is much more complex. For although certain employers did mount a campaign from the bastion of the church to

For statistics on Rochester churches and labor activists, refer to tables 6.1–6.6.

establish control over the rapidly changing social order that they themselves had wrought, a portion of the working class developed its own independent religious vision of the Good Society, sometimes from within the church itself, and in the process challenged the prerogative of their "betters" to rule unimpeded.[8] The opening salvo in this warfare came in the late 1820s with an Evangelical attempt to proscribe the behavior of Rochester workers, provoking in turn fierce opposition from a wide spectrum of dissenters. Among these dissenters were champions of "primitive Christianity": together with a minority of anti-Christian Freethinkers, they mounted a two-front war, one on secular issues concerning Rochester workers, the other on the terrain of religion. As we shall see, the two issues were never quite separate.

The line of battle in this labor-religion conflict shifted by the mid-1830s with the simultaneous proliferation of religious revivals on the one hand and institutions of organized labor protest on the other. Labor activists continued to articulate criticisms of the church and orthodoxy, but they often carried on the fight from within the church itself. For though the Evangelical attempt at coercion largely failed, the evangelical revival succeeded in dramatically increasing church membership. In the process, the church drew in not only those loyal to an emerging system of capitalist relations, but also those who rebelled against it. Rochester workers thus found ways to resist from both outside and inside the church—often in a critical stance, but almost always within a Christian framework.

Evangelicals vs. Their Enemies:
The Battle for the Soul of Rochester, 1828–36

Antebellum Rochester "was a peculiarly Puritan city," resident George Humphrey remembered later: the Sabbath was sacred time, when walks for recreation were "not quite respectable," cooking was kept to a minimum, and the novel was put aside in favor of Scripture.[9] But, to hear some contemporaries tell it, antebellum Rochester was anything but a place of grace. The editor of the local paper insisted in 1824 that "probably no place in the Union of the size of Rochester is so much infested with the dregs and outcasts of society as this village."[10] Indeed, through the 1820s, increasingly so as the decade wore on, a chorus of voices warned of the state of Rochester's soul.[11]

As the burgeoning village began processing the agricultural surplus of its rich Genesee hinterland, fabricating consumer products for its growing population, and acting as a key entrepôt along the Erie Canal, Rochester took on a decidedly picaresque character. Overnight, it seemed, it was filled with adventurers and other ambitious young men, immigrant laborers and boatmen, journeymen mechanics and mill workers, peddlers and traveling showmen. And, accompanying this heterogeneous and rowdy lot, the pious noted with alarm, came all sorts of viciousness and vice—profanity and disrespect, drunkenness and gambling, theater and the circus, and, most especially, Sabbath-breaking.[12] Emblematic of this retrograde state was the spontaneous fight in the town center that drew a crowd of some one thousand onlookers in 1830.[13]

In addition to an allegedly degenerate population—perhaps because of it, moralists thought—there was organized hostility to the community's religion institutions. For Rochester was host to a vigorous heterodoxy, with some half dozen or more newspapers loudly critical of prevailing orthodox religious belief and practice, several societies of "Free Enquiry" or "Liberal" discussion, and public celebrations of Thomas Paine's birthday. A year after the town brawl came an event even more alarming: the largest public meeting in the town's history, billed as a gathering against "kingcraft, priestcraft, and monarchists," missionaries and tract distribution societies, the prohibition of the Sunday mails (as a threat to the separation of church and state), and imprisonment for debt.[14] In the 1820s and 1830s, Rochester was perhaps the major outpost of anti-Evangelical fervor in the nation's interior.[15]

Partly for this reason, it also became a center of the Second Great Awakening, with a series of intense revivals beginning in 1831.[16] The man most responsible, Charles Grandison Finney, helped turn the place into "the most thoroughly evangelical of American cities."[17] His goal was to remake Rochester in the image of the New England village, in great measure because the initial inhabitants had failed at it.[18] The Genesee region had been populated by New England farmers since the 1790s, but Rochesterville itself was founded in 1812 by Maryland land speculators.[19] They built a southern town, with two broad streets running east-west and north-south, in a gridiron with no public common, unlike the neighboring communities of Geneva, Batavia, Canandagua, Bath, and Buffalo, all of which were built around a public square.[20] From the beginning, then, Rochester lacked the common core that characterized the New England town. Moreover, though the overwhelming majority of the early inhabitants were Yankees—New Englanders from the Connecticut River Valley or transplanted New Englanders from the Hudson and Mohawk region of upstate New York—the continual influx of newcomers on the canal rendered the re-creation of the New England model a perennial problem. As for organized worship, at the time of settlement only an estimated 10 percent were churched, and the problem dogged pious community boosters throughout the early years.[21] In a double sense, Rochester had to *practice* its religion.[22]

The result was intense conflict: if the Evangelicals believed that Freethought signaled the erosion of community, a longtime resident on the other side of the religious divide lamented that his townsfolk now had to prove how much they loved God "by showing with what delightful animosities, we hate each other."[23] Though carrying a religious signature, these divisions were rooted in class issues, with all sides vying for the working class as the prized constituency. For the competing visions of proper thought and behavior that emerged during the

1820s and 1830s arose out of dramatic economic and social changes. Rochester was the "junction of the East and West," not merely because of its location astride a major travel route; it also was a center of capitalist development, and it experienced the aristocracy of wealth and democracy of poverty and exploitation attending such development. As a consequence, a vibrant and variegated movement for labor's rights emerged here, rendering the town one of the leading arenas of class conflict in upstate New York.

An organized workingmen's movement did not emerge in Rochester until late 1829 and 1830.[24] Earlier, though, a pro-worker sentiment can be glimpsed in the opposition to attempts by Rochester elites to tame the village's increasingly autonomous and defiant working class through temperance and, especially, Sabbath laws.[25] At a public meeting in early 1828, the Sabbatarians resolved to patronize only those stage and canal-boat lines that operated on a six-day week.[26] At about the same time, a local flour miller and prominent member of the Third Presbyterian Church, Josiah Bissell, Jr., established a Sabbath-keeping and temperance-observant stage-and-canal operation called the Pioneer Line. When the proposed ban on Sunday travel was blocked locally by those claiming it would hinder the mails, Bissell and his Evangelical benefactors organized a nationwide campaign. Rochester thus became the national focus of a far-flung Evangelical movement centering on enforcing the Sabbath as a day of "proper observance."

A response from those who disagreed was not long in coming: just two weeks after the first meeting of the Rochester Sabbatarians, some four hundred townspeople met in protest, vowing to boycott the boycotters. The nature of this opposition was diverse, but it included a dissenting Christian element that spoke for working people against certain employers and their clerical allies. One outlet for that voice was the *Plain Truth* (*PT*), a semimonthly started by "Heterodox men" that appeared on the day Bissell's Pioneer Line began in the spring of 1828.[27] Subtitled *A Religious Work: Devoted to the Defense of Primitive Christianity, and to the Exposing of Frauds Committed Under the Garb of Religion,* the *PT* was a Christian sheet that opposed Sabbatarianism and the "ministry (and missionary) system" in the name of the "mild and benignant religion of Jesus."[28] The proprietor was a Quaker who championed "plain" Christianity: the "Benevolent Empire" ("a few mad religionists"), he said, was producing a "fanatical and intolerant spirit, equally at war with the Christian Religion, and civil liberties," enabling ambitious men to acquire wealth and lay the foundation for an American hierarchy, which would "tread with the 'weight of a war elephant' upon the necks of a prostrate people."[29] Here was a paper that linked the struggles against religious and temporal tyranny, raising the issues of inequality and material oppression in a religious context, condemning "worldly gain and clerical ambition," demanding a return to the principles of Christianity's founder—just as antebellum labor activists would throughout the Northeast before the Civil War.[30]

In language that anticipated the radical mill girls in Lowell during the 1840s, the *PT* declared in 1828, "Christian Religion, simple and beautiful in its original character, has . . . been subjected, ever since it was first preached by its great founder, to perversion by the designing and the crafty."[31] Thus, the paper rejected Paine, who had mistaken the "impure workings of a spurious religion" for "a most excellent faith," pronounced the whole system of Christianity a "cunningly devised fable," and opened the world to the floodgates of licentiousness.[32] Alternatively, the anti-Sabbatarian *PT* advocated Sabbath schools—and, in general, keeping the Sabbath—while opposing the Benevolent Empire for what it had made of such institutions.[33] For the *PT,* the issue was not Christianity, but how best to promote it.

In early 1829, about three months before the *PT* folded, another paper emerged as an advocate of both religious liberty and the material rights of the poor and downtrodden. As with the *PT,* the *Craftsman* (1829–31) linked religious, political, and economic tyranny, and championed the "sincere Christian," the poor, the worker.[34] Indeed, the religion of editor Elijah J. Roberts and his correspondents was a plain-style Christianity based on good works for the dispossessed, in the spirit of the original Christians, grounded in biblical principles.[35] Established ostensibly to defend Masonry from the withering attack of the Antimasons, the *Craftsman* also ran reform pieces that advocated street maintenance, abolition of imprisonment for debt, changes in prison administration, and temperance; printed temperance notices for a series of lectures by Frances Wright; placed on its masthead the "Farmers', Mechanics' and Workingmen's" candidate for governor; and reprinted poetry and essays from mechanics' papers like the New York *Working Man's Advocate* and the Albany *Mechanics' Mirror.*[36] Also, under the banner "Tolerance and Equal Rights" were reprinted articles from the *Episcopalian Watchman,* religious instruction from the *Lady's Book,* and Col. Richard M. Johnson's Senate Report rejecting petitions for a prohibition of Sunday mails.[37]

Like those at the *Plain Truth* and in the emerging American labor movement then in gestation, Roberts opposed government-coerced religious observance, which, he said, defaced the beauty of the faith taught by "its great founder," which was without "desire of political ascendancy."[38] Anticlerical but avowedly Christian, he distinguished between the "*character* and *abuses*" of churches.[39] In this, he followed the tradition prevalent among antebellum reformers in contrasting "professed" and "practical" Christians: "How many Christians *profess* Christianity, are called Christians, but are the veriest knaves and hypocrites that ever disgraced the altar," who force upon "the pure and unadulterated worshipper . . . rules by which they are to profit."[40] Similarly with the clergy, whose involvement in politics would inevitably lead to "opposition to the church itself."[41] Roberts's was a defense of the faith, of "pure" Christianity.[42]

The joining of resistance to Evangelicals with the advocacy of the rights of the poor and working population was not limited to dissenting Christian newspapers like the *Plain Truth* and the *Craftsman;* it also appeared in the Mutual Association, a group composed primarily of artisans from the building trades. Growing out of the "hard times" of 1828–29—a national economic downturn that hit Rochester with particular force—and emerging amidst both the temperance and the Sabbatarian crusades mounted by town elites, the group agitated for more than a year against the specific scourges of imprisonment for debt, unemployment, and the payment of wages in store orders, or "duebills."[43] The association's targeted enemy was the "Shylock Association"— local creditors, led by members of the Third Presbyterian Church, who published a monthly list of those who owed them money, demanding repayment and pledging no further credit to the delinquent. In response, the Mutual Association collected dues to care for indigent members, boycotted the creditors, published its own list of "shavers" (swindlers), and led a petition campaign for a state law abolishing imprisonment for debt.[44]

Among the leaders of this upstart movement were churchgoing workers— two were Methodist leaders (one a lay exhorter) who would help mount the local carpenters' effort to win the ten-hour day in the early 1830s. Freethinkers could be found in the association's leadership as well, though their presence should not be taken as evidence of the movement's opposition to religion. For the Mutual Association claimed to speak for all "men and christians" outraged by the publishing of the debtors' lists, and it accepted only those of "good moral character."[45] In their ranks were the apparently nonchurchgoing but pious editors of the *Spirit of the Age,* a local labor paper, which advocated the demands of the Working Men's movement.[46] As the champion of the poor against the rich, the paper protested emerging inequality with a decidedly religious bent, denouncing the "usurpation by man of the prerogative of the Creator," locating equality in "the charter of Heaven, sealed by the Maker of the universe," and demanding for workers those privileges "a wise and beneficent Providence saw fit to bestow." These editors were anti-Evangelical Christians, pillorying Josiah Bissell in terms consonant with the philosophy of the Mutual Association: the "creditor who owns the Pioneer Line" was a man badly in need of "practically learning some of the most essential lessons of Christianity himself."[47]

This movement—prolabor, anti-Evangelical, Christian—gained momentum with the coming of Charles Finney, whose revival was largely a response to the failure of Bissell's Sabbatarian campaign. In January 1831, smack in the midst of Finney's spiritual "harvest," the "Friends of Liberal Principles and Equal Rights," which numbered upwards of a thousand in at least one of its meetings, announced opposition to Sabbath laws, religious oaths, Bible, tract, and missionary societies, and imprisonment for debt, and advocacy of a system of "moral, liberal, and practical education" that would give the children of the poor equal opportunity with that of the rich.[48] The group's linking of religious and temporal oppression during its several meetings in early 1831—railing at "wealth and Priestcraft," for example—marked it as a direct descendant of the *Plain Truth* and the *Craftsman,* the Mutual Association, and the Working Men.[49]

The Friends of Liberal Principles' activities proved short-lived, apparently petering out after a few meetings. But in the aftermath of the Finney revival, as his army evangelized among the working class, the movement found another voice.[50] Early in 1832, about the same time that another revival was sweeping Rochester's churches, Obediah Dogberry brought out the *Liberal Advocate,* dedicated to "equal rights and free discussion."[51] Here, from 1832 to 1836, Dogberry and his correspondents carried on the fight for victims of "wealth and Priestcraft." They championed the cause of the poor and ordinary against an aristocracy of politicians, clergy, and wealthy—and most especially "patent Christians."[52] Pledged "without distinction of sect or party" to labor for "suffering humanity," for those forced into "hard labor" because of the "'pressure of the times,'" the paper reprinted articles from the labor press, applauded the campaigns against prison labor and imprisonment for debt, and called on Rochester's mill workers to emulate the striking mill girls of Lowell. At the same time, it warned of the creation of a "national church party."[53] The *Advocate* made explicit what had been at the very heart of early dissent in Rochester: the conjoining of prolabor advocacy and opposition to the Evangelicals.[54]

Dogberry emblazoned his paper's masthead with the words of the Enlightenment poet Alexander Pope: "Know thyself, presume not God to scan! The proper study of mankind is man." Despite his worldliness, Dogberry, like Pope, was not a critic of religion per se.[55] Like others among Rochester's early religious dissenters—and some elsewhere in the early American labor movement—he advocated a noncoercive, rationalist, morally based, anticlerical, "primitive Christianity."[56] Railing against the sectarianism of contemporary Christianity, he also rejected the sectarianism of those who professed liberalism while imposing beliefs on others.[57] Though he opposed the Sabbatarians, he deplored tavern going on the Sabbath.[58] Though he rejected contemporary temperance societies as "a cloak" for "cold-water, pale-faced, money-making men" who ground the face of the poor, he advocated temperance in all things.[59] Like George R. McFarlane, his fellow Paineite in the Wilmington-Philadelphia area, Dogberry sought a moral revolution, condemning drinking, boarders rushing to dinner "like hungry dogs after a love," young men cavorting with "wanton" ladies, fathers swearing in front of their children and mothers gossiping before their daughters.[60] And, again like McFarlane, this quest for moral reformation always had a working-class edge, as Dogberry also lamented that butchers "sell meat to the rich, and the bones to the poor."[61]

Only one paper in this battle justly earned the label "infidel"—and by the time it appeared, the intensity of the conflict had subsided.[62] Published in 1836 by a materialist named Luke Shepard, the *World As It Is* printed essays that went

beyond denying revelation and the divinity of Jesus.[63] Shepard and his correspondents railed against the Bible (particularly the Old Testament), priests,
sects, Sabbath schools ("sinks of corruption and houses of ill fame"), revivals,
and all forms of religious creed, dogma, fashion, superstition, and bigotry.[64]
The *World* did have in common with the anti-Evangelical press that had preceded it the linking of spiritual and temporal forms of tyranny ("the priest and
the aristocrat have always been, and always will be inseparably connected")—
only here with far greater emphasis on temporal than spiritual salvation. When
Shepard condemned low wages, the duebill system, and exorbitant rent as the
work of the orthodox ("enemies of equal rights"), he called on "mechanics and
working men" together under the banner of "Liberalism and Equal Rights."[65]

Despite its position on the extreme edge of Rochester's religious spectrum,
though, the *World* did focus more on the abuses of religion than on its
essence—by the mid-1830s, the standard position of Rochester's social and
religious dissenters. Thus, the Bible was sometimes condemned for being anti-
religious, revivals for being only a temporary expedient that would not prevent
inevitable backsliding, and ministers for being the direct emissaries of Satan.[66]
Thus, too, articles contained references to man's "God-like form," which was
contrasted to that of the "pretenders," priests, and kings.[67] Even Shepard
himself defended the advocates of the "pristine Christian faith . . . as taught
and believed in the Apostolic age" who were branded as "Infidels, Deists,
Atheists, by the ephemeral clergy, and their fawning sycophants."[68] Those who
wrote for the *World* did evince a belief in God and the societal importance of
religiously based morality, just as their predecessors at the *Plain Truth,* the
Craftsman, and the *Liberal Advocate* had. Even on this fringe of the Rochester
community, the importance of religion, in the struggle against "aristocrats"
and "priests" on behalf of "mechanics and working men," rose inexorably to
the surface.

Labor and Rochester Churches

Freethinkers maintained an organized presence in Rochester into the 1840s,
but their heyday had passed by the mid-1830s. Moreover, as journeymen
craftsmen began to organize on a more permanent basis, beginning with the
carpenters' movement for the shorter workday, the locus of the intimately
connected religious and labor struggles shifted to unions and citywide associations articulating working-class demands. The record of these activists' religious beliefs is sketchy, but they appear to have shared many of the religious
traditions glimpsed in the dissenting press of the late 1820s and early 1830s,
even though they often carried on the fight from inside the churches of
Rochester—sometimes the very churches that had been "revived."[69] Indeed,
one irony of the post-Finney religious and social history of Rochester is that

although the Evangelical attempt to impose a legal framework of enforced morality was defeated, the cumulative effect of the revivals rendered church involvement and religious rhetoric ubiquitous among social and labor reformers from the 1830s onward—not exactly what the Evangelicals had in mind.[70]

Though available church records are fragmentary—especially for the Methodists, the largest denomination in town by the mid-1830s—at least one-quarter of the activists identified for the antebellum period were church members at the time of their involvement in labor protest, again with a higher percentage among the leadership.[71] Reflecting Rochester's volatile population, these churchgoers were a diverse group: some were native born, others were English, Irish, Scottish, or German immigrants; some had been living in town as early as the 1810s, others had just arrived. But New Yorkers and transplanted New Englanders constituted the dominant element. And few were recent converts; many were longtime members. Labor reform in Rochester was the creation in some measure of the same kind of church members we have seen elsewhere.

They could be found in the array of Rochester's Protestant churches: Presbyterian, Episcopalian, Methodist, Baptist, and, to a lesser extent, Unitarian and Universalist; in certain groups, they could be found in the Catholic Church as well. But, as elsewhere, activists were attracted to certain congregations over others. As we shall see, in the Journeymen Carpenters' and Joiners' Society (JCJS) were a number of Methodist leaders, plus some members of the Second Presbyterian (Brick) Church.[72] The faithful among the printers in the Rochester Typographical Association (RTA) who struck for higher wages at the end of the 1830s were primarily Baptists and Presbyterians, a couple of the leaders having been involved in a Presbyterian revival just before their involvement in the movement; the church-affiliated clerks who petitioned for shorter hours during the 1840s were predominantly Presbyterian.[73] Overall, the most popular churches among the labor activists here were the First Methodist and Brick Presbyterian, the two Rochester churches whose revivals, in the wake of Finney's harvest, dwarfed the great revivalist's earlier efforts.[74] The evangelical revival in Rochester played a role in working-class as well as middle-class formation.

As elsewhere in the early American labor movement, carpenters and joiners were in the forefront of union organization and working-class agitation here. Though we know little about the carpenters' religious beliefs, because of the absence of written documents, or about their relationship with the forces of religious dissent, we know enough about them to give us pause when pondering the standard models used to understand religion and class during the 1830s.[75] Here, while some sought to convert the working class, in an effort to turn a class division into a religious one by allying evangelical workers with their employers against their unchurched brethren, the front line of militant working-class protest was organized and led by churchgoers, many of them evangelicals.

Amidst the housing construction boom of these years, the merchant capitalists and subcontractors worked gangs of building tradesmen from dawn to dusk without surcease.[76] Beginning in 1832 or 1833, and continuing for several years, the carpenters demanded the ten-hour day, their greatest effort coming with the start of the building season in the spring of 1834.[77] In April, the JCJS pledged themselves to the "TEN HOUR SYSTEM" beginning on the 15th, essentially announcing a strike for the shorter workday.[78] The chairman of the meeting was a steward of the First Methodist Church.[79] Indeed, among the JCJS officers and some ninety-one signers of the strike announcement were twenty-one (and possibly as many as thirty-three) area church members.[80] In the leadership—a majority of whom were local congregants—were a number of well-known, active, church leaders.[81] Timothy C. Haskell, a member of Brick Presbyterian, had been converted with his first wife in the revival of June 1827.[82] Willis Tuttle, who had come to Rochester from Connecticut in 1825, was a "leading and efficient" member of the Methodist Church, who "carried his Christianity always with him, in his business, in his family, and in all relations with his fellow-men."[83]

The carpenters occupied center stage in the Rochester labor movement of the 1830s, which was, as everywhere, decimated by the depression that followed the Panic of 1837. In the winter of 1839–40, however, just after the crest of these "hard times," a new force emerged to take their place—the printers of the city's several newspaper and book establishments.[84] Formed in late September 1839, the Rochester Typographical Association outlined its case in its constitution: complaining of low employment, an inability to obtain "just remuneration," and the employment of those who degraded the profession, they called for resisting encroachments on the "unalienable rights" of the profession by establishing a uniform scale of prices, a benefit fund for distressed members, and an employment bureau for out-of-work printers. While advocating the "mutual benefit of the employer and the employed," the association set its sights on winning higher wages from the city's printing employers, by striking if necessary.[85] And strike they did. Excluding all masters, the RTA pledged in October 1839 to work only at the union wage scale.[86]

Unlike the carpenters,' the printers' worldview is available to us, because they established their own daily newspaper, the *Working-Man's Advocate* (*WMA*), which ran articles discoursing on low employment, low wages (and the notorious duebill system), long hours and poor health conditions, high rent and squalid living conditions, and prison labor.[87] Its principal editor bears some looking into, as Henry Church Frink was an evangelical and regular churchgoer.[88] About thirty years old, Frink was a New Englander, a native of Northampton, Massachusetts. In later years he waxed eloquent about life in this New England village—he called it a "mountain paradise"—stressing the importance of family, neighbors, ministers, schools, and most especially the local church. Such villages had but one church, he remembered, which constituted the core of the community; indeed, he conjured up the community itself as a "congregation."[89] Well-read in the Bible and the classics, with a grasp of at least five languages, and having traveled extensively as a young man, Frink had seen the world and then some by the time he arrived in Rochester as a printer's apprentice in 1831, the year of the Finney revival. The following year, he was apparently swept up in the revival at the Brick Church, then under the spell of the evangelist Jedediah Burchard, and became a "professor of religion." The experience changed his life, sending him back to the verities of his youth; later in life, he would be certain that without such a "born-again" experience, there could be no real change, in the individual or in society.[90]

Frink supported Bible classes and Sabbath schools, he regularly quoted Scripture, and he clearly believed he lived in—should live in—a "Christian community."[91] And yet, he sometimes sounded like the religious dissenters of a decade earlier—and Christian labor activists in New England like Seth Luther, Sarah Bagley, and William Young—in his inveighing against the hypocrisy of contemporary congregations (and their ministers), condemning the "many in the visible church" who professed but did not practice. Dress underlay the "claims of respect" within the contemporary church, he charged, while "cant phraseologies" held sway in church discourse, resulting in the worship of Mammon, the encouragement of vanity and profligacy, and the creation of social divisions—all at the expense of the poor. Rather than reforming the world, these professors judged not persons but possessions. The interest of "every practical mechanic," therefore, lay in "a thorough reformation."[92]

The basis of this evangelical's Christianity—which he shared with radical Quaker Benjamin Webb and many of Rochester's early religious dissenters— was morality, the essence of which he called "genuine charity."[93] For greed was the bane of society. Thus, during the winter of 1839–40, Frink praised the ladies of St. Luke's Episcopal Church for the charity fair they had organized, and, noting his intention to attend, urged his readers, quoting Scripture, " 'go and do likewise.' "[94] Two weeks later, he recounted how, during each winter he had lived in Rochester, he had seen "ragged, starved, bare-headed and barefooted children" collecting chips and shavings from building sites, while "the carriages of the wealthy . . . pass by with no sympathy for such woes." "Can this be Christianity?" he asked, followed by the familiar charge: " 'By their fruits shall ye know them,' is the appropriate standard by which infallibly to test the prevalence of avarice, and vanity, and pride."[95]

Interestingly enough, Frink and the other editors of the WMA deliberately avoided theological discussions, just as the Working Men had earlier in the decade—and, like them, they endorsed a working-class Christianity in the process. Typically, their avoidance of what they called "theological disputation" was of a piece with their overweening aversion to discord of all kinds.[96] But those associated with the *WMA* did feel free to admit beliefs—indeed, they found it necessary.[97] So, while rejecting discussion of "Old School and New School (Presbyterian) doctrines," for example, they insisted that "the great principles universally assented to of virtue and morality, will meet our steady support and approbation."[98] They advertised religious volumes and ministerial engagements and carried religiously inspired poetry.[99] In one short editorial column entitled "The Comforts of Religion," they declared that in times of trouble, "religion shall sustain the just."[100] Their movement was self-consciously Christian.

There were differences among them over the precise role of religion in society, a topic at the heart of Frink's Thanksgiving Day editorial for 1839. Though the historical record is silent on the position Frink was arguing against in this editorial, some Rochester laborites evidently were too suspicious of mixing religion and politics to accept the virtue of even a day of thanksgiving. For Frink went to great lengths here to justify his celebration of public religion. Endorsing "our customary season for returning thanks to Divine Providence for his merciful dispensations toward us," he reminded his readers that the principal object of their Puritan ancestors had been "'liberty of conscience in the worship of God, and the establishment of a Christian church, according to the apostolic pattern.'"[101] Frink readily admitted that the Puritans had established a theocracy, which he regretted as an "error," but he reminded his constituents that "it was the sole intention of the first founders of the Republic, to dedicate a nation to God in its infancy, as well as in its maturer age." If they had been too enthusiastic about that mission, that only demonstrated their sincerity. Frink also acknowledged that, though prayer was advisable, it would be both "imprudent and illegal" for politicians to enforce observance of religious rites.[102] Still, he would brook no obstruction by those who would interfere with the liberty to engage in those rites.[103] If Americans acknowledged God's existence and thanked their Maker for their political blessings, then could they not voluntarily pray on their day of thanksgiving? Frink accepted labor's first principle of separation of church and state, but speaking for the more orthodox within the labor movement, he also insisted that America was a Christian nation.

Despite the apparent opposition to Frink on the public celebration of religion, notices in the *WMA* for church services and meetings at local churches offer at least indirect evidence that much of the paper's readership was traditionally religious.[104] Moreover, the RTA was home to significant numbers of local church members, particularly among its most important leaders, who again could be found in a range of churches.[105] The key organizer of the group was William H. Beach, a resident of Rochester for fifteen years and a pew holder in the Unitarian Church. Among the three members of the publishers' committee of the *WMA* were two Baptists and a Quaker.[106] During a revival several months before the founding of the printers' union, publisher William S. Falls was baptized in Rochester's First Baptist Church. A recent arrival from the Albany area, Falls became a lifelong labor and reform activist after his involvement with the printers: in addition to his activities as a trade unionist, he was a leading abolitionist, temperance advocate, and opponent of vice—a reformer of the evangelical variety.[107] George T. Frost, an Englishman who had come to Rochester in 1833 just before his fifteenth birthday, joined the Second Baptist Church and remained a member until his death fifty-eight years later.[108] The Quaker was Cornelius S. Underwood, who transferred to the Rochester Meeting from Saratoga, New York, in 1836.[109]

This basic pattern—church members as labor activists—characterized the city's increasingly diverse labor movement during the 1840s as well. In the early part of the decade, three different but not wholly separate campaigns were organized by local activists and their allies. The most timid of these efforts was mounted by the city's clerks, who petitioned their employers in 1841 and 1844 for early closing of stores and offices—essentially a demand for the shorter workday.[110] By the 1830s, clerking was no longer a stepping-stone to a substantial business; their numbers expanding and their work increasingly burdensome, clerks now faced the prospect of permanent wage-earning status. One solution was church membership, which was sometimes rewarded with occupational mobility.[111] By 1841, four years into relatively depressed economic times, another was collective action to improve labor conditions. For at least a quarter of the clerks who petitioned for early closing, the two solutions were not mutually exclusive.[112]

Among them was James L. Elwood, who worked in Rochester from the mid-1830s until the late 1840s. Shortly after arriving in the city and taking a position as a bookkeeper and discount clerk at a local bank, he wrote to his brother in Lockport, New York. Apologizing for a long delay in writing, he referred to "the multiplicity of duties which devolve upon me in my new situation," with only Sundays offering any time to write. A temperate and dedicated worker, Elwood took the Sabbath seriously enough to purchase a pew in the new Unitarian church of Rochester, just months after he signed the 1841 petition asking for earlier closing of business to allow more time in the evening for the clerks' "moral and intellectual improvement."[113]

More militant were the activists who in the same year began the first in a long series of campaigns against paying wages in "store orders." In the context of the hard times of the early 1840s, the practice provided a convenient symbol and rallying cry for an increasingly destitute and angry populace, and it took the struggle into the streets of Rochester and, eventually, into the political arena.[114] Led by journeymen and small masters in the shoemaking and building trades, and supported by local shopkeepers and petty professionals, the agitation against what they called the "Duebill System of Robbery" represented something more than just a demand for a more reliable currency; it was a response to increased unemployment (exacerbated by the use of prison labor), reduced wages, and longer hours.[115] In the summer of 1841, a call to "journey-men mechanics in general" resulted in the formation of the Workingmen's Benevolent and Equal Rights Society (WMBERS).[116] Early the following year, as hard currency disappeared and the use of the "Grocery Shin-Plasters" in-creased, the society threatened a general strike against offending employers and store owners, pledging to "starve if needs be."[117] On March 21, inaugurating "such a 'Strike' as never before witnessed in this city," some two to three thousand citizens marched through Rochester behind the American flag and the WMBERS banner, a man standing atop a pile of duebills with the inscrip-tion, "ARE WE NOT ALL FREEMEN?" The immense assemblage elicited a hasty promise of support from the mayor and three aldermen, after which the group burned a lot of bills and retired for the evening.

But the duebills did not disappear. In 1843, the movement turned violent, as years of pent-up frustration finally exploded in what some at the time called the "Due Bill War."[118] For a week and a half in the middle of June, Rochester was rocked by rallies and riots. On June 9, after declaring that the moral suasion of the previous two years had been more than enough, angry workers surrounded the grocery of one alleged offender.[119] Two were arrested, and the local militia was called into readiness. On the 11th, several Rochester groceries were painted with the slogan, "STOP YOUR DUE BILLS, OR BLOOD!"; on the 13th there was more violence and more arrests. The next day, a handbill appeared with the title, "MONEY OR BLOOD," inviting all opponents of the system to arm themselves and take vengeance. Though disavowed by WMBERS leaders, these incidents prompted the impaneling of a grand jury. Meanwhile, the night the handbill appeared, another huge gathering of several thousand in Market Square spilled over into one of the principal commercial avenues in the city, with violence done, it appears, to both citizens and stores.[120] At some point, a false cry of "fire!" went up and, as the engines arrived, the crowd dispersed in confusion. The "war" was over.[121]

We know the names of only a few activists in the society—a handful of leaders and supporters—but it appears that church members were important in this movement, too. Both the president and secretary of the initial 1841 organizing meeting, for example, were Brick Presbyterians. At least one other—and as many as ten—of the fifteen men known to have been directly involved in this movement, and at least four and as many as seven of their eleven supporters whose names appeared in the local press, were church mem-bers.[122] Little wonder that these activists spoke of the Creator as the source of liberty, quoted the Bible and employed its florid language to make their case, and condemned the purveyors of duebills in Rochester as enemies of God and emissaries of Satan.[123]

Among these churchgoers was William C. Bloss, a prominent Rochester reformer and a dedicated evangelical.[124] Bloss spoke at the giant "general strike" meeting in 1841 and appeared at other mechanics' meetings during the decade. Editor of the abolitionist *Rights of Man* in the 1830s and a leading advocate for total abstinence, educational reform, woman's suffrage, and moral reform, Bloss was also a come-outer who rose from his seat in church one day to partake of sacrament with the separated blacks in the congregation. A transplanted New Englander from western Massachusetts and of Pilgrim ancestry, he was a member of the Third Presbyterian Church who promoted strict Sabbatarianism and taught Sabbath school in area prisons and in Presbyterian missionary churches. Armed with a ready knowledge of Shakespeare and the Bible, he was, in his capacity as a spiritual and social reformer, a man who "so mixed religion with his politics, his politics with religion, that one cannot tell which was which," as one of his eulogizers put it—in this case on behalf of a working class.

The anti-duebill agitation may have fed off the Millerite mania that swept through Rochester during the early 1840s, though the precise connections between the two movements remain cloudy.[125] The early 1840s witnessed revivals similar to those of the early 1830s.[126] In the spring of 1842, Burchard set fire to the Brick Presbyterian, and Finney returned to hold forth at the Bethel Presbyterian. By the following year, there were meetings on all sides, with many turning to the evangelist William Miller as his April date for the end of the world approached. Even after the day of reckoning came and went, as the leadership readjusted its calculations, the movement continued to draw hundreds, perhaps thousands, to the fold. By late June, the great Miller Tent opened just outside Rochester; said to hold five thousand, the tent measured some 120 feet in diameter and 360 in circumference. In mid-summer 1843, just a couple of weeks after the main event of the duebill war—the "MONEY OR BLOOD" meeting in Market Square—"WORKER" wrote to a local newspaper on behalf of the anti-duebill movement.[127] He requested that the editor do a favor for the "working portion of this population" by announcing the coming appearance of the "Mechanic Advocate," which would, consonant with the Millerite practice of using charts and maps to illustrate the visions of Daniel and St. John, offer "cuts and illustrations of the symbols of Millerism applied to currencies, and the Declaration of Rights . . . against the Due-bill system."[128] Given the WMBERS's evangelical rhetoric, it is possible that some in it were also swept up in the apocalyptic moment when the ex-Baptist minister was predicting an imminent end to the world.

Closely associated with the anti-duebill movement, and similar in social makeup, was the "Democratic Working Men's Equal Rights Anti-Duebill Club," or Working Men's Club. In 1843–44, the club sought to elect officials who would represent the interests of the "Mechanics and Working Men of Rochester" by opposing any legislation aimed at aiding "capitalists to enrich themselves by wrongfully oppressing the Workingman."[129] Of eighty-nine Working Men candidates and their public supporters, at least eighteen and as many as thirty-nine were church affiliated. Though including for the first time significant numbers of immigrants, this movement looked very much like those that preceded it: the churchmen in the group, of diverse origins, were stable and longtime members of the Christian community.[130]

Much the same can be said, finally, of the labor activists of the late 1840s. George W. Parsons, a leader of the movement for ten-hour legislation in 1848, was a tax collector, city school trustee, and official of the missionary Bethel Free Presbyterian Church.[131] One of his compatriots was Carlton Dutton, a long-time leader and officer of the Universalist Sabbath school; another was Daniel Graves, a resident of Rochester since 1818 and vestryman in St. Paul's Episcopal (Grace) Church with a reputation as a Christian who "lived and walked by faith and prayer."[132] Other activists joined the Mechanics' Mutual Protection Association, the national union of skilled journeymen and small masters centered in upstate New York. Presiding over one of their festivals in 1849 was the young harnessmaker and saddler Moses R. Fassett, a New Yorker who had been in town for at least five years and was the treasurer of the First Universalist Society. One of the speakers was master shoemaker John Alling, another New Yorker who had lived in Rochester since 1822; he had been a member of the Presbyterian Church for the better part of twenty years. And there was yet another New Yorker, state secretary of the New York MMPA, Farrington Price.[133] Price had been living in Rochester for nearly a decade, always as a boarder, working first as a grocer, then as a clerk, finally as the owner of a hat store. A member of the local Unitarian Society, his toast at the festival came appropriately enough from the Bible: "the laborer is worthy of his hire."[134]

From the beginning, labor protest and religious commitment (including church membership) were intimately connected in Rochester. Though critical of "professing" Christians who arrayed themselves against the working population—and particularly those who sought to use the church and religion to compromise individual freedom of conscience—the first generation of working-class dissenters in this community generally adhered to a religious faith, advancing Protestant morality as the essential ingredient in creating and maintaining the Good Society, often as members of local congregations. As we shall see, this fidelity to both the doctrines and institutions of Christianity would inform the nature of their labor protest. To be sure, as everywhere, the particular role that religion played in Rochester was unique to that community. Of one matter, though, there is little doubt: when Rochester workers resisted attempts by Christian employers to subordinate them, they often did so on religious grounds, from within the church as well as outside it. Religion, that is, was less a club used by one side to beat the other into submission than a contested piece of cultural territory that workers as well as their employers fought in (and over) in the dialectical process of class formation.[135]

Chapter 7. Meetinghouses and Ministers: The Church and Clergy Contribution

The intimate connection between religious and class conflict in antebellum America ensured that not just Christianity but the institutions and representatives of Christianity would play a part in labor struggles. The picture of the church and clergy as the voices of moderation and order, as forces seeking to dampen the fires of working-class protest, is a familiar one. The "Journeymen Mechanics" of Oswego, New York, certainly felt the brunt of church opposition in 1836 when local Presbyterians deliberately blocked their efforts to establish the ten-hour workday by refusing them access to their church bell, the only one in the town.[1] Meanwhile, labor activists knew well the likes of the Reverend Flavel S. Mines, the New York City preacher who denounced "the pompous doctrine that 'all men are born free and equal,'" declaring that it was "infidel, not Christian, and strikes at all that is beautiful in civil, or sacred in divine institutions."[2]

Such antilabor sentiments and actions emanating from the Christian community are, as already noted, a common staple of the working-class historiography of the period.[3] Moreover, historians of religion and reform insist that even antebellum church reformers were "conservative and self-serving," dedicated to resurrecting a passing social order; they were vehement opponents of labor legislation, unions, and strikes, and outspoken advocates of individual moral reformation through personal salvation, education, and benevolent reform.[4] To be sure, there are critics of this "social control" argument who suggest that reform-minded churchmen were not self-conscious agents of a particular class interest, but rather "humanitarians" trying to "adjust" to an egalitarian age through interclass reform, or "brokers between classes" promoting a "shared ideological framework" on behalf of a rising middle class, or concerned traditionalists simply trying to "guide" society through the troubled waters of rapid social change.[5] Both the "social control" historians and their critics, however, assume that the ministry was the instrument of interclass harmony alone, usually for the sole benefit of the capitalists and their allies. None of the literature allows for the possibility of clerical attempts to control from below, for "adjusting," "brokering," or "guiding" expressly in the interest of the working class.

In fact, there were ministers and congregations that championed the cause of labor in antebellum America. Throughout these years, and throughout the country, labor meetings and strike rallies were held in a variety of local Protestant churches. More important, its spokesmen, the clergy, were key figures in the community. Particularly in the New England countryside, a small but significant number of clergymen actively promoted the cause of workers' rights. In this age of religious revivalism, these ministers became, in effect, evangelists for labor. In addition to making church facilities available to the labor movement, their activities ran the gamut from offering prayers before workers' meetings to speaking at rallies, writing pamphlets or articles for the local press, editing labor newspapers, organizing local and regional associations, and donating badly needed funds. They headed labor reform associations and even led strikes.[6]

These prolabor ministers, identifying themselves with working people who sought to remake society in their own image, had a distinctly different social agenda than other religious figures of their day: though they drew upon shared Christian traditions, they reshaped those traditions on behalf of a developing labor movement from within the movement itself. To be sure, as we shall see, their role was intrinsically ambiguous. On the one hand, they took the side of the workers in communities where workers and employers were increasingly divided. By offering the fledgling labor movement a powerful and authoritative religious critique of an emerging class system of exploitation and oppression, and by bestowing divine sanction on protest against that system, these ministers helped sharpen class division and conflict. On the other hand, their religious concerns undermined class antagonism in the movement, thus muting class division and conflict. For, as Christian ministers, they insisted that the interests of all God's children—workers and employers alike—were the same: the purging of sin and the formation of moral character. Still, in the end, what is most significant about these activist clergymen is their positive and active support for the antebellum labor movement.[7]

The Church as Meetingplace

As we have seen, life in many antebellum communities revolved around the Protestant meetinghouse, a social and spiritual center in which politics and religion intersected.[8] Here, townspeople worshiped God and struggled over public issues, because they believed that social arrangements were fundamentally religious matters. Thus, the major reform movements of the period— antislavery and temperance—were nurtured in the church. Sympathetic ministers invited lecturers to address their congregations, and parishioners formed local associations and held their meetings in the church vestry. Activists some-times encountered opposition within the congregation, but they insisted that social reform was a Christian mission undertaken on behalf of the entire community. It was only proper, they said, that they do their work in the community center, the Protestant church. When the minister was sympathetic—or sufficiently cowed—that is precisely what happened.

The antebellum labor movement arose in this culture, which recognized the meetinghouse as the appropriate arena for airing community concerns, and, where they could, activists made effective use of church buildings to further their cause. Holding labor meetings at local churches legitimated the move-ment by lending Christian sanction to a potentially controversial cause. Vilified by employers and often by the local press, activists could prove they were Christians acting in the community's interest by using that community's spir-itual and social center as their headquarters. Moreover, with the meetinghouse as their base, they could attract church members and clergymen.

Labor's use of church space depended upon the nature and composition of the movement, the religious elements in the community, and, of course, the attitude of the local clergy. Laborites in certain towns, many of whom were communicants, sought the aid and support of their churches. When these activists campaigned for broad social change through a program of labor reform, they sometimes found a sympathetic minister willing to provide that assistance. So far as we know, though, the practice was rare in Boston and even rarer outside of New England, where laborites usually met in taverns, clubs, and public buildings. Fear of stirring up religious dissension within the community and, more important probably, the indifference or hostility of the clergy, help explain this pattern. Foreign-born workers, striking for specific demands like wages and working conditions, were almost never able to gain ready access to local churches. Only when workers could make the claim to being integral to the community—and were willing to exert that leverage—could they fashion a movement from inside the institutions of Christianity.

The particular churches in which activists met also depended upon a variety of factors. Sympathetic ministers, dissenting traditions within congregations, and available space elsewhere each played a role in determining an appropriate meetingplace. Generally, the poorer and less-established churches, which ac-tively sought converts among the working population, provided the most consistent support for labor's cause. In antebellum New England, for example, the Universalists and the Freewill Baptists occupied the radical fringe of the Christian community; these churches provided the most consistent support for labor.[9] Still, there were progressive congregations and clergymen among all Protestant denominations during this period, especially in the smaller towns.

Protesting workers met in a wide range of churches. In 1830, the Working Men of Buffalo, New York, gathered in a Baptist church to celebrate the Fourth of July.[10] In 1832, at the start of an attempted regional strike for the ten-hour day organized by the New England Association of Farmers, Mechanics and Other Working Men (NEA), some eight hundred people jammed into the Universalist Chapel in Pawtucket, Rhode Island, to hear an address by the congregation's minister, Jacob Frieze, who would shortly become editor of the the association's newspaper, the *New England Artisan*.[11] At the end of that year, local workers founded the "Pawtucket Producing Classes Saving Society," a consumers' cooperative, this time at a Methodist church.[12] The General Trades' Union of New York City celebrated their first anniversary at a Presbyterian church.[13] In 1835, the city hosted a meeting of the National Trades' Union at a local Bethel Baptist church.[14] When mill women "turned out" in Amesbury, Massachusetts (1836), and again in Saco, Maine (1841), they marched to Baptist churches to pass strike resolutions.[15]

The practice continued in the 1840s and beyond. In 1842, the Mechanics' Association of Syracuse met at a local Presbyterian session room; a year later, the Franklin Typographical Society in Cincinnati met in "Reverend Grundy's Room" to protest the firing of two journeymen printers.[16] In 1844, the workers of Manchester, New Hampshire, met at the Episcopal Chapel to form the Mutual Benefit Association.[17] And in 1847, a prolabor utopian socialist, H. H. Van Ameringe, told a national gathering of activists in New York City that his group had held meetings in a variety of churches throughout the Northeast, including, he said, Pittsburgh, Pennsylvania; Winsted, Connecticut; and Troy and Plainfield, New York.[18] Thus, when the female shoefitters of Haverhill, Massachusetts, held strike meetings in the local Freewill Baptist church during the massive shoe strike of 1860, they were continuing a tradition at least a generation old.[19]

Fitchburg and Fall River provide important case studies of this phenomenon. In the former, where organized religion had always provided the focus of cultural, political, and spiritual life, the FWA often met in a local Congregational church. When Fitchburg was incorporated in 1764, the heart and lifeblood of the community had been Thomas Cowdin's tavern, where townsfolk gathered for town meetings, judicial proceedings, and Sunday worship; the blending of religion and politics continued into the nineteenth century when, as one town historian remarked, "church and town affairs were almost inextricably intertwined."[20] The reform impulse there thus emanated from the town's churches. In the winter of 1834–35, for example, members of the Calvinistic Congregational Church sparked an antislavery campaign when they invited a Lane Seminary abolitionist to lecture before the congregation and, though there was sharp disagreement among the congregation, the church became the meetingplace for Fitchburg's antislavery advocates. When internal dissension led to the formation of the Third Congregational (Trinitarian) Church in 1842, the new church hosted local antislavery meetings.[21] The temperance movement in town followed the same pattern.[22]

As did the workingmen's movement. The FWA was founded at the town hall and met on occasion at a local tavern and an old schoolhouse, but its regular meetingplace was the Trinitarian vestry, the minister and a number of his parishioners being members of the FWA. To be sure, lack of funds played a part here, for the group apparently could not raise the money to rent a local public building.[23] But, legitimacy was also a key issue, which a church meetingplace would address, as it appears that the association was not well received in the town. Just before these working men and women began meeting at the Trinitarian vestry, the group found it necessary to release a "Circular to the Inhabitants of Fitchburg and Vicinity" that sought "to make a correction of wrong views and impressions which have gone out in this vicinity."[24] When these activists proclaimed their movement the cause of "philanthropy and Christianity," they did so from the house of God.[25]

As in Fitchburg, Fall River's religious institutions constituted the vortex of the community, serving as a public arena for citizens' meetings, reform activities, and holiday celebrations. Though by 1812 the community boasted a separate town hall, numerous schoolhouses, and a variety of public buildings, some townspeople continued to promote their "secular" endeavors in the church. Here, too, antislavery and temperance advocates met in a range of local churches.[26] And, again, clerical and congregational support was critical. During the ten-hour agitation of the early 1830s, local ministers expressed little open support for labor, and protesting workers held their meetings in a local schoolhouse and in Lyceum Hall.[27] During the 1840s, however, when several progressive working-class ministers held pastorates in the town, the Baptist, Methodist, Christian, and Universalist churches opened their doors to labor activists. By this point, as we have seen, many local activists were communicants of those ministers' congregations; their movement regularly sponsored clerical lectures on contemporary social issues. Even after the Mechanics' Association had equipped its own Mechanics' Hall during the summer of 1844, the group continued to meet in the Berean Temple, the meetinghouse of the Universalist Society.[28]

Labor's Quest for Clerical Support

The real prize here, though, was not the church itself but its emissaries. The value activists placed on clerical support—revealed, as we shall see, in the time and energy expended to cultivate it—reflected the deep strain of piety in this movement. It also reflected the simple fact that in antebellum America— among labor activists as well as in the broader community—what the clergy said and wrote *mattered*. Even in this age, marked by the rise of the ministry as a profession, ministers retained their traditional role as educators and as guardians of morality, and their support could be crucial for a fledgling movement.[29]

In its dealings with the clergy, though, labor faced a serious dilemma. Venerated in the community, ministers could lend legitimacy to controversial demands, and their literary and rhetorical skills could provide valuable service in promoting labor's cause. But, should they be unsympathetic, which all-too-often was the case, their opposition could be devastating. Consequently, activists were deeply concerned with ministers who defended employers or simply ignored labor's plight. And yet, for a self-consciously Christian movement in a fervently religious society, it was not at all clear how to challenge the preponderant indifference and often outright opposition of the ministry. Should activists condemn the contemporary clergy as betrayers of the gospel for their failure to support labor, or should they solicit that support? Just how far could the movement go in criticizing Christian ministers without exposing itself to that dreaded charge of infidelity?

Like their attitude toward the church in general, labor's attitude toward the clergy was complex and often ambivalent, particularly at the regional or national level where leaders had to consider a variegated constituency as well as the general public. As we saw in chapter 3, most activists agreed that the contemporary ministry had largely abandoned the reforming impulse and humanitarianism of early Christianity—the dignity of labor "is a cause which the Christian ministry . . . has long ceased to understand" was how the *Mechanics' Mirror* put it—but they differed on what labor should do about it.[30] Those who rejected institutional Christianity (though not necessarily Christianity itself) as an ally of the employers argued that the clergy should be openly condemned for their complicity with evil forces, an anticlericalism that began with Jesus himself and was rejuvenated in the Protestant Reformation.[31] These laborites, in the interest of their movement, sought to draw workers out of the minister's den, which they perceived as wholly corrupt. The majority of activists in the antebellum labor movement argued, however, that the movement should make every effort to enlist clerical support by encouraging the church to adhere to its original charter. They curried ministerial favor and welcomed their support, even as they were also outspokenly critical of churchmen who were indifferent or hostile to the cause.[32] In any case, for this embryonic movement—self-consciously Christian in a self-consciously Christian community—clerical support or opposition made a difference.

The tensions over the issue of clerical support surfaced in 1847 at the second convention of the Industrial Congress, a national gathering of labor activists and other reformers.[33] Fanny Lee Townsend of Providence, the labor reformer who later would organize an open-air working-class church in Philadelphia, offered a resolution condemning the clergy's delinquency in supporting humanitarian causes and denouncing ministers as "speculators" and "monopolists."[34] Urging adoption of her motion, Townsend reminded the assembly of the "power which the church and clergy exert against the interests of the laboring classes." Several members of the assemblage opposed the resolution and, after some debate, it was tabled. The following day, three delegates offered an amended version of the proposal, which read in part: "That while we fully appreciate the labors of all in behalf of suffering humanity, we are constrained to declare *more in sorrow than in anger,* that the great body of the so-called Christian Church and Clergy of the present day are fearfully recreant to the high and responsible duties upon them."[35] If the clergy wanted to be faithful to the principles they preached, the resolution continued, they should "infuse their teachings and practice more of truth, justice and regard for the rights of humanity."[36]

Despite this softening of the resolution, though, many delegates continued to oppose it as alienating to both the clergy and the movement's constituency. In doing so, they revealed just how important was religion—and the religious—to this movement. J. K. Ignalls, New York land reformer and anti-slavery advocate, argued that since clergymen were not the movement's worst enemies, they should not be singled out for condemnation. Indeed, he believed that ministers represented a "class of laborers" themselves who, with few exceptions, taught the true word of God. The president of the Congress, H. H. Van Ameringe, feared that the resolution would alienate "many religious men engaged in this cause." Even deist George Henry Evans thought the motion imprudent. Since an attack on the clergy would look like an attack on religion, he said, it would deprive the movement of many supporters, particularly among women. Another delegate argued that the influence of the ministry was great and "should not be arrayed against us unnecessarily." Moreover, Van Ameringe reminded the convention, the movement would be deprived of the valuable use of church space for its meetings.[37]

Significantly, proponents of the resolution included not only those who rejected the church entirely but also those who sought to goad the clergy into supporting the cause. A Boston activist labeled ministers "instruments of slavery" and tools of the capitalist, insisting that the movement had nothing to lose by condemning an institution that had already become a deadly enemy of reform. He proposed that the people establish their own church and their own government. Another Boston reformer supported the resolution in the same vein, contending that ministers could not be trusted because they moved "as the wind." Other delegates believed that clerical support was both desirable and possible. Lewis Masquerier, another New York land reformer, supported the motion as a good way to "remind the clergy of their duty." Boston's Charles Hosmer, prominent member in the New England Labor Reform League, insisted that the resolution was not anti-Christian, but rather "condemned only pseudo-Christianity." Since ministers had betrayed Christ's teachings, he thought the movement should "admonish them and call upon them to adopt a better course." His remarks, in fact, reflected the view of most antebellum labor activists, who condemned the contemporary clergy in an attempt to place Christianity on the side of progressive movements. Even Townsend herself embraced this position, proclaiming to her fellow delegates that she knew "no greater reformer than Jesus Christ." The problem was clergymen who had betrayed Christ's legacy by failing to carry out his program of social reform. It was not Christianity that she opposed, Townsend insisted, but the contemporary "sham-institutions" of Christianity.

In the end, the convention rejected the amended resolution, reflecting the prevailing view that the clergy were too important to the movement and its constituents to risk even the appearance of infidelity.[38] At regional gatherings in New England, activists followed a similar course, consistently avoiding outright condemnations while encouraging support. The fate of two NEWA resolutions illustrates the strategy. In 1846, during a debate over the rumored possibility of war with Great Britain over the Oregon country, ex-Methodist minister John C. Cluer offered a resolution attacking the clergy for promoting the conflict: "let the ministers of the gospel who pray for the success of armies go fight themselves and let humane men preach." The motion provoked considerable opposition in the assembly—the only one of several introduced that day to elicit debate. John G. Kaulbach, Jr., cooperationist, founder of the Boston Working Men's Mutual Benefit Society, and agent for the *Voice of Industry*, argued that the community owed a debt to the ministry and that it was unjust to single them out for special condemnation. And, although a Lynn minister in attendance averred that he took no offense at the statement, the assembly voted it down.[39] In contrast, at the following convention, a second Cluer resolution was unanimously adopted. This time, though, he courted rather than condemned men of the cloth, expressing "gratitude to the ministers of the Gospel who have attended its session," and asking their cooperation "in the great work of Humanity."[40]

At the local level, the issue surfaced repeatedly.[41] In Boston, with an organized Freethought movement and a generally antilabor ministry, the theme of betrayal dominated labor's attitude toward men of the cloth. A letter to the *New England Artisan* accused ministers, once "the fast friends of the people, the able and willing defenders of equal rights," of abandoning the "worldly interest."[42] Another letter warned workers not to heed clergymen, for these "false, proud and selfish ministers of a Divine Master, He whose conspicuous virtue was a most perfect abnegation of self, have often sold themselves to Tyrants."[43] When the local clergy denounced a ten-hour strike in 1835, they were excoriated by the radical Universalist preacher Theophilus Fisk: "How much the heart of the christian bleeds to witness conduct so strangely inconsistent with the gospel of Christ. How deeply injured is the cause of the Redeemer of his friends, by misguided advocates."[44] Workers in the industrial towns were also vocal in their condemnations. Lowell's Sarah Bagley denounced any minister who sanctioned a system "*not sanctioned* by Him, whose follower, he proposes to be."[45] "The pulpit could do much," lamented a factory worker in Manchester, New Hampshire, "but the clergy are ever the enemies to reform."[46] As a Fall River activist put it, "the parsons apostrophize on *religion*, while they are all the while cooperating with society to degrade and brutalize humanity."[47]

But, in most places, activists were more interested in attracting the clergy than in condemning them, typically distinguishing good from bad clergymen. Claiming the Christian mantle, such laborites naturally sought the support of the representatives of that faith in the community. Fall River's "A Working Man" was typical. After denouncing labor's clerical opponents, he assured the readers of the *Mechanic* that he had "many friends among the sable coated worthies and many whom I esteem very highly for their works sake." Seeking support, he claimed only to be exposing the errors of those ministers who neglected the ten-hour struggle. "God forbid that I should derogate in aught the worthier part of the order," he wrote; "many among them are worthy of all honor, on account of their disinterested labors in behalf of the oppressed."[48]

And when clergymen did speak out, labor activists loudly praised their efforts, upholding sympathetic ministers as examples worthy of emulation. When a Rhode Island Congregationalist minister publicly supported the ten-hour movement in 1846, the *Voice* heartily thanked him for "his fidelity in this truly humane and religious cause." "O, that ministers everywhere would imitate his noble example," editor (and ex-Universalist minister) John Allen intoned, expressing his wish that just one of Lowell's ministers would support the labor movement.[49] Several months later, his prayer was answered: a Baptist minister became the first Lowell clergyman to speak out against the long-hours system. Allen immediately expressed the hope that more would follow: "Let it not be said that he is the only christian minister in this place."[50] Thus, while labor remained critical of a generally unsympathetic clergy, it nevertheless actively sought clerical support.[51]

Clerical Support for Labor

Ministers who answered the reformers' call engaged in a wide variety of activities on behalf of labor, editing the *New England Artisan* and its successor, the *Boston Reformer,* opening their churches and speaking to organizing meetings of the NEWA, and donating money to the strike fund of the Boston tailors.[52] But, as important as all this was, there was one service that only a clergyman could perform: the blessing of workers' gatherings with prayer.[53] A common feature of antebellum gatherings—clergymen opened labor meetings with a devotional exercise in Boston in 1835, in Fitchburg in 1844, and in Haverhill in 1860—these offerings helped establish the legitimacy of labor's cause in the Christian community and no doubt strengthened the participants' sense of religious mission.[54] Antebellum activists so valued this ritual that they even held up their proceedings to ensure its observance. When it was discovered that no ministers were in attendance at the first NEA convention in Boston in March 1832, a committee was chosen to fetch one. While the convention waited, a delegation called on Methodist minister Edward Thompson Taylor, the former sailor, farm laborer, shoemaker, and tin peddler who pioneered the vernacular, evangelical style of modern American revivalism from his pulpit at the Boston Seamen's Bethel Church. For a workers' movement drawing on the faithful of many denominations, the choice of Taylor was apt: well respected by churchmen throughout the city, even among the Unitarians, this man, who had been illiterate until the age of eighteen, presided over a congregation where the worker was the equal of his master. And, was it not appropriate to seek the inspiration of a minister whose prayers, according to his biographer, were "not made by him, but through him"? So, after this "Shakespeare of the sailor and the poor," as Emerson called him, offered an "appropriate prayer" to the gathered delegates, they invited him to take a seat at their meeting.[55]

The most concentrated clerical support for labor struggles came with the wave of protest that swept across scores of New England communities in the mid-1840s—nowhere more so than the place where that upsurge began, Fall River.[56] As everywhere, of course, there was opposition to labor within the churches of Fall River. In the spring of 1844, Fall River building tradesmen pledged to enforce the ten-hour day on all local construction projects. Now came the "foul calumny," repeated by some "officers in our churches," said the *Mechanic*, that the movement was the work of "strangers" and "the Rabble."[57] It was in this context that the Mechanics' Association formed a special committee to solicit local ministers to lecture before the organization on the current "long hours system." Recognizing the power their opponents held in many of the local congregations, the editors of the *Mechanic* issued this entreaty: "We pray God that [the minister]) may yet overcome the fear which he now has of the aristocracy in his church, and be ennobled to speak out boldly and as effectually upon this evil."[58]

Not all did.[59] Labor's most troublesome church opponent here was a Quaker named Jacob Viney; the way local activists handled his opposition underscores the importance they attached to religious support for their movement. During the summer of 1844, Viney helped a local Friend import carpenters who were willing to work more than ten hours per day.[60] While his defenders insisted that he sought only to help an associate, ten-hour advocates accused him of conspiring with the "wealthy and mighty influences of our village against a measure of mercy for the benefit of the laboring classes."[61] One night in mid-July, a group led by a *Mechanic* editor confronted Viney. Reports of the confrontation differed among activists and their opponents, but a Mechanics' Association committee later found it necessary to publicly deny that they had threatened the preacher in any way, taking the opportunity to express their shock and dismay that he would oppose their movement.[62] No doubt Viney believed his own cause righteous, one labor advocate quipped sarcastically, "as much as (did) Paul when he held the clothes of the young men who stoned the martyr Stephen."[63]

In fact, labor activists would garner significant support from the clergy in and around Fall River.[64] As early as 1841, the town's Universalist, Methodist, and Baptist pastors were lecturing before labor reform associations; in the next few years, Christian, Freewill Baptist, Episcopalian, and Swedenborgian clergymen joined them. By 1844, they were serving as orators, organizers, and even officials of a burgeoning regional movement; preachers had become some of the town's leading labor spokesmen. That summer, the Mechanics' Association joined local temperance societies in sponsoring a Fourth of July rally. Some two thousand townspeople assembled in a nearby grove—traditionally used during the warm months for religious revivals—to advocate the ten-hour day and general labor reform. The rally opened with a prayer by a Christian pastor, followed by the reading of the Declaration of Independence. Of the six speakers who addressed the crowd on that sunny July afternoon, five were clergymen.[65]

In preaching the gospel of labor in the section of town used for revival meetings, these ministers (and their working-class sponsors) had appropriated on behalf of labor reform the dominant method of advocacy of their day—Protestant evangelicalism. And, like contemporary revivalists, they combined the efforts of settled clergy with those of itinerant evangelists. In the summer of 1844, the Mechanics' Association organized a "street meeting" in the town center, with local and Rhode Island clergymen preaching from a wagon to the assembled on the virtues of the shorter workday.[66] Alternatively, when the association began its campaign for a regional workers' organization later that summer, it sent Universalist minister Simon C. Hewitt to tour New England's industrial communities. Hewitt held pastorates in several Massachusetts communities during these years; in 1844, he was what can only be described as an itinerant preacher for the labor movement. In his travels to towns and factory villages in Rhode Island, Massachusetts, and Connecticut, he spread the ten-hour gospel, establishing labor associations and promoting the regional meeting slated for the fall. Along the way, he located several preachers "very favorable" to the cause. In the Blackstone Valley of Rhode Island, for example, clergymen not only opened their churches for labor meetings but also joined Hewitt in the pulpit to advocate workers' rights.[67]

Who were these prolabor clergymen? Some were prominent and longtime residents. In Asa Bronson, as already noted, local activists enjoyed the support of an established and respected member of the Christian community, with a strong commitment to social justice.[68] Another lecturer before the Mechanics' Association was George Randall, pastor of the Episcopal Church since 1838 and a school committee official.[69] But other sympathetic clergymen were more recent arrivals. Two ministers of the Christian Connexion, H. P. Guilford and A. M. Averill, who became prominent speakers at outdoor rallies and labor meetings, settled in the area in 1843.[70] Benjamin Phelon, an immigrant from Yorkshire, England, came to town in the same year after nearly a decade of preaching in Rhode Island and New Hampshire mill towns and in Boston. In

Fall River, he organized a Freewill Baptist church, spoke at labor rallies, and wrote a series of important articles for the *Mechanic*.[71] Universalist J. B. Dods had been pastor of the Taunton Universalist Church in the early 1830s; shortly after he arrived in Fall River in 1841, he spoke before the local ten-hour society, the Association of Industry.[72] His successor, John Gregory, fresh from Quincy, Massachusetts, served on Mechanics' Association committees, was a delegate to regional workingmen's conventions, advocated labor's rights at ten-hour rallies and from his pulpit, and even hosted a quarterly meeting of the NEWA at his church. He claimed to have given the first lecture sponsored by the Mechanics' Association and to have been "among the foremost who started the project" in Fall River.[73]

What accounts for the involvement of these particular ministers in this labor movement? It is tempting to seek a denominational explanation. In the region generally, the most consistent support for labor does appear to have come from the Universalists, and to a lesser extent the Freewill Baptists, which might be explained by the doctrine, structure, and social composition of these denominations.[74] In embracing the notions that sin was voluntary and that salvation was open to all, their anti-Calvinist theology implied that collective sin could be eliminated on earth. The Universalists especially, with their emphasis on freedom of conscience, individual interpretation of Scripture, and, most important, the "final holiness and happiness of all men," encouraged participation in antebellum reform causes, and the same tendencies may have led some of their clergymen to support labor reform as well. The Universalists' democratic church polity may have also contributed to their progressive position on labor issues. And both churches held a kind of "outsider" status in antebellum society: they were often poorly educated and "socially despised," occupying the radical fringe of the Christian community.[75]

Ministers of these denominations were indeed prominent in the Fall River labor movement. But prolabor clergy could be found as well among the town's Methodists, Baptists, Christians, Episcopalians, and even Swedenborgians. Their involvement might be explained by their churches being generally the poorer, less established, dissenting churches in the community, whose congregations contained many of the movement's activists. These prolabor clergy may have been motivated in part by their desire to attract and maintain membership, a central concern of any pastor. Beyond this, though, such ministers had little in common. Some were Calvinist, others not; some possessed a democratic church polity, others a hierarchical one; some adhered to an established creed, others to the credo of no creed at all. Nor can marginality fully explain clerical support, for some of the churches that yielded prolabor pastors were small and recently established in Fall River (Universalists, Freewill Baptists, Swedenborgians), others were products of the revivals of the 1820s and 1830s (Methodists, Christians), and still others were well established (Baptists).

In fact, there was no single denominational pattern of clerical support for labor; local conditions and individual personality often played the critical roles.[76] There was one characteristic that a number of the prolabor clergy shared, however, which may explain their involvement more than any other single factor: their own experiences with manual labor. Fall River ministers often remarked on that fact, as when John Gregory told the Fourth of July rally in 1844 that he "believe[d] the Ministers in this place, who have espoused the ten hour system, have been mechanics." Phelon, Hewitt, and Bronson all professed a background in manual labor; George Randall, though the son of a Rhode Island judge, experienced poverty as a youth and had originally apprenticed as a printer. Gregory himself had completed a seven-year apprenticeship in "fancy painting" before joining the ministry. He made clear that there was a causal connection between his background and his current activism. "Having been mechanics ourselves," he said, "we know the wants of our laboring brethren, and we sympathize with them, in their struggles for reform." His colleagues concurred.[77]

With this knowledge and sympathy, these clergymen tapped into a common dissenting tradition in American Protestantism that transcended denomination, a tradition that, as we shall see, was fierce in its condemnation of avarice, that insisted on the equality of all God's children, and that invoked God's authority to challenge the authority of men. Out of this, they developed a powerful argument for labor reform. Ironically, that argument was fraught with ambiguity and paradox in some measure precisely because of their working-class origins. Listen, for example, to Asa Bronson in a sermon to the "Ladies' Mechanic Association" of Fall River. "I know what it is to eat bread in the sweat of my brow," he told these women who were actively engaged in the struggle for the shorter workday. Their demand made sense to him, he said, because he had known "what it was to pant for useful instruction and long to turn over the pages of some interesting book, while my hands grasped the tools of the artizan or the implements of the agriculturalist."[78] For our understanding of the clerical contribution to antebellum labor activism, it is more important that Bronson was no longer a worker than that he had once been one. For he had escaped the hardships of a life of toil, and as a supporter of labor reform he delivered a complex message of moral uplift through spiritual and intellectual cultivation to those who had not. To comprehend the various elements of that message, its complex character, and its meaning for working-class protest, we must turn to an analysis of the prolabor clergy's views on the labor question.

The Clergy on the Labor Question

As churchmen concerned with humanity's spiritual condition, these prolabor ministers endorsed labor reform first and foremost because they believed that prevailing social conditions promoted infidelity. Convinced that salvation—

and proper Christian devotion such as family worship, Sabbath observance, and church attendance—were impossible so long as poverty, excessive toil, and general social misery prevailed, they directed much of their fire at the men they held primarily responsible for those conditions: the employers. Their emphasis on the spiritual dangers of exploitative working conditions constituted a potent indictment of one class in a self-consciously Christian community, drawing a line between the followers and the defilers of God's will. When Fall River mill owner Nathaniel Borden, a Unitarian, insisted in a local newspaper that competition and the profit motive would not permit a reduction in the length of the workday unless employers elsewhere did likewise, Asa Bronson replied that God, not competition, must determine human arrangements. "God has told us," he chastised Borden with biblical authority, "'whether ye eat or drink, or whatsoever ye do, do all the glory to God.'" What shall govern business and the conditions of labor, he demanded, "God, or 'competition'?" For Bronson, the answer was self-evident and incontrovertible: "Jehovah's law must be our guide." "My first principle," he declared, "is, that God has an undoubted right to reign over the world he has made; and that his laws should be most sacredly regarded and faithfully obeyed in all our business operations." And God had not intended, Bronson insisted, that people should work more than ten hours a day. Borden's rejection of that demand made him, in Bronson's eyes, a defiler of Christianity.[79]

The moral authority invested in such condemnations of Christian employers was heightened by the scope of the prolabor clergy's social analysis, which went beyond a mere censure of oppressive working conditions to a general condemnation of an emerging social order. Here though, in offering labor a social analysis grounded in Christian concerns, they placed in workers' hands a double-edged sword. Prolabor ministers were concerned with the decline of moral character, and the consequent decline of religion, that accompanied capitalist development generally. But who was to blame for this predicament? Prolabor ministers accused employers of hindering spiritual development by promoting the sin of avarice, and in this way placed the blame for prevailing social misery squarely on the shoulders of those employers. Thus, Benjamin Phelon attacked "the competition, or selfish system" as a detriment to religion since the "acquisition of property" required men to abandon Christian principles.[80] But, according to such clergymen, this problem applied not to employers alone, for greed infected workers as well. The emphasis on the universal effects of avarice suggested a harmony of interests between the classes, who were victims of the same disease and therefore presumably interested in the same cure. Similarly, by focusing on greed as the fundamental social evil of the day, the prolabor clergy sometimes left the impression that the solution to social problems lay primarily in moral and spiritual renewal rather than in institutional reform.

The ambiguity of this message is evident in a series of articles written by

Benjamin Phelon for the Fall River *Mechanic*.[81] Here, this Freewill Baptist preacher focused on the general effects of the "selfish system," which set man against his brother.[82] As an evangelical, he located the roots of social misery in the unregenerate human heart, the remedy in regeneration. "Unless the working people love their neighbor as themselves," he wrote, "their sorrows and deprivations will not be diminished." Ultimately, their continued suffering rested on their own shoulders, for the perpetuation of social ills stemmed directly from the contagion of selfishness.[83] Now, this was not simply a plea for personal moral reform over institutional change, as the purveyors of the "social control" thesis might have it, because Phelon actively supported the labor reform movement in Fall River. Indeed, he was trying to ensure the success of that movement by stressing the importance of unity and commitment. "If the workingmen's efforts to redeem themselves fail," he predicted, "it will be principally through selfishness,—through selfishness which has defeated many wise and good enterprises." Still, by insisting that social ills were ultimately spiritual problems, Phelon suggested that change would automatically follow if all Christians would practice what he called the "cult of universalist benevolence."[84]

Phelon's articles, conspicuously displayed in the editorial column of the *Mechanic* for several weeks, formed a kind of jeremiad that focused on the social and cultural effects of capitalist development, chastising both employers and workers for their contributions to the "selfish system" and exhorting them to rectification and ultimate redemption.[85] Though the critique was leveled in defense of the workers' movement and against employers, it nevertheless condemned sin and its social effects at the same time that it attacked the sinful employer; despite the minister's advocacy of workers' rights and workers' organizations, ultimately he offered benevolence as the proper path for all Christians of whatever class, rather than advocating the rights of labor over capital. In other words, as Christian ministers concerned with salvation, these clergymen softened the antagonisms between workers and owners at the same time that they enunciated a strident condemnation of the latter on behalf of the former. Their primary concern was the formation of moral character; they could not distinguish among God's children in that enterprise. In their advocacy of labor reform, therefore, they spoke on behalf of the working class but in the interests of all Christians.

This stance explains in part why the shorter workday drew most of the prolabor clergy's attention.[86] For these churchmen, the demand represented far more than simply a call for better working conditions: it was a prescription for good morals and religion among the laboring classes and in the community at large. Their argument was rooted in their particular interpretation of God's "design." It was God's will, they explained, that men and women use their God-granted time on earth to cultivate not only their physical, but also their mental,

moral, and spiritual faculties; any labor system that denied workers the opportunity to fulfill this divine plan therefore violated God's laws. Thus, George
Randall on the ten-hour day, in a lecture before the Fall River Mechanics'
Association: it would promote "cultivation of the moral and intellectual nature
of man in obedience to the laws of his Maker."[87] And, after all, as far as these
clergymen were concerned, the purpose of life on earth was to serve the Lord.
This is how Asa Bronson explained it: though God had decreed that all should
labor, that same God created laws of health as well; the Creator had given his
children malleable minds for which there were also laws; and most important,
God had ordained a "moral law." By this ordinance, Bronson declared, we must
"examine ourselves, read the Bible, worship God, do good works, and educate
our children. We cannot do these things, in obedience to God, if we labor more
than ten hours per day."[88]

Once again, as with their condemnation of Christian employers generally, in
their advocacy of the ten-hour day the prolabor clergy drew a line in the
community between the faithful and the defilers of the faith. H. P. Guilford, for
example, told a ten-hour gathering at the Universalist Berean Temple that "he
wished the line to be drawn so straight through the community, as to oblige
every individual to take sides either for or against the Ten Hour System."[89] But
the clergy's argument for the shorter workday exposed a fundamental paradox
in their overall message, rooted in the contradiction between their working-
class background and their escape from it: labor was divinely ordained, but the
real purpose of life was spiritual. The thinking was most clearly set forth by the
Reverend James M. Davis, a Congregationalist minister in Woonsocket, Rhode
Island, where Hewitt had been successful in organizing for the Fall River
Mechanics' Association. In 1846, Davis wrote an important series of articles on
the hours of labor for the weekly newspaper in Woonsocket, winning praise
from local and regional labor activists for his efforts.[90] "No more interesting
subject can engage the thoughts of Ministers of the Gospel" than the subject of
labor, he maintained, because "God is active" and made humans in their
Maker's image, thus dignifying labor. To be sure, Davis said, one of the consequences of Adam's fall was that his descendants must exert themselves to live
("In the sweat of thy face"), but excessive toil must be condemned along with
idleness because both were based on the same false and pernicious principle—
selfishness. And look what such selfishness had wrought. Although the "Providential design of all (the) wonderful improvements in machinery" was the
reduction of toil, and although the Bible foretold a time when "'instead of the
thorn shall come up the fir-tree, and instead of the brier the myrtle tree,'" the
long hours of labor had turned Rhode Island factories into "living tombs—
great charnel houses of the living dead." Moreover, no time to "cultivate the
powers of the immortal mind, and to meet the high claims of God Almighty,
and immortality" meant "a desecrated Sabbath, and abandoned sanctuaries

and broken down family altars," as all yielded to "the exorbitant demons of the golden God." Again, in this rendition, the ten-hour day was not so much a working-class demand as a Christian one.

Concern over religious and social duties, then, dominated the clerical critique of what they called the "long-hours system." The ten-hour day would be the savior of the individual, the family, and the Christian community. As Guilford told an assembly at his church, "no man could, consistently with Christian duties, labor more than ten hours per day, and do justice to himself, his family and his God." Phelon pressed a similar theme regarding wages in the mills. Factory workers could not afford to purchase clothes, he said, and they "absent themselves from meeting on this account." Typically, Davis put it in the most florid terms. As a result of the long hours of labor, he wrote, "a gradual and far-reaching decay begins to wither up everything green and blooming among the faculties of the mind, and the graces and virtues of the heart. A blight falls upon the social circle."[91]

For these clergymen, the successful application of the ten-hour day presaged the fulfillment of Christian perfection on earth. As Hewitt declared in one of his orations, the movement sought "to develop [the laborer's] spiritual elements in harmony with the physical" so that "the influx of divine and perfect life may show itself most beautifully in all external condition." Here, shorter hours represented only "*a first step*" in this process. Time would allow cultivation of the higher instincts, he said, resulting in "an elevation of man's whole nature." In this way, God's design would be fulfilled: "cultivation and perfection of the earth, by the developement and energetic exercise of the varied faculties and powers of man's being."[92]

On the hours question, then, as on the labor question generally, these clergymen advocated working-class demands, but in doing so they articulated working-class interests as those of the broader Christian community. The effect of this was to simultaneously lend a crucial measure of legitimacy to the cause while diluting the class content of their advocacy. For, in the hands of these ministers, advocacy of the shorter workday was precisely what Phelon had argued true labor reform advocacy had to be: a form of religious benevolence. As Asa Bronson told the ladies' auxiliary, the target of their work should be their "souls and the great salvation." Toward that end, he encouraged them to continue agitating for shorter hours, so that the "recording angel" would say, "'she hath done what she could,' to suppress evil—to alleviate human suffering—to elevate human character—to promote human welfare—to honor Christ—to glorify God."[93] Bronson's exhortation was a prescription for social action, but as Christians, not as workers with a distinct class interest.

This same ambiguity is evident in the prolabor clergy's call for workers to do battle against employers. Activists were surely buoyed by ministers who spoke of the "righteousness" of labor reform as a "moral movement," and especially when men like Benjamin Phelon told them, "if I have any prevailing power with God, you have my prayers."[94] In fact, these preachers directed their audience's attention to the movement's "final victory," the apparently inevitable result of a great struggle between the forces of good and evil, and thus offered their listeners a stark and presumably irresistible choice.[95] "On the one hand is seen the oppressed, and on the other the oppressor," Hewitt wrote in the *Mechanic,* "on the one hand those who are laboring to promote a general interest, and on the other those who are endeavoring to secure the supposed interest of only a few. In one party is Philanthropy, in the other Avarice: in one is seen the narrow contracted, selfish Aristocrat, and in the other the whole souled Republican." Again, though, this language was designed to appeal to labor activists not as workers but as Christians who were actors in the unfolding of a sacred historical design, in a drama whose conclusion had already been determined.[96]

More important, while this kind of rhetoric could invest labor struggles with Christian sanction, significantly the rhetoricians generally insisted that only "Christian means" be employed in the battle. A Christian mission must be carried out in the spirit of Christian brotherhood, they contended. As most of these ministers took the New Testament as their guide to action and belief, they condemned violence—indeed even the *spirit* of antagonism—in the pursuit of labor's rights. The dictum "love thy neighbor as thyself" expressed not only their goal but the means to achieve it as well. Here perhaps most of all, the clergy imparted a problematic message to workers who were in conflict with their employers.

Fall River's Asa Bronson was typical. Though a staunch supporter of labor reform, workers' associations, and even at times strikes, he counseled against any means other than those of the practicing Christian.[97] Always taking great care to aver respect for the employers' rights as Christians, he cautioned workers against violating those rights. Thus, Bronson to the ten-hour women: "Treat your employers with entire respect. Learn in all things to respect yourselves. Resort not, I beseech you, to acts of violence." For Bronson, the means to the laborers' goal was education (the cultivation of the mind) and the gospel (the salvation of the soul). His model was that of religious conversion: having pledged themselves to a sanctified life, workers would carry out their reform mission in the spirit of the reform itself.[98]

Writing to the *Mechanic* during the building trades' strike of 1844, Bronson warned Fall River workers against any antagonistic action. Praising the paper as *"a winged herald"* and applauding the movement in general, he remarked that "it would be wonderful . . . if [the laborers] did not manifest some impatience to have the whole work 'cut short' in righteousness and done up at once, and thus rush into hasty and precipitate measures to attain their end." Typically, he emphasized the workers' moral character as the key to success. The only danger in the present movement, he said, was the possibility that "the working classes . . . will not sufficiently respect themselves and stand aloof from some means

and measures which will, if employed, *most surely defeat their own* object."
Typically, though Bronson supported the building tradesmen's refusal to continue working on the long-hours system, he cautioned against the antagonistic
climate that labor strife often engendered. Referring to labor agitation elsewhere, he warned the workingmen to avoid "a whole moral hemisphere of
'kick ups,' and 'turn outs,' or anything, that looks like *mobocratic violence.*"
Instead, Bronson held out the surety of victory if the workers followed
Christian principles. For, "if they seek diligently to understand their rights," he
wrote, "and in a calm and respectful, but *decided* and *manly* tone, assert them;
they will be heard and their cause will triumph."[99]

But the prolabor clergy's approach to the question of "means" was more
complex than the foregoing suggests, revealing just how much their role resists
easy generalization. Phelon's appeal to Fall River employers illustrates the point.
His entreaty began by invoking the familiar Christian refrain that all God's
children were equal in their Maker's eyes: "Though the employers are superior
in rank to myself, there is one point of equality in which many of them and
myself agree—the rank of Christian brotherhood. As a Christian, I wish to
address them in the language of our holy religion." In this single bold stroke,
the preacher rhetorically stripped away the temporal power of the employer,
holding him accountable to universally recognized standards of conduct.
Though he did not counsel violence, he did speak of divine retribution for
earthly crimes, warning: "Your lives and your possessions are in the hands of
God. If you refuse the entreaties of suffering humanity, you may be suddenly
summoned before God. . . . Various are the ways in which God may disap-
point you, if you trample his laws."[100] Though he insisted that "it is not my
purpose to destroy peace," he also reminded his readers that true peace could
be achieved only if social evils were eradicated. And though he conceded that
the operatives had only prayers in their defense, he cautioned that "the employers ought to remember that these prayers are heard in heaven, and may be
answered in the destruction of [the employers'] gain." Naturally, though, following the logic of his evangelicalism, Phelon held out the possibility that the
owners' lives might be spared if they reformed. "May the Divine wrath be
averted," he said, "by their rendering to the laborer his just hire."[101]

Here, too, since the sin of the "selfish system" was universal, infecting
workers as well as bosses, the entire community faced the prospect of divine
retribution if employers did not yield. Indeed, Asa Bronson attributed just such
significance to the devastating fire that swept through Fall River in the summer
of 1843. When Borden, the Unitarian mill owner, rejected the demand for a
shorter workday on the grounds that Fall River's prosperity depended upon the
manufacturers' ability to compete in the marketplace, the Baptist minister
responded angrily: "Yes! And a righteous God may bring it down suddenly!
Have we forgotten the lesson? *It was written in fire!*" In a speech at the Pearl
Street Christian Church on the first anniversary of the 1843 conflagration,

Bronson told the Ladies' Mechanic Association that the destruction had reminded the people of Fall River "of that coming day" when

> The heavens, being on fire shall be dissolved, and the heavens shall melt with fervent heat. . . . [When] the Lord Jesus Christ shall be revealed from heaven with his mighty angels, in flaming fire, taking vengeance on them that know not God, and that obey not the gospel of our Lord Jesus Christ. Who shall be punished with everlasting destruction from the presence of the Lord and the glory of his power; when he shall come to be glorified in his saints, and to be admired by all them that believe.[102]

And, in fact, fiery retribution might even be by man's hand as well as by God's. For, though they were always careful to warn workers that the rights of all should be protected, these ministers also reminded their constituents to "guard their rights with vigilance."[103] Indeed, the clergy's homilies on violence and vigilance were sometimes just ambiguous enough to allow for a variety of interpretations. In the midst of the building trades action, Guilford explained his position on the question of means to a gathering of labor advocates. After affirming that his religion prohibited fighting, he told a fable about a Quaker traveling unarmed in dangerous lands. Though he refused to carry a gun, this Friend had agreed to take a hot poker from a family with whom he had spent the night. Sure enough, only a few miles from the house, a robber accosted him. With feigned innocence, the Quaker asked the man to hold the poker while he reached for his money. Still hot, the piece of iron burned the highwayman and foiled the robbery attempt. Assuring his audience that as a Christian he could not fight, Guilford added that "he was ready to offer the hot end of a poker to those who are endeavoring to rob the Mechanic of his rights." He left his audience to determine just how they might offer "the hot end of a poker" to their employers.[104]

Hewitt imparted a similarly ambiguous message on labor tactics. Like the others, he claimed that the workers' movement "conflicts with evil, but with no man's real rights and interests." Though he was accused of setting one class against another, he insisted that his role was "to fill up the awful chasm which is already existing between the laborer and the capitalist—to heal the breach which their present antagonism is continually making more alarming." And yet, he did accept some responsibility for the enmity between employer and employed, for a diseased body "must sometimes be made to feel the *greater disagreeable effects of medicine*" for a short time. In these cases, he pointed out, an apparently greater evil signaled returning health. Applying the same principle to the "*social* body," Hewitt accepted class antagonism and its effects in the short term. For this minister, the conflict engendered by the labor movement was necessary as it merely exposed the true source of contemporary social strife, namely the "unnatural" organization of human relations.[105] Though

Hewitt looked forward to a future without class, he accepted the reality of class struggle as necessary to get there.

Some prolabor ministers, then, did acknowledge the reality of social conflict in the struggle for workers' rights. Though they prayed for harmony, their support for the labor movement necessitated at least a limited acceptance of the *"greater disagreeable effects of medicine"* needed to cure an ailing social body. Though they counseled against the spirit of dissension in the tradition of New Testament morality, their advocacy of this "holy cause" of "labor's sacred rights," as they called it, meant that they had indeed taken sides in a dividing community.

Though a distinct minority in the antebellum New England pulpit, prolabor ministers lent critical support to the nascent labor movement of the era—for which leaders and rank-and-file alike were outspokenly appreciative—and, in the process, they helped sharpen emerging class lines in American society during these years. They accomplished this by advancing an essentially working-class interpretation of their religion. They condemned as contrary to God's will not only prevailing labor conditions but also a consequently immoral and chaotic social system, identifying employers as the principal culprits in the matter. They also provided inspiration and confidence for the soldiers of "the laboring classes" by proclaiming, as emissaries of the Lord and the church, that labor's cause had the sanction of God and the Christian religion—indeed, that labor reformers were engaged in a battle of light and darkness whose end had already been determined.

At the same time, the prolabor clergy's contribution to the development of class consciousness among their constituents was fraught with paradox; the ministers offered the labor movement a deeply problematic language of resistance.[106] In some measure, the ambiguity of their message can be traced to these ministers having entered the fray as churchmen first and workingmen second. Though they spoke of the dignity of labor, for example, ultimately they promised escape from it in order to cultivate the "higher" instincts of humanity. They articulated a powerful indictment of the "competition, or selfish system," but their focus on individual morality undercut calls for concrete action and institutional change in favor of testimony and spiritual renewal. In the same way, harsh condemnations of contemporary social arrangements could be used to advocate a natural harmony of interests over the prevailing clash of interests, when such arrangements were seen as the collective personal sins of God's children—workers and employers alike. And, finally, though the prolabor ministers called on workers to fight for their rights—indeed, assuring them of victory by investing labor struggles with divine sanction—they generally insisted on employing only "Christian means" in the course of battle. In other words, while engaged in a conflict of classes on the side of the workers, these clergymen also softened that very antagonism by elevating Christianity over class. For, ultimately, they expressed a Christian concern that transcended the social misery caused by prevailing labor conditions. From these ministers' perspective, the labor movement brought workers together not on the basis of their specific material interests as workers but as Christians concerned with the moral and religious character of their community.

At the same time, their voice harmonized with that of their constituency.[107] Indeed, much of the religious authority of the clerical message—and its ambiguity—can be seen in the language of labor during these years. In this sense, the ministers, though seeking to transcend class, were nevertheless lending their voice to one side in an expanding clash of classes. Thus, while the prolabor clergy saw the laborer, as well as the employer, as souls to be saved, in their labor evangelism they registered a resounding protest against an emerging system of exploitation that prevented salvation because it was, in their view, fundamentally unchristian: the long hours of labor allowed no time for devotion, and a social order based on avarice bred sin and immorality. Even more crucially, their preoccupation with immorality and sin in the new industrial community was clearly more a criticism of capitalism and capitalists than of the workers who increasingly made up the majority of the population.[108] Although the prolabor clergy may appear to have shared the concerns of other Protestants because of their common vocabulary, they generally attached different meanings to similar language, and their social agenda clearly set them apart from the mainstream.

Precisely the same must be said of the "mind of antebellum labor," the ideology and program of the labor activists themselves.

Part 3.
The Mind of Antebellum Labor: Religion and the Development of an American Working-Class Consciousness

Chapter 8. Sources of Inspiration

Over the last two decades, historians have identified the republican heritage of the American Revolution as the big gun in antebellum labor's ideological arsenal.[1] But labor activists throughout this period entered the public debate over the course of their nation's development speaking the language of radical Christianity as well as of working-class republicanism. Invoking religion to bolster their own morale, to exhort other workers to join the struggle, and to appeal for community support, they christened the labor movement a "holy cause" sanctioned by God, the Bible, and Christianity. In this way, religion formed an essential ingredient in labor's "call to arms" during the period. Indeed, as we shall see in chapters 9, 10, and 11, labor activists developed a thoroughgoing critique of contemporary social arrangements, sketched an expansive vision of an alternative future, and articulated various strategies and tactics for promoting their movement's goals, all in accordance with what they insisted were the dictates of their religion.

To be sure, the Revolution did figure prominently in their emerging sense of themselves as a class with an agenda for the nation. But even in this tradition laborites found religious significance. In the 1830s, with the memory of the Revolution kept fresh by living veterans, the "spirit of '76" symbolized for many labor activists religious suffering and Christian promise, and imparted meaning to their struggle and a beacon of hope for the future. During the 1840s, when millennialist expectation swept the nation, the language of republicanism blended almost imperceptibly with the language of Christianity—indeed, became subsumed within it—as activists frequently perceived the hand of God in contemporary events and gained strength from a sense of their movement's providential destiny to realize in America what they called the "good time coming." Here, the vision of a laborite Republic was one heavily laden with Christian imagery, language, and doctrine, and the labor movement itself became a religious crusade. Appealing to its constituency as Christian republicans, the early American labor movement was in a fundamental sense driven as much by the demands of the spirit as of the flesh.

The Appeal to Christian Duty:
"The Cause of God, of Christ and Humanity"

Perhaps the most important inspiration for antebellum labor, a key ingredient in creating a tradition of working-class resistance in America, was the fulfillment of Christian duty. Coming of age in an evangelical culture, often deeply enmeshed in the church life of their communities, and spurred on by the pious pronouncements of sympathetic clergy, antebellum labor activists not surprisingly made their appeal for support—to other workers and the broader community as well—on religious grounds. Labor protest, they said, was divinely inspired, their movement's goals divinely assured. In Philadelphia, the citadel of antebellum Freethought, and in rural New England, the land of the Puritans, among skilled male artisans and female mill operatives, and on both sides of the Panic of 1837, labor voices invoked God, the Bible, religious imagery, and spiritual precept to justify their activities, to steel themselves for battle, and to attack their opponents as defilers of the faith. Such invocations had different meanings in different hands—sometimes in the same hands—as activists drew on both the gentle and angry traditions in their religion, thus evincing some of the same ambiguities and ambivalences we have seen in the rhetoric of the prolabor clergy. Whatever the differences in rhetorical usage, though, such appeals were not merely calculated attempts to promote the cause of labor; they reflected a religious worldview that underpinned the labor ideology of an emerging working class.

In May 1845, the Fitchburg Workingmen's Association published the first issue of the *Voice of Industry,* which would soon become the organ of the New England Workingmen's Association and the mouthpiece of New England labor reform. Under the editorship of NEWA leader William F. Young, the paper claimed biblical authority for its right to speak—to be a voice—emblazoning its masthead with a motto taken from the Book of Job: "Hearken to me, I also, will show mine opinion."[2] At the top of the editorial page, the paper justified the other part of its name: "What We Labor For.—The abolition of idleness, want and oppression; the prevalence of industry, virtue and intelligence." In the *Voice,* these demands for sweeping changes in the workplace and in the community were also defended on specifically Christian grounds. Thus, "Industry's" attempt at defining the paper's editorial goals proclaimed *"The Abolition of Oppression"* a Christian duty: "For this, the Savior came; for this, he suffered; for this, he labored; for this, he died and rose again. To relieve oppression is, therefore, *christian*—is the cause of God, of Christ and humanity."[3]

The language typified New England labor reform in the 1840s, activists sounding like contemporary evangelists as they exhorted their minions with the Old and New Testaments to do battle "in the name of God" on behalf of a "righteous" and "holy" cause. "Gird up your loins, ye working men!" cajoled the fiery exhorter John Gibson, editor of the Lynn *True Working Man.*

Stand in your lot and place, and do your duty. Agitate the great questions of the rights of man . . . for your redemption draws nigh; the reign of universal justice—of peace on earth, good will to man. . . . Up! drones! and do your duty; for God is mighty and will prevail. Lift up your hands ye poor men, and all you that are oppressed; for the Lord God of earth resigneth; and the wicked, and all those that oppress, shall perish from the earth.[4]

Meanwhile, nearby mill girls roused their constituency in the same fashion, "Juliana" assuring her sisters in the women's column of the *Voice,*

Let the thought that we are engaged in a *good* work nerve us on to duty. The battle is not to the strong, nor the race to the swift—but to the righteousness of the cause. In the strength of Elijah's God, the God of Right, let us march boldly on to the conquest. Let us take no rest until the shout shall rend the earth and heavens—"Goliath is fallen!"[5]

The rhetorical appeal was peculiar neither to New England nor to the 1840s. In Philadelphia a decade earlier, "An Enemy to Banks" enlisted his brethren "in the righteous cause," "the good work," of the *Mechanics' Free Press;* the Journeymen Tailors' Association called on all producers "to come out of Babylon." In New York City, the Typographical Association called on area printers "as from Holy Writ" to "cast in thy lot among us"; factory operatives called their efforts a "cause alike sacred to all the human family."[6] In Rochester, the Equal Rights Party, radical Democrats with a labor constituency, called on the citizenry to come to the polls as "friends of righteous principles," engaged in a "just and righteous cause" to "redeem [the] country."[7] Two months later, the Carriers' Address of the *National Laborer* read:

Nobly they stand, and nobly let them fall—
God for their right, and Justice for their all.

For *Equal Justice* and for *Equal Laws,*
Man's charter'd rights, and Nature's holy cause.

And proud Oppressor, tottering from her throne,
Proclaims the virtue of *thy will be done.*[8]

In New York City, Christian workingmen addressed "Men and Brethren" with the entreaty, "we call upon you to unite with us for man, for righteousness, for God!"[9]

Sometimes, this language may have simply been a reflexive use of religion. In 1834, striking carpenters in Rochester adopted a resolution which announced, "we will not put our hand to the plough and look back"; nine years later, a meeting of the Working Men's Benevolent and Equal Rights Society proclaimed it the duty of all citizens of Rochester to "watch with Argus eyes" any system that "defraud(s) the laborer of his hire."[10] At other times, calculation was clearly involved. When the self-styled Old Testament prophet, "Isaiah," chose to head his letter to the *MFP* with "Rivers shall break forth and streams in the desert," he put biblical prophecy on the side of labor: "their swords shall be beat into ploughshares, and their spears into pruning hooks."[11] In any case, the *effect* of such appeals was to announce the movement as religiously inspired.

In some measure, the appeals worked because they were often couched in the prevailing anti-Calvinist theology of the age. These activists, after all, were demanding that workers step forward and change their lives, just as the contemporary revivalist called on sinners to take steps toward their own religious salvation. In a major address to the New England Labor Reform League (NELRL) in 1847, later reprinted as a pamphlet, Charles Hosmer drew the connection between the temporal and spiritual worlds of antebellum America for the assembled labor reformers:

> We have been taught that our condition was 'ordained,' and that we should be 'contented with our lot.' But blessed be God, this theology is passing away. Content with your lot! What is this but the old dogma of unconditional submission, new vamped to suit the altered social and political state of our time; suited, in fact to the new form which the 'divine right' has assumed? Contented with your lot! Be not contented, suffer not men to preach to you to be contented, to be dissatisfied, so long as the present frightful advantages exist.[12]

In this rendition of religious responsibilities, eliminating social evils was a Christian duty, justifying labor reform *and* requiring the support of all Christians.[13]

Much of the rhetoric here was for internal consumption: by promoting labor's cause as a fulfillment of divine mandate—by invoking their religious identity as a movement—these activists were steeling themselves for continued struggle.[14] Thus was the movement buoyed at crucial moments in time—even by some deists, though their rhetoric often drew upon sources other than Scripture. As the Wilmington Working Men prepared for local elections in 1830, George McFarlane quoted Shakespeare to provide divine sustenance for labor struggle, reminding that "what though aristocratical and lordly oppressors frown upon you, fear them not;

> Be just, and fear not:
> Let all the ends ye aim at be *your country's,*
> Your GOD's and TRUTH's; then if ye fall,
> Ye fall as blessed Martyrs.[15]

Other activists simply invoked the sacred nature of their protest to cheer their fellows with visions of eventual victory, as when Rochester's "Citizen" reminded striking printers in 1839 that "the aspirations of a heaven-born spirit—are now triumphing over the cravings of . . . an unholy passion."[16]

Such assurances were particularly useful in moments of disappointment or despair. Persevere, the *National Laborer*'s Thomas Hogan told his readers on the eve of hard times in the late 1830s, and you will not "'long endure the vulgar dominion of ignorance and profligacy,'"; persevere, and the "'avenging hour will at last come'—'the banditti will be scourged back to their caverns.'"[17] In the next phase of national labor agitation, after a failed carpenters' strike in Cincinnati during the spring of 1844, the editors of the *People's Paper* wished the men "God-speed in their holy cause."[18] Four years later, contemplating the tenuous fate of the European revolution, the horror of black slavery in America's capital and the "Armies of white slaves" in America's cities, and the coming of a cholera epidemic, Philadelphia's George Lippard reminded his readers, "there are three words which solve all problems, and make sunshine even in the grave—TRUST IN GOD."[19]

Activists also sought support in the broader community, and religion was a powerful tool of legitimation in this culture. When William Young announced in the first issue of the *Voice* that "our platform is humanity, from this our Voice will echo in all directions wherever the image of God is known," he put the broader community on notice that only those who did not know God could resist his movement's call.[20] Thus, too, the call to Christian duty could be a potent weapon against opponents, who could be tarred as betrayers of the faith—usually in such loaded Christian terms as "the *proud* oppressor," or "the *proud* aristocrat."[21] Sometimes, this was as simple as condemning certain employers as sinful, as when the editor of the *National Trades' Union* urged the master tailors of New York to "forsake their evil ways and sin no more."[22] Sometimes, the exposition was more detailed, as when "Poor Mechanic" offered a series of articles bearing on the question for the *MFP*.[23] The first installment set forth "a rule for all professed christians to measure their actions by," what might be called "Labor's Rule," given how often they used it: "Do unto others as you would have others to do unto you."[24] "That spirit in religion that is not productive of this pure and everlasting righteousness, is not the right spirit," he warned, yet few "professors" adhered to it. William Young used the same language, quoting Scripture directly, when he asked unsympathetic clergymen in 1845 if they had forgotten the biblical injunction, "'as ye would that others should do unto you, do ye even so unto them'"; he asked factory owners—"the professed embassadors of him who has commanded us to 'love our neighbors as ourselves'"—if they had "any humanity; any manhood?—aye christianity?"[25] By thus proclaiming labor reform a Christian duty, and criticizing those who neglected that duty as sinful, activists both sanctioned their cause and stripped legitimacy from the system they sought to topple.

In all of this, Jesus proved a particularly potent model. Young, for example, concocted a powerful appeal for Christian support when he noted that his activism had brought down the censure of the truckling politicians, the anathemas of the time-serving christian, and the cry of 'infidel' from those who are feasting upon the laborers, bones and sinews of God's poor, under the garb of religion; still with one of old, I can say, 'Father, forgive them for they know not what they do'—they are crucifiers of the spirit of truth.[26]

Leonard Cox, labor editor, secretary of the Boston Mechanics' Association, and NEWA officer, employed a similar rhetorical technique in his condemnations of Christian employers.

Tell us, ye who claim to be followers of Him who 'though he was rich yet for your own sake became poor,' tell us, do ye love your brethren as ye love yourself? Do ye never despise or avoid a brother because he is poor, and are ye ever ready to give of your abundance to supply his immediate need? Tell us, ye rich, do ye always use your wealth to increase the sum of human happiness? do ye never look unmoved upon a brother's suffering, for you, the recompense he has earned? If he asks for bread, do ye never give a stone, and if he seeks your aid, do ye never place obstructions rather than succor in his way?[27]

For, one Lowell mill girl insisted, in an echo of Wilmington's Benjamin Webb, Rochester's Henry Frink, and Lowell's Sarah Bagley, "is it not the very work our savior laid out for us, to love our neighbor as ourselves—to visit the widow and the fatherless, in their afflictions—to break the fetters of those that are bound, and let the oppressed go free?"[28] Here was the voice of New Testament labor protest, demanding support from all professors.

Especially in the 1840s, such activists spoke to "christians and philanthropists."[29] In a letter to the *Voice* that Young entitled, "A Word to Philanthropists," FLRA secretary Huldah Stone called on the "charitable and christian" to support her group's "holy enterprise."[30] The preamble to the FWA constitution, written by a committee that included a churchgoing Baptist and Congregationalist, declared that since prevailing social conditions frustrated the "design" of the "*Allwise Author* of the *Universe*," it was the duty of all "christians and philanthropists" to reform society.[31] The Fall River *Mechanic,* whose editors were also members of local churches, addressed "Mechanics, Philanthropists and Christians."[32] Unlike the twentieth-century conception of philanthropy as alms giving, here the term referred to active involvement in humanitarian and Christian causes such as the labor movement. Antebellum activists were not speaking to those who gave to charities or to the benevolent rich, but to the lover of humankind and, in their terms, the good Christian.[33] Thus, in a call to labor activists, Huldah Stone appealed to "every philanthropist [to] exert all the powers God hath to circulate the *Voice*."[34] In identifying themselves as religious humanitarians, such laborites inspired those already engaged in the struggle, while promoting the cause in the broader community.

There was another religious voice that inspired antebellum labor and informed its public appeal, though it too blended easily with the apocalyptic language of contemporary evangelical fervor: the angry cry of Christians at war with the forces of darkness. As we have seen, some were not above condemning their opponents as the very agents of the devil. The Rochester WMBERS, for example, declared in an 1842 resolution that any who continued to engage in the duebill system "ought to be held as aliens to God—reserved for no higher employment than to do His Satanic Majesty's most dirty work."[35] Others, like New York's "Veritas," warned of the "hosts of darkness" and, insisting that "the time is at hand," goaded workers to be "steeled for the combat between *unholy oppression* and *equal rights* for all," and "with the united cry of the God of Right and justice for *assistance,* go up—fear not—the arm of Almighty God is not shortened that it cannot save!"[36] Unsurprisingly, this angrier Christian appeal drew on the Old Testament, as can be seen in the powerful rhetoric of Seth Luther, who made no attempt to speak to "christians and philanthropists."[37] "Let our motto be, 'Vox Populi, Vox Dei.'—*The Voice of the people, is the voice of God,*" he said, announcing that the people would soon awaken from a thousand years of slumber and "hurl their chains at their oppressors." Reminding his listeners of Babylon, Luther cautioned tyrants to prepare for the coming change. "It will be well for our oppressors to stand back," he warned in an Independence Day address in 1836, "when the mighty phalanx shall roll on and sweep from the land every vestige of domestic tyranny. . . . The flame of liberty, like the pent up fires of a volcano, has broken forth, and threatens to overwhelm thrones and dominions and principalities and powers, in one widespread ruin and desolation."[38]

Thus, the language and imagery of Christianity could be turned to a variety of uses when rendering labor's appeal. While some solicited the support of "christians and philanthropists," others offered a stern warning to the wealthy and powerful. But some combined both tendencies, resulting in a studied ambivalence. Robert McFarlane of the Mechanics' Mutual Protection Association, for example, frequently insisted that he sought no class war between employer and employee, and yet:

> Oppressors of mankind, ye who rob the poor of their bread—who reap the fruit of the working-man's toil, that you may flaunt in your gilded chariots and bask in the glories of earth-born splendors, beware, remember the scathing language of the great Law-giver, "Thou shalt not, therefore, oppress thy neighbor, but thou shalt fear the Lord thy God."[39]

Labor's appeal was also ambiguous when editors stoked workers to a fiery defiance and then—sometimes immediately afterward—reminded them of their Christian obligations to kindness and mercy. In 1833, the Baltimore *Mechanics' Banner and Working Men's Shield* praised striking journeymen hatters who had "risen up in the majesty of their strength" for their "spirit of holy enthusiasm" and for having said "to those who would question their heaven-born and blood bought privilege to think and act for themselves, 'so far shalt thou come and no farther." In the next breath, though, the editor warned them that while some might advise, "'kick against the pricks,'" he would "spread the mantle of charity, and simply say, 'Do unto others as ye would they should do unto you.'"[40]

For the mill girls of the mid-1840s, alternating appeals to a God of justice and a God of love may have reflected strategic considerations.[41] When they spoke of their blessings in general, or appealed for support from the larger community, the mill women spoke in the mild tones of the merciful and forgiving God they found in the New Testament. When they faced their enemies, though, they often solicited instead the aid of the "God of Right and Justice" they found in the Old Testament. Thus, in her first column during her short solo editorship at the *Voice,* Sarah Bagley sounded a note of militancy uncharacteristic of that paper's editorials, before or after her tenure. Speaking to her constituency and announcing herself to her enemies, Bagley chastised a textile agent who had threatened to discharge an FLRA member: "We will make the name of him who dares the act, stink with every wind, from all points of the compass."[42] When she addressed the NEWA convention as FLRA president the following fall, however, she insisted that her cause was one in which every philanthropist should take an interest, reminding her audience to "be true to the sympathies and emotions of piety which a God of Infinite Love has implanted in every human soul."[43]

The strains of militancy and conciliation in labor's appeal, rooted in religion, in varying ways provided encouragement for a fledgling movement and condemned those who stood in the way. As Christians seeking the ear of other Christians, these activists sought to remind themselves as well as others of their religious duties in order to advance the cause. Still, in the process, activists articulated two different Christian appeals—or, perhaps, one ambiguous appeal—and thus, like the prolabor clergy, communicated two quite different messages to workers and the broader community.

The Revolution, Republicanism, and Religion

The other principal source of inspiration for antebellum labor radicals—the republican heritage of the Revolution—was often cast in religious imagery. Indeed, Christianity and the Revolutionary tradition intermingled during these early years, forging a powerful heritage of resistance that rendered the "spirit of '76" sacred and irresistible with the transcendent authority of God and religion. Typical was the meeting in 1836 of Philadelphia workers, whose president reported that they had met "to assert their rights in the rear of that venerable fane [Independence Square], where liberty first drew breath, where the sages of '76 shook off from their necks the tyrant's yoke, and swore on the altar of God to be free or die in the attempt.:—the blood of thousands sealed the decree."[44] Labor's rendition of the republican tradition and its meaning for a new generation varied within the movement and changed with the passage of time—just as the appeal to Christian duty did—but it rarely surfaced as a source of inspiration without some reference to Christianity. Eventually, it would meld into an explicitly millennialist vision of a laborite Republic.

A secret ceremony of Boston building tradesmen in 1835 illustrates the spiritual watering of the tree of liberty in the opening years of antebellum labor agitation.[45] During the early morning hours of July 4 of that year, a contingent of journeymen housewrights and stonemasons gathered in Trades' Union Hall to celebrate a ten-hour victory in Philadelphia and to rededicate their own efforts, over a decade in the making, to establish a shorter workday.[46] Conceived as a tribute to Philadelphia's mayor for his signing of a municipal ten-hour ordinance in early June, the building tradesmen timed their celebration to coincide with the birthday of American Independence. For the organizers of the event, this earlier struggle for basic human rights clearly constituted a source of inspiration, guidance, and strength. Indeed, their actions here reflected a kind of ritual reenactment of the Revolution, a reliving by the sons of their fathers' experience. In this way, they invested the struggle for labor's rights with the force and power of the Revolution.

In their elaborate arrangements, these workers sought to resurrect the memory of the Revolution, to relive the suffering it entailed, and to exalt the principles it embodied. After completing their preparations late in the evening of July 3, the "joint committee on the Tribute" slept on the floor of Trades' Union Hall, bringing "forcibly to their minds the far greater hardships our fathers endured, lying on the ground under no shelter but the canopy of heaven." Rising in the middle of the night so that their "Tribute" could be duly executed at sunrise on July 4, the artisans called their meeting to order at 3:30 A.M. The chairman of the proceedings, a leader of the local stonemasons' union named Jethro Snow, took his seat on the podium, with the meeting's secretaries and the joint committee seated on either side of him. The stage itself had been elaborately arranged. Busts of Franklin, Lafayette, and Washington stood on fluted columns, and the Declaration of Independence graced the wall behind the platform. At each of the table's four corners were beautifully ornamented china vases filled with white and red flowers. But suffering rather than beauty was the theme of the artisans' labors. To one side of the table stood a shell work depicting the miseries of the masses in vivid detail. This sculpture showed a multitude of workers supporting a single man (symbolizing "National Glory . . . based on National Misery"), whose weight caused blood to pour from their eyes and mouths.[47]

But the most elaborate aspect of the unionists' preparations was a triangular sculpture formed by the rear edge of the table and two walking sticks. One of

these canes, belonging to chairman Snow, had been constructed from fragments of the old Bunker Hill monument, "erected to the memory of Warren,
and the Farmers, Mechanics, and other workingmen, who fought and fell on
the glorious 17th of June, 1775." The other implement had been fashioned
from the wood of the USS *Constitution*. At the sculpture's apex was a cannon-
ball that had been "thrown into the *Town of Boston* from Dorchester Heights by
the investing Forces under Washington, previous to the '*Evacuation*' by General
Howe March 17, 1776." Traversing each walking stick, arranged like muskets at
a charge, were five eagle feathers. Their tips had been dipped in gall which,
mixed with the wormwood in the china vases, was to represent "the cup of
bitterness our fathers drank while grappling with tyrannical power." In the
center of this construction was an English Bible printed in 1631 and containing
a copy of the act "which drove the Pilgrim Fathers from their native land."[48]
The Bible was presented by the chairman's father, a veteran of the Revolutionary War; it had been in their family for more than a century.

The proceedings centered on this sculpture, which embodied the essence of
the artisans' culture of resistance. Its symbolism was steeped in Revolutionary
tradition, bringing together artifacts from the war and those who had actually
participated in the event. In this way, the workingmen identified their movement with the military struggles of the Revolutionary generation. Furthermore,
by explicitly noting that the Revolution itself had been fought by the "Farmers,
Mechanics, and other workingmen," the artisans directly linked their struggle to
that of their Revolutionary forbears.[49] For these workers, labor activism was an
expression of fidelity to the "fathers"—in Jethro Snow's case, literally so.

Obviously, there was a religious component to the sculpture as well. Indeed,
religious symbolism and imagery characterized much of the ritual itself, forming a kind of undertone to the ceremony, a subtheme that enhanced the
Revolutionary motif. The gall and wormwood signified the cup from which
Jesus drank on the cross. By linking the Crucifixion to their fathers' experience,
the artisans invested the Revolutionary heritage with Christian meaning. In
this way, the feathers of the eagle, symbol of both military strength and the
father, bestowed the power and courage of the ancestors upon their descendants. The Bible itself, the sculpture's centerpiece, represented the historic
struggle for religious liberty. Here, the artisans' tradition of resistance embraced the Pilgrims, as well as the Revolutionary generation, condemning
religious as well as political and economic oppression. As an example of religious tyranny, the artifact served to remind fiercely anticlerical artisans in
urban New England of their Puritan heritage of resistance. Moreover, the fact
that the Bible had been in the Snow family for several generations reflected the
centrality of Scripture in New England culture; its role in the ritual provided a
graphic representation of the continuity in piety from the seventeenth to the
nineteenth centuries.

Most significant of all, perhaps, the pyramidal structure bore a striking resemblance to the symbolism of Freemasonry. Indeed, the prominent display of Masons Washington and Franklin, the centrality of Scripture, and the highly ritualistic and secretive nature of the event suggest some kind of Masonic influence. The Masonic Order's emphasis on universal brotherhood, its strict moral code, and its religious catholicity likely appealed to these urban artisans. In Boston, where the church and clergy generally opposed the labor movement, activists may have also been attracted by the anticlericalism and dissenting traditions among the Masons. And like many of their contemporaries, these workers may have perceived the order as a religious denomination or even as an alternative to organized religion. A fraternal association with strong links to the Revolutionary generation, which required adherence to the simplest of moral and spiritual creeds while rejecting temporal authorities, Freemasonry suited the urban laborites of the 1830s.[50]

The artisans carried out their meeting like good sons of the Revolution. Calling them to order, Jethro Snow distributed an eagle feather to each of the presiding officers and committeemen. At sunrise, "under the discharge of Artillery," the "Tribute" to the mayor of Philadelphia was signed by all those present. When everyone had affixed his signature, the radical clergyman Theophilus Fisk offered a short prayer, and Snow addressed the assembly.[51] The unionists then paraded out of their hall and through Boston's downtown streets to the city post office, where they completed their commemoration by depositing their "Tribute" for delivery to Philadelphia.

The "Tribute" ritual illustrates the inspirational power of the Revolution for labor activists of the 1830s, but it was a "call to arms" powerfully shaped by Christian imagery, the Bible, and prayer. Children of the Revolutionary generation, these workers were self-consciously Christian freemen. A week before the Independence Day celebration, for example, the Boston housewrights issued a circular explaining their demand for the ten-hour day. Declaring their confidence that the struggle would soon be achieved "by a glorious triumph over our oppressors," they called for community support in the names of "posterity," "country," and all "benefactors of man." "Shall it be said of Boston that she guilty as she is, of, we had almost said, immolating her sons upon the altar of avarice refused to heed the cry of humanity?" The appeal was to humanity, but the renunciation was formulated in the language of the Bible. The image of "Boston . . . immolating her sons upon the altar of avarice" would surely catch the eye and ear of anyone familiar with the excoriations of contemporary preachers. And, in the spirit of Christian exhortation, the strikers called on their fellow workers to heed this cry of humanity and return the community to its designated course. In this effort, they appealed to the Revolutionary mantle, charged with the Christian spirit of redemption. "Has the redeeming spirit of '76 which watched over [humanity's] destinies during that dark period, fled from her borders, and gone forth to tell the melancholy tale of degradation?— We trust not."[52]

After the Philadelphia victory, Boston artisans petitioned their own mayor and aldermen for a ten-hour ordinance on municipal works. When the city refused, a number of building trades' unions formed the Ten Hour Association and went out on strike. The group's constitution invoked both the Revolution and religion in its appeal for support. Maintaining that "virtue and intelligence" were the only safeguards of "civil and religious liberty," they demanded time for "intellectual and moral cultivation." "A system which demands uniform, unceasing toil," the association insisted, "should be equally deprecated by the Patriot, Philanthropist, and the Christian."[53] Theirs was a movement that demanded the attention of all citizens and Christians.

This interlacing of Christian and republican language as a source of inspiration, blending biblical tradition and the spirit of 1776, was the hallmark of this movement's greatest speechmaker, BTU leader Seth Luther.[54] In Luther's oratory, Revolutionary events gained religious sanction as symbols of American freedom: Bunker Hill was "that *Holy Hill* where Warren fell," the "Sinai of *American Liberty*."[55] And he used this imagery explicitly to exhort his audiences. Drawing on God's authority and warnings of divine wrath, he told workers that the Revolutionary heritage had been betrayed. Proclaiming the unfinished monument at Bunker Hill a "mockery of a monument," he suggested that its tardy construction should cause "no wonder," since "the curse of almighty God must rest at its base, mean heaven-daring hypocrisy." He hoped that it would remain unfinished, he said, to stand "as a monument to our unfinished independence," in a land where "the name of freedom is reproached and heaven's laws are violated."[56] Here the two traditions joined, fusing the spirit of the Revolution and the dictates of God.

In Luther's hands, these traditions imparted a legacy of militancy, tapping the righteous Christian anger that also imbued his appeal to Christian duty. Reminding workers of their duties to their Father and their fathers, Luther declared:

> To day the united shout of millions ascends to the blue concave of heaven's high arch, proclaiming in exulting accents the national joy. It is our duty to lift our hearts in thankfulness to the God of armies who so manifestly bared his right arm and assisted our revolutionary sires in giving birth to a nation of FREEMEN; our bosoms ought to glow with the pure flame of gratitude to those who suffer every privation that we might be free.[57]

He warned of any negligence in the defense of that freedom. Freedom depended upon intelligence, wisdom, virtue, purity, and patriotism, he said, and if workers were not vigilant, the nation would fall into ignorance, poverty, and vice. Then, he said, the "sun of liberty will have set in endless night."

> When posterity shall visit the hallowed grounds where liberty was gained with blood poured out like water, they will put sackcloth on their loins and ashes on their heads. They will weep, bitterly mourn for lost freedom never

to be regained. Then will the experiment we are now trying have failed. Must it be so? God forbid![58]

Since the Revolutionary heritage was sacred, any betrayal of that heritage constituted a sin. "We now warn the aristocracy of our country to stand off," he announced; "keep your distance: touch not the ark of our liberties with unholy hands, lest you find them withered by the scorching indignation of a brave and virtuous people, who know their rights and are determined to maintain them if we wade knee deep in blood in so doing."[59] The language evoked the avenging God of the Old Testament, in a powerful call to battle.[60]

Here, activists like Luther were appropriating the Revolutionary mantle much as they appropriated the Christian mantle: they were the faithful, their adversaries were the infidels. And, their rhetorical stance here forms a striking parallel to the way they used the appeal to Christian duty as a weapon. In its Fourth of July editorial in 1836, for example, the *NTU* disqualified "the aristo-cratic" from enjoying this "day sacred to the memory," for they prostituted it to "selfish or party purposes," they buried "the proud and holy feelings," they disregarded "righteous principles." The friends of Equal Rights, though, "avoid the carousal, the parade, and the clamorous rejoicings . . . , and spend the day in devotion to Him who led the armies of our country through their perilous struggle, and strengthened their hearts and arms to fight and conquer till the Star Spangled Banner waved in victory."[61] Being true to the Revolutionary heritage was thus invested with a moral and religious significance that rendered labor republicanism more than a mere "secular" language of resistance.

During the 1830s, it was not uncommon for laborites to speak of "this enlightened republic" and "this Christian community."[62] There were frequent references to the Revolution ("act as our forefathers who rejected the stamp act," "remember there were tories in our Revolution," and so on), but many could not separate the language of republicanism from that of Christianity.[63] By the mid-1840s, the Revolution was increasingly muted in labor rhetoric.[64] To be sure, some did continue to make reference to the founding fathers, as when a section of the National Reform Association in New York City main-tained that the workers were "contend[ing] for the rights that God gave the race and the possibility of those rights guaranteed to us by the Declaration of Independence and handed down to us by our Fathers," but, with the passing of the Revolutionary generation, republicanism blended into the Christian world-view of most labor activists.[65] *Voice* editor John Allen struck the keynote of the 1840s when he condemned prevailing labor conditions as "subversive of all religion and christian principles."[66]

But it was his predecessor who established the basic rhetorical frame. Sel-dom referring to the Revolution directly, William Young melded republicanism and religion into one source of inspiration, typically speaking of "a true Christian Republic" and the importance of defending "the doctrines of

Christian Republicanism."[67] For Young, the Revolution and its principles were significant sources of inspiration because they embodied the fundamental truths of biblical Christianity, because the Revolutionary fathers had fought as Christians for basic Christian rights. Any system that abrogated the "great and vital truths" that *all men are born free and equal,* and entitled to life, liberty and the pursuit of happiness must be anti-republican and anti-christian."[68] And, anyone who violated those Revolutionary principles could not be "true friends to their God and their race."[69] Alternatively, he demanded (for "all who lay claim to patriotism and christianity") "that prerogative which our fore-fathers deemed so essential to the prevalence of true christian intelligence among men . . . the *universal* and *undisputed* right to think, act and speak, according to the age in which we live, and the light which nature's God has revealed to us."[70] Remaining true to the founders' legacy was a Christian responsibility.

Activists in the 1840s thus identified republican with Christian liberty. In his essay, "Religion—Freedom," MMPA founder Robert McFarlane exemplified the tendency, reminding the readers of the *Mechanics' Mirror* that Christ had preached "pure liberty," the seed of freedom from which "the tree of liberty shoots up." In this way, McFarlane at once called workers and the broader community to the cause of labor reform and condemned those who opposed that effort as betrayers of both the nation and the national faith. Alluding to Labor's Rule—the Golden Rule, which labor had adopted as its own—he reminded Americans that "all freedom is condensed in the brief but infinitely expressive words, 'Do unto thy neighbor as thou wouldst have thy neighbor to do unto thee,' this is the foundation of our freedom—this is the spirit of the Declaration of Independence." Moreover, all departure from this law in spirit or action, is a departure from the principle of liberty; and just as a man is guided in his action by this rule, just so far do I esteem him as a true republi-can, a true American, and just so far as he departs from this law, do I consider him a recreant to his God, his country, and his fellow man."[71]

In the 1840s, this blending of religion and republicanism amounted to more than the sum of its parts, for activists like Young and McFarlane were inspired by a vision of their movement's providential destiny that at times rendered that movement a kind of religious crusade, in which Christian workers saw the reformation of their communities as a prelude to the redemption of human-ity.[72] A mild version can be glimpsed in a letter to the *National Reformer* by a member of the Rochester MMPA, who wrote, "Heaven seems to prosper our noble work."[73] But, the sentiment took a much more dramatic form among many labor radicals, who exhibited a near-absolute faith in the imminence of radical change. The belief itself, by this time deeply rooted in the cities and towns of a revival-swept nation, grew out of the spiritual enthusiasm that inflamed the country during these years. The desire to escape the unattractive features of commercial and industrial development, most dramatically displayed in the Panic and depression, and the growing sense of America's great potential for economic and territorial growth, combined to engender millennial expectations throughout the society.[74] Millerite adventists, communitarians, and a host of social and economic reformers offered visions of a new world using biblical eschatology and Christian imagery.[75]

The labor movement reflected these broader currents, particularly in New England, where a massive revival engulfed the region in 1842 and 1843. In towns like Fitchburg, where this enthusiasm brought business to a standstill and swept hundreds into its whirlwind, the sense of danger and impending change gave special impetus to labor organization. Before every FWA meeting, the group's constitution was read aloud, the preamble to which painted a picture of contemporary social conditions in horrific hues and spoke of "eradicat[ing] these evils and all other systems of seductive error."[76] Among the committee that wrote the document were a Baptist and a Trinitarian Congregationalist. Just as the revivalists of these churches preached a message of salvation from darkness that would be sudden, cataclysmic, and overwhelming, the Workingmen's Association announced a coming change in social relations that would be immediate, total, and irreversible.

The labor activism of the mid-1840s embodied this revivalist spirit, even in antichurch Boston. South Boston's Albert Wright, early president of the NEWA, recalled later that the movement had been concerned with "moral subjects." Wright, a leading member of an evangelical church who had declared that the millennium was near in 1845, at the end of the decade repudiated the initial labor enthusiasm as nothing more than "beating the air." His recollections of the mid-1840s, though, accurately portrayed the spirit of those years. In the labor press and at workers' meetings, he recalled, "fanaticism and enthusiasm combined to create a horrid picture of the condition of laboring people." As "the thermometer of zeal was raised to a high temperature," activists put forward plans to "work out a deliverance for the people." "The 'good time coming' had been prophesied," Wright recalled, "and a sort of prelude to those times would be enjoyed occasionally during the excitement of a great public meeting."[77]

For labor's goal in this enterprise, Young had explained in 1846, was "the final redemption of the human family from their present false and unnatural relations."[78] And this particular faith in a coming Millennium, more than just a general sense of divine favor, provided a way for activists to convince themselves of not only the righteousness but also of the assured success of their undertaking, thus spurring them on to continue their efforts. Here, the perennial tension between confidence and anxiety in antebellum political and social thought, a tension in many respects rooted in evangelical religion, could be a kind of motor for action, rather than a source of social paralysis. Like most antebellum Americans, labor activists believed that Americans had a mission in the world, that the "experiment" of this Republic would figure prominently in the course of human development, but they worried whether they had the moral and spiritual fortitude to fulfill their mandate. Their religion sometimes gave them a comforting answer to any self-doubts. "God be praised!" shouted Sarah Bagley in her NEWA speech, exhorting her compatriots with words from Longfellow, reminding them that they could count on divine aid: "Act—act, in the living present, Heart within, and God o'erhead."[79] And Christ also. Though laborites might express alarm at their society's parlous course, they could take courage in the faith that "the captain of salvation" watched over their movement.[80]

Despite the failure of prior attempts, then, these activists were confident that their enterprise would be different. Again, the point of reference was often the Revolution, but invested with religious significance. Thus, the first major NEWA address to American workers ended with this announcement:

> The sacred spirit of liberty is again revisiting the earth; the undaunted zeal of the fathers once more re-animates the sons, and the marshalled hosts are gathering for a glorious contest and a bloodless victory. Through the once darkened future, the glow of hope is seen, which tells of the coming of the broad day of freedom, when man shall stand erect in all the dignity of his nature—in the darkness of the past—when labor shall be disenthralled—the supremacy of humanity asserted, and the workingman stand forth confessed as EARTH'S TRUE NOBLEMAN.[81]

The language—visitation, zeal, gathering hosts, coming, confession—was unmistakably evangelical, the imagery pitting light against darkness, with the confidence that salvation lay within labor's grasp. As Young put it, though evils abounded, the age was "big with tendencies of a glorious future."[82] He did express reservations about "'special visitations and judgements,'" but he insisted that his age was "prophetic."[83] His successors at the *Voice* concurred: John Allen insisted that labor's victory was "as sure as the reign of Providence," while John Orvis called the movement a "child of Providence."[84] But it was South Boston's Albert Wright who best exemplified this confidence in labor's ultimate triumph, in his presidential address to the NEWA in 1845. "If we can judge future effects by present causes," he declared, "the signs of these times are indicative of the long-looked for millennium."[85]

This optimistic vision, then, did not simply give labor the hope of victory; like the appeal to Christian duty generally, it offered the assurance of success.[86] And again, faith buoyed hopes when the cause seemed least hopeful. After a poorly attended NEWA meeting in Nashua, New Hampshire, during the fall of 1846, a delegate invoked "a certain promise left by the Great Reformer." The meeting had convened "in the name of humanity's God, and the God of truth," reminded this activist, and "God can bring light out of darkness and order out of confusion."[87] Even as the movement teetered on the brink of collapse in 1848, the dedicated maintained their confidence and hope in the knowledge that they were engaged in God's work. After what would be the last quarterly meeting of the NELRL, in March 1848, Huldah Stone reported that although their numbers had been small, "still we felt to thank God, and take courage, for the true spirit was with us."[88]

There was also the problem of false hope, however. For while faith in "a good time coming" might strengthen the resolve of many, the promise of a Millennium could easily lead to disappointment. The failure to effect immediate and total change could result in rapid dissipation of interest and eventually cause the movement to collapse. And, indeed, the movements of this period are notable for their rapid rise and precipitous fall. More important, perhaps, while the surety of ultimate victory through biblical prophecy and divine favor galvanized forces and fortified morale, it also discouraged realistic strategies. As one operative exhorted the *Voice* in 1847, seeking inspiration in the early Christians:

> Be thou like the first Apostle; be thou like
>   the pious Paul;
> If a free thought seeks expression, speak it boldly,
>   speak it all.
> Face thine enemies—oppressors, scorn the prison,
>   rack or rod;
> And if thou hast truth to utter, speak!—and leave
>   the rest to God.[89]

This worker called for speaking out against injustice, but she implied that the motor of change was divine rather than human. As God's kingdom was coming, in this fashion Christian labor activists could condemn contemporary arrangements, exalt the brotherhood of humanity, and leave the rest to God.

There was also something profoundly ahistorical about this stance. For though the awareness that this was a historic experiment heightened their sense of being on "trial"—a notion not unrelated to the revivalist concept—and thus inspired them to act, they understood "experiment," as Rush Welter has pointed out, in the sense of "making a known principle manifest."[90] Their vision of achievement in the future thus meant remaining true to the past— though not to history, from which they assumed they had escaped. Their religion added a special quality to this ahistorical perspective, for as Protestant millennialists they believed they were part of an unfolding sacred historical design that had *already been determined at the beginning of time*.[91] The belief could strengthen resolve in the face of adversity, but it could also lead to flights of fancy.

Some activists were aware of the problem and tried to counter it. Wilmington's George Reynolds, while warning against frustrating "righteous ends" by a "whittling away of principles," advised "unwearied patience." Can we expect to eradicate all at once, he asked, referring to the abandoned promises of the Revolution, "the abuses which have been for half a century under-mining our republican institutions"?[92] For this Hicksite Quaker, righteousness demanded steadfastness to the cause, while haste led to compromise. In Phila-delphia, an *MFP* correspondent also advocated a gradual approach to what he called the "great and glorious work of reformation," reminding his brethren after a series of articles outlining his plan for redemption, "I have many things to say unto you, said Christ unto his disciples, but you cannot not hear them now."[93] In these hands, religion was marshaled for the long-term task of building a movement for radical social change.

Labor's religious "call to arms" amounted to more than cynical calculation. The various appeals discussed in this chapter in fact reflected a religious world-view, rooted in a commitment to do God's will. At the most basic level, this meant obeying God's law, which Christian laborites believed pointed the way to remedying existing evils. As one writer put it in 1830, rules for the distribution of land, a universal scale of wages and standard for working hours, and the collectivization of machinery should be "founded on reason and justice, and the law of God, which teaches us to do as we would be done by."[94] Above all, though, these activists insisted upon duty to God, because, like the prolabor clergy, their religion taught that fulfilling God's will on earth constituted the most noble of all endeavors. "Listen to the voice of your conscience in the chambers of your own heart," Young told his readers, for it would reveal that "there is only one stream that is pure, and that stream flows from the throne of God." This was Asa Bronson's argument in his debate with Nathaniel Borden: the one true path in life was to serve God, and only that could be the basis of both public and private behavior. "It is that one which Jesus Christ has marked out in his word, and which leads to glory," wrote Young. "Live for God," he advised, "give your powers to Him . . . seek His honor in all you do."[95] Only in a culture that accepted as axiomatic that, as a member of the Rochester MMPA put it, ["there is] no superior power, save that of the Father of all mercies," could workers thus advance the notion that they would *gain* power by *giving* it to God.[96]

And since they believed that serving God meant promoting the Christian faith and serving humanity, these activists, as religious and secular reformers, consistently linked spiritual and temporal responsibilities: labor reform, the FWA claimed without privileging one over the other, was "the cause of God and humanity."[97] To grasp precisely what they meant by that, we need to take a closer look at what they thought was wrong in their society and what they wanted to do about it.

Chapter 9. Labor's Critique: The Degradation of Work and the Rise of Inequality

To understand the role religion played in the critique, vision, and praxis of antebellum labor activists—in the emergence of a consciousness of working people's interests *as a class*—we must return to where we began, to the central place that the Holy Bible occupied in their mental, moral, and spiritual universe. For a wide range of laborites found in Scripture convenient tools for advancing many interests on behalf of many constituencies.[1] Ultimately, in a kind of rhetorical class conflict over the Bible—a battle that mirrored the more general religious debate we have seen in communities like Fall River, Wilmington, and Rochester—they fashioned a sharply different interpretation of that book than did their opponents. On this contested biblical terrain, antebellum workers produced a distinctive brand of class consciousness.

The nature of the clash over Scripture can be glimpsed in a dispute that surfaced in the pages of the Rochester *Working-Man's Advocate*. In 1840, the women of the Third Presbyterian Church, a center of the Finney revival, announced their sponsorship of a fair at Market Hall, the proceeds of which were to go to their Sabbath school library and to the library of the local Young Men's Association (YMA), organized in 1837 as an alternative to the Mechanics' Literary Association (MLA).[2] For "S," the Presbyterian women's fair was a good idea, and he advised his fellow mechanics to patronize it, but he wondered why the money could not be forwarded to the MLA, on behalf of the *mechanics'* cause.[3] "T" reminded "S" that, unlike the MLA, the YMA was a public institution serving all the citizens of the city. To clarify their positions, "T" then invoked Scripture: "S" was of the "argus-eyed, fault-finding class," who, like "one of old," asked why the ointment had not been sold for a hundred pence and given to the poor, an allusion to the Gospel story in which Jesus utters the famous words, "the poor ye have with you always."[4] For "S," though, the Bible held a different meaning. The scriptural allusion of "this second Daniel," he answered, is really nothing more than, "great Diana of the Ephesians," referring to the Book of Acts in which Asian silversmiths give their allegiance to the Greek goddess rather than listen to the proselytizer Paul, because they had become rich rendering shrines in her image. Here was the

Bible used by both parties, one preaching fatalism and restraint to the poor, the other preaching renunciation of wealth to the rich.

If Scripture could be used by both sides in an argument, it could also serve more than one purpose for those on labor's side of that argument. Radical mill women like Huldah Stone, for example, took up the Bible to defend working women in particular. After a professedly sympathetic machine shop boss had refused to purchase a subscription from this itinerant evangelist for the *Voice of Industry*, because "'females are out of their *place* while soliciting names to a workingman's paper,'" Stone wrote a long letter to the *Voice*, reminding both him and her sisters of the role one woman had played in biblical times.

> Only think of it, girls, how very unfeminine and "out of place" it would have been in this gentleman's eyes, had he lived in Christ's day, for Mary to have gone alone to the scepulcre where none but *Jesus* slept. No *ladies* there? Why in all probability he would not have received the news of the glorious resurrection from her lips had it been what his soul was panting to hear; for, O shameful to relate, a *female* had dared to presume to know for herself somewhat of that blessed "truth" which was to elevate and make good and happy the race, and had even stepped out of *her place* (the *back kitchen* I suppose he meant) so far, as to go out and ascertain whether Christ was indeed risen, and to proclaim the glorious news to her friends and her kindred![5]

True to her namesake, the Old Testament prophetess Huldah, this was a woman who rejected the "place" set aside for those of her sex.

Biblical exegesis in the antebellum labor movement involved matters from the most lofty to the most mundane. The Bible, said some, formed the very basis of American freedom. Keep the "spirit-stirring, that transforming virtue, which breathes in the pages of the book of God," the NEA president told his membership in 1834, "that virtue, which our Pilgrim Fathers inculcated and practised, and to which, more than to all else, let me tell you, we owe that portion of liberty, we now hold in possession."[6] Scripture also had much to offer regarding the more mundane aspects of daily life. Thus, in their attempt to discredit the vegetarianism of the Bible-wielding health reformer Sylvester Graham—who lectured in the churches of Rochester during the "hard times" winter of 1839–40—the editor and correspondents of the *WMA* marshaled voluminous scriptural citations to prove that it was not unchristian to eat meat.[7] Declaring that Graham's system could be accepted only when "both the Old and New Testaments [are] destroyed," Henry Frink also rejected his prohibition on tea and coffee, citing the proclamation in Ecclesiastes 2:24, "there is nothing better for a man, than that he should eat and drink, and that he should make his soul enjoy good in his labor."[8]

There were disputes over biblical interpretation within the labor movement, of course, but that they read the Bible and used it on behalf of their nascent movement, there can be no doubt—even in the American citadel of Free-thought, in the heyday of Freethinking.[9] Here, the *Mechanics' Free Press* was filled with biblical language. As already noted, there were editors and readers of this paper who counted themselves infidels, or at least found authority in places other than Scripture. Indeed, a new editorial board in the spring of 1831, heading one of its editorials with a quotation from the Book of Matthew, found it necessary to begin with the caveat, "Our readers must not be astonished that we speak from Scripture."[10] Still, the frequency of biblical headings at the top of articles and letters, and the use of such biblical pseudonyms as "Genesis," "David," "Moses and Aaron," "Caleb and Joshua," "Jehu," and "Isaiah," suggest that probably few required the warning.[11] Of course, some of these writers may have used the Bible simply to counter their Christian opponents. "Paul," for example, declaring "'*I will condemn thee with thy own words,*'" cited the Sermon on the Mount and Paul's epistles in an argument concerning usury, though he was not a Christian himself.[12] "Paul," however, was the exception.

The context of biblical usage in the antebellum labor press makes that clear. Take the editor of the *National Laborer,* who frequently cited Scripture to make his case. To be sure, Thomas Hogan once acknowledged that he employed Old Testament justifications for land reform because only in that way could a demand that is "esteemed the rankest heresy of levellers" be advocated without fear of "reproach." But, at the very least, as his appeals to workers demonstrate, Hogan believed the Bible carried weight with his constituency, and he himself spoke in the tongue of the Christian labor activist.[13] Though obviously among the better educated in the movement, Hogan and other major labor editors of the age—in Wilmington (*Delaware Free Press*), Rochester (*Working-Man's Advocate*), Albany (*Mechanics' Mirror*), Boston (*Laborer*), and Fitchburg and Lowell (*Voice of Industry*)—were Bible-quoting Christians who represented a Bible-reading constituency.[14]

When one of the *MFP's* most prolific correspondents recommended frequent reading of the Old and New Testaments, he sounded a note that would reverberate through the labor movement for years to come. Advising the readers of America's first labor paper to read "*each part with the other,*" without the "construction of others," and "according to the rational conception with which the individual is blessed by an all-wise and bountiful Creator," "Peter" tapped both the rationalist currents in Enlightenment thought and the Reformation emphasis on the individual's ability to apprehend the "plain testimony" of Scripture.[15] In this way, he spoke to—and for—a movement that literally found its voice in the language of the Bible. As early as 1829, Scripture provided much of the doctrine, imagery, and style of a rising, increasingly self-conscious working class. When these workers sought to make sense of the rapid economic and social changes they faced, particularly what they saw as the degradation of work (and those who performed it) and the consequent growing inequality in their communities, it was to Holy Writ that they turned first.

God's "Design" and the Promulgation of Divine Law

Christian labor activists in antebellum America based their critique of society upon what they called God's "design."[16] Throughout the period, among the rank-and-file as well as the leadership, along the religious spectrum from deists to evangelicals and Arminians to Calvinists, in New England, New York, and the Mid-Atlantic states, in big cities and village hamlets, laborites pointed to this design for authority and guidance as they raised a host of issues and concerns. The articulation of the belief took many forms, in its many hands. In 1835, "A Working Man" in Pennsylvania reminded his fellows that "Providence, in the formation of man, evidently designed him for a social and improved state of existence"; the New York Journeymen House Carpenters announced that they were forming a grand phalanx against "*overgrown capital*" because it was "perpetually wringing from the honest and industrious that portion of comfort and happiness which the God of Nature designed them to enjoy."[17] Ten years later, in the mill towns of New England, labor leaders sought to help men and women live "as they were designed to" by "plac[ing] them upon the platform of equal rights, which freemen and christians alone can occupy," while the operatives sought restoration of rights, "which God and nature designed you to enjoy."[18]

Among the evangelicals operating within this paradigm was Robert McFarlane, for whom God's involvement in the affairs of the world was quite direct. In discussions of the mechanical arts, he spoke of "the hand of a righteous Deity," "the Preserver and Governor, as well as the Creator of His Works," "the design of the wonderful Creator" evident in nature.[19] There was also, though, "a distinct Revelation": "For the creatures which He has made, He will fix and has ordained certain laws, and that design of His creation, and laws, are for some important purpose."[20] From this, McFarlane articulated a social philosophy in tune with the Arminian currents in antebellum American Protestantism.[21] The Creator made the individual free and moral, he said. Thus, in the beginning, as a kind of child, he tried to become God, rebelled against his Maker, and in this "hellish passion" of pride fell from his "high estate." But, McFarlane continued, having universally fallen, man had been given another chance, for Revelation also "bringeth the glad tidings; that he will yet become universally free." Moreover, he had been given the proper rule by which to live, Jesus' most famous command to his followers, and antebellum labor's favorite biblical injunction: "do thou unto thy neighbor as thou wouldst have thy neighbor do unto thee." McFarlane looked forward to the day when that injunction would be obeyed, and humanity saved, because that is how it had been intended. "That the time will come," he assured his followers, "when man shall be redeemed and ransomed from slavery, we believe, is certain and is the design of God."[22] Thus alerting fellow Christians to God's design, activists like

McFarlane could enjoin the entire community to obey the "laws" upon which that plan depended.

Others were not as sanguine as McFarlane, nor did all Christian labor activists draw on the same religious doctrines, but they did articulate their social philosophy within the framework of a laborite interpretation of God's design and the laws that followed from it. The "Address to the Working Men of Massachusetts," written by an NEA committee in 1834, pictured religion itself as a casualty of the contravention of divine intent: the teachings of Christian charity were advanced in vain, while the "merciful dispensations of Providence" had actually become a curse, as a result of current "law."[23] Here, the remnants of a Calvinist emphasis on human depravity found its way into the logic of the argument. For the committee began by stressing the roots of social domination in human nature itself. "The great evil in the business of government," they declared, "has consisted in placing the whole power in the hands of a few. All men are tyrants. God has made them so. And it is not in the nature of man to possess power, without abusing it."[24] Similarly, while most hewed to a belief in humanity's basic goodness, some in the movement insisted on a system of human laws in strict accordance with God's law because of, as one activist put it, humanity's basic selfishness, love of tyranny, betrayal of the weak, and love of power.[25]

Whether they believed in innate goodness or depravity, whether they drew on moral ability and a glorious destiny or the need to regulate passions, the overwhelming majority of antebellum laborites would have agreed that present arrangements defied divine purpose. Thus, as with their appeal to Christian duty, a range of labor activists used the idea of hewing to God's law as a way both to encourage their constituency to demand their rights and to single out their opponents as sinners. At the height of the ten-hour struggle in Fall River, the *Mechanic* published an article entitled, "Christian Principle By Example," in which a correspondent praised a local foreman who had been fired for refusing to require long working hours. "He could not in principle any longer resist God," the writer declared, "and set at naught the divine and holy laws."[26] Here was something on which all activists could agree: the solution to the problem of resisting God's design was a change in current arrangements—"a rebuke of sin," the NEA called it—so they would be aligned with those of God and Christianity.[27] And this condemnation of labor conditions as sinful formed a powerful indictment of contemporary society, especially since it equated obeying divine laws to obeying God generally. When William Young labeled Lowell a "wilderness of sin" where the "holy and divine laws of God are disregarded," he arraigned an entire community on the most serious charges that could be leveled against Christians.[28] Like other antebellum reformers, these laborites sought to rise above earthly law, calling for the establishment of God's law in its stead. "It is time to give the government to God," a Fall River operative declared in 1845. "Let his law, as expounded by his Son, be proclaimed and acknowledged supreme above all the earth."[29]

This call for the establishment of God's law on earth, of course, must not be confused with the movement for religious legislation and a "Christian party in politics," which, as we have seen, labor fought tooth and nail. Christian laborites were always careful to distinguish between obeying the laws of God in social relations and dictating in law specific religious observances. They would do so while articulating a division of the external from the internal spheres of life that bore a superficial resemblance to the emerging insistence among capitalists that the business world operated on different laws than the spiritual world. The resemblance was superficial only. When Cornelius Blatchley argued that things civil and political were external and involved duties among men, while things religious and divine were internal and involved duties owed to God, he was arguing against the unity of church and state—the "impious interference of state and rulers with the internal dominion of God."[30] A committed Christian, this inspiration for early American labor was not arguing against the application of Christian principles in temporal relations. To the contrary, he insisted on Moses' law—the moral law derived from God—as the basis of external relations. Similarly, Blatchley's Quaker compatriot in Wilmington, Benjamin Webb, saw religion as crucial to political and social life, but not specific religions and their particular trappings. For, Webb wrote, when the founding fathers excluded God from their legislative councils, their concept of God was not "the universal spirit that fills all space," but something voted in or out of a house, an image or idol (therefore, anti-Christian), and conveyed through "kings, Priests, and Professors of holy rites and ceremonies."[31] Blatchley, Webb, and the overwhelming majority of Christian laborites opposed specific religious beliefs governing *religious practices, politically,* for that would have been fundamentally anti-Christian to them. By the 1840s, as a result of the defeat of this religio-political movement, labor activists would not need recourse to this argument, advancing instead the notion of God's law as an antidote to the devastating secular law of supply and demand on which the capitalist revolution was based.

For those aggrieved by the rapid social and economic changes attending that revolution, God's design offered not only a standard for judging right from wrong but a vision of a world where they could live as "freemen and christians." In such a society based on divine law, labor would claim its "rightful power and influence" in the community, and the laborers would reclaim that dignity and respect for which God intended them.[32]

Labor

In the spring of 1845, William F. Young, then a twenty-three-year-old harnessmaker working at Hale's Carriage Shop in Fitchburg, launched his half-century career as an American labor reformer with a speech to the local Working Men's Association, of which he was an officer. He had addressed the group before, both as a debater and as a lecturer, but this was the first time he had crafted a full-scale rendition of his views on what would become known as the "labor question." He entitled his remarks, "On the Existing Evils of Society."[33] Like all labor activists of the period, he began with a condemnation of working conditions, declaring that under the prevailing system, "labor becomes disreputable."[34] The industrious were robbed and the idle rewarded, he pointed out, thus demeaning both the laborer and his work. And yet the latter preached incessantly to the former on the virtues of hard work! The resolution to the paradox, according to Young, lay in the creation of a truly Christian system of production and distribution, in which everyone worked and shared equally in the fruits of that work. The current degradation of labor, hindering productive activity and denying the producer the product of his toil, Young insisted, frustrated the "great design of Creation."[35]

In this way, drawing easily upon biblical commandments, activists like Young were able to condemn those who lived by the labor of others as violators of divine law. Unlike other antebellum Christians who counseled industry to ensure a loyal and tractable work force, these laborites sought to expose the hypocrisy of "drones and hangers-on in society" who sang the praises of industry to others. Here similar language among classes masked quite different class messages.[36] In their birthday announcement "To Their Fellow Mechanics and Laborers Throughout the United States," the NEWA declared, "We believe our present system of labor is false in principle. In the decree 'in the sweat of thy face thou shalt eat bread,' we trace the original design of the Creator."[37] But some were eating in the sweat of *others'* faces. The *Voice* correspondent who chose the name "Industry" specified the problem. Heading a list of his movement's goals with "The Abolition of Idleness," he noted that the laborer's "opulent *pensioner* or temporal lord has broken both the commands to obtain his bread by the 'sweat of the brow,' and to *abstain from eating* when he *abstains from working*." These nonproducing rich had betrayed the widely recognized canons of a Christian community.[38]

Again, the language transcended time, geography, and religious denomination. The *Mechanics' Free Press,* exhorting Philadelphia workers to the polls in the fall of 1829, asked if any could harbor "so impious a sentiment, as to believe that our Maker ordained one set of men to live on the loaves and fishes, on the very fat of the land, at the expense of another."[39] The next year, drawing on the Gospels, George Reynolds excoriated employers "who like the 'lilies of the valley, toil not neither do they spin," and "'are arrayed in purple and fine linen and fare sumptuously every day.'" With the liability to illness, "want of employment," and most employers seizing every pretext to lower wages, just how were workers to "earn their bread by the sweat of their brow"?[40] Fifteen years later, farther north in New England, William Young frequently attacked the idle rich, in similar if more explicitly Christian tones: "If labor is a christian duty are those christians, who live without it, or are engaged in vocations, useless and injurious to society?" Here, too, Labor's Rule applied: "That labor is a christian duty, cannot be denied," he wrote; "it is embodied in the great law of love, that 'whatsoever ye would, that men should do unto you, do ye even so unto them.'"[41] In Albany, Robert McFarlane offered the same argument, in virtually the same language. "We have always been the zealous advocates of 'honest industry,'" he began an editorial endorsing the ten-hour day for factory operatives. "We have endeavored upon every suitable occasion to preach the holy doctrine 'the laborer is worthy of his hire.'" And yet, in America in 1846, McFarlane lamented, "no precept of Scripture is more often and more audaciously violated than this, and believing as we do that the violators of this precept fall under the fearful sentence, 'extortioners of God's will judge,' it is our duty to warn all those who trespass against the majesty of *Heaven's course.*"[42]

Still, the exaltation of labor signified more than a simple condemnation of idle employers, and here we glimpse a tension embedded in this working-class appropriation of religion, a tension between the enhancement and often simultaneous attenuation of class struggle that pervaded Christian labor thought in this period. For though Marx was surely right that religious virtues in a society that contradicts them are subversive of the prevailing social order, those virtues often serve several purposes at once.[43] Since many of these activists had imbibed Protestant injunctions about the importance of "useful industry" as an essential support for a virtuous Christian life, they sought to remind workers, too, of their duties in this regard.[44] While Young distinguished Lowell's industry from a "virtuous and christian . . . system of labor," he did exhort the operatives of that city to be hard-working Christians. Indeed, the paper he founded, aptly titled the *Voice of Industry,* was filled with homilies on the blessings of honest labor and the evils of idleness. The editor reprinted articles exalting the manual labor of biblical figures from Adam to the apostle Paul, published poetry that extolled work as "noble and holy," and, of course, constantly reminded his readership that being productive, active, and industrious was part of the Creator's design.[45]

Such paeans to labor and warnings about idleness can be found in abundance in the era's labor press. "Holy writ expressly condemns [sloth]," Charles Douglas told the readers of the *New England Artisan* in 1832, "and both by precept and narrated example, teaches us that it is in itself one of the greatest vices."[46] In 1837, Thomas Hogan ran an editorial in the *National Laborer* entitled "Anything But Work," derisively using the biblical heading, "'Get money—*honestly* if you can, but by all means get money.'"[47] A decade later, the editors of the Fall River *Mechanic* reminded their subscribers that "labor is most emphatically ordained by God." "Man was never intended to be idle," they cautioned. "Inactivity frustrates the very design of his creation; whereas an active life is the guardian of virtue, and the greatest preservation of health, of body and mind. Nor can a person expect to rest in eternity, unless he labor for God here."[48] As one writer to the *Mechanics' Mirror* put it in a little piece of doggerel in 1846:

> God, in his wisdom has decreed, that all
> For bread shall labor, whether great or small
>
> .   .   .   .
>
> No! God has made us for a noble end,
> And wiser purpose, than our lives to spend
> Like some, in idleness and dissipation;
> Such men are but a tax upon the nation.[49]

McFarlane concurred, insisting that one could not be a Christian without also being industrious. Reminding his readers that the Bible said that those who did not work should not eat, he advised them, "'That ye study to be quiet, to do your own business, and to work with your hands, that ye may walk honestly toward others, and that ye may have lack of nothing.'"[50] For these activists, an individual could not be true to his origins, his God, or his religion if he were not industrious.[51]

In this sense, there was an echo of what employers were preaching to workers. But what these Christian laborites were arguing here was still more complex, for their message was to the community as a whole, rather than merely to employers or employees. The editors of the *New York State Mechanic* explained the issue in a biblical exegesis under the heading, unsurprisingly, "The Sweat of the Brow."[52] "Every dispensation of God" was a blessing, even those that were punitive, they reminded their Christian readers. For God's saying, "cursed be the ground for thy sake," meant not only to punish sin but also to provide a way to mitigate its consequences. And yet God's children had not heard. "There is no arrangement of Providence against which man has more universally rebelled than that which ordains that he shall eat his bread by the sweat of his brow," the editors instructed. Thus far, the lesson was unexceptional by antebellum Protestant standards. But here, the editors made clear just how different was their view from that of the mainstream Christian moralists of their day. In a trenchant criticism of America, they insisted that though Americans might be an active people, they were also a lazy bunch in the manner in which they had arranged their economic relationships: "our activity is to acquire the fruits of the industry of others." That kind of "restlessness," insisted the editors of the *New York State Mechanic*, was a rebellion against the law, "He that will not work, neither shall he eat." And, though things were hardly as they should be, they promised that the "time will come when all will learn, and all will be laborers."

What these workers were fashioning was a religiously based version of the labor theory of value that was at least implicitly anticapitalist. "Labor is the

Creator of all wealth," the editor of the (Manchester) *Operative* reminded his readers in 1844. "It was ordained by God as a universal condition."[53] Hence the laborer ought to enjoy the fruits of his toil. John Allen found ample support for that demand in the Bible. "'Whatsoever a man *sows,* that shall he also reap,'" he intoned. "Such is the law of distributive justice ordained by Almighty God, and sustained by the commonsense of mankind."[54] By thus exalting labor's creative power, activists not only laid claim to their product but also regained a sense of dignity and pride in a world where, as Young had put it in his FWA speech, "labor becomes disreputable." Thus, for South Boston's Albert Wright, "God honors labor"; for Vermont farm girl Huldah Stone, the divine hand of "the Great Eternal" was evident in the grand, magnificent works in nature; for the itinerant Seth Luther, "labor, the source of all wealth" must be rewarded according to "the golden rule, 'whatsoever ye would that men should do unto you, do ye even so unto them.'"[55] What all these diverse elements of the early American labor movement were creating was a religious foundation for the elevation of workers *as a class.*

For, if labor were honorable and the source of all wealth, then the laborer should be an exalted figure in the community. After all, had not Jesus and his disciples—exemplars for antebellum Christian laborites—been common workingmen? He had come to teach by example, Robert McFarlane said, to show the way to freedom, to strike at aristocracy and tyranny, to produce goodwill on earth—but most of all, to teach industry. "The Son of God," he reminded the readers of the *Mechanics' Mirror,* "labored as a common mechanic, and selected his disciples from among the fishermen of Galilee."[56] After all, it was Jesus himself who had elevated the laborer to great status in society, by proclaiming him "worthy of his hire." Though that Carpenter had referred to work done on God's behalf, labor activists conflated the two purposes. So, "the laborer is worthy of his hire" graced the masthead of the *NEA;,* it was Leonard Cox's watchword when he launched the *Laborer* on behalf of the Boston Mechanics' Association; and it was the motto of the Mechanics Mutual Protection Association.[57] So, too, labor's adoption of the appellation, "hewers of water."[58] In this fashion, with the Bible as a guide, much of the antebellum movement proudly wore the label, "the laboring classes."

Indeed, here we see the rudiments of a class stance by first-generation American labor reformers, with the Bible as their authority. In 1835, Philadelphia operatives declared their "common feeling" with striking carpenters in Boston, with "the rights of all who earn their substance by the 'sweat of their brow.'"[59] The following year, mill women in Rockdale, Pennsylvania, voiced their support for striking boot- and shoebinders in Philadelphia, recommending the cause "to all females who earn their bread by the sweat of their brow."[60] In 1842, the Rochester WMBERS noted "two classes of this community," the employers and the "better class . . . whose daily labor by the sweat of his brow is his only income or inheritance."[61] When Young began publishing the *Voice* three years later, he proclaimed that his paper would be supported exclusively by those who "'earn their bread by the sweat of the brow.'"[62] There was, of course, much more to a class analysis of American society, as we shall see, but here was a diverse array of antebellum workers beginning to articulate a basis for class unity whose source of legitimacy was Holy Scripture.

Equality

As these labor activists saw it, it was the unjust labor system, in which some ate bread in the sweat of others' faces, that had produced radical disparities of wealth and power in the community—another clear violation of the design of a God who was, as they insisted by quoting Scripture, "no respecter of persons." Generally, though again their theological orientations varied, they agreed that their Lord was basically benevolent and fair and had implanted similar tendencies in humanity. In their view, the prevailing inequities of capitalism as it was emerging in America flew in the face of that benevolence and fairness.

At the outset of his presidential address to the NEA in 1832, Charles Douglas offered the keynote of the age on the question of equality. Sometimes exhibiting deist tendencies, sometimes sounding like an evangelical Protestant, Douglas invoked God's design and the language of the Bible:

> Has the great Author of our existence scattered blessings with a partial hand? Has he resolved that one portion of his creatures, made of the same materials, and subject to the same laws of our common nature, should riot in wealth and luxuriate on his bounties, while the great numbers should be poor and miserable, the hewers of wood, and the drawers of water to their more fortunate but less honest oppressors? No—never, never was this the design of the great Governor of the Universe, whose ways are just.[63]

Seth Luther, the former Baptist who was Douglas's compatriot in the association, answered the question in the same manner. "A man who tells you that the great Author of our existence designed that the many should be poor and miserable, in order that the few may roll and riot in splendid luxury," he told Brooklyn workers, "would pick your pocket if he had a good opportunity."[64] Discoursing on the "distinctions of wealth," which he called "walls of separation," the Presbyterian churchman Henry Frink declared at the end of the decade, "We believe that man—*every* man, was created for a more noble purpose, than to be thus on earth made the sport of accident; and that *wisdom,* and *goodness,* and *power,* implanted by the Almighty in the human breast, constitute its *only* just claims to approbation; and are in themselves of a character too sacred to suffer, with impunity, the present neglect of the multitude."[65] A decade later, Robert McFarlane, another Presbyterian, put it much more

simply when he reminded the people of New York that God, being "no respecter of persons," had decreed equality among men: "Let him that is greatest
among you be as if he were least."[66] But that decree had been defied in the
present social arrangements of the young American Republic.

To be sure, as numerous historians have noted, some also found a vision of
equality in the Declaration of Independence, which could be used to criticize
the growing inequality they perceived around them. But their articulation of
that vision—like their recourse to the republican heritage of the American
Revolution—was typically based on a faith in God and Christianity. Thus, a
group of Christian workingmen in New York City during the 1830s reminded
their audience that the Declaration of Independence had appealed to the "im-
mutable justice of God" and, in setting forth the principle that all men were
created equal, had affirmed "the sacred words of Revelation, that 'God is no
respecter of persons, that all are equal in his sight.'"[67] A decade later, an FWA
circular began: "It is believed that all men are created equal; endowed with
capacities and privileges for the pursuit of social and intellectual happiness, and
that these are the gifts of God, dispersed to all mankind with equality." These
gifts, in this rendition, "the Creator intended should be cultivated for his glory
alone." And again, such notions transcended denomination: the five-man committee that wrote the circular included two Congregationalists, a Baptist, and
two deeply pious but unattached activists. What they all agreed on was that a
vigilant concern for equal rights constituted fidelity of God's design.[68]

In describing a growing chasm between rich and poor in America, laborites
painted a horrific picture of contemporary society, cast in the dramatic images
of good and evil they had imbibed from the Bible. Even in the 1830s, the
inequities seemed so great to some that matters appeared to be approaching
critical proportions. For Boston trade unionist and labor editor Aaron Wood,
America in 1836 was reminiscent of Old Testament Israel. In those ancient
times, he said, the trumpets of Jubilee sounded "and the bond men were
declared free, the chains of the captives were unloosed, the heritage of the poor
was restored, and a vast nation were sharers in the Nation's wealth." Wood
suggested that a similar restitution might be necessary in his own time, "a
restraint similar to that imposed by the Theocracy of that ancient day."[69] On
the other side of the depression of the late 1830s and early 1840s, the sense of
crisis had deepened. Complaining of the "present state of extreme luxury and
affluence and miserable want and poverty" that cast "a night of gloom over
many of the finest portions of God's universe," William Young warned, "we are
fast becoming beggars, dependants and slaves."[70] The picture was stark indeed.

Underlying these lamentations about a wealthy few lording over an im-
poverished, enslaved multitude was a yearning for equality, for a world where
there was "no Master but God."[71] Once again, the idea was grounded in
Christian tradition transcending denomination.[72] Charles Hosmer explained
the Christian logic behind the claim to worker equality simply: "He, in His

infinite wisdom as in goodness never intended that one man should be thus dependant upon another for his daily bread. He created all *equal*."[73] Others tapped the universalist idea of humanity's common destiny, exemplified in the Association of Industry circular to the employers of the Fall River in 1840: "We are brethren, 'of one flesh and blood.'" Pointing to the use of child labor, the churchgoing authors reminded the owners that "the laborer's daughter is equally dear to him as yours to you; equally destined to immortality; equally the child of the same Universal Parent."[74] In the same vein, Boston labor leader Philip B. Holmes told a rally of Charlestown, Massachusetts, workers a month later, "Before God, all men are equal, are children of a common parent, for one God hath made them all, and all are his offspring." The vision apparently derived from the specifics of this carpenter's faith. Accepting the doctrine of the General Atonement, Holmes insisted that Christ's mission on behalf of all humanity proved that everyone was equal in the eyes of God: "Before the Gospel all men are equal for one and the same Savior hath died for them all; and the same faith, repentance, and means of salvation are preached to them all, and declared to be equally necessary to them all." Here the activist appropriated the style and language of contemporary revivalists, who called on Americans to embrace Christ and seek salvation, though in his hands the demand was for equal rights for all workers.[75]

For some, like Hosmer, the problem of inequality suggested a utopian socialist solution. With workers' cooperatives, he said, would come "equal distribution of the profits of labor," and "with that we will build our own houses, and our own churches; we will found our own schools, and buy our own Bibles."[76] Even when denying adherence to such radical solutions— commonly called "agrarianism" in that day—some found religious sanction for the spirit behind them. Thomas Hogan, for example, found it astonishing that the doctrine was viewed with such horror by "men . . . who profess the principles of that religion which teaches this as a fundamental doctrine; and we cannot understand why men should attempt to destroy the liberties of a large portion of the people, lest a doctrine might obtain which christianity acknowledges and insists upon."[77] Praising the National Trades' Union declaration that cooperatives were "our only hope," he declared, "we say to every working man in the words of Holy Writ—'Take fast hold of it, let it not go—keep it, for it is thy life!'"[78] The alleged agrarianism of Fanny Wright was defended in the same manner by the New York *Man*, which asked its readers, "did not Jesus Christ himself advocate this principle, and had not the first Christians all things in common?" For good measure, the editors added, "those who deny this know little of their bibles."[79] Though one of those wielding an editorial pen at the *Man* was the deist George Henry Evans, the comment was both telling and typical: the most readily available justification for rejecting a social system based on competition and embracing one based on cooperation was the example of the early Christians found in Scripture.

For most Christian labor activists, the religious condemnation of inequality, while implicitly (and sometimes explicitly) anticapitalist, did not mean rejecting property rights per se, which once again reveals the tension in Christian labor thought that simultaneously drew workers away from their employers and toward them. Henry Frink spoke for many when, in the midst of an attack on the social inequities of depression-era Rochester, he singled out those "who are willing to reap where others have sowed, without putting their hands to the plow," but took care to remind his readers that he "condemn[ed] not the possession, but the *abuse* of wealth."[80] Hogan, too, voiced the dominant view when he reminded "the Aristocracy," which saw a threat to property in the National Trades' Union, that his movement was in fact "most anxious that property should be protected, for [we] have suffered most from its violation." Moreover, understanding that, "under the present order of things," an equal division of property would within three months put workers in a worse situation than before, "all are perfectly willing that those who have should keep." "Who are they that hold up the anti-republican, and anti-christian spirit of illiberality, inequality and proscription of opinion?" Hogan asked rhetorically. It was not the National Trades' Union but its opponents "who preach and practice the doctrine that 'unto him that hath shall be given, and to him that hath not shall be taken away even that which he hath.'"[81] Here was a scriptural condemnation of inequality, though not of property per se.

Even for utopian socialists like Hosmer, who flatly rejected "the whole system of labor for wages," there were limits to the Christian laborite critique of inequality.[82] Like their exaltation of labor, the activists' vision of equality gave workers a sense of worth, encouraging them to build a movement based on "equal rights," while suggesting a certain harmony of interests between laborer and employer. Hence the Association of Industry's appeal to the Fall River mill owners: "We believe all men to be the off-spring of One Being, whom the enlightened mind worships and adores as the Father; unlike the product of all other creative efforts, we are declared to be found in the image and likeness of GOD." It followed that "Our highest and true relation, is . . . that of brother; we are brethren. Our interests, then, must be identical, when properly understood."[83] If all were equal in God's eyes, with the same origins and the same destiny, the antagonism between employer and employee might be eradicated by the two recognizing their common interests.

Nevertheless, the critique itself was potent in great measure because of its religious underpinnings. For here, labor's views on work and equality dovetailed, as the Christian embrace of private property by labor activists became a celebration of the labor theory of value. As one anonymous writer put it in New York's *Young America* in 1845, property was "founded on the law of justice and Christian love. The right of property, then, secures to every man the just fruits of his own labor."[84] Moreover, there was an unmistakable leveling character to the Christian laborite attack on inequality that rendered it radical despite its harmonizing tendencies. Benjamin Webb, Working Man and radical Quaker, saw in the movement for social and spiritual freedom of his age—a kind of second revolution to the political revolution of 1776—a harbinger of an end to all forms of authority. "Even from parents to children," he prophesied, "master and servant shall be on terms of equality, and the laborer assume the rank in society to which his services so justly entitle him." This was a prediction—a *call*, really—for a leveling that was every bit as "radical" as that attached to the hated term, "agrarian."[85] And, for Webb as for laborites throughout the nation during this period, the basis of this egalitarianism was a *Christian* vision.

Chapter 10. Labor's Critique:
The Decline of the Moral Community
and the Rise of Social Chaos

If unjust working conditions and inequality formed the basis of labor's critique, activists expended most of their energies inveighing against what they perceived as the inevitable consequence of this "selfish" or "competition" system: moral dissipation and social chaos. In Rochester, Henry Frink noted an alarming increase in crime "against the laws of men and of God"; in Fitchburg, William Young pointed to the "alarming extent, and rapid increase of sordid, selfish and isolated avarice . . . which are filling our fair world . . . with sin, disease, war and contention with their concomitant train of seductive vices and heartless crimes," while the local Workingmen's Association pictured "VICE and CRIME walking abroad beneath the noonday sun—their naked daggers drawn, murdering at will, VIRTUE, MERCY and TRUTH"; in Pittsburgh, Samuel Fleming spoke of his community as a "sink of pollution," "hoary headed and venerable with corruption and crime."[1] Here was the voice of the outraged Christian, shouting alarm at the corrupting influence of sin in the community.

Christianity was thus fashioned into a weapon of class struggle, as in the explicitly religious formulation of the era's principal labor demand, the ten-hour day. But these activists developed their critique and program on broader terrain. Though they placed much of the blame on employers and their allies, as secular *and* religious reformers, they concerned themselves with nothing less than the reestablishment of a moral community based on Christian harmony. In this rhetorical framework, workers themselves could not escape responsibility. In the process, the tension in the language of labor emerged once again, between the Christian desire to elevate workers as a class and the concerns of workers as Christians to elevate the entire Christian community.

Moral Community

"That money is not our only object in our pilgrimage on this earth, but the welfare of the rising generation, is worthy of our regard." This resolution of ten-hour operatives in Manchester, New Hampshire, captures much about the early American labor movement.[2] The central issue here was not what a later generation of historians and social analysts would call "bread and butter" issues, though these activists certainly sought to improve the material conditions under which they lived and worked. Rather, they were concerned first and foremost with their moral condition, which most of them believed was contingent on their spiritual condition, and that of their children and descendants.[3] Thus money figured prominently in their concerns—as something to be wary of, not worshiped. This matter was at the heart of their alarm that what they were witnessing was the decline of the moral community.

The root of the problem, they said, was the sin of human selfishness—from a Christian perspective, the first mortal sin.[4] Again, Christianity was their guide, proffering the proper antidote to rampant individualism, namely, love of humanity. In an early argument for a system of education that would produce "perfect equality" (one of the central demands of the Working Men's movement) a Philadelphia activist reminded the readers of the *Mechanics' Free Press:*

> sordid and selfish education says, love thyself alone; domestic education says, love your family; the national, love your country; but religion says, love all mankind without exception. A new commandment give I unto you, that ye love one another.[5]

This biblical precept, rooted in Hebrew tradition but explicitly part of Jesus' message, was a watchword for many antebellum activists, another aspect of their quest for "union," of their struggle against the egoism that divided the human family.[6]

The selfishness that most concerned them was the spirit of avarice they perceived swamping their communities, that ancient lust for wealth so roundly condemned in Scripture, which the editor of the Lynn *Awl* called the "god of gold." Avarice loomed large in Seth Luther's social critique, for example, forming the basis of one of his most important speeches, *An Address on the Origins and Progress of Avarice,* published in pamphlet form in 1834. "I have arrived at the conclusion that Avarice is *not* implanted in the human breast by the Great God of heaven and earth," Luther declared, for it could not have derived from "that being whose ways are just." Reminding his audience that "the love of money . . . is the root of all evil," and that only proper education and moral training could prevent avarice from infecting everyone, his discourse on the evils of greed sounded like the moral denunciations of an evangelical minister.[7] But he departed from the overwhelming majority of chastising evangelicals of his day in leaving no doubt about just who was ultimately to blame for this ruinous spirit—the wealthy and powerful. "A spirit of monopolizing avarice, cold, heartless, insatiable avarice," he told a gathering of workers, "is the real governor, the veritable tyrant which holds unlimited and uncontrollable sway over every hall of legislation in the United States."[8] And though, like a censorious minister, he might also appeal to God to strike the evil from the nation, as a voice of labor Luther issued a call that no doubt struck fear into the hearts of many professedly patriotic and devout "leading citizens." "God of heaven," he prayed before these workers, "how long must the sword of avarice disgrace and destroy this people? How long Father of mercy, how long must this nation be deceived with the gorgeous splendor of *national* wealth, *national* glory, and national independence?"9

A couple of months after Luther's New York speech, the Lowell mill girls "turned out" to protest a cut in their wages. Comparing their resistance to that of their Revolutionary fathers, they too inveighed specifically against the sin of greed. "As our fathers resisted unto blood the lordly avarice of the British Ministry," one of their pronouncements declared, "so we, their daughters, *never will wear the yoke* which has been prepared for us."10 Meanwhile, their supporters at the *National Laborer* in Philadelphia denounced their oppression as "avaricious brutality."11 In all these ways, attention to avarice was a tool labor used to condemn the wealthy and powerful.12

Still, the movement's declamations here, like their equally condemnatory statements about the evils of idleness, were often directed at workers them-selves, revealing again the tension within this religiously based class conscious-ness. When the editor of the Lynn *Awl* warned that the "devilish spirit [of avarice] would make man barter away his *Savior,*" he was speaking to his working-class readership; the activist in the mill village of Hooksett, New Hampshire, wrote "The Blindness of the Age" to warn the readers of the *Voice* to stop *their* avaricious quest after gold; South Boston trade unionist George Robinson implored workers to check the "insatiable spirit of *avarice* that is making slaves of so many of our citizens," warning that they would find happiness "just in proportion to *their* advance in moral excellence."13 The battle against greed and selfishness was part of a larger battle to root out sin and immorality in themselves, not just in their enemies.

A similar tension can be seen among the era's female factory workers, who, both as wage-earners and as women, had special concerns in this regard. It is well known that the mill girl's morality was a chief interest of the mill owners, the clergy, and the internationally famous *Lowell Offering,* a literary magazine written by and for female textile operatives in the early 1840s; but it was also a major preoccupation of female labor reformers, who reported that mill towns contained thousands of "young, unsuspecting females, who are thrown upon the charities of a cold, unfriendly world, in helpless childhood, and compelled to earn their daily bread somewhere or perish in the streets!"14 For labor reformers, the resultant sin derived not from individual moral failing, but from "the division of labor consequent upon the introduction of machinery," a position that set them apart from defenders of the system.15 Still, they were in agreement that women had a unique moral obligation that could be fulfilled only through marriage and motherhood. Thus, at the top of "Juliana's" list of the "Evils of Factory Life" was the destruction of "all love of order and practice in domestic affairs." Female operatives, future wives and mothers, were "incarcerated within the walls of a factory, while as yet mere children . . . surrounded on all sides with the vain ostentation of fashion, vanity and light frivolity—beset with temptations without [and] the carnal propensities of natures within."[16] The attack on the factory system here was radical, but the view of women—predicated on traditional notions of Christian morality—was conventional indeed.

There were different views on the question of morality within the labor movement, sometimes reflecting different religious, though not necessarily denominational, orientations. Among the Rochester printers, there was disagreement over working-class patronage of the theater. Chafing over the number of notices in his paper for such entertainment, and likely responding to complaints about it from some readers, the evangelical editor of the *Working-Man's Advocate* detailed his opposition to the institution. First, Henry Frink said, when funds for relieving real distress were squandered at such places, thus ignoring the need to exercise what he called the faculty of susceptibility to the suffering of others, "the intentions of the Deity are contravened." Second, theaters promoted licentiousness: "nakedness, dancing, kissing, the indecency of allusion, and the ungodly air of recklessness." And finally, calling them "unholy and unclean," Frink reminded his readers of the biblical warning, "Broad is the way that leads to death."[17] By contrast, Cornelius Underwood, a member of the *WMA*'s publishing committee and a longtime Quaker, favored the placing of the notices, and though he received letters from both sides, he claimed the majority were, like him, proponents of the practice.[18]

On less controversial moral issues, such as the injunction to be charitable, there was more harmony among labor activists. Once again, the authority was the Bible, as when "E——h" discoursed on poverty and religious duties in the *Delaware Free Press*. Beginning with the scriptural truism that a tree is known by its fruits, this activist reminded the Wilmington community that actions and not profession demonstrated faith.

> If thy brother is *needy* give him, if he is naked clothe him, if he is hungry feed him. This is doing to others as we would they should do unto us. . . .
> Thou shalt not *lord* over *God's* heritage.
> The race is not always to the swift nor the battle to the strong; but the honest laborer will surely have his *reward*.
> Thou shalt not grind the face of the *poor;* the needy require assistance; the helpless orphan and the motherless children are objects of divine compensation.

The point: give to the poor. But, "these things cannot be where there is such a hollow profession of religion."[19] Six years later on the eve of hard times, Philadelphia's "C" offered *National Laborer* readers, "A Plea for the Suffering

Poor," castigating those who failed to live by Christian principles with a rendition of the Gospel of Matthew, "'I was an hungered and ye gave me no meat—I was thirsty and ye gave me no drink—I was a stranger and ye took me not in—sick and in prison, and ye visited me not."[20] Seven years later in Cincinnati, just after the last effects of the depression had subsided, the People's Paper criticized the distribution of Bibles and tracts to the indigent without a like distribution of "bread, soup and potatoes," for while the soul was the "most essential part of man," it could only be reached through the body, ears, and eyes.[21]

The demands for Christian charity were aimed at the wealthy and powerful, who were seen as falsely pious and the principal obstacles to social reform, which may explain, at least in part, the consensus among activists on the issue. Again, though, their Christian perspective necessitated subjecting everyone to the same obligations. The goal was to make the community Christian by building a movement of workers who adhered to Christian principles and precepts. Thus, Henry Frink's biblical advice to Rochester workers in the winter of 1839: "'then's the time to remember the poor.'"[22] Or William Young, following his address on the "Existing Evils of Society" to the FWA, presenting the "destitute circumstances of a family in the neighborhood" and taking up a collection for them.[23] As much as the efforts on behalf of shorter hours, higher wages, and better working conditions, such activities were an essential ingredient of labor reform. Deeply concerned with both individual and social salvation, these Christian labor activists sought to recreate a moral community in a world witnessing "the immolation of the whole higher nature, of all the higher sensibilities and passions of the soul upon the altar of mammon, to them an 'unknown God'."[24]

For the abandonment of Christian morality prevented spiritual development.[25] Here, once again, we glimpse the intertwining of the secular and the religious, yet another meaning to the search for union—the re-union of the spirit and the flesh. Young again: "spiritual and temporal welfare . . . are so inseparably connected that if one is violated the other must suffer"; "every act is either religious or irreligious"; there can be no "religious" or "secular" duties, only a faithful obedience to God's laws in all activities. Invoking labor's insistence on a "practical Christianity," which harmonized the physical and the spiritual according to religious teaching, he called on workers (and their employers) to be "religious through the week, not only at church, but in your workshops." The practice of true Christian virtue, in a moral community, was the only route to salvation.[26]

Harmony

Along with immorality, the "competition" system produced the decidedly unchristian spirit of antagonism. Perhaps more than anything else, the fear of social chaos and the yearning for concord and unity dominated the era's labor rhetoric.[27] In this, and in their ambivalence toward change, labor activists were quintessentially American. As citizens who sought reform—some even said "revolution"—they embraced "progress" while fearing it, or at least its negative, disordering effects. Like the mainstream revivalists and other reformers of their age, these Christian laborites, as "*progressive* conservatives," reflected the tension between "memory and desire" many have noted in antebellum Americans. Their search for unity—which added still another dimension to their quest for *union*—was really a reaffirmation of solidarity in the face of the divisiveness wrought by capitalist development.[28] As we shall see, that division was not just between workers and employers but, the workers believed, a generalized condition in the community. The job of the labor movement, in this sense, was literally to put a shattered community back together again.

Here was one major reason these activists so vehemently rejected sectarianism in religion and politics; they condemned the spirit of party in the language of the censorious Christian who saw it tearing the community apart. Certainly, party division had proved to be a hindrance to the cause of labor, and early on. In 1830, George Reynolds spoke of "the usurpations of ambitious political aspirants and the blood-sucking of unprincipled office hunters" who had sacrificed labor's dearest principles on "the altar of party spirit." It is up to you, the "bone and sinew of the body politic," he told Wilmington workers, to say to "this foul spirit of party excitement, . . . 'thus far shalt thou go, and no further.'"[29] But, for many, the problem went deeper, and it was destructive of the social fabric itself. The solution to the social ills of the day, said a Boston activist after reviewing the miserable state of the manual trades in 1836, lay "in laboring for the good of all—in doing away, as inconsistent with Christianity; all factitious distinctions in society, striving to induce all to live together in harmony, as becometh the children of one common Father, and that the one God."[30] The call was to the whole community of citizens to end all divisions—religious, political, social—and find happiness in the solidarity preached by their religion, to bring order out of disorder, unity out of discord.

These themes pervaded the labor rhetoric of the entire age, but they were especially salient during the 1840s.[31] With the seemingly unbridled growth in industry and commerce, and the concomitant shock of depression, activists of many stripes, at the editor's desk and in the workshop, painted dramatic scenes of dissipation and the decline of Christian values. Typical was an anonymous writer in the *Voice* who spoke of discord, strife, confusion, and selfishness everywhere in the world, as professed Christians "set at defiance" the command to "'love thy neighbor as thyself.'"[32] Unsurprisingly, many therefore looked toward an era of tranquility, in the express recognition that chaos would continue and deepen until the dawning of a new day of Christian brotherhood and harmony, "until human nature is perfect," one labor editor wrote, "and every man becomes so thoroughly civilized and christianized as to make laws and restraints unnecessary, until all men shall seek to do good and to do unto others as we wish them to do unto us."[33] Here was Labor's Rule once again, now used to buttress the argument for harmony over discord.

This quest for harmony was, naturally, particularly significant in towns undergoing rapid economic and social change, among workers who felt that their lives and their communities had been disrupted by those changes. When small, rural towns like Fitchburg, for example, experienced the rise of mills and machine production, the coming of the railroad and the Irish, and the influx of farm emigrants and new consumer goods, the ideal society was often the peaceful and quiet village of the past.[34] Labor activists here perceived an erosion of community in the emergence of an unjust labor system, the scramble for riches in commerce and industry, the proliferation of worldly vices such as drinking and gambling, and sectarianism in religion and politics. Though they sought a major transformation in human organization, they were alarmed at the chaos of contemporary economic, political, and community life. Their watchword was harmony through adherence to Christianity, for without sound moral and religious institutions, the self-interested human heart would "revel without restraint in wild disorder."[35]

Such was the plaint of many a revivalist in this age, only here it was from the mouth of FWA vice president William Wilder. The themes of order and disorder played as critical a role in his view of the world as they did in that of the era's leading religionists. A longtime resident of Fitchburg, who was alarmed that what he remembered as his once quiet and simple community had been shattered by the disruptive forces attending commercial and industrial development, Wilder vociferously denounced those aspects of contemporary society that promoted strife. Sectarianism, of any sort, was the bête noire of this churchgoing Baptist. A professed democrat, he defended equal rights but no particular party; a churchgoing Baptist, he defended the gospel but no particular sect or creed ("religious partyism" should be replaced by the "pure principles of the gospel"). His most cherished object was harmony, and his vehicle for promoting that end was labor reform.[36] William Young, unlike Wilder new to Fitchburg, was also concerned that rapid social and economic change had disrupted an older, orderly, and morally just community. A product of the rapidly changing landscape of rural New England in the 1820s and 1830s, Young's early life typified many in his generation of labor activists: the son of native-born Americans, he was raised in the New England countryside and gravitated to the emerging mill towns of the region as a young adult. Coming of age during the depression years of the late 1830s and early 1840s, he had trouble establishing his independence, drifting from farming to dentistry to harnessmaking.[37] As an activist, he perceived dissension everywhere—between employers and employees, among nations, within communities, even within families—which prevented the individual from understanding his true interest: to become a "friend to his God, his neighbor, and himself."[38]

The analogy such activists used to describe this social condition was the biblical world of the Ishmaelites, tribal descendants of the illegitimate son of Abraham and an Egyptian servant girl. Conjuring up the image of a caravan of traders whose only common bonds were the acquisition of goods and a life of dishonesty, bloodshed, and strife, the analogy expressed in scriptural terms their concern with the erosion of the moral community. "The God of nature designed mankind to live as a band of brothers for the mutual good of all," an FWA resolution declared, "but the laws and customs of men have rendered them a gang of Ishmaelites."[39] Often drawing a direct link to the rise of capitalism—"anarchical competition and organized selfishness . . . converts the members of every trade into Ishmaelitish enemies," John Allen charged— activists perceived "Ishmaelitish strife" everywhere and thus developed a truly radical social vision.[40] Like their condemnations of idleness and exhortations to manual labor, their denunciations of antagonism and calls for brotherhood reflected their belief that the problems of contemporary society touched every-one and every aspect of life, even in the laborer's own family. As editor of the *Voice*, for example, Young printed stories, articles, and pithy exhortations on the virtues of the home and hearth, vociferously condemning the dissension he perceived there. In his first issue, he carried a short piece entitled, "Household Love," designed to discourage conflict in the home. Here, he related the story of Ishmael himself, "the youth who was sent into the wilderness of life with his bow and arrow, 'his hand against every man, and every man's hand against him.'" "God forgive those who turn the household altar to a place of strife!" Young railed. "Domestic dissension is the sacrilege of the heart."[41]

The alternative was Christian harmony and brotherhood, a transcendence of the prevailing social order for worker and capitalist alike.[42] Young told the men and women of the FWA that the labor movement sought to "redeem man from the disruptive thraldom of accidental fortunes which is swaying him to and fro in the world, perverting his nature, stifling his conscience, and making him the creature of circumstances . . . and place him upon nature's platform of christian intelligence, in accordance with the laws of his being, in harmony with external creation, and consistent with revelation."[43] "Man" here referred to both the individual Christian and the Christian community, as God's design did not distinguish between the individual and humankind, one's progress depending upon the other. Each individual's fulfillment depended upon one's neighbor's, because God found pleasure in the harmony of the human family and the cultivation of its cooperative nature.

While this stance could lead to advocating a harmony of interest between employer and employee, it also had leveling tendencies. In the hands of a labor reformer like Young, the notion that each depended upon the other was inex-tricably linked to the demand for equal rights and responsibilities and repre-sented at least an implicit rejection of an emerging ideal of happiness that allowed the boss to accrue material comforts through the exploitation of the worker. Young had something else in mind. Underlying his wish to redeem his fellows from current circumstances was a vision of a world not only without contention and strife, but also without the social arrangements that created such discord. The vision itself was biblical in origin, and Young's rendition of it was designed to remind workers of life's true purpose as disclosed in their Bibles. "Did you ever, amid all this rancor," he asked, "think the real intention of 'Creative Wisdom' was that mankind should be bound together by nature's golden chain of attractive affinity into one harmonious whole—no slaves—no servants—no masters—no oppressed, and no oppressors—but in the language of Christ—'For one is your master, and all ye are brethren?'"[44] Here Young brought together the major themes of the Christian laborite critique under the rubric of unity before God: all divisions of condition, wealth, and power were false to the religion that both workers and employers professed.

In this way, a number of antebellum laborites came to articulate a kind of Christian socialism. *Voice* editor John Orvis called on those who were weary of the present-day "Ishmaelitish strife" to renew "before God the primitive bond of Unity." Born and raised on a Vermont farm during the 1810s and 1820s, Orvis harkened back to a "'Golden Age,'" or "the remembrance of a state of innocence, peace and happiness," which he called "Edenism." Destroyed by humanity in its quest for control over the environment, this state could be reestablished on a higher plane by promoting cooperation and mutuality through labor reform, he claimed. The labor movement, therefore, was a "child of PROVIDENCE," a step toward "the age of Harmony on Earth . . . a PARADISE REGAINED."[45]

Orvis's vision, like Allen's, Young's, and that of the Fitchburg Workingmen—particularly in their near-obsessive fear of disorder and yearning for harmony—echoed the language of Associationism, the American adaptation of Charles Fourier's utopian socialism. During the 1840s in the Northeast and Middle West, the Associationists established twenty-five communities (or "phalanxes") and "unions" in a like number of cities and towns.[46] A significant minority of this movement were workers, among whose ranks were numerous labor reformers.[47] Its attraction was its critique and vision, which expressed the anxieties and needs of men and women searching for solutions within a Christian framework.[48] In labeling "prevailing relations" "unnatural"—or, simply, "reversed"—Fourierists suggested a perversion of some prior plan. They described the competitive organization of society as "false," because it degraded labor that God had intended for noble purposes, allowed a few to monopolize natural resources granted by God to all, and promoted strife among those whom God had designed to live as brothers and sisters—that is, it was false because it degraded labor, fostered inequality, and generated conflict, precisely those issues of most concern to labor activists. In its stead, they proposed a harmonious and cooperative order that would usher in the "brotherhood of man" spoken of in Scripture. For Christians who sought justice and order, this vision offered an alternative way of life consistent with the principles and spirit of their religion—indeed, it tapped into a Judeo-Christian tradition of realizing cooperation over self-seeking that rendered socialism a kind of "brotherliness" made constitutional.[49] In thus imagining in religious tones a world that was the mirror image of the "competition system"—a world without selfishness, a *moral community*—Associationism fit the needs and sentiments of the Christian laborite in the 1840s more closely than any other available utopian vision.[50]

The Hours of Labor

These religio-moral themes—the sins of selfishness and contention, the reestablishment of a harmonious Christian moral community—dominated labor's arguments for the shorter workday, just as it did for the prolabor clergy.[51] As it was articulated by activists in this period, the demand had to do with lessening the physical requirements of labor only insofar as it would allow attention to what they called the "higher purposes." Though some did stress the physical burdens of the long-hours system, and very few ignored that aspect of the issue, the crux of the argument was not about what a later generation of labor reformers (and historians) would called "leisure time."[52] Like their clerical allies, these activists saw in the demand for the ten-hour day nothing less than a path to Christian salvation for both the laborer and the community. Indeed, rejecting a distinction between physical happiness and spiritual health, insisting that one could not survive without the other, they too sought the "cultivation" of the physical, mental, moral, and spiritual "faculties" of humankind according to God's "design."[53] Only in this way could the race realize its true destiny, they said. And for that, they needed time.

This movement's vision of the laborer's proper station in life entailed more than simply the "useful industry" they advocated for all citizens. While they exalted manual labor, demanding the fruits of their work and the respect of society, activists insisted upon their God-given right to time without toil as well. For, though God had told Adam "'in the sweat of thy face thou shalt eat bread, until thou shall return to the ground,'" Christ had commanded God's creatures to labor not simply for the "'meat which perisheth, but for that meat which endureth into life everlasting.'"[54] To truly achieve their "rightful place" in society, laborers had to be more than merely workers; they had to become citizens and Christians as well.

The major pronouncements of the ten-hour advocates in Fall River reflected this view. In its appeal "To the Employers of Fall River," the Association of Industry announced that "a number of Operatives and others residing in this village, have united together . . . for the purpose of 'securing to themselves and their families, *Opportunity* for mental, Moral and Religious Improvement'" and reminded employers of biblical injunction in the matter: "'Man doth not live by bread alone'; neither ought he to be so confined to earn bread alone." Humanity was therefore duty bound to cultivate its higher instincts, they declared, "by the dispensation under which we live."[55] Three years later, the local Mechanics' Association opened its "Circular to the Mechanics of New England" by declaring "that the long established, unjust and prevailing system of labor in this country, is at war with the real interest of man's physical, intellectual, social, moral and religious being." Beginning with the physical hazards of the long-hours system—the "*first cause*" of laborers' deaths was "attributable, either directly or indirectly, to the prevailing system of labor by which we are governed"—they reminded their readers that the system also extinguished "the intellectual fire which heaven designed should burn and blaze *upon* and *in* every soul of man." Thus, they advocated a "new system of labor by which our sacred rights may be secured, and in the adoption of which, man, 'the noblest work of God,' may more fully and effectually answer the *end* and *object* of his being."[56]

Ten-hour advocates in the Wilmington area during the late 1840s proffered virtually the same arguments. Writing in the reform-oriented *Blue Hen Chicken* in November 1847, "Youngster" noted that while "man is [or at least ought to be] a reasoning being, formed for high and holy purposes, created after the image of his Maker, and endowed with moral and intellectual feelings," the "vast majority" of the laboring class were "slaves." With labor-saving machinery, the ten-hour day would "leave ample time for the exercise of his higher powers."[57] A month later, at a gathering of ten-hour operatives in Brandywine,

> [Thomas Roberts] showed that [the long hours system] was alike opposed to the dictates of Nature, Humanity and Religion, inasmuch as it in a great degree incapacitates man for fulfilling the high and noble destiny assigned him by his Creator; which was a subject of far greater importance than the mere acquisition of dollars and cents. He trusted, therefore, that every humane, Christian man would lend his aid to the movement.

The speech was repeatedly applauded by the assembled operatives, and large numbers enrolled in the ten-hour association at the end of the meeting.[58]

Labor activists everywhere stressed this desire for spiritual development in their advocacy of the shorter workday. Nowhere was this more true than among the mill girls who, in many factory areas, led the fight for the ten-hour day in the 1840s. "Call ye this *life*?" Huldah Stone cried out from Lowell in the biblical style she generally affected. Insisting upon the necessity of cultivating moral and religious capacities, she called for a reduction in the hours of toil as the only way for humanity to "honor the Great Creator."[59] Having grown up in the farmlands of southern Vermont under the tutelage of a mother who "found counsel, wisdom and strength" in Scripture, Stone typified antebellum laborites who demanded more time to cultivate their "higher sensibilities," for whom enlightenment and religion were intimately connected.[60] She found in books, "Treasures, which are full of blessedness, flowing from a true knowledge of the Great Author of all mind and matter, the holy laws by which he governs and upholds the universe." In Stone's worldview, the ultimate aim of life was to cultivate and harmonize the mind and soul. "Life!" she cried, "what is it, but the power of appreciating and adorning the Source of all life, light and intelligence!"[61] Here, Stone pressed toward a definition of "life" that, while taking account of the material world, in fact transcended it.

Stone's sisters in the Lowell mills echoed her demand for spiritual cultivation, even as they demanded "happiness" for themselves, again making no necessary distinction between doing for oneself and doing God's will. "If one thing may be more clearly demonstrated than another it is this," wrote "One of the Sufferers," "that the Divine Being wills the happiness of all his creatures." Toward this end, the Creator had endowed humanity with powers of mind and body, for whose development the long-hours system allowed no time. The laborer has no opportunity, this self-consciously Christian worker said, "to sing the praises of Jehovah," to "revel in nature," to "read God's word" or "learn his revealed will."[62] Happiness here was to be found in the cultivation of the soul.

The need to fulfill specific devotional obligations formed another common argument in labor's advocacy of the shorter workday, though as we have seen, there was little consensus among workers about exactly what those obligations were. That was of little import for most in the movement, however, as they advanced the argument on the broadest possible grounds. "I cannot devote more than ten hours per day to physical labor," a Fall River worker maintained in 1844, "and appropriate sufficient time to the regular, faithful, solemn discharge of the religious duties binding upon me."[63] In this way, labor activists articulated a conception of the proper Christian life that reflected a consensus in the community at large.[64]

The shorter workday, then, was a religious demand for many activists, as it was for the prolabor clergy, a demand for the intellectual, moral, and spiritual cultivation of humanity in harmony with the physical. Though material conditions had everything to do with the demand, the issue was not about money, at least not for the outspoken Christian laborites of the day. Boston's Leonard Cox put it this way: "The question we do not conceive to be, do the mechanics of New England work a greater number of hours than they receive adequate payment for but, are they compelled to devote to toil any portion of that time which should be given to the cultivation of their minds and hearts?"[65] For this reason, the movement conceived the ten-hour day as a symbol of a larger struggle in which they were engaged, an opening wedge to the moral and spiritual reformation they sought for the community at large. In their New Year's message for 1845, the editors of the Fall River *Mechanic* reminded local workers that the shorter-hours demand was merely a "stepping stone to higher ground": "the redemption of your rights."[66] The Lowell mill girls soared higher still, seeing the ten-hour day as a step toward the recovery of "primitive Christianity."[67] Such activists focused on the shorter workday because they believed that long hours destroyed religion. Unhealthy in body, mind, and spirit, workers had become ignorant, family life had deteriorated, and the moral character of the community had declined. Rather than the "christians and moralists" their God had designed them to be, they had become reflections of the system in which they worked and lived: selfish, contentious, immoral.

In their lamentations about rising immorality and their call for moral reformation, principally through the adoption of the shorter workday, labor activists drew upon the same language as did most antebellum Protestants concerned with the unrestrained self-interest that accompanied the expansion of capitalism and the rise of industry. But laborites did not draw upon the same social philosophy that many of their fellow Christians did. Men like Fitchburg's William Wilder sought to reestablish the Christian spirit by freeing workers from a burdensome labor system and a morally corrupt social system. Like contemporary churchmen, he expressed concern over the corrupting influence of the theater, gambling, and drink, but he insisted that these evils had been spawned by an unjust society and had to be eradicated through labor reform as well as moral reformation—for him, one and the same.[68] He was obsessed with strife and contention in his community and he yearned for harmony and peace, but his "search for order" represented a means of "social control" from below, not from above. His goal, Wilder claimed, was to defend and protect the rights of the masses: "Social Rights, Individual Rights, Moral Rights, Religious Rights, Physical Rights, Intellectual Rights and Legal Rights."[69] The program was rooted in Christian language and doctrine, but the social philosophy upon which it was based was rooted in at least a rudimentary class analysis of American society.

   Still, the movement's religio-moral stance closed off certain avenues of analysis, just as it opened others. The notion that moral character determined as well as reflected the course of material life, for example, inevitably led to some confusion—if not in the speaker, then potentially in his or her audience—over the causes of social ills, and hence to confusion over their possible remedy. Take their contention that people could only be "brotherly" if their community was so organized. Here, they tapped an ancient religious notion, running back to the Hebrews and extended by the early Christians, that love of God was linked to love of humanity; hence, the commands to "love thy neighbor" and "do unto others."[70] But, in this perspective, where was the locus of social and spiritual salvation—in the neighbor or the neighbor*hood*? At times, labor activists seemed to suggest that it was "false" social arrangements that had set individuals against one another in a race for the earth's wealth, thus perverting the divine natures of those involved and preventing the commonwealth for which all of God's children had been designed. At other times, however, ignoble qualities became causal factors in themselves. Boston WMP leader and area trade unionist Samuel Whitcomb, in an 1831 speech before the Working-Men's Society of Dedham, Massachusetts, traced the cause of social problems to an unequal distribution of wealth, but he insisted that the taproot of such ills was a failure of moral character. "Luxury, love of show, imitation of nobility; these are the true causes of poverty in our productive country," he told his working-class audience. Whitcomb acknowledged that it was the rich who promoted this condition, substituting fashion and extravagance for "moral excellence, honour, purity, integrity, independence, and frugality," but he insisted that no one could escape its debilitating spirit.[71]

In a similar vein, an FWA circular singled out "lust for power" as the cause of "a false and pernicious policy in the organization of society at the present day," rather than the reverse. Adding to the conceptual confusion, these workingmen located this "lust" in "various forms of aggrandizement, wealth and pride," which mixed activity with result.[72] Was the "lust for power," then, to be found in wealth or in the process of attaining it? For if the pursuit of wealth were lustful in itself, the seeker—whether an employer *or* a worker—could be indicted as an enemy of the community. Here, as with Whitcomb, the force of the class analysis embedded in the Christian laborite critique was diluted. The onus to be virtuous fell to the workers themselves, and attention was deflected from their opponents, just as when Christian laborites discussed the importance of work or the need to live in harmony with all, regardless of temporal differences.

The confusion of cause and effect led, in turn, to confusion over solutions, with the same result. As Christians, these labor activists believed that change began in the individual's sinful heart.[73] With this faith as their point of departure, they envisioned change in their society. When a Fall River operative called for a "government of God" in 1845, he found its greatest obstacle in "ignorance, selfishness and pride." "The moral sentiment is corrupt, and our social system is all wrong," he declared. In this view, a purification of the first would rectify the second, suggesting that moral reformation would change the world.[74] Sometimes calling themselves "good Washingtonians," in reference to temperance advocates who promoted their movement by publicly pledging their sobriety, laborites often devoted their energies more to testimony and exhortation than to concerted actions against their employers.[75] Here, their religio-moral worldview defused the explosive potential of their class analysis.

The movement's moral concerns also discouraged a careful assessment of the problems labor faced, rendering their analysis and program more problematical still. While their dramatic portraits of a morally corrupt community offered a compelling indictment of society, designed to jolt other workers and the community at large, it was also exaggerated and vague. Reflecting a Manichean worldview drawn from Christian imagery, it conjured up forces of good and evil without identifying the characters in the drama, which explains in part why these laborites often seemed incapable of identifying their particular enemies as a class, to be fought as such.[76] Combined with the New Testament tradition of hating the sin while loving the sinner, this way of looking at the world allowed laborites to fight—or at least *appear* to be fighting—a spirit rather than an actual enemy. In this, they once again reflected broader currents in an America that, from its very inception, had seen itself slaying the enemies of Christ as the principal player in an unfolding sacred drama set forth in Revelation. As Ernest Tuveson has noted, this mind set, nurtured by the post-Reformation militants who had colonized the North American coast in the seventeenth century, had become nearly universal by the nineteenth century and revealed itself even among the most "secularized" in the society.[77] As in the abolitionist and other reform movements of this period, the activists of the labor movement, many of them self-styled heirs to the Reformation Protestants, were ripe for the flowering of the kind of language and imagery that rendered their opponents "larger than life."

If it was unclear exactly *who* they were fighting, their apocalyptic rhetoric ignored the precise state of their society, making it difficult to determine exactly *what* they were fighting, as well. The Fitchburg Workingmen's Association, for example, argued variously that evil forces threatened the community, that they were in the process of destroying it, and that they already reigned supreme. Though most antebellum activists typically painted the picture of an endangered society on the precipice of irreversible disaster, the excesses in their rhetoric must have made it difficult, at least sometimes, to tell just where things stood. When the FWA constitution declared that the group had come together after "looking over the *world* and view(ing) the rapid progress and direful effects of *insatiable avarice vicious & bloated luxury squalid poverty, privation and wretchedness*," they surely inflated as well as voiced the fears, anxieties, and expectations of their constituency.[78] Thus, while these laborites forthrightly condemned prevailing social ills, as activists *and* Christians they were as vague and inconsistent about the enemy and conditions they faced as they were about the causes of and solutions to social ills. In seeking to combine an attack on society with a harsh accounting of individual morality, they called for a moral reformation of the community that sometimes left unclear precisely how such a transformation would come about.

To understand the ambiguities in their vision and the ambivalences in their attempts to make that vision a reality, we now turn to labor's ideas about its own redemption and to the debate they carried on amongst themselves over the means by which they would be redeemed.

Chapter 11. The Road to Redemption: Labor's Christian Vision and the Question of Christian Means

Armed with a Christian critique of antebellum America that began with the social relations of production and broadened out to include a withering attack on the state of the family, church, politics, and community life, antebellum labor activists looked to a new social order based on their conception of "practical Christianity." But the vision they developed, and the means they advocated for inaugurating it, reflected the inevitable tensions that have arisen whenever Christians have engaged in class conflict. Their idea of redemption was, at the same time, secular and religious, collective and individual, historical and prophetic, proletarian and universal. It was a class vision that sought to transcend class. In similar ways, as suggested at the end of the last chapter, the religious discourse on strategy and tactics led in a number of different directions. Some drew on their religion to discourage militancy, conflict, even the spirit of antagonism embedded in certain kinds of actions and words; others stressed different religious traditions or gave the same traditions different meanings, to justify even violence in achieving labor's goals. Neither element, moreover, despite their best intentions, was entirely free of the other's point of view. All this made for an enormously complex mix of thought and action, the class consciousness embedded in both ineluctably shaped by the religious currents that no antebellum American could escape.

Redemption

That the community needed to be reformed—in their terminology, "redeemed"—Christian laborites had no doubt. In 1848, a member of the Rochester Mechanics' Mutual Protection Association spoke for many when he called for the "redemption" of the mechanics and workingmen. It was a common refrain in the labor rhetoric of the age.[1] But what, exactly, did it mean? One notion is revealed in a Manchester, New Hampshire, factory girl's "A Dream: I had a dream which was not *all* a dream." In her vision, on Judgment Day, sinners are arrayed in groups "like criminals," with the agents and owners

of the Amoskeag Manufacturing Company, the largest mill corporation in the
city, standing before their Maker. As on earth, in the dream the agents speak for
the employers.

Judge. What were you doing on Sunday, the-day-of-1844?
Agent. Attending church.
Judge. But I am informed that you were blasting rocks.
Agent. Oh, ah, ye-yes-I, we employed some common people to do that for
   us, *I* attended church *myself.*
Judge. You must go below.

Then, a factory girl from one of the mills appears.

Judge. What were you doing on Sunday the-day-of-1844?
Girl.   I attended church in the morning and in the afternoon I rambled off
   into the woods.
Judge. How came you to ramble in the woods on Sunday?
Girl.   I had no time on weekdays.

After eliciting information on her working hours and the time remaining
"for relaxation, religious and moral instruction, reading, social visiting and
intercourse with your family," the judge decided this factory girl's fate.

Judge. You may go to Heaven.
Girl.   What seat shall I take?
Judge. Any of the upper seats that you like.

Resonating with the power of Christ's prediction in the Book of Matthew that
"the last will be first, and first last," this vision surely served to remind the mill
girls—and, perhaps, their employers—that their day would come.[2]
   But for many, "redemption" meant more than just a promise to be fulfilled
on the Day of Judgment. Labor's vision of the moral community was rooted in
a version of Christian perfectionism: through the cultivation of their God-
given faculties, men and women could eventually attain perfection.[3] Hence, the
demand for shorter hours, which would: "assimilate us to God and the Angels,"
allow development of "that which unites us to the great Architect of the
Universe," to "draw near to the Father" until "assimilated" with the Creator,
"to subdue to low, the animal nature, and elevate, ennoble and perfect the
good, the true and God-like which dwell in all the children of the common
parent."[4] William Young articulated a similar vision, rejecting the claim that
human nature was imperfect and that society would remain flawed. In the
tradition of St. Paul, he opposed the notion that evils like the long-hours
system were necessary to create good. A sin such as the fourteen-hour workday
was no less a sin than stealing, for there could be no distinction between
individual and collective violations of God's law. "God's laws are perfect. They
operate equally upon all classes of society and by strict obedience to these laws,

all would be fed, clothed and educated." "We believe," he continued, "that it would be better, cheaper and more economical, for men to do right, than wrong; that by so doing, the blessings of life, and the products of industry, would be so abundant that none would want." This was Young's notion of "elevating the race": the full development of human powers for "useful production." Then, he predicted, "the world will be filled with plenty and peace, for avarice . . . will be converted into a ministering angel to the brotherhood of Man."[5]

The ideal of human perfection through labor reform provided a vision of a happy and harmonious world beyond the prevailing misery and strife of contemporary society. In her NEWA speech, Sarah Bagley announced that labor's spirit had been aroused and would not cease "until Righteousness, with its peaceful regenerating streams shall flow through every vale."[6] Huldah Stone told the operatives of Manchester, New Hampshire, to "be active, firm, and united in every good work, until Righteousness shall be established throughout the length and breadth of Columbia's land."[7] With the inauguration of this Christian righteousness, said Young, would come a world in which both the individual and society would be transformed, a "total change" within nations, states, churches and individuals, when "men will prefer peace and harmony to litigation, industry to idleness, temperance to dissipation, virtue to vice, and true piety to hypocrisy and deceit."[8] "Where once was contention, hatred and discord," he promised, "will be peace, love and harmony."[9]

Surfacing in the 1820s and 1830s and flowering on a national scale in the 1840s, this vision of a new world, founded upon Christian precept and biblical eschatology, tapped the popular antebellum belief in the coming Kingdom of God on earth known as the "Millennium."[10] Here, labor's critique and vision came together in its most developed form, as millennialism embodied both a critique of this world and a vision of a new one. Though the rhetoric again transcended denomination and religious orientation, common to its various manifestations was an evangelical rendition of labor's notion of God's design: here in the Kingdom, William Young promised, men and women would live "as God intended [they] should be."[11] And, at the heart of Reformation Protestantism to which these early wage earners were heir, this millennialist expectation hardly required a learned theological exegesis. Calling for "a radical reformation" in the *Mechanics' Free Press* in 1830, a "poor mechanic, scarcely able to put my ideas together" declared himself "willing in this day of revival, and struggle, for the cause of righteousness on earth, to contribute all in my power to assist it."[12] He located that new world in prophetic sections of Scripture, pointing to "one of the Prophets alluding to a more glorious day of knowledge . . . and John in his vision saw a new Heaven and a new Earth, for the first Heaven and the first Earth had passed away, and all things become new."[13]

The vision flourished in the 1840s. In Lowell, Huldah Stone envisioned a world where "the wandering, sin-enslaved, wretched and lost ones of Our

Father's family" would be reclaimed, when "man [would] be redeemed, God glorified, and earth a paradise become."[14] In Allegheny County, Pennsylvania, an NEWA supporter reminded *Voice* readers that the "good book" had prophesied "every man . . . under his own vine and fig tree with . . . none to molest or make him afraid."[15] In Boston, Albert Wright looked toward "the redemption of this world from ignorance and oppression," a "day of millennial rejoicing which is in store for our fruitful earth and the inhabitants thereof."[16] In New York, "Shawmut" prophesized that "Justice will be done and the kingdom of Heaven will be established on the Earth."[17] And Young, drawing upon the Gospels, reminded the rich to "seek first the kingdom of God and his righteousness, and all things shall be added"; he told workers to labor for that "beautiful world 'wherein dwelleth righteousness,'" where "justice dwells among men and the pure principles of Christianity be made practical."[18] Young's labor movement was the harbinger of this new kingdom, he insisted, a movement that would "bring the 'bread of life' and [open] the living fountain to the thirsty, panting, husked souls of men," ushering in "a day when the gallows shall be exchanged for the platform of christian intelligence, and the halter for the golden chain of pure friendship—when oppression shall flee away, and the prison house be turned into the abode of liberty and contentment."[19]

As these images suggest, this was a social vision, which sought not individual redemption alone but the deliverance of humanity. To be sure, the social philosophy began with the individual and, in that, it reflected antebellum social and political thought. The primary duty of all was to regenerate the self; however, this was to be carried out as part of a process of social transformation. Here, the personal and the corporate met, for laborites insisted that individualism as it was then flowering in America was the root of the problem. On this, John Orvis reminded the readers of the *Voice* of Paul's words to the Romans: "we are every one members of one another." Hence, "there can be no such thing as a merely *individual* Redemption for man." Rejecting the Calvinism of an older time, he insisted upon the common fate of the race: "We must suffer or rejoice, be saved or damned together."[20] Individual happiness was a collective pursuit.

Here again was the vision of Christian brotherhood that underlay the entire edifice of this movement for *union,* a movement that spoke not only for the laboring classes but for the community as a whole.[21] This stance may have provided labor reformers with a measure of moral legitimacy, but it also once again linked them to their employers, as did their universalist application of religious strictures concerning work, equality, morality, and harmony. And thus, the same problematic tension emerged here as in other areas of their thought. The problem was not so much that activists attempted to speak for humanity rather than their class, claiming that their class represented the interests of all humanity—for even revolutionary "scientific socialists" on the

European continent would do that—but that these activists defined this mission in specifically religious terms.[22] Here, after all, was a movement advancing the interests of a particular class engaged in a battle with forces that had exploited them as workers, and yet they held to a worldview concerned foremost with the salvation of all sinners before God. The combination of this reality with the way they thought about it created a kind of schizophrenia in their thought: their ostensible reason for being was the conflict between workers and employers, and yet for them the world was ultimately divided between believers and nonbelievers; they sought material change on earth in real historical time, and yet they envisioned a total transformation amounting to a new heaven and new earth based on prophesies that were, in the most fundamental sense, outside of time.

Still, the vision of the coming kingdom as articulated by antebellum labor activists was a leveling one, in accordance with biblical prediction. In his catalog of the movement's goals in 1845, "Industry" exhorted the readers of the *Voice* to seek "*The Abolition of Want.*" "God labors for this," he declared; "'He openeth his hand and satisfieth the desires of every living thing.'" Reminding workers that "God provides a plenty," this activist called on them in biblical language to "lift higher and swell louder your 'Voice,' till the pampering haughty are brought to a level with thee, and thou aboundest with the fat of the land."[23] However problematical for the articulation of a consistent class analysis of American society, this religious vision, like the Manchester mill girl's vision of Judgment Day, was a powerful tool in the hands of antebellum labor activists. How they would wield that tool—what it meant for working-class behavior—was yet a final question on which, despite their common faith, they would disagree.

Means

Christian tradition allowed for a variety of strategies and tactics. Most antebellum laborites invoked the gospel teachings of the New Testament to renounce violence, indeed often the very spirit of antagonism.[24] Other workers found a tradition of defiance, even vengeance, in Christianity, drawing upon Old Testament imagery and the more militant passages of the New Testament. Sometimes, activists imparted different meaning to the same language. Though both elements claimed the Christian mantle, their interpretations of the faith often led them down different paths of labor action.

"Brotherly Action, Christian Action"

For many, the vision of redemption embedded in Christian millennialism could only be realized through what they sometimes called "Christian means."

Here, the invocation of labor's cherished Golden Rule served some well. As an NEA convention was instructed in 1834, "if ever the philanthropist or the Christian sees, (and see he will!) his expected millennium, he will owe it more than to all else, to that spirit which says to you and to me, 'do unto all men, as ye would they should do unto you.'"[25] In their pursuit of labor reform, many Christian laborites did in fact adhere strictly to New Testament dictates against violence, insisting on only pacific measures in pursuit of their goals.

Of course, they were quick to condemn first and foremost the violence of the enemy. A case in point is "David," another of the *MFP* correspondents who took a biblical name. After denouncing employers, banks, and landlords as "giants" like those described in the Bible, he concluded, "the earth as of old is filled with violence, which a just Creator must behold with abhorrence." However, violence was not to be met with violence. Instead, "I trust, [God] will raise up men whose energies will cement the working classes."[26] But how? Many Christian activists were crystal clear on this point. In his opening editorial at the *Voice,* William Young denounced "gun-powder, grape-shot and cannon" in favor of "the sword of truth and the whole armor of christian justice."[27] Similarly, the FWA circular forthrightly rejected any actions "other than those which are in strict accordance with the spirit and doctrines of Christ."[28] Drawing upon the parts of Scripture that stressed mercy, kindness, and forgiveness, these activists reminded their compatriots of the power of Christian love. As Young told his readers, quoting Proverbs: "A SOFT ANSWER TURNETH AWAY WRATH."[29] Moreover, violence could lead only to disaster. For "'they that take the sword shall perish with the sword.'"[30] Only by embracing the warm and humanitarian spirit of Christianity could workers achieve their goals.

In this way, such activists assured employers and the general public that they sought only what the Bible and Christianity commanded, thus appealing for community support while insisting on reciprocal treatment from their employers. In launching the *Wachusett Independant* in 1845, FWA members William Wilder and E. R. Wilkins asked their readers to speak out "if anything in our movement is unreasonable or unscriptural," pledging to cooperate with any whose principles were "truth and righteousness."[31] This pose involved more than a strategy for dealing with the public and with labor's enemies, however; it constituted their prescription for the proper Christian life.[32] Young located the essence of true religion in the Gospels, frequently exhorting his listeners to "love thy neighbor" and "do unto others." He insisted that since the movement sought only "brotherly love" and "mutual interests," all activists should exercise "the spirit of charity toward those who are opposed to them."[33] Similarly, the FWA pledged, "'whatsoever ye would that men should do to you, do ye even so unto them,'" is the rock upon which we have planted the standard of our Truth," promising to work "IN THE SPIRIT OF LOVE AND KINDNESS, BY AN UNTIRING ACTIVITY FOR THE WELFARE OF EACH OTHER."[34] Here, the gospel of Jesus provided general rules for relations within the community.

The notion was common in labor circles throughout the nation. In Wilmington, Benjamin Webb insisted to the readers of the *Free Press* that "that principle which leads us to do good, and to love all men, 'even our enemies,' must in itself be good; and so proceed from God."[35] In Rochester, Henry Frink offered essentially the same argument as those in the FWA, rooted in his adherence to Christian prescriptions for the good life. While many believed that only bloodshed would bring change, he wrote, these were people who despise "the bonds which should connect mankind." Frink maintained that the light labor shed "alone is necessary to dispel the illusion" of prejudice that all mechanics suffered under.[36] Elsewhere in New York, Robert McFarlane insisted "ours is not the spirit of the French Revolution . . . ours is the intelligent spirit of true Christianity which seeks to elevate the lower, without envying any other."[37]

These laborites were not simply repudiating violence here; they were repudiating the spirit of antagonism as well.[38] As Wilder and Wilkins advised their public in 1845, "if there should be, here or there, an individual who in his hasty zeal for the cause, should at any time express himself in too strong language, we hope it may be imputed to an error of the head rather than the heart."[39] True Christians, for this Baptist and Congregationalist, should harbor only kindness and warmth for their fellows. Contentious and hostile sentiments violated Christian law, harmed the individual's Christian spirit and, ultimately, retarded the course of Christianity in the community. In this way, antagonism—a principal source of their alarm at the "competition system"— ran directly counter to their movement's goal.

The rejection of conflict and adherence to New Testament morality stemmed from a deep-seated fear of chaos and strife in the community, an abiding faith in the power of the moral spirit and the overlordship of God, and a Christian insistence on the mutuality of interest among all God's children. Having formulated their critique and vision in response to what they perceived as rising antagonism in contemporary society, these activists sought a consistency of means and ends. The last thing they desired was an increase in social tensions. William Young reminded his readers that while he hated "the present state of manufacturing," he opposed "that vague clamor" and the "desire to keep society in fomentation and broil." His goal, rather, was "to reconcile and harmonize the antagonizing interests among men, and eradicate the causes from which they spring." Thus, he called for a "peaceful industrial revolution . . . a revolution inspired by the principle of love and *right* instead of passion and *might*."[40] The path to labor's goal lay in the benevolent and humanitarian promptings of the gospel, not in the contentious spirit of present-day life.

Thus, for example, independent political action was often regarded as a moral danger. The labor movement possessed a "moral power" that stood above the "party contention and lustful ambition" of contemporary politics, Young maintained.[41] By entering the political arena, labor would be forced to appeal to the "passions and selfish feelings" of workers, the quest for power would become its primary object, and, once successful, the movement would be corrupted.[42] Furthermore, Young reminded, "'political action' . . . wears the demagogic stain," rendering it an unfit pursuit for a movement of "christians and philanthropists." Politics, he pointed out, implied "unholy, sectarian controversy, factional aspirancy and jacobinal usurpation."[43] If labor were to remain pure, it had to stand above the fray of politics. And, for people like Young, so deeply concerned with rising sin and corruption in their communities, the labor movement was nothing if not pure. Here again, by seeking to elevate his movement above the self-interested strife of contemporary society, Young invested it with moral legitimacy. At the same time, by implying that political power was morally corrupting, he suggested that labor would have to achieve its goals without resorting to political means. Since human strife, rooted in human selfishness, constituted the Christian community's great enemy, it was the duty of Christian labor activists to seek harmony through peaceful and harmonious measures. In this framework, labor action beyond testimony and debate might lead to conflict within the community, and thus was suspect.[44]

The preference for bearing witness rather than taking concrete action stemmed from faith in the power of Christian morality. Young insisted that coercion could never match the spirit of justice and right found in Scripture; legal coercion was not only ineffectual but wrongheaded.[45] In the same spirit, he insisted that labor's moral principles had to be disseminated throughout society before real change could be effected. Like other Protestants, he sought a propagation of the gospel, advocating "intelligent action and moral power." "Let us have some terms more pure," he suggested, "*rational, intelligent, brotherly action,* christian action, terms upon which the friends of truth and goodness can unite." Only in this way could the movement "build to heaven the noble structure of humanity's brotherhood."[46] For Young, the means labor employed would testify to the kind of society the movement sought to create.

The faith in moral power, in turn, hinged on a recognition of God's control over human affairs, the sine qua non of the Christian labor critique. Again, while this invocation of divine favor provided assurance of victory, it also could discourage action against employers, either political or economic.[47] Many activists believed that change was imminent, but they rarely indicated how that change would come about. Some suggested that merely stepping forward might be enough. As one of the Fitchburg mill women put it:

> Strife and discord send away
> Trust in God, he'll set you free
> Rouse then brothers—sow, TO-DAY
> Ye are MEN, then why delay.[48]

More important, these activists insisted that the actual righting of wrongs was the responsibility of God alone. Thus, a Fitchburg laborite opposed capital punishment by invoking the New Testament declaration, " 'vengeance is mine, I shall repay.' "[49] For Young, who consistently exalted the merciful injunctions of the New Testament gospel, this was the only acceptable form of retaliation.[50] Like the prolabor clergymen, he believed that sin would not go unpunished; like most of them he, too, believed that the punishment would be not by mortal hands, but by God's.

Ultimately, labor's adherence to "christian action" rested upon the Christian commandment to hate the sin but love the sinner. Insisting that conflicting class interests stemmed from the "unnatural" conditions of a sinful society, these activists repudiated class hatred and, therefore, class struggle.[51] Not that they denied the existence of class or the conflict of classes, nor did they always shrink from the contest.[52] To the contrary, the advent of a movement for workers' rights in this period clearly signaled the rise of class in American society.[53] Labor activists recognized the existence of class distinctions; they simply refused to accept their legitimacy.[54] Still, Christian laborism did tend to retreat from any analysis that proffered a life-and-death struggle between classes for hegemony in American society.[55] Though Young believed that workers constituted a "class" whose immediate interests were in direct opposition to "the capitalists and non-producers," he called for warfare against the "false" system that produced these classes, not against capitalists themselves.[56] "Let it be understood," he declared, "that the workingman's warfare is not against *individuals* but *systems*."[57] Thus, he asked workers to harbor "no jealousies or cynical animosities toward those who stand in a hostile position to *our* true interests—treating those who are working against us as a class, *as men*, and demanding the same treatment from them."[58] In the end, all interests were mutual.

As Christians, activists like Young could accept the idea that one group unjustly stood in the way of another's interests, but they rejected the notion that the interests of the Christians involved were fundamentally different.[59] Under the prevailing labor system, in this view, the rich suffered as well as the poor. While the latter were robbed of the "means of cultivating the common gifts of God," the former were robbed of the ennobling relations of the "family circle" and "true" Christianity.[60] The interests of capital and labor, like the interests of all God's children, were ultimately not antagonistic but harmonious and mutual. If society were organized according to "correct principles," said Young, everyone would see that their interests lay in "brotherly love."[61]

And, after all, their opponents were almost always Christians just like themselves, which tended at crucial moments to take the edge off their social activism. In 1839, amidst the printers' strike in Rochester, a member of the RTA wrote to the union's paper, expressing shock that two recalcitrant boss printers, "persons who are practical printers and *professing Christians,* refuse 'the laborer his proper hire.'" It only proves, said this Bible-quoting journeyman, that the "pursuit of gain and the worship of Mammon, drown ever better impulses." To this stinging attack on recalcitrant Christian employers, the editors responded that one of the bosses was "a sincere Christian; and, as such, he is respected by us." Though they acknowledged that he necessarily must bear censure for submitting to his partner so long as he was a tacit participant in opposing the journeymen, they attributed his behavior to "his head rather than his heart."[62]

For many activists, then, the goal was a peaceful revolution consistent with the spirit and doctrines of the New Testament. Rejecting violence, destruction, and even the spirit of antagonism, they advocated change through "Christian means" alone. In their view, the labor movement could be successful only if its votaries reflected in their actions the brotherhood they sought to create. These laborites were caught in a dilemma, though: as Christians they abhorred conflict with their enemies, but, as activists they advocated radical changes in the "present organization of things." Engaged in a struggle of classes and class interests, they insisted that all interests were ultimately the same. Promising to "cherish brotherly love" in all their activities, they repudiated the antagonism in those activities.[63] As a result, they sought a social transformation, without, it seemed, the means to achieve it.

Christian Vengeance

But the Bible, and Christianity, could be turned to many uses. Invocation of Labor's Rule, for example, was not always a way of dampening down labor militancy. "M" was a militant living in New Bedford in 1832. He told the readers of the *New England Artisan* that the spreading workers' societies of his region should use the language of "patriots of old, when they cried 'Liberty or Death,'" urging them to be "as determined on the overthrow of the present system, as was Washington to gain the liberty of his country." Then, reminding them to take care to abide by the rule, "do unto others, as they wish others to do by them," he advised them to take over their employers' shops![64]

These were antebellum activists—often church members and operating within the broad parameters of the Christian laborite tradition—who had little trouble moving from moral suasion to concrete action. Take the distinction Young made between the interests of certain social groupings, which could be antagonistic, and the interests of the Christians involved, which were not. In Young's hands, as we have seen, the distinction discouraged class confrontation. Others, though, accepted the distinction and then bent it to entirely different ends. Boston's Philip Holmes discussed the issue openly in his speech to the Charlestown, Massachusetts, workingmen in 1840. After declaring that the interests of capital and labor "stand in direct opposition to each other," he reminded his audience that men and women possessed a variety of interests, some reflecting their status as human beings (as children of God) and others reflecting their roles in the workplace and in the community. "As men," Holmes asserted, "no doubt their interests and ours are the same; but their interests as capitalists, and ours as laborers, are directly opposite, and mutually destructive." Since the interests of capitalist and worker were "hostile and irreconcilable," it was ludicrous for the latter to seek salvation from the former. In this way, some labor activists could accept the mutuality of interests among all Christians and yet rely on their class alone in the battle against the capitalist. Looking to the employer for salvation, Holmes maintained, was as fruitless as the poor of Christ's day expecting the gospel "from the scribes and pharisees, the chief priests and elders, who crucified Jesus for proclaiming it."[65]

Sometimes, activists shifted their stance on class conflict in the course of struggle, perhaps reflecting a calculated public posture, but perhaps simply reflecting their frustration. The Rochester WMBERS, for the better part of two years in the early 1840s, acted the part of praying Christians asking for mercy from employers and store owners in ridding their community of the duebill system. In early 1842, after many months of meetings and entreaties, they addressed the community in apparently soothing tones. To eradicate duebills, they said, as well as the "increasing distrust between the employers and the employed, we appeal to the moral sense of the public once more."[66] Resolutions the following month echoed the basic position: the practice violated the principles of "honor and morality," was "conceived in cupidity, and sustained by the avaricious propensities," and in general ran against the interests of a "moral community."[67] And, despite their "general strike" against the system that spring, including a massive rally and march of several thousand that culminated in the burning of the reviled currency, this movement of good Christian activists exhibited no signs of violence. The following year, however, the society had reached its limit. At a meeting in June 1843, it resolved "that it is the duty of all to PRAY for the removal of all such men, by persuasion *or some other means.*" Evidently the real sentiment of the gathering was located in the second half of the resolution, for a later one announced that the reasoning and moral suasion of the previous two years had been enough to induce honest men to desist in their perpetuation of duebills, and it advised the people to cease wasting their money on hiring rooms to hold meetings and "meet under the broad canopy of heaven" until their grievances were removed. The result was the street violence and near riot called the "Due-Bill War."[68]

Sometimes, such violence—or, at least, the threat of it—was accompanied by an explicitly religious rationale for militancy. For the Bible antebellum Americans read, of course, spoke of retaliation as well as forbearance, retribution as well as forgiveness. If Christianity inculcated sympathy, kindness, and mercy in some, it authorized anger, militancy, and a strict sense of justice in others. Indeed, even some of those who could speak the language of the former also reminded labor's opponents that the Christian worker's patience had its

limits. Thus, Robert McFarlane declared, typically citing Old Testament strictures, "we have always spoken in courteous language but we have never, and
never shall want moral courage to say 'woe unto you ye scribes and pharisees!'"[69] McFarlane's contemporary George Lippard advocated the overthrow
of the current system (of "Bankers, Land Monopolists, and Monied Oppressors"), peacefully if possible but violently if necessary. In Lippard, as head
of the secret Brotherhood of the Union, we can see most clearly the facile ability
of antebellum labor activists and social radicals to shift between various
Christian traditions. "When the few will not listen to the voice of Justice, nor
the Gospel of Nazareth," he proclaimed, "then we would advise Labor to go to
War, in any and all forms—War with the Rifle, Sword and Knife." "The War of
Labor—waged with pen or sword," declared Lippard, "is a Holy War."[70]

Thus, too, in contrast to those who advocated "the spirit of love and kindness" in the struggle for labor reform, Seth Luther spoke for the angry
Christian worker who demanded retribution for prevailing crimes. Born into
the home of devout Rhode Island Baptists, he had imbibed a militant interpretation of the Bible. In "that good old fashioned book," he told workers, "the
laborers' rights are plainly laid down."[71] In the Old Testament—in the stories
of the Babylonians, the Philistines, and the Israelites—he found useful analo-
gies to antebellum America.[72] Unlike William Young, who found in Scripture a
gentle message of charity and forbearance that stressed a mutuality of interest,
Luther found a powerful indictment of rich oppressors despising, cheating, and
exploiting the poor.[73] From the New Testament, he blended the gentle and the
harsh to fashion an angry language of Christian vengeance. Again, we see the
plastic nature of biblical precept and imagery in the hands of these labor rebels.
In a speech in Providence, he declared:

> We believe in the golden rule, "whatsoever ye would that men should do
> unto you, do you even so unto them." We plead the cause of the widow and
> fatherless; the poor and the needy.

Then, without pause, Luther continued his litany of biblical quotations, moving in an entirely different direction.

> We say to the rich, who have obtained property dishonestly, and by oppres-
> sion, "Why do ye grind the faces of the poor?" Ye sell the poor for silver, and
> the needy for a pair of hoes. Yea, ye sell the refuse for wheat; "Behold the hire
> of the laborers, who have reaped down your fields, which is of you, kept
> back by fraud, crieth, and the cries of them that have reaped, and labored for
> you, in building your splendid luxurious abodes of opulence, have entered
> into the ears of the just governor of the Universe. Your riches are corrupted,
> and your garments are motheaten."[74]

Here, in Luther's hands, the Golden Rule—Labor's Rule—seamlessly became a
rallying cry of the poor, demanding justice from their Christian overlords.

Juxtaposing that commandment with the angry accusations in the Books of Isaiah and James, he fashioned a blistering indictment of labor's opponents.[75]

Luther's Christianity, in fact, did not even exclude the use of violence, as he reminded his audiences that force alone had restored popular rights in the past.[76] Social evils would be remedied, he assured his audience, "'peacefully if we can, forcefully if we must.'"[77] Frequently referring to the Revolution, this son of a Revolutionary War veteran warned employers that workers would maintain their rights "proclaimed in blood with our own blood."[78] Luther was quite specific about the meaning of this pledge, announcing, "We will try the ballot box first"—"If that will not effect our righteous purpose, the next and last resort is the cartridge box."[79]

Unlike Young, then, Luther spoke of conflict, not harmony. Though he did assert on at least one occasion that the "interests of all classes are invested in the *intelligence* and *welfare* of those who labor," he evinced little concern for the alleged sufferings of the rich.[80] He always described himself as a "plain mechanic" and insisted that he spoke for that class alone.[81] Since human history had been characterized by "oppression on our part," Luther sought to rouse workers to battle against their oppressors.[82] He declared it "the duty of all men to resist tyranny, if need be, sword in hand," "the duty of every man, rather to die on the last ditch and never surrender his birthright."[83] Proclaiming "'*we are the Majority,*'" Luther articulated the interests of a class at war against a mortal enemy.[84]

If Seth Luther's message represented the angry Christian counterpart to William Young's gentle gospel, the militancy of the Fall River labor movement contrasted sharply with the mild and merciful activism of the FWA. Important differences between the two towns distinguished the movements that emerged there. In a more industrialized setting, with a larger and more heterogeneous population, the Fall River activists stressed equal rights more than harmony. Having lived with the factory system for a generation, their concerns focused less on a return to the putative peace and quiet of the past than on ridding the community of the inequities wrought by that system. Moreover, a history of struggle for labor's rights and a strong tradition of Baptist dissent gave rise to a militant interpretation of the Bible and Christian tradition. Although they generally repudiated violence, Christian workers in Fall River took direct action against their opponents, exhibiting a far different temperament than their brethren in Fitchburg.

Whereas the FWA expended its energy mostly in testimony and debate, the Fall River Mechanics' Association sponsored a ten-hour strike among building tradesmen in the spring of 1844, which, in turn, led to physical confrontation between workers and their opponents.[85] During the early summer, local activists destroyed the tools of several employers and laborers working on the long-hours system, causing quite a stir in the community.[86] The movement's stance regarding this action revealed a malleable Christian perspective on the question of "means": while publicly proclaiming their faith in moral force here, they came close to legitimating such direct action in the course of their struggle.

At a Mechanics' Association meeting convened to discuss the issue of the recent disturbance, several members persuaded their compatriots that the organization should repudiate violence, since the movement "had always maintained an untarnished character."[87] Consequently, the group issued a public statement that advocated "the use of MORAL POWER which is mighty to overturn long cherished systems of oppression and wrong." Insisting that they could not "under any circumstances countenance resort to violence or the destruction of property," the mechanics pledged to "scrupulously regard the rights of others." This statement represented the association's public posture. As citizens of the Christian community engaged in what they regarded as a "just, humane and righteous cause," it would have been unthinkable for these activists to openly condone violence.

But in a *Mechanic* editorial introducing the statement, association secretary Thomas Almy suggested a more militant approach to the issue. Though he, too, condemned "wanton violations of 'Law and Order,'" maintaining that "such acts as these deserve the severest censure of every good citizen of the place," he added, "we cannot but believe that they are the *legitimate fruits* of the very system which these professed christians . . . are trying to perpetuate."[88] When employers crush the "finer sensibilities of the soul" of the laborer, he warned, they should not be surprised "if, when his feelings are outraged, and insult is heaped upon injury, he should, in his blindness, commit deeds of violence." Legitimating direct action in this way, Almy went on to condemn the behavior of labor's opponents in still harsher terms. Referring to the importation of labor to break the ten-hour movement, he reminded his readers that "such acts as THESE also, *deserve the severest censure of every good citizen of the place.*" In Almy's view, ten-hour advocates had shown enormous restraint compared to their opponents, and he stated his position in terms any Christian could understand. "Certain we are," he wrote, "that the *crime* of the latter as much exceeds that of the former, as the wickedness of Satan does that of a Christian." In this vein, how much of a crime could the dumping of scabs' tools be?

In general, Fall River labor activists drew upon a tradition of Christian defiance and vengeance that was apparently missing in Fitchburg. "Will you not come forward," the *Mechanic* editors exhorted their readers at the outset of the ten-hour strike in 1844, "and stand between your rights and those who would wrest them from you, and draw the line, and say to them, 'thus far shalt thou come and no farther?'"[89] The rhetoric suggested confrontation. While more pacific laborites drew upon the mild gospel of Jesus, Fall River workers often looked to the Old Testament, where examples of retributive justice abounded. "When Haman conspired the death of Mordecai, and then got hung on his own gallows," the editors wrote, "has not universal nature, in all ages, cried out,

'Right—jest what the wretch deserved'?"[90] The sentiment expressed the anger of workers who demanded not only justice but retribution as well.

These activists rejected the notion that the message of Christianity was forbearance and mercy alone. With respect to tactics, then, they defied the basic message of the prolabor clergy, whose favor they curried and whose numbers were greater in Fall River than anywhere else in antebellum America. A local factory operative, who in fact shared the fears of a local minister about the dangers of anarchy, cautioned his brethren that "this should never deter us from the use of such means as we believe will effect the greatest amount of good." In this view, God sanctioned a variety of means. When systems are wrong, the operative declared, "treat them as God deals with His disobedient children;—by love—by pointing them to Calvary—and if this does not answer, He tries them by the threatenings of His wrath—by the thunderings and lightenings of Sinai." Under certain circumstances, then, direct action—perhaps violence—were justifiable within the Christian worldview. "If we cannot induce men to do right by the mild sunshine of truth," this Fall River mill worker maintained, "we must bring to bear upon them the blast of the looming and surcharged war cloud. Like the farmer who espied the little thief in one of his apple trees, we will first try the effects of grass, and if that will not bring him down, we must try what virtue there is in stones."[91] More than a decade later, this rhetoric echoed the either/or language of Seth Luther.

Now, to be sure, there were also activists in Fall River who drew upon the gentler message of Christianity, pledging, as one said, to "cultivate a spirit of forbearance and brotherly love" toward their enemies.[92] But most stressed justice, not charity. The dominant voice of the Fall River labor movement was a voice of Christian defiance that called the faithful to what some saw as a life-or-death struggle between good and evil, typically blending the religious and Revolutionary traditions of this generation of Americans. As "A Mechanic" exhorted his brethren in the spring of 1844, at the start of the ten-hour strike:

> Arm! arm, ye brave, a noble cause;
> The cause of RIGHT demands your zeal!

Fellow Mechanics! Now is your time. At this instant the decisive blow must be struck. The strong arm of wealth is rising on every side to crush you. But TRUTH is stronger—Nay, it is Omnipotent. Therefore stand to your principles; again, take arms, and be resolved to *conquer or die.*[93]

Epilogue

Beginning in the late 1840s, immigrants dramatically altered the composition of the American work force, particularly in port cities like Boston and key industrial towns like Fall River. Although an in-depth study of religion and immigrant workers is beyond the scope of this book—and any judgments must be rendered in the most tentative terms—it appears that at least their initial use of religious language was different from what we have seen among groups of predominantly native-born Protestant workers. Typically, the latter were rooted in relatively homogeneous communities; they spoke of redeeming a pious community they could call their own. The foreign-born were new-comers, often Catholic, and from diverse social and cultural backgrounds: they did not at first identify their interests with those of the Protestant communities in which they lived and worked, and instead concentrated on specific labor reforms. Rather than offering elaborate religious arguments for their demands, they more often simply stated the facts of their case. They did occasionally employ imagery and biblical precept in their rhetoric, but in doing so they seem to have been seeking public attention and support rather than a sweeping religious reformation.

Evidence for such a contrast emerges from immigrant wage strikes in Fall River and Boston during these years. In Fall River, these struggles evinced a style of labor activism distinct from, say, the early ten-hour struggles there. Take, for example, the block printers' strike at Andrew Robeson's calico dye works in 1840, a walk-out prompted by a reduction in their wages.[1] At a strike meeting in Firemen's Hall, the men drafted a public letter to their employer, outlining their grievances and appealing to his sense of generosity. Neither the meeting's resolution nor the open letter made any reference to God or religion in defense of their claims.[2] A strikers' circular issued the following month evinced a similarly secular style. Explaining that they were "conscientiously and firmly resisting the unprincipled encroaches of a monied aristocracy, who are tyran-nically attempting to make war upon our just rights," these workers reviewed the history of wage reductions in Robeson's mills since 1826. The only religious reference in the document regarded the manufacturers who had refused to

214

follow Robeson's lead, the block printers calling these employers honest men, "the noblest work of God." Unlike the circular of the Association of Industry issued the following year, the nature and thrust of the block printers' public appeal was simple and direct, with recourse to no other authority than the facts of their case. They claimed, simply, that they had been treated unjustly.[3]

In general, immigrant strikers in Fall River focused on working conditions, usually invoking the name of God or Christianity only at the end of their letters and speeches.[4] When they employed religious language, it rarely formed an essential part of their argument, as it clearly did for activists in the Mechanics' Association of 1844–45. The secretary of a strike meeting in 1867, for example, invoked the same biblical precepts used in the early years, but he did not use these quotations in the way his predecessors had. "God has told us that by the sweat of our brow we are to earn our bread," W. B. McAuley reminded, but "while our employers wish us to labor they must remember that the 'laborer is worthy of his hire.'" "It takes all we can earn to keep body and soul together," he railed, as the employers proposed to reduce the workers' wages still further. McAuley's message was directed at native employers on behalf of immigrant workers, demanding fair treatment from professed Christians: "We left the old country and came to America to get a living like honest, hard-working men and women, and I believe, if this reduction takes place, Fall River will lose the best help that ever came into its limits."[5] Aware of their status as outsiders, immigrants like McAuley did not claim to be redeemers of the entire community.[6] They merely asked for Christian justice.

Something similar happened in Boston. In the summer of 1849, local tailors quit work over a reduction in their wages, beginning the largest and most protracted strike in the city before the Civil War.[7] Many of these strikers were new to America, Irish peasants forced off the land by population pressure, the decline of handicraft industries, and a series of potato blights that culminated in the great famines of 1846 and 1848.[8] Mostly Catholic, they fashioned a religious language of anger and determination that was at once more militant than the rhetoric of many native-born Protestant labor activists and less focused on religious reformation of society. For the tailors spoke *to* a community from which they sought support, rather than *for* a community that they sought to represent. Thus, Journeymen Tailors' Society vice president Philip Walsh assured his fellow strikers that they "had but to tell the truth to the American people and they would sustain them." If that support was not forthcoming, he warned, the tailors would return to the "miserable despotism from whence they came."[9] The threat distinguished immigrants from native-born workers, who spoke as standard bearers of the community. When the tailors appealed to the public, their rhetoric reflected more an attempt to draw attention to their plight than an airing of their religious views. As a result, their use of religious language appears to have been selective; it played little role in the logic of their arguments.[10]

One of the tailors' key spokesmen, Bernard S. Treanor, reflected this rhetori-cal style. A Young Irelander who immigrated to Boston during the late 1840s, Treanor was not himself a tailor, but he maintained very close ties to the strikers: he was the only outsider to attend their meetings and the main organizer of support rallies for them. Though he stressed that social evils resulted from the "unnatural struggle of capital and labor" and called for cooperative enterprise as the ultimate solution to the tailors' problems, he insisted that the "first object" was to win the strike. Show the "purse-proud aristocrats" that the workers have the real power, he exhorted them. Employing a fierce biblical style, he condemned these "aristocrats" as " 'oppressors of the poor,' and 'robbers of the widow and fatherless.' " "They add house to house and field to field, with wealth stained with the blood of thousands," he railed. "They must, and shall be defeated, if there be manhood and truth amongst them; for their iniquities cry aloud to Heaven for vengeance." Speaking for "the Carneys and the Mahoneys," Treanor voiced the outrage of immigrants forced to work under oppressive conditions.[11]

When the tailors themselves used religious shibboleths in their public pro-nouncements, they rarely advanced a Christian rationale for their strike.[12] When they announced the first in a series of public support meetings, they headed the notice with the commonly used gospel dictum, "the laborer is worthy of his hire."[13] The body of the advertisement did not offer a biblical defense of labor, however. It appears that the heading was designed to attract the attention "of every man in the Commonwealth," to whom the notice was directed. Similarly, the tailors' manifesto to the public ("To the Mechanics and Workingmen of the United States of America") invoked Scripture, but again it did not present a religious argument in defense of their cause.[14] The circular, issued in response to the employers' repeated attacks on the strikers in the press and the announcement of a blacklist, was entitled "Resistance to Tyrants is Obedience to God."[15] This invocation of divine authority could not have been lost on an American public weaned on the Bible, striking a chord of resistance running back to 1776, and even farther to the Puritan Revolution.[16] And, for emphasis, the tailors placed under the title a scathing attack on the rich based on the Epistle of James:

> Go to now ye rich men, weep and howl in your miseries which shall come upon you. Your riches are corrupted and your garments are moth-eaten. Your gold and silver are cankered; and the rust of them shall be a testimony against you, and shall eat your flesh like fire. You have stirred up to your-selves wrath against the last days. BEHOLD THE HIRE OF THE LABORERS, who have reaped down your fields, *which by fraud has been kept back by you, crieth! and the cry of them hath entered into the ears of the* LORD OF SABAOTH.

Other antebellum activists, including Seth Luther in the 1830s and the Fall River building tradesmen in the 1840s, had made good use of the same passage, but the tone of the tailors' message was atypical of antebellum labor rhetoric.[17] More important, the language and its location in the circular appears to have been designed to catch a Christian community's eyes and ears; it did not state the strikers' case. The purpose of the document, the tailors made clear at the outset, was to "appeal to you, the people of this great and free republic, and that you may understand the matter at issue between us (the tailors and their employers), we will narrate briefly the facts of our case." The authors then detailed the declining wages in their trade and the honest and just course of their strike. They employed religious language only when they framed their appeal for support. "Mechanics and workingmen of America," they declared, "we are fighting your battle—the battle of laborers' rights. Shall that holy cause be sacrificed in our persons? . . . No: a thousand times no. . . . The sacred cause of labor is in our care, and that we swear never to give up, but with our lives." A plea for help rather than a promise of redemption, the language gave legitimacy to a specific demand, not to a religious crusade to remake the world.

However, redemptive Christian labor activism did endure in certain sectors of the American labor movement in the late 1840s and 1850s. Indeed, when the Boston tailors' struggle broadened into a more general one for workers' cooperatives in late 1849 and 1850, they would be part of a movement speaking the language of religious labor radicalism that so typified antebellum labor struggles. That language was noticeable, for example, among native-born activists like John Orvis, who voiced support for the Boston tailors, pushing them toward cooperative enterprise as a solution to their problems. His resolution at a strike rally that condemned "Grab-all-ism" (a reference to the greed of recalcitrant clothing employers) as "antichristian in spirit and the primary cause of our social evils." Since "the wise and good of all ages (had) spoken in their prayers of a christian brotherhood," it continued, "cooperative fraternities" might realize that brotherhood "in our shops, our workhouse, and in all our social relations."[18]

Orvis's approach was typical of the cooperative movement known as Protective Unionism, which emerged out of the mid-1840s upsurge in New England. In 1845, a committee of the Boston Mechanics' and Laborers' Association whose members were active in the NEWA established the Working Men's Protective Union, initially a consumer cooperative and mutual benefit society.[19] Another group influenced by Associationism, these activists sought to elevate the entire community in the spirit of Christian redemption: in the name of "Industrial Association," they looked forward to a cooperative and harmonious system based on Christian principles that would replace the current competitive and contentious social order.[20] Reminding their audiences that their efforts involved more than simply "monetary savings," they insisted that the "social feature" of their movement brought workers together as brothers and put an end to the prevailing "grabbing of throats and Ishmaelites."[21] For, under present conditions, Albert Wright declared in defense of Protective

Unionism, there was "no bond of brotherhood," no "connecting link between one laborer and another to make them realize the truth that 'we are all brethren,'" while cooperation offered the promise of redemption in the face of "the present commercial Babylon."[22] "If this organization takes deep root in the moral and social structure," the *Journal of the New England Protective Union* proclaimed a decade later, "it will become a vital, living spirit, and do much, not only to mitigate present wrongs and privation, but also render important services to the cause of man's permanent social, moral and political eleva- tion."[23] And, like the NEWA out of which it emerged, the Protective Unionists accepted only those of "good moral character."

By the late 1840s, now a regionwide movement concentrating on consumer cooperatives, the New England Protective Union (NEPU) joined forces with a producer cooperative movement among Boston trade unionists, many of them immigrants, in the "Uprising of 1850." A national explosion of union organiz- ing, strikes, and producer cooperatives among urban workers from Ohio to Virginia to Vermont, the rising brought together advocates of shorter hours, land reform, Associationism, trade unionism, and cooperationism in a move- ment for general labor reform.[24] In Boston, trade union agitation began among the printers with the formation of the Boston Printers' Union (BPU) in 1848, followed by a wage strike, a producers' cooperative under the direction of the Boston Printers' Protective Union, and a newspaper called the *Protective Union,* which became the mouthpiece of the upsurge in New England.[25] The tailors struck and then founded a cooperative in the fall 1849; others followed.[26] With the aid and assistance of the NEPU, the movement was in full swing by the spring of 1850.[27]

This movement bore many of the hallmarks of its predecessors.[28] Speeches at rallies, resolutions at meetings, and especially editorials and correspondence in the *Protective Union* recapitulated the religious language of antebellum labor reform: the attack on the hypocrisy of professing employers and sectarian religion (while allowing a range of religious views to be aired), alongside the claim that cooperative workshops represented "christianity grown practical"; the recourse to God's "design" and the frequent invocation of God, Jesus Christ, heaven, and the righteousness of the movement (even warnings to resist the "power of the beast"); the use of biblical injunction, particularly from the Gospels; and the articulation of a millennial vision of labor reform variously described as the "Emanuel of Labor," the "Workingmen's Jubilee," the "New Jerusalem," and, of course, the "Good Time Coming."[29]

A similar style was evident in the New England Industrial League, a kind of workers' cooperative congress established at the height of this upsurge in the spring and summer of 1850. The league drew especially from the printers and tailors, but also cabinetmakers, sailmakers, and machinists, with the support of the Protective Unionists and the Associationists.[30] With veterans Charles Douglas, Henry Trask, N. W. Brown, and William Young taking leading roles in the effort, the league's rhetoric bristled with the religious language so common in the 1830s and 1840s. Treanor wrote the group's constitution, but here he spoke in a different tongue than when speaking on behalf of the tailors nine months earlier: the "practical exemplification of the great idea of Christianity, in the common brotherhood of the race—can only be made manifest by Union and Association, rather than isolation." In announcing the group's formation, the *PU* editors followed the lead, exhorting their constituency: "Workingmen rally. The harvest is ready for the tiller, see that you reap in due time."[31]

Similarly with the league's successor, the Massachusetts Ten Hour Conventions of 1852 and 1853.[32] Drawing their inspiration from previous struggles, this movement for a legal reduction in the workday crystallized in their public statements the religious arguments that shorter-hour advocates had been erecting for nearly a generation. Those involved here included Young, fellow *Voice* editor John S. Fletcher, itinerant NEWA agitator John C. Cluer, Fall River ten-hour supporter James Borden, South Boston cooperationist Hilton P. Langley, and Boston machinist Henry P. Trask.[33] In their famous "Hours of Labor" address, they reiterated the most basic of the antebellum arguments for the shorter workday: "God has created man with moral, intellectual and social capacities, and with these endowments, He has imposed corresponding duties, which cannot be properly performed without due mental and moral cultivation." Those duties were religious as well as social. Staking their claim on higher law principles—the workers' right to their "due portion" of the day was "an inalienable birthright of every human being, a right not dependent upon the sanction of human laws and customs, but proclaimed by an ordinance of God, written in the moral and physical constitution of man"—these activists promised religious salvation if their program were enacted. Here once again was the argument that "practical Christianity" would flourish only if workers had time to cultivate their souls. "As the religion which Christ taught does not consist of mere blind conformity to prescribed forms and ceremonies but of practical deeds of righteousness, proceeding from purified hearts and elevated moral sentiments, time for daily study and contemplation of God's word and works is necessary for religious progress and improvement." On this foundation, they demanded the support of all Christians in the community for this "just and righteous project."[34]

Nor, finally, was this a phenomenon confined to the land of the Puritans. Take, for example, a little-studied movement that appeared in Philadelphia during the early 1850s, sometimes calling itself the "Jubilee Association of the Daughters and Sons of Toil," sometimes simply the "Association of Working Men and Women." The group sponsored two textile cooperatives employing several hundred spinners, weavers, and dyers, an emigration association that resettled factory families in the West, a reading room, a 150-man militia, and a monthly magazine (*Monthly Jubilee*) with a boasted circulation of ten thousand

and more than a thousand exchanges in the United States and Europe.[35] They also called themselves "Pioneers of the Second Coming of the Savior"; they looked forward to the "coming millennium, latter day glory" or "the good time coming," drawing hundreds to open-air Sabbath meetings ("the Jubilee Church") at a plot just outside Philadelphia ("Jubilee Grove"). Anthony F. C. Wallace, among the very few historians of the era to note the existence of this remarkable group, labels them "a labor union of a new style," in great measure because of their appeals to God and the Millennium, but it would be more accurate to call the movement a radical resurgence of an old style, from their condemnations of contemporary Christianity to their biblically suffused critique and vision.[36]

The Philadelphians advocated a wide range of reforms and practices—free land, shorter hours, women's rights, peace, universal suffrage, the secret ballot, direct democracy, beards, regular bathing, and the use of human feces as fertilizer. Employing the entire range of biblical imagery and arguments from the Old and New Testaments used by their predecessors, their advocacy rarely strayed from those texts. In one especially telling moment, at the seventh Industrial Congress meeting in 1852, their leader John Sidney Jones expressed his hope for "a Jubilee Industrial Congress for the elevation and emancipation of Labor from the thraldom and oppression of Capital," and with thinly veiled allusion to Revelation and the Book of John, he declared, "And *I, John,* foretell the coming of this 'Jubilee.' In the beginning was the word, and the word was with God, and the word was God!"[37]

Interestingly enough, John and other biblical figures like Moses, Elias, Peter, and Paul were not the only icons in these particular activists' pantheon of heroes. As in nearby Wilmington, the ghost of Thomas Paine loomed large, too, though it was hardly the Paine of the rationalist late eighteenth century. At a Jubilee Association celebration of the Englishman's birthday in 1853, with Jones presiding, pictures of Paine hung next to pictures of the Crucifixion (with an inscription containing Labor's Rule, "do unto others as ye would they should do unto you"). Saying grace before the supper, Jones spoke of humanity's powers of improvement bestowed by God, "the same God that sent Moses into the world, that sent Jesus Christ the Savior of mankind into the world, that sent Thomas Paine into the world."[38] Linking biblical times to the Revolution, singing the praises of what they called "Christian Democracy," the movement carried into a new era the language of religious radicalism introduced by an earlier generation of labor activists.

The Pioneers were a reprise of the 1830s and 1840s: like Seth Luther, they condemned churches where "every seat [was] . . . stuffed, covered and cushioned with damasks; and here the rich men will loll at ease, in purple and fine linen, while the poor will be refused the crumbs that fall from their tables."[39] Like William S. Wilder and the Fitchburg Workingmen, they denounced "fake, sectarian Christianity."[40] Like Sarah Bagley and the Lowell mill girls, they indicted the "christian employer" who "profess(ed) christianity with the spirit of satan," by forcing those who earned their bread "by the sweat of their brow" to work "according to the times."[41] Like the seeker William Young and the Presbyterian churchman Henry Frink, they rejected the "churchianity" of doctrine for a Christianity of works.[42] Like Wilmington's Benjamin Webb, they championed free inquiry and the rights of individual conscience within a devoutly Christian framework. Seeing themselves as evangels of a new labor gospel—"missionaries of the jubilee"—they held their Sunday meetings out-doors, just as activists did in Fall River ten years earlier, only here they elected speakers of the day by voice vote, while, in Quaker fashion, allowing any to speak "according the dictates of conscience." Mixing politics with the tradi-tional sermon (while Townsend, as editor of the *Jubilee,* banned discussions of sectarian religion and party politics), these affairs were, in their own words, "religio-political exercises." Like earlier labor activists in New England, upstate New York, and nearby Wilmington, these men and women championed a "practical Christianity" based on the gospel teachings of Jesus and the example of the early Christians.

As a language of protest, religion provided antebellum workers with a clarion call to battle and a compelling social critique and vision, bequeathing to later generations a protean legacy of rebellion. Of course, religion could be a source of division—at times a fatal one—but the Christian dissenting tradition fash-ioned by some antebellum labor reformers was embraced by many as a univer-sal faith that could transcend theological differences.[43] After the Civil War, in the National Labor Union, the Knights of Labor, and the American Federation of Labor, evangelical Protestantism was often grasped as a tool of universal liberation, exalting the common humanity of all working people and con-demning all intolerance and bigotry as antithetical to the Christian spirit—just as before the Civil War. Though it had its different uses in different hands, this religion offered a legitimating framework for labor protest in nineteenth-century America, as it cast popular struggles in the language of the dominant culture: the workers, their champions shouted, were the redeemers of the Republic.

Notes

Preface

1. In this sense, the project was directly informed by Werner Sombart's famous question, "Why is there no socialism in the United States?" a concern that in the broadest sense had generated interest among historians and social commentators long before the publication of the essay of the same name—indeed, at least since the early days of the American labor movement, beginning in the 1820s. Much has been written on questions of this type, with many recent attempts by American labor historians to move on to other issues, but Sombart's query remains a principal concern, for good reason in my view. Note that it is the point of departure for the first attempt to synthesize the "new labor history" of the nineteenth century (Bruce Laurie, *Artisans into Workers: Labor in Nineteenth-Century America* [New York: Noonday Press, 1989], intro.).

2. In this book, as in this paragraph, I use the terms labor *reform* and labor *radicalism* interchangeably. The words can convey very different meanings, of course, regarding the extent, nature, and purpose of the change proposed. Indeed, much of the book examines just how far religion could carry labor dissent in antebellum America. However, for reasons that will become clear in the pages that follow, conventional distinctions like that between *reformer* and *radical* simply do not accurately capture the realities of labor activism in this era. Hence, in a letter to a union of Fall River textile operatives in early 1848, Lowell labor leader William Field Young advocated "one great plan of reform," insisting that "nothing but a thorough, intellectual and radical reform in our political, social and industrial laws and customs, can effect any permanent good." People like Young were reformers *and* radicals, and I have treated them as such. ([Fall River, Mass.] *All Sorts*, 4 Mar. 1848). To make the usual labels even more problematic, these labor activists also thought of themselves as conservatives, as they demanded that their society live up to the time-worn principles on which that society was allegedly based—a pose that can be quite radical. See, e.g., Rhys Isaac, "Radicalised Religion and Changing Lifestyles: Virginia in the Period of the American Revolution," in Margaret and James Jacobs, eds., *The Origins of Anglo-American Radicalism* (London: Allen and Unwin, 1984), 257–67.

3. Doris Kirkpatrick, *The City and the River* (Fitchburg: Fitchburg Historical Society [FHS], 1971) 1:166–69; Ebenezer Foster Bailey, "An Early Workingmen's Association of Fitchburg," *Proceedings of the FHS* [hereafter, *FHS Proceedings*] 4 (1908): 242–52. Although an audience for labor reform survived in the aftermath of the FWA, apparently no such independent movements emerged before the Civil War. See (Boston) *Herald*, 22 Oct. 1852. For more on Fitchburg, see chap. 4.

4. Hereafter, "FWA Record Book."

5. Before relocating to Boston to edit the *New England Artisan (NEA)*, Douglas was editor of the *Political Observer and Working Man's Friend* in his hometown of New London.

6. On the historiography, see intro.

7. (Pawtucket, Providence, and Boston) *NEA*, 8 Mar., 15 Aug., 11 Oct. 1832; (New York) *Young America* (*YA*), 21 Mar. 1846; (Boston) *Reformer*, 11 Aug. 1836; (New York) *Man*, 20 Feb. 1834; (New York) *Working Man's Advocate* (*WMA*), 3 Mar. 1832. A month after Douglas came to Brownson's defense, he wrote to a friend in Philadelphia that if the "producers" would learn to take care of themselves as "consumers," "old things would be done away, and all things would become new," ending his epistle, "God grant that this blissful period may shortly arrive" ([Philadelphia] *National Laborer* [*NL*], 1 Oct. 1836). For more on Douglas and Brownson, see chap. 4.

8. For an introduction to recent efforts in this area, see the following works by David R. Roediger: *The Wages of Whiteness: Race and the Making of the American Working Class* (London and New York: Verso, 1991); *Towards the Abolition of Whiteness: Essays of Race, Politics, and Working Class History* (London and New York: Verso, 1994); and "Race and the Working-Class Past in the United States: Multiple Identities and the Future of Labor History," *International Review of Social History* (Supplement) 38 (1993): 127–43.

Introduction

1. (Fitchburg, Lowell, and Boston, Mass.) *Voice of Industry*, 9, 16, 23 Apr. 1847. The New England Labor Reform League (NELRL) was successor to the New England Workingmen's Association (NEWA), organized in 1844; they constituted the regional institutions of a major labor upsurge in the mid-1840s. Norman Ware calls this particular meeting "the peak of the [movement's] swing away from working-class purposes and methods," but Frances Early has shown that the spring of 1847 was precisely one of those moments when "the worker and the reformer merged together to become the 'labour-reformer' of this era" (Ware, *The Industrial Worker, 1840–1860: The Reaction of American Industrial Society to the Advance of the Industrial Revolution* [orig. publ., 1924; repr. ed., Chicago: Quadrangle Books, 1964], 221; Early, "A Reappraisal of the New-England Labour-Reform Movement of the 1840s: The Lowell Female Labor Reform Association and the New England Workingmen's Association," *Histoire Sociale [Social History]* 13 [May 1980]: 34–35, 50). For more on the debate among historians over the character of the NEWA/NELRL, see n. 30 below.

2. Also spelled "Tukesbury." The editor of the *Voice* at the time, William F. Young, referred to him as the late editor of "a rum organ," "not a Reformer, by any means" (*Voice*, 16 Apr. 1847).

3. Ibid., 23 Apr. 1847.

4. The five-member resolutions committee at this convention included two women (ibid., 9 Apr. 1847).

5. Lawrence and Appleton were prominent New England industrialists.

6. Thus, what Lincoln said of the sectional struggle during the Civil War must also be said of the class struggle before it: "Both read the same Bible, and pray to the same God; and each invokes His aid against the other" (Second Inaugural Address, *The Collected Works of Abraham Lincoln*, Roy P. Basler, ed., vol. 8 [New Brunswick: Rutgers Univ. Press, 1953], 333).

7. See David Brody, "The Labor Movement," in *Reader's Companion to American History*, Eric Foner and John Garraty, eds. (Boston: Houghton Mifflin, 1991), 627; Leon Fink, "American Labor History," in Eric Foner, ed., *The New American History* (Philadelphia: Temple Univ. Press, 1990), 239. For two influential monographs on antebellum labor that stress republicanism, despite the authors' own evidence suggesting important religious strains in labor rhetoric, see Alan Dawley, *Class and Community: The Industrial Revolution in Lynn* (Cambridge: Harvard Univ. Press, 1976), 2, 9; Thomas Dublin, *Women at Work: The Transformation of Work and Community in Lowell, Massachusetts, 1826–1860* (New York: Columbia Univ. Press, 1979), 86, 114, 119, 131. See, too, Amy Bridges, *A City in the Republic: Antebellum New York and the Origins of Machine Politics* (New York: Oxford Univ. Press, 1984); Steven J. Ross, *Workers on the Edge: Work, Leisure, and Politics in Industrializing Cincinnati, 1788–1890* (New York: Columbia Univ. Press, 1985), chaps. 3, 7; Brian Greenberg, *Worker and Community: Response to Industrialism in a Nineteenth Century American*

City, Albany, New York (Albany: State Univ. of New York Press, 1985), chap. 1. For texts and recent surveys and reviews, see Ronald L. Filippelli, *Labor in the USA: A History* (New York: Knopf, 1984), e.g., 29, 46–47; Sean Wilentz, "The Rise of the American Working Class, 1776–1877: A Survey," in J. Carroll Moody and Alice Kessler Harris, eds., *Perspectives on American Labor History: The Problem of Synthesis* (Dekalb: Univ. of Illinois Press, 1989), 85, 88–90, 104; Friedreich Lenger, "Beyond Exceptionalism: Notes on the Artisanal Phase of the Labor Movement in France, England, Germany and the United States," *International Review of Social History* 36 (1991): 16, 18. Even in an important new book that identifies evangelical religion as the root of all radical insurgency in Jacksonian America, the antebellum working-class insurgency is treated as if it were somehow different. See Charles G. Sellers, *The Market Revolution: Jacksonian America, 1815–1846* (New York: Oxford Univ. Press, 1991), chap. 9, esp. 284–85, passim. For what is probably a premature postmortem on republicanism, see Daniel T. Rodgers, "Republicanism: The Career of a Concept," *Journal of American History* 79 (June 1992): 11–38.

8. For some disparate examples, see James P. Hanlan, *The Working People of Manchester, New Hampshire, 1840–1886* (Ann Arbor: UMI Research Press, 1981), 63; William S. Pretzer, "'The British, Duff Green, the Rats and the Devil': Custom, Capitalism, and Conflict in the Washington Printing Trade, 1834–36," *Labor History* 27 (winter 1985–86): 6, 8–9, 23–26, 28; Christopher Clark, *The Roots of Rural Capitalism: Western Massachusetts, 1780–1860* (Ithaca: Cornell Univ. Press, 1990), 206; David G. Hackett, *The Rude Hand of Innovation: Religion and Social Order in Albany, New York, 1652–1836* (New York: Oxford Univ. Press, 1991), 148–52. Ironically, a recent review of the crisis in the writing of labor history analogizes its current condition to religious history itself: "an outmoded subdiscipline consigned, if not to the rubbish bin of history, then at least to the laws of nature wastage so far as staff replenishment [is] concerned" (Verity Bergmann, "The Strange Death of Labour History," in Bob Carr et al., *Bede Nairn and Labour History* [Sydney, 1991], quoted in Marcel van der Linden, intro. to "The End of Labour History?" *International Review of Social History* [Supplement 1] 38 [1993]: 1).

9. Katherine Paterson, *Lyddie* (New York: Penguin, 1991), 5–6, 57–58, 69, 80, 84–85, 90–93. Betsey, a cynic not involved in the labor protests of the age, does exclaim at one point, "Against the Bible to fight injustice? Oh, come now, Amelia, I think you've got the wrong book at that church of yours" (93).

10. Ware, *Industrial Worker,* 157; Ten-Hour Convention, "The Hours of Labor," *Address of the Ten-Hour Convention* (Boston, 1852).

11. Hannah Josephson, *The Golden Threads: New England's Mill Girls and Magnates* (New York: Russell & Russell, 1949), 269; *Voice,* 23 Jan. 1846. The language here echoes the favorite slogan of French utopian socialist Etienne Cabet, a contemporary: "Communism is Christianity in its original purity" (Christopher H. Johnson, "Communism and the Working Class before Marx: The Icarian Experience," *American Historical Review* 76 [June 1971]: 669).

12. Before the 1980s, a partial exception is Paul Faler's *Mechanics and Manufacturers in the Early Industrial Revolution: Lynn, Massachusetts, 1780–1860* (Albany: State Univ. of New York Press, 1981), based largely on his 1971 dissertation ("Workingmen, Mechanics and Social Change: Lynn, Massachusetts, 1800–60" [Ph.D. diss., Univ. of Wisconsin, 1971]). In the book, Faler argues that the Lynn shoemakers were drawn to Methodism because of its democratic style and doctrine. Still, he insists that Christianity played a minor role in the ideology of most labor activists in Lynn, relative to republicanism and especially when compared to later activists. "Unlike native-born American workingmen of the post–Civil War period who used Scriptures to comprehend what was happening to them," he writes, "the Lynn journeymen used the secular tradition of the Revolution. They occasionally used quotations from the Bible, but their world view and sense of history were not those of the evangelical Protestant" (*Mechanics and Manufacturers,* 46–48, 185). Faler's reference to the later period derives from the work of Herbert Gutman, noted below (n. 23). Mary Blewitt mistakes Faler's discussion of Methodism and the new industrial morality in Lynn as an "argument that evangelical religion in Lynn supported labor protest," an argument that he does not make (*Men, Women, and Work: Class, Gender, and Protest in the New England Shoe Industry,*

1780–1910 [Urbana: Univ. of Illinois Press, 1988], 367, n. 35). More positive than Faler's is Mike Davis's assessment in his 1980 overview of the American labor movement ("Why the U.S. Working Class is Different," *New Left Review*, no. 123 [Sept.–Oct. 1980]: 20): "Like the analogous English Methodism, evangelical religion could be a two-edged sword, and working men could appropriate its egalitarian side to advocate good, Protestant justifications for trade unionism, and the Ten Hour Day." Davis offers no evidence for the claim; his view may reflect his closeness to the European historiography, also discussed below (n. 22). See, too, Roediger's brief remarks on the ways "revivalist religion . . . came also to be part of the arsenal of the ten hour movement" in pre–Civil War America, in "The Movement for a Shorter Working Day in the United States Before 1866" (Ph.D. diss., Northwestern Univ., 1980).

13. *Artisans into Workers*, 95. The 1846 "Declaration of Independence" emerged from correspondence between the Lowell FLRA and mill women in Pittsburgh who had unsuccessfully struck for the shorter workday the previous September. The planning began in the fall of 1845 and was formally proposed at a meeting in Manchester, N.H., in late December by a recent immigrant from Scotland, ex-Chartist and itinerant labor agitator John Campbell Cluer. Josephson calls the idea a "feeble device" (*Golden Threads*, 267); Ware refers to it as a proposed "general strike" (*Industrial Worker*, 139–42). For reasons that are not entirely clear, the strike never materialized. It is true, as historians have pointed out, that the Lowell mill women and others in the New England labor movement of the 1840s appear to have been less willing to strike than earlier in the period, and, as discussed in chap. 11, their religion undoubtedly played some role in engendering that reluctance. At the same time, the FLRA constitution (art. 9) did not disavow strikes; indeed, it insisted on any means necessary once moral suasion had been tried ("The members of this Association disapprove of all hostile measures, strikes and turn outs until all pacific measures prove abortive, and then that it is the imperious duty of every one to assert to maintain that independence which our brave ancestors bequeathed us, and sealed with their blood," *Voice*, 27 Feb. 1846). Moreover, the militancy exhibited by some self-consciously Christian workers throughout the period suggests that we need a more nuanced picture of religion's radical potential during these years. For more on Cluer (also McCluer, McClure), a temperance and antislavery as well as labor reformer, see ibid., 30 Jan. 1846; *Herald*, 7 Feb. 1849; *South Boston Gazette*, 6 Jan. 1849; 22, 29 Nov., 6 Dec. 1851; *WMA*, 24 Aug. 1844.

14. Paul Johnson, *A Shopkeeper's Millennium: Society and Revivals in Rochester, New York, 1815–1837* (New York: Hill & Wang, 1978).

15. Ibid., 202, n. 4. Here Johnson cites three works from the early 1970s: Paul Faler's "Cultural Aspects of the Industrial Revolution: Lynn, Massachusetts Shoemakers and Industrial Morality, 1826–1860," *Labor History* 15 (summer 1974): 367–94; Bruce Laurie's "Nothing on Compulsion: Life Styles of Philadelphia Artisans, 1820–1860," *Labor History* 15 (summer 1974): 337–66; and David Montgomery's "The Shuttle and the Cross: Weavers and Artisans in the Kensington Riots of 1844," *Journal of Social History* 5 (summer 1972): 411–46. But, on the question of "helplessness" and the turn inward, he might also have cited John R. Commons et al., *History of Labour in the United States* (orig. publ., 1918; repr. ed., New York: Augustus M. Kelley, 1966), vol. 1, part 3, chap. 6.

16. Faler, *Mechanics and Manufacturers*; idem and Alan Dawley, "Working Class Culture and Politics in the Industrial Revolution," *Journal of Social History* (June 1976): 466–80; Laurie, *Working People of Philadelphia, 1800–1850* (Philadelphia: Temple Univ. Press, 1980), esp. part 2.

17. Johnson, *Shopkeeper's Millennium*, 6. Interestingly enough, even those critical of Johnson's lack of attention to worker agency here have missed this possibility. Instead, they suggest, for example, that Johnson and others "overstress the imposition of more rigorous morality on workers, *scanting their own willing embrace of it*" (James Turner, *Without God, Without Creed: The Origins of Unbelief in America* [Baltimore: Johns Hopkins Univ. Press, 1985], 287, n. 16 [emphasis added]). A more recent account of how middle-class manufacturers allegedly used religion to impose new industrial work values on a pliant work force, though again without giving much attention to the workers' side of the story, can be found in Judith A. McGaw, *Most Wonderful*

Machine: Mechanization and Social Change in Berkshire Paper Making, 1801–1885 (Princeton: Princeton Univ. Press, 1987), 60, 81–88, 256–75, 377–80. For sources on the "social control" argument, see chap. 7, n. 4, 5.

18. Anthony F. C. Wallace, *Rockdale: The Growth of an American Village in the Early Industrial Revolution* (New York: Knopf, 1978), parts 3, 4, esp. 367, 372–373.

19. Montgomery, "Shuttle and the Cross." On religion as a unifying force among manufacturers and a divisive force among workers, see John B. Jentz, "Industrialization and Class Formation in Antebellum America: A Review of Recent Case Studies," *Amerikastudien* 30 (1985): 303–25.

20. Laurie, *Working People,* chaps. 4–6, 140–47, 168–77. Sean Wilentz's work on the New York City working class during the same period (*Chants Democratic: New York City & the Rise of the American Working Class* [New York: Oxford Univ. Press, 1984]), while paying less attention to religion, exhibits the same virtues and liabilities as Laurie's book. On the use of Johnson's work among these historians, see ibid., 277–81; Laurie, *Working People,* chap. 2, esp. 50–52. In her study of working women in New York City during this period, Christine Stansell finds revivalism the religion of the rising commercial and industrial bourgeoisie, Jeffersonian and Paineite "freethought" the language of the literate journeymen, and little trace of Christian invocation or exhortation among either male or female unionists before 1845 (*City of Women: Sex and Class in New York, 1789–1860* [New York: Oxford Univ. Press, 1986], 66–67).

21. Melvin Dubofsky seems to follow the same dichotomizing in his recent short overview, "The Origins of the Labor Movement in the United States: Themes from the Nineteenth Century," *Pennsylvania History* 58 (1991): 273. Meanwhile, consumers of labor history working in other fields have little else to work with. For one such example, see Eric Lott, *Love and Theft: Blackface Minstrelsy and the American Working Class* (New York: Oxford Univ. Press, 1993), 130–31, chaps. 5, 6.

22. Although Britain has been more the exception than the rule—until recently. For a discussion of the German case, with remarks on religion and working-class formation generally, see Willfried Spohn, "Religion and Working-Class Formation in Imperial Germany 1871–1914," *Politics & Society* 19 (March 1991): 109–32. In England, arguments concerning Methodism's role in hindering or promoting social protest date from the period itself. Among historians, the place to begin is Elie Halévy, *A History of the English People in the Nineteenth Century—I: England in 1815,* E. I. Watkin and D. A. Barker, trans. (orig. publ., 1913; 2nd rev. ed., London: E. Benn, 1961), part 2; J. L. and Barbara Hammond, *The Town Laborer, 1760–1832: The New Civilization* (New York: Longmans, Green, 1925); Robert F. Wearmouth, *Methodism and the Working Class Movements of England, 1800–50* (1937). During the 1950s and 1960s, E. J. Hobsbawm and E. P. Thompson exyended the discussion onto the broader terrain of religion and class formation. See Hobsbawm, "Methodism and the Threat of Revolution in Britain" and "Labour Traditions," in *Labouring Men: Studies in the History of Labour* (New York: Basic Books, 1964), 23–33, 371–85; idem, "The Labour Sects," in *Primitive Rebels: Studies in Archaic Forms of Social Movements in the Nineteenth and Twentieth Centuries* (orig. publ., 1959; repr. ed., New York: W. W. Norton, 1965), 126–49; E. P. Thompson, *The Making of the English Working Class* (New York: Pantheon, 1963), esp. chap. 11. Hobsbawm's and especially Thompson's views on religion's radical potential and limitations have been subjected to widely varying interpretations, and ultimately both resist categorization as either entirely "positive" or "negative" readings of religion's historical role. For some interesting remarks on the debate generally, see Hugh McLeod, *Religion and the Working Class in Nineteenth-Century Britain* (London: Macmillan, 1984), 22–24, 49–52. For a recent argument that stresses religion-as-opium in both English and American labor historiography, see B. H. Moss, "Republican Socialism and the Making of the Working Class in Britain, France, and the United States: A Critique of Thompsonian Culturalism," *Comparative Studies in Society and History* 35 (April 1993): 396, 398–401, 412.

23. Herbert G. Gutman, "Protestantism and the American Labor Movement: The Christian Spirit in the Gilded Age," *American Historical Review* 72 (Oct. 1966): 73–74.

24. Louis Hartz, "Seth Luther: The Story of a Working Class Rebel," *New England Quarterly* 13

(Sept. 1940): 402, 413–15. Arthur Schlesinger, Jr., though stressing ways the forces of religion were aligned against labor in Jacksonian America, also recognized that even in this age "Christianity was, potentially, the most radical of all faiths" (*The Age of Jackson* [Boston: Little, Brown, 1945], 359). Indeed, even if we eventually conclude that religion was a yoke around the neck of the early American working class, its lower-class (and rebellious) origins should not be difficult to discern. As one observer noted over forty years ago, "In religion as in politics, an idea which is to disarm discontents must at some time, in some sense, have seemed both to friend and foe an idea of rebellion. We are only held securely by fetters we have helped to forge ourselves; no one else can tell the exact fit of our wrists and ankles" (V. Kiernan, "Evangelicalism and the French Revolution," *Past and Present* 1 [Feb. 1952]: 45).

25. For provocative remarks on the reluctance of American intellectuals to take religion seriously, see Gary Wills, *Under God: Religion and American Politics* (New York: Simon and Schuster, 1990), esp. 15–16.

26. Ware, for example, was not a Marxist but knew his writings and was sympathetic to him as a social critic, a recent biographical sketch asserts. See Thomas Dublin's intro. to a new edition of Ware's *Industrial Worker* (Chicago: Ivan R. Dee, 1990), vii.

27. In the last twenty years, liberation theology and Islamic revivalism, for example, have dramatically heightened contemporary awareness of religion's radical, indeed revolutionary, potential. For an introduction, see the essays in "Religion and the Left" (special issue), *Monthly Review: An Independent Socialist Magazine* 3 (July–Aug. 1984); Lonnie Kliever, ed., *The Terrible Meek: Essays on Religion and Revolution* (New York: Paragon House, 1987); Bruce Lincoln, ed., *Religion, Rebellion, Revolution: An Interdisciplinary and Cross-Cultural Collection of Essays* (New York: St. Martin's Press, 1985). See, too, Guenter Lewy, *Religion and Revolution* (New York: Oxford Univ. Press, 1974). Marx's views on religion were much more complex than one might assume from the oft-quoted "opium" phrase. See Louis Dupré, "Religion as Alienation, Ideology and Utopia in Marx" (unpubl. paper, n.d., in possession of the author). For the phrase in context, see Marx, intro., *A Contribution to the Critique of Hegel's "Philosophy of Right,"* Annette Jolin and Joseph O'Malley, trans., Joseph O'Malley, ed. (New York: Cambridge Univ. Press, 1970). For an example of what he was talking about—"*religious* suffering is at the same time an *expression* of real suffering and a *protest* against real suffering"—see Teresa Anne Murphy, *Ten Hours' Labor: Religion, Reform, and Gender in Early New England* (Ithaca: Cornell Univ. Press, 1992), chap. 4. See too, Karl Marx and Friedrich Engels, *On Religion* (New York: Schocken Books, 1964). Note, though, Eric Hobsbawm's comment that while the "ambiguity of Christian teaching is not beyond the power of suitable exegesis or casuistry to spirit away . . . it remains an obstacle to the construction of a consistently social-revolutionary doctrine" ("Labour Sects," 148–49).

28. Dublin, intro., *Industrial Worker*, viii–ix.

29. The latter are allegedly distinguishable from the former by their personal characteristics (occupation, wealth, education, standing in the community, etc.) and/or their beliefs. On the problems with this dichotomizing, see part 2 below.

30. The locus classicus of the worker–reformer dichotomy can be found in succinct form in Commons's *History of Labour* 1:18–19. For citations on the 1820s and early 1830s, see chap. 5, n. 10. On the 1840s, see ibid., esp. 537–39; Charles E. Persons, "The Early History of Factory Legislation in Massachusetts," in S. M. Kingsbury, ed., *Labor Laws and Their Enforcement* (New York: Logmans, 1911), 32–35; Helene S. Zahler, *Eastern Workingmen and National Land Policy, 1829–1862* (New York: Columbia Univ. Press, 1941), 61–63; Philip S. Foner, *History of the Labor Movement in the United States* (New York: International, 1947) 1:202–07; Josephson, *Golden Threads,* 263–65. In Ware's influential account of the 1840s (*Industrial Worker*, chap. 14), for example, middle-class reformers (mainly communitarians and land reformers) vied for control of the NEWA with worker representatives who sought shorter hours, higher wages, and workers' cooperatives. Here, the former spoke for a harmony-of-interests and universal reform, while the latter were militant and *pragmatic.* The problem is, as historians of both reform and labor have now shown, the overlap in both personnel and ideology was simply too great to make such

distinctions in most cases. For an alternative view, from someone in a position to know, see George E. McNeill, ed., *The Labor Movement: The Problem of Today* (orig. publ., 1887; repr. ed., New York: Augustus M. Kelley, 1966), 91. Also, Dawley, *Class and Community,* chap. 2; Early, "Reappraisal of the New-England Labour-Reform Movement"; Philip Foner and David Roediger, *Our Own Time: A History of American Labor and the Working Day* (Westport, Conn.: Greenwood Press, 1989), 62–63; Carl J. Guarneri, *The Utopian Alternative: Fourierism in Nineteenth-Century America* (Ithaca: Cornell Univ. Press, 1991), chap. 11.

31. The problem has affected the way historians of the middle class have written the history of this period as well. Thus, for example, Jonathan Glickstein (*Concepts of Free Labor in Antebellum America* [New Haven: Yale Univ. Press, 1991]) remarks that "some if not most of the spokesmen of the mid-nineteenth century labor organizations to which skilled wage-earners belonged had dubious worker credentials or backgrounds; they were often either disgruntled master craftsmen or radicals of even more undisputed middle-class status" (297). At one point, he goes beyond even this, declaring that those "who may have been of undisputed working-class background" were in fact atypical [of, presumably the "real" workers] "the moment they took up a pen" (493).

32. The literature here is enormous. Sample Perry Miller, *The Life of the Mind in America From the Revolution to the Civil War* (New York: Harcourt, Brace and World, 1966); Sidney E. Ahlstrom, *A Religious History of the American People* (Garden City, N.Y.: Doubleday, 1975), vol. 1, part 4; William G. McLoughlin, *Revivals, Awakenings, and Reform: An Essay on Religion and Social Change in America, 1607–1977* (Chicago: Univ. of Chicago Press, 1978), chap. 4; Randolph A. Roth, *The Democratic Dilemma: Religion, Reform, and the Social Order in the Connecticut Valley of Vermont, 1791–1850* (New York: Cambridge Univ. Press, 1987); Gordon S. Wood, *The Radicalism of the American Revolution* (New York: Knopf, 1992), 330–32; Joel H. Silbey, *The Partisan Imperative: The Dynamics of American Politics Before the Civil War* (New York: Oxford Univ. Press, 1985); Ernest Lee Tuveson, *Redeemer Nation: The Idea of America's Millennial Role* (Chicago: Univ. of Chicago Press, 1968). For a recent overview insisting on the widespread influence of evangelical Protestantism on antebellum society, see Curtis D. Johnson, *Redeeming America: Evangelicals and the Road to Civil War* (Chicago: Ivan R. Dee, 1993). Cf. Jon Butler, "Born-Again History?" (unpubl. paper, 1992, in possession of author).

33. William G. McLoughlin, "Pietism and the American Character," *American Quarterly* 17 (summer 1965): 163–86.

34. For a fuller discussion of these religious doctrines in American Protestantism, see chap. 1.

35. On the "democratic" thrust of nineteenth-century evangelical Protestantism generally, see Nathan O. Hatch, *The Democratization of American Christianity* (New Haven: Yale Univ. Press, 1989).

36. Despite numerous cross-currents, ambiguities, and complexities, antebellum protest is not comprehensible apart from the powerful influence of evangelical Protestantism. Again, the literature is enormous. See Ronald G. Walters, *American Reformers: 1815–1860* (New York: Hill & Wang, 1978); Whitney R. Cross, *The Burned-Over District: The Social and Intellectual History of Enthusiastic Religion in Western New York, 1800–1850* (Ithaca: Cornell Univ. Press, 1950); Ian R. Tyrrell, *Sobering Up: From Temperance to Prohibition in Antebellum America, 1800–1860* (1979); Valarie H. Ziegler, *The Advocates of Peace in Antebellum America* (Bloomington: Indiana Univ. Press, 1992); Nancy Hewitt, *Women's Activism and Social Change: Rochester, New York, 1822–1872* (Ithaca: Cornell Univ. Press, 1984); Stephen Nissenbaum, *Sex, Diet, and Debility in Jacksonian America: Sylvester Graham and Health Reform* (Westport: Greenwood Press, 1980); Guarneri, *Utopian Alternative;* Christine Bolt and Seymour Drescher, eds., *Anti-Slavery, Religion, and Reform: Essays in Memory of Roger Amstey* (Hamden, Conn.: Archon Books, 1980).

37. Albert Raboteau, *Slave Religion: The "Invisible Institution" in the Antebellum South* (New York: Oxford Univ. Press, 1978); Eugene Genovese, *Roll, Jordan, Roll: The World the Slaves Made* (New York: Knopf, 1974), part 4. See, too, David Walker, *David Walker's Appeal,* Charles M. Wiltse, ed., 3rd ed. (Boston, 1930; New York: Hill & Wang, 1965).

38. Tuveson, *Redeemer Nation,* 59.

230   NOTES: INTRODUCTION

39. Jeremy Rifkin with Ted Howard, *The Emerging Order: God in the Age of Scarcity* (New York: G. P. Putnam, 1979), 128 (my emphasis).

40. For evidence buried in recent scholarship, see Gary Kulik, "Pawtucket Village and the Strike of 1824," *Radical History Review* 17 (spring 1978): 17; Jonathan Prude, *The Coming of Industrial Order: Town and Factory Life in Rural Massachusetts, 1810–1860* (New York: Cambridge Univ. Press, 1983), 154; Cynthia Shelton, *The Mills of Manayunk: Industrialization and Social Conflict in the Philadelphia Region, 1787–1837* (Baltimore: Johns Hopkins Univ. Press, 1986), 128–33, 137, 150, 153, 158–62. For scholarship more directly related to this issue, see Lazerow, "Spokesmen for the Working Class: Protestant Clergy and the Labor Movement in Antebellum New England," *Journal of the Early Republic* 13 (fall 1993): 323–54; idem, "Religion and the New England Mill Girl: A New Perspective on an Old Theme," *New England Quarterly* 60 (Sept. 1987): 429–53; idem, "Religion and Labor Reform: The World of William Field Young," *American Quarterly* 38 (summer 1986): 265–86; Murphy, *Ten Hours' Labor;* idem, "Work, Leisure, and Moral Reform: The Ten Hour Movement in New England, 1830–1850," in Gary Cross, ed., *Worktime and Industrialization: An International History* (Philadelphia: Temple Univ. Press, 1988), 59–76; idem, "Religious Authority and Labor Protest Among Antebellum Working People" (unpubl. paper, 1986, in possession of author); Mark S. Schantz, "Piety in Providence: The Class Dimensions of Religious Experience in Providence, Rhode Island, 1790–1860" (Ph.D. diss., Emory Univ., 1991); idem, "Religious Rhetoric and Resistance to Industrialization: New York City's *Working Man's Advocate,* 1829–1845" (unpubl. paper, 1984, in possession of the author); Gregory L. Kaster, "'We will not be slaves to avarice': The American Labor Jeremiad, 1827–1877" (Ph.D. diss., Boston Univ., 1990); idem, "'Not for a Class?' The Nineteenth-Century American Labor Jeremiad," *Mid-America* 70 (Oct. 1988): 125–39. For a similar line of argument on the post-Revolutionary era, though based on rather thin evidence and narrowly focused on rationalist currents, see Ronald Schultz, "God and Workingmen: Popular Religion and the Formation of Philadelphia's Working Class, 1790–1830," in Ronald Hoffman and Peter J. Albert, eds., *Religion in a Revolutionary Age* (Charlottesville: Univ. Press of Virginia, 1994), 125–155.

41. Murphy, *Ten Hours' Labor,* argues that this was a distinctly New England phenomenon, and muted before the 1840s. Others, like Bruce Laurie in his Philadelphia study, have contrasted the "rationalism" of the 1830s with the "revivalism" of the 1840s, while also noting the peculiarities of New England. To be sure, geography and time made a difference, as discussed below, but what we glimpse in groups like the NELRL was part of a national antebellum pattern. On the ubiquity of religious rhetoric, see, for example, Schantz ("Religious Rhetoric and Resistance") and Kaster ("'We will not be slaves to avarice'").

42. There are many ways to define *evangelicalism,* though spiritual rebirth through a conversion experience distinguished it. In suggesting that evangelicalism powerfully influenced antebellum labor radicalism, I have employed the term loosely to denote a religious style—as opposed to any particular theological tendency—a style that affected virtually all denominations of this period. See, for example, Ann C. Rose's remarks on the Unitarians in her *Transcendentalism as a Social Movement, 1830–1850* (New Haven: Yale Univ. Press, 1981), esp. chap. 1. Clearly, the labor language of this period was evangelical in that its critique was filled with the imagery of sin (immorality, irreligion, political turmoil, strife, decay) and its vision was of a "good time coming." Moreover, the emphasis on free moral agency, a strict moral code, and an imminent millennium typified antebellum labor reform, as it did the growing evangelical Protestant consensus of antebellum America. There is, in fact, a body of scholarship dealing explicitly with precisely how to define *evangelicalism.* See Donald W. Dayton and Robert K. Johnston, eds., *The Variety of American Evangelicalism* (Nashville: Univ. of Tennessee Press, 1991). For a typology of evangelicalism—rooted in class determinants, though without reference to labor activism—see Johnson, *Redeeming America,* passim.

43. According to Murphy, it also facilitated women workers' access to the labor movement in a way that working-class republicanism, with its masculine characteristics, could not; once in, she argues, they challenged and reshaped gender boundaries (*Ten Hours' Labor,* esp. chap. 8). For a

model, see Blewitt, *Men, Women, and Work*. Murphy suggests as well that many New England labor activists made their way into a movement for the shorter workday via a religio-moral dispute with their employers. The central class-based religious battle of the age, she says, was over the meaning and uses of "free moral agency," the very heart of early-nineteenth-century evangelicalism. When employers defended longer hours of labor, for example, on the moral and paternalistic grounds that workers would turn to vice if they had too much free time, while at the same time promoting a new theology that stressed individual conscience and internal rather than external restraints, they inadvertently undermined their own authority and control, she argues. For labor activists then launched their own moral reform movement around the ten-hour day, insisting that they control the amount of time they worked, in order that they be able to fulfill God's design, as they interpreted it. See, too, her "Work, Leisure and Moral Reform."

44. Tuveson makes a similar point about the impact of millennialism on American foreign policy (*Redeemer Nation*, 213).

45. Murphy also argues for religion's differential impact on women and men, and among New England communities (*Ten Hours' Labor*, chaps. 6–8, esp. 141–42, 173–74, 210–12); though the distinctions are sometimes strained and the causal relationships sometimes unconvincing, the speculations are provocative.

46. See part 3.

47. Murphy traces the noncoercive aspects of New England labor radicalism to these workers' Arminianism, to their need to demonstrate choice in human behavior (*Ten Hours' Labor*, chap. 6, and esp., "Religious Authority and Labor Protest"). But struggle, and even violence, were not precluded by evangelical Christianity; they were simply deemphasized in many instances. In fact, as discussed in chap. 11 below, religion was sometimes used by antebellum activists to justify militant action. For a modern example of Christianity's militant potential, see Huey P. Newton, "The Son of Man," *Radical Religion* 2 (1975): 68–72. In any case, as Eric Hobsbawm has pointed out ("Labour Traditions"), it is not violence that marks a movement as revolutionary, but the "political way" violence is used. The role of religion in social and political movements is clearly complex: witness the course of the Islamic political revolt in contemporary Jordan, or the divisions among Christians in the Salvadoran civil war of the 1980s, both of which suggest that it is not the religion but its use, by certain groups in particular historical circumstances, that explains its role.

48. For this phenomenon among American Protestants generally, see Tuveson, *Redeemer Nation*.

49. This view may be unduly harsh. For an alternative, which sees both universalist and class tendencies in antebellum labor language, see Kaster, "'We will not be slaves to avarice.'" Still, see Michael Jimenez's treatment of the liberation theologians in Latin America, whom he compares to the English Puritan radicals, spiritual ancestors of the antebellum laborites. Seeking better conditions and the defeat of one's oppressors is one thing, Jimenez notes, but a real program for winning is quite another when one's religion teaches that politics is about the dissolution of power, rather than the acquisition of it ("Citizens of the Kingdom: Toward a Social History of Radical Christianity in Latin America," *International Labor and Working Class History*, no. 34 [fall 1988]: 3–21).

50. Something similar might be said of the era's capitalists as well, but that subject is outside the purview of this study.

51. The attempt to do the latter can be seen in Laurie's use of my portrait of William Young to criticize Norman Ware's dichotomous view of the 1840s (i.e., middle-class reformers versus militant, class-conscious workers). Accepting Ware's claim that Young was the "real voice and spirit of the workers" in this period, I sought to show just how religious this working-class leader was, in order to demonstrate that, while his religion sometimes dampened militancy and limited class consciousness, it was a path to radicalism and labor protest. My point: working-class radicals, like middle-class reformers and the opponents of labor, could be deeply religious, too. In Laurie's hands, though, all this is reversed. According to Laurie, Ware was wrong, because Young was no more militant than the middle-class reformers! Filtered through Young's evangelical lens, as Laurie

tells it, the Industrial Revolution pitted light versus dark, not producer versus accumulator. And so, Young was not, in fact, representative of the putative militant, class-conscious worker; this ideal type thus remains a staple of the labor historiography. But, as I tried to point out, Young proves that the assumptions underpinning these "types" are all wrong. For this worker, as for so many others of these years, the battle of producer and accumulator *was* a battle of light and dark, because their radicalism was grounded in religious symbol, language, and rhetoric. See Laurie, *Artisans into Workers*, 94–95; Lazerow, "Religion and Labor Reform"; Ware, *Industrial Worker*, 22–23.

52. I have chosen to call this product "class consciousness," because, however ambivalent these workers were, no other term captures the essence of their worldview as well. All things associated with class are matters of fierce debate, of course; I take the same ground as Wilentz in his "Against Exceptionalism: Class Consciousness and the American Labor Movement, 1790–1920," *International Labor and Working Class History*, no. 26 (fall 1984): 5–6.

53. Kliever, *Terrible Meek*, xv.

54. Compare the work on religion and the working class in England, which has emerged from nearly a century of serious historical investigation, discussed in McLeod, *Religion and the Working Class*.

55. Indeed, the parallels with what Gutman found for the late nineteenth century are striking ("Protestantism and the Labor Movement").

56. What Alfred Young notes regarding the memory of Oliver Cromwell among American workers after the Revolution—"when we get a glimmer of it early in the nineteenth century, we seem to be in the presence of a much older cast of mind"—applies to their use of religious tradition as well. See "English Plebeian Culture and Eighteenth-Century American Radicalism," in Jacobs and Jacobs, *Origins of Anglo-American Radicalism*, 197.

57. Dubofsky suggests we should see the history of labor in the nineteenth century generally as a cyclical rather than a linear story, in "Origins of the Labor Movement," 270, 272, passim.

58. For a similar perspective on middle-class ideas about work in this period, see Glickstein, *Concepts of Free Labor*, esp. 21. See, too, David Zonderman's discussion of working-class ideas about the Industrial Revolution in *Aspirations and Anxieties: New England Workers and the Mechanized Factory System, 1815–1850* (New York: Oxford Univ. Press, 1992).

59. *Voice*, 23 Apr. 1847.

60. Ibid.

Chapter 1

1. The reader should note that the discussion in this chapter focuses on native-born activists, who were, until the late 1840s, the mainstay of both the leadership and rank-and-file of most American movements of labor protest.

2. And from this, as we shall see, came weapons of resistance. A newspaper captured the phenomenon in a description of a southern textile strike a hundred years later.

> The strikers today went back to the fundamentals which they brought with them from the mountains. . . . H. J. Crabtree, minister of the Church of God, prayed for divine guidance of the strike. As the old man prayed a group of strikers stood with bowed heads and as he came to the close fully a dozen joined in the "Amen."

(Baltimore) *Sun*, 29 Apr. 1929, quoted in Liston Pope, *Millhands and Preachers: A Study of Gastonia* (New Haven: Yale Univ. Press, 1942), 276.

3. The extent and nature of that piety is a matter of some dispute among religious historians of the eighteenth century. See Patricia U. Bonomi's review of Jon Butler's *Awash in a Sea of Faith: Christianizing the American People* (Cambridge: Harvard Univ. Press, 1990) in the *William and Mary Quarterly*, 3rd ser., 48 (Jan. 1991): 118–24. See also the Bonomi and Butler essays in Hoffman and Albert, *Religion in a Revolutionary Age*, the intro. to which remarks on the "rich variety and

enormous complexity of the role of religion in America's Revolutionary age" (xii). For general remarks, see Wood, *Radicalism*, 329–30. One aspect of the ongoing debate over religion and the Revolution is discussed in Ruth H. Bloch, "Religion and Ideological Change in the American Revolution," in *Religion and American Politics: From the Colonial Period to the 1980s*, Mark A. Noll, ed. (New York: Oxford Univ. Press, 1990), 44–61.

4. This was true in varying degrees, depending upon local and personal circumstances, more so in rural New England and in small towns and villages. But, this was a religious society, by any contemporary measure, with the most religious elements enjoying substantial influence over the culture at large. Particularly relevant to the study of antebellum labor activists is the fact that the curriculum of the nation's schools at the time of the Revolution was strongly permeated by religion ("worshipping God, according to His revealed will"), with most of the reading material written by rural New Englanders who evinced a distinct New England bias (Ruth Miller Elson, *Guardians of Tradition: American Schoolbooks in the Nineteenth Century* [Lincoln: Univ. of Nebraska, 1964], 5–7, 34–35, 45; Monica Kiefer, "War with the Devil," in *American Children Through Their Books, 1700–1835* [Philadelphia: Univ. of Pennsylvania Press, 1948]; Ahlstrom, *Religious History*, 1:169; David DeLeon, *The American as Anarchist: Reflections on Indigenous Radicalism* [Baltimore: Johns Hopkins Univ. Press, 1978]). For a different emphasis, see Jack P. Greene, *Pursuits of Happiness: The Social Development of Early Modern British Colonies and the Formation of American Culture* (Chapel Hill: Univ. of North Carolina Press, 1988).

5. Henry May, *The Enlightenment in America* (New York: Oxford Univ. Press, 1976). Tocqueville observed that in America the Enlightenment had not brought an end of religious zeal but rather the opposite (*Democracy in America*, J. P. Mayer, ed. [Garden City, N.Y.: Archor Books, 1969], 295). As a whole, in fact, the Enlightenment was really more about reforming religion than destroying it.

6. Outside the seaboard and particularly on the frontier, the key threat to orthodoxy was indifference, not Enlightenment ideas. See Turner, *Without God, Without Creed*, 74. Also, Butler's discussion of religious indifference in "Coercion, Miracle, Reason: Rethinking the American Religious Experience in the Revolutionary Age," in Hoffman and Albert, *Religion in a Revolutionary Age*, 18–20, in which he emphasizes church membership.

7. The latest general study is Ruth H. Bloch's *Visionary Republic: Millennial Themes in American Thought, 1756–1800* (New York: Cambridge Univ. Press, 1985), but see, too, Tuveson's older but brilliant study, *Redeemer Nation*, esp. chap. 4. Nathan Hatch argues that in the aftermath of the Revolutionary era, ordinary Americans began addressing the apocalyptic themes that in the eighteenth century were really the province of rational "gentlemen and scholars" (*Democratization of American Christianity*, 184). On the origins of America's "civil religion," which blended Puritan and Enlightenment themes, see Catherine Albanese, *Sons of the Fathers: The Civil Religion of the American Revolution* (Philadelphia: Temple Univ. Press, 1976).

8. Turner, *Without God, Without Creed*, 42. Tuveson argues that the idea of progress expressed here was in fact religious in origin and bears little resemblance to the secular notion that became dominant only in the nineteenth century. Whatever the sources of the idea, though, the concept of human betterment, for those born at the end of the eighteenth century, came wrapped in religious garb. The millennial mode of thought also blended easily with republicanism in this period. See Eric Foner, *Tom Paine and Revolutionary America* (New York: Oxford Univ. Press, 1976), chaps. 3, 4; James T. Kloppenberg, "The Virtues of Liberalism: Christianity, Republicanism, and Ethics in Early American Political Discourse," *Journal of American History* 74 (June 1987): 9–33.

9. Wills, *Under God*, part 8.

10. G. Adolph Koch, *Republican Religion: The American Revolution and the Cult of Reason* (New York: Henry Holt, 1933); Herbert M. Morais, *Deism in Eighteenth Century America* (New York: Columbia Univ. Press, 1934); Kerry S. Walters, intro., *The American Deists: Voices of Reason and Dissent in the Early Republic* (Lawrence: Univ. Press of Kansas, 1992), esp. 26–32.

11. Stanley Johannesen, "American Republicanism and Christian Piety," in Kliever, *Terrible Meek*, 15–17. Nor should one entirely discount the possible significance of the drafters of the

Constitution dating that document, "in the year of our Lord one thousand seven hundred and eighty-seven," though they excluded the Deity from the document itself. During the 1820s, advocates of a ban on Sunday mails pointed to this phrase as evidence of the Christian nature of the founding. See James R. Rohrer, "Sunday Mails and the Church–State Theme in Jacksonian America," *Journal of the Early Republic* (spring 1987): 53–76. Consider, too, a modern-day calculated use of such religious language: the deliberate Christianizing of America's first landing on the moon. As a Nixon speechwriter in 1969, William Safire, along with other White House aides, wrote the words for the sign to be left on the moon by the Apollo astronauts, deliberately *though surreptitiously* inserting religion in the message. "July 1969 A.D.," the *New York Times* columnist wrote later, "was a shrewd way of sneaking God in: the use of the initials for *Anno Domini*, in the year of our Lord, would tell space travelers eons hence that earthlings in 1969 had a religious bent." For good measure, they also made sure that copies of both the Old and New Testaments were included in the cargo. See "Of Nixon, Kennedy and Shooting the Moon," *New York Times,* 17 July 1989. As we shall see below, first-generation Americans did not keep God out of their state constitutions. Alternatively, it has been argued, the fact that the founders "dissembled their unbelief" is itself evidence of the power of religion in American society (John M. Robertson, *A History of Freethought in the Nineteenth Century* (orig. publ., 1929; London: Dawsons of Pall Mall, 1969) 1:378–79. Hamilton was alleged to have said that the founders simply "forgot" to include God in the Constitution. Perhaps it is a measure of the relative power of religion in Revolutionary America that whereas Safire had to sneak religion into the moon landing in 1969, the founders had to justify excluding it. For Hamilton's remark, see Wood, *Radicalism,* 330. On religion at the state versus national level, see Butler, "Coercion, Miracle, Reason."

12. The term *stripped down* Christianity is Turner's (*Without God, Without Creed*, xi–xii, 42–52). For the range of religious belief subsumed under the deist label, see Gordon Stein, ed., *The Encyclopedia of Unbelief* (Buffalo: Prometheus Books, 1985) 1:134–37.

13. Paine, much revered by some antebellum labor activists, did reject Christianity, which he condemned as "more derogatory to the Almighty, more unedifying to man, more repugnant to reason, and more contradictory in itself" than any other religion. But he did not reject religion, much less God. He wrote his famous anticlerical tract, *The Age of Reason* (the "deist's Bible"), in order to stem the tide of atheism, "lest in the wreck of superstition, of false systems of government and false theology, we lose sight of morality, of humanity, and of the theology that is true" (Foner, *Tom Paine,* 116–17, 245–47, 252; Robertson, *History of Freethought,* 1:377).

14. In addition to the works cited in n. 10, see Albert Post, *Popular Freethought in America, 1825–1850* (New York: Columbia Univ. Press, 1943). Walters argues for a significant deist presence at the turn of the century in *American Deists.* On schoolbooks, see Elson, *Guardians of Tradition,* 44.

15. Martin Marty, *The Infidel: Freethought and American Religion* (Cleveland, Ohio, and New York: Meridian Books, World Publishing, 1961), 194. These attacks sometimes had the effect of pushing unorthodox leaders—Thomas Jefferson, for example—closer to the religion of Jesus (Wills, *Under God,* 357).

16. Post, *Popular Freethought,* chap. 1. As Foner remarks (*Tom Paine,* 256–57), Revolutionary hero Paine fell out of favor in America in the 1790s not, as one might expect, because of his vociferous republican diatribes against the immensely popular George Washington, but because of his attacks on organized Christianity in *The Age of Reason.* Foner also points out that, in general, the nineteenth-century labor movement preferred Jefferson to Paine, because the former was less tainted with anticlericalism than the latter.

17. Perhaps, increasingly so. See B. Edward McClellan, *Schools and the Shaping of Character: Moral Education in America, 1607–Present* (Bloomington: ERIC Clearinghouse for Social Studies/Social Science Education and the Social Studies Development Center, Indiana Univ., 1992), chap. 2. Given the fragmentary nature of the sources that detail the precise nature of the religious culture into which individual antebellum activists were born, here I have attempted a composite sketch drawn from a range of materials about everyday religious life.

18. R. Freeman Butts and Lawrence A. Cremin, *A History of Education in American Culture* (New York: Holt, Rinehart and Winston, 1953), 237. This was particularly true in rural New England, from which came most early labor activists of that region. See Joseph F. Kett, "Growing Up in Rural New England, 1800–1840," in Tamara K. Haraven, ed., *Anonymous Americans: Explorations in Nineteenth Century Social History,* (Englewood Cliffs, N.J.: Prentice Hall, 1971), 3–5; idem, *Rites of Passage: Adolescence in America, 1790 to the Present* (New York: Basic Books, 1977), chap. 3. Most of the retrospectives Kett examined for the late eighteenth and early nineteenth centuries placed religion at the center of childhood experience.

19. Aramantha, "The Last Evening at Home," *Lowell Offering* 4 (Feb. 1844): 78. The profound reverence for "home" is clear in the writings of dissident operatives as well; e.g., Amelia, "Some of the Beauties of Our Factory System—Otherwise, Lowell Slavery," *Factory Tracts,* no. 1 (Oct. 1845). (*Factory Tracts* was published by the Lowell FLRA.)

20. Butts and Cremin, *History of Education,* 238.

21. Joseph Packard, *Recollections of a Long Life* (Washington, D.C.: B. S. Adams, 1902), 10–31 (emphasis in original).

22. The practice was later carried forward by voluntary societies. Earlier, the government of colonial Massachusetts had sent out inspectors to make sure each family owned a Bible and that each child knew the catechism (David D. Hall, "Introduction: The Uses of Literacy in New England, 1600–1850," in William L. Joyce et al., eds., *Printing and Society in Early America* [Worcester: American Antiquarian Society, 1983], 26). On Connecticut, see Benjamin Trumbull, *A Complete History of Connecticut* 1:238, 240–42, cited in Richard D. Shiels, "The Feminization of American Congregationalism, 1730–1835," *American Quarterly* 33 (spring 1981): 58–59.

23. William J. Gilmore, *Reading Becomes a Necessity of Life: Material and Cultural Life in Rural New England, 1780–1835* (Nashville: Univ. of Tennessee Press, 1989), 27, 257. Gilmore's remarkable study draws on materials from several Vermont and New Hampshire counties in the upper Connecticut River Valley, but he makes a convincing case for its representativeness in the rural Northeast as a whole during the period.

24. Kiefer (*American Children Through Their Books,* 50–51), in her study on children's books in early America, quotes a popular contemporary verse in this regard.

> That sacred book inspir'd by God,
> In our own tongue is spread abroad;
> That book may little children read,
> And learn the knowledge which they need.

25. Diary of Sarah Snell Bryant, 3 Feb., 20, 28 Mar., 12 Apr. 1796, cited in Mary Beth Norton, *Liberty's Daughters: The Revolutionary Experience of American Women, 1750–1800* (Boston: Little, Brown, 1980), 258.

26. Lucy Larcom, *A New England Girlhood* (orig. publ., 1889; repr. ed., Gloucester, Mass.: Peter Smith, 1973), 150.

27. Ibid., 44. The Boston newspaper editor Joseph Buckingham, born and raised in the Connecticut countryside in the late eighteenth century, learned to read in the same manner. See *Personal Memoirs and Recollections of Editorial Life,* quoted in Hall, "Uses of Literacy," 22–23.

28. Gilmore, *Reading Becomes a Necessity of Life,* 259, 261. This is how Buckingham described the "library" of his childhood home: "The Bible and Dr. Watt's Psalms and Hymns were indispensable in every family, and ours was not without them. There were, also on the 'book shelf,' a volume or two of Sermons, Doddridge's 'Rise and Progress of Religion,' and a very few other books and pamphlets, chiefly of a religious character." Buckingham, *Personal Memoirs,* quoted in Hall, "Uses of Literacy," 1. The boyhood home of William Miller, titular head of a premillennialist mass movement during the 1840s, contained just three books: the Bible, a hymnal, and a prayer book (Johnson, *Redeeming America,* 167). On the importance of religious materials, such as catechisms, psalmbooks, and primers, but especially the Bible, in the acquisition of literacy in late-eighteenth-century America, see ibid., 24–26.

29. Hall, "Uses of Literacy," 22.

30. Samuel Goodrich, *Recollections of a Lifetime,* cited in ibid.

31. Thomas Wentworth Higginson, *Cheerful Yesterdays* (Boston: Houghton Mifflin, 1898); Peter Tolis, *Elihu Burritt: Crusader for Brotherhood* (Hamden, Conn.: Archon Books, 1968), 4–5; William J. Gilmore, "Orestes Brownson and New England Religious Culture, 1803–1827" (Ph.D. diss., Univ. of Virginia, 1971). Lowell mill operative Huldah Stone, a key activist in the New England labor upsurge of the 1840s, also remembered that the old family Bible, a source of "counsel, wisdom and strength," had occupied a prominent place on the common room table of her childhood home (*Voice,* 8 May 1846).

32. Butts and Cremin, *History of Education,* 236, 272. See, too, Elson, *Guardians of Tradition,* vii, 16; Larcom, *New England Girlhood,* 45.

33. Norton, *Liberty's Daughters,* 281–82, 86, 90; Butts and Cremin, *History of Education,* 118–21. See, too, Jack Larkin, *The Reshaping of Everyday Life , 1790–1840* (New York: Harper & Row, 1988), 34.

34. Elson, *Guardians of Tradition,* 59–60.

35. "Betsey," "Recollections of an Old Maid," *Lowell Offering* 1 (Mar. 1841): 49 (emphasis added). Larcom notes the use of the Bible in her childhood schoolroom in *New England Girlhood,* 45.

36. Elson, *Guardians of Tradition,* 41–46.

37. See Gilmore, *Reading Becomes a Necessity of Life,* chap. 1. The same might be said of the shift in advice on child-rearing during the same period from an emphasis on conversion to an emphasis on character-building. See Mary P. Ryan, *Cradle of the Middle Class: The Family in Oneida County, New York, 1790–1865* (New York: Cambridge Univ. Press, 1981); Kett, *Rites of Passage.* On the book as a "vehicle of far-reaching dissent" as well as an "agent of control," see Hall, "Uses of Literacy," 17–20.

38. Lucy Larcom began attending church at the same age she began reading the Bible (*New England Girlhood,* 48–49).

39. See, especially, Packard, *Recollections;* Larkin, *Reshaping Everyday Life,* 275–78.

40. Albert B. Hart, ed., *Commonwealth History of Massachusetts* (New York: States History, 1828), 1: 8–13; Richard Eddy Sykes, "Massachusetts Unitarianism and Social Change: A Religious Social System in Transition, 1780–1820" (Ph.D. diss., Univ. of Minnesota, 1966), 36–38.

41. E.E.T., "Childhood's Home," *Offering* 1 (Apr. 1841): 69. See, too, Angeline, "The Old Village Church," ibid. 5 (July 1845): 163–64. For similar remarks by Rochester printer Henry Frink, born and raised in western Massachusetts in the early nineteenth century, see his apparently autobiographical temperance tract, *Alow and Aloft: On Board and on Shore* (Rochester, 1842). On Frink, see chap. 6 below.

42. Quoted in Lewis O. Saum, *Popular Mood of Pre–Civil War America* (Westport: Greenwood Press, 1980), 221. In his study of thousands of diaries and letters of ordinary folk in the generation before the Civil War, Saum concludes (38) that antebellum Americans were "inveterate churchgoers."

43. Patricia U. Bonomi and Peter R. Eisenstadt, "Church Adherence in the Eighteenth-Century British American Colonies," *William and Mary Quarterly,* 3rd ser., 39 (Apr. 1982): 275, and the largely speculative Douglass H. Sweet, "Church Vitality and the American Revolution: Historiographical Consensus and Thoughts Towards a New Perspective," *Church History* 45 (Sept. 1976): 341–57. For a different reading of the same evidence, see Butler, "Coercion, Miracle, Reason," 18–21. In his study of everyday life in the early Republic, Larkin (*Reshaping Everyday Life,* 300–301) concludes that Americans were increasingly likely to worship on the Sabbath, particularly in the smaller cities and towns where it often took the place of other amusements. The exceptions, he suggests, were the very edge of settlement and working-class areas of major urban centers. In a rare quantitative analysis, Randolph Roth (*Democratic Dilemma,* 98, chap. 3, and passim) concludes that the churches gained throughout the post-Revolutionary era, especially among the poor and young. See, too, Schultz, "God and Workingmen." For a full discussion of church membership, with statistics, see part 2.

44. Though, at least in the abstract, no American believed it was necessary to go to church to keep the Sabbath properly. As descendants of the Radical Reformation, theirs was a religion of the heart (and head), not one dependent on "outer garments." For the Reformation, in challenging the church and its emissaries, had set in motion a movement away from the institutional church, doctrines, and creeds toward an emphasis on personal faith, devoutness, and piety (Turner, *Without God, Without Creed,* 8–14, 22–23).

45. As John Thomas pointed out years ago, the era's reform activism had many sources, including the antitheocratic but nevertheless Christian and perfectionist assaults of the Owenites, and the revolt of liberal theology from Unitarianism to Transcendentalism ("Romantic Reform in America, 1815–1865," *American Quarterly* 17 [winter 1965]: 656–81). Here, I stress the more important development of evangelical Protestantism. As for the broad sketch I paint of this complex phenomenon: clearly, evangelical Protestantism could—and did—lead individuals and groups in antebellum America in many directions. I wish only to indicate those tendencies that portended the possibility for radical thought and action, in this case for working people.

46. The terms *First* and *Second Great Awakening* are constructs of religious historians and, as such, have been a matter of some debate. The precise dates of both phenomena—indeed, their precise nature—are hard to pin down. Important reinterpretive essays are Jon Butler, "Enthusiasm Described and Decried: The Great Awakening as Interpretive Fiction," *Journal of American History* 69 (1982–83): 305–25; and Nathan Hatch, "Redefining the Second Great Awakening: A Note on the Study of Christianity in the Early Republic," in *Democratization of American Christianity,* 220–26.

47. On the revivals, in addition to the works cited elsewhere in this section, see Frank G. Beardsley, *A History of American Revivals* (Boston: American Tract Society, 1904); David M. Ludlum, *Social Ferment in Vermont, 1791–1850* (New York: Columbia Univ. Press, 1942); Charles R. Keller, *The Second Great Awakening in Connecticut* (New Haven: Yale Univ. Press, 1942); Miller, *Life of the Mind,* book 1. Alexis de Tocqueville, who in 1835 labeled America the place "where the Christian religion has kept the greatest real power over men's souls," had observed a society at the height of revivalist activity during his visit several years earlier (*Democracy in America,* 291). "The religious atmosphere of the country was the first thing that struck me on arrival in the United States" [in the spring of 1831] (295).

48. See Curtis Johnson, *Islands of Holiness: Rural Religion in Upstate New York, 1790–1860* (Ithaca: Cornell Univ. Press, 1989). For urban revivals in the 1840s and 1850s, and their connection to social reform, see Timothy L. Smith, *Revivalism and Social Reform: American Protestantism on the Eve of the Civil War* (Nashville: Abingdon Press, 1957).

49. Trollope, "Domestic Manners," in Edith I. Coombs, comp., *America Visited* (New York: The Book League of America, n.d.), 84.

50. One thing is clear from the recent studies of the Second Great Awakening: it was an incredibly complex and varied phenomenon, which cannot be attributed to any one cause, tied to any one class, or associated with any one theology or social perspective. In this section, I bring together several of the most important tendencies evident in the Awakening in order to emphasize its radicalizing potential. For a provocative attempt by a sociologist to explain the meaning of nineteenth-century revivalism, see George M. Thomas, *Revivalism and Cultural Change: Christianity, Nation Building, and the Market in the Nineteenth-Century United States* (Chicago: Univ. of Chicago Press, 1989).

51. Hatch, *Democratization of American Christianity,* 30–34, chap. 4, and passim, quotation on 127. Cf. Thompson, "The Transforming Power of the Cross," in *Making of the English Working Class,* 350–400.

52. The process, while neither simple nor unilinear, was nonetheless inexorable. Ahlstrom provides an overview in *Religious History of the American People,* 469–614.

53. The democratization of American culture during the late eighteenth and early nineteenth centuries has been noted by numerous historians, including Richard D. Brown, in *Modernization: The Transformation of American Life, 1600–1865* (New York: Hill & Wang, 1976), chap. 5; and

James A. Henretta, *The Evolution of American Society, 1700–1815: An Interdisciplinary Analysis* (Lexington: D. C. Heath, 1973), chap. 6.

54. For a fascinating discussion of this process, which explores how the evangelicals involved simultaneously injected sacredness into the public agenda, thus Christianizing the idea of progress, and conflated the will of God with the good of man, thus secularizing Christian eschatology, see Turner, *Without God, Without Creed,* 83ff.

55. McLoughlin, "Revivalism," in Edwin C. Gausted, ed., *The Rise of Adventism: Religion and Society in Mid-Nineteenth Century America* (New York: Harper & Row, 1974); Nathan Hatch, "Millennialism and Popular Religion in the Early Republic," in Leonard I. Sweet, ed., *The Evangelical Tradition in America* (Macon: Univ. of Georgia Press, 1984), 113–30; James Moorhead, "Between Progress and Apocalypse: A Reassessment of Millennialism in American Religious Thought, 1800–1880," *Journal of American History* 71 (1984): 524–42; Timothy L. Smith, "Righteousness and Hope: Christian Holiness and the Millennial Vision in America, 1800–1900," *American Quarterly* 31 (spring 1979): 21–45; Sacvan Bercovitch, "The Typology of America's Mission," *American Quarterly* 30 (summer 1978): 133–55; Perry Miller, "From Covenant to Revival," in *Nature's Nation* (Cambridge: Harvard Univ. Press, 1967), 90–121; Tuveson, *Redeemer Nation,* 77, passim.

56. For an example of someone who took much of the foregoing in a very different direction than the radical reformers, see Newell G. Bringhurst, *Brigham Young and the Expanding American Frontier* (Boston: Little, Brown, 1986), 23–25.

57. Smith, "Righteousness and Hope." Cf. Richard D. Birdsall, "The Second Great Awakening and the New England Social Order," *Church History* 39 (Sept. 1970): 345–64. On the relationship between revivalism and social reform during this period, see Cross, *Burned-Over District.*

58. For an example of an antebellum reformer who exhibited a distinctive evangelical style even as he moved away from the church—and eventually from Christianity itself—see Lawrence B. Goodheart's *Abolitionist, Actuary, Atheist: Elizur Wright and the Reform Impulse* (Kent, Ohio: Kent State Univ. Press, 1990).

59. Karl Polanyi, *The Great Transformation: The Political and Economic Origins of Our Time* (orig. ed., 1944; Boston: Beacon Press, 1957). The literature on the rise of capitalism and the Industrial Revolution in America—what an increasing number of historians call the "Market Revolution"—is now quite vast, if also quite contested. For a useful short summary, with a selected bibliography, see Sean Wilentz, "Society, Politics, and the Market Revolution, 1815–1848," in Foner, ed., *New American History,* 5–71. See, too, William L. Barney, *The Passage of the Republic: An Interdisciplinary History of Nineteenth-Century America* (Lexington, Mass.: D. C. Heath, 1987), chap. 1; Sellers, *Market Revolution;* Allan Kulikoff, *The Agrarian Origins of American Capitalism* (Charlottesville: Univ. Press of Virginia, 1992). Stephen Innes cautions against slighting production for the market in the period before 1820 in "Fulfilling John Smith's Vision: Work and Labor in Early America," in *Work and Labor in Early America,* (Chapel Hill: Univ. of North Carolina Press, 1988), 34–41. For estimate of wage labor force, below, see Christopher L. Tomlins, "Law, Labor and Ideology in Colonial and Antebellum America" (unpubl. paper, 1992, in possession of the author, 1992), 14n.

60. *Wachusett Independant* [*WI*] (Fitchburg), 8 Feb. 1845.

61. As we shall see, there were significant theological differences both between labor reformers and their opponents and within the ranks of the labor movement itself. However, such distinctions can obscure as much as they reveal. The dichotomy that Laurie draws in his portrait of the pre-1837 Philadelphia, for example, between rationalist "Universalism and Free Thought" in the labor movement and "orthodoxy and reformed Protestantism" outside it, erects ideal types that conceal the diversity in both and distort the changes then going on in their ranks. The emphasis on reason and science, for example, was hardly alien to the evangelical mind by the 1820s and 1830s, as James Turner and others have shown. Indeed, in antebellum America the hallmark of public rhetoric was the blending of rational and evangelical currents. Moreover, the most vociferous attack on orthodoxy in this period came from within reform Protestantism rather than from

without. Meanwhile, there was a significant evangelical strain in American Universalism itself—and challenges from within to its own "orthodoxy." Finally, the label "Free Thought" papers over an enormous array of viewpoints. What needs to be investigated are the specific ways various religious perspectives were used in the service of labor radicalism. See Laurie, *Working People*, 69–71; Turner, *Without God, Without Creed*, 103–4; Herbert Hovenkamp, *Science and Religion in America, 1800–1860* (Philadelphia: Univ. of Pennsylvania Press, 1978); Steven A. Marini, *Radical Sects of Revolutionary New England* (Cambridge: Harvard Univ. Press, 1982); Russell E. Miller, *The Larger Hope: The First Century of the Universalist Church in America, 1770–1870* (Boston: Unitarian-Universalist Association, 1979).

62. (Cincinnati) *People's Paper* (PP), 11 Jan. 1845; (Fall River) *Mechanic*, 22 June 1844; (Philadelphia) *MFP*, 26 Dec. 1829; *NEA*, 20 June 1833.

63. Nathan Hatch, "*Sola Scriptura* and *Novus Ordo Secularum*," in Hatch and Mark A. Noll, eds., *The Bible in America: Essays in Cultural History* (New York: Oxford Univ. Press, 1982), 59–78. See, too, Ernest Sandeen, ed., *The Bible and Social Reform* (Baltimore: Scholar's Press, 1984), 7.

64. Quotation from "Concord"'s "Profession vs. Practice," *Voice*, 5 Dec. 1845. As Gilmore has pointed out regarding Brownson, early Bible training in basic moral values among reformers does not constitute proof of any causative link between upbringing and later activities ("Orestes Brownson," 50–51). It does, however, explain a great deal about the style and content of social activism.

65. Among the many habits early Bible reading imparted to later labor activists was the fascination with eschatology. As Gilmore observes, "one of the central features of the rural Bible was to provide a complete explanation for human history" by inculcating the belief in God's providence as the master of human actions and offering a "sacred history" that spoke of the end of "things earthly" (Gilmore, *Reading Becomes a Necessity of Life*, 260).

66. Mary Adams to Thomas Braden, 17 December 1832, repr. in Jo Anne Preston, "'To Learn Me The Whole of the Trade': Conflict Between a Female Apprentice and a Merchant Tailor in Ante-Bellum New England," *Labor History* 24 (spring 1983): 264.

67. *NEA*, 19, 12 July 1834.

68. Massachusetts Bureau of Statistics of Labor (MBSL), *Second Annual Report* (1871), 570ff. For the importance of the Bible and church in the life of discontented workers and labor activists during the early 1850s, see "J.S.," "Letter from a Factory Operative," *Workingman's Journal* (Newport, R.I.), 8 Mar. 1853.

69. Labor's battle with these evangelicals is discussed in chaps. 2, 3.

70. Though the tendency was not confined to that region or period. For comparable use of the evangelical style for radical purposes among the English Chartists of these years, see Eileen Yeo, "Christianity in Chartist Struggle, 1838–1842," *Past & Present*, no. 91 (May 1981): 109–39.

71. *Voice*, 12 June 1846. The editors' call here should not be confused with the attempt by some Freethinkers during this period to cynically adopt the language and tactics of their opponents in order to skewer them. Always under the control of pious activists during its three years as New England's leading labor oracle, the paper was originally the organ of the FWA, set up in May 1845 by a committee of that group with association secretary William Young as its editor. In the fall, it moved to Lowell as the official voice of the NEWA. Young remained its sole editor until the following spring, when he was forced to take a temporary leave due to illness. At this time, for a short period in May and June of 1846, local activists Sarah Bagley, Joel Hatch, and John S. Fletcher assumed editorial responsibilities. They were succeeded after six weeks by Boston Associationist John Allen. Young returned in the fall of 1846 for a year and then turned the presses over to Lowell artist and Associationist D. H. Jaques, who was soon joined by cooperationist and fellow Associationist John Orvis. Having published in both Lowell and Boston from late September 1847, Jaques and Orvis moved the paper to the latter city in November. Orvis took sole editorial responsibility in mid-April 1848 but brought out only one issue, which turned out to be the last under the *Voice* masthead. From the same offices, in early June, Orvis published the first edition of a short-lived paper called *The New Era of Industry*. See also chap. 3, n. 91.

72. *Mechanic,* 8 June 1844.

73. *Voice,* 8 May, 20 Feb. 1846.

74. Ibid., 17 Apr. 1846.

75. Ibid., 12 Feb. 1847.

76. Ibid., repr. in *YA,* 28 Feb. 1846.

77. Ibid., 10 Apr. 1846. For similar language, see their earlier report in ibid., 23 Jan. 1846.

78. *NEA,* 3 Oct. 1833.

79. (New York) *NTU,* 26 Mar. 1836.

80. For more on the Pioneers and their journal, see the epilogue.

81. *MFP,* 6 Feb. 1830.

82. For an extended discussion of labor and the clergy, see chap. 7.

83. *Voice,* 1 May 1846.

84. Ibid., 14 Nov. 1845. For Young's stance toward the church, see chap. 3.

85. Ibid, 29 May 1845. For Young's advocacy of what he called "practical Christianity," see ibid., 29 May, 6 June, 3 July, 7 Aug., 4 Sept., 14 Nov., 5, 11 Dec. 1845; 30 Jan., 6 Mar., 3, 10 Apr. 1846. On faith and works among antebellum evangelicals generally, see the discussion in Johnson, *Redeeming America,* chap. 3.

86. *MFP,* 17 May 1828.

87. *Voice,* 12 June 1846. For the same language among leading antebellum labor activists John C. Cluer, Huldah Stone, John Allen, and Albert J. Wright, see ibid., 7 Aug.; 26 Dec. 1845; 3 July 1846; *South Boston Gazette,* 1 July 1848. The phrase "practical Chistianity" transcended geography and denominational affiliation. Cluer was a former Methodist preacher from Scotland, Stone came from a Congregationalist background in northern rural New England but apparently eschewed church membership in Lowell; Allen was a member of the Boston Religious Union of Associationists, and Wright was a leading evangelical churchman in South Boston. Cluer: *Voice* 30 Jan. 1846; Stone: ibid., 17 Apr., 8 May 1846; Allen: Sterling F. Delano, "A Calendar of Meetings of the 'Boston Religious Union of Associationists,' 1847–1850," in Joel Myerson, ed., *Studies in the American Renaissance, 1985* (Charlottesville: Univ. Press of Virginia, 1985), 188; Wright: Phillips Church, *Alphabetical List of Members* (Boston, 1872).

88. For parallels among Washingtonian temperance advocates of the era, see Murphy, *Ten Hours' Labor,* 120–30; but note that the phenomenon was not confined to the 1840s.

89. *Voice,* 8 May 1846.

90. Ibid., 17 July 1845.

91. Seth Luther, *An Address on the Origins and Progress of Avarice* (hereafter, *Avarice*) (Boston, 1834), 34.

92. In the same spirit, as we shall see in chap. 3, they condemned the contemporary church. A working man in Fall River put it simply: "Religion and the factory system, as now established, cannot thrive together" (*Mechanic,* 14 Dec. 1844). The argument here was straightforward: the church mirrored prevailing conditions, and, like society at large, its problems demanded rectification. Loyal defenders of the faith, as they claimed to be loyal defenders of the community, these activists sought reform—even revolution—in the church as well as in the social order.

93. (Albany) *Mechanics' Mirror [MM],* Jan. 1846, 8.

94. "Religion—Freedom," *MM,* Apr. 1846, 80–81. Most of his biographers agree that, after spending his youth in the parish schools and dye works of Glasgow, Scotland, McFarlane came to the United States in 1835 or 1836, founding the MMPA as a secret society in Buffalo in 1842. John R. Commons, ed., *A Documentary History of American Industrial Society* (Cleveland: A. H. Clark, 1910–11), 8:251n; Dumas Malone, ed., *Dictionary of American Biography* (New York: Scribner, 1946) 11:43–44; James Grant Wilson and John Fiske, eds., *Appleton's Cyclopaedia of American Biography* (New York: D. Appleton, 1888) 4:115; *Who Was Who in America* (rev. ed., Chicago: Marquis Who's Who, 1967); Cynthia Maria Little, *History of the Clan MacFarlane,* 227–29; A. J. Parker, *Landmarks of Albany County, New York* (1897), part 3, 31; Clifford K. Yearling, *Britons in American Labor: A History of the Influence of the United Kingdom Immigrants on American Labor,*

1820–1914 (Baltimore: Johns Hopkins Univ. Press, 1957), 34–36. The dates in Ray Boston's *British Chartists in America, 1839–1900* (Manchester: Manchester Univ. Press, 1971), app. A, 93 are almost certainly wrong. McFarlane, at the time of his editorship of the *MM* (Apr. 1846, 97), claimed to be a "practical (journeyman) mechanic."

    95. *Voice*, 23 Jan. 1846. For the context and their precise language, see intro.

    96. Ibid., 17 July 1845.

Chapter 2

    1. The creed of America's pious in this period differed in intensity, tone, and character: despite the increasingly Christian character of this society, it was richly diverse, engendering a bewildering array of religious perspectives among the citizenry. By the 1830s, in addition to the wide variety of Protestant sects, non-Christian forms of theism had also emerged onto the American theological landscape, stressing spirituality and morality without Christianity. One popular form grew out of the belief that one could know God through nature. Some, like the Transcendentalists, took this one step further, and declared that nature *was* God (Butler, *Awash in a Sea of Faith;* Turner, *Without God, Without Creed,* 164–65).

    2. I have capitalized *Freethinker* (and *Freethought*) where they denote those actually involved in an anti-Christian movement. The problem with such labels, of course, is that they have multiple meanings. The key distinction for the purposes of this book is that between the general and the specific theological connotation. Thus, *freethinker* here refers not only to the unorthodox, but also to those forming their opinions independent of authority and/or established doctrine, sometimes expressed in terms of religious doubt as well as denial. That latter definition would characterize both large numbers of antebellum labor activists who considered themselves Christians but either joined dissenting churches or eschewed institutional affiliation entirely, and also those who opposed orthodoxy but also rejected deism and anti-Christian doctrines like materialism or atheism. *Infidelity,* which means lack of (religious) faith, was a term of abuse. For the origins, definitions, and historical uses of such terms, see Robertson, *History of Freethought,* 1:1–5; David Tribe, *One Hundred Years of Free Thought* (London: Elek Books, 1967), 7, 31–32, 43; Edward Royle, ed., *The Infidel Tradition From Paine to Bradlaugh* (London and Basingstoke: Macmillan, 1976), xvi; Marshall G. Brown and Gordon Stein, *Freethought in the United States: A Descriptive Bibliography* (Westport: Greenwood Press, 1978); Stein, *Encyclopedia of Unbelief.* Stein (ibid. 1:247–48) distinguishes "free thought" (opposition to religious dogma) from "freethought" (*organized* opposition to institutional religion), essentially the same distinction I have made here.

    3. This was the second such campaign of the postwar era; the first was 1814–17.

    4. The phrase, which became notorious during this period, came from a sermon by Philadelphia Presbyterian minister Ezra Stiles Ely. Ironically, Stiles's sermon was actually a pro-Jackson attack on his presidential opponent, President John Quincy Adams, as a Unitarian. The mail campaign, mounted by extant evangelical societies and the newly formed General Union for Promoting the Observance of the Christian Sabbath, sought repeal of congressional legislation that required post offices to hold Sunday hours. See Rohrer, "Sunday Mails and the Church–State Theme," 53–76; Bertram Wyatt-Brown, "Prelude to Abolitionism: Sabbatarianism and the Rise of the Second Party System," *Journal of American History* 63 (1971): 316–41. On the Benevolent Empire—sometimes referred to as the "evangelical united front"—see esp. Charles I. Foster, *An Errand of Mercy: The Evangelical United Front, 1800–1860* (New Brunswick, N.J.: Rutgers Univ. Press, 1960).

    5. For the suggestion that the antipathy to evangelical religion may also have been rooted in working*men*'s fears for their familial authority, see Murphy, *Ten Hours' Labor,* 97.

    6. James Turner, the foremost authority on the subject, finds evidence of skepticism and even a "fair number" of "quiet disbelievers in Christianity" in antebellum America, though the deists were, by 1830, "aging relics and shrill outcasts." Moreover, he finds very few cases of outright

atheism, concluding that the labels of the day obscure the "freakishness of out-and-out disbelief before the 1860s" (*Without God, Without Creed,* 101–2). The worship of Paine in the antebellum labor movement did not always mean an abandonment of Christianity; for one example, see the epilogue.

7. The Freethought sentiment that emerged in America in the mid-1820s and flowered at the end of that decade was largely sparked by British immigrants who had arrived in the country after the Panic of 1819. The deist celebrations of Paine's birthday they organized were largest and most militant among the urban plebian classes. Meanwhile, the first burst of American labor politics, the Working Men's movement (1828–34), enjoyed significant support from a number of Freethinkers. The nature of Freethought's connection to early labor activism is discussed in Post, *Popular Freethought in America,* esp. chaps. 1–4. For New York, see Wilentz, *Chants Democratic,* 153–57.

8. "Atheism in New England," *New England Magazine* 7 (Boston, 1834).

9. Hubbard Winslow, *The Means of the Perpetuity and Prosperity of Our Republic,* and Alonso Potter, *Political Economy; Its Objects, Uses and Principles,* quoted in John Ashworth, *"Agrarians" and "Aristocrats": Party Political Ideology in the United States, 1837–1846* (Cambridge: Cambridge Univ. Press, 1987), 196. For similar views among Whig politicians, see Schlesinger, *Age of Jackson,* 352–54. Note, too, the claim at the time of its founding that the NEWA was "attacking the institutions of patriotism and religion" ([Boston] *Bee,* 17 Oct. 1844).

10. As, indeed, it is to gauge the reality of the threat many activists and others perceived in the "political religion" of the Benevolent Empire. For an argument that the threat was more fantasy than reality, see Rohrer, "Sunday Mails."

11. Saum found a society with an "enormous appetite" for religion—the "one thing needful"—with an "indiscriminate religious fascination." Indeed, he found nineteenth-century commoners much like the Puritans in their attitudes toward the individual and society (*Popular Mood,* 29, 36, 109). See too, Post, in *Popular Freethought,* who asserts that, despite the numbers of Boston and New York workers who were attracted to Freethought, most of the American masses clung to their traditional beliefs.

12. "Loose Thoughts–No. II," *MFP,* 21 Nov. 1829. Post (*Popular Freethought,* chap. 7) notes that foreign visitors to the United States disagreed on the point.

13. See, for example, the comments by prominent theologian Nathaniel Emmons on the spread of infidelity in New England by the 1820s, quoted in Paul G. Goodman, *Towards a Christian Republic: Antimasonry and the Great Transition in New England, 1826–1836* (New York: Oxford Univ. Press, 1988), 72–73. Goodman points out (67) that, while Theodore Dwight and his compatriots in the 1790s had seen external threats to the church, a generation later the religious Antimasons feared the danger within.

14. For examples throughout the country, see (Wilmington) *Delaware Free Press* [*DFP*], 28 April 1832; (Rochester) *Liberal Advocate (LA),* 6 April 1834; (Rochester) *World As It Is,* 14 May 1836. On the other hand, Post notes (*Popular Freethought,* chap. 7) that some self-proclaimed infidels, proud of the label and their movement, did cite some of the hyperbole favorably.

15. For more on this movement, see chap. 5.

16. *Woodstock Observer* in *WMA,* 31 July 1830, quoted in Commons, *History of Labour* 1:293.

17. *Courier,* 11 Aug. 1830, cited in ibid.

18. Ibid., 211–12, 272–74; Foner, *History of the Labor Movement* 1:129, 132, 137; *New York Evening Post,* 31 Oct. 1829, quoted in William Randall Waterman, *Frances Wright* (New York: Columbia Univ. Press, 1924), 203.

19. (New York) *Commercial Advertiser,* 17 July 1829, quoted in Commons, *History of Labour* 1:272–74; (New York) *Courier and Enquirer,* 3 Nov. 1829, quoted in Foner, *History of the Labor Movement* 1:132.

20. Typical was the resolution of the Boston Working Men in 1830, which declared their group's "abhorrence [with] every attempt to disturb the public peace by uniting with political doctrines any question of religion or anti-religion." Similarly, a *WMA* correspondent warned against any interference with the laborer's political or religious loyalties, while a lecture series

welcomed all topics *but* religion (and local politics) [*Courier,* 28 Aug. 1830, quoted in Commons, *History of Labour* 1:293; *WMA,* 4 Dec. 1830; 20 Aug. 1831]. For examples from other cities, see Commons, *History of Labour* 1:211, 212, 272.

21. Quoted in *NL,* 2 July 1836.

22. On antiparty sentiments in early American history, see Richard Hofstadter, *The Idea of a Party System: The Rise of Legitimate Opposition in the United States, 1780–1840* (Berkeley and Los Angeles: Univ. of California Press, 1969); Ronald P. Formisano, "Political Character, Antipartyism and the Second Party System," *American Quarterly* 21 (winter 1969): 683–709. On this sentiment among Christian labor activists, see chaps. 5, 6.

23. For a more in-depth discussion of labor's aversion to sectarian schism generally, particularly that rooted in political division, and its desire for both purity and unity, see part 3.

24. *NTU,* 27 June 1835 (emphasis in original).

25. Eric Foner is thus only half right when he notes, in his ruminations on the fate of Paine in the American labor movement, that labor organizations in the 1830s were "conspicuously silent on questions of religion" (*Tom Paine,* 267).

26. See, for example, the common ground between the radical Hicksite Quaker Benjamin Webb of Wilmington and the evangelical Presbyterian Henry C. Frink of Rochester (chaps. 5 and 6).

27. (Utica) *Mechanics' Press* [*MP*], 30 Jan. 1830.

28. Cited in Schantz, "Religious Rhetoric," 9.

29. Ibid., 10. This stance stemmed from these activists' attachment to the *public* tradition in Christianity. On the Christian laborite distinction between the temporal and spiritual spheres of life, see part 3.

30. Post, *Popular Freethought,* 195.

31. *Man,* 17 Dec. 1834. In fact, the "infidel" label was used by more established Protestants to stigmatize Freewill Baptists, Hicksite Friends, Unitarians, and Universalists, and, in the political arena, by Whigs to denigrate Jacksonians. See Post, *Popular Freethought,* chap. 7; Schlesinger, *Age of Jackson,* 353.

32. Quoted in Schantz, "Religious Rhetoric," 15.

33. Dickinson to Bancroft, 27 Jan. 1835, Bancroft Papers, Massachusetts Historical Society, Boston.

34. The term referred to redistribution of property to achieve at least a measure of material equality, but it was used as a catchall for radical social restructuring, and for alleged infidelity as well.

35. *MP,* 30 Jan., 12 Dec. 1830.

36. Huldah Stone, in the *Voice,* 8 May 1846 (emphases in original).

37. Ibid., 7 Nov. 1845.

38. Marty, *Infidel,* 194.

39. That presence, or at least their program, was largely purged from the labor movement after a brief flirtation between 1828 and 1832. After the 1830s, activists remembered well the opprobrium they endured as a result of having such Freethinkers in their midst. In his history of the American labor movement, labor leader George McNeill would write about how the New York City Working Men, by passing a resolution calling the church's tax exemption a "positive robbery of the people," had frightened away many "church-going conservative wage-laborers" and allowed the press to stigmatize the movement as "infidel" (*Labor Movement,* 76). Organized Freethought in America would enjoy some resurgence with the influx of German "Forty-Eighters" at midcentury, but it would not enjoy the kind of presence it had in the early years until after the Civil War. By then, however, the evangelical style was firmly entrenched as the language of American radicalism, including in labor reform. See Post, *Popular Freethought;* Turner, *Without God, Without Creed;* Gutman, "Protestantism and the American Labor Movement."

40. Again, Marty (*Infidel,* 8): "anti-church, anti-christian, or anti-religious movements in the United States have not been widespread or profound."

41. Post, *Popular Freethought;* Roderick S. French, "Liberation from Man and God in Boston: Abner Kneeland's Free-Thought Campaign, 1830–1839," *American Quarterly* 32 (summer 1980): 207.

42. Detailing the proceedings, the editor of *WMA* commented: "Among the reasons given for the rejection of Mr. Seaver, was, that he was a member of the Working Men's Association of Boston, which was already represented in the Convention, but we fear that sectarian prejudice was the principal cause" (*WMA,* 19 Oct. 1844; Commons, *History of Labour* 1:537n). The vote on Seaver was close (76–64), however.

43. *Voice,* 12 Mar. 1847.

44. Ibid., 26 Feb. 1847.

45. Ibid., 21 May 1847.

46. Ibid., 20, 27 Mar. 1846.

47. Ibid., 10 Apr. 1846.

48. *MFP,* 17 July 1830, cited in Commons, *History of Labour* 1:273n.

49. See chap. 6.

50. Though Wilentz (*Chants Democratic*) finds some evidence of evangelical fervor harnessed to the cause of labor activism in New York during these years, he downplays both the power and significance of the religious critique when contrasted to "working class republicanism." Schantz offers an important corrective in "Religious Rhetoric," his brief study of the *WMA* cited above.

51. "Except for a few leaders and their coterie in the movement," Walter Hugins concludes in his study of New York labor in the 1830s, "the Workingmen do not appear to have been fundamentally committed to anticlericalism or skepticism" (*Jacksonian Democracy and the Working Class: A Study of the New York Workingmen's Movement, 1829–1837* [Stanford: Stanford Univ. Press, 1960], 135, 110).

52. Usually associated with abolitionists during this period, who "came out" of their churches to protest the countenancing of slavery, "come-outers" could be found among laborites as well. On the phenomenon generally, see Lewis Perry, *Radical Abolitionism: Anarchy and the Government of God in Antislavery Thought* (Ithaca: Cornell Univ. Press, 1973). The term comes from Rev. 18:4: "And I heard another voice from heaven, saying, Come out of her, my people, that ye be not partakers of her sins, and that ye receive not of her plagues."

53. "A.G.," *MFP,* 27 Mar. 1830.

54. The paper was the official organ of the Mechanics' Union of Trade Associations, the nation's first citywide union of trades, and the Working Men's Party (WMP), the nation's first labor party. See Laurie, *Working People;* idem, *Artisans Into Workers,* 68.

55. For the quotation, see "White," *MFP,* 28 Nov. 1829. For the presence of various denominations in the movement, see, e.g., "An Apprentice" (Universalist), 1 May 1830; "No Sectarian" (Episcopalian), 3 July 1830; "R.B.V." (Methodist), 7 Aug. 1830.

56. Laurie depicts Philadelphia's labor leaders as "rationalists" in *Working People,* 70.

57. *MFP,* 1 Aug. 1829 (emphases in original).

58. Ibid., 31 Oct. 1829 (my emphasis). See, too, 14 Aug. 1830. The paper did publish favorable reviews of Wright on occasion, though not necessarily of her religious views, a distinction labor editors of the era often were at pains to make.

59. The editors sometimes employed a biblical style and even quoted the Bible to make their point. E.g., ibid., 24 July 1830.

60. Ibid., 6 Feb. 1830.

61. Laurie claims (*Artisans Into Workers,* 68) that the most important member of the publishing committee, William Heighton, revered Paine, belonged to several "rationalist" groups, and called himself an infidel. Schultz dissents in "God and Workingmen," 152–55.

62. Ibid., 7 Aug. 1830.

63. "A Citizen," ibid., 7 August 1830.

64. Ibid., 14 Nov. 1829 (emphasis added). This labor activist would deliver a Fourth of July address the following year in which he opposed religious coercion ("the intemperate zeal, the

overweaning ambition of those deluded minds, which would despoil the sanctity of religion . . . by claiming legislative enactment in her support"), while at the same time insisting that workers knew "no master but their God" (ibid., 17 July 1830).

Chapter 3

1. As it did in the case of some other antebellum reformers. Elizur Wright, whose religion led him to reform activity, found it necessary to leave the church in order to his continue his activities. See Goodheart, *Abolitionist, Actuary, Atheist.*

2. Perry, *Radical Abolitionism,* 93. Charles Rosenberg remarks on the "peculiarly American variety of anticlericalism" in *The Cholera Years: The United States in 1832, 1849, and 1866* (Chicago: Univ. of Chicago Press, 1962), 51. Many Americans attributed infidelity to the machinations of the clergy, or "priests." So, Jefferson: "There would never have been an infidel if there had never been a priest" (quoted in Wills, *Under God,* 358).

3. Wright called the "true" Christian church "outside Christianity" (Goodheart, *Abolitionist, Actuary, Atheist,* 125).

4. The former phrase was written by a Lowell mill girl who objected to her employer's admonitions about Sabbath church attendance. "God is a spirit," she reminded her readers, "and they that worship acceptably must worship in spirit and truth. The accompanying sacrifice is not a change of garments but a change of hearts" (*Voice,* 2 Apr. 1847). The condemnation of religion that consisted of "unmeaning phrases, forms and ceremonies" is from Charles Douglas (*Reformer,* 11 Aug. 1836).

5. *Chronotype,* 18 Dec. 1847. This paper was edited by Elizur Wright, during the one phase in his long reform career when he advocated labor rights. By then, ironically, when the labor movement in the region came to resemble a religious crusade, Wright had rejected Christianity and was well on his way to an atheist position (Goodheart, *Abolitionist, Actuary, Atheist,* 128–31).

6. See chap. 1. When Abraham Lincoln's opponent accused him of infidelity in the 1846 congressional race, for example, the Illinois lawyer issued a handbill admitting that he did not attend meeting but professed a firm belief in God and the Bible (Stephen B. Oates, *With Malice Toward None: The Life of Abraham Lincoln* [New York: New American Library, 1977], 83).

7. For a brief discussion of regular church attendance as a condition of employment in the so-called boardinghouse mills—and mill operative opposition to it—see Lazerow, "Religion and the New England Mill Girl," 437–38.

8. *Voice,* 2 Apr. 1847. See also Laura S. Brigham, ed., "An Independent Voice: A Mill Girl from Vermont Speaks Her Mind," *Vermont History* 61 (summer 1973): 142–46.

9. On the abolitionists who did this, see Ronald G. Walters, *The Antislavery Appeal: American Abolitionism After 1830* (Baltimore: Johns Hopkins Univ. Press, 1976), chap. 3.

10. Jack Larkin, "Remembering the Sabbath," *Old Sturbridge Visitor* 20 (winter 1980–81): 5; idem, *Reshaping Everyday Life,* 275–78.

11. For complaints about the need to market on Sunday morning because of Saturday pay, see letter of "Workingman," (Wilmington) *Blue Hen Chicken,* 24 Nov. 1848.

12. The available evidence on the changing nature of Sabbath observance during the early antebellum period presents some interesting cross-currents, which perhaps explain, at least in part, why it became such a fractious public issue. On the one hand, as Paul Goodman has pointed out, by the 1820s the Puritan idea of the Sabbath (two or three trips to the meetinghouse, with Bible reading and family devotion during the rest of the day) was becoming anachronistic for increasing numbers of Americans. On the other hand, with the success of the Second Great Awakening, proportionately more Americans were likely to worship on Sunday after 1820 than before (Goodman, *Towards a Christian Republic,* 68; Larkin, *Reshaping Everyday Life,* 300; Rohrer, "Sunday Mails," 58–59).

13. *MM,* Oct. 1846, 236–39.

14. On the Knights of Labor, see Susan Levine, "Labor's True Woman: Domesticity and Equal Rights in the Knights of Labor," *Journal of American History* 70 (Sept. 1983): 323–39.

15. For strikingly similar complaints about Sabbath labor by Indian whalers in mid-seventeenth-century Nantucket, see Daniel Vickers, "The First Whalemen of Nantucket," *William and Mary Quarterly,* 3rd ser., 40 (Oct. 1983): 581.

16. In a sentiment "cordially assent[ed] to" by the editors of the *MFP,* "A Mechanic" wrote that such a law "is as directly opposed to true christianity as is darkness to light" (3 Apr. 1830). Meanwhile, "Senex"—whose views ("upon a second reading") convinced the editors that they should make an exception to their stated rule of refusing articles involving theological disputation—opposed Sabbatarianism with this qualifier: "nothing is farther from my intention than to say or insinuate anything in derogation of the primitive and evangelical canon, adopted by general consent throughout the Christian world, of devoting one day in seven to acts of social worship and public instruction; but on the contrary to recommend and enforce it in the way most congenial with the mild, gentle, and tolerant spirit of the Gospel" (21 Nov. 1829). The labor motto "no legislation on religion" was conceived as a defense of religion rather than an attack on it. To be sure, there were significant disagreements among activists over the sanctity and nature of the Sabbath—Must it be Sunday? Were the Ten Commandments part of the Christian code? What, exactly, constituted proper observance?—but these disagreements were regularly articulated in explicitly Christian terms. For examples, see ibid., 12 June, 26 Apr. 1830; 21 Nov. 1829.

17. Activists' complaints about Sabbath labor extended to all forms of religious worship. "Pray tell me, ye who enforce the old system of labor and profess to love God's Holy Book," "Encourager" asked the employers of Fall River, "*how* can the poor mechanic, and the operative in the mill, search the scriptures daily and fruitfully, and at the same time compelled to labor '*fourteen hours*' per day?" (*Mechanic,* 25 May 1844 [emphasis in original]).

18. *Voice,* 12 June 1846. See also, ibid., 23 Jan. 1846.

19. Ibid., 9 Oct. 1846.

20. "An Operative," intro., *Factory Tracts.* The *MFP* (31 Oct. 1829) made the same argument regarding domestic servants. Here, activists echoed an antichurch animus evident among large numbers of antebellum workers. Typical—and to the point—was the comment of one factory girl in Clinton, Mass., in 1851: "our churches," Lucy Ann wrote her cousin Charlotte, are marked by "desecration" and "mockery" (29 June 1851, quoted in Saum, *Popular Mood,* 30–31).

21. Bagley's father was a tithingman when Sarah was ten; his obituary noted "his righteous life and Christian demeanor." Helena Wright, "Notes and Documents: Sarah G. Bagley: A Biographical Note," *Labor History* 20 (summer 1979): 401–02, 412, 414; Philip S. Foner, ed., *The Factory Girls: A Collection of Writings on Life and Struggles in the New England Factories of the 1840's* (Urbana: Univ. of Illinois Press, 1977), 58–60; Ware, *Industrial Worker,* 212–13; Early, "Reappraisal of the New-England Labour-Reform Movement," 44, 49.

22. *Voice,* 12 June 1846 (emphasis in original). See also, letter of "Octavia," *Factory Girl,* 1 Mar. 1843. *Offering* editor Harriet Farley also noted that "some girls" complained of not being able to afford the pew rent or a proper dress (3 [July 1843]: 240). Murphy suggests (*Ten Hours' Labor,* 211–12) that such complaints were peculiar to mill women, but the problem of social distinctions in church life was commonly remarked upon by activists of the period.

23. *Voice,* 1 May 1846.

24. Luther claimed to have covered forty-five thousand miles in fourteen states and Canada (*Avarice,* 38–40). Along the way, he met white pioneers and Indians in the West and slaves in the South. He also claimed to have lived for years "among Cotton mills, worked in them, traveled among them" (*New England Address,* 35). In the course of these travels, exercising what he called his "constant habit of observation," Luther developed his biting critique of contemporary society. By 1832, at the age of thirty-seven, he had returned to his native Providence, R.I., where he helped launch the New England Association of Farmers, Mechanics and Other Working Men (NEA); in the middle years of the decade, he was a leading light of the Boston Trades' Union and National

Trades' Union. While working sporadically as a carpenter in Boston during these years, he continued to travel, this time in service of the labor movement. For sources, see n. 87 below.

25. Luther, *Avarice*, 34.

26. *MFP,* 23 Jan. 1829.

27. Ibid., 5 Dec. 1829.

28. *Mechanic,* 29 June 1844.

29. Ibid. Jacob Frieze, *The Elements of Social Disorder: A Plea for the Working Classes in the United States* (Providence, R.I.: B. F. Moore, 1844), 31, 34; *Lowell Offering,* 2nd ser., no. 2 (1842): 120. See also, letter of "An Operative," *Voice,* 22 Jan. 1847; Bagley's letter, ibid., 8 Sept. 1846.

30. *MFP,* 3 July 1830.

31. Ibid., 31 Oct. 1829.

32. WMA, 2 Jan. 1830, quoted in Schantz, "Religious Rhetoric," 11.

33. *All Sorts,* 6 Feb. 1847.

34. *Voice,* 5 Dec. 1845.

35. (Philadelphia) *Jubilee,* Sept. 1855, 124.

36. See, e.g., "An Operative," *MFP,* 27 June 1829.

37. Ibid., 27 Mar. 1830.

38. Ibid., 21 Aug. 1830.

39. Ibid., 4 Sept. 1830.

40. Ibid., 4 Sept. 1830. Sometimes, though, labor spoke in a matter-of-fact manner about the church's longstanding opposition to the interests of the worker, without apparently needing to specify the nature of its crimes. Thus, the *NEA* (19 Apr. 1832), on a successful strike of building tradesmen who were converting a Providence theater into a church: "it is pleasant to reflect that there will be at least one church in Providence prepared for Divine Worship without the aid of oppression practiced on the workmen."

41. The words are "A.G."'s in *MFP,* 27 Mar. 1830.

42. Ibid., 27 Mar. 1830.

43. *Voice,* 8 May 1846.

44. It also stemmed from the emergence of denominationalism as the American religious orthodoxy of the early Republic. For those thoroughly disenchanted with the state of the church, creed became a principal target. See Perry, *Radical Abolitionism,* 94.

45. Hatch, "*Sola Scriptura,*" 59–78.

46. *Reformer,* 6 Jan. 1837.

47. *Voice,* 29 May 1846.

48. *MFP,* 3 July 1830.

49. *Voice,* 10 Apr. 1846.

50. (Fitchburg) *Sentinel,* 7 Sept. 1841.

51. Ibid., 30 June, 12 Aug. 1841.

52. Ibid., 2 Sept. 1841.

53. Note that Philadelphia's "No Sectarian" claimed lifelong membership in the Episcopal Church (*MFP,* 3 July 1830).

54. "A.G.," *MFP,* 27 Mar. 1830.

55. Brownson, "Laboring Classes," excerpted in (Fall River) *Patriot,* 30 July 1840. Some, in the Christian tradition of hating the sin but loving the sinner, were careful to distinguish between the clergyman and the clergy. George Lippard, founder of the secret Brotherhood of the Union and editor of the prolabor reform newspaper, the (Philadelphia) *Quaker City* [*QC*], insisted that his anticlerical animadversions were denunciations of an institution—those in society "who, instead of preaching the gospel to the poor, attack some imaginary evil, or make their complacent hearers feel very comfortable, by picturing the vices of the Socialists, Novel Writers and other dreadful persons" (*QC,* 28 Dec. 1848; 6, 20 Jan. 1849; Roger Butterfield, "George Lippard and His Secret Brotherhood," *Pennsylvania Magazine of History and Biography* 79 [July 1955]: 292).

56. *Reformer,* 11 Nov. 1836.

57. Idem.

58. For late-eighteenth-century antecedents of this virulent anticlericalism among ordinary Americans, welling up from within the church itself, see Hatch, *Democratization of American Christianity,* 25–45. Hatch notes that popular American journals between 1800 and 1830 were filled with anticlerical invective. One of these, the Philadelphia *Reformer* (1820–35) reprinted articles from the *MFP.* For examples of popular poems and songs from that period, "severely anticlerical yet overtly Christian" and bearing a striking resemblance to antebellum laborite anti-clericalism, see "A Sampling of Anticlerical and Anti-Calvinist Christian Verse" (ibid., 174, 176–77, 227–43). Among these is the Baptist preacher John Leland's "False Prophets Contrasted with the Apostle Paul" (240), which captures precisely labor's suspicion of the clergy in the warning, "Beware of prophets false and greedy / Those ravening wolves who rob the needy."

59. "Mechanic," 5 Feb. 1844, ms., Fall River Historical Society (FRHS).

60. "Avaricious professing Christian" is from "Cooperative Unions," by I[srael] Y[oung], *NL,* 6 Aug. 1836.

61. *MFP,* 27 June 1829.

62. *Voice,* 8 May 1846 (emphasis in original). On Stone, see ibid., 17 Apr. 1846; Early, "Reappraisal of the New-England Labour-Reform Movement," 44, 49; Foner, *Factory Girls,* 100.

63. Quoted in Schantz, "Religious Rhetoric," 9.

64. Ibid., 6.

65. *Gleaner,* 4 Apr. 1846.

66. *MFP,* 27 June 1829.

67. *Voice,* 4 Sept. 1846. On the "Sabbath Labor Christians," a shadowy group about which little is known, see ibid., 19 June, 9 Oct. 1846; 8 June, 9 July, 3 Sept. 1847.

68. Ibid., 2 Apr. 1847 (citations refer to Babylon, as characterized in Rev. 18:4).

69. Ibid., 9 Oct. 1846.

70. Ibid., 8 May, 12 June 1846.

71. Bagley became a member of the First Universalist Church of Lowell in 1840; extant church records do not indicate her affiliation thereafter (records in possession of Laura Husted, Lowell). Though her attitude toward local religious institutions apparently became less sanguine as she actively protested the factory system (see her early piece, "Pleasures of Factory Life," *Offering* 1 [Dec. 1840]: 26), her concern for the "cultivation of the mental and moral faculties" remained (see the preamble to the FLRA constitition, which she likely wrote, *Voice,* 27 Feb. 1846).

72. "Hours of Industry," *MM,* Nov. 1846, 277. See, too, "Religion—Freedom," no. 4, ibid., July 1846, 153. For McFarlane's religious history, see Little, *History of Clan MacFarlane,* 227–29; G. R. Howell et al., *Bi-Centennial History of Albany: History of the County of Albany* (1886), 607.

73. On the *Mechanic's* encouragement of clerical support, see 15 June, 27 July 1844; 25 Jan. 1845. The senior member of the publishing committee of the paper, Thomas Almy, was a leader of the Fall River Church of the New Jerusalem (Swedenborgian) when it was organized in the 1850s. While active in the mechanics' movement, he may have been a member of a small circle of Swedenborgians who had been meeting in the town since the late 1830s (*Journal of the Massachusetts Association of the New Jerusalem* [Boston, 1855], 429; D. Hamilton Hurd, *History of Bristol County, Massachusetts, with Biographies of Many of its Pioneers and Prominent Men* [Philadelphia: J. W. Lewis, 1883], 383). On Fall River, see chap. 4.

74. The resolution is contained in the "FWA Record Book." On the sponsors' (Ebenezer and Goldsmith Bailey) church affiliations, see chap. 4.

75. *Chronotype,* 18 Dec. 1847.

76. *Voice,* 2 Apr. 1847.

77. King's story is detailed in Fred Landon, "Extracts from the Diary of William C. King, A Detroit Carpenter, in 1832," *Michigan History Magazine* 19 (winter 1935): 65–70.

78. Ibid., 67.

79. Ibid., 68.

80. Ibid., 69.

81. Monte A. Calvert, "The Allegheny City Cotton Mill Riot of 1848," *The Western Pennsylvania Historical Magazine* 46 (Apr. 1963): 97–133.

82. Foner, *History of the Labor Movement* 1:241.

83. "Religion—Freedom," nos. 3, 4, *MM,* 104–05, 153. McFarlane made the remark about the "rotten" condition of American Christianity (Feb. 1846) in observing that some seven-eighths of the prisoners at the Clinton County (N.Y.) State Prison were of Christian parents, and one-third belonged to Christian churches.

84. By 1858, now living in Boston, he was part of the Parker Fraternity, a benevolent association connected with Theodore Parker's Unitarian congregation. After the Civil War, relocating to Wakefield, Mass., he joined the First Universalist Society there. A lifelong advocate of labor and social reform, he remained a churchgoing Universalist until his death in 1900. See *Voice,* 29 May 1845; (Boston) *Globe,* obit., 20 Aug. 1900; (Boston) *Transcript,* obit., Aug. 20, 1900; (Wakefield) *Daily Item,* obit., 20, 22 Aug. 1900; *Biographical Sketches of Representative Citizens of the Commonwealth of Massachusetts* (Boston: Graves and Steinbarger, 1901), 690–92; Twenty-Eighth Congregational Society, *The Parker Fraternity* (Boston, 1864); "Records of the Clerk of the First Universalist Society of Wakefield" (1858–1900, 1900–1934), Harvard Divinity School Library, Cambridge, Mass. Young may have been exposed to the preachings of Orestes Brownson, who was a Unitarian minister in one of Young's pre-adolescent homes (Walpole, N.H.).

85. In 1824, nine years after his admission, Luther was excluded from the Baptist Church for "disorderly walking," an evangelical term connoting straying from the path of righteousness, as in "walking in the path of the Lord." Carl Gersuny misidentifies this phrase as referring to drunkenness in "A Biographical Note on Seth Luther," *Labor History* 18 (spring 1977): 241.

86. Luther, *Avarice,* 29–30.

87. In the 1840s, Luther emerged as a leader of the Rhode Island free suffrage movement, for which activities he landed in prison. After several months' incarceration, he set out on yet another tour. Although he was now losing his mental faculties, for which he blamed his brief imprisonment, Luther played an active role in the NEWA meeting at Nashua, N.H., in April 1846. During the summer, he was arrested for attempting to rob the State Street Bank in Boston (in the name of President Polk and the Mexican War effort) and was committed to an asylum in East Cambridge. He died at the Brattleboro Retreat in 1863. Foner, *History of the Labor Movement* 1:106; Edward Pessen, *Most Uncommon Jacksonians: The Radical Leaders of the Early Labor Movement* (Albany: State Univ. of New York Press, 1967), 87; Hartz, "Seth Luther"; Gersuny, "Biographical Note"; Marvin E. Gettleman, *The Dorr Rebellion: A Study in American Radicalism: 1833–1849* (New York: Random House, 1973); *WMA,* 16 Nov. 1844; 5 Apr., 17 May 1845; *Chronotype,* 11 June 1846.

88. Hatch (*Democratization of American Christianity,* 167–70) discusses forms of "primitivism" in nineteenth-century American Protestantism.

89. "Paul," in *MFP,* 17 May 1828; *Voice,* 9 Oct. 1846.

90. "No Sectarian," ibid., 3 July 1830.

91. Letter of "C," (Boston and New York) *Harbinger,* 13 May 1848. On the Associationists, their religion, and the labor movement, see Guarneri, *Utopian Alternative,* esp. chaps. 3, 4, and 11; and below, chaps. 4, 7, 9 and 10. The cross-denominational nature of this movement can be seen in Delano, "A Calendar of Meetings," 260 n. 11.

92. *Voice,* 10 Apr. 1846.

93. Ibid., 1 May 1846.

94. (Lowell) *Vox Populi,* repr. in *YA,* 18 Oct. 1845.

95. FLRA report to the Industrial Congress (Oct. 1845), ibid., 7 Nov. 1845; 29 May 1846.

96. Ibid., 19 June, 9 Oct. 1846.

97. "Progress of Reform—The Redemption of the Masses," *Peoples Rights,* repr. in *WMA,* 28 Sept. 1844. The address has not survived.

98. *Voice,* 20 Feb. 1846.

99. Ibid., 18 Feb. 1848.

100. *Jubilee,* Dec. 1852, 93. For more on Townsend and this movement, see the epilogue.

101. *Herald,* 8 June, 20, 21, 27 July, 14 Dec. 1855; *Voice,* 30 Jan. 1846; *Transcript,* obit., 10 Sept. 1886. Cluer engaged in similar activities during the 1840s, though indoors. In late 1845 and 1846 he toured industrial towns in Massachusetts and New Hampshire; his topic, according to the *Voice,* was "the application of true Christianity to the pursuits of life," or "practical Christianity" (5, 26 Dec. 1845; 2 Jan. 1846). For Cluer's description of one such "lecture," see chap. 7, n. 40.

102. Calvert, "Allegheny City 1848 Riot," 114.

Chapter 4

1. For more on this movement, see chap. 5.

2. In western Massachusetts, Sylvester Judd echoed numerous movement voices when he recorded in his diary that many Working Men were "orthodox christians in good standing" (quoted in Ronald P. Formisano, *The Transformation of Political Culture: Massachusetts Parties, 1790s-1840s* [New York: Oxford Univ. Press, 1983], 446, n. 56). In Albany, N.Y., a recent study reports, the proportion of church members among Working Men's political leaders was the same as for the city's political leadership generally (one-third) [Hackett, *Rude Hand of Innovation,* 144–45]. For the Woodstock figures, see Roth, *Democratic Dilemma,* 158–61, which seems to assume that such religious affiliation precluded a radical program for these activists, given that they, unlike their urban counterparts, did not support Freethought, women's rights, unions, cooperatives, land reform, or the ten-hour workday. As we shall see, churchgoing was hardly a disqualifier for radical labor advocacy in antebellum America.

3. Shelton, *Mills of Manayunk,* 128–33, 137, 150, 153, 158–62.

4. John B. Andrews and W. D. P. Bliss, *History of Women in Trade Unions* (orig. publ., 1910; reprint ed., New York: Arno Press, 1974), 42–43.

5. Names also appear on such lists as Sabbath school "scholars," pew rentals, building committees, and charitable collections. When such individuals appear in the tables, they are identified as such. Often, though, the majority of these were members of the congregation. In any case, names combined do not accurately reflect the universe of attenders. Whitney Cross (*Burned-Over District,* 41) found that the "overwhelming majority of western New Yorkers sympathized with the churches and attended meeting regularly," but relatively few "professed" religion, attended communion, or belonged to the church proper. Winthrop Hudson (*Religion in America* [New York: Scribner, 1965], 129) estimated that in the country generally during these years, "the number attending a Sabbath service was usually three times as large as the membership." For a Working Man who was a regular churchgoer but not a member, see "Truth," "An Abuse in Church," in *DFP,* 27 Feb. 1830.

6. Cross makes the same point in *Burned-Over District,* 41–42. For another example, see the Hodgson letters in Thomas Dublin, ed., *Farm to Factory: Women's Letters, 1830–1860* (orig. publ., 1981; 2nd ed., New York: Columbia Univ. Press, 1993), 39–58. See, too, Harriet Robinson's story of being ostracized in Lowell for being a Congregationalist while attending Universalist meeting (*Loom and Spindle; or, Life Among the Mill Girls* [New York: Thomas Y. Crowell, 1898], 31). On Clark, see Red Clay Creek Presbyterian Church Records, 1827–1971, microfilm, Delaware Historical Society (DHS); Kelso Records, DHS.

7. On abolitionism, John R. McKivigan, *The War Against Proslavery Religion: Abolitionism and the Northern Churches, 1830–1865* (Ithaca: Cornell Univ. Press, 1984); on Antimasonry, Goodman, *Towards a Christian Republic,* 60, 62–63. See also Sellers's cross-denominational "antinomian Come-outerism" in *Market Revolution,* 158–59, and P. Jeffrey Potash's description of church membership patterns in *Vermont's Burned-Over District: Patterns of Commercial Development and Religious Activity, 1761–1850* (Brooklyn: Carlson, 1991). On the effective shattering of theological boundaries between denominations in this period, see Turner, *Without God, Without Creed,* passim, esp. 107. For a reading of the evidence that finds familial tensions in denominational choice, see Murphy, *Ten Hours' Labor,* 89–90.

8. *Voice,* 27 Oct. 1847.

9. The secretaries of the NEA's first meeting were George W. Light of the Salem Street Congregationalist Church in Boston (received, Aug. 1831), and Jacob Frieze, minister of the First Universalist Society of Pawtucket in 1829. Frieze's church affiliation in 1832 is unknown, but his popular 1844 pamphlet, *Elements of Social Disorder,* reveals a self-proclaimed Christian still very much in the Universalist mold. The convention was chaired by P. N. Tillinghast, received by letter (i.e., from another church) into the First Baptist Church of Fall River in 1836; he remained a labor reformer while a member of that congregation. Unsurprisingly, article 2 of the NEA constitution confined membership to "persons of good moral character" (Commons, *Documentary History* 5:192–95; *The Articles of Faith and Covenant of the Salem Street Church* [Boston, 1848]; *A Brief History of the First Baptist Church, of Fall River, with the Declaration of Faith, the Church covenant, and a List of Members* [Fall River, 1872]). An excellent discussion of the association can be found in Murphy, *Ten Hours' Labor,* chap. 2.

10. The following account pertains almost exclusively to male activists, because little is known of the women who participated in the movement. The latter's role in the 1840s seems to have been as "auxiliaries" to the main, male-dominated "mechanic" movement. Although a Fall River delegate report to the NEWA singled out two supportive "classes," the clergy and "the ladies," few of the women's names have surfaced. In 1844, local activists formed the Ladies' Ten Hour Association (also, Ladies' Mechanic Association), but only the names of the president and secretary are known. Some ten women's names appeared on the ten-hour petition lists of the early 1840s; the only other female name linked to this movement is Mary Reed, a "factory girl" who spoke at an NEWA meeting in Fall River in 1845. Fifty female weavers struck the Massasoit Factory in February 1842, but local press reports did not reveal any of their names ([Boston] *Laborer,* 26 Oct. 1844; [Fall River] *Weekly News,* 11 Sept., 1845). We do know, though, that the women spoke in the same voice as their male counterparts. See, e.g., "A Ten Hour Woman," encouraging striking building tradesmen in the *Mechanic,* 28 Dec. 1844:

> Woman is upon your side,
> Full armed for moral fight,
> For brother's aye, and sister's wrongs,
> For God and human right.

The role of the clergy in Fall River is discussed in chap. 7.

11. Fall River's prominence as an industrial center during the post-Civil War period is well known: Philip T. Silvia, "The Spindle City: Labor, Politics, and Religion in Fall River, Massachusetts, 1780–1905" (Ph.D. diss., Fordham Univ., 1973); John T. Cumbler, *Working-Class Community in Industrial America: Work, Leisure, and Struggle in Two Industrial Cities, 1880–1930* (Westport: Greenwood Press, 1979). For the early period, see Arthur Sherman Phillips, *The Phillips History of Fall River* (Fall River: Dover Press, 1944–46), vol. 2; Henry M. Earl, *Centennial History of Fall River, Massachusetts* (New York: Atlantic, 1877); Henry M. Fenner, *History of Fall River* (New York: F. T. Smiley, 1906); Robert K. Lamb, "The Development of Entrepreneurship in Fall River, 1813–1859" (Ph.D. diss., Harvard Univ., 1935); Thomas Russell Smith, *The Cotton Textile Industry of Fall River, Massachusetts: A Study of Industrial Localization* (New York: King's Crown Press, 1944); Mary Christopher Loughram, "The Development of the Church in the City of Fall River From the Beginning Until 1904" (Master's thesis, Catholic Univ. of America, 1932), 6–8, 12; *Fall River and Its Manufactories, 1803–1878: With Valuable Statistical Tables, From Official Sources,* 5th ed. rev. and enl. (Fall River: Benjamin Earl, 1878), 5–9; Alanson W. Borden, ed., *Our Country and Its People, A Descriptive and Biographical Record of Bristol County, Massachusetts* (Boston: Boston History, 1899), 422–24, 449–71, 481–502, 554–602. "Struggling hamlet" is Borden's phrase (460). Statistics on the Fall River work force were computed from John G. Palfrey, *Statistics of the Conditions and Products of Certain Branches of Industry in Massachusetts, for the Year Ending April 1, 1846* (Boston: Dutton and Wentworth, 1846), 275–77.

12. *NEA*, 16 Feb., 1, 8, 15, 29 Mar., 10 May, 11 July, 11 Oct. 1832; 10, 31 Oct. 1833; *WMA*, 3 March 1832; (New York) *Man*, 17 June 1834; Lamb, "Development of Entrepreneurship," 10–11; (Fall River) *Recorder*, 31 Oct. 1832; (Fall River) *Monitor*, 9 Nov. 1833. Benjamin Wood Pearce (*Recollections of a Long and Busy Life, 1819–1890* [Newport, R.I.: B. W. Pearce, Newport Enterprise, 1890], 42–43) claimed that the Satinet owners had lengthened the workday due to a large order, but the timing suggests a connection to the ten-hour agitation. On the NEA, see Commons, *History of Labour* 1:302–25; Foner, *History of the Labor Movement*, 1:104–6.

13. Likely the first organized labor agitation in New England after the onset of the depression, the group met under various names beginning in September 1840, adopting "Association of Industry" (AI) six months later. These activists provided a base for the dramatic upsurge of the mid-1840s. Although nothing is known of its membership, several AI leaders were prominent in subsequent labor struggles. See *Patriot*, 3 Dec. 1840; (Fall River) *Archetype*, 21, 28 Jan., 4, 11, 18, 25 Feb., 1, 29 Apr., 1 July, 12 Aug. 1841; *Monitor*, 23 Jan., 25 Sept. 1841; 26 Feb. 1842; (Fall River) *Gazette*, 27 Jan., 26 Feb. 1842. There is a reference to a workingmen's association having been founded five years earlier in Worcester in *Voice*, 5 Dec. 1845.

14. *Monitor*, 9 Mar., 6 Apr. 1844. The group began meeting in December 1843 and organized as the Mechanics' Association in March 1844. Dominated by carpenters, the leadership included a printer, an iron worker, and two shopkeepers, while a number of factory workers took leading roles in activities sponsored by the group. Like the regional movement it helped to create, the association advocated the shorter workday as an opening wedge to a broad transformation of the workplace and the community. In their newspaper, the *Mechanic*, activists discussed workers' cooperatives, land reform, utopian socialism, abolition of capital punishment, antislavery, and a host of other social reforms. On the ten-hour demand as a "stepping stone" to a more general reformation, see chap. 10.

15. *All Sorts*, 16 Mar. 1844; *Monitor*, 13 Apr. 1844; *Mechanic*, 27 Apr. 1844.

16. The NEWA was officially organized at Lowell in March 1845, though its initial gathering took place six months earlier at Boston, in response to calls for a regional association by local mechanics' organizations in Fall River and Lynn. See Persons, "Early History of Factory Legislation," 28–29; Ware, *Industrial Worker*, 202–22; McNeill, *Labor Movement*, 101–2, 104–11; Foner, *History of the Labor Movement* 1:202–7; Commons, *History of Labour* 1:537–40; Murphy, *Ten Hours' Labor*, chap. 6. In Fall River, several groups participated in the mid-1840s upsurge, including the Workingmen's Reform Association (WRA), founded by local shopkeepers and artisans apparently to involve mill workers. By spring 1845, with imported "scab" labor and internal dissension sapping the strength of the ten-hour strike, and active mill-owner opposition to the demand for a ten-hour law pressing on the movement generally, the activity expired. The town remained a center of labor agitation, with strikes among weavers, spinners, machinists, painters, and nailors, but these conflicts differed significantly from those of the early years in being increasingly immigrant affairs (n. 17). See *Mechanic*, 11 May, 7, 9, 21 Sept., 27 Apr., 13 July 1844; 1 Apr. 1845; Silvia, "Spindle City," chap. 2; Charles H. Mullen, "Textile Labor Movement: Nineteenth Century Fall River, Massachusetts" (unpubl. paper, 1964, Fall River Public Library [FRPL], 1964); Robert Howard, "Progress in the Textile Trades," in McNeill, *Labor Movement*, 215–16.

17. At least nine of thirteen leading laborites during the early 1830s were born in Massachusetts or Rhode Island; during the early and mid-1840s, only five of thirty-five identified leaders were foreign born. With no systematic ethnic survey of the town before 1865, no city directory until 1853, and only scattered and fragmentary mill records, it is impossible to determine the precise immigrant composition of the work force for the pre-1850 period, but all available quantitative evidence suggests that the work force was overwhelmingly native born and would remain so until the late 1840s. There were Irish in the area as early as 1774; a number came during the 1820s from the "Coal Pits" of Portsmouth, R.I. The English and Scots, most of them skilled textile workers or mechanics, had been in nearby Pawtucket and Providence since the 1780s; they, too, were working in Fall River by the 1820s. By this time, the work force also included Irish-born workers who had learned their textile trade in England (either in Lancashire or Yorkshire). Still, the only significant concentration

of immigrant workers before midcentury was in the calico print works industry, which employed large numbers of British operatives from its inception in Fall River during the 1820s. Unsurprisingly, the only labor agitation with significant numbers of immigrant workers before 1848 was a strike at Andrew Robeson's calico print works; for discussion of this strike, see the epilogue. On work force composition, see Victor S. Clark, *History of Manufactures in the United States* (New York: McGraw-Hill, 1929) 1:398; *Monitor*, 17 Feb. 1827; Massachusetts General Court, *House Document*, 1842, no. 4; *Senate Document*, 1842, no. 56; Alice Brayton, *Life on the Stream* (Newport, R.I.: Wilkinson Press, 1962) 1:54–57; Silvia, "Spindle City," 16, 28–29, 37; *Patriot*, 28 May 1840; *Monitor*, 30 May, 22 Aug., 2 Sept., 17, 24 Oct., 7 Nov., 5, 12 Dec. 1840; 27 Feb., 31 July, 2 Oct. 1841; 3 Dec. 1842; 7, 14 Jan., 11 Mar. 1843; 31 May, 25 Oct., 27 Dec. 1845; *News*, 22 Oct. 1846.

18. *Monitor*, 31 Jan. 1846; Orin Fowler, *Historical Sketch of Fall River* (Fall River: Benjamin Earl, 1841), 56. Intending to "call on every family" and visiting 2,038, the committee found only 262 (or 13 percent) "destitute." In 1830, the editor of the *Monitor* (14 Aug. 1830) claimed he knew no other "village" "where public worship [is] more generally attended, or the Sabbath better observed."

19. Ibid., 27 June 1840. Not enough work has been done on church participation during these years—general estimates are notoriously inexact, and criteria vary widely—but recent studies suggest an upward trajectory of the number of church members reaching roughly one-fifth to one-third of the adult population by midcentury. See Roger Finke and Rodney Stark, "Turning Pews into People," *Journal for the Scientific Study of Religion* 25 (June 1986): 180–92; Johnson, *Redeeming America*, 4, 10; idem, *Islands of Holiness*; David W. Kling, *A Field of Divine Wonders: The New Divinity and Village Revivals in Northwestern Connecticut, 1792–1822* (University Park, Pa.: Pennsylvania State Univ. Press, 1993), 190 and n. 75; Butler, *Awash in a Sea of Faith*, 283–84; Potash, *Vermont's Burned-Over District*; Terry D. Bilhartz, *Urban Religion and the Second Great Awakening: Church and Society in Early National Baltimore* (London and Toronto: Associated Univ. Presses, 1986); Glenn C. Altshuler, "Varieties of Religious Activity: Conflict and Community in the Churches of the Burned-Over District," in *Revivalism, Social Conscience, and Community in the Burned-Over District: The Trial of Rhoda Bement*, Altschuler and Jan M. Saltzgaber, eds., (Ithaca: Cornell Univ. Press, 1983), 148–49 and n. 9. For important remarks on criteria, see Hudson, *Religion in America*, 129–30.

20. Brayton, *Life on the Stream* 1:50–51.

21. *Monitor*, 5 Mar. 1846.

22. I have assumed here that the 603 townspeople who signed ten-hour petitions in 1842, 1843, and 1845 represent a fair sampling of the movement's constituency. The 1845 petition may have contained some with an electoral interest, however, as the movement had resolved to support for office only those who signed (*Mechanic*, 16 Nov. 1844).

23. Similarly with some immigrant Baptists: Englishman John E. Carr had been a member of the Fall River Baptist Church since 1834; Scot John C. Milne had attended regularly from 1835 (Adams, "Autobiography, 1816–1836," FRHS; Edward S. Adams Papers, FRHS; *Globe*, obit., 3 Apr. 1990; U.S. *Seventh Census* (1850); "Biographical File," FRHS.

24. Some leading Unitarians, usually professionals, shopkeepers, and sympathetic master artisans, became prominent movement figures. Hotelkeeper Horatio Gunn, a Unitarian officer, was the secretary of the AI and president of the WRA. Thomas D. Chaloner, a founder of the Fall River Unitarians, was the local *NEA* agent and a member of the Fall River Association of Mechanics and Workingmen in 1832; he was an NEWA officer in 1845. A carpenter who once worked in Fall River's mills, by the mid-1840s Chaloner was established enough to be chosen selectman and town representative to the Massachusetts General Court (Sykes, "Massachusetts Unitarians and Social Change, 129–30; "Payroll Records," "Time Books," Fall River Iron Works Collection, FRHS; *NEA*, 16 Feb. 1832; *Recorder*, 31 Oct. 1832; *Monitor*, 12 Mar. 1832; 9 Nov. 1833; 11 Nov. 1843; 21 June 1845; *News*, 5 June 1845; *Mechanic*, 1 Apr. 1845; *All Sorts*, 31 Jan. 1846; Edward S. Adams, *History of the Unitarian Church* [Fall River, 1932]).

25. *First Baptist Church, Fall River, Massachusetts: Centennial Anniversary, February 15, 1881*

(Fall River, 1881); *The Sesqui-Centennial History of the First Baptist Church of Fall River, Massachusetts, 1781–1931* (Fall River: Monroe Press, 1932), chap. 6; *Manual of the Second Baptist Church of Fall River, Massachusetts, 1881* (Fall River, 1897); Frank Wolcott Hutt, ed., *A History of Bristol County, Massachusetts* (New York: Lewis Historical, 1924) 1:355; *News*, 21 Feb. 1856; Margaret Russell Johnson, *Annals of the Church of the Ascension, Fall River, Massachusetts* (n.p., n.d.); Fowler, *Historical Sketch*; Lamb, "Development of Entrepreneurship," 14–19; Pearce, "Recollections"; Borden, *Our Country*, 276–81, 502–7; Sykes, "Massachusetts Unitarianism and Social Change," 129–30.

26. The Christian Church emerged at the turn of the nineteenth century from three separate but related movements: among Kentucky, southern Indiana, and North Carolina Baptists, Virginia Methodists, and New England Baptists. Taking the name "Christian" to avoid all partisan labels, these movements sought an end to hierarchy, formalism, and dogma in their churches. They stressed democracy, simplicity, and the right of each individual to interpret the Bible without mediation: the covenant of the First Christian Church of Fall River declared Jesus its only leader and the Bible an infallible guide to faith, order, and discipline. Similarly, the North Christian Society insisted upon just three principles at its formation: nonsectarianism, Christian character as the only test of fellowship, and the Word of God interpreted by the individual as the sole standard of doctrine. See *Rules of Government and Covenant of the First Christian Church of Fall River, Massachusetts, Organized April 9, 1829* (Fall River: Almy and Milne, 1877); "Membership Book," North Christian Society, in possession of Albert Canedy, Fall River. On the Christians generally, see Lester G. McAllister and William E. Tucker, *Journey in Faith: A History of the Christian Church* [Disciples of Christ] (St. Louis: Bethany Press, 1975); Milo True Morrill, *A History of the Christian Denomination in America, 1794–1911* (Dayton, Ohio: Christian Publ. Association, 1912); David E. Harrell, Jr., *Quest for a Christian America: The Disciples of Christ and American Society to 1866* (Nashville: Disciples of Christ Historical Society, 1966); Nathan Hatch, "The Christian Movement and the Demand for a Theology of the People," *Journal of American History* 67 (Dec. 1980): 545–67; idem, *Democratization of American Christianity*, 68–81.

27. As for the other congregations that appealed to the less affluent here, the Episcopalians and Presbyterians maintained relatively small congregations of mostly British textile workers; the Universalists, Freewill Baptists, Millerites, and Swedenborgians left no records. See Johnson, *Annals of the Church of the Ascension*; Fenner, *History of Fall River*, 117; *Journals of the Proceedings of the Conventions of the Episcopal Diocese in Massachusetts* (Boston, 1836–50); *The One Hundredth Anniversary of the United Presbyterian Church in Fall River, Massachusetts* (Fall River, 1946); personal communication, Iain Murtin to the author; Benjamin Wilbur, "Life of Benjamin Wilbur," FRHS; Historical Records Survey, *An Inventory of Universalist Archives in Massachusetts* (Boston, 1942); Adams Papers; *Monitor*, 9 Apr. 1836; 1 Aug. 1840; 6 Mar. 1841; 15 Oct., 19 Nov. 1842; 14 Jan., 9 Dec. 1843; 1, 22, 24 Oct. 1846; 26 June 1847; *Patriot*, 9 Aug. 1838; *All Sorts*, 24 Sept. 1843; 21 Nov. 1846; *News*, 24 June 1847; 13 Sept. 1849; *Mechanic*, 14 Dec. 1844; the Reverends G. A. Burgess and J. T. Ward, *Free Baptist Cyclopedia: Historical and Biographical* (n.p.: Free Baptist Cyclopedia, 1889), 523–24; *Rhode Island Freewill Baptist Pulpit* (Boston: Gould and Lincoln, 1852), 246–49; Hutt, *History of Bristol County*, 1:369; F. Sidney Mayer to the Reverend William Worcester, 9 Jan. 1910, "Fall River Society of New Church" File, Swedenborgian Library, Newton, Mass.; *Fifteenth Anniversary of the Society of the New Jerusalem at Bridgewater, Massachusetts, May 29, 1883* (Boston, 1883), 24–26; *New Jerusalem Magazine* 27 (1854–55): 401; Hurd, *History of Bristol County*, 361, 383.

28. *Monitor*, 9 Apr. 1836; 29 Feb., 7, 14 Mar. 1840; *Patriot*, 27 Feb. 1840.

29. *Sesquicentennial-History*, 13; "Source Material Book" (1781–1949), First Baptist Church; Bowen Scrapbook, FRHS; *Moments in History: Bicentennial Souvenir Booklet*, First Baptist Church, 5; *First Baptist Church, Fall River*, 36–39; (Fall River) *Evening News*, obit., 1 Dec. 1866; 1 July 1893; (Boston) *Commercial Gazette*, 13 Aug. 1835; *Monitor*, 23, 30, Aug. 1834; 13 Feb., 9 July 1836; 16 Dec. 1837; 1 Jan. 1842; 13, 20 June, 8, 15 Aug. 1846; *Patriot*, 6 July 1837; 20 Sept. 1838; 4 July 1839; Earl, *Centennial History*, 241; *Massachusetts Annual Baptist Convention, 1876*, 65–66.

30. Although a church member later claimed that a second congregation became necessary because the parish area was "too wide" for one meetinghouse, all other accounts indicate that disputes over social issues prompted the division. According to the historian of the Second Baptist Church, Bronson's "decided views and agitation for" the ten-hour demand provoked a "slight discord," resulting in his resignation and removal to the First Baptist Church of Albany, N.Y. Moreover, at its founding in the summer of 1846, the Second Baptist Church adopted a plan for free seats and voluntary contributions; the words scrawled in the front of its church minutes book illustrate its reputation in their community: "Dr. Thomas says Radicals." Though a number of important labor activists did remain with the original group, it does not appear that the two groups of activists represented opposing points of view or different constituencies within the labor movement. Among the nearly five hundred congregants of the First Baptist Church, fifty-three had signed ten-hour petitions. Moreover, like their counterparts in the Second Baptist Church, several of these activists were leaders of the congregation: the treasurer and five trustees of its Bible Society in 1836, all ten-hour men and including Philip and Elisha Smith (see below), remained in the First Baptist Church after 1846. See "Source Material Book"; Abram G. Hart, "Historical Sketch of the Second Baptist Church," in *Manual of the Second Baptist Church;* "Minutes Book of the Second Baptist Church of Fall River," in possession of Barbara Bogle, Fall River; *The One Hundredth Anniversary of the Baptist Temple Church, 1846–1946* (Fall River, 1946); *A Brief History of the Second Baptist Church of Fall River, Massachusetts* (Fall River: William S. Robertson, 1881), 5–10; *All Sorts,* 13 June 1846; *Monitor,* 13, 20 June, 8, 15 Aug. 1846; *News,* 1 Oct. 1846.

31. Twenty-two members had signed ten-hour petitions.

32. *Manual of the First Baptist Church; NEA,* 16 Feb. 1832; *Recorder,* 31 Oct. 1832; *Monitor,* 9 Nov. 1833; 10 Apr. 1841; 2 Dec. 1843; AI, "To the Employers of Fall River" (11 Oct. 1841), FRHS; "Record Book of the Fall River Workingmen's Protective Union," FRHS; "Payroll Records," Iron Works Collection; *Patriot,* 14 Sept. 1837; *News,* 2 Oct. 1851; 28 Oct. 1852; Bowen Scrapbook, 7. Smith apparently drew no distinction between social activism in the community and social activism in the church. In 1842, during the furious debate over slavery within the Baptist denomination, he offered a resolution in meeting that declared, "slavery is one of the grossest sins against God." Smith's wife was also involved in church-related social activities. In 1828, shortly after joining the congregation, she and several other women founded the "Ladies Benevolent Society" to aid the church's poor ("Source Material Book"). Elisha Smith, another machinist in this church, was a prominent speaker at labor meetings, presiding over the largest ten-hour rally of the period, on July 4, 1844. He was also active in the WRA and later became an officer of the New England Protective Union, a regional network of consumer cooperatives. Joining the Baptists in 1834, he became trustee of its Sunday school two years later and remained a leading member of the congregation through the 1840s (*Manual of the First Baptist Church;* Wilbur, "Life of Benjamin Wilbur"; *Mechanic,* 6 July, 14, 21 Sept. 1844).

33. Samuel J. Carr was a product of the same Baptist revival; he subsequently became a clergyman in that denomination (*Manual of the First Baptist Church;* Hart, "Historical Sketch"; "Minutes Book of the Second Baptist Church"; *Mechanic,* 22 June 1844; *Monitor,* 25 Oct. 1845; U.S. *Seventh Census*).

34. Born in Scotland in 1824, Milne was raised in the strictly religious household of his grandfather, a Baptist preacher, who brought him to North America in 1832, settling first in Nova Scotia where young Milne worked in the family printing office. Three years later, the family moved to Massachusetts, following relatives who had found employment there. Arriving in Fall River shortly thereafter, at the tender age of twelve Milne went to work in Andrew Robeson's calico dye works, while he continued his childhood practice of regular church worship at Bronson's meetinghouse. In 1838, he accepted an offer to return to the printing trade as a compositor at the local Democratic paper, the *Patriot.* Here he met Thomas Almy, who would soon become a prominent labor leader. The two young printers continued to work together on a number of short-lived Democratic papers after the *Patriot* folded in 1840. During the spring of 1844, as Mechanics' Association members, they collaborated on the *Mechanic.* Although Milne was a consistent worshiper in Bronson's congrega-

tion, he did not become a member until the founding of the Second Baptist Church in 1846. Still, as a young man in his late teens, he seems to have been quite close to his minister. When Milne left Fall River in search of work after the *Mechanic* folded in April 1845, he went to Albany, where Bronson had taken up another ministry. With the pastor's help, Milne secured several months' employment as a printer in New York City. Late in 1845, he returned to Fall River to help Almy edit a new Democratic paper, the *Weekly News*. When discontented local Baptists formed a new congregation with Bronson as their pastor, Milne was in the forefront of the movement. See Borden, *Our Country*, 776–78; Biographical File, FRHS; Lamb, "Development of Entrepreneurship," 14; *News*, 10 Apr. 1845. Milne was later a leading activist in the cooperative movement.

35. "Book A," "Book B, Board of Stewards and Leaders of the First Methodist Church in Fall River, May 13, 1844," "Record Book No. 1, 1827–37," "Constitution and Records of the Sunday School Society of the First Methodist Episcopal Church, Fall River, Massachusetts, September 6, 1847," "Account Book, 1827–38," First Methodist Church, United Methodist Church, Fall River; "Subscription Book, 1851–64," "Record Book No. 1," Second Methodist Church, United Methodist Church; *Voice*, 12 June 1845; *Mechanic*, 4 Jan. 1845.

36. "Membership Book I, 1829–53," First Christian Church of Fall River, FRHS; *Mechanic*, 4 Jan. 1845; 20 July 1844.

37. *The One-Hundredth Anniversary of the United Presbyterian Church in Fall River*, 3.

38. Johnson, *Annals of the Church of the Ascension;* "Parochial Register of the Church of the Ascension," 1841–42, 1842–43, Church of the Ascension, Fall River.

39. "Membership Book," "Minutes Book," North Christian Society.

40. *Mechanic*, 8 Feb. 1845.

41. The FWA met for a mere six months in late 1844 and early 1845. However, as noted in the preface, the surviving record of its activities and personnel is unique: a complete membership list, all of the group's official pronouncements (including its constitution and all resolutions passed by the body), and the minutes of its weekly meetings have been preserved in the "FWA Record Book."

42. Also, Wilkens.

43. "FWA Record Book"; Bailey, "Early Workingmen's Association," 246. The phrase "nature's God," often associated with deism, was also used by churchgoing Christians in the FWA, like Baptist William S. Wilder. Nothing is known of Birch's activities in Fitchburg, save that he worked as a shoemaker in Horace Hayward's shop on West Main Street.

44. The phrase "Christians and philanthropists," a label commonly adopted by antebellum labor reformers, appeared in the preamble to the FWA constitution ("FWA Record Book"). On the use and meaning of the appellation, see chap. 8.

45. On Fitchburg's early industrial development, see Kirkpatrick, *City and the River* 1:81–83, 120–24, 147–55; D. Hamilton Hurd, *History of Worcester County* (Philadelphia: J. W. Lewis, 1889) 1:208; William A. Emerson, *Fitchburg, Massachusetts: Past and Present* (Fitchburg: Blanchard and Brown, 1903); *Globe*, 28 Apr. 1878.

46. Palfrey, *Statistics*, 100–102.

47. By 1850, only 25 percent of Fitchburg's work force was engaged in agriculture; its industrial growth did not compare to some of the larger mill towns of this era. In Fall River, for example, farming accounted for less than 3 percent of the work force in 1850. Statistics compiled from U.S. *Seventh Census*.

48. The native born accounted for this growth in population. Although Irish workers helped build the railroad to Boston (some forty-five miles away) during the early 1840s, barely 5 percent of the population was foreign born in 1845 (Kirkpatrick, *City and the River* 1:191; [Fitchburg] *Sentinel*, 12 Sept. 1845).

49. Ibid., 22 July 1840.

50. "FWA Record Book." Two of the five writers were church members: Hosea Proctor (Baptist) and Daniel Wilkins (Trinitarian Congregationalist). Two others would soon edit papers in which they explicitly identified themselves as Christians: William F. Young (*Voice*) and E. R. Wilkins (*Wachusett Independent*).

51. The textile mills employed an average of 35 workers, the paper mills only 7. By contrast, Lowell's textile mills employed an average of 229 workers. Compiled from Palfrey, *Statistics*, 59–62, 100–102.

52. Fitchburg paper manufacturer Alvah Crocker and others campaigned for the road in neighboring communities during the winter of 1841–42. In an effort to raise funds and convince a suspicious populace, Crocker spoke more than a hundred times, often to shouts and ridicule. In the latter part of 1842, a fire of suspicious origin destroyed his mill. His brother Samuel, whose factory also went up in the fire, claimed the blaze was "incited by prejudice" stemming from the railroad project (Kirkpatrick, *City and the River* 1:177–78; Henry A. Willis, "The Early Days of Railroads in Fitchburg," *FHS Proceedings* 1 (1895): 27–49).

53. Seventy of the 131 members were traced in the 1850 census. Sixty-five (92.8 percent) were born in New England—fifty-five (78 percent) in Massachusetts and New Hampshire.

54. By "leadership," I am referring to FWA officers, delegates to labor conventions, and those who participated in debates or discussions within the organization. Of 131 members, 21 fell into one or more of these categories.

55. This last figure understates the presence of factory workers and ordinary laborers in the FWA. A number of the women in the group whose occupations could not be determined were probably mill hands, and those who left no record of their work were more likely unskilled than skilled. At the same time, *non*factory workers clearly dominated the group; the group's meeting time was 6:30 in the evening. There was some discussion of holding Saturday evening meetings "to accommodate those who are denied the privilege of attending other evenings of the week," but the idea was rejected because the cost of renting a hall on that day was considered too high (Kirkpatrick, *City and the River* 1:163; "FWA Record Book").

56. Walter A. Davis, comp., *The Old Town Records of the Town of Fitchburg, Massachusetts* (Fitchburg: FHS, 1907) (hereafter, *Old Records of Fitchburg*), vol. 6; *Sentinel*, 13 Mar. 1839; 3 Mar., 7 July 1841; 15 Apr. 1842; 10 Mar., 1 Dec. 1848; First Parish Church of Fitchburg, "Valuation of Polls and Estates" (1844), FHS.

57. "FWA Record Book."

58. Ebenezer Foster Bailey, "Reminiscences Relating to the Second Meeting-House in Fitchburg," *FHS Proceedings* 4 (1908): 52–64; "Obituaries, 1878–1883," FHS Scrapbook, 19–20; E. F. Bailey, "Mr. Shelton's School," in Bailey Papers, FHS, 37; idem, "History of Fitchburg Notes," FHS.

59. Bailey, "Mr. Shelton's School," 38; idem, "Reminiscences"; George Alfred Hitchcock, *A History of the Calvinistic Congregational Church and Society* (Fitchburg: Sentinel, 1902).

60. Topics included, for example, "the effect of manufacturing on the physical and moral nature of mankind."

61. Kirkpatrick, *City and the River* 1:192; *Sentinel*, 2, 9, 30 Jan. 1846. Other FWA members, such as printer and bookbinder Charles Shipley and law student Milton Whitney, also participated in Lyceum debates. Like the Bailey brothers, Shipley and Whitney were members of the Calvinistic Congregational Church.

62. Hitchcock, "Camera View of Early Homes," FHS, 22; *Old Records of Fitchburg*, vol. 6; *The Principles and Rules, with the Articles of Faith and Covenant, of the Trinitarian Church, Fitchburg; With a List of the Officers and Members* (Fitchburg: W. J. Merriam, 1843). Kinsman's grandfather had been elected to Fitchburg's school committee in 1789; the family had been involved in the Congregational Church in Fitchburg at least since 1805 (Hitchcock, *History of the Calvinistic Congregational*).

63. "Important" Scrapbook, FHS, 52; *Sentinel*, 8 May, 12 June 1839; "Records of the Baptist Church of Fitchburg," FHS.

64. *Old Records of Fitchburg*, vol. 6; "Records of the Baptist Church"; "Valuations of the Town of Fitchburg" (1844), Fitchburg City Hall.

65. Here, I have used the percentage of the over-sixteen population in 1840 (42 percent) to determine the eligible communicant population in 1845 and calculated the proportion of churchgoing Fitchburgers as of 1844. For figures, see tables 4.4–4.8.

66. Hitchcock, *History of the Calvinistic Congregational.* In 1815, financial troubles led to a temporary reunion of the Calvinists and Unitarians, who had kept the original name of the congregation, the Church of Christ; they split again in 1823, the Unitarians now calling themselves the First Parish Church.

67. Methodists, Universalists, and a few Freewill Baptists also worshiped in the town from the mid-1780s. The Universalists held public services in the town hall as early as 1837, but they did not organize a society until the fall of 1844. The Freewill Baptists, always few in number in Fitchburg, played no known role in the association. The Methodists are discussed in detail below. The Millerites held outdoor meetings in local groves and open fields in the early 1840s; by 1845 they had disappeared entirely from the area. There is no evidence of any support for this group within the FWA. See Kirkpatrick, *City and the River* 1:126, 193; Hart, *Commonwealth History of Massachusetts* 1:8–13; Hurd, *History of Worcester County* 1:253; Kendall Brooks, *Historical Sketch of the Baptist Church in Fitchburg* (Fitchburg, 1861); *History of the First Universalist Society of Fitchburg, Massachusetts* (Fitchburg: Blanchard and Brown, 1894); "Garfield" Scrapbook, FHS, 131; *Sentinel,* 5 Aug. 1842; 6 Sept. 1844; 18 July 1845.

68. Martha D. Tolman, "An Historical Sketch of the Third Congregational Trinitarian Church of Fitchburg," *FHS Proceedings* 5 (1914): 45–68.

69. "FWA Record Book." On Pettibone and the FWA's use of his church, see chap. 7.

70. Even this figure does not tell the entire story. Two Methodists who joined the Baptist Church in 1843–44 and two others who were "on trial" in the Methodist Church were never received into full communion. With the addition of these four, Methodists and former Methodists accounted for 46 percent of the FWA communicants. For sources, see "Records of the First Methodist Episcopal Church," Faith United Parish, Fitchburg.

71. On 20 Feb. 1845, at an FWA meeting in Pettibone's vestry, the group "voted to choose a committee consisting of one from each religious society in town to invite the clergymen to lecture" ("FWA Record Book"). Like all the other ministers in town, the Methodist pastor refused the invitation.

72. N. T. Whittaker, *History of the First Methodist Episcopal Church, 1794–1897* (Fitchburg: Sentinel, 1897); D. Dorchester, "Early History of the First Methodist Episcopal Church in Fitchburg"; (Ashville, N.C.) *Methodist,* 17, 18 Dec. 1888; Kirkpatrick, *City and the River* 1:193–95.

73. Whittaker, *History of First Methodist; Sentinel,* 3 Feb. 1843.

74. "Records of First Methodist"; "Records of the Baptist Church"; *Sentinel,* 19 Aug. 1842; William A. Emerson, *A Centenary Discourse, Delivered in the Meeting House of the Calvinistic Congregational Church, in Fitchburg, Massachusetts* (Fitchburg: Kellog and Simons, 1868), 16; Hitchcock, *History of Calvinistic Congregational,* appendix.

75. "Records of First Methodist." By contrast, the Baptists received 102 converts into a congregation of more than 150, and the Calvinists received 108 into a congregation of several hundred. It does not appear that the Unitarians, Universalists, or Freewill Baptists participated in the revival in any substantial way, the first because of its traditional aversion to revivalism, the latter two because of their insignificant size. Unfortunately, there is little evidence concerning the Millerites, who did participate in the enthusiasm. Indeed, the historian of the Fitchburg Methodist Church maintained later that only the Methodists were able to "contend successfully" with the Millerites, whose presence may be glimpsed from one of their camp meetings in early september 1844. Here, the *Sentinel* reported, some 50 females sat on the "anxious seat." The editor did not say how many others attended the gathering, nor how many were merely curious observers like himself, but clearly this sect caused quite a stir in Fitchburg (Whittaker, *History of First Methodist; Sentinel,* 6 Sept. 1844).

76. "Records of First Methodist."

77. Again, the number of laborers and factory workers among the Methodists was probably higher, since seven of the fifteen women in the FWA were Methodists. See n. 55.

78. Ten FWA members who joined the Methodists during the revival have been identified by occupation; seven were factory workers or ordinary laborers, only one a skilled artisan.

79. "Valuations of Fitchburg" (1844).

80. *Sentinel*, 5 Jan., 16, 23 Feb. 1844.

81. "Records of First Methodist"; "Valuations of Fitchburg" (1844, 1845).

82. "Records of First Methodist"; "Valuations of Fitchburg" (1844); U.S. *Seventh Census.*

83. George Clark Baker, Jr., *An Introduction to the History of Early New England Methodism, 1789–1839* (Durham, N.C.: Duke Univ. Press, 1941); James Mudge, *History of the New England Conference of the Methodist Episcopal Church, 1796–1910;* John Leland Peters, *Christian Perfectionism and American Methodism* (Nashville, Tenn.: Abingdon Press, 1956); Charles G. Steffen, *The Mechanics of Baltimore: Workers and Politics in the Age of Revolution, 1763–1812* (Urbana: Univ. of Illinois, 1984), chap. 12; Russell E. Richey, *Early American Methodism* (Bloomington: Indiana Univ. Press, 1991).

84. The only Methodist to appear in the "FWA Record Book" was the delegate chosen to solicit that church's minister to speak before the association. The thirteen communicants among the group's twenty-one leaders belonged to other congregations: four Calvinists, three Trinitarians, three Baptists, two Unitarians, and one Universalist.

85. *WI,* 8 Feb. 1845.

86. Before midcentury, Boston's economy was largely commercial and financial, serving as an entrepôt for manufactured goods and as a source of capital for factory and railroad building. Comparatively poor waterpower and a scarcity of cheap labor kept its manufacturing sector small and localized; with the exception of glass and iron, there was little machine production in the city. The best overview is still Oscar Handlin's *Boston's Immigrants: A Study in Acculturation* (Cambridge: Harvard Univ. Press, 1941), chaps. 1, 3. See also Carroll Wright and Horace Waldin, "Industries of the Last Hundred Years," in *The Memorial History of Boston,* Justin Winsor, ed. (Boston: Ticknor, 1880), vol. 4, chap. 3; Eric Lampard, "Afterword," in Peter R. Knights, *The Plain People of Boston, 1830–1860: A Study in City Growth* (New York: Oxford Univ. Press, 1971).

87. Seth Luther, *An Address Delivered Before the Mechanics and Working-Men of the City of Brooklyn* [hereafter, *Brooklyn Address*] (Brooklyn, 1836), 25–26. For other, similar remarks on this incident, see *NEA,* 12, 19 July 1834.

88. I have identified 561 Boston labor activists from local and labor newspaper reports, all of whom must be considered leaders of one sort or another: officers of labor organizations, convention delegates, speakers, and strike leaders.

89. By 1860, there were more than a hundred church congregations in Boston, rendering the labor–church membership linkage far more difficult here than in the other communities studied. Therefore, the Boston figures are probably understated. However, I did obtain at least partial records for nearly three-quarters of these congregations. See the source notes for table 4.9.

90. *Hollis Street Church from Mather Baylies to Thomas Starr King, 1732–1861* (Boston, 1877); *NEA,* 11 Oct. 1833; 10 Oct. 1832.

91. *Articles of Salem Street Church; The Articles of Faith and Covenant of the Bowdoin Street Church* (Boston, 1836); *The Articles of Faith and Covenant of the Hanover Street Church* (Boston, 1826); *Phillips Church, Alphabetical List of Members* (Boston, 1872); *Reformer,* 3 Nov. 1834; (Boston) *Post,* 9 July 1835.

92. *Articles of Salem Street Church; NEA,* 23 Feb., 5 Apr., 5 July 1832.

93. "Membership Book of the High Street Methodist Episcopal Church, 1820–1854," Boston Univ. Theology Library; *Post,* 7 May 1835.

94. French, "Liberation from Man and God in Boston."

95. Many of these subscribers lived outside of Boston, however. By 1832, Kneeland had fifty-five agents in nine states, and in Canada as well (ibid, 208).

96. Ibid., 208, 212, 215, 218.

97. Citing Handlin's observation that laborers flooded into the city during the 1820s and 1830s, taking the places of those who had moved West, French suggests that Kneeland's Boston audience consisted of workers who had recently migrated from "depressed rural areas of New England." But he offers no evidence that Freethought was particularly popular among these

newcomers. While other students of the movement concur that Freethought societies were sustained by the so-called lower classes, most believe that the recruits were more likely urban bred than recent farm migrants. As Post points out (*Popular Freethought in America*, chaps. 1, 3), the infidel movement of the late 1820s and 1830s concentrated in larger cities, particularly New York, Philadelphia, and Boston, precisely because these were the most secularized communities in the society. As for Freethought strength in Boston, shortly after Kneeland began lecturing there, he switched his Sunday morning service to the afternoon, probably, as French suggests (208–9), to "accommodate those who wished to attend church services as well as his meetings."

98. *NEA*, 12 Sept. 1833. Two months earlier (18 July 1833), Douglas reprinted a letter from an anticlerical friend of labor who asserted that the clergy's betrayal of "equal rights" had "allowed Irreligion to become the order of the day." "The truly orthodox are only those who dare to oppose this vicious conspiracy for priestcraft and political jugglers," he insisted.

99. Arthur Schlesinger, Jr., *Orestes Brownson: A Pilgrim's Progress* (Boston: Little, Brown, 1939), 34, 50–60; Americo D. Lapati, *Orestes A. Brownson* (New York: Twayne, 1965), 31, 55. The church, which continued to meet until 1844, drew audiences of three to five hundred for Sunday services but apparently never established a stable and regular membership in the city.

100. *Reformer*, 11 Aug. 1836.

101. "Ten Hour Circular," in Commons, *Documentary History* 6:94–99.

102. *A Sketch of the History of the Boston Society of the New Jerusalem* (Boston, 1873).

103. *Reformer*, 6 Jan. 1837. On Wood, see chap. 3.

104. *Brooklyn Address*, 26.

105. *Phillips Church, Alphabetical List of Members*.

106. Despite Wright's laments, his church claimed a membership of 250 in 1850 (*South Boston Gazette*, 22, 29 Jan., 3 June 1848; 2 Nov. 1850).

107. *Laborer*, 18 May 1844.

108. MBSL, *Seventh Annual Report* (1877), 73.

109. *Voice*, 28 Jan. 1848. As noted (chap. 1, n. 71), Orvis and Jaques were Associationists; they embraced Christianity while rejecting the contemporary church. Orvis's parents were Hicksite Quakers, but he stopped going to meeting when he was young. According to one acquaintance, however, Orvis never abandoned "that conception of life" (Lindsay Swift, *Brook Farm: Its Members, Scholars, and Visitors* [New York: Macmillan, 1900], 175; (New York) *Harbinger*, 11, 27 Feb., 23 Oct., 27 Nov., 3, 25 Dec. 1847).

110. Boston workers, labor activists among them, surely attended Orestes Brownson's "Church of the Future" in the 1830s, packed public halls to hear the radical Unitarian reformer Theodore Parker in the 1840s, and gathered in city parks to hear evangelical "street preachers" in the 1850s. But we have little evidence of just *who* these adherents were.

Chapter 5

1. (Wilmington) *American Watchman*, 31 Aug., 3, 7, 10, 14, 17, 24 Sept., 1, 8, 12, 15 Oct. 1824; *Lafayette in Delaware* (n.p., 1934), 11–14; A. Levasseur, *Lafayette in America in 1824 and 1825; or, Journal of a Voyage to the United States* (Philadelphia: Carey and Lea, 1829), 159–61; Anna T. Lincoln, *Wilmington, Delaware, Three Centuries Under Four Flags, 1609–1937* (Rutledge, Vt.: Tuttle, 1937), 198–201. The *Watchman's* description of the visit ("Lafayette's Visit to Delaware," 8 Oct. 1824) can be found in Charles E. Green, *History of the M. W. Grand Lodge of Ancient, Free and Accepted Masons of Delaware* (Wilmington.: William N. Cann, 1956), 67–71.

2. For information on church membership—Robinson and Brobson: "Wilmington Monthly Meeting of Friends: Marriages, Births, Deaths, to 1830. First Membership List" [hereafter, Friends List] (copied from original records by Gilbert and Anna C. Cope, 1906), DHS; Corbit: J. Barton Cheaprey, "Daniel Corbit" (typescript, 19 June 1936), 1, in Jeanette Eckman Collection, Daniel Corbit File, Box 6, DHS; Henry C. Conrad, *History of the State of Delaware* (Wilmington: Publ. by

the author, 1908) 3:907–9; Chandler: "Every Evening," *History of Wilmington: The Commercial, Social, and Religious Growth of the City During the Past Century* (Wilmington, 1894), 26; Gibbs: Sunday School Class Book, subscriber, Prayer Book, 1827, St. James Episcopal Church (Stanton), DHS; Clark: Family History File, Clark Family, DHS, 12–14.

3. On Alrichs and Webb, see Friends List; J. Thomas Scharf, *History of Delaware, 1609–1886* (Philadelphia: L. J. Richard, 1888), 2:639. For Siddal's role in initiating what became the Brandywine Manufacturers' Sunday School, see Frank W. Zebley, *The Churches of Delaware* (Wilmington, n.p., 1947), 123; Longwood Manuscripts, Group 9, Series A, Hagley Museum and Library. Two other participants, John McClung and John Hedges, were involved in labor reform activities in Wilmington, surfacing in 1847 as president and vice president, respectively, of the Convention Reform Association, a largely working-class organization dedicated to a general program of labor reform to be initiated mainly by changes in the state constitution. They, too, were church members—McClung: Records of the First Presbyterian Church of Wilmington, 1838–1920 (microfilm, DHS); Hedges: Lincoln, *Wilmington, Delaware*, 168.

4. Carol E. Hoffecker, *Delaware: A Brief History* (New York: W. W. Norton), 8–13.

5. After the English had established permanent control in the 1660s, competing claims by Lord Calvert of Baltimore and William Penn cast a shadow over the area for the better part of another century. In the end, Maryland significantly shaped the lower part of Delaware (Kent and Sussex Counties), and Pennsylvania exerted the more profound influence over the upper part (New Castle County). See Scharf, *History of Delaware* 2:629; Hoffecker, *Delaware*, 4, 19–23, 77; idem, *Wilmington, Delaware: Portrait of an Industrial City, 1830–1910* (Charlottesville: Univ. Press of Virginia for the Eleutherian Mills-Hagley Foundation, 1974), 3.

6. Ibid., 3–4; John A. Munroe, *History of Delaware* (1st ed., 1979; 2nd ed., Newark: Univ. of Delaware Press, 1984), 110.

7. Scharf, *History of Delaware* 2:630–33; Hoffecker, *Delaware*, 27–28, 78–79; idem, *Wilmington*, xiv, 7.

8. To be sure, by midcentury, a sort of "second phase" of economic development began, with the emergence of heavy industry, such as the fabrication of railroad cars, boilers, cast-iron ships, and rolled iron and steel. Even in these endeavors, though, production was often accomplished by small groups of skilled workers. A "third stage" of economic development began after 1890 with the decline of industry and the rise of management and research. For sources, see n. 9.

9. Hoffecker, *Wilmington*, xiv, 4, 15–28, 30–31, 71; idem, *Delaware*, 29–49; Mary Durham Johnson, "Madame E. I. DuPont and Madame Victorine DuPont Banduy, the First Mistress of the Eleutherian Mills: Models of Domesticity in the Brandywine Valley During the Antebellum Era," in Glenn Porter and William H. Mulligan, eds., *Working Papers from the Regional Economic History Research Center* (Wilmington: Eleutherian Mills-Hagley Foundation, 1982), vol. 5, nos. 2 and 3, 28. In 1805, Jedediah Morse thought the region would soon become the greatest seat of manufacturing in the United States; by 1829, the key industrial area of the state was Christiana Hundred, which included Wilmington. See Richard Lynch Mumford, "Constitutional Development in the State of Delaware, 1776–1897" (Ph.D. diss., Univ. of Delaware, 1968), 152; Roger A. Martin, *A History of Delaware Through Its Governors, 1776–1984* (Wilmington: McClafferty, 1984), 158.

10. Known by various names, but most commonly as the "WMP," this movement was complex and diverse in both membership and program. Much of the historical literature concerns its "authenticity." To be sure, some of those involved came from outside the ranks of labor—typically opportunistic politicians and businessmen—with other goals in mind than simply the advancement of workers. And, for that reason, working-class activists in the movement sought to keep out large employers and capitalists and to remain independent of "designing" politicians. Meanwhile, the WMP's demands, ranging from mild reform to radical social transformation, generated tension over means and ends. But historians' consequent obsession with the "authenticity" issue has blinded many to the importance of this movement. Typical of early American labor movements, the WMP was a mixed affair; as the first supralocal expression of organized labor protest in the nation's history, it deserves careful scrutiny in its various manifestations, not dismissal because it

fails the test of some essentialist version of working-class agitation. On "authenticity," see Pessen, *Most Uncommon Jacksonians* (13–14), which is framed around the question of whether these were "true" Working Men's parties or "fraudulent" " 'associations of so-called workingmen.' " A particularly forceful recent argument that such parties, in one place at least, were a "front" for ambitious capitalists can be found in Marc Ferris, "The Workingmen's Party of Hampshire County, 1811–1835," *Historical Journal of Massachusetts* 28 (winter 1990): 37–60. But see, too, Formisano, *Transformation of Political Culture,* chap. 10, which stresses the greater influence of politicians and employers in the Working Men's *party* as opposed to the broader Working Men's *movement.* In any case, as Pessen points out (27), despite similarities among various groups, no two were precisely the same. On the various names used, see ibid., 10. On the movement generally, see Helen L. Sumner, "Citizenship," in Commons, *History of Labour* 1:169–332; Foner, *History of the Labor Movement* 1:97–106, 121–42; Laurie, *Artisans into Workers,* 79–83. The best local treatment is Wilentz, *Chants Democratic,* chap. 5. On New England, see Arthur B. Darling, "The Workingmen's Party in Massachusetts, 1833–34," *American Historical Review* 29 (Oct. 1923): 81–86.

11. The NEA fielded its last candidates in the Massachusetts gubernatorial campaigns of 1833 and 1834. In other places—in New Jersey and New York City, for example—the Working Men continued to run for political office in the mid-1830s, but this was long after the party itself, *as a movement,* had dissipated. See Pessen, *Most Uncommon Jacksonians,* 26, 32.

12. Foner, *History of the Labor Movement* 1:103; Commons, *History of Labour* 1:287–90. "Yorick," an *MFP* correspondent in Wilmington, claimed in late 1829 that the paper circulated among the "Working class" there "perhaps" more than any other (*MFP,* 17 Oct. 1829).

13. (Wilmington) *Delaware Register,* 20, 27 June 1829.

14. Ibid., 25 July 1829.

15. Ibid., 15 Aug., 19, 26 Sept. 1829. Following the traditional historiography, the only modern historian of the AWPNCC (sometimes, "Working Men's Association of New Castle County") insists that the group was "not made up of *real* workingmen, but rather of skilled artisans whose level of education was a cut above the average" (Thomas Dew, "Delaware's First Labor Party: A History of Working People of Newcastle County, 1829–1832" [Master's thesis, Univ. of Delaware, 1959], 24 [my emphasis]). Matters were a good deal more complex. To be sure, there was concern in the ranks about infiltration by elements not of the working class. "A Mechanic" warned, "I think that we had better beware of men of capital, as we have had application from such men to join this society"; AWPNCC founder George McFarlane warned of the wolf in sheep's clothing, asking, "have not men come in among you, who are not of you?" (*MFP,* 24 Oct. 1829; McFarlane, *An Address Delivered Before the Association of Working People of New-Castle County, at the Town Hall, Wilmington, April 3, 1830, To Which is Added, Sundry Resolutions, Stating the Objects of the Association* [Wilmington, 1830], 19). Interestingly enough, for Dew, McFarlane was not an "authentic" worker himself, being an iron founder and well versed in Shakespeare—even though he was active in the labor movement of Philadelphia and would soon become the first president of its General Trades' Union, "the most impressive city central union in Jacksonian America" (*DFP,* 10 July 1830; Laurie, *Working People of Philadelphia,* 87; Leonard Bernstein, "The Working People of Philadelphia from Colonial Times to the General Strike of 1835," *Pennsylvania Magazine of History and Biography* 74 [1950]: 335). An AWPNCC supporter provided one answer to such characterizations when he chastised a local editor for assuming that one of his correspondents ("A Journeyman Mechanic") was not in fact a worker because his letter was well written (*DFP,* 18 Sept. 1830).

16. On Philadelphia, see Laurie, *Working People of Philadelphia,* 85. To be sure, as elsewhere, here too many of the candidates came from outside the ranks of the movement itself, and only three of some fifty Working Men nominees were known leaders of the association (Jacob Alrichs, AWPNCC president; Francis Sawdon, host of an organizing meeting; and John Walker, AWPNCC committeeman). But the organizers and political platform of the WMP make clear just how close were the two organizations. The prolabor *DFP* (29 May 1830) maintained that the Working Men nominated only those who were friendly to the association's program and spirit.

17. Commons, *History of Labour* 1:287–88. "Hundreds" are geographical divisions roughly equivalent to "townships."

18. McFarlane, *Address*, 25–26; *DFP*, 8, 22 May 1830. Essentially the same program appeared during the late summer and fall (and again the following year) in the pronouncements of a group fielding candidates for state offices under the rubric "Farmers, Manufacturers, Mechanics, and Other Working Men." This group was likely little more than the association meeting under a different name. The members of the committee to prepare the electoral ticket in 1830, for example, were all AWPNCC leaders. Indeed, throughout the fall campaign, the party's two secretaries were key AWPNCC figures: McFarlane, principal organizer, orator, committeeman, and secretary; and Pusey, committeeman, secretary, and vice president. Moreover, in announcing itself to the public and always addressing the "working men," the party disavowed connection to any organization but the association (Ibid., 21 Aug., 11, 18 Sept. 1830; 20 Aug., 10, 17 Sept., 1 Oct. 1831).

19. Ibid., 8 May 1830; 24 Sept. 1831.

20. Ibid., 1 Oct. 1831.

21. Unfortunately, we have the names only of the leaders of this movement (we do not even have any estimates of the total numbers involved). Moreover, the absence of town or city directories between 1814 and 1845 precludes any precise accounting of even these leaders' occupations. However, with evidence from the 1850 U.S. *Seventh Census* and scattered literary sources, a rough profile of the leadership is possible, based however on those who lived in the area for a long time.

22. The evidence on the association's relationship with mill workers is mixed. On one hand, their meeting on Saturday morning, as they did during the summer of 1830, suggests the absence of mill workers, at least at that time. However, the group met on Saturday nights in the summer of 1829, Tuesday evenings from fall 1829 to spring 1830, and then, beginning in fall 1830, on Monday evenings. And, as noted earlier, the group did address itself to "operatives," among others. On the other hand, there is indirect evidence of the movement's nonfactory character in its stated target audience for the Savings Fund Society in 1831: tradesmen, mechanics, laborers, and domestics (ibid., 13 Aug. 1831).

23. Approximately one-third of the activists involved were located in the 1850 U.S. *Seventh Census;* only one was born in Europe. Once again, the figures here are biased toward persisters.

24. That is, they generally fit the prevailing standard that workers were those who performed "honest toil" (Pessen, *Most Uncommon Jacksonians,* 28) Though the precise definition was perpetually shifting, the excluded were usually "nonproducers" (bankers, speculators, and sometimes lawyers, clergymen, etc.) and employers of large numbers of workers. In New York City, the WMP eventually decided to elect no leaders other than journeymen; in Philadelphia, at first employers could attend meetings but not hold office, though this may have been dropped later (ibid., 28–29).

25. The quotation is from "Address of the Association of Working People of Newcastle County, to the Mechanics, Manufacturers and Producers, of Newcastle County, State of Delaware, as adopted by the Association," reprinted in the (Wilmington) *Farmers', Manufacturers' and Mechanics' Advocate* [*FMMA*] 24 Oct. 1829.

26. McFarlane, *Address*, 25–36; *FMMA*, 24 Oct. 1829.

27. Which is not to say that their demands were strictly "economic." Pessen (*Most Uncommon Jacksonians,* 23): "it would be an economic determinism of a very rigid sort, indeed, to insist that authentic labor organizations confine their programs to economic issues advantageous only to workers."

28. *FMMA*, 24 Oct. 1829.

29. McFarlane, *Address*, 25–26.

30. On the WMP's demands elsewhere, see Pessen, *Most Uncommon Jacksonians,* 21ff. What Pessen has concluded about WMPs in major cities can be said as well of the Wilmington movement (28): "it was formed by workers or men devoted to the interests of workers, explicitly sought workers as members or at least supporters, devised programs promoting the causes and welfare of workers, and entered politics in the hope of goading the major parties to concern themselves with important reforms heretofore ignored." Moreover, "the authenticity of the party was not com-

promised when, evincing no interest in their social status or the size of their bankrolls, it backed candidates who promised support of the Working Men's program or important elements of it." Benjamin Webb, AWPNCC officer and *DFP* editor, claimed that the movement was originally established on behalf of the "producing classes" alone but was subsequently modified to include all who were favorable to its object, which, he said, was education. The association, Webb contended, was "nothing more than an education party." But this argument was advanced in the heat of the 1830 elections, in defense of a WMP under fire. After all, the AWPNCC's second organizing meeting in August 1829 had called on not just "mechanics and operatives," but "manufacturers" as well. Moreover, Webb's assessment was less an accurate reflection of reality than a rationale for his social philosophy: on religious grounds, he rejected "class" politics. See chap. 11 for a discussion of the problem of class in the Wilmington movement and elsewhere.

31. "J[onas] P[usey]," *DFP,* 9 Oct. 1830.

32. McFarlane, *Address,* 17.

33. According to Sumner, "perhaps the most important" factor in destroying the movement in Wilmington "was the charge of religious 'infidelity'" (Commons, *History of Labour* 1:289–90). Foner lists public denunciations—infidelity chief among them—as one of six factors contributing to the movement's failure (*History of the Labor Movement,* 1:140–41). In fact, later generations of laborites were well aware of the role that the charge had played in this first blush of American labor activism, and they were determined not to let it happen again. In the 1880s, for example, George McNeill would note in his history of the labor movement that although the Free Enquirers' sympathy for the efforts of the "poor and oppressed" made them welcome at labor gatherings half a century earlier, they also frightened away many "church-going wage-laborers" and allowed the big newspapers of the day to stigmatize labor as a movement of infidels *(Labor Movement,* 76).

34. *DFP,* 2 Jan., 10 Apr. 1830.

35. Ibid., 15 May, 11 Sept. 1830.

36. Ibid., 9 Jan. 1830. On the charge, and the response, see also ibid., 18 Sept. 1830.

37. Ibid., 12 Feb., 1831; 19 Jan., 2, 9 Feb., 2, 9, 16, 23, 30 Mar. 1833. It appears that McFarlane traveled back and forth between Philadelphia and Wilmington in 1829–30. As for other "Free Enquirers," though there is no evidence that Frances Wright played a direct role in organizing the Wilmington Working Men, she did deliver a "course of lectures" there in May 1829, just before the founding of the association; and, workers in the labor movement defended her from the inevitable censure of some local citizens (*Delaware Register,* 23, 30 May 1829; *MFP,* 31 Oct. 1829). On one such defense, see n. 85.

38. *DFP,* 19 Jan. 1833.

39. Ibid., 23 Mar. 1833.

40. Ibid.

41. McFarlane, *Address,* 10–11.

42. E.g., ibid., 24.

43. E.g, ibid., 11, 19.

44. Ibid., 8 Jan. 1831.

45. E.g., "Yorick," *MFP,* 21 Nov. 1829; B[enjamin] W[eb], *DFP,* 24 Mar. 1832.

46. Again, generalizations about these activists' participation in the church applies to the leadership, not to the movement itself.

47. As table 5.2 indicates, the actual figure might have been higher. For sources on church membership among Working Men elsewhere, see chap. 4, n. 2.

48. By 1832, when Wilmington incorporated as a city, there were more than a dozen churches serving a population of approximately sixty-five hundred (Hoffecker, *Wilmington,* 72).

49. Henry C. Conrad, *History of the State of Delaware,* 3 vols. (Wilmington, 1908), 2:745; Zebley, *Churches of Delaware,* 7–8.

50. In the late eighteenth and early nineteenth centuries, there were crowds outside this church nightly; indeed, evening services typically began early in order to dismiss the assembled before

dark! The problem became so acute that, in 1800, a three-man committee from the congregation found it necessary to take out an advertisement in the local press demanding an end to the depredations of the "infidel rabble" that, the committee said, had been regularly breaking windows, stoning preachers, and "casting nauseous reptiles, insects, and other filth in at the windows among the female part of the congregation." The persecution ended, however, and the growth of the congregation twice necessitated the enlargement of the church, in 1811 and again in 1828. See Munroe, *History of Delaware,* 89–90; Zebley, *Churches of Delaware,* 7, 30–31, 90; Hoffecker, *Delaware,* 74–78. Lincoln, *Wilmington, Delaware,* 74–76, 163–65.

51. Scharf, *History of Delaware,* 2:710–11; Lincoln, *Wilmington, Delaware,* 159; Zebley, *Churches of Delaware,* 10.

52. Ibid., 8–9.

53. Hoffecker, *Wilmington,* 77.

54. (Wilmington) *Blue Hen Chicken,* 17 Dec. 1847.

55. Sumner declared the paper "not primarily political but . . . a free-thought paper," being, according to her, similar to Owen and Wright's *Free Enquirer* in containing much discussion of religious issues (Commons, *History of Labour* 1:288, n. 20). The same, though, could be said of the *MFP,* which Sumner called "the earliest labour paper of which any numbers have been preserved" (186). Mumford identifies the paper as the "voice of the mechanic and working man"; in addition to advocating education, abolition of debt, and other Working Men's demands, the paper objected to the exclusion of certain "undesirable" elements from the Wilmington Town Hall ("Constitutional Development in the State of Delaware," 163–64, 411 n. 44). For indirect evidence that the editors themselves thought of their paper as more a Working Men's publication than a Freethought one, see Webb's response to the *Batavia People's Press,* in *DFP,* 28 Aug. 1830.

56. *DFP,* 2, 23 Jan. 1830. According to an article in the *MFP* (17 Oct. 1829, cited in Commons, *History of Labour* 1:288), the need for a Working Men's press became palpable after the disastrous elections of fall 1829.

57. At least six men edited the *DFP* at different times and in different combinations from early 1830 until mid-1833. The only one who was involved from first issue to last, and clearly the leading light of the operation, was Benjamin Webb ("B.W."). He was ably assisted by George Reynolds ("G.R."). Henry Wilson ("H.W."), publisher for the first year and a half, occasionally signed editorials, as did McFarlane ("G.R.M'F"). J. D. Coleman and William W. Baker ("W.W.B.") shared editorial responsibilities for a short period in 1830 and 1831, respectively. Of these, four (Webb, Reynolds, Wilson, and McFarlane) were involved with the Working Men's movement: all were AWPNCC committeemen; Webb and McFarlane were, at different times, secretary of the organization; Wilson was librarian of the Working Men's Reading Club (WMRC). Moreover, though there is no evidence of their direct involvement, Coleman and Baker were clearly favorable to the cause. From time to time, other initials appeared under editorial columns, but I have been unable to identify them.

58. The relationship between the AWPNCC and the *DFP* was so close, in fact, that those involved sometimes had to take care to separate them, inasmuch as they were not synonymous. When one editor used the appellation "we" in reference to the paper's hostility to "secret associations," one of his colleagues reminded him that some in the AWPNCC and some of the editors belonged to such organizations (*DFP,* 3 July 1830). It is also true that there was tension at the paper over labor versus "strictly" religious questions. By the third issue, there were complaints about the abundance of religious articles in the paper; by the end of the first month, the editors noted that "our friends, the working men" had complained that not enough space had been devoted to them, noting too that of the "one hundred communications" they had in hand, none was from them (ibid., 16, 30 Jan. 1830). While all this reminds us to use anonymous articles and letters with caution, two key facts should be kept in mind: one, a number of those who were published in the early weeks—and certainly thereafter—identified themselves as some kind of worker or advocate of workers; and two, a number of the original editors were, in fact, members of the association. The

complaints, in other words, may have reflected a sense that "strictly" Working Men's issues were not being aired in the paper, while potentially divisive theological subjects, the bane of the early Working Men's existence, were.

59. Not, the editors hastened to point out, free of charge or providing license for attacks on others.

60. "The liberality we wish to cultivate," wrote one editor early on, "will not depend on the *opinions* a man believes it right for him to hold, but on the *disposition* he manifests towards others enjoying the same privilege" (ibid., 13 Feb. 1830). Thus, for Benjamin Webb, the main principle of the paper was neither skepticism nor orthodoxy, but liberty of conscience. Its only goal: "rectify error, and establish truth" (11 June 1831, 31 July 1830).

61. For reprints of Blatchley's writings, see, e.g., ibid., 14 May 1831. For his obit., ibid., 21 Jan. 1832. On Blatchley and the labor movement in antebellum New York City, see Wilentz, *Chants Democratic,* 159–61, 193, 196, 199, 200; Walter Hugins, *Jacksonian Democracy,* 98. David Anthony Harris misses the importance of Blatchley's Christian perspective in *Socialist Origins in the United States: American Forerunners of Marx, 1817–1832* (Assen: Van Gorcum, 1966), chap. 2.

62. *DFP,* 2 Jan. 1830; also, "W.W.," 16 Jan. 1830. Sumner noted the phenomenon (*History of Labour* 1:272): at the time "the most violent prejudice existed against speculative opinions which denied the truth of any religion."

63. In an early editorial, the *DFP* announced a ban on religious disputes in its pages, though correspondents could write on religious subjects, if they wished. The distinction reflected the pervasive antebellum fear of sectarianism. One group responding to the AWPNCC's call to organize declared that they would never "meddle with religion, or suffer to make it any part of our consideration in the Society, and by this means endeavor to keep clear of polemic disputes" (preamble to the constitution of the "Local, Republican, Educational Association of Working Men, of Brandywine and Red Clay Creek, and their Immediate Neighborhoods, in this State Delaware," ibid., 28 Aug. 1830). Sometimes, this position reflected a fear of interfering with preexisting loyalties. See "Memorial of the Association of Working People of New Castle County," petition to the Delaware legislature, 1830, Delaware State Archives (DSA), Dover. Others feared dividing workers who had not yet made up their minds on certain religious issues (for, in matters of religion, "men might agree about the one, when they would differ about the other," *DFP,* 6 Mar. 1830).

64. Ibid., 4 Dec., 13 Feb. 1830.

65. Ibid., 9 Jan. 1830.

66. Ibid., 12 May 1830 (editorial comment).

67. Ibid., 27 Mar. 1830; 26 May, 1832; 22 May 1830. The pseudonym "Mosheim" may have been taken from Ruprecht Von Mosheim, a sixteenth-century religious enthusiast who believed himself commissioned by God to unite the various religious branches of the Reformation era to lay the foundation for a new Jerusalem. Rejecting the prevailing creeds of his day as anti-Christian and severely critical of the clergy, he prayed for another reformation to unite all the followers of Jesus. His heresy landed him in prison, where he died in 1546. According to the foremost authority on the Hicksite Quakers, Larry Ingle, the reference is more likely to Johann L. Mosheim, a religious historian popular among certain Quakers of this era (personal communication with the author).

68. See, e.g., *DFP,* "Luther," 28 Jan. 1830.

69. "H.N.," ibid., 1 Jan. 1831; "Medicus," ibid., 16 Jan. 1830.

70. Ibid., 6 Mar. 1830.

71. Ibid., 7 May 1831.

72. Ibid., 23 June 1832. *Social* prayer, in the context of protracted meetings, was contemporary evangelical Protestantism's answer to the problematic of human ability and the dispensation of grace (Johnson, *Shopkeeper's Millennium,* 95–97).

73. *DFP,* 15 Nov. 1831.

74. As Webb announced in November 1830, the *DFP* was partly owned and edited by Friends (ibid., 6 Nov. 1830).

75. Ibid., 13 Mar. 1830. On Reynolds, see Wilmington Friends Meeting Records, 3 vols., DSA; *American Watchman*, 21 Oct. 1823.

76. AWPNCC officer Jacob Alrichs was also a trustee of the African School Society; *DFP* editor William W. Baker was also a director of the Temperance Society; Webb's son, James, WMRC treasurer, was also an organizer of the Free Produce movement. All were Quakers.

77. As we shall see in chap. 6, this was precisely the stance of trade unionist Henry Frink of Rochester, a Presbyterian.

78. *Delaware Gazette*, 28 Feb. 1851. Quaker "from youth up" is from Webb, *DFP*, 6 Aug. 1831.

79. Ibid., 23 Oct. 1830. Christ was the way to salvation for Webb: "we learn in Scripture, 'what is known of God, is manifested within,' and promulgated by Jesus of Nazareth, being sufficient, if attended to, to lead him aright" (9 Jan. 1830). Still, he used various terms to describe "the savior," including the "word of the Lord," the "spirit of improvement," the "moral emotion," the "voice of truth."

80. Ibid., 10 Dec. 1830.

81. "All the reason on earth," he said, "will not convince a man of the existence of God." He had to *feel* the "holy and benign influence" (ibid., 23 Jan. 1830).

82. Ibid., 1 May 1830.

83. Ibid., 7, 21 Apr. 1832; 22 June 1833.

84. Ibid., 10 Dec. 1831; also, 9 Oct. 1830.

85. Ibid., 10 July 1830. Though he quoted the Bible frequently and with reverence, he did not embrace it as the Word of God. "I value the Bible like other books," he said; "I value it for the truth it contains, and for nothing else" (ibid., 4 Aug. 1832). See, too, 17 Dec. 1831.

86. Ibid., 7 May 1831. In articulating this social religion, like Charles Douglas, Webb steered between extremes, insisting, "I equally fear the sectarian heretic, and the fanatical believer." "I dread irreligious sects or combinations as much as I do those formed of orthodox or religious opinions" (31 July 1830). A self-proclaimed "free enquirer," he was no infidel. Though he often defended his era's most notorious infidels, Robert Dale Owen and Frances Wright, he did so as a nonsectarian Christian who believed in liberty of conscience, rather than from any agreement with them. And he always forthrightly condemned any intolerance on their part toward those who held differing religious views (but he believed both had been unfairly accused of irreligion, pointing out that most of what they expressed was doubt or agnosticism rather than conviction.); ibid., 21 Apr. 1831, 22 June 1833.

87. The split was also known as the "Liberal schism." The Hicksite label was the more popular, deriving from the reform movement's principal leader, Elias Hicks.

88. The following paragraphs on the Hicksite schism are based on Larry Ingle's fascinating account in *Quakers in Conflict: The Hicksite Reformation* (Knoxville: Univ. of Tennessee Press, 1986). See also, Robert Doherty, *The Hicksite Separation: A Sociological Analysis of Religious Schism in Early Nineteenth Century America* (New Brunswick, N.J.: Rutgers Univ. Press, 1967).

89. In some ways, this schism marked one of this era's many battles pitting tradition against modernity. On one side were Hicks's followers, who saw the Quakers as the most Protestant of all sects, because they took the doctrinal centerpiece of the Reformation to its logical extreme: religious faith came directly and immediately from one's own experience of the divine Word. Though they emphasized the crucial role of reason, implanted in the breasts of all God's children, they avoided what they saw as the deist trap of intellectualizing faith. Indeed, for most Hicksites—and there were many differences among them—revelation activated reason. For these traditionalists, the only true way to God was through the Inner Light, through the personal mystical experience of the Holy Spirit, just as George Fox had proclaimed two centuries earlier. On the other side of the schism were those who saw value in the message of turn-of-the-nineteenth-century evangelicalism (soon to become a new orthodoxy) that if Christianity were to survive the onslaught of deism (or worse), it needed to simplify and propagate its message through the establishment of a creed, while it also shored up its internal mechanisms of control. In a more fundamental sense, though, the Hicksite schism was merely one outcome of the tension in Protes-

tant (and Enlightenment) thought between the individual and government, autonomy and community, liberty and order. For the new orthodox, insistence on the divinity of Christ and the authority of Scripture was a way of reigning in dangerous tendencies. For those who saw themselves as heirs of the Reformation radicals, though, maintaining the traditional Quaker belief that individual experience was the ultimate basis of spiritual understanding became at once an act of rebellion and fidelity to the faith—indeed, a renewal of the covenant, a new reformation, to finish the one only begun by Martin Luther. As they saw it, theirs was a truly unmediated religion, in the best tradition of Reformation Protestantism.

90. Larry H. Ingle, "'A Ball that Has Rolled Beyond Our Reach': The Consequences of Hicksite Reform, 1830, As Seen in an Exchange of Letters," *Delaware History* (fall/winter 1984): 127–37.

91. On the conflict, we have only the later testimony of the antagonists. See ibid.; idem, *Quakers in Conflict; DFP,* Jan.–Apr. 1831. Interestingly enough, some Quaker leaders in Wilmington rejected the term "Hicksite" in the midst of the battle with Webb and his friends. See the comments of Jonathan Pierce at Webb's disciplinary hearing before the Wilmington Yearly Meeting of Friends, in ibid., 17 Sept. 1831. *DFP* editor J. D. Coleman remarked that he would not be surprised to see Gibbons "renounce his erroneous Hicksite views, and become a zealous convert to and defender of orthodoxy" (ibid., 13 Mar. 1830).

92. Ibid., 29 Oct. 1831. According to Webb, the trouble with Gibbons began in 1825, when Webb was general agent for the *Berean.* The final straw at the journal came two years later when, as editor, and "taught in the school of William Gibbons," Webb directly confronted his mentor by refusing to attack Owen. According to Gibbons, the genesis of the trouble was Webb's denial in meeting, "as is typical with young skeptics," of parts of Scripture (ibid., 29 Jan. 1831; Ingle, "'A Ball that Has Rolled Beyond Our Reach," 133).

93. The group was founded by New Light Presbyterian minister E. W. Gilbert; according to Baker, he and Webb were the only Friends in the circle (*DFP,* 2 July 1831). Gibbons's compatriot, Benjamin Ferris, had debated the young Gilbert in a series of letters in Robert Porter's *Christian Repository* early in the 1820s. The views Ferris presented in this public forum marked some of the opening shots in the Quaker war of that decade. On Gilbert and Ferris, see Hoffecker, "Benjamin Ferris and the Perils of Liberal Religion," *Quaker History* 77 (spring 1988): 33–37.

94. Then, they had opposed such proceedings. The disciplinary meetings mounted by Gibbons and others against Webb and his friends in the early 1830s were worse, though, according to the latter, because anyone could initiate them on even the slightest pretext.

95. *Exposition of Modern Skepticism, in a letter addressed to the editor of the Free Enquirer* (Wilmington: R. Porter, 1829). In the space of a few months, the pamphlet went through four printings, in part because of the mistakes noted by Webb and his associates. *DFP,* 30 Jan. 1830; 29 Oct. 1831.

96. According to Baker, the paper came out only after Webb sought an audience with Gibbons at the house of fellow Friend Ira Jackson (ibid., 29 Oct. 1831). Moreover, it was the *DFP's* view that it was the *Exposition* that had been the root cause of the problem (ibid., 3 Dec. 1831; 7 July 1832).

97. *Exposition,* 133, 135.

98. *DFP,* 24 Mar. 1832.

99. Ibid., 24 Mar. 1832. Ingle misleadingly attributes the line to Webb and his associates alone (Ingle, *Quakers in Conflict*).

100. *DFP,* 24 Mar. 1832. Gibbons, of course, saw matters differently. Having recently read *Anarchy of the Ranters* (1675), which identified the principal danger of Quakerism as the tendency for the individual experience of the Deity to resist all authority, he insisted on the need for *some* discipline, *some* government, without which society would collapse (Ingle, "'A Ball that Has Rolled Beyond Our Reach,'" 136). Ferris, though, seemed to understand at least part of the problem. In a letter to Gibbons in September 1830, he admitted that "some of us" had helped excite the younger and inexperienced among them to free inquiry and had treated "sacred subjects" with "great freedom," thus giving impetus to "a ball that has so rolled beyond our reach." He counseled patience and rejection of the spirit of violence (ibid., 131–32).

101. *DFP,* 30 Apr. 1831.

102. Ibid., 2 Jan. 1830.

103. Thus: the enemy was simply using the Christian label; real reformers sought to do good, not because it was written in the Bible but because the impulse had been implanted in their hearts by the Author of existence; all should be treated in the spirit of Jesus and the issue left to God; Owen and Wright had defended Jesus as a reformer, who was tolerant of others, who had been an opponent of rites against others who had impugned him; and so on. As for being followers of Fanny Wright, a group calling itself "MANY FRIENDS" claimed in the *DFP* that not a single Quaker had adopted her views, believing that "'God alone is the Sovereign Lord of conscience'" (ibid., 23 Jan. 1830).

104. Ibid., 11, 25 Feb. 1832.

105. Ibid., 28 Jan., 4, 11 Feb. 1832.

106. Ibid., 18 June 1831.

107. Letter of "A Friend to Truth," in ibid., 28 Jan. 1832.

108. The charges against Webb shifted over time, and his opponents had somewhat differing views of the precise nature of his crimes. Ferris, for example, insisted that it was not Webb's writings that were at issue but those of others that he had published in his paper (ibid., 26 Mar. 1831). The indictment seems to have had two basic components: the calling into question of Christianity in the *DFP* (principally, the Bible as revelation and the divinity of Jesus), and the misrepresentation of the proceedings of the Wilmington Monthly Meeting, at which a discussion took place on freedom of the press (ibid., 9 Apr. 22 Oct. 1831). A good overview of the entire affair can be found in William Baker's series of articles in ibid., Sept.–Dec. 1831. After "conviction," Webb appealed to both the quarterly and yearly meetings, to no avail (ibid., 19 Nov. 1831).

109. Ibid., 16 Apr., 10 Sept. 1831.

110. Ibid., 16 Apr. 1831.

111. Baker's ouster came six months after Webb's; others were ousted, or kept out. See, for example, the fate of female preacher Elizabeth M. Reeder of Philadelphia and her allies in the Wilmington Meeting in 1832 (ibid., 25 Feb. 1832; Diary of Daniel Byrnes, 13, 14 May 1832, DHS). One local casualty, Welcome Gray, would receive a favorable obit. in the *Voice of Industry,* 19 June 1846 (on Gray, see *DFP,* 29 Dec. 1832; Friends List).

112. Ibid., 12 Mar. 1831; 9 June 1832 (source of names: the remonstrance for equal treatment in examining Gibbons as well as Webb and the request for a meeting on *all* matters). The schism within a schism occurred outside Wilmington as well and followed a pattern similar to the original split, occurring first in Philadelphia and Wilmington, and then spreading to Ohio, Indiana, and Baltimore, Maryland (Ingle, *Quakers in Conflict; DFP,* 9 Apr. 1831). On the trouble elsewhere, see, e.g., ibid., 2 Oct. 1830.

113. Ibid., 11 June 1831. Webb's cause was apparently quite popular among certain elements within the society. See, for example, the description of the Concord Quarterly Meeting ("filled with young people") in ibid., 19 Nov. 1831. Also, Baker's recapitulation of the case argues that, though sometimes in the majority, the reformers, in a kind of replay of the earlier split, were regularly outmaneuvered by the "orthodox Hicksites" (ibid., 3 Sept. 1831), rather than, one assumes, outnumbered.

114. I am indebted to Larry Ingle for pointing out this example.

Chapter 6

1. Hawthorne also described Rochester as "an instantaneous city" (*Tales, Sketches and Other Papers,* quoted in Dorothy S. Truesdale, "American Travel Accounts of Early Rochester," *Rochester History* [*RH*] 16 [Apr. 1954]: 14).

2. Whitney R. Cross, "Creating a City: Rochester, 1824–1834" (Master's thesis, Univ. of Rochester, 1936), 315. Truesdale noted (5) that "every traveler who passed through [after 1825] . . .

remarked on its clatter, its bustle, and its general air of being in constant motion"—as, for example, U.S. Bureau of Indian Affairs head Thomas McKenney (1827) (8): "The Place is in such motion, and is so unmanageable as to put it out of one's power to keep it still long enough to say much about it. It is like an inflated balloon rolling and tumbling along the ground, and which the grapple itself cannot steady."

3. Only an estimated 15 percent of those living in the town in 1827 were still there six years later, a persistence rate that was low even for the restless standards of antebellum America; the rate for workers was lower still (Blake McKelvey, *Rochester: The Water-Power City, 1812–1854* (1945), 101–2; Johnson, *Shopkeeper's Millennium,* 37). The turnover rate slowed only slightly in the following decade. See Hewitt, *Women's Activism,* chap. 2.

4. Truesdale, "American Travel Accounts," 14; Jesse W. Hatch, "Memories of Village Days: Rochester, 1822 to 1830," *RH* 4 (1925): 242; McKelvey, *Rochester: The Water-Power City,* 69–70, 103; Cross, "Creating a City," 69–70. Despite Truesdale's account, Rochester actually retained much of its villagelike character well into the 1830s; though it dropped the "ville" with the charter revision of 1826 and became a city in 1834, residents continued to refer to their community as a "village" ([Rochester] *Liberal Advocate* [*LA*], 10 May 1834).

5. Ibid., 14 Apr. 1834.

6. My purpose here is to explore the relationship of pervasive religious excitement to early labor protest in Rochester, not to explain the *cause* of the religious ferment. For a contemporary view of the social origins of Rochester's religious battles, see the analysis by editor Obediah Dogberry in ibid., 6 Apr. 1834.

7. I have chosen to use a capital "E" in this chapter to distinguish between those church elements seeking to impose their religious practices on others, through political and other coercive measures, and the larger membership of the evangelical churches in Rochester, among whom, as we shall see, were some in the local workers' movement.

8. The best recent studies of antebellum Rochester (Paul Johnson and Nancy Hewitt), which have much to say about religion and social reform, focus exclusively on the middle and upper classes (though Hewitt does write of those at the "bottom rungs of the city's new middle class," 36). Much of the working class is invisible in these studies. Johnson argues (127–29) that the Finney revival and its aftermath transformed an emerging class conflict into a religious one. In the late 1820s, he argues, the town divided along class lines between owners and workers (over proper behavior) and along ideological lines among the elite (over how to handle the resistance of workers to attempts to induce such behavior). The Finney revival then melted the latter division (reuniting the elite), and the subsequent elite-sponsored revival among the working class transformed the conflict into Christian versus non-Christian rather than boss versus worker. The evidence in this chapter reveals not only a continued class battle in the 1830s and beyond, but overlapping religion and class conflicts as well. For more on Johnson's thesis, see intro.

9. George H. Humphrey, "Old East Avenue Days," *Rochester Historical Society Publications* (*RHSP*) 6 (1927): 247–48. For memories similar to Humphrey's, see Porter Farley, "Rochester in the Forties," *RHSP* 4 (1925): 265.

10. *Telegraph,* 10 Feb. 1824, quoted in William F. Peck, *History of the Police Department* (Rochester: Rochester Police Benevolent Assoc., 1903), 33.

11. Johnson, *Shopkeeper's Millennium,* 84ff. There had been concern in earlier years—both the Episcopalians and Presbyterians had established missions to the poor, intemperate, and ungodly in the 1810s—but concern turned to alarm in the 1820s (Hewitt, *Women's Activism,* chap. 2).

12. McKelvey, *Rochester: The Water-Power City,* 133; Joseph W. Barnes, "Obediah Dogberry: Rochester Freethinker," *RH* 36 (July 1974): 3; (Rochester) *Craftsman,* 17 Feb. 1829. On crime in Rochester during the 1820s, see Cross, "Creating a City," 183–85; (Rochester) *Paul's Pry,* 24 Apr. 1828.

13. Cross, "Creating a City," 70–71.

14. Post, *Popular Freethought,* 113–14, 148–49, 158, 161–62; McKelvey, *Rochester: The Water-Power City,* 131, 134, 196–97; (Rochester) *World as It Is,* 20 Feb. 1836; *Craftsman,* 19 Jan. 1831;

Cross, "Creating a City," 138–39; *Proceedings of the Friends of Liberal Principles and Equal Rights, in Rochester . . . January, 1831* (Rochester: S. H. Salisbury, 1831). Paine's birthday celebrations: *Rochester Daily Democrat* (*RDD*), 6 Feb. 1835; *World*, 2 Apr. 1836; *Rochester Republican* (*RR*), 10 Jan. 1837; (Rochester) *Working-Man's Advocate* (*WMA*), 28 Jan. 1840. The Freethought movement continued, though with less force, into the 1840s. See (Rochester) *Circumstance*, 20 Dec. 1845.

15. Much to the chagrin of local Evangelicals, one of whom had a very different memory of these years than did Humphrey. He recalled later that at the time, "Rochester was not a particularly religious or evangelical village. On the contrary, a large infidel club held meetings in which Thomas Paine's 'Age of Reason' was extolled as more worthy of credit than the Holy Scriptures" (Cross, "Creating a City," 124–25, quoting an anonymous source). Moreover, such complaints about rampant Freethought, as well as those concerning the alleged collapse of moral order attending commercial and industrial development, remained a staple of local discourse into the 1840s. See, for example, Schermerhorn Letters, 31 July 1841, Rochester Public Library (RPL).

16. These revivals brought religious passions to a boil in Rochester; Humphrey's memory of a powerful church may have been, in part, a reflection of that zealotry.

17. The phrase is Johnson's, *Shopkeeper's Millennium*, 14. Although there were religious stirrings in 1816–17 and 1826, it was the Finney revival of 1831 that sparked a virtually uninterrupted awakening through the 1830s and into the 1840s. According to McKelvey, Finney turned Rochester from the "hot spot of Western New York" into the state's most active center of Sabbath schools and Bible societies (Blake McKelvey, *Rochester: A Brief History* [New York and Toronto: Edwin Mellen Press, 1984], 13, 276; Farley, "Rochester in the Forties," 265; Orlo J. Price, "One Hundred Years of Protestantism in Rochester," *RHSP* 12:259–61; Cross, "Creating a City," 134; Barnes, "Obediah Dogberry, 2; correspondence of Edward Paine, Jr., *World*, 2 July 1836). Note the local Freethinkers, "Henry," an ex-Presbyterian who found himself "viewed by my friends as a sort of non-descript anomaly in nature," and "Stupio," who used a variety of pseudonyms when writing in the Freethought press because "I could do more good with less injury to myself than to have come out with my own name, knowing as I do the persecution of religion" (ibid., 30 Apr. 1836).

18. McKelvey, *Rochester: The Water-Power City*, 133.

19. Prominent among them was Nathaniel Rochester. On the background, see Cross, "Creating a City," 31–3; Johnson, *Shopkeeper's Millennium*, 17, 24–27; McKelvey, *Rochester: The Water-Power City*, 16–26, 35–37, 69. In McKelvey's formulation (69), Rochester was a child of Genesee County settlement, but the grandchild of New England, with southerners giving it a diversified flavor.

20. Ibid., 36–37; Turpin C. Bannister, "Early Town Planning in New York State," *New York History* 41 (Apr. 1943): 185–95; Blake McKelvey, "The Physical Growth of Rochester," *RH* 13 (Oct. 1951): 3.

21. Price, "Hundred Years of Protestantism," 241, 244, 246.

22. This underlying and persistent problem of creating and maintaining a pious community was nowhere better expressed than in the proposal of a minister attending a regional Sabbath convention in Rochester in 1842, after more than a decade of revival. Read the Bible for at least a half-hour three times a week, he counseled—a little piece of advice that surely would have made an earlier generation of American Protestants squirm, for whom Scripture was the lifeblood of home, hearth, and community (Cross, "Creating a City," 114; *Proceedings of the Sabbath Convention, Held at the City of Rochester, July 20th and 21st, 1842* [Rochester, 1842]).

23. Letter of "Zero," *LA*, 22 Sept. 1832.

24. The first stirrings came with a journeymen tailors' cooperative, countywide agitation for a mechanics' lien law, and a short-lived Working Men's electoral ticket. In 1831, boat caulkers demanded a raise in their daily wage; then carpenters began the fight for the ten-hour day (and higher wages), joined later by caulkers, masons, painters, and coopers. During these years, too, a vigorous anti-prison-labor movement emerged that would occupy Rochester workers for the better part of the century. And, finally, in these early years, workingmen helped found the Mechanics' Literary Association (MLA), which established a library, reading room, and debating club

for "the laboring class." See Commons, *History of Labour* 1:262; *MFP*, 1, 15, 22 May 1830; *Rochester Daily Advocate and Telegraph* (*RDAT*), 17 Mar. 1831; Cross, "Creating a City," 180; Alan H. Gleason, "The History of Labor in Rochester, 1820–1880" (Master's thesis, Univ. of Rochester, 1941), chaps. 1, 2; Blake McKelvey, "Organized Labor in Rochester Before 1914," *RH* 25 (Jan. 1963): 2; *RDD*, 10, 13, 20 Apr. 1835; 28 Mar., 7 Apr. 1836; *NTU*, 16 Apr. 1836.

25. The temperance and Sabbatarian crusades in Rochester are described in Johnson, *Shop-keeper's Millennium*, 79–88.

26. Their pledge launched a national organization, the General Union for Promoting the Observance of the Christian Sabbath.

27. *Paul's Pry*, 24 Apr. 1828. The paper appeared for approximately one year, merging later with the Lockport, N.Y., *Priestcraft Exposed* (*PT*, 21 May 1829; Henry Bradford Smith, "Rochester Printing, 1816–1834" [Master's thesis, Syracuse Univ., 1969], 26, 48).

28. Smith, "Rochester Printing"; *PT*, 5, 19 June 1828; *Craftsman*, 31 Mar. 1829. The paper's intent, the editor wrote, was a "tender regard . . . for the *genuine* principles of Christianity, whilst the licentious scoffer at Revelation, as well as the intolerant and Pharisaical *bigot* will be held up to the publick view, and deserved reprehension."

29. *PT*, 5 June 1828; Smith, "Rochester Printing," 26, 48. Similarly, in the prospectus for vol. 2 (19 Mar. 1829), the proprietor condemned Bible societies as a "specious show of false charities" to "entrap the credulous, beguile the simple, and create a monied aristocracy." Cross ("Creating a City," 242–43) listed the paper among those early publications of Rochester (with the *LA* and *Paul's Pry*) "in fundamental sympathy" with "the rights of labor."

30. *PT*, 21 May 1829; 21 Aug. 1828. From the *PT* office during the economically depressed winter of 1828–29, for example, came a circular signed "Reason and Common Sense," which took note of the hundreds of needy families in this "favored seat" for the operations of the "'*clerical begging fraternity.*'" Why hadn't the clergy set aside Thanksgiving Day to take up contributions for the sick, naked, and hungry, the writers asked, instead of taking bread from the destitute to clothe the priesthood in fine cloth? (4 Dec. 1828). *PT* writers traced the problem to Old Testament days, when the prophets of Israel had denounced priests, then to India and Africa, through the blood-stained pages of European history; despite the "overwhelming flood of light . . . shed upon the world," the problem remained very real, even in America, where men planned to move the clergy once again into the realm of politics. Moreover, the very idea that God's power was somehow contingent upon the "'*prayers*, the *charities* and *energies* of his forces in the christian world,'" as the pastor of a local Presbyterian church had put it, was, in the *PT*'s view, a violation of divine sovereignty: "what God willeth, that he will do, the perverseness of man to the contrary notwith-standing" (17 July 1828).

31. Ibid., 5 June 1828 (mill girls' statement in intro.).

32. Ibid., 18 Sept. 1828. By contrast, fellow Quaker Benjamin Webb, while not agreeing entirely with Paine on religion, defended him as an advocate of free enquiry (*DFP*, 24 Mar. 1832).

33. *PT*, 17 July, 21 Aug. 1828. The paper applauded a Lowell group that opposed the Union for Sabbath Observance while endorsing individual observance of the Sabbath as essential to order, morality, and piety. Violators of the Sabbath were answerable to a "higher authority than man," while a union of church and state would be "prejudicial" to both (ibid., 16 Oct. 1828).

34. Ibid., *Craftsman*, 17 Feb., 3 Mar. 1829.

35. Ibid., 6, 13 Oct. 1829. Roberts's tribute to the "Almighty Dispenser of all good" on Thanksgiving Day, 1829 (1 Dec. 1829), echoed what the *PT* had said the year before, declaring the occasion a day to visit the sick, comfort the afflicted, and minister to the poor. Shortly after, "Civil Rights" criticized a local minister's Thankgiving sermon, because it had failed to adhere to the biblical injunction to charity (ibid., 10 Mar. 1829).

36. Smith, "Rochester Printing," 50–51; Johnson, *Shopkeeper's Millennium*, 62–71, 75–77; *Craftsman*, 3, 10 Mar., 6, 20, 27 Oct., 24 Nov. 1829; 31 July, 4 Sept. 1830; 19 Jan., 16 Feb., 1 May 1831. Roberts claimed only to be "Anti-Anti-Masonic," calling Antimasonry "an inquisition of the most hideous character." He claimed later that his paper was never designed to defend Masonry as

such, but rather to oppose that faction that had been trying to misdirect the "honest feelings of the community," and, by an extensive and evil combination, rise to power. Roberts also denied being in the WMP but insisted that he would not allow it to be slandered without a hearing, for no man could "reprobate their principles" (ibid., 10 Feb., 3 Mar. 1829; 4 Sept. 1830).

37. Ibid., 2 Feb. 1831; 23 Mar. 1830.

38. Ibid., 28 Apr. 1830. On the avoidance of sectarian disputes, see ibid., 6 Apr. 1829.

39. Ibid., 28 Apr. 1830.

40. Ibid., 2 Feb. 1831; 17 Feb. 1829. Roberts made his remarks on professing Christians in response to a letter writer who had angrily criticized his paper for reprinting the proceedings of the Rochester "Liberal Meeting" of 1831 (discussed below), claiming the gathering had been mis-named. Reversing the criticism, Roberts pointed out that "names do not indicate principles," and took the opportunity to hoist those who called themselves Christians—like this correspondent, Josiah Bissell, and Charles Finney—with their own petard.

41. Ibid., 28 Apr. 1830. Roberts made ample use of biblical quotation to demonstrate the historic Christian aversion to politics (e.g., 13 Oct. 1829). As Protestants, writers for the *Craftsman* endorsed the Reformation, while criticizing the passions it excited and the divisions it engendered; they sang the praises of the Pilgrims, for their defense of freedom of opinion, but warned against the radicalism of the Puritan Revolutionaries; they defended the clergy against attacks by the Antimasons, but opposed the "false Christs and false prophets" predicted in Scripture (29 Sept., 6 Oct., 29 Dec. 1829).

42. Addressing "all pure Christians," he insisted that they would "readily perceive, that they can hope for the extension of the gospel only, when the channels through which its limpid stream flows, are pure" (ibid., 6 Oct. 1829). Roberts even refused to publish anti-Christian sentiments in his pages. "It is not our intention to attack the church," he wrote in response to one anti-Christian correspondent. "We revere religion, and shall exert ourselves to divest it of its impurities, and uphold it in its native loveliness" (ibid., 3 Mar. 1829). "To christians, (not in profession but practice,)" he wrote on another occasion, "I would say, I do not intend to attack the church, nor the humble and devout teachers of God's word; for no one respects them more than I do" (ibid., 6 Oct. 1829).

43. Also called "Grocery Shin-Plasters"; the system itself was generally referred to as the "order" system. An employer would purchase store credits at discount prices (15–35 percent), to be redeemed within a certain period of time, and then he would use them to pay his workers. The store owner, in turn, not only was ensured a steady business but also took another cut by discounting the notes when the workers brought them in for redemption in goods. The employer, in addition to reducing his labor costs, received a discount and credit at the store issuing the bills, as a kind of kickback for providing the owner with customers. Meanwhile, the laborer's wages were reduced and he could only trade at certain stores, usually at high prices. The best description is in John C. Chumasero, *Life in Rochester, or Sketches from Life; being Scenes of Misery, Vice, Shame, and Oppression in the City of the Genesee* (Rochester, 1848), 41–47. See also, Gleason, "History of Labor," chap. 2. For the use of the system elsewhere in New York, see David A. Gerber, *The Making of an American Pluralism: Buffalo, New York, 1825–60* (Urbana: Univ. of Illinois Press, 1989).

44. *Minutes and Proceedings of the Mutual Association, of the Village of Rochester, Together with its Constitution; and a List of the Members of the Shylock Association* (Rochester, 1829); *Craftsman*, 10, 24 Feb., 10, 24 Mar., 4 Aug., 15 Sept. 1829; 26 Jan. 1830. It is not entirely clear whether the meetings at which the idea for a petition campaign was hatched were sponsored by the association. However, the chair and secretary of the first such meeting, as well as four of the five committeemen chosen to prepare a statement on the issue, were members of the group.

45. As did both the NEA and NEWA.

46. For the relationship of the editors (C. Fischer Ames and Thomas B. Barnum) to the labor movement, see Cross, "Creating a City," 42; *MFP*, 6 Feb., 10, 24 Apr., 1, 22 May 1830; the prospectus for the *Spirit* (20 Oct. 1829); *Craftsman*, 31 Mar. 1829; *MP*, 17 Apr. 1830; Smith, "Rochester Printing," 52. No issues of the paper have survived.

47. *Spirit* prospectus; *MP,* 17 Apr. 1830; *MFP,* 10 Apr. 1830.

48. Despite the large numbers involved in this short-lived movement, we know the names of only the twelve leaders of the Committee to Prepare an Address and Resolutions, a mixed group occupationally, including two artisans, three grocers, two professionals, and two brokers. The first of their meetings was in late December 1830, at which they requested that the state legislature abolish imprisonment for debts of less than fifty dollars; two days later, at their first meeting under the "Friends of Liberal Principles" label, they formally petitioned for such a law, which passed on 16 Apr. 1831 (Cross, "Creating a City," 149–52). Both the chair and secretary of the first meeting had been members of the Mutual Association. As it had covered the latter's meetings, the *Craftsman* regularly reported on the Friends' proceedings.

49. Anti-Evangelical believers, the Friends of Liberal Principles insisted that the right of conscience (to believe or not) was the "first right of man as a moral agent" derived from "the same Omnipotent Being that organized the human mind." Similarly, they did not object per se to the distribution or sale of Bibles or tracts, nor to missionary work, but rather to the clergymen who might use the money as a means to temporal power. As for Sabbath laws: "When and where have the people delegated to their representatives the right to determine for them what day is holy?" (*Craftsman,* 26 Jan. 1831; Cross, "Creating a City," 149–52; *Proceedings of Friends*).

50. Johnson, *Shopkeeper's Millennium,* 116–19.

51. After a stint as editor of the Palymira *Reflector* in 1829 and 1830, where he was the first to take on Joseph Smith and his nascent Mormon movement, Dogberry came to Rochester and flung himself full tilt into battle: in his first editorial, he compared the revivalism then sweeping the community with the Salem witch trials (Barnes, "Obediah Dogberry"; Post, *Popular Freethought,* 59; *LA,* 23 Feb. 1832; M. Hamlin Cannon, "Contemporary Views of Mormon Origins [1830]," *Mississippi Valley Historical Review* 31 [Sept. 1944]: 261). Dogberry was the pseudonym of John L. Stevens; he died in 1837.

52. *LA,* 23 Feb., 12 July 1834.

53. Ibid., 31 Mar., 3 July, 15 Sept. 1832; 23 Feb., 3, 7, 22 Mar., 6 Apr., 7 June, 14 June, 9 Aug., 12, 20 Sept., 5 Oct. 1834.

54. When a "deacon of this village" had one of his former workmen arrested and jailed for a small debt, "R" wrote, "Verily, 'by their fruits ye shall know them'" (ibid., 22 Mar. 1834).

55. Ibid., 23 Feb. 1832. Cannon, one of the few historians to notice Dogberry, identified him, incorrectly, as "irreligious" ("Contemporary Views," 265). Elsewhere (266), he calls him "free-thinking," which, as I have used the term in this book, accurately describes the man.

56. "W.A.P."'s series, "The Primitive Churches," insisted that the Christian Church had, virtually from the beginning, deviated entirely from the original doctrine of Christ and his disciples (*LA,* 21 June 1834). Notably, the author identified this primitive religion with "Free Thought" (14 June 1834).

57. Ibid., 6 Apr. 1834. Here, Dogberry apologized if he himself had exhibited such "illiberalism." It was in great measure this aversion to dissension—as it was for so many of Dogberry's labor-reform contemporaries—that he insisted it would do no good to debate the fine doctrinal points of religion. On his "religious creed"—"if we have any"—Dogberry insisted that "we have never said a word about it."

58. Ibid., 28 Apr. 1832. Dogberry's correspondents could be found on both sides on the question of Sabbath schools (e.g., 28 Apr. 1832; 4 Oct., 22 Nov. 1834).

59. Ibid., 14 June 1834; 3 Mar. 1832.

60. Dogberry even ran columns on the Evangelical employer's cherished "Frugality" (27 Nov. 1833). For his correspondents' views on this point, see, e.g., "Consistency's" lament of the decline of "good manners" (14 June 1834).

61. Ibid., 21 June 1834. To be sure, there were anti-Christian—though not atheistic—voices in these pages. "Carlos," for example, while not denying the existence of a Supreme Power or an original design in nature, did embrace the sobriquet "free enquirer," rejecting the Old Testament story of creation, the divinity of Jesus Christ, and even Christianity itself (14 June 1834; 6 Apr.

1834). For an embrace of the infidel label, see "An Infidel," 26 July 1834. Deism got a full airing in the paper as well (e.g., "Clotair," 10 May 1834). Still, it was the church—"a resort for pride and vanity" filled with "frigid misanthropes among the professors of the day"—not Christianity, that troubled most of those who wrote in the *LA* (14 June 1834; 27 Nov. 1833).

62. Bissell, the man who had brought Finney to Rochester, died in the spring of 1831; the following fall, the Evangelicals' mouthpiece, the *Observer*, folded. By mid-1834, Dogberry noted that the Finney crisis had "nearly dissipated"; shortly afterward, his paper folded as well (*LA*, 21 June 1834). During this period, there was also the atheist Delazon Smith's New York *Watchman* (1838–39), but no copies have survived (Post, *Popular Freethought*, 48–49, 64–65).

63. Ibid., 60. Shepard called Christ a "demagogue" and an "impostor" (*World*, 7 May 1836).

64. Ibid., 20 Feb., 9, 26 Mar., 23, 30 Apr., 4 June, 16 July 1836. For his correspondents' condemnation of Christ, see 30 Apr. 1836.

65. Ibid., 30 Apr., 9, 26 Mar. 1836.

66. On the Bible as "calculated to degrade religion," see ibid., 20 Feb. 1836; on revivals, 20 Feb. 1836; on the clergy, 2 July 1836.

67. Ibid., 20 Feb. 1836.

68. Ibid., 26 Mar. 1836.

69. Among those traditions was taking on orthodox employers for betraying the faith. In 1840, for example, "A Mechanic" attacked a local masterbuilder for reducing his journeymen's wages: "our celebrated Architect and puritannical fellow-citizen" was "grinding the faces of the poor," violating the biblical precept, "'love our neighbor as ourselves.'" "As a people," the mechanic acknowledged, "we should indeed feel grateful to our heavenly Benefactor, for rendering our fields prolific and our harvests redundant; but shall it be said, because the Giver of all Good is kind to us, that our neighbors, through selfishness, must interfere and afflict us on that account?" A local builder, assuming he was the target of this attack, retorted, "The gentleman makes use of a variety of small 'fixings' which is rather foreign from his general character, that would seem to indicate some specific standard for morality and religion, which he would assume the responsibility of establishing." (In fact, the "Architect" who responded, Col. Jason Bassett, was not the builder in question.) See (Rochester) *WMA*, 16, 21, 25 Mar. 1840.

70. For evidence of the defeat of the Evangelicals, though with a different conclusion, see Johnson, *Shopkeeper's Millennium*, 128–35. See, too, Wallace's *Rockdale*, 322ff, for the "evangelical counterattack" that allegedly defeated the Freethinkers and united employers and employees on the basis of Christian individualism. Some Rochester workers no doubt did join area churches to advance themselves in employment. As one clerk told Luke Shepard in 1836, "'Ha! I don't care a d——n; I get five dollars more in a month than I did before I got religion,'" continuing, "'Who in h——l wouldn't have religion for that much; and have to work as hard as I do?'" (*World*, 9 Apr. 1836). This may have been the result of employers' cajoling during and after the Finney revival (Cross, "Creating a City," 117).

71. If one includes those who were "church affiliated" (using the church for birth, marriage, or death, or belonging to a church-sponsored society) and those for whom there is evidence of later church involvement, the total may have been closer to 50 percent. In none of the ten labor groups analyzed was the figure below 20 percent. The percentages here, in other words, are roughly comparable to those found for Fitchburg, Fall River, and Wilmington. As for how such figures compare to the proportion of church members in the general population of Rochester, we have precious little statistical work on which to base comparisons. But, it appears that the Rochester laborites—like their brethren in New England and the Mid-Atlantic states—were fairly typical antebellum Americans in this regard. Johnson (*Shopkeeper's Millennium*, 119) estimates that one-quarter of Rochester journeymen were Protestant church members in 1837, though only about one in seven appears in the extant records.

72. Probably many more of the carpenters were Methodists than the records reveal, for we know the names only of Methodist leaders here. The eight Methodist leaders who were carpenters represent about one-fourth of all leaders in that church during this period.

73. The Episcopalians appear in a concentrated fashion only among these clerks, discussed below.

74. Johnson, *Shopkeeper's Millennium,* 118–19, 156. These congregations may have been dominated by the "middle class," but neither were middle-class "missions" (like the Free Presbyterian, Bethel Presbyterian, or Second Baptist); in any case, membership and participation obviously did not preclude labor protest.

75. The carpenters had no organ as an outlet for their views—religious or otherwise.

76. Johnson, *Shopkeeper's Millennium,* 41–42.

77. There is disagreement among historians about just when the carpenters entered the fray: Cross and McKelvey say 1833, Gleason late 1832 (see n. 24 above). The building boom was fueled in part by two fires and a hurricane in the winter of 1834. See Jesse Hatch, "The Old-Time Shoemaker and Shoemaking," *RHSP* 5 (1926): 245; Maj. Wheeler C. Case, "In the Looking Glass of 1834," ibid., 11:159.

78. Case, "Looking Glass," 167; Gleason, "History of Labor," 194; Cross, "Creating a City," 180; McKelvey, "Organized Labor," 2; Maurice Isserman, "A Profile of Identity: Rochester Journeymen and Masters in the 1830s" (unpubl. paper, n.d., in possession of author), 6; *RDD,* 9 Mar. 1833; 9 Mar., 30 Apr. 1835; *RDA,* 9 Apr. 1834; 17 Jan 1835. The 1834 circular ("To Journeymen Carpenters and Joiners who may hereafter come to this village with a view of obtaining employment") asked for resistance to their masters' call for workers, which, given the city's position astride the Erie Canal, was the principal weapon of local employers in this period. The carpenters, and their mason and caulker allies, were ultimately unsuccessful.

79. Jesse Croshaw (Creshaw): "Steward's Book" (1832–47), First Methodist Church, Asbury-First Union Methodist Church, Rochester. The secretary, Isaac Hellins (Helms, Hellums, Hellems, Holmes), was a trustee of the First Universalist Society at its founding in 1846. See *History of the First Universalist Church of Rochester, New York* (n.p., n.d.), 3; "Records of the First Universalist Society" (typescript), Records of the County Clerk of Rochester, RPL; Henry Clifford Spurr, "Highlights of Universalism in Rochester, 1833–1946," in *A Century of Liberal Leadership, 1846–1946* (First Universalist Church, Rochester, 1946), 7.

80. Though 102 carpenters signed the 1834 circular, 5 signed using only a first or last name and 6 more could not be positively identified in the documentary record because of the commonality of their names, leaving 91. Four of the 8 identified leaders (1833–35) did not sign the petition.

81. Methodists could be found among other craft unionists of the 1830s. William Lovecraft, one of a three-man committee in 1836 that sought to exclude out-of-town coopers who worked under scale, was a lay "exhorter" in the First Methodist Church ("Trustees' Records" [1820–1881]; "Stewards Book"; "Quarterly Conference" [1821–1848], Asbury-First).

82. *RDA,* obit., 24 Jan. 1840; *RDD,* obit., 24 Jan. 1840; *RR,* obit., 28 Jan. 1840; Brick Presbyterian Records, PHS.

83. Edwin Scranton, Old Citizen's Letters, no. 123, RPL, 189; "Trustees' Records," Asbury-First (quotations from his obituary). In the aftermath of the strike, the organization continued to draw its leadership from the ranks of local congregations. The president in 1835, Joel Chaffee, was a Universalist, as was the society's secretary, Schuyler Moses; the chair of an 1836 carpenters' meeting was Methodist steward and class leader Archibald McArthur (*RDD,* obit., 14 Feb. 1840; First Methodist "Steward Book," "Quarterly Conference"). We know a lot about Moses. A native of Connecticut (where his ancestor John Moses had settled in 1632), Schuyler Moses was a longtime resident of Rochester, having arrived from Madison County, N.Y., in 1817 at the age of nineteen. He was "early in life" a Universalist (the Universalists began meeting in Rochester in 1833; he was thirty-eight in 1835); in 1840–41, the only year for which we have records, he was a teacher in the Sabbath school. An artisan from a long line of artisans (John Moses's blacksmith tools were still in his possession when Schuyler died in 1889), Moses helped build Rochester (Biographical Catalogue [BC], RPL; William F. Peck, *Semi-Centennial History of the City of Rochester* [Syracuse: D. Mason, 1884], 661–63; "Tengwall Scrapbook," RPL, obit., 1:335; "Barton's First Obituary Book" [B1OB], RPL, 180; [Rochester] *Democrat and Chronicle* [*DC*], obit., 31 Dec. 1888; 14 Mar.

1889; "Records of the Sabbath School of the First Universalist Society Rochester" [1839–52], Book 5, First Universalist Society, Rochester).

84. The effects of this national depression were relatively slight in Rochester. Although industry and commerce there did not fully recover for several years, the worst of it was over by the spring of 1838 (Gleason, "History of Labor," 29–30).

85. *WMA,* 19 Oct. 1839.

86. Ibid. The RTA expelled members for working under scale, calling them "rats": "it will be our object to ferret out all such vermin" (26 Oct., 12 Nov. 1839). The printers claimed shortly after the strike began (31 Oct. 1839) that the RTA numbered eighteen, a majority of the trade in the city. Gleason ("History of Labor," chap. 2) places their number at twenty-two but offers no evidence for the figure.

87. *WMA,* 19, 23, 26 Oct., 25 Nov., 16, 26 Dec. 1839; 15, 22 Feb. 1840; Gleason, "History of Labor," 36–38. Prompted by the strike, and intended as a temporary publication, the paper— "devoted to the interests of the working-classes generally"—became the voice of Rochester labor. It also had links to earlier American labor protest. The paper's initial motto was the same as the *DFP*'s ("We have asked for nothing but what is RIGHT——we will submit to nothing WRONG"), although its readership was well aware of their namesake, the labor paper of the same name published earlier in New York City by George Henry Evans. To prove his support for the paper, one resident sent, as a gift, back issues of the New York City *WMA* (ibid., 19 Nov., 23 Dec. 1839).

88. Frink, member of the RTA founders' committee and subsequently its president, was listed as editor beginning 20 Nov. 1839, a month after the paper first appeared. His religion was not a product of a later conversion, as might be suggested by his *Alow and Aloft* (see chap. 1, n. 41). On his evangelicalism, see *WMA,* 2 Dec. 1839.

89. In *Alow and Aloft,* the pivotal temperance meeting takes place in a local church and opens with a minister's prayer.

90. There is some confusion about precisely when Frink joined the Presbyterian Church. His obituary says 1832. The available Presbyterian records say only that he was received into the Brick Church by letter, from New York, in 1834; at another point, there is the notation "since 1835." The obituary is probably correct, the letter from New York probably reflecting a relocation to that city before returning to Rochester. Frink remained a member of the Brick congregation until he returned to New York in 1844, just before his death (*RDD,* obit., 18 Aug. 1845). His evangelical belief in the importance of virtue in a sinful world can be seen in one of his editorial ditties (*WMA,* 23 Nov. 1839): "A virtuous man who has passed through the temptations of the world, may be compared to a fish which lives all the time in salt water, yet is still fresh." See, too, the 18 Nov. 1839 issue, where he praises the words, "there is but one way of access for all sinners to the favor of God"—namely, the heart.

As for the church he joined, Johnson (*Shopkeeper's Millennium,* 194, n. 20; 120–21) acknowledges a class component to Jedediah Burchard's preaching at the Brick Church in 1832, but the premises on which his analysis is based do not allow for someone like Frink. Johnson recites the story told by one Rochester memorialist of Burchard, during one of his sermons, singling out a prominent mill owner by name and asking him to come forward and be saved; Johnson suggests that the journeymen and clerks in the "back pews" may have (silently) reveled in this moment, as they enjoyed their spiritual superiority over such wealthy and powerful men. But, in the context of his argument that workers joined evangelical churches solely because of economic or familial ties, the potential for a more far-reaching analysis of the class tensions here dissipates. Johnson recognizes that some workers adopted the mantle of "respectability," rejecting the drink and amusement of the rougher elements of their class, and from that cultural orientation became involved in sustained labor organization and agitation during these years; here, though, he assumes that these workers did so outside the walls of the church (citing the work of Montgomery, Laurie, and Faler as evidence of this division elsewhere). In this context, he points to the vigorous Freethought press of Rochester (misreading it as irreligious), which, he says, joined anti-evangelicalism to support for the workingmen. In other words, there were radical workers in Rochester, but, by definition, they could not be members of evangelical churches. The fact that things were otherwise should send us back to basic assumptions, both in Johnson's work and in the work he cites to support his case.

91. *WMA*, 18 Nov. 1839. On his quoting of the Bible, see, e.g., ibid., 31 Oct., 13 Nov. 1839; 7, 31 Jan. 1840. On living in a Christian community, see, e.g., ibid., 28 Jan. 1840.

92. Ibid., 10 Jan. 1840.

93. Frink once praised a lecture before a local Young Men's Association for advancing the notion that all citizens had an obligation to promote the diffusion of gospel morality (ibid., 1, 3 Feb. 1840).

94. Ibid., 17 Dec. 1839; 6 Jan. 1840.

95. Ibid., 30 Dec. 1839.

96. They rejected involvement in partisan politics, for example, because it placed particular over national interest and thereby replaced harmony and goodwill with contention and persecution. Politics was corrupt, associated with "contamination, and all things disagreeable to the moral sense" (ibid., 23 Oct. 1839; 25 Jan. 1840). For similar reasons—both practical and principled—they claimed neutrality in religion as well, refusing, as Frink put it, to "enter into theological discussions" (14 Nov. 1839). In essence, in religion as in politics, the activist printers of Rochester eschewed party in favor of advocating for their class. On politics, see chaps. 9, 11.

97. Ibid., 19 Nov. 1839. There is nothing in the *WMA*, it is true, about sects or denominations, but of Christian morality and virtue, there is plenty.

98. Ibid., 19 Nov. 1839.

99. For examples, ibid., 26 Oct., 4, 20 Dec. 1839; Feb., Mar. 1840. Although the editor declared his intention of gratis printing of any meeting notices (13 Mar. 1840), not all received equal treatment in the pages of his paper, as the controversy over theater advertisements discussed below makes clear.

100. Ibid., 6 Nov. 1839.

101. Editorial, "Church and State," ibid., 27 Nov. 1839.

102. Similarly, "although believing in a Divine Being and revelation," Frink nevertheless rejected the exclusion of atheists from giving testimony in court: "Religion needs not the aid of civil enactments" (ibid., 14 Nov. 1839).

103. As the Friends of Liberal Principles had earlier in the decade, Frink cited the state constitution in support of his position, but unlike the Friends, who sought to guard against religious legislation, he sought to remind his readers that New York was a Christian state: "We, the people of the state of New York, acknowledge with gratitude, the grace and beneficence of God in permitting us to make a choice of our form of government, do establish this constitution."

104. Ibid., Feb.–Mar. 1840.

105. Two of them, at least, were involved in a March 1839 revival, some six months before the founding of the organization and newspaper, though again most were not recent converts.

106. Beach, who had arrived in Rochester with his parents in 1825, was expelled from the RTA in late 1839 for working under scale. But he turned up on a printers' committee in the trade union upsurge of 1853, and as vice president of the Rochester Typographical Union the following year (*WMA*, 28 Oct. 1839; [Rochester] *Union and Advertiser* [*UA*], obit., 9 Dec. 1879; Leases B, Unitarian Church, Rochester). By contrast, Joseph Curtis, another member of the RTA founders' committee, had just arrived in town. He was also a founder and early trustee of the Unitarian Church Society, which occasionally met in schoolhouses in the 1830s, established a permanent organization in 1840, incorporated in 1841, and erected a church edifice in 1843 (Price, "One Hundred Years," 258; "Subscription Book" [1840], "Subscribers, 28 Sept. 1842," "Deeds" [1843], "Treasurers' Accounts" [1842–48], "Treasurers' Book of the Rochester Unitarian Society From 1843 to 1850," "Records of the Treasurers of the Unitarian Church of Rochester, New York, 1841–67," all at the University of Rochester Library [URL]).

107. Another member of the RTA founders' committee and, eventually, vice president, Falls was president of the Rochester Typographical Union in the 1850s and still active in the 1860s. Typical of his evangelical style, as corresponding secretary of the local Washingtonians (tem-

perance) in 1843, Falls called on his fellow citizens to bring their intemperate friends to a lecture by Baltimore's John Hawkins, "if you want them SAVED" ([Rochester] *Daily Democrat* [*DD*], 13 July 1843; "Mrs. George W. Fischer Scrapbook," RPL; "A Few Leaves from the Diary of an Underground Railroad Conductor" [*DC*, 20 June 1881], 24; B1OB, 100; *UA*, 10 Sept. 1866; obit., 28 Apr. 1884; Jane [Marsh] Parker, *Rochester: A Story Historical* [New York: Scranton, Wetmore, 1884], 256–58). Baptized with Falls on the same day in March 1839 was another member of the founders' committee, Alonzo Bennett ("Records of the First Baptist Church of Rochester," First Baptist Church).

108. Yet another RTA founder and subsequently recording secretary, Frost also remained active in union activities, showing up in 1848 as the vice president of the local printers' society (*RGLA*, marriage announcement, 2 Apr. 1838; *UA*, obit., 20 Apr. 1895; "Barton's Second Obituary Book" [B2OB], RPL, 116; "Tengwall Scrapbook," 1:58; "Records of the Second Baptist Church," First Baptist Church). Seceders from the First Church, the Second Baptists were zealously evangelical, antislavery, and temperate.

109. Corresponding secretary of the RTA, Underwood was dismissed from the Quaker meeting in late summer 1840 because he "neglected meeting and attended theater" ("Records of the Society of Friends," Monroe County, N.Y., c. 1740–1920, Cornell Univ. Library).

110. Agitation for early business closing began in the late 1830s; the city's businessmen relented a decade later, though only for the winter months. See Johnson, *Shopkeeper's Millennium*, 123, 197; McKelvey, *Rochester: The Water-Power City*, 302; Gleason, "History of Labor," 42; *WMA*, 15 Nov., 21 Dec. 1839; *RDA*, 1 Oct. 1841; 5 Oct. 1844; 17 Dec. 1852; *RR*, 30 Nov., 7 Dec. 1848; *RDD*, 8 Dec. 1851.

111. See n. 70.

112. These clerks may seem like strange characters to label labor activists. Certainly, they articulated their demand in the most circumspect manner. Their address to the city's merchants "respectfully represent[ed]" that they could not "faithful[ly] discharge our duties" under the prevailing system of 9:00 P.M. closing and asked for an end to the practice "if practicable" and "without sacrifice of principle on our part, and without detriment to your best interest." Their goal was to avoid associating with "the profligate and abandoned of both sexes" because they retired from work too late and were therefore unable to associate with those women "whose restraining influence would at once relieve our manners and purify our hearts." More broadly, they sought to preserve their energy for mental cultivation and general improvement: more time would make them better workers. They also expressed their hope that they had not overstepped the bounds of propriety in raising the issue in such a public way. Still, these clerks did raise the issue publicly, in precisely the manner it had been raised by the carpenters a decade earlier, if in more self-effacing language. Moreover, when the clerks raised the issue a second time—during the same week that other activists organized the Working Men's Club (see below)—the class nature of their demand was quite evident. Insisting once again that an earlier closing hour was in the interest of both employer and employed, they nevertheless resolved that "the remainder of the evening ought and should belong to ourselves." As for their emphasis on improvement, as we shall see in chap. 10, the crux of the shorter-hours movement in this period was the desire for what workers of the age typically called "cultivation"—material, mental, moral, and spiritual. And, most important for our purposes, the clerks' church membership patterns are remarkably similar to that of other Rochester unionists and labor activists, suggesting that the labor-church relationship was not substantially altered by the nature of labor protest in Rochester.

113. Elwood to E. Bushnell, 15 Dec. 1838, URL; Unitarian Leases B; Temperance Pledge (1836), V. R. Jackson Folder, RPL; *RDA*, 1 Oct. 1841.

114. McKelvey, *Rochester: The Water-Power City*, 220; Gleason, "History of Labor," chap. 2; *RDA*, 1 July, 18 Aug. 1841; 4 Feb., 15, 21, 22, 23, 26 Mar. 1842; 10, 13, 15, 20 June 1843; 5 Oct. 1844; (Albany) *New York State Mechanic*, 2, 5 Apr. 1842; *RR*, 2 Apr. 1842; 20 June 1843; *RDD*, 12, 13, 15, 16 June, 18 July 1843; Schermerhorn to wife, 14 June 1843, photostat letter, RPL.

115. "Duebill System of Robbery" from a notice in *RDA*, 5 Apr. 1842.

116. Originally called the Mechanics' Benevolent Association.

117. This was a demand for currency without depreciation, these activists averred, not for a raise in wages (ibid., 21 Mar. 1842).

118. In 1842, the movement had been praised by the local press for its "sobriety and good order."

119. The grocer, Samuel Hamilton, issued a card the next day denying that he had sold duebills below their value and, in any case, vowed never to issue another one except in exchange for those already in circulation (ibid., 10 June 1843).

120. There is some discrepancy about the nature of the violence on this night. The *Republican* called it "mob violence" directed against citizens and store windows, while the *Advertiser* was unsure whether the windows had been broken by design or by accident (*RR*, 20 June 1843; *RDA*, 16 June 184).

121. Rallies continued in 1844, but the practice of issuing duebills for wages was not eliminated in Rochester until after the Civil War; as late as 1860, Rochester ironworkers went on strike against their iron bosses over the practice.

122. And again, some were leaders in their congregations. William W. Shephard (Shepherd, Shepard), a society committeeman in 1841 and 1842 and a prominent local reformer, was an elder in the Free Presbyterian Church who had gone to the Fourth Presbyterian in 1838. Among the grocers who joined the movement in 1842—helping to draft a resolution on their behalf—was Samuel Finley Witherspoon, who was confirmed in the St. Luke's Episcopal Church in April 1842, a month after he announced his public support for the abolition of the duebill system. See "Session Minutes, 1838–1846, with register of members, 1828–1862," Fourth Presbyterian Church, PHS. Witherspoon—a leading evangelical in the Rochester church community—participated in the Sabbath convention of 1842 and, later in the decade, was on the board of directors of the Society for the Promotion of Evangelical Knowledge. In the 1850s, he became a vestryman in the Trinity (Episcopal) Church. See Episcopalian Church Records, 1820–1851, 2 parts (Rochester Genealogical Society, 1982); *RDA*, 24 Mar. 1842; 15 May 1848; *Sabbath Convention*.

123. Indeed, the preamble and resolutions of the great March 21 meeting—which spoke of two classes in the Rochester community, those who earned their "daily labor by the sweat of [their] brow" and "emissaries of the devil" who deprived the former of their "heaven-born privileges"— was drafted by a committee with a significant representation of local churchmen. Two were Presbyterians (T. H. Patchin, William Shephard), one is listed in the records of the First Baptist Church in 1843 (George G. Ritchie), and another had just been denied his appeal for a new trial in the Methodist Church (Justin B. Jones). A fifth, a William Morgan, may very well have been a member of St. Luke's Episcopal Church, though there was more than one William Morgan in Rochester during this period (*RDA*, 23 Mar. 1842; see, too, ibid., 18 Aug. 1841; 4 Feb., 15, 22, 26 Mar. 1842; 20 June 1843; *RR*, 20 June, 4 July 1843; Brick Records; Records of the First Baptist Church, First Baptist Church; First Methodist "Quarterly Conference").

124. *RDA*, 22 Sept. 1841; 23 Feb. 1850; *RDD*, 22 Apr. 1844; *UA*, obit., 20 Apr. 1863; (Rochester) *Post-Express*, 23 Sept. 1893, in "Peck's Scrapbook," RPL, 48; John Devoy, *A History of the City of Rochester From the Earliest Times* (Rochester: Post Express, 1895), 173–74; "Tengwall Scrapbook" 11:54; ibid. 4:190.

125. Michael Barkun, *Crucible of the Millennium: The Burned-Over District of New York in the 1840s* (Syracuse: Syracuse Univ. Press, 1986); Parker, *Rochester: A Story Historical*, 251–52. Rochester eventually became the center of Millerism in the West.

126. The following is taken from Scranton, Old Citizen's Letters; *RDD*, 17, 23 June 1843; letter of Warren Mason, *DC*, 9 Sept., 1894, in "Samson Notebook," RPL, 52:92.

127. For the letter, see *RDD*, 12 July 1843.

128. This paper did appear in 1843, but no copies of have survived. The "Declaration of Rights" is a reference to a document drafted by elements of the anti-duebill movement and first read at a rally in Court House Square on July 4, 1843. No copies of this proclamation have survived, either. See ibid., 4, 18 July 1843.

129. *RDA*, 5, 10 Oct. 1844. See, too, *RDD*, 10 Apr. 1843; Gleason, "History of Labor," chap. 2. The movement turned to politics in July 1843, when the society reported gathering 2,212 signature pledges against the duebill system and resolved to oppose any candidates for office who continued to support it.

130. Lewis Rice, a member of the vigilance committee for the Fourth Ward in 1844, was born in upstate New York in the 1790s, fought in the War of 1812, and moved to Rochester in 1817. A journeyman mason, he was baptized in the First Baptist Church in 1830 and was one of the founders of the Second Baptist Church in 1834 (*UA*, obit., 8 Apr. 1876; B1OB, 46; Records of First Baptist). One of the Methodist members of the vigilance committee for Ward Seven was Daniel C. Stocking [Stockings, Stroking], Jr., a native of Connecticut who came to Rochester as an adult in 1831 to establish a pumpmaking business. A founder and steward of the Asbury Methodist Church, he "lived and died in the Christian faith as a Methodist" (*UA*, obit., 23 Apr. 1868; "Steward's Book," Asbury-First). And Ward Five's Joseph Schutt, a Prussian who arrived in Rochester in 1836 at the age of twenty and soon established himself as a local dealer in looking glasses and picture frames, was a "deeply interested" member of St. Joseph's Catholic Church (*UA*, obit., 9 Feb. 1881; Records of St. Joseph's Church, St. Joseph's Church, Rochester). Most of the Catholics among the labor activists were in this WMC cohort.

131. Also known as Central Presbyterian. Parsons supported the carpenters during the union upsurge of the early 1850s, too (*RDU*, 31 Mar. 1853; Rochester, New York Central Presbyterian Church Records, PHS, 1:271–72; Records of Bethel, Washington Street, Central and Sunday School, vols. 1, 2, PHS; Bethel Sabbath School Minutes, 1836–1843, vols. 1–4, PHS).

132. *UA*, obit., 20 June 1862; Records of the First Universalist Sabbath School; *UA*, 14 Feb. 1859; John Kelsey, *The Lives and Reminiscences of the Pioneers of Rochester and Western New York* (Rochester, 1854), 43–44; "Samson Notebook," 8:58–59.

133. *RDA*, 1 Jan. 1849. Price also turned up frequently as a speaker at shorter-hour meetings (*UA*, obit., 28 Oct. 1890; B1OB, 105–6; *RR*, 4, 9 Nov., 7 Dec. 1848; *RDA*, 1 Jan. 1849).

134. Immigrants participated in the festival as well, but they too were often well integrated into the Rochester community. Englishman John F. Lovecraft, one of the toastmasters, arrived in Rochester in the mid-1830s as a carpenter and joiner. Within a year of his arrival he was acting as an agent for a radical Democratic paper, the *Rochester Intelligencer and Mechanics' and Working Men's Advocate*. In 1844, he was chosen to the vigilance committee for the Second Ward of the WMC. In 1850, he was elected secretary of the meeting to choose Rochester delegates for a statewide mechanics' meeting in Syracuse. Though not apparently a church member, Lovecraft was married and baptized his children in the Episcopal Church. The same was true of another Englishman, Joseph Lovecraft, a Devonshire artisan (master cooper) who had come to Rochester in 1831: his wedding (1839), the baptism of his daughter (1843), and his funeral (1850) all took place at St. Paul's Church. See *Rochester Intelligencer,* 17 Oct. 1836; *Episcopal Church Records; UA,* obit., 16 Apr. 1877; ibid., obit., 8 Nov. 1879. On the shorter-hours movement of the late 1840s, see Gleason, chap. 2; "Raymond Scrapbook," RPL (1848), 68; *Rochester Daily Advertiser* (*RDA*), 5 July 1847; 18 Sept., 2, 3, 4 Nov. 1848; *RR*, 26 Oct., 9 Nov. 1848. On the Rochester MMPA fight against duebills, see (Rochester) *National Reformer* (*NR*), 7 Dec. 1848.

135. The Rochester story thus dramatically reveals the need to revise the loyalist-traditionalist-rebel typology first advanced by Paul Faler (see intro.).

Chapter 7

1. *Reformer,* repr. in *NL*, 21 May 1836.

2. *The Church, the Pillar, and Ground of the Truth,* 11, 12, cited in Schlesinger, *Age of Jackson,* 353. On clerical opposition to labor in Philadelphia in this period, see *Pennsylvanian,* 9 May 1834, cited in William A. Sullivan, *The Industrial Worker in Pennsylvania, 1800–1840* (Harrisburg: Pennsylvania Historical and Museum Commission, 1955), 147–48.

3. Typical is Norman Ware's mention of the Reverend Henry Miles's rosy account of the factory system in Lowell in *Industrial Worker*, 95–97.

4. For the "social control" argument applied to the working class and the labor movement, see Charles C. Cole, Jr., *The Social Ideas of the Northern Evangelists, 1820–1860* (New York: Columbia Univ. Press, 1954), 187–89. The classic rendition of the general interpretation can be found in Charles I. Foster, "The Urban Missionary Impulse, 1814–1860," *Pennsylvania Magazine of History and Biography* 75 (Jan. 1951): 45–65; idem, *An Errand of Mercy*.

5. Lois W. Banner, "Religious Benevolence as Social Control: A Critique of an Interpretation," *Journal of American History* 60 (June 1973): 23–41; James Moorhead, "Social Reform and the Divided Conscience of Antebellum Protestantism," *Church History* 48 (Dec. 1979): 427–28; Walters, *American Reformers*, 34–35. Two earlier works that discovered a nascent "social gospel" among the antebellum clergy, though with little to say about labor, are Gordon A. Riegler, *Socialization of the New England Clergy, 1800–1860* (Greenfield, Ohio: Greenfield, 1945), and Smith, *Revivalism and Social Reform*. For essays questioning the "social control" concept, see William A. Muraskin, "The Social Control Theory in American History: A Critique," *Journal of Social History* 9 (summer 1976): 559–68; Lawrence Frederick Kohl, "The Concept of Social Control and the History of Jacksonian America," *Journal of the Early Republic* 5 (spring 1985): 21–34.

6. Salome Lincoln, lay Freewill Baptist preacher, led a mill turn-out in Taunton, Mass., 1829 (Carolyn B. Owen, "Vignettes, No. 66," Taunton Historical Society; [Taunton] *Columbia Reporter and Old Colony Journal*, 6 May 1829); Hiram Stevens, Freewill Baptist preacher, headed the Dover, N.H., FLRA, 1846 (*Voice*, 16 Apr. 1847). See, too, *Herald*, 15 June 1853; James Hutson, "Facing an Angry Labor: The American Public Interprets the Shoemakers' Strike of 1860," *Civil War History* 28 (Sept. 1982): 208–9; (Haverhill) *Gazette*, 16, 23 Mar. 1860; (Haverhill) *Tri-Weekly*, 1, 17, 27 Mar. 1860; *Courier*, 27, 28 Feb. 1860, cited in Foner, *History of the Labor Movement*, 1:244–45; George Rogers Taylor, *The Transportation Revolution 1815–1860* (New York: Harper & Row, 1951), 285.

7. In all this, historical context is crucial. In Poland, for example, when Solidarity began in the early 1980s, the Catholic Church was in general support, at least to an extent, of a radical movement of rank-and-file socialist workers. By late 1989, cut loose from its working-class base, Solidarity moved openly toward a capitalist stance, though again with the blessing of the church. In other words, the meaning of church support changes as conditions change.

8. Especially in New England, church affairs and social concerns had been closely intertwined since colonial times. Often, church worship and town meetings were conducted under the same roof in a building called simply the "meetinghouse." By the second quarter of the nineteenth century, the erection of town halls and other public buildings rendered the multifaceted meetinghouse unnecessary, while the emergence of denominationalism made it unacceptable. Still, churches remained a common arena for public gatherings. Indeed, until the late 1840s, places of worship were often called "meetinghouses" rather than the more modern term "churches."

9. Possible reasons for the involvement of these particular churches are discussed below.

10. *Buffalo Bulletin*, 26 June 1830, cited in Dirk Hoerder, "Some Connections between Craft Consciousness and Political Thought among Mechanics, 1820s to 1840s," *Amerikastudien* 30 (1985): 340. The "Mechanics and Working Men" of New York City held their celebration in a Bethel Baptist church; the Philadelphia Working Men held theirs at Zion Church in Southwark (*MFP*, 10, 31 July 1830).

11. Frieze (1789–1880) remained a supporter of labor struggles into the 1840s, though his relationship to the Universalist church after 1829 is unclear (*NEA*, 22 Mar. 1832; [New York] *Christian Leader*, 10 June 1880; Miller, *Larger Hope*, 268–69, 758–59; Frieze, *Elements of Social Disorder*).

12. *NEA*, 29 Nov., 13 Dec. 1832.

13. *NTU*, 27 Sept. 1834; also, *NEA*, 4 Oct. 1834.

14. Ibid., 12 Aug. 1835.

15. *Transcript*, 25 Mar. 1836, cited in Josephson, *Golden Threads*, 240; Zonderman, *Aspirations and Anxieties*, 205.

16. *PP*, 22 Dec. 1842; *New York State Mechanic*, 22 Oct. 1842.

17. *Operative*, 14, 21 Sept. 1844.

18. *Voice*, 25 June 1847.

19. *Tri-Weekly*, 27 Mar. 1860; *Mechanic*, 21 Sept. 1844.

20. Kirkpatrick, *City and the River*, 1:99–101; Hurd, *History of Worcester County* 1:223, 246.

21. Bailey, "History of Fitchburg Notes," FHS; *Sentinel*, 10 July 1839. The Trinitarian Church was the organizing center for abolitionists who emigrated to Kansas in 1855. Their leader, Dr. Charles Robinson, became Kansas's first governor (Tolman, "Historical Sketch").

22. In September 1841, itinerant temperance advocate and former alcoholic John Hawkins came to speak to the Calvinists. Following his lecture, 130 citizens signed the Washingtonian Total Abstinence pledge and proceeded to organize a temperance society. After the 1842 schism, they held most of their meetings in the Trinitarian church (Bailey, "Reminiscences of the Old Town Hall," *FHS Proceedings* 4 [1908]: 72–73; Kirkpatrick, *City and the River* 1:196).

23. For this reason, the association abandoned a plan for meetings aimed at mill workers on Saturday evenings.

24. "FWA Record Book"; *WI*, 8 Feb. 1845.

25. There were limits to the Trinitarians' welcoming of labor reformers, however, which may have reflected conflicts within the congregation. When John Cluer came to town on his lecture tour in late 1845, his talk at the church engendered fears among at least some of the congregation's leaders because of charges that the Scotsman was an infidel (letter of "S.S.S." to *Voice*, 9 Jan. 1846 [incorrectly dated 22 Dec. 1846, rather than 1845]). There were other issues concerning Cluer's "character," but his attacks on the church seem to have been the sticking point for labor activists: Ware, *Industrial Worker*, 140–41. For similar problems in some sympathetic Fall River churches at about the same time, see below.

26. On the use of local churches by antislavery activists, see *Monitor*, 8 Feb. 1834; 9, 30 July 1836; 16 Dec. 1837; 13 Apr., 18 May 1844; *Patriot*, 6 July, 14 Dec. 1837; 20 Sept. 1838; 4 July, 21 Nov. 1839; *Argus*, 5 Jan. 1843. For the temperance movement, see *Monitor*, 13 Feb., 10 Apr., 12 June 1830; 13 June, 11 July, 31 Oct. 1835; 19 June 1841; 16 July 1842; *Recorder*, 20 Feb., 3, 10 Apr., 3, 10 July 1833; *Archetype*, 25 Feb., 24 June 1841.

27. *NEA*, 16 Feb. 1832; *Recorder*, 31 Oct. 1832; 27 Mar. 1833; *Monitor*, 9, 27 Nov., 11 Dec. 1833.

28. In Fall River, as in Fitchburg, native-born activists with deep roots in an overwhelmingly Protestant community mounted these struggles; articulating a program based on the elevation of that community, they organized within its churches and were supported by them. Workers who were not part of the dominant churchgoing community, like the Fall River immigrants who led mill strikes during the late 1840s and 1850s, found the local churches far less sympathetic to their struggles. In 1848, striking weavers were denied the use of Town Hall and local public buildings; they met on the steps of local Protestant churches, in the streets, and in nearby groves. During the 1850–51 mill strike, the Freewill Baptist Church and Asa Bronson's Second Baptist Church opened their doors to striking weavers, but the walkout did not enjoy the massive clerical support the ten-hour movement had garnered in the 1840s. By the 1860s, mill workers like the mule spinners had procured their own meetinghall, while other, less skilled immigrants held their meetings outdoors during the warmer months and rented public buildings during the winter. See *Voice*, 10 Mar. 1848; *News*, 2, 23 Jan, 13, 20 Feb. 1851; 4 Apr., 3 Nov. 1866; 11 July, 19 Aug., 7 Sept. 1870; 26 July, 5 Aug. 1875; *Monitor*, 7 Dec. 1850; 22 Feb. 1851; (Fall River) *Herald*, 21 Oct. 1878; (Fall River) *Labor Standard*, 1880, passim.

In Boston, the nearly universal opposition of the local clergy and the availability of numerous public buildings in the downtown area (taverns, clubs, and public halls) generally discouraged labor's use of the church. Sometimes, in the neighborhoods, a meetinghouse might open its doors for a workers' meeting, as when Charlestown workers used the Reverend Walker's Methodist vestry to organize a cooperative in 1833 (*NEA*, 21 Feb. 1833). More common was the BTU's experience in 1834, discussed in chap. 4. Wilmington and Rochester were more like Boston than Fall River and Fitchburg. In Wilmington, where there is little evidence of secular groups meeting in local churches, the Working Men met at taverns and inns, the town hall, and a local schoolhouse used in the antebellum period by all sorts of groups. See *Delaware Register*, 25 July, 15 Aug. 1829; *DFP*, 17 Apr., 15, 29 May, 19 June, 17, 30 July, 21 Aug., 11, 18, 25 Sept., 16 Oct., 4 Dec. 1830; 30 July, 10, 24 Sept., 1 Oct. 1831; Carol E. Hoffecker, *Brandywine Village: The Story of a Mining Community* (Wilmington: Old Brandywine Village, 1974), 62–65. In mid-1830, after nearly a year of agitation, the AWPNCC established the "Working Men's Reading Company" with it own room, but the group continued to meet in other public buildings and commercial establishments. In Rochester, activists met at local hotels and taverns, the Court House, and, by the 1840s, Mechanics' Hall and various other "rooms" in town. See *Craftsman*, 10, 24 Feb., 10 Mar. 1829; *RDAT*, 17 Mar. 1831; *RDA*, 1 July, 18 Aug. 1841; 28 Mar. 1842; 4 Oct. 1843; 5 July 1847; 18 Sept. 1848; 23 Feb. 1850; 19, 23 Apr. 1853; *RDD*, 6 Mar. 1835; 24 Feb. 1836; 22, 28 Mar., 8 Apr. 1853; *RDU*, 31 Mar. 1853.

29. Donald M. Scott, *From Office to Profession: The New England Ministry, 1750–1850* (Philadelphia: Univ. of Pennsylvania Press, 1978). Alexis de Tocqueville, among other discerning visitors to America during these years, noticed the central role clergymen played in regulating the community by influencing its manners and morals (*Democracy in America*, 290–301). See also, Francis Trollope, "Domestic Manners," excerpted in Coombs, *America Visited*, 73.

30. *MM*, July 1846, 285.

31. For remarks on the traditional American ambivalence toward the clergy, see Daniel Calhoun, *Professional Lives in America: Structure and Aspiration, 1750–1850* (Cambridge: Harvard Univ. Press, 1965), 7; Richard Hofstadter, *Anti-Intellectualism in American Life* (New York: Vintage Books, 1962), part 2.

32. This particular brand of "anticlericalism" may in great part explain why historians have not paid much attention to the prolabor clergymen discussed in this chapter. A recent example of the traditional view, by a historian who recognizes the positive role religion sometimes played in nineteenth-century labor protest, can be found in Clark Halker, "Jesus was a Carpenter: Labor Song-Poets, Labor Protest, and True Religion in Gilded Age America," *Labor History* 32 (spring 1991): 277–79. For an important caveat about the nature of American anticlericalism generally, relevant to this discussion, see Sidney Mead, "The Rise of the Evangelical Conception of the Ministry in America, 1607–1850," in H. Richard Niebuhr and Daniel D. Williams, eds., *The Ministry in Historical Perspective* (New York: Harper & Row, 1956), 233–36.

33. The idea for a national Industrial Congress (IC) was proposed at an NEWA meeting in May 1845. Land reformers in the National Reform Association submitted a resolution calling on all workers and reformers to join together on a platform of broad social reform. In September, the two groups jointly issued a call for "farmers, mechanics and producers, friends of reformers" to meet in New York City the following month. Composed of delegates elected by local societies, the congresses were to act in an advisory capacity only, with "Industrial Brotherhoods" carrying out political action and providing sickness and burial benefits. Although employers could not join and the IC program centered on the land and hours questions, some historians have questioned its labor orientation (see the similar issues regarding the WMP, chap. 5). Ware, for example, described the IC as a platform for "pet schemes" (*Industrial Worker*, 217–18, 222–26). Zahler (*Eastern Workingmen*, 64–66) offers a more balanced account. She notes that "none of the Industrial Brotherhoods was a federation of skilled workers untainted by the presence of utopian reformers," but she also points out that in antebellum America, "it was not yet the accepted notion that labor organization is properly concerned only with improving the worker's position as a wage earner." In these years, she writes, many workers' associations went beyond immediate issues "and considered remedies for fundamental evil." Though organized labor did not dominate the congresses (which met annually, 1845–56), unions were represented and several important labor leaders participated

in the proceedings, among them Sarah Bagley, Huldah Stone, and William F. Young. See McNeill, *Labor Movement*, 104, and Guarneri, *Utopian Alternative*, chap. 11.

34. *Voice*, 25 June 1847. Unless otherwise noted, all direct quotations from this debate are found in this issue.

35. Emphasis in original.

36. McNeill, *Labor Movement*, 110.

37. It was here that Van Ameringe pointed out that he had spoken at churches in numerous cities during his lecture tours (*Tri-Weekly*, 27 Mar. 1860; *Mechanic*, 21 Sept. 1844).

38. For a similar rejection of come-outerism among abolitionists as not likely to advance the cause of antislavery and as a threat of "subversion of established institutions through revolution and bloodshed," see *PP*, 28 Nov. 1843.

39. *Voice*, 23 Jan. 1846; (Lynn) *True Workingman*, 31 Jan., 7 Feb. 1846, repr. in Commons, *Documentary History* 8:113–16.

40. *Voice*, 10 Apr. 1846. Cluer himself was a Christian labor reformer, as can be glimpsed from his speaking tour in 1845–46. When attacked by a Manchester newspaper editor for "advocat[ing] the theology of Tom Paine from a text of Scripture," the Scot went on the offensive, calling his accuser "a dishonest atheist." This is how Cluer described his speech: having first read a chapter from the New Testament and sung a hymn, he then discoursed on, "For the wages of sin is death," in which he sought to prove the existence of "the law-giver" by science and divine revelation. A benevolent Deity who was no respecter of persons, God required obedience, with suffering and misery the consequence of disobedience. Cotton dust, heated rooms, short meals, long workdays, bad housing—these hallmarks of the factory system had forced people to sin against their Maker (ibid., 9, 16 Jan. 1846). Cluer claimed direct experience with such crimes, recalling childhood factory labor of sixteen hours per day (*Chronotype*, 8 Apr. 1847). For Young's defense of Cluer (he had shown the Manchester newspaper editor to be an "enemy of true religion, temperance and the prosperity of our people as a Christian and Republican nation"), see *Voice*, 18 Dec. 1845.

41. The lines of debate were rarely neat. See, e.g., the discussion of Lynn's John Gibson in Murphy, *Ten Hours' Labor*, 188–89, n. 56.

42. *NEA*, 18 July 1833.

43. (Boston) *Independent Chronicle and Reformer* [*ICR*], 4 July 1835.

44. Ibid., 8 Aug. 1835. Although sometimes identified as an ex-Universalist minister by the time of his involvement in labor activity (e.g., Schlesinger, *Age of Jackson*, 169–70), Fisk [also Fiske] did not abandon the pulpit (he was forced out, really) until 1838 (see the *Universalist Register and Almanac* for 1836, and 1837). See, too, "A Working Man," *MFP*, 21 Aug. 1830, for a religious condemnation of ministers who disparaged the morality and piety of journeymen mechanics. A few months later, the editors of the *MFP* declared flatly, "Wherever the Clergy as a body have been allowed connection with the government in this country, they have *always* been found arrayed on the side of tyrants against the rights of the people" (ibid., 1 Jan. 1831).

45. *Voice*, 23 Jan. 1846.

46. Ibid., 11 Sept. 1845.

47. Ibid., 7 Apr. 1848.

48. *Mechanic*, 22 June 1844. For their part, the editors offered frequent and favorable comment on "our minister friends," taking care to distinguish between those who "acted as sheep" and listened to "rich men," and those who sided with the oppressed (ibid., 15 June, 27 July 1844). In Lowell, William Young pleaded with his town's ministers, as "public men" of great influence in the community, to take up labor's cause. If they would only open their eyes, he told them, they would see a "world-wide moral revolution" mounted by "true" Christians, in the interest of Christianity. Imploring them to join the struggle against widespread social misery, for "pure and undefiled" religion could not flourish in a society that denied basic rights, he reminded them of their "duty to your God and your fellow-men" to speak out against contemporary injustices (*Voice*, 30 Jan. 1846; also, 21 Nov. 1845). Prolabor clergymen similarly pressed their brethren: *Mechanic*, 25 May

(Christian Henry P. Guilford); 13 July 1844 (Universalist John Gregory); (Woonsocket) *Patriot,* 12 June 1846 (Congregationalist James Davis).

49. *Voice,* 19 June 1846. Allen left the ministry in 1841 over the slavery issue (Swift, *Brook Farm,* 181–82).

50. *Voice,* 9 Oct. 1846.

51. Early the following year, the *Voice* carried a special report by one of its traveling correspondents, veteran Manchester operative and labor organizer Mehitable Eastman, on a Unitarian sermon preached in Concord, N.H., by the Reverend William P. Tilden. What caught Eastman's attention about this ex-artisan, who described himself as having entered the ministry in 1840 as "a mechanic with hard hands" (and later as "a ship-carpenter minister"), was his view that the clergy had an "exalted mission . . . to strike . . . against wrong and in behalf of right," and should never "gloss over any evil for the sake of being popular." If there were more preachers like Tilden, wrote the founder and president of the Manchester FLRA, "we should soon see less of vice, more of Christianity and a better state of things generally" (ibid., 5 Mar. 1847; *William Phillips Tilden: Autobiography and Personal Tribute* [Boston, 1891], 72, 84). For more examples, see *Voice,* 30 Jan., 19 June 1846; 16 July 1847. On Eastman, ibid., 10 Sept., 31 Dec. 1847; see Foner, *Factory Girls,* 100; Early, "Reappraisal of the New-England Labour-Reform Movement," 49.

52. In North Andover, Mass., during a trip to promote the NEWA, a *Voice* editor secured a local church and enlisted the aid of a sympathetic pastor from a neighboring town, who addressed the assembly on the Christian's duty to defend "man's" "natural rights, upon which hangs his life, liberty and spiritual elevation" (ibid., 27 Feb. 1846). In Fitchburg, Congregationalist minister Philo C. Pettibone used the same tactic, bringing a pastor from nearby Sterling to speak before the FWA ("FWA Record Book"). Frieze was the first editor of the *NEA;* editors of the *Reformer* included the Unitarian Orestes Brownson and two Universalists, Linus S. Everett and Theophilus Fisk. A number of Boston's Unitarian ministers participated in NEWA meetings, while Episcopal minister E. M. P. Wells supported striking tailors by speaking at labor rallies and by donating to their strike fund (*Post,* 25 Aug., 7 Sept. 1849; *Herald,* 7 Sept. 1849).

53. Unfortunately, we do not know the precise nature of these prayers because none has survived. If the use of such exercises in other nineteenth-century gatherings is any guide, though, these prayers were likely substantial. The offering of the presiding clergyman at Gettysburg in November 1863, for example, took substantially more time to deliver than Lincoln's famous address (Gary Wills, *Lincoln at Gettysburg: The Words That Remade America* [New York: Simon and Schuster, 1992]).

54. *Post,* 6 May 1835; *ICR,* 11 July 1835; "FWA Record Book"; *Gazette,* 16 Mar. 1860. Also, Woburn: *Harbinger,* 12 July 1845; *Voice,* 10 July 1845; North Andover: *Voice,* 27 Feb. 1846; Boston: *Herald,* 30 Sept. 1852.

55. *NEA,* 11 Oct. 1832. On Taylor, see Robert Collyer, *Father Taylor* (Boston: American Unitarian Association, 1906), 4, 5–7, 21–23, 25, 54, 58. For his influence on Emerson, as well as other writers of the so-called American Renaissance, see David S. Reynolds, *Beneath the American Renaissance: The Subversive Imagination in the Age of Emerson and Melville* (Cambridge: Harvard Univ. Press, 1988), 19–21, passim.

56. Several factors likely contributed to the intensity of ministerial interest during these years. First, the depression of the late 1830s and early 1840s produced a new awareness in the pulpit of social problems produced by deteriorating labor conditions. Second, the revivalism that accompanied that depression carried a message of impending apocalypse. While some converts, like the Millerites, waited for the physical coming of Christ to inaugurate the Millennium, many looked to the establishment of God's kingdom through the perfection of earthly institutions. Since this latter spirit characterized a significant tendency within the labor movement, some ministers saw labor reform as a harbinger of the Light. Third, the growing numbers of churchgoing workers converted during the depression revivals made the clergy sensitive to popular demands among the laboring population. Fourth, a new breed of Christian perfectionism infused the ministry during the late 1830s and early 1840s. Some, like Fitchburg's Philo Pettibone, for example, had been exposed to an

abolitionist upsurge in the seminaries. Fifth, many of these ministers had been workers themselves and, therefore, identified more readily with labor's demand for shorter hours and better working conditions. And finally, the labor movement of the mid-1840s endorsed broad labor reform centered on the demand for the shorter workday. Embracing anyone who sought in elevation of the laboring classes and of humanity as a whole, the movement's universalist approach and Christian character attracted many clergymen.

57. *Mechanic,* 25 May 1844.

58. Ibid., 15 June 1844.

59. Orin Fowler, pastor of First Congregational, professed support for the ten-hour demand, while denouncing the agitation engendered by it, particularly the actions of local building tradesmen. His colleague at the Central Congregational Church, the Reverend Samuel Washburn, said nothing publicly about either shorter hours or the labor movement. Though labor activists counted Fowler among their enemies, they believed that Washburn was merely indifferent. The pastor of the Unitarian Society, John R. W. Ware, opposed the movement, even though several prominent members of his congregation were labor advocates. Like Washburn, Ware took little part in the public debates over the issue, but, like Fowler, he claimed to support the demand while rejecting the tactics of its proponents ([New York] *WMA,* 22 June 1844). Fall River's Catholic priest, Father Edward Murphy of St. Mary's Cathedral, professed his sympathy but withheld his active support. When a ten-hour committee requested his church for meetings and invited him to lecture on the hours question, he refused, claiming instructions from his bishop to open the chapel for worship only. The activists were unconvinced. It appears that "the Catholic Priest," one wrote, "has got a bedstead to which he ties himself up" (*All Sorts,* 14 Aug. 1844).

60. *Mechanic,* 29 June 1844.

61. *All Sorts,* 24 July 1844.

62. *Monitor,* 20, 27 July 1844.

63. *All Sorts,* 24 July 1844.

64. Though activists would continue to confront clerical and church opposition. As noted, at the height of the agitation in 1844, Bronson was forced to relinquish his pastorate and leave town for a time. A. M. Averill encountered problems when he tried to speak before the Mechanics' Association, though he was not removed from his position for doing so and his support for the movement continued. On Averill, see *Mechanic,* 15 June 1844.

65. Ibid., 6, 13 July 1844. Little wonder that one of Fall River's delegates to the preliminary meeting of the NEWA in Boston that October identified the clergy as one of his movement's principal allies (*Laborer,* 26 Oct. 1844). According to the *Post* (18 Oct. 1844), four of the delegates at the Boston meeting were clergymen. See, too, "A Working Man" to the *Mechanic:* "the clergy generally (speak) in favor of your holy enterprise" (1 June 1844).

66. Ibid., 15 June 1844.

67. Ibid., 31 Aug. 1844. For his weekly reports, see ibid., Aug. 1844; Philip Foner, "Notes and Documents: Journal of an Early Labor Organizer," *Labor History* 10 (spring 1969): 205–27. Hewitt headed Universalist congregations in Wrentham, Mass. (1840–43), and Providence, R.I. (1844), before going to work for the Mechanics' Association; he would hold several other pastorates in Massachusetts during the 1840s and 1850s (Dighton [1845–46], Amesbury [1848–50], Salem [1851], and Cambridge [1852–54]). See Historical Records Survey, *An Inventory of Universalist Archives in Massachusetts* (Boston, 1942); A. B. Grosh, ed., *The Universalist Companion, with an Almanac and Register* (Utica: A. B. Grosh, 1840–45). Murphy (*Ten Hours' Labor,* 139) incorrectly implies that Hewitt did not become a minister until after his activities on behalf of the Mechanics' Association.

68. On Bronson, see chap. 4.

69. On Randall (1810? 1812?-73), see "Diary of George Maxwell Randall, 1839–1854," FRHS; *Biographical Encyclopedia of Representative Men of Rhode Island,* 361; *National Cyclopedia of American Biography* (New York: James T. White, 1883). Randall left Fall River in 1844 to become rector of Boston's Messiah Church.

70. On Alexander McCormick Averill (1820–1904), see Clara A. Avery, comp., *The Averell-Averill-Avery Family: A Record of the Descendants of William and Abigail Averell of Ipswich, Massachusetts, 1637–1914* (n.p., 1914), 1:4, 582; 2:807, 935; *General Catalogue of the Theological Seminary, Andover, Massachusetts, 1808–1908* (Boston, n.d.); *Transcript*, obit., 23 Nov. 1903. Little is known about Henry Pittman Guilford (b. 1816? 1818?), who seems to have moved almost yearly in the 1840s and 1850s. Born in Lynn, he was in Fall River in 1843 and 1844, and again in 1848. In between he surfaced in Haverhill and New Brunswick, Canada. Thanks to Professor Henry B. Leonard for the information on Guilford.

71. On Phelon (1806–82), see G. A. Burgess and J. T. Ward, *Free Baptist Cyclopedia: Historical and Biographical* (n.p.: Free Baptist Cyclopedia, 1889), 523–24; A. D. Williams, *Rhode Island Freewill Baptist Pulpit* (Providence: National Biographical, 1881), 246–49. This preacher also addressed a convention of the NEWA (*Harbinger*, 27 Sept. 1845).

72. *Archetype*, 12 Aug. 1841. John Bovee Dods (nee Jerome Bonfils) (1795–1872), later a famous spiritualist, was in Fall River for only a short time in the early 1840s. *Dictionary of American Biography* (New York: Scribner, 1946); *National Cyclopedia of American Biography*; Samuel Hopkins Emery, *The Ministry of Taunton* (Boston: J. P. Jewett, 1853), 147; Miller, *Larger Hope*, 224–25.

73. *Mechanic*, 7 Sept. 1844; *Voice*, 18 Sept. 1845; *Monitor*, 7, 14 Dec. 1844; Hon. John Gregory (1810–81), *Centenary Proceedings and Historical Incidents of the Early Settlers of Northfield, Vermont* (Montpelier, Vt.: Argus and Patriot, 1878), 167–69; Edith Fox MacDonald, *Rebellion in the Mountains: The Story of Universalism, and Unitarianism in Vermont* (Concord, 1926), 147; *Transcript*, obit., 3 Oct. 1881. A decade later, during a subsequent movement for the ten-hour day, the principal speaker at a major strike rally was another Universalist minister, the Reverend Benjamin Hill Davis (1813–1903). See *News*, 28 Oct. 1852; 20 Oct. 1853; *Transcript*, obit., 10 July 1903; *Universalist Register* (1904), 102–3; *Universalist Leader*, 18 July 1903, 916; Necrology, *General Convention Annual Report* (Universalist), 1903, 82; *Weymouth Gazeteer, 10 July 1903*; Legislative Biography Card, State House Library, Boston.

74. Three of the four Blackstone Valley pastors who helped Hewitt, for example, belonged to these two churches. The Freewill Baptist was Blackstone's Maxcy Whipple Burlingame (1805–79), who was actually on the payroll of the Blackstone Manufacturing Company in the late 1830s; the Universalists were John Nelson Parker (1814?-1906) of Pawtucket and John Boyden, Jr. (1809–69), of Woonsocket, who also opened his First Universalist Church to meetings of the local Mechanics' and Laborers' Association. Boyden's church was organized in 1843, but the Woonsocket Universalists had been holding services in mill lofts in that factory town for nearly twenty years. Before coming to Rhode Island in 1840, he had held a pastorate in the mill town of Dudley, Mass., for six years. The denomination of the fourth minister, a Reverend Fish, is unknown. See *Mechanic*, 25 Jan. 1845; (New York) *WMA*, 8 Feb. 1845; Murphy, *Ten Hours' Labor*, 81–82; Edgar J. Allair, "History of Woonsocket" (unpublished ms.), 115; Wallace C. Boyden, A. M. et al., comps., *Thomas Boyden and His Descendants* (Boston, 1901), 127–28.

75. The phrase is Bertram Wyatt-Brown's ("Prelude to Abolitionism," 334). An important treatment of the New England Universalists and Freewill Baptists, though for an earlier period, is Steven Marini, *Radical Sects of Revolutionary New England* (Cambridge: Harvard Univ. Press, 1982).

76. For a similar perspective on the denominational support for abolitionism and utopian socialism in this period, see McKivigan, *War Against Proslavery Religion*, 24–25; Guarneri, *Utopian Alternative*, 68–74, 168–69. In Lowell in the 1840s, support for labor came from two ministers, a Baptist (Lemuel Porter, 1809–64) who had held a pastorate there for over a decade, and a recently arrived Episcopalian (Thomas P. Smith). In Lynn in 1860, it was a Unitarian graduate of Harvard (Charles Chauncey Shackford, 1815–91), along with an African Methodist and a Catholic priest. And, in Fitchburg, the clerical supporter of labor activism (Philo Columbus Pettibone, 1815–70) was converted in the early 1830s when the fires of the Finney revivals "burned over" upstate New York; a Congregationalist, he had originally been ordained in the Presbyterian Church. On Porter,

see *Illinois Baptist Anniversaries, 1864,* 10–11; *General Catalogue of the Newton Theological Institution, 1826–1943* (Newton Centre: Newton Theological Institution, 1943), 47. On Shackford, see N. F. Carter, *The Native Ministry of New Hampshire* (Concord: Rumford, 1906) 648–49; *General Catalogue of the Theological Seminary of the Officers and Graduates, 1636–1930* (Cambridge, Mass., 1930), 235; *Proceedings of the 63rd Annual Conference of the Iowa Unitarian Association, Held in the First Unitarian Church, Iowa City, Iowa, October 21, 22, 23, 1940; Transcript,* obit., 28 Dec. 1891. On Pettibone, see "FWA Record Book"; Tolman, "Historical Sketch," 56–58; *General Catalogue of the Theological Seminary, Andover,* 184; Samuel Bates, *History of Mercer County: Its Past and Its Present* (Chicago: Brown, Runk, 1888); Necrology, *Congregational Quarterly* 13 (Boston, 1871): 328–30. For examples of the dangers of using theory to explain denominational patterns, see Laurie, *Working People,* chap. 3 and Schultz, "God and Workingmen," 143–44.

77. *Mechanic,* 13 July 1844. On Hewitt and Phelon, see ibid., 4, 11 May, 20 July 1844; 22 Feb. 1845. Jacob Frieze, who was in the Universalist pulpit at the time of his initial involvement in labor reform, had been "brought up to, and labored in a mechanical profession" (*NEA,* 5 Jan. 1832, quoted in Murphy, *Ten Hour's Labor,* 35). Boston Universalist Linus S. Everett, labor reform editor and frequent speaker at strike rallies for the ten-hour day in 1835, had been a sign painter. Sebastian Streeter, another Boston Universalist who supported area laborites during these years, was of humble birth; at least three others (Boyden, Burlingame, and Dods) had farming backgrounds before entering the pulpit. Guilford's father was a cordwainer. Finally, the Unitarian William P. Tilden (1811–1890), praised in 1847 by labor organizer Mehitable Eastman for his insistence that ministers "stand against wrong," had been a fisherman and ship carpenter. See n. 51, above; *Post,* 6, 8 May 1835; Miller, *Larger Hope,* 58, 176, 191, 204–7, 288–89, 303–4, 537, 596–97; *Reformer,* 11 July 1835; *Universalist Register* (1868), 75–77; *Woonsocket Weekly Patriot and Rhode Island State Register,* obit., 1 Oct. 1869; *Representative Men and Old Families of Rhode Island* (Chicago: J. H. Beers, 1908) 2:926–27; *Free Baptist Cyclopedia,* 86–87; Williams, *Freewill Baptist Pulpit,* 171; Tilden, *William Phillips Tilden,* 11, 42–46, 57–63, 72, 77, 84, 88, 113–14.

78. Bronson, *An Address on the Anniversary of the Fire, Delivered in the Pearl Street Christian Chapel, July 2, 1844; Pursuant to a Request from the "Ladies' Mechanic Association"* (Fall River, 1844); *Monitor,* 13 Apr. 1844. See, too, "Source Material Book," 23, describes Bronson as a "man of peculiar power and efficiency, remarkable for strength, soundness, richness, gospel resources, and a warm heart, rather than for polished rhetoric," perhaps because of his background in manual rather than mental labor.

79. The exchange between Borden and Bronson was part of a two-month-long public debate in the pages of the Fall River *Monitor* (13, 20, 27 Apr., 4, 11, 18, 25 May, 1, 8, 15 June 1844; Borden: 13, 27 Apr., 25 May, 8 June; Bronson: 18 May, 1, 15 June 1844). Though it was a Baptist minister squaring off against a Unitarian employer, the issue was not a denominational one. Recourse to the laws of God over the laws of man was common among a range of Christian labor activists, behind the pulpit and in front of it. For a Universalist minister's use of the same argument, in this case in a diatribe against the tariff, see *NEA,* 26 July 1832. See, also, the remarks of Methuen's "Rev. Chase" (*Voice,* 27 Feb. 1846); an anonymous minister (*NEA,* 30 Aug. 1834); and Frieze, *Elements of Disorder,* iii–iv, 66–69, 92–94. In part, the (ex?)Universalist Frieze sought here to discredit his denominational rivals in the Benevolent Empire. But his critique was not primarily a product of internecine religious warfare; it was, rather, part of a broader attack on what he saw as the hypocrisy of Christian capitalists in antebellum America.

80. *Mechanic,* 1 Feb. 1845. For similar remarks by Averill, see ibid., 8 June 1844.

81. Ibid., 18, 25 Jan., 1, 8, 15, 22 Feb. 1845.

82. Phelon's thoroughgoing opposition to selfishness was, in fact, part of his theology. See his "Sermon: Criminal Prayer," *Zion's Herald* (1841), repr. in Williams, *Rhode Island Freewill Baptist Pulpit,* 250–55.

83. In particular, he blamed greed for workers leaving their jobs so frequently, insisting that they often sought more money when their present wages were sufficient. This pursuit of wealth, he reminded the readers of the *Mechanic,* sent men to early graves. "Where are the aged men, whose

lives have been preserved though they have engaged in trade?—They are very few." More than that, perhaps, the pursuit itself harmed others, for "selfishness *desires not the happiness of others*" (*Mechanic,* 1, 8 Feb. 1845).

84. Ibid., 1, 15, 22 Feb. 1845.

85. The role of the jeremiad in American culture is the subject of Sacvan Bercovitch's *The American Jeremiad* (Madison: Univ. of Wisconsin Press, 1978).

86. Ironically, one of the very few histories that noted "social gospel" sentiment among some antebellum New England clergymen found "a notable absence of comment on long working hours" (Reigler, *Socialization of the New England Clergy,* 137). On religious elements in the shorter-hours demands in this period, see chap. 10.

87. *Mechanic,* 11 May 1844. The argument echoed a familiar theme of clerical labor advocacy in the period. For Frieze's discourse on the question while editor of the *NEA,* see 19 Apr. 1832.

88. *Monitor,* 15 June 1844.

89. *Mechanic,* 8 June 1844.

90. The articles appeared in the (Woonsocket) *Patriot,* 22, 29 May, 5, 12, 19, 26 June 1846. Toward the end of the series, a meeting of local workingmen rendered thanks to Davis for "the bold, manly, and able manner in which he has indicated the rights of the laborer, in the pulpit and through the press." Reprinting the resolutions of the meeting from the *Patriot,* the editor of the *Voice* in Lowell joined the Rhode Island workers in thanking him for "his fidelity in this truly humane and religious cause." "O, that ministers every where would imitate his noble example," William Young sighed (*Voice,* 19 June 1846). Little is known about Davis. On his church in Woonsocket, the Globe Congregational, see Richard M. Bayles, ed., *History of Providence County, Rhode Island* (New York: W. W. Preston, 1891) 2:351–52.

91. *Mechanic,* 25 May; 25 Jan. 1845; *Patriot,* 5 June 1846. For similar remarks by Averill, see *Mechanic,* 8 June 1844.

92. *Mechanic,* 11 July 1844.

93. Bronson, *Address on the Anniversary of the Fire.*

94. *Mechanic,* 11 Jan. 1845, 3 Aug. 1844. For similar remarks, see Jacob Frieze (*NEA,* 19 Apr. 1832); Everett (*Post,* 8 May 1835); Fisk (*New York Evening Post,* 6 Aug. 1835 and "Labor the Only True Source of Wealth" in *Orations on the Freedom of the Press* [orig. publ. 1837; repr. ed., New York: Arno Press, 1970], 6); Bronson (*Address on the Anniversary of the Fire*); Averill (*Mechanic,* 8 June 1844); Phelon (ibid., 15 June, 13 July 1844); Bristol, R.I., "Rev. Sanborn" (ibid., 15 June 1844); Gregory (ibid., 13 July 1844); Hewitt (ibid., 31 Aug. 1844).

95. *Mechanic,* 31 Aug. 1844. For Phelon's remarks in this vein, see ibid., 13 July 1844, 11 Jan. 1845.

96. Ibid., 18 May 1844. For similar language and imagery, see ibid., see 3 Aug. 1844 (Hewitt); and, in the 1830s, *NEA,* 30 Aug. 1834 (anonymous Boston minister).

97. In an early *NEA* editorial, Jacob Frieze assured employers "in the sight of God and man" that the NEA harbored no hostility toward their interests (15 Mar. 1832). Similarly, Everett hoped the striking masons he supported in Boston would "be careful not to endeavor to accomplish their purpose by brute force—let it be accomplished by *mind*—by harmonious action—and not endanger our defeat by rashness" (*Post,* 8 May 1835).

98. Bronson, *Address on the Anniversary of the Fire.* See, too, *Post,* 8 May 1835 (Everett).

99. *Mechanic,* 18 May 1844.

100. In an imaginary dialogue in one of his newspaper articles, the Reverend Davis has a prolabor manufacturer warn others that one day the "judge" would review the "*murdered time, and crushed intellect,* and *obliterated affections,* and *smothered aspirations,* and *perished hopes,* and *blighted joys,* and *corrupt morals*" that resulted from the antebellum factory system (*Patriot,* 12 June 1846).

101. *Mechanic,* 18, 25 Jan. 1845.

102. Bronson, *Address on the Anniversary of the Fire.*

103. *Mechanic,* 8 June 1844.

104. Ibid., 25 May 1844. There is some evidence that Fall River workers themselves opposed physical confrontations in principle while they managed to countenance it in practice, all the while maintaining a "Christian" stance. See, for example, how local activists handled the destruction of "scab" tools during the 1844 building trades' strike discussed in chap. 11.

105. Ibid., 17, 24 Aug. 1844. The language here is redolent of Associationism, of which Hewitt was a devotee (*Harbinger,* 7 Feb. 1846).

106. Moorhead notes this phenomenon in antebellum reform generally, labeling it the "divided conscience of antebellum Protestantism." Although they were very different, what he says of Finney could be said as well of the prolabor clergy: both offer "fruitful insight into nineteenth century evangelicalism's explosive potential for reform and its equally powerful tendency to limit and contain that impulse" ("Social Reform and the Divided Conscience of Antebellum Protestantism," 428).

107. Moreover, it will not do to make these men of a piece with most evangelical reformers of their age, despite some superficial similarities. For the sympathies of the prolabor clergymen lay first with the laborer. Compare, for example, the reform sentiments of the leading evangelical of the day, Charles Finney, who opposed shorter-hours legislation (ibid., 428). Nor should the prolabor clergy be confused with the Social Gospel ministers of a later age, even those who became actively involved in union activity, again despite some superficial similarities. For the Social Gospel clergy generally came from outside the ranks of the labor, whereas their ancestors before the Civil War emerged organically from a nascent working-class movement. More important, the former sought more to tame the working class than to advocate on behalf of it. Like their predecessors, they may have been motivated by the desire to promote social justice and the Christian religion, but their major concern was what they perceived as the threat of organized socialism, something the earlier generation did not confront (Kenneth Fones-Wolf, *Trade Union Gospel: Christianity in Industrial Philadelphia, 1865–1915* [Philadelphia: Temple Univ. Press, 1989], esp. 95–96, 114–19, 120; Gutman, "Protestantism and the American Labor Movement," 113–17).

108. Certainly these clergymen were a far cry from such "critics" of the factory system as the Reverend Joseph Cook of Lynn, who, in 1871, advanced a "middle class" moral critique of industrial capitalism that was more critical of workers than it was of employers (John T. Cumbler, *A Moral Response to Industrialism: The Lectures of Reverend Cook in Lynn, Massachusetts* [Albany, N.Y.: State Univ. Press of New York, 1982]).

Chapter 8

1. For references, see intro., n. 7.

2. *Voice,* 29 May 1845. After Job's friends advised him to repent of his sins, a younger man named Elihu spoke:

> I am young, and ye are very old: wherefore I was afraid, and durst not shew you mine opinion.
> I said, Days should speak, and multitude of years should teach wisdom.
> But *there is* a spirit in man: and the inspiration of the Almighty giveth them understanding.
> Great men are not *always* wise: neither do the aged understand judgment.
> Therefore I said, Hearken to me; I also will shew mine opinion.
> Job 32:6–10 AV

The first issue of the *Voice* appeared four days after the last meeting minute entry in the "FWA Record Book," but the editorial page identified the paper as "published by an Association of Workingmen," the editor was an FWA officer, and the local distributors and agents were FWA members. The *Voice*'s last Fitchburg issue was 9 Oct. 1845; after a month's hiatus, it began publishing again in Lowell under the same editorship but with a new motto, "Organ of the New England Workingmen's Association."

3. Ibid., 11 Sept. 1845. In this appeal for—indeed, declaration of—divine favor, activists typically referred not only to God, the Creator, the Almighty, and Christ, but also more generally to the "Omnipotent Power" and the "All-Seeing Eye" (notice of NELRL meeting [*Voice*, 26 Feb. 1847]; "J.R." [ibid., 9 Oct. 1846]; "Mary Ann" [ibid., 28 May 1846]; Sarah Bagley's speech at the NEWA convention [ibid., 11 Sept. 1845]; Huldah Stone's letter to Manchester operatives [ibid., 26 Dec. 1845]; *Literary Wreath and Factory Girls' Album* [Exeter, N.H.], 10 July 1845, repr. in Foner, *Factory Girls*, 217–18).

4. "Agitate! Agitate!" repr. in *YA*, 22 Nov. 1845. On Gibson, see Murphy, *Ten Hours' Labor*, 182–82, 188–89.

5. *Voice*, 12 June 1846. For other examples, see, in *Factory Tracts*, "Amelia's" "The Summons":

> Yea, be thou strong—there yet remains
> A promise sure to thee.
> That God will break the oppressor's chains,
> And set the prisoner free.
> That righteousness and truth shall reign,
> Through all the peopled earth,
> And heaven repeat the exulting strain,
> Which hailed creation's birth.

Also, Mehitable Eastman at a labor rally in Manchester, N.H.: "Let us remember that the children of Israel did not arrive at the promised land, save through a journey of forty years in the wilderness" (*Voice*, 4 Sept. 1846).

6. *MFP*, 28 Feb., 23 May 1829; *NTU*, 6 Sept. 1834; 15 Aug. 1835. To call attention to their clothing cooperative, the tailors used the heading, "Great Revival." During the political season the following year, a journeyman mechanic calling himself "Spirit of '76" called on Philadelphia workers to join those "who have already come out of political Babylon": "Come out from the support of those who consult the interests of the rich and not the poor" (*MFP*, 9 Oct. 1830).

7. *Rochester Intelligencer and Mechanics' and Working Men's Advocate*, 8 Nov. 1836. See, too, *NL*, 3 Dec. 1836.

8. Carriers' Address, 1 Jan. 1837, in the folio of the *NL*, Library of Congress. A poem in the previous month (ibid., 3 Dec. 1836) addressed "To Mechanics" ended:

> Our god proclaims our cause is just,
> Strike! strike for Freedom—all who trust
> In God for Liberty.

9. (New York) *WMA*, 28 Sept. 1844.

10. *RDD*, 18 Apr. 1834; 4 July 1843. The carpenters' language drew on the ninth chapter of the Book of Luke, which contains a lesson about following in the path of the Lord. On his journey to Jerusalem, Jesus confronts many potential devotees who, though professing their desire and willingness to follow him, beg his leave to first do some other chore. To a man who asks that he be allowed first to say goodbye to his family, Jesus says, "No man, having put his hand to the plough, and looking back, is fit for the Kingdom of God" (Luke 9:62 AV). The message could have been lost on neither the pious employers and citizenry of Rochester nor the Christian elements within the carpenters' movement. For church participation in the two groups cited here, see chap. 6.

11. *MFP*, 2 May 1829 ("Then shall the lame *man* leap as an hart, and the tongue of the dumb sing: for in the wilderness shall waters break out, and streams in the desert" [Isa. 35:6 AV]). See, also, Young's editorial for 1846, in *Voice*, 2 Jan. 1846; and Bagley's NEWA speech, ibid. 3 Apr. 1846.

12. [Charles H. Hosmer] *The Condition of Labor* (Boston, 1847), 3–4. The speech was delivered at the league's quarterly meeting. An Associationist and at one time a resident of Brook Farm, Hosmer introduced the address as a pamphlet at the spring convention and almost certainly was its author (Early, "Reappraisal of the New-England Labour-Reform Movement," 50, n. 98).

13. See, too, "Agency" by "Caleb and Joshua," *MFP,* 31 Jan. 1829. Under the biblical heading, "And shall not thee save Ninevah," the author(s?) exhorted Philadelphia workers with an Old Testament tale of the citizenry altering the course of prophecy by their own actions, reminding readers that man's free agency was recognized by legislators, rulers, and fathers "in their rewards and punishments," rendering him "the mortal image of the deity."

14. When Huldah Stone encouraged William Young in a letter to the editor with the salutation, "God speed thee in thy holy mission gentle 'voice,'" she was doing precisely what her compatriot Sarah Bagley had done at the first official meeting of the NEWA when she reminded the assembly that they were in the forefront of "the holy cause of human rights and human equalities" (*Voice,* 31 July, 12 June 1845). See, too, George Lippard in *QC,* 14 Apr. 1848, cited in Butterfield, "George Lippard," 297; "Letter from a Young Reformer," *YA,* 27 Sept. 1845.

15. McFarlane, *Address,* 19.

16. (Rochester) *WMA* , 22 Nov. 1839. See, too, the insistence of the WMBERS that the duebill system deprived workers of "heaven-born privileges" (*RDA,* 4 Feb. 1842). Similarly, when the Mutual Benefit Society of Journeymen Cordwainers of Lynn issued their call for a national shoemakers' convention in 1844, they closed with the prayer, "may the God of light, truth, and justice, aid us onward in our cause!" ("Objects of the Mutual Benefit Society of Journeymen Cordwainers," (Lynn) *Awl,* 17 July 1844, repr. Commons, *Documentary History* 8:234).

17. *NL,* 17 Dec. 1836.

18. *PP,* 4 Mar. 1844.

19. *QC,* 28 Dec. 1848. A week later, Lippard chastised those who were "croaking piteously" about the end of republicanism in France: "the man who imagines for a moment, that the cause of human rights goes backward either in France or throughout the world, commits an involuntary blasphemy upon the goodness of Providence. . . . All the Napoleans in the world cannot stop the movement whose force is derived from the strength of Omnipotence" (ibid., 6 Jan. 1849). The flip side of this appeal to religious faith, and serving the same purpose, was threatening divine wrath. In 1830, an *MFP* correspondent—choosing the biblical name "Genesis" and using the heading, "If thou doest well, shalt thou not be accepted, and if thou doest not well, sin lieth at the door"— recalled the story of Cain and Abel (*MFP,* 27 Mar. 1830). Four years later, drawing on the very same biblical passage (Gen. 4:7), the president of the NEA warned, "if you fail, the sin will be at your own door" (*NTU,* 4 Oct. 1834).

20. *Voice,* 29 May 1845. The pages of Young's paper are replete with his appeals to "christians, friends and brothers" (e.g., 12 June, 17 July, 7 Aug. 1845). For Young's appeal to clergymen in these terms, see ibid., 30 Apr. 1846.

21. E.g., meeting of the "Journeymen Mechanics" of Utica, N.Y., in *NTU,* 30 Jan. 1836.

22. Ibid., 26 Mar. 1836.

23. The series appeared under the title, "An Observer," in *MFP,* 24 July, 14, 21, 28 Aug. 1830.

24. Probably the most frequently cited message from the Bible in antebellum labor rhetoric (Matt. 7:12; Luke 6:31), this injunction formed the basis of the Christian laborite worldview. See, e.g., the resolution of a meeting of carpenters in Hartford, Conn., to establish the General Trades' Union there in 1836: "That wishing to be guided by the grand rule 'do as you would be done by,' we will take the course pursued by our landlords" (*NTU,* 2 Feb. 1836). In the hands of labor activists, the "rule" was employed for a variety of purposes. Robert McFarlane, for example, found in it the meaning of self-ownership (as distinct from the ownership of property)—in his view the essence of the American experiment—"that every man should be ruled in his actions, of doing unto his neighbor as he would have his neighbor to do unto him" ("Religion—Freedom," *MM,* May 1846, 104). Others took it as a prescription for a happy life. In 1834, the New York *Man* reprinted the "Catechism of the Society for Promoting National Regeneration," which declared happiness as their objective, "in obedience to the divine command—'whatsoever ye would that men should do to you, do ye even so to them'" (*Cobbett's Register,* repr. in *Man,* 25 Feb. 1834). For different uses of this injunction—such as buttressing arguments for the importance of labor, equality, harmony, charity, and morality in general, for descriptions of the coming Kingdom of God, and so on—see below.

25. *Voice,* 14 Aug., 25 Sept. 1845; also, 19 June, 10 July 1845. An ordinary factory girl in Exeter, N.H., would make the same point a year later: "The man who is unkind to his female help cannot be a christian, if he is a church member, a deacon, or even the carrier round of the contribution box" (*Factory Girls' Album,* 14 Feb. 1846). It was also Robert McFarlane's argument in his opening editorial in the *MM:* "It is our Christian duty that our mechanics and laborers should be paid for their labor"; "If we ignore our fellow man, we injure ourselves for God has said that we are 'to love our neighbor as ourselves'"; "Can Christians of any station, nay can any man be a Christian, who forgets the solemn declaration 'bear ye one another's burdens'?" ("America," Jan. 1846, 8). See also, Stone, "Improvement of Time" and Ada, "The Universal Brotherhood," *Voice,* 7 Aug. 1845; 6 Feb. 1846.

26. Ibid., 1 May 1846. Laurie misses the power of this use of biblical analogy in his discussion of Young in *Artisans into Workers,* 95. In fact, activists throughout the period made good use of this potent passage. Remarking on a notice she saw about extra pay for hard-working (read: slave-driving) overseers, a Manchester, N.H., "Weaver" declared, "Father, forgive them, they know not what they do." Then, after noting how they drive their workers, she asked God to have mercy on those who would countenance such a thing. Here, the citation was less a call for forgiveness than for censure ([Manchester] *Democrat,* 13 Jan. 1847). Nearly two decades earlier at the *DFP,* radical Quakers Benjamin Webb, his son James Webb, and D. C. Coleman used it to condemn the spirit of persecution among their opponents (9 Jan., 29 May 1830; 4 Feb. 1832). Like Lincoln's use of scriptural quotation in the famous passages of his second inaugural address, the surface appearance of Christian magnanimity thinly masked devastating censure. On Lincoln, see *The Collected Works of Abraham Lincoln,* Roy P. Basler, ed., (New Brunswick: Rutgers Univ. Press, 1953), 8:332–33.

27. *Boston Laborer,* 18 May 1844.

28. *Voice,* 13 Mar. 1846. Bagley had written a month earlier that the "religious part of the community should be the *first* to engage in the work in improving the operative, physically." Who are the followers, *practically,* of the Maker who left examples? she wanted to know. Then, reminding her readers of their Savior's injunction, she concluded, "'By their fruits ye shall know them'" (ibid., 6 Feb. 1846). See, too, Rochester's "Citizen": lamenting the state of labor relations in 1839 and the failure of the community to ameliorate it, he reminded local residents in language Fall River's John Gregory would use five years later, "there are men who have eyes and do not see—who have ears and will not hear" ([Rochester] *WMA,* 22 Nov. 1839). At about the same time, the *WMA* condemned two New York papers, then engaged in a battle with journeymen printers of that city, for violating the principle, "'the laborer is worthy of his hire'" (ibid., 31 Jan. 1840).

29. The language was common to the 1840s, but it was used by some in the previous decade as well. See, e.g., the extract of the Address to the Trades' Union of Washington, D.C., at City Hall, Washington, 4 July 1834, *NTU,* 30 Aug. 1834; the Address of the President of the NEA, *NTU,* 4 Oct. 1834; and the appeal of the New York Female Bookbinders Union Association, ibid., 4 July 1835. Labor adapted the rhetoric from the prevailing customs of the day. See, e.g., the notice of the Monroe Circuit Grand Jury to the citizenry on a proposed meeting of the New York State Temperance Society, which addressed "every Patriot, every Philanthropist, every Christian, and every friend to his country" (*Craftsman,* 8 Sept. 1829).

30. *Voice,* 3 June 1846.

31. "FWA Record Book." See, too, the resolution of two FWA members, Congregationalists E. F. Bailey and G. F. Bailey: "That the Workingman's Caus is one of philanthropy and Christianity and as christians and citizens we are bound to sustain it."

32. *Mechanic,* 29 June 1844.

33. Laurie (*Working People,* 146–47) misunderstands the use of the term *philanthropist* in his book on Philadelphia workers during these years.

34. *Voice,* 9 June 1846.

35. *RDA,* 23 Mar. 1842. The Rochester Working Men's Club, with close personnel and ideolog-

ical ties to the Equal Rights Society, echoed this rhetoric a year later when it declared that its members had for many years felt the grinding oppression of the duebill system by which the workers had been "wickedly ground down by the iron heel of a heartless, unfeeling, and unprincipled clique of beings, wearing the human form" (ibid., 5 Oct. 1844). The language of the WMBERS should not surprise us: on its resolutions committee were two Presbyterians, a Methodist, and an Episcopalian. The chair of the meeting was apparently not a member of a local church; the secretary was a Baptist. For a simple assertion that the duebill system was "an enemy of God," see the resolutions of a Buffalo artisans' convention in (Buffalo) *Weltburger,* 4 May 1839, quoted in Gerber, *Making of an American Pluralism,* 246. On the use of Satan's image in the labor movement, see "Address to the Working Men of Massachusetts, by the Committee Appointed for that Purpose By the Northampton Convention [of the NEA]," *NTU,* 1 Nov. 1834; letter of Martha Hollingsworth, *YA,* 23 Sept. 1848.

36. *Voice,* 25 Sept. 1845.

37. Like African-American slaves, some labor activists found inspiration in the Old Testament story of Exodus. One *MFP* correspondent, likening himself to a "modern Moses and Aaron" calling on "the flocks of the working men," compared the master carpenters of Philadelphia who held out against the ten-hour strike of 1827 to "the Egyptian monarch [who] contended for arbitrary power, even against the wisdom and justice of Almighty God." "I think the time has come," he told *MFP* readers, "when the Lord God of Israel again declares, 'Let my people go.' . . . 'Thus saith the Lord God of Israel let my people go'" (20 Dec. 1828). This activist spoke the language of the Bible but understood the divisions of his world to be sociological rather than political or theological. "Whether Calvinist or Arminian," he insisted, "Catholic or Quaker, Unitarian or Trinitarian, Federal or Democrat, Jackson or Antimason men, if they are opulent, they, with Pharoahs, will unite in declaring to us, You are idle, you are idle,; get you to your daily tasks!" Subsequent pieces by "Caleb and Joshua" (31 Jan. 1829) and "David" (7 Feb. 1829) may have been penned by the same individual, as the language and argument are strikingly similar. A year later, "Jonathan" told *MFP* readers, "the present state of merchandising may be very aptly compared to Egyptian bondage." Insisting that only workers could effect the radical change he deemed necessary, "Jonathan" intoned the scriptural analogy: "Your case has now become even worse than were the children of Israel under Pharaoh, who commanded them to make bricks without straw." "Arise then," he concluded, "there is another door for your redemption . . . hanker not after the fleshpots of Egypt" (12 Dec. 1829). For other references to the Old Testament, see *NTU,* 12 Mar. 1836.

38. Seth Luther, *An Address on the Right of Free Suffrage* [hereafter, *Suffrage*] (Providence: S. R. Weeden, 1833), 25; idem, *Avarice,* 7; idem, *Brooklyn Address,* 18. Luther's use of the Bible and God possessed little of Young's gospel message. While Young insisted upon charity and kindness in his exhortations, Luther was angry and avenging. A letter Luther penned while in prison for his part in the Dorr War of the early 1840s illustrates the idea of justice he held throughout his life as an activist:

> There is much gall in this pen; notwithstanding sweet and flowery words flow from it, it can scorch and burn like the glowing coal or the wrathful lava from the flaming mountains side. All I ask is justice and justice I will have, from friend and foe. Woe unto that man high or low, rich or poor who by a course of cowardly duplicity, and mean underhanded baseness wrongs any human being within my knowledge.

Luther to Walter S. Burgess, 5 Sept. 1842, John Jay Library, Brown Univ., Providence. For more on the contrast between Luther and Young, see chap. 11.

39. *MM,* Apr. 1846, 81. Here, McFarlane also intoned God's rebuke to Israel: "ye have not hearkened unto me, in proclaiming liberty every man to his brother, and every man to his neighbor; behold I proclaim a liberty unto you saith the Lord, to the sword, to the pestilence, and to the famine; and I will make you to be removed unto all the nations of earth."

40. Editorial repr. in *NEA,* 3 Oct. 1833.

41. See Bagley's editorial, *Voice,* 15 May 1846; Mehitable Eastman's report to the NELRL, ibid., 12 Feb. 1847; Huldah Stone's letter to the Manchester operatives, ibid., 26 Dec. 1845; Bagley's NEWA speech, in ibid, 9 Nov. 1845; letter of "Juliana," in ibid., 7 May 1847.

42. Ibid., 15 May 1846. Bagley was a member of the publishing committee of the *Voice* for its first six months in Lowell (Oct. 1845-Apr. 1846), one of several editors in Apr. 1846, and solo editor in May and June 1846.

43. Ibid., 9 Nov. 1845. Note, too, Stone's encouragement to editor William Young in the summer of 1845. Hoping his efforts would "cause the flinty heart to quake, the stubborn knee to bow, before the mighty and all conquering power of Eternal Truth and Justice," Stone also defined the *Voice's* "holy mission" in the language of Christ's mission: "Mayest thou speak comfort to the despairing—whisper *Hope* to the ear, and pour balm into the heart lacerated and festering with the cankering cares of life." This was the language of Christian benevolence (ibid., 31 July 1845).

44. *NL,* 27 Aug. 1836. See, too, "Nicholas," *MFP,* 9 Oct. 1830, who spoke of "the holy fire of honorable patriotism that glowed upon the altars of the heroes and statesmen of 76."

45. Especially in the 1830s, the living memory of the Revolution, nurtured by surviving "fathers" and heightened by the imminence of their passing, focused special attention on the "spirit of '76" as a heritage of resistance. Moreover, in the minds of the "sons" and "daughters," the death of the "fathers" coincided with the threatened extinction of Revolutionary principles. Incantations of the legacy thus had special poignancy for early labor activists, who sensed that the promise of that historical event had been betrayed. See Paul C. Nagel, *One Nation Indivisible: The Union in American Thought, 1776–1861* (New York: Oxford Univ. Press, 1964), chap. 6.

46. The following account and all quotations are drawn from a report of the event that appeared in the *ICR,* 11 July 1835. Although no author is given, it may have been written by the paper's editor at the time, the Reverend Theophilus Fisk, who participated in the ceremony.

47. Note here the hostility to politicians so prevalent in the labor movement of the day. Also, compare this graphic depiction of wealth and misery with Edward Bellamy's famous analogy of capitalist society as a stage coach in *Looking Backward, 2000–1887* (orig. publ. 1888; repr. ed., New York: New American Library, 1960), 27.

48. This English statute, "An Act for the Uniformetie of Common Prayer and Service of the Church, and Administration of the Sacraments," was passed in 1552 to stem the local power of the Puritans.

49. That is, they referred to the Revolutionaries in the language laborites used to describe themselves, as in the NEA, the progenitor of the BTU.

50. The beginnings of Freemasonry are obscure, but most scholars trace the order to the English and Scottish stonemasons of the early Middle Ages. The movement's worldwide proliferation began with the formation of the first grand lodge in London in 1717. A study of the Connecticut Order between the Revolution and 1830 argues that it served as a platform for religious and political dissent, as well as a common fraternal bond among those whose "marginality" separated them from the broader community. Although not an irreligious movement, Connecticut Freemasonry represented a dissent from New England Congregationalism, embodying a "latitudinarian frame of reference" (Dorothy Ann Lipson, *Freemasonry in Federalist Connecticut* [Princeton: Princeton Univ. Press, 1977], 77 and passim).

51. The address has not survived.

52. *Proceedings of the Government and Citizens of Philadelphia, on the Reduction of the Hours of Labor, and Increase of Wages* (Boston, 1835). Among the five-man committee that produced this circular was Jethro Snow. More generally, activists typically joined their religion and their nationalism, as when the president of the NEA told his people that the destiny of the country was "emphatically (under God) in your hands" (*NTU,* 4 Oct. 1834).

53. *ICR,* 8 Aug. 1835. On the course of the Boston ten-hour movement in 1835, see Commons, *History of Labour* 1:388–89, 393; Pessen, *Most Uncommon Jacksonians,* 42–43. For many, the

Revolution was not finished but continued as a holy cause. "The Producer's Hymn" (*Man*, 19 July 1834), dedicated to the working classes by "The Poor Man's Poet," announced:

> Nor is the holy glow extinct,
> Columbia shall be free!
> Defying native, foreign knaves,
> To sap her liberty.
>
> . . . .
>
> Shall we, in *Freedom's* cradle nurs'd,
> Forsake her holy cause.

54. The intermingling of republicanism and religion in labor's public appeal was common throughout the nation in these early years. In the Wilmington Working Men's movement, one religious republican urged his fellows to ensure their representation at the constitutional convention of 1831 and "show their brethren and the world, they are not unworthy of the trust committed to them by Heaven and the valor of their sires" ("To the Working People," by "Independent and Liberal," *DFP*, 30 July 1831). In Philadelphia, an *MFP* correspondent exhorted his working-class brethren, "Americans, the eyes of the world are on you!" "Raise! Raise the standard of righteousness . . . unrighteousness is a reproach to a republic" ("An Observer," *MFP*, 28 Aug. 1830). Ten years later, we can glimpse the joining of the two inspirational traditions in an exchange in the Rochester *WMA*. "A Mechanic," castigating an opponent for reducing his journeymen's wages, arraigned the masterbuilder on both republican and Christian grounds. Referring to him as "this tyrannical nabob" who sought to make his workers "serfs" by keeping them in "abject and cringing dependence" in "this republican country," he also sarcastically addressed him as "our pious and exemplary citizen," "a humane, generous and Christian individual" who was "grinding the face of the poor" while "professing to live under the genial influence of that religion which teaches us to 'love thy neighbor as ourselves.'" "A Mechanic" considered himself both a republican and a Christian: asking for the "ear of every American freeman," he also spoke reverently of "our heavenly Benefactor" and "the Giver of all Good" (*WMA*, 16 Mar. 1840).

55. Seth Luther, *An Address to the Working-Men of New England* [hereafter, *New England Address*] (Boston, 1832), 6; idem, *Suffrage*, 14.

56. Idem, *Brooklyn Address*, 14–15.

57. Ibid., 4.

58. Ibid., 10.

59. Ibid., 18.

60. For Luther, the Revolution was but the latest and most dramatic event in an age-old, divinely inspired struggle for human freedom that had dominated human history from the Israelites of the Old Testament to the Revolutionary "sires" of 1776. Thus, he found inspiration in the Protestant Reformation as well: the pope had cautioned Martin Luther not to promote excitements, but that religious rebel had declared that "the Pope was not the viceregent of God on earth, and he did not feel disposed to kiss the great toe of his holiness" (*Suffrage*, 25; also, *New England Address*, 27–28). The nineteenth-century Luther also pointed to the example of the pious English colonists, reminding his audience of the "republican simplicity, the manly independence, and contempt of hardship and poverty which characterized our Pilgrim ancestors" (*Avarice*, 35). Most crucially, God's Word animated the Revolutionary tradition: the "Good Book" proclaimed, "'God is no respecter of persons, but he has created of our blood all the nations of the earth'; in accordance with this truth the Declaration of our Independence declares the equality of the rights of man" (ibid., 23). Like most antebellum laborites, though, Luther ascribed several meanings to the Revolution, sometimes in the same speech. Most often, he insisted that workers were responsible for redeeming a tradition that had been betrayed. As he told the Brooklyn rally, a "worm has been gnawing at the root of the liberty tree" (*Brooklyn Address*, 16). At other times, he portrayed the Revolution as an unfulfilled promise, calling for an application of Revolutionary principles to

contemporary circumstances ([Boston] *Post,* 7 May 1835). At still other times, he depicted the war with Britain as a struggle for political independence to be followed by a social revolution (*Brooklyn Address,* 17, 23). Benjamin Webb offered a version of the third perspective in his "Present Condition of Liberty," *DFP,* 21 Jan. 1832. For the various meanings workers have ascribed to the Revolution, see Philip Foner, ed., *We, the Other People: Alternative Declarations of Independence by Labor Groups, Farmers, Women's Rights Advocates, Socialists, and Blacks, 1829–1975* (Urbana: Univ. of Illinois Press, 1976).

61. *NL,* 2 July 1836.

62. See, e.g., Henry Frink's editorial, "Titles of Honor," (Rochester) *WMA,* 28 Jan. 1840.

63. For references to the Revolution in Rochester, see carpenter circular, *RDD,* 9 Mar. 1835; printer editorial, *WMA,* 19 Oct. 1839. See, too, part of a resolution of a mass meeting of the WMBERS, summer 1843: "Whereas our forefathers opposed British taxation on tea and stamped paper, by turning Indians, and throwing the former overboard. And their seed is living yet" (*RR,* 20 June 1843). For the mixing of the Revolution and religion, see "Orlando's" letter in the *WMA:* hard times threaten "our loved asylum of the free and oppressed," while some, "'clothe himself in purple and fine linen'" (17 Dec. 1839). See, too, "J"'s "Aristocracy," ibid., 11 Dec. 1839; "Address to the Patrons of the Workingmen's Advocate," ibid., 1 Jan. 1840; "A Mechanic's" "Sociability," ibid., 15 Nov. 1839; editorial, "Ten Hours System," ibid., 27 Dec. 1839; exchange between "A Mechanic" and Col. Jason Bassett, ibid., 16, 18, 21, 25 Mar. 1840.

64. But see, e.g., "Veritas," *Voice,* 25 Sept. 1845: "Let every soul feel as did the fathers of the Revolution, that they will undertake no work, which they do and cannot ask God to assist and bless."

65. Quoted in Schantz, "Religious Rhetoric and Resistance," 23. Part of this, of course, was a confluence of religion and nationalism, but the rhetoric reflected a distinctive republican worldview. On "God and country," see, e.g., "Letter of a Young Reformer," *YA,* 27 Sept. 1845.

66. *Voice,* 21 Dec. 1847. FWA officer and labor editor William Wilder spoke of "the standard of eternal truth" that he said could be found in Scripture, while Lowell's Sarah Bagley told workers to "be true to the sympathies and emotions of pity which a God of Infinite Love has implanted in every human soul" (*Sentinel,* 5 May 1841; *Voice,* 6 Mar. 1846).

67. Ibid., 26 Feb. 1847; 23 Jan. 1846. Thus, manufacturing in Lowell was "false, antirepublican and unchristian," which produced "seductive errors" that were "poisoning our philosophy and republicanism and perverting and neutralizing all our christianity and religion" (ibid., 7 Nov. 1847). Similarly, regarding land reform: "Is not the whole spirit of Republicanism and Christianity, opposed to land monopoly?" (ibid., 16 Jan. 1846)

68. Ibid., 7 Nov. 1845.

69. Ibid.

70. Ibid., 14 Nov. 1845; 29 May 1845. Even his insignia on the *Voice* masthead—the quotation from the Book of Job noted earlier—blended Christian determination with the popular libertarian spirit of 1776.

71. *MM,* May 1846, 104–5; July 1846, 152.

72. This sense of providential destiny should be distinguished from the general belief in Providence adhered to by deists, particularly in the early 1830s. See, for example, George McFarlane's use of phrases like, "the Power which first called man into existence," "that Power who presides over the affairs of nations," and "the guardianship of an over-ruling Providence," in his *Address,* 10–11.

73. *NR,* 7 Dec. 1848.

74. Labor activists sometimes referred specifically to the Second Coming of Christ, but I have used the term "millennial" in a broader sense here, referring to a religious vision of a coming age of human perfection on earth.

75. George Rogers Taylor identifies several factors that contributed to the utopian spirit of the 1840s: a postdepression search for refuge, humanitarian currents in the Western world, and the "spirit of adolescent enthusiasm" accompanying America's economic and territorial growth. He

asserts that the "mass impulse to embrace magic nostrums for social ills" mostly affected what he calls the "middle class," but he finds four movements that "appreciably" influenced working people during these years: Associationism, land reform, cooperation, and the ten-hour day. Although I think he has distorted these movements by distinguishing cooperation and shorter hours as "closer to reality," Taylor has correctly elucidated the utopian character of labor protest—and some of its sources—in the 1840s. See *Transportation Revolution*, 277–78.

76. "FWA Record Book." See, too, "Circular of the Workingmen's Association of Fitchburg to their fellow Mechanics and Workingmen," *WI*, 8 Feb. 1845. Young, a member of the committee that wrote the preamble, used the phrase "seductive errors" in reference to Lowell's manufacturing system in late 1847, and "seductive vices" in his description of social conditions generally (see n. 67; chap. 10; chap 11, n. 45).

77. *South Boston Gazette*, 11 Aug. 1849. The phrase, "There's a gude time coming," originally appeared in Sir Walter Scott's *Rob Roy*, but these activists probably took the quotation from *The Good Time Coming* by Charles MacKay. For other uses, see the article on the Brandywine coopers' strike in *Blue Hen Chicken*, 29 June 1848; Robert McFarlane's comments in "Mechanical Reform," *MM*, Jan. 1846, 290 ("'a better day is about to dawn upon the mechanical classes'"); and "America," ibid., 8 ("Many questions of Justice, between man and man are left unsettled in this world, but there is a day coming when those questions will be settled between man and his God'").

78. *Voice*, 23 Jan. 1846.

79. Ibid., 12 June 1846. "Our light has not gone out in the altar, nor our exertions abated," she declared on another occasion, "and by the blessings of Heaven, we mean to fight on till a complete victory crowns our efforts" (ibid., 11 Sept. 1845).

80. Ibid.

81. "An Address of the Mechanics and Laborers, Assembled in Convention at Faneuil Hall, Boston, October 19, 1844, To Their Fellow Mechanics and Laborers throughout the United States," (Boston) *Bee*, 30 Oct. 1844.

82. *Voice*, 29 May 1846. On the *Voice's* six-month anniversary (11 Dec. 1845), Young assured his readers that humanity's true interests had been revealed "by the genial rays of the great fountain of light and life, which begins to beam in upon the darkness and superstition of the world, chasing away the dogmas and relics of barbarism which have preyed upon the rights of mankind; and like angels of destruction, cast a blight and gloom over the face of the Earth, and confusion, religious doubt and mysticism upon the minds of the race." He then expressed his confidence that the cause would progress and "*restore* to *Man* self-government, to Labor its true dignity and just rewards, and to humanity the Heavenly impress, of which sin, and oppression has robbed it."

83. Ibid., 26 Feb. 1847.

84. Ibid., 3 June 1847; 4 Feb. 1848.

85. Quoted in McNeill, *Labor Movement*, 102.

86. When a Manchester, N.H., operative sought to cheer her sisters in 1847, she reminded them of the "'good time coming'" when oppression and tyranny would cease. Although she voiced uncertainty that she would see that "day of great change," she was certain that it was coming. "Let our prayers ascend that our labors may be blessed," she told her fellow workers, "and that God, in his own good time, will crown our labors with success" (*Democrat*, 15 Sept. 1847).

87. Repr. from (Lynn, Mass.) *Vox Populi* in *Voice*, 6 Oct. 1846.

88. *Voice*, 31 Mar. 1846. Young also remained optimistic about his movement's prospects during periods of adversity, steadfastly holding to his faith in its providential destiny. In February 1848, a committee of striking textile operatives from Fall River came to Lowell in search of support. In a letter to them cited earlier (preface, n. 2), Young apologized for the "present depressed feelings" among Lowell workers that had rendered "the recent visit of your delegates rather fruitless." Indeed, he lamented, all efforts against "incorporated wealth" in his city had proved "fruitless." But he did not mean to imply by this that no progress had been made. "On the contrary," he maintained, "a most healthy change is going on, that betokens the 'good time coming'" (*All Sorts*, 4 Mar. 1848).

89. *Voice,* 19 Feb. 1847.

90. Rush Welter, *The Mind of America, 1820–1860* (New York: Columbia Univ. Press, 1975), quotation in text, 23.

91. David W. Noble, *Historians Against History: The Frontier Thesis and the National Covenant in American Historical Writing Since 1830* (Minneapolis: Univ. of Minnesota Press, 1965); Fred Somkin, *Unquiet Eagle: Memory and Desire in the Idea of American Freedom, 1815–1860* (Ithaca: Cornell Univ. Press, 1967); Tuveson, *Redeemer Nation;* Major L. Wilson, *Space, Time, and Freedom: The Quest for Nationality and the Irrepressible Conflict, 1815–1861* (Westport: Greenwood Press, 1974); Bercovitch, *American Jeremiad.* Welter suggests that Americans of the era believed they had "escaped" history in a "macro" sense, while they faced very pressing problems in a "micro" sense (*Mind of America,* part 2).

92. *MFP,* 5 Mar. 1831.

93. "An Observer," ibid., 24 July, 28 Aug. 1830.

94. "An Observer," ibid., 14, 21 Aug. 1830.

95. *Voice,* 3 Apr. 1846. On the centrality of duty to God in Young's view of the proper life, see ibid., 13 Feb., 1 May 1846.

96. *NR,* 7 Dec. 1848.

97. *WI,* 8 Feb. 1845. See, too, Charles Hosmer's call for the NELRL to organize "by all you hold most dear, as you value your own nature, by your duty to yourselves and your god, by your duty to your children, to your country and to humanity" (*Condition of Labor,* 29). Also, Young's NELRL resolution pronouncing the unceasing advocacy of labor's demands "a sacred duty which the laboring people of this country, owe to themselves, to posterity and to the cause of Christian progression" (*Voice,* 9 Apr. 1847).

Chapter 9

1. To be sure, antebellum labor activists drew their rhetorical fire from numerous sources—Greek mythology, Shakespeare, Bacon, Byron—but it is striking, especially in light of the historical literature, how frequently they turned to Scripture.

2. The MLA had established a library, reading room, and debating club in the belief, they said, that it was the duty of all mechanics and laborers to perpetuate equality by the diffusion of knowledge. Not an integral part of the labor movement per se, the MLA attracted a number of local activists. See *RDD,* 28 Mar. 1836; *NTU,* 16 Apr. 1836; McKelvey, *Rochester: The Water-Power City,* 273; Cross, "Creating a City," 263–64.

3. For the letters described here, see *WMA,* 5, 7 Mar. 1840. "S" may be the "Mechanic" who engaged in a series of exchanges with the "Architect" (see chaps. 6, 8). Support for the charitable efforts of local churches was not unusual for this paper; see chap. 6.

4. In the story (Mark 14:3–7 AV), Jesus defends a woman criticized for pouring over his head perfume that might have been sold and the proceeds given to the poor. Jesus reproaches her critics: "For ye have the poor with you always, and whensoever ye will ye may do them good: but me ye have not always."

5. *Voice,* 13 July 1847.

6. *NTU,* 4 Oct. 1834.

7. *WMA,* 26 Nov., 28 Dec. 1839; 7, 11 Jan. 1840.

8. Ibid., 11 Jan. 1840; 13 Nov. 1839. In 1830, Cornelius Blatchley, radical Quaker and inspiration for some of the Wilmington Working Men, called for the abandonment of the credit system in America on the ground that it was a religious duty, which every follower of Jesus was bound to adhere to and which had been established by the religious command, "owe no man anything" ([Alabama] *Spirit of the Age,* cited in *DFP,* 9 Oct. 1830). Land reform was also generally advanced as a biblical right. See, e.g., "Progress of Reform—The Redemption of the Masses," *People's Rights,* cited in (New York) *WMA,* 28 Sept., 1844 ("'The land is *mine,* saith the Lord, and ye are sojourners with me'"; "'The land shall not be sold forever'").

9. See, for example, the dispute over the scriptural foundation for capital punishment between "A Subscriber" and "Yorick"—both Christian laborites—in *MFP*, 12, 19, 26 Mar. 1831. The debate centered on whether or not God's dealing with the individual in a manner "best calculated to answer his own divine purposes" changed the "government of that Being, one of whose attributes is said to be immortality." Deist George McFarlane used the Bible as well. The last line of his Wilmington address in 1830 was from the First Epistle of Paul the Apostle to the Thessalonians: "Let us 'prove all things, and hold fast to that which is good'" (*Address*, 24).

10. "W" editorial, *MFP*, 23 Apr. 1831.

11. For the use of scriptural headings, see, e.g., ibid., 15 Nov., 20, 27 Dec. 1828; 2 May 1829; 27 Mar., 29 May 1830; 23 Apr. 1831. Moreover, the *MFP* consistently refused to publish the correspondence of infidels, criticized the skeptical (like George Henry Evans of New York) for "exciting" feelings, and wrote directly to "Christian readers." See chap. 3.

12. "A none [non?] professor is commonly much more candid," "Paul" wrote, as he has no reason to falsify the New Testament but reads it as he would "any other history" (*MFP*, 4 Sept. 1830).

13. For example, he once described the Philadelphia labor movement, putatively some ten thousand strong, as united by a tie, "strong, holy and unchanging"; alternatively, he thought of his movement as one "against unholy combinations of capital and avarice." For his land reform argument, Hogan cited Lev. 35 and Isa. 5:8 (*NL*, 21 May, 17 Dec., 2 Apr., 26 Mar. 1836).

14. The same seems to have been true in the late nineteenth century. See Gutman, "Protestantism and the American Labor Movement."

15. "Frequent Reading of the Old and New Testaments recommended," *MFP*, 26 Dec. 1829.

16. In this, they marked themselves not as peculiar but typical, for, as studies of contemporary schoolbooks reveal, the existence of God and divine design in the earthly world were taken for granted in early-nineteenth-century America. It is for this reason that so much of early American labor reform was based explicitly on the goal of *elevation* (i.e., in a material as well as spiritual sense, but rooted in the religious notion of *uplift*).

17. (Penn.) *Germantown Telegraph* [*GT*], 28 Aug. 1835; *NTU*, 12 Dec. 1835.

18. *Voice*, 29 May, 31 July, 14 Nov. 1845; 24 Apr. 1846. See, too, 18 Sept. 1845; 26 Nov. 1847. Similarly, notices for the Lowell FLRA welcomed anyone who wished to place the working woman "in that elevated station . . . which a bountiful Creator designed for her to occupy in the scale of being" (ibid., 9 Jan. 1846). The Ladies' Branch of the Cordwainers' Society of New York resolved in 1844 to join with those who sought to elevate the working class "to that position which God and Nature intended they should occupy" ([New York] *WMA*, 13 July 1844). By the 1840s, labor activists were invoking this putatively divine plan to advocate of a wide range of reforms—from antislavery to abolition of capital punishment to land reform. See *Voice*, 5 June, 24 July, 11 Sept. 1845; 16 Jan., 16 Oct. 1846; 25 June, 3 Dec. 1847; *MFP*, 3 May 1828; *YA*, 27 Sept. 1845; 31 Jan. 1846.

19. "Religion—Freedom," *MM*, Apr. 1846, 15.

20. Ibid., 79. On this foundation, McFarlane articulated his view of the proper relations among men, beginning with the insistence that the very basis of the Author's purpose was "for man to love his Creator as his father, and his fellow man as his brother—as himself" (80).

21. Not all those who believed that God's design could be located in revelation were evangelicals, of course. Nevertheless, there was a general acceptance of the sin-redemption model that was at the heart of the evangelical paradigm.

22. *MM*, 80.

23. *NTU*, 1 Nov. 1834. See, too, the NEA presidential address of 1834: "The law of God, emphatically the Magna Carta of all civil and religious liberty, has held but a feeble influence over the minds of men" (ibid., 4 Oct. 1834). By "law," these activists meant not simply prevailing legislation but the way things were then organized. Indeed, their acceptance of the "moral government of God" was a recognition that God's sovereignty took precedence over humanity's. For antebellum activists' expositions on "the present organization of things," see chap. 11, and for the moral government of God, see below.

24. *NTU,* 1 Nov. 1834.

25. Human beings were unable to escape the "Omnipotent curse of man's cupidity," declared an address of a land reform meeting in Albany, N.Y., without "some fixed and definite political-social principle" to underlie all institutions. That principle clearly came from God, as all Christian laborites would have agreed, but for the writers of this address, the reason for the necessary laws rested on a particular interpretation of human nature. See "Address approved by the National Reform Convention, Albany, New York," signed by chair of committee on address, William J. Young, repr. in *Voice,* 9 July 1847.

26. *Mechanic,* 25 May 1845.

27. *NTU,* 1 Nov. 1834.

28. *Voice,* 6 Mar. 1846.

29. *Mechanic,* 8 Mar. 1845. On the recourse to the "government of God" in American abolitionism, see Perry, *Radical Abolitionism.* On the "higher law" tradition in American radicalism, see especially, Staughton Lynd, *Intellectual Origins of American Radicalism* (New York: Random House, 1968); DeLeon, *American as Anarchist.*

30. Blatchley to Isaac Sherwood of New York, repr. in *DFP,* 3 Sept. 1831.

31. "Present Condition of Liberty," *DFP,* 21 Jan. 1832.

32. *NEA,* 26 Sept. 1833.

33. Young reprinted his speech in the first two issues of the *Voice* (29 May, 5 June 1845).

34. In the most fundamental sense, labor constituted both the beginning and the end of Christian laborite analysis during this period. For, if the issues of the age, particularly the 1840s, spoke to the momentous issues of humankind—peace, liberty, economy, land—the key to the entire period was, as one activist put it, the "distribution of profits of labor."

35. In the previous decade, from Philadelphia to Rochester, activists articulated virtually the same argument, and on the same basis. A meeting of Philadelphia workers in 1835, called to express the group's solidarity with striking carpenters in Boston, announced, "we cannot believe that the Divine Author of our existence ever designed any part of the human family to live in idleness, on the fruits of the labor of those who possess the same natural rights" (*NTU,* 15 Aug. 1835). Four years later, Presbyterian printer Henry Frink proclaimed, "The author of our being intended that every individual should labor for his support, but obstacles in the present organization of society" prevented it—specifically the "*contempt of laborious pursuits*" and "*the abuse of wealth*" ("Idleness and Industry," *WMA,* 22 Nov. 1839). See, too, Schantz's review of the New York labor press in the 1830s and 1840s, which verifies, in broad outline, the analysis below ("Religious Rhetoric and Resistance," 19–20).

36. A similar divergence in meaning can be seen in the preoccupation with the mill girls' morality common to both mill-owner paternalists and radical mill women, though, as we shall see, there was a significant area of overlap. See Lazerow, "Religion and the New England Mill Girl," 450–51, and chap. 10.

37. *Bee,* 30 Oct. 1844. Laborites frequently pointed to this particular biblical injunction (Gen. 3:19) in their denunciations of employers and their allies who, they said, lived off those who labored. At the second meeting of the FWA, Young offered a resolution that reminded the local community, "the injunction, 'In the sweat of thy face thou shall eat bread' is as *true* and *binding* now as when uttered by our Creator" ("FWA Record Book"). Similarly, the editor of the Lynn *Awl* called for a society in which everyone worked and none lived off his neighbor, a society that followed the "divine command," "in the sweat of thy face, shalt thou eat thy bread" (repr. in the *Voice,* 9 Oct. 1845).

38. Ibid., 11 Sept. 1845. For other uses of this Pauline injunction, see, e.g., "A Working Man," *GT,* 28 Aug. 1835: the Maker never intended that the employer should take the role of the master and the employee that of the slave, even though "He that will not work, neither let him eat," is an old maxim. On the producerist ethic among labor activists during this period, see Faler, *Mechanics and Manufacturers.*

39. *MFP,* 10 Oct. 1829. Precisely the same language appeared in the letter of "A Working Man," dated 21 Aug. 1833 (likely a misprint), in *GT,* 28 Aug. 1835.

40. *DFP,* 13 Nov. 1830. Two days earlier in the Philadelphia *Working Men's Gazette,* "Jehu," taking his pen name from the king of Israel (c. 842–815 B.C.) who led a revolution against the house of Omri, remarked on the number in his city who had to obtain their bread for their families "by the 'sweat of the brow'" (quoted in *MFP,* 11 Nov. 1830). This writer chose his biblical name carefully. Before the emergence of the Omride rulers, small peasant farmers had ruled in Israel; with their ascension came the rise of a merchant class and a consequent dramatic contrast between rich and poor.

41. *Voice,* 21 Aug. 1845.

42. "Hours of Industry," *MM,* Nov. 1846, 277. Regarding labor, he insisted that the precept was most flagrantly violated in the "common practice [of] rob[bing] the laborer of his just reward" (ibid., Nov. 1846, 280).

43. For a modern articulation of this insight, see Frederick Hastings Smyth, "Religion and Socialism," *Monthly Review* 1 (July 1949), repr. in ibid., 40 (Feb. 1989): 35–44.

44. The evenhandedness was typical of antebellum labor ideology. Robert McFarlane: "To get as much labor out of the working man as possible, has been and is the only aim of money making capitalists, and to do an easy day's labor, and get as much for it as possible, is too much the aim of journeymen" (*MM,* Aug. 1846, 197).

45. *Voice,* 27 Feb., 6 Mar. 1846; 9 Oct. 1845; 27 Feb. 1846; 21 Aug. 1845.

46. *NEA,* 15 Nov. 1832.

47. *NL,* 4 Feb. 1837.

48. *Mechanic,* 18 Jan. 1845.

49. Adam Rennie, "The Mechanic," *MM,* Sept. 1846, 218.

50. Ibid., "Religion—Freedom," July 1846, 153.

51. Such exhortations, as much else here, echoed the teachings of prolabor ministers. When Pettibone invited one of his colleagues to lecture before the FWA, the Reverend Proctor of nearby Sterling declared, with supporting evidence from the Old and New Testaments, "Labor (is) a divine calling." Two FWA leaders reported later that his address had been "well-timed" and a correct reading of both revelation and nature in showing "the true dignity of manual labor": everyone must labor, they said, for those purposes "so evidently designed by the Creator in the sentence pronounced upon Adam: 'In the sweat of thy brow shalt thou eat bread'" (*WI,* 8 Feb. 1845).

52. *New York State Mechanic,* 19 Mar. 1842.

53. *Operative,* 31 Aug. 1844.

54. *Voice,* 3 July 1846.

55. *South Boston Gazette,* 26 May 1849; *Voice,* 20 Mar. 1846; Luther, *Avarice,* 40–42.

56. "Religion—Freedom," *MM,* May 1846, 104. The habit of identifying with Jesus and his disciples was common among antebellum laborites, as it has been for assorted rebels and revolutionaries throughout modern history. "We must not forget," McFarlane told an audience of mechanics at the Broadway Tabernacle in New York City in 1847, "that the Reformer of Judah labored as a Carpenter, and those whom he chose for his followers were men of toil" (Commons, *Documentary History* 8:256). Similarly, Philadelphia radical George Lippard reminded his readers that Christ was "the Carpenter of Nazareth," in the "Mechanic's gaberdine" at work in his father's shop. "He is thinking of the Workmen of the World," he wrote in *Washington and His Generals,* "the Mechanics of the earth, whose dark lot has been ever and yet ever—to dig that others may sleep—to sow that others may reap—to coin their groans and sweat and blood, into gold for the rich man's chest, into purple robes for his form and crowns for his brow" (quoted in Butterfield, "George Lippard," 288–89).

57. *Monitor,* 13 Apr. 1844; *MM,* July 1846, 164. Also, "Observer," *MFP,* 27 Dec. 1828; "Address to the Working People of Manayunk, Pennsylvania," 28 August 1833, in Commons, *Documentary*

History 5:330–34; 8:258; Carriers' Address, *NL,* 1836; *Voice,* 27 Nov. 1846. The Female Industrial Association, the principal labor organization of women outside New England in the 1840s, began one of its pronouncements: "whereas the young women attached to the different trades in the city of New York, having toiled a long time for a remuneration totally inadequate for the maintenance of life, and feeling the truth of the Gospel assertion, that 'the laborer is worthy of his hire'" ([New York] *WMA,* 8 Mar. 1845, repr. in Commons, *Documentary History* 8:226–31 and *Voice,* 5 Sept. 1845).

58. See, e.g., NEA presidential address, *NTU,* 4 Oct. 1834; WMBERS reference to the carpenters of Rochester in *RDA,* 15 Mar. 1842; ten-hours resolution, ibid., 18 Sept. 1848. See also its use in a derogatory sense—i.e., hewers as drones—in the address and resolutions of the Farmers, Mechanics and Working-Men in Albany, 16 Apr. 1830, *MP,* 24 Apr. 1830.

59. *NTU,* 15 Aug. 1835.

60. *NL,* 7 May 1836.

61. *RDA,* 23 Mar. 1842. See, too, George Reynolds, *DFP,* 13 Nov. 1830: to eradicate existing evils, to "place things upon their proper footing," and produce equality would be to "begin anew, and would require A COMMUNITY OF WORKING MEN."

62. *Voice,* 20 Mar. 1846. A generation later, in response to a question about the membership of the Knights of Labor, Grand Master Workman Terrence Powderly declared, "We take all men who obey the divine injunction 'By the sweat of thy brow shall thou eat bread'" (quoted in David Montgomery, "Labor in the Industrial Era," in Richard B. Morris, ed., *The American Worker* [Washington, D.C., 1976], 120).

63. *NEA,* 11 Oct. 1832.

64. Luther, *Brooklyn Address,* 7.

65. *WMA,* 6 Dec. 1839.

66. "Religion—Freedom," *MM,* July 1846, 152. See, too, address to New York workers by New York Journeymen House Carpenters, *NTU,* 12 Dec. 1835.

67. *WMA,* 28 Sept. 1844.

68. *WI,* 8 Feb. 1845. Activists made the same kind of argument about their right to freedom, focusing more on the religious argument in the Declaration than its author might have. "Liberty is granted to man from the Creator," declared a meeting of the Rochester WMBERS in 1841 (*RDA,* 18 Aug. 1841). See, too, George Reynolds, "Address to the Working People of Delaware," *DFP,* 21 Aug. 1830: the American worker "is heir to the choicest gift of Heaven—LIBERTY." The unattached activists were Young and William Elleck. For a sampling of the latter's use of religious imagery, see "Sonnet: Address to Wachusett," *WI,* 8 Feb. 1845.

69. *Reformer,* 30 Dec. 1836.

70. *Voice,* 29 May 1845; 9 Jan.; 20 Nov. 1846.

71. (New York) *WMA,* 28 Sept. 1844.

72. This attachment to the ideal of human equality—expressed in what was perhaps the most common labor cry of the age, the demand for "equal rights"—owed virtually nothing to the conflating of liberty and equality, in the form of equal economic *opportunity,* that Rowland Berthoff has identified as the term's principal definition in the public arena during the early Republic ("Conventional Mentality: Free Blacks, Women, and Business Corporations as Unequal Persons, 1820–1870," *Journal of American History* 76 [Dec. 1989]: 758–59). Though labor's usage did not generally suggest "agrarian" leveling (see chap. 10), it did, often, imply an equality of condition. More important, though, when antebellum Christian laborites spoke about "equality," they echoed the more radical scriptural meaning of the idea, particularly that found in the Gospels, which stressed the commonality of all God's children. See, too, idem, "Independence and Attachment, Virtue and Interest: From Republican Citizen to Free Enterpriser, 1787–1837," in Richard L. Bushman et al, eds., *Uprooted Americans: Essays to Honor Oscar Handlin* (Boston: Little, Brown, 1979). For numerous distinctions of the term, see J. R. Pole, *The Pursuit of Equality in American History* (Berkeley and Los Angeles: Univ. of California Press, 1978).

73. *Condition of Labor,* 21. Hosmer maintained that the prevailing system of domination was

"the root of all evils" (7). "The good God never intended a part of his creatures to live thus at the mercy of the rest," he declared. "He created them all EQUAL, socially equal" (8).

74. Association of Industry, "To the Employers of Fall River" (11 Oct. 1841), FRHS; (Fall River) *Gazette,* 27 Jan. 1842. The broadside was signed by two association officers, Horatio Gunn (a Unitarian) and Philip Smith (a Baptist).

75. *Third Grand Rally of the Workingmen of Charlestown, Massachusetts, Held October 23d, 1840* (Boston, 1840).

76. Hosmer, *Condition of Labor,* 24.

77. *NL,* 26 Mar. 1836.

78. Ibid., 17 Dec. 1836.

79. Cited in Schantz, "Religious Rhetoric and Resistance," 15.

80. (Rochester) *WMA,* 22 Nov. 1839. See, too, "Yorick," writing from Wilmington, "Loose Thoughts—No. II," *MFP,* 21 Nov. 1829. Condemning unbounded wealth while others were steeped in poverty, "Yorick" insisted that he was not advocating that the rich divide their wealth equally with the poor. Still, he reminded his readers "that the Creator of Man created no other distinctions but male and female," and that therefore the sum of the "overflowing coffers of the rich" should render comfortable the "evening of life to the aged and sorrow-stricken sons of poverty." For a typical display of "Yorick's" use of the Bible, see ibid., 18 Sept. 1830.

81. "Property," *NL,* 9 July 1836. The language is biblical; see Matt. 25:29. For the prevalence of the argument that wage labor robbed the worker of his "property," see Wilentz, "Against Exceptionalism"; idem, *Chants Democratic.*

82. Hosmer, *Condition of Labor,* 21.

83. Association of Industry, "To the Employers of Fall River."

84. Cited in Schantz, "Religious Rhetoric and Resistance," 19.

85. "Present Condition of Liberty," *DFP,* 21 Jan. 1832.

Chapter 10

1. (Rochester) *WMA,* 5 Nov. 1839; *Voice,* 29 May 1845; 24 Apr. 1846; *WI,* 8 Feb. 1845.

2. *Democrat,* 1 Sept. 1847, repr. in Foner, *Factory Girls,* 269.

3. Thus, the artisans of Buffalo called for an end to the duebill system "in the name of Christian morality" (*Weltburger,* 4 May 1839, quoted in Gerber, *Making of an American Pluralism,* 249).

4. As the editor of the Cincinnati *People's Paper* put it, so long as selfishness reigned supreme, so there would always be the "war of conflicting interests" (30 Nov. 1843). Like the prolabor clergy, the term this generation of activists used for commercial and industrial capitalism was the "competition," "competitive," or "selfish" system.

5. "A Friend to Emancipation," *MFP,* 6 Feb. 1830.

6. It was, for example, a motto of the MMPA (*MM,* July 1846, 164; Oct. 1846, 247).

7. Luther, *Avarice,* 19, 34–37.

8. Idem, *Brooklyn Address,* 7.

9. Ibid., 16.

10. *Norwich Advertiser,* repr. in *NL,* 29 Oct. 1836. Typically, historians have noted the republican connection in such statements, but not Christian sources of the opposition to avarice. See, for example, Dublin, *Women at Work,* 93. For other condemnations of avarice, see *NL,* 9 July 1836.

11. *NL,* 15 Oct. 1836.

12. For other condemnations of avarice, see *MP,* 29 May 1830; extract from Fourth of July Address of A. F. Cunningham before the Trades' Union of Washington, D.C., at City Hall, Washington, 4 July 1834, *NTU,* 30 Aug. 1834; Address to New York workers by the New York Journeymen House Carpenters, ibid., 12 Dec. 1835.

13. Repr. in *Voice*, 9 Oct. 1845; ibid., 23 Apr., 15 Oct. 1847; 10 Dec. 1845 (emphasis added).

14. *Voice*, 19 Feb. 1847.

15. Ibid., 15 May 1846 (the words are Bagley's).

16. *Factory Tracts*. See also Clariette, "The Ten Hour System," *Factory Girls' Album*, 11 Apr. 1846.

17. *WMA*, 26 Feb. 1840.

18. Underwood's position did not sit well with the Monroe County Society of Friends; they excluded him in late summer of 1840 because he "neglected meeting and attended theater."

19. *DFP*, 18 Jan. 1830.

20. *NL*, 21 Jan. 1837. Interestingly, for the heading of his piece, "C" chose the biblical passage (Mark 14:7 AV) traditionally used by defenders of the status quo: "'*Ye have the poor with you always, and whensoever ye will, ye may do them good.*'"

21. "Benevolence and Cold Weather," *PP*, 6 Dec. 1843. See, too, ibid., 13 Dec. 1843; 20 Jan. 1844.

22. *WMA*, 16 Dec. 1839.

23. "FWA Record Book." The meeting appointed him to deliver the money himself.

24. Hosmer, *Condition of Labor*, 6. Here he used Labor's Rule: America's Christian communities were "in defiance of that sublime precept which he spoke, so exact, so infallible, of so universal application, the sum of all morality, 'As ye would that others should do to you, do ye even so to them'" (25–26). Also: "As a professor of the religion of Jesus Christ," trumpeted a labor voice in Plainfield, N.Y., "it is my bounden duty to do all in my power to discourage vice and immorality and encourage virtue and morality" ("Letter from a Young Reformer," *YA*, 27 Sept. 1845). See, too, Lippard's remarks on brotherhood at an IC meeting in Philadelphia, quoted in Butterfield, "George Lippard," 297. For other uses of "Mammon," see *Voice*, 26 Dec. 1845; *RR*, 20 June 1843; *NL*, 12 Nov. 1836.

25. The argument clearly reflected the religiously rooted notion that such evils damaged the entire community, rich and poor, which again could enhance or attenuate class conflict, depending upon how it was used and interpreted. Thus, "E——h" concluded his plea for eliminating poverty with the assertion that Christian injunctions against it will never be followed "where the rich are debased by luxury and the poor want for the comforts of life; where the rich man is known for his riches, and the poor man despised for his poverty: for all these things proceed from the *evil* of the *heart* of man" (*DFP*, 18 Jan. 1830).

26. *Voice*, 30 Jan. 1846. Because of the general triumph of Protestantism (without control in the political realm) over the residual forces of Freethought, Young and others apparently felt no need to make the argument, advanced by their predecessors in the late 1820s and early 1830s, that the external and internal realms of life should be distinct. For that argument, see above, chaps. 2, 9. By the 1840s, as the Christian critique in labor circles reached full blossom, activists generally echoed Young in declaring the two realms one and thus seeking a "higher" plane of development.

27. Not all those working within a religious paradigm in this period saw the problem as strictly a product of their own time, however. "From the morning of creation" brute force has ruled the world; "the first born of men, who slew a brother, more righteous than himself," gave "sad presage" of what would follow. "As then, so since, from age to age the cries of a brother's blood have risen up to him, who sitteth in the heavens" (NEA presidential address, *NTU*, 4 Oct. 1834).

28. A phenomenon noted during the period by Tocqueville, the phrase "memory and desire" is Fred Somkin's (see chap. 8, n. 91). For a recent study, one among many, noting antebellum ambivalence toward change, see Randolph Roth, *Democratic Dilemma*.

29. *DFP*, 2 Oct. 1830. Earlier in the year, Reynolds claimed his AWPNCC had been formed to "overturn the altar of the demon party spirit," to "cleanse the polls from pollution" (ibid., 2 Jan. 1830).

30. *ICR*, 12 Aug. 1836.

31. For the rejection of the "party spirit" in the 1830s, see, e.g., *DFP,* 26 June 1830 (Benjamin Webb); *NTU,* 4 Oct. 1834 (NEA president). On anti-partyism in the movement generally, see chaps. 2, 11.

32. *Voice,* 31 Dec. 1847. The language here, of course, was heavily biblical. In politics, the writer said, the people have divided into parties, following demagogues ("wolves in sheep's clothing") in a rush after the "'loaves and fishes' of office," while in religion, churches divided into sects, creating discord, strife, and confusion, where goodwill, harmony, and love should reign.

33. Quoted in McNeill, *Labor Movement,* 111.

34. The longing for harmony and order manifested itself in a deep reverence for and exaltation of nature, a peaceful realm in which many activists found the spirit of God. See, for examples, FWA leader William Ellick's "Sonnet: Address to Wachusett," *WI,* 8 Feb. 1845; anon. Fitchburger, "The Sunshine," *Voice,* 11 June 1847. The same was true for the radical mill women of this era, many of whom came out of the countryside into the urban factories; in an attempt to cope with that wrenching experience, they romanticized nature, particularly the natural surroundings of their childhood homes. In this, they found order and wholeness in contrast to the chaos and division they faced in their new working lives. Thus, for activists like Huldah Stone, "the green hills and fertile vales . . . where the pure air of heaven, gave life to the whole being" became not only a sanctuary to which to retreat, but, under certain circumstances, a standard by which to judge their present condition (ibid., 25 Sept. 1846).

35. *Sentinel,* 7 Apr., 2 Sept. 1841.

36. Ibid., 6 Jan. 1841; *WI,* 22 Mar. 1845. For Wilder's religious biography, see chap. 4.

37. A systematic and exhaustive search of federal, state, and local records failed to yield any reliable information on the Young family before William Field's appearance in Fitchburg in 1843. Consequently, for early biographical material, I have relied upon several obituaries and one published biographical sketch. For sources, see chap. 3; *Globe,* obit., 20 Aug. 1900; *Transcript,* obit., 20 Aug. 1900; (Wakefield) *Daily Item,* obit., 20, 22 Aug. 1900. Although there is no corroborating evidence, *Biographical Sketches of . . . Massachusetts* (690–92) identifies his father as having been "engaged in the manufacturing business." The authors are silent on the precise nature of that involvement.

38. *Voice,* 29 May 1845.

39. "While the spirit of the New Testament teaches us to teach and pray for each other," proclaimed another resolution, "the customs of men requires us to *prey upon each other*" ("FWA Record Book").

40. *Voice,* 31 Dec. 1847.

41. Ibid., 29 May 1845. See, too, Elizur Wright's comments on the *Voice* in *Chronotype,* 11 Feb. 1847. Such editorial sermonizing of the masses was not peculiar to New England. See, for example, *PP,* 30 Nov. 1843. For other uses of the Ishmael image, see Blatchley's letter to Isaac Sherwood in *DFP,* 3 Sept. 1831; William Lloyd Garrison to Thomas Shipley, quoted in McKivigan, *Proslavery Religion,* 59. For echoes of this rhetoric among American laborites and social radicals in a later period, see, for example, Bellamy, *Looking Backward,* 212.

42. William Sewell depicts a similar phenomenon among French workers in the early nineteenth century in *Work and Revolution in France: The Language of Labor From the Old Regime to 1848* (Cambridge: Cambridge Univ. Press, 1980).

43. *Voice,* 29 May 1845.

44. Ibid., 5 June 1845.

45. Ibid., 4 Feb. 1848. On Orvis's life, see (Boston) *Labor Leader,* obit., 8 May 1897.

46. Although Charles Fourier began articulating his vision in 1808, his ideas did not gain currency in America until Albert Brisbane translated his work from French into English in 1840; when New York *Tribune* editor Horace Greeley gave Brisbane a column in 1842, a Fourierist movement quickly developed in the United States. The definitive work is Guarneri's *Utopian Alternative,* which demonstrates strong connections between Associationism and labor reform, connections that most labor historians have discounted because of Fourierism's putative "middle

class" and "reformist" orientation. See, e.g., Ware, *Industrial Worker*, chap. 11. But see, too, Zahler, who pointed out that the Fourierists had a strong following in the New England labor movement (*Eastern Workingmen*, 54).

47. Orvis claimed that "all the editors of the *Voice of Industry* have, from the beginning, been earnest and active Associationists"; John S. Dwight, a Brook Farm resident during its Fourierist phase, proclaimed that the "*Voice* has always been friendly to our movement." Although there is no evidence of William Young's membership in Fourierist organizations, he was openly sympathetic, for example praising the efforts of *Voice* editors John Allen and John Orvis—both of whom lived for a time at Brook Farm—when they toured Vermont on behalf of the American Union of Associationists during the fall of 1847. Young reported favorably on lectures he had heard by Brisbane and New England's leading Fourierist, Unitarian divine William Henry Channing. He looked upon Brook Farm "with interest and hope," telling his readers that it deserved the sympathy of all "true reformers." Other *Voice* editors who participated in the movement included Sarah Bagley, Huldah Stone, Mehitable Eastman, D. H. Jaques, and T. G. Pierce. Also involved, or at least supporters of a Fourierist solution to the labor problem, were John Cluer; S. C. Hewitt; Jacob Frieze; Lewis Ryckman, first president of the NEWA; Charles Hosmer, a leader of the NELRL; and Henry P. Trask, Boston cooperationist and trade unionist. In Rochester, Associationism caught on in 1843, coinciding with the shorter-hours struggle of the city's clerks and the cresting of the duebill excitement. Among the Fourierists here were WMBERS activists Hiram Carmichael, E. A. Theller, M. F. Whitney, William Morgan; A. K. Amsden (clerk leader); and George Morgan of the MMPA. See *Voice*, 27 Nov. 1846; 7 May, 23 Apr. 1847; 13 Mar. 1846; 14 Apr. 1848; *Harbinger*, 18 Sept. 1847; *Herald*, 7 Feb. 1849; Gleason, "History of Labor," 46–49; *RR*, 7 Nov. 1843; *RDD*, 18 Apr. 1843; *RDA*, 3 Nov., 25 Dec. 1843.

48. Like the labor movement generally, Fourierism was tarred with the infidelity brush. One Rochester Fourierist resolution, unanimously adopted, denied the charge of being anti-Christian, proclaiming, "on the contrary, [we] believe the system of Industrial Association . . . is strictly in harmony with the precepts of the gospel," and for that very reason gave it approval (*RDD*, 18 May 1843). See, too, the defense of Fourierism from charges of infidelity and Owenism by a "Friend of Social Reform," in the (Rochester) *Evening Post*, 27 Mar. 1843; and the address by S. A. Clemons before the Rochester Fourier Society, entitled "The Religious Tendencies of Associationism, in *RDA*, 6 June 1843.

49. On this tradition in Jewish and Christian thinking, see Smyth, "Religion and Socialism."

50. More than any other movement of this era, Associationism represented the Christian spirit in social reform: its mission was to realize "practical Christianity" by unifying religion with life. See *Harbinger*, 14 June 1845; 28 Nov. 1846; 27 Jan 1849; *Phalanx*, 27 July 1844, repr. in Commons, *Documentary History* 7:261; *Voice*, 5 July 1845; 6 June 1846; 7 May 1847; 14 Jan. 1848; William A. Hinds, *American Communities* (Oneida, N.Y.: Office of the American Socialist, 1878), 222–23. For the use of religion by Rochester labor activists among the Fourierists, see *RDD*, 18 Apr. 1843.

51. The first modern study of the shorter-hours movement is Foner and Roediger, *Our Own Time*. One of the very few insightful discussions of the logic behind the demand, in this case on the 1860s, can be found in David Montgomery, *Beyond Equality: Labor and the Radical Republicans, 1862–1872* (New York: Knopf, 1967), chap. 6.

52. On the later period, see, e.g., Roy Rosenzweig, *Eight Hours for What We Will: Workers and Leisure in an Industrial City, 1870–1920* (New York: Cambridge Univ. Press, 1983). Historians of antebellum labor have stressed the physical and generally ignored the spiritual arguments for the shorter workday. Murphy finds the ten-hour movement concerned with control of leisure as opposed to control over work (*Ten Hours' Labor*, chap. 2, 224).

53. As we shall see, though they perceived an inexorable link among these various aspects of human nature, these activists clearly privileged the spiritual and moral over the physical and mental. For the prolabor clerical view, see chap. 7.

54. *Voice*, 20 Mar. 1846. See, too, the Boston laborite who pointed out that although the "beneficence of the Creator" offered many blessings, the community could not overlook "the true

character of man, his divine origin, his sublime and transcendent destination"—a warning to employers who "erase the image of the divinity from the human soul" of their employees (*NEA*, 18 Oct. 1832). For the insistence on "time to develop God-given capacities" by Buffalo artisans, see *Weltburger*, 4 May 1839, quoted in Gerber, *Making of an American Pluralism*, 246.

55. Association of Industry, "To the Employers of Fall River." In this opening statement, they were apparently quoting from their "Preamble and Resolutions," drafted at the group's first meeting in October 1840 (*Patriot*, 22 Oct. 1840).

56. *Mechanic*, 29 June 1844. The circular was drafted by a committee of four, two of whom belonged to local congregations. A third, Thomas Almy, may have been part of a local Swedenborgian circle. The Association of Industry circular, as noted, was signed by two church members.

57. *Blue Hen Chicken*, 12 Nov. 1847.

58. Ibid., 10 Dec. 1847. Politicians picked up this rhetoric and echoed it when appealing to workers for votes around election day. In November 1848, the Wilmington Democrats issued a circular that declared in typically verbose fashion: Citizens, they cajoled, vote Democratic, if you wish restraints applied to the "murder of soul, mind and body" perpetrated on our fellow-men by the "monstrous manufacturing system of this country," which tends to destroy the "moral, mental and physical energies" by "overtaking their powers and depriving them of the necessary leisure required by God for Devotion, by Nature for Rest, and by the Mind for Reflection and Improvement" (my paraphrase of [Wilmington] *Delaware Gazette*, 10 Nov. 1848).

59. *Voice*, 18 Sept. 1845.

60. Ibid., 8 May 1846. On Stone's background, see ibid., 17 Apr. 1846.

61. Ibid., 7 Aug. 1845.

62. Ibid., 26 Nov. 1847.

63. *Mechanic*, 25 May 1844.

64. This was an argument made throughout the period and in many different communities. During a period of intense ten-hour agitation in Boston in 1835, for example, a meeting of building tradesmen posed this question to the city's clergy: "Is it, in your opinion, compatible with the social, moral, and religious duties men owe to God, to society, to themselves, and those dependent upon them, to labor during the period of thirteen hours per day?" (*ICR*, 4 July 1835) See, too, the meeting of the "Journeymen Mechanics" of Utica, N.Y., in *NTU*, 30 Jan. 1836: laborers "ought in justice to ourselves, the duty we owe to our friends, our country and our God, not to perform more than ten hours labor in a day."

65. (Boston) *New England Mechanic*, 8 Mar. 1845.

66. *Mechanic*, 4 Jan. 1845.

67. See intro.

68. A wide range of antebellum labor activists, both evangelicals and non-evangelicals, resembled Wilder in this regard. For Young's views on moral vices and their solution, see *Voice*, 11 Sept. 1845; 3, 24 Apr., 1 May 1846. For the 1830s, see Charles Douglas's similar expressions in *NEA*, 4 Apr. 1833; 15 Sept. 1834. Wilder's position may be gleaned from the *Sentinel*, 5, 12 May, 2 June, 28 July, 21 Oct. 1841.

69. *WI*, 8 Feb. 1845.

70. Smyth, "Religion and Socialism."

71. Samuel Whitcomb, Jr., *Address Before the Working-Men's Society of Dedham* (Dedham, Mass., 1831).

72. *WI*, 2 Feb. 1845.

73. On the importance of this impulse among antebellum reformers, see Walters, *American Reformers*, intro. and passim.

74. *Mechanic*, 8 Mar. 1845.

75. On the implications of labor's moralism for working class action, see chap. 11.

76. For more on this, see chap. 11.

77. Tuveson, *Redeemer Nation*. This conjuring up of dragons to be slain probably owes something as well to the themes of "subversion and counter-subversion" in American life that

David Brion Davis has uncovered ("Some Themes of Countersubversion: An Analysis of Anti-Masonic, Anti-Catholic, and Anti-Mormon Literature," in idem, ed., *The Fear of Conspiracy: Images of Un-American Subversion from the Revolution to the Present* [Ithaca: Cornell Univ. Press, 1971], 9–22). On the need to destroy the "Monster Bank" in this era, see Marvin Meyers, *The Jacksonian Persuasion: Politics and Belief* (New York: Vintage, 1957).

78. "FWA Record Book."

Chapter 11

1. "H.H.," *NR*, 7 Dec. 1848.

2. *Democrat*, 5 Sept. 1845, repr. in Foner, *Factory Girls*, 81–82; see, also, Bagley editorial, *Voice*, 8 May 1846.

3. Based on the Gospels and the Pauline letters, Christian perfectionism preached the possibility of perfection in earthly life, an entire sanctification of the soul through a cleansing of sin and a renewal of Christ's spirit; see Peters, *Christian Perfectionism*. Gutman was right about the significance of Christian perfectionism for discontented workers. See his "Protestantism and the American Labor Movement," 83.

4. *Voice*, (Lowell) 7 May, (Hooksett) 23 April 1847; (Bagley) 9 Nov. 1845.

5. Ibid., 3 Apr. 1846; 29 May 1845.

6. Ibid., 3 Apr. 1846.

7. Ibid., 26 Dec. 1845.

8. Ibid., 29 May 1845.

9. Ibid., 31 July 1845.

10. On millennialism in moments of crisis, see Tuveson's description of Julia Ward Howe's "The Battle Hymn of the Republic," in *Redeemer Nation*, 197–202.

11. *Voice*, 11 June 1847. See, also, remarks of Pittsburgh's Samuel Fleming, ibid., 20 Feb. 1846.

12. "An Observer—No. 1," *MFP*, 24 July 1830.

13. Ibid., 28 Aug. 1830 (allusion to Rev. 21:1). "Caleb and Joshua" spoke of "the promised land," Wilmington's George Reynolds spoke of "'flee[ing] the wrath to come,'" BTU leader Aaron Wood spoke of "the city of your God, of which glorious things are spoken," and Seth Luther spoke of "a paradise of bliss" (ibid., 31 Jan. 1829; *DFP*, 13 Nov. 1830; *Reformer*, 25 Nov. 1836; Luther, *Avarice*, 43).

14. *Voice*, 31 July 1845.

15. This was "the will of the Almighty," she wrote (ibid., 12 June 1846), repeating the prophecy, without quoting it, in a subsequent letter (ibid., 14 Apr. 1848; allusion to Micah 4:4). Luther also drew on the Book of Micah in this decade, offering a resolution at an NEWA meeting that expressed his hope for "that glorious time when every man, woman, and child, shall sit under their own fig tree, with none to molest or make afraid" (ibid., 10 Apr. 1846). He invoked the same vision in *Brooklyn Address*, 10. Also, *NL*, 26 Mar. 1836, quoted in Commons, *History of Labour* 1:363; NEA presidential address, *NTU*, 4 Oct. 1834.

16. *South Boston Gazette*, 16 Sept. 1848.

17. *Voice*, 14 Jan. 1848.

18. Ibid., 5 June, 31 July 1845.

19. Ibid., 1 May 1846.

20. Ibid., 17 Dec. 1847.

21. Young sought "the elevation of the whole human family to that condition which nature and God designed they should occupy; that they be made what they are capable of being; a land of brothers, instead of a gang of enemies and oppressors" (ibid., 29 May 1846).

22. On Marx, see, e.g., Ralph Miliband, *Marxism and Politics* (New York: Oxford Univ. Press, 1977), 32–33.

23. *Voice*, 11 Sept. 1845.

24. In this regard, free white labor activists were very different from radical blacks of this age. Cf., e.g., David Walker's *Appeal,* which bore numerous rhetorical similarities to antebellum labor language—from the critique of hypocritical Christians to the use of the Golden Rule—while containing a militancy rare among whites. Still, as we shall see, Christianity could justify violence in certain working-class hands; moreover, even Walker's militancy was tempered by his American (as opposed to strictly African-American) nationalism. See Wilson Jeremiah Moses, *Black Messiahs and Uncle Toms: Social and Literary Manipulations of a Religious Myth* (University Park: Pennsylvania State Univ. Press, 1982), 38–46, 81–82, passim; David Howard Pitney, *The Afro-American Jeremiad: Appeals for Justice in America* (Philadelphia: Temple Univ. Press, 1990), 13, chap. 2.

25. *NTU,* 4 Oct. 1834.

26. *MFP,* 7 Feb. 1829.

27. *Voice,* 29 May 1845.

28. *WI,* 8 Feb. 1845

29. *Voice,* 14 Nov. 1845.

30. Ibid., 4 Sept. 1845.

31. *WI,* 8 Feb. 1845.

32. At its base, the sentiment was religio-moral. As Robert McFarlane put it in his opening editorial, the remedy for existing ills was "moral"—"the balm is in Gilead" ("America," *MM,* Jan. 1846, 7).

33. *Voice,* 31 July, 7 Aug. 1845.

34. *WI,* 8 Feb. 1845.

35. *DFP,* 23 Jan. 1830.

36. (Rochester) *WMA,* 15 Feb. 1840. Implicit in Frink's stance here, of course, is the existence of those in the movement who did advocate something more than mere "light."

37. "America," *MM,* January 1846, 8. Elsewhere, McFarlane said, "we war against no class, but seek the elevation of our own" (ibid., Aug. 1846, 199). Wilmington's Thomas Roberts, after outlining a classically religious rationale for the ten-hour day before Brandywine operatives in 1847, advised that he would not injure the interests of any class of the community. Use "every proper effort," he told the gathering, and "avoid as far as possible, giving offence to any class of our fellow citizens" (*Blue Hen Chicken,* 10 Dec. 1847). Typically, he claimed to advocate specifically on behalf of workers; he simply insisted that nothing he sought was aimed at injuring any other group in the community. For another notice of his speech, see chap. 10.

38. In this spirit of non-antagonism, they were really no different from the other "romantic reformers" of the age (Thomas, "Romantic Reform in America").

39. *WI,* 8 Feb. 1845. For such rhetoric among the Rochester printers, see below.

40. *Voice,* 7 Nov. 1845.

41. Ibid., 28 Aug. 1845.

42. Ibid., 28 Aug., 21 Nov. 1845; 2 Oct. 1846.

43. Ibid., 28 Aug. 1845.

44. This stance did not preclude all political activity, but it did make such efforts deeply problematical. For similar problems, with similar roots, see Leon Fink's discussion of the Knights of Labor in "The Uses of Political Power: Toward a Theory of the Labor Movement in the Era of the Knights of Labor," in *Working-Class America: Essays on Labor, Community, and American Society,* Michael H. Frisch and Daniel J. Walkowitz, eds. (Urbana: Univ. of Illinois Press, 1983), esp. 117–18.

45. As a temperance advocate, for example, Young counted himself among the "moral suasionists." Praising a lecturer in Fitchburg who called for moral action against intemperance, he maintained that the speech had done more for the cause than "all the lawyers, sheriffs, constables and houses of correction in christendom." Those who advocated legal enactments against liquor, he asserted, had "more faith in man than God, more faith in law than moral power" (*Voice,* 29 May, 5 June, 21 Aug. 1845; 4 Dec. 1846; 22 Jan. 1847; *Herald,* 5 Mar. 1857). In fact, Young had firsthand experience with the evils of alcohol. Refusing to speak at a printers' festival in Fitchburg

because the hotel hosting the event served liquor, he declared: "I have sworn eternal enmity to the demon intemperance—he disturbed my childhood days—robbed me of early privileges, and poisoned the home of youth with disappointment and sorrow" (*Voice*, 22 Jan. 1847).

46. Ibid., 2 Oct. 1846.

47. In Fitchburg, for example, the Workingmen's Association undertook no course of direct action to remedy the "evils" it identified in contemporary society. Its constitution called for the use of "all *laudable* measures to eradicate these evils and all other systems of seductive error"; the group's principal activities were internal debate, resolution making, and sending delegates to regional and national labor meetings. Its public agitation involved sponsoring speakers and spawning the publication of two labor newspapers, the *Wachusett Independant* and the *Voice of Industry*. For quotation, see "FWA Record Book."

48. *Voice*, 12 June 1845.

49. Ibid., 11 Sept. 1845.

50. A "day of retribution will surely come," he told his readers in 1847, when all violations of God's law would be "avenged" (ibid., 26 Feb. 1847).

51. Given their religiously inspired antisectarianism, advocating a "class" or particular interest would have run counter to the entire project in which these activists were engaged.

52. Young, for example, did not repudiate strikes. See his letter in *All Sorts*, 4 Mar. 1848.

53. See, e.g., the comment on "grades of Society" in "Qui Capit Ille Faut," *DFP*, 6 Feb. 1830.

54. When a letter writer attacked the *DFP* for professing to be free of sectarianism while addressing itself exclusively to the mechanic and working classes, editor William Baker responded that most of the papers of the day were "aristocratic." The *DFP* sought to promulgate laws that formed the basis of "all practical righteousness," he claimed, to elevate the "poor, illiterate," not to tear down the well-to-do; to support the oppressed, not to diminish the oppressor; "except in so far as relieving the one may detract from the other." Thus, Benjamin Webb could advocate the cause of the worker while insisting, "we are as much opposed to a combination of working men against the non-producer, as we are of the non-producer against the laboring man," and disavowing any intention to "raise the hue and cry of the poor against the rich, for a division of property." In defense of his activism, Webb maintained that he was more a friend of the poor than the nonproducer because the latter did not enjoy his God-given equal rights and therefore needed to be "elevated" (ibid., 24 Apr., 26 June 1830).

55. Indeed, a small minority of labor advocates, while recognizing that it was the "higher classes" that had caused class conflict—strikes, for example—by trampling the rights of those below them, nevertheless accepted the necessity of class distinctions in society, calling only for mutual respect among the various (unequal) parties. See, e.g., *PP*, 30 Nov. 1843.

56. *Voice*, 31 July 1845. A similar perspective could be found early in the period as well as late, in New York and Delaware as well as in New England. Benjamin Webb, fifteen years before Young, drew similar conclusions from his religious philosophy. Thus, regarding Quaker select meetings at which he and his compatriots were arraigned for their "heresies," he reminded his readers of the "necessity of censuring the system, and not the individuals who are the unfortunate victims of such a delusion" (*DFP*, 17 Dec. 1831). His social philosophy flowing from his religion, Webb's stance here went considerably beyond the theological matters at stake between he and his persecutors. He told the Philadelphia Yearly Meeting in the spring of 1832 that if he had sinned against charity and benevolence and against honesty with his fellows, injured others' characters to build his own reputation, gathered where he had not strewn, oppressed the poor and ground the face of the needy for price and selfishness, neglected the truth, not visited the widow and fatherless, not fed the hungry, not clothed the naked, not done to others as he would be done by—if he had done any of this, he said, then he would accept that he had strayed from the Quakers and violated the principles of Christianity. If not, though, then he insisted that he remained a member in good standing of a Society bound by good works. But, if the Society and its religion were not engaged in benevolence and social duties, guided by the "Light within," then "am I neither Quaker nor Christian" (ibid., 7 Apr. 1832). Note, too, Robert McFarlane's vision of a coming elevation of the

workers, "without enmity to any class, but *evildoers*" (emphasis added) in "Religion—Freedom," *MM*, July 1846, 153.

57. *Voice*, 28 Aug. 1845. Though seeking to transform society as a whole, Christian labor activists like Young advocated a reformism that was, at bottom, highly individualistic. As one of Young's successors at the *Voice* put it succinctly, "men are anterior to systems."

58. Ibid., 29 May 1845. Note the position of the *pro-revolutionary* Nicaraguan bishops in 1979 ("Pastoral Letter of the Nicaraguan Episcopate," 17 Nov. 1979, quoted in Penny Lernoux, "The Church Revolutionary in Latin America," *Nation*, 24 May 1980, 623):

> With respect to the class struggle, we think that one thing is the dynamic fact of the class struggle which ought to produce a just transformation of societal structures, and another thing is class hatred which is directed against persons and contradicts radically the Christian obligation to conduct oneself with love.

59. Turning this logic in another direction, though, some labor activists, as we shall see in the next section, accepted this distinction and still advocated a kind of class warfare.

60. *Voice*, 30 Jan. 1846.

61. Ibid., 24 Apr. 1846; 31 July 1845.

62. *WMA*, 26 Oct. 1839.

63. Quotation from "FWA Record Book."

64. *NEA*, 15 Mar. 1832.

65. Holmes, *Third Grand Rally*, 12–13.

66. *RDA*, 4 Feb. 1842.

67. Ibid., 23, 26 Mar. 1842.

68. *RR*, 20 June 1843.

69. *MM*, Nov. 1846, 286. While imploring workers to expose existing evils "always in a manly, dignified, and open, honest manner," McFarlane also reminded them (and, at the same time, their enemies) that "the day of justice cannot always be delayed" (ibid., Nov. 1846, 281). Though hardly a proponent of violence, McFarlane tapped the tradition of Christian retribution readily available to activists of this age. This Presbyterian church leader, in a warning to America for the miseries accumulated since the Revolution, described in his opening editorial how the Spanish had been punished for *their* cruelty in the New World: "by the unerring laws of Divine Providence, which for the infringement of the *golden rule* ultimately bringeth punishment upon the perpetrators" ("America," ibid., Jan. 1846, 6).

70. *QC*, 29 Sept. 1849, quoted in Butterfield, "George Lippard," 286.

71. Luther, *Brooklyn Address*, 23.

72. Idem, *Avarice*, 7, 14, 15.

73. Idem, *Brooklyn Address*, 12–13.

74. Idem, *Avarice*, 42.

75. The context of Luther's remarks made all the difference. Contrast his remarks here with the call for charity to the widowed and fatherless in the ideology of Wilmington's Benjamin Webb (Quaker) or Rochester's Henry Frink (Presbyterian), discussed in chap. 10.

76. Luther, *Suffrage*, 23, 6.

77. Ibid., 21.

78. Idem, *Brooklyn Address*, 17.

79. Ibid., 18.

80. Idem, *New England Address*, 5.

81. Ibid., 3; idem, *Suffrage*, 5.

82. Idem, *Brooklyn Address*, 12.

83. Idem, *Suffrage*, 21.

84. Idem, *New England Address*, 31.

85. The Christian laborite position on strikes was complex. Robert McFarlane, for example, rejected such actions as "unwise and impolitic," and always injurious to both parties, but acknowl-

edged that there was often no other remedy against an arbitrary employer, as operatives were
blacklisted for their activities (*MM*, Nov. 1846, 279–80).

86. *Mechanic,* 29 June 1844; *Monitor,* 20 July 1844.

87. Quotations in this paragraph and the next are from *Mechanic,* 29 June 1844.

88. My emphasis.

89. *Mechanic,* 11 May 1844.

90. Ibid., 18 May 1844.

91. Ibid., 1 Feb. 1845.

92. Ibid., 25 May 1844.

93. Ibid.

Epilogue

1. Having dominated the calico printing trade in Fall River since the 1820s, English, Irish, and
Scottish workers made up the leadership of the 1840 strike, though some native-born workers were
involved (see Lazerow, "A Good Time Coming: Religion and the Emergence of Labor Activism in
Antebellum New England" [Ph.D. diss., Brandeis Univ., 1983], 170–72, n. 55). Although English
mule spinners probably participated in the struggle for the ten-hour day in the early 1830s, no
evidence of their involvement has survived.

2. *Monitor,* 11 Apr. 1840.

3. *Patriot,* 28 May 1840.

4. A weavers' turnout in response to wage reductions in 1848 led to violence against strike-
breakers and the arrest of two strike leaders, but the participants left no record of their speeches or
resolutions. The massive spinners' and weavers' strike of 1850–51, on the other hand, produced
several public pronouncements, which focused on working conditions and demanded fair treatment from the mill owners. A weavers' circular ("To the Inhabitants of Fall River and Vicinity")
contained no specifically religious references. It called the attention of "justice lovers" to the
"cupidity and avarice" of the manufacturers and declared it a "duty" to resist the encroachments of
employers, but it did not offer a religious rationale for the strike. When they publicly thanked their
supporters in February 1851, they apparently found no need to make any reference to religion or
God then, either. "Rather than see our children compelled to follow in our miserable, slave-ridden
life," they declared, "we are prepared to sacrifice all but our honor and virtue." When the strikers
did employ religious rhetoric, it was to expose their employers' hypocrisy. A weavers' meeting at
the Free Will Baptist Church, perhaps with the aid of its minister, adopted a resolution announcing
that it viewed "with surprise and disapprobation, the unjust and unchristian conduct of the Cotton
Manufacturing Companies of Fall River." Generally, however, the strikers simply argued their case
by disseminating information about their miserable working conditions. This style of protest
characterized mill workers at least into the 1870s. A typical pronouncement can be found in the
"spinners' committee" letter that appeared in the local press (*News,* 16 Aug. 1870), offering hours
and wage statistics for Fall River and elsewhere. Only in the last paragraph did the spinners invoke
a broader purpose: claiming to represent the workers in their trade, they declared, "we have Truth
and Justice on our side, and we pray God defend the right." For the 1850–51 strike, see ibid., 19
Dec. 1850; 27, 20, 6 Feb. 1851.

5. Ibid., 1 Jan. 1868.

6. The very nature of their status as an imported work force required immigrant workers to
cast a different appeal than that of their native counterparts. During a weavers' strike in 1875,
union leader D. B. Harriman remarked, "we find (local manufacturers) the same as their Puritan
ancestors, who fleeing from persecution became sorry persecutors over here in America." Later
that year, at a weavers' meeting in a local park, a speaker called upon the assembled workers "to
imitate their English brethren in standing firmly against a violation of their rights" (ibid., 8 Mar.,
26 July 1875).

7. During the late 1840s, the invention of Howe's sewing machine and the rapid influx of Irish immigrants facilitated factory production of ready-made clothing in Boston, eclipsing custom work and the skilled tailor in a remarkably short period of time, and allowing employers to repeatedly reduce piece-rate wages. In response, members of the trade organized the Journeymen Tailors' Society (JTS) in 1847. Although the union expressed increasing concern over wage reductions, it took no direct action until 1849. In late June of that year, the JTS offered employers a new "price list," to which nearly half acceded. Most of the large wholesalers in the city resisted, however, and in the first week of July the tailors walked out. Estimates of the number of workers involved ranged from five to eight hundred. It is not clear precisely when the strike ended, but the last press reports of activity appeared in late September. See Handlin, *Boston's Immigrants*, 74–77; (Boston) *Pilot*, 24 Apr. 1847; 22 Sept. 1849; *Herald*, 2 Oct. 1848; 10, 19 July, 6 Aug., 11 Sept. 1849; *Chronotype*, 1 Sept. 1849.

8. In the late 1840s, the number of tailors in Boston increased more than threefold (from 473 to 1,547); by 1850, two-thirds were Irish. Precise dates of arrival could be determined for only four strikers, however. The president and one of the secretaries of the JTS had lived in Boston since 1844 and 1843, respectively; another secretary and a speaker at a strike rally apparently came in 1848 (Handlin, *Boston's Immigrants*, 76; *Herald*, 19 July, 3, 7 Aug. 1849; *Stimson's Boston Directly* [Boston: Charles Stimson, 1840–49]; U.S. *Seventh Census* (1850); William V. Shannon, *The American Irish* [New York: Macmillan, 1966], 19–24; Oliver MacDonough, "The Irish Famine Emigration to the United States," *Perspectives in American History* 10 [1976]: 373–78). Eleven of the twelve strike leaders identified in local press reports had Irish names: Joseph McMullen, Philip Walsh, John Fleming, William Hennessey, Thomas McGee, Hugh O'Brien, Thomas Adams, William Kelly, Thomas Rowan, Patrick Burns, and Patrick Cannon.

9. *Herald*, 3 Aug. 1849.

10. Handlin's portrait of the Boston Irish during these years suggests some reasons for the tailors' distinctive activism. On one hand, certainly, their rhetoric reflected their sense of themselves as outsiders in a strange and often hostile community. More important, it may be that as Catholics who lived in the "bitter atmosphere of poverty and persecution," they found it difficult to embrace the perfectionist reform spirit that animated many antebellum activists. On the other hand, these strikers were hardly Irishmen who had, in Handlin's words, "a deep respect for class distinctions" with no "firm appreciation of the equality of man" (*Boston's Immigrants*, 125, 131, passim).

11. *Herald*, 3, 15, 22 Aug. 1849. On Treanor, see *Post*, 7 Sept. 1849; Handlin, *Boston's Immigrants*, 29, 160, 210; Commons, *Documentary History* 8:281–83. On Catholicism and these Irish, see especially David W. Miller, "Irish Catholicism and the Great Famine," *Journal of Social History* 9 (1975): 81–98.

12. Even though, in the course of their protracted struggle, the strike became a community issue, eventually involving the city's trade unionists and other labor advocates, the mayor and the courts, the press and the general public. Shortly after the walkout, some employers offered a "compromise bill" of wages; when their employees returned to work, however, they found the old wage system intact. The tailors then organized a "watch" (picket line) of forty strikers at each establishment, which led to several confrontations involving strikers, working tailors, employers, and customers. At least one of these incidents, in which a striking journeyman accused an employers' agent of assault, led to litigation in the Boston courts. In late July, the tailors solicited the mediation of Mayor John Prescott Bigelow, who agreed to help as a private citizen. When only one employer deigned to attend, trade unionists and other activists in the city mounted several large meetings and marches in support of the strike. Meanwhile, the tailors drew up placards indicating which employers had acceded to their demands and which had refused, carrying them through the city's streets. For the early course of the strike, *Herald*, 11 Sept. 1849; tailor picketing, ibid., 30 July, 28 Aug., 5 Sept. 1849; *Bee*, 27 Aug. 1849; tailor's [James Hern] suit against Naham Wetherbee, *Herald*, 5 Sept. 1849; tailors' meetings with Mayor Bigelow, ibid., 9, 11, 14 Aug., 1 Sept. 1849; support meetings, which drew the support of Irish leaders, local clergymen, and coopera-

tionists, as well as trade union activists, ibid., 15, 22 Aug., 7 Sept. 1849; *Post*, 7 Sept. 1849; *Pilot*, 22 Sept. 1849.

13. *Herald*, 11 Aug. 1849.

14. Ibid., 11 Sept. 1849. In early August, the tailors pledged to appeal to the public if the mayor's mediation efforts failed to resolve the dispute. They had not done so to this point, they claimed, because they feared the "spirit of strike" it might engender. Later that month, they resolved to publicly address the "workingmen and citizens of Boston and the neighborhood," though they did not compose the document until early September (ibid., 9, 16 Aug. 1849).

15. The JTS claimed that the employers assailed them in the press—including the libel that the strikers were "'idle, profligate, drunken Irish jours'"—as they "felt the force of public indignation." The blacklist came in early September, when forty clothing dealers placed an advertisement in the *Post* that denounced the tailors "daily stationing a guard over our place of business," called their insults to workers and customers "obnoxious and disgusting," and pledged not to hire anyone known to be a JTS member (*Herald*, 11 Sept. 1849; *Post*, 10 Sept. 1849).

16. The title of the circular was adopted as a motto by Thomas Jefferson, who believed it was the credo of one of Charles I's executioners. Actually, the quotation came from an inscription on a cannon near the grave of John Bradshaw (1603–59), who presided at the trial of the deposed king in 1649 (H. L. Mencken, comp., *A New Dictionary of Quotations on Historical Principles From Ancient and Modern Sources* [New York: Knopf, 1942], 1009; Burton Stevenson, comp., *The Home Book of Quotations: Classical and Modern* [New York: Dodd, Mead, 1967], 1682).

17. Quotation from James 5:1–4. For Luther's use of the passage, see *Avarice*, 42; for the Fall River Mechanics' Association and the *Mechanic*, see (New York) *WMA*, 29 June 1844; *Mechanic*, 22 June 1844. There may be a Chartist connection here (Treanor was an ex-Chartist): in 1839, during a crackdown on workers' meetings, English labor activists assembled on the Sabbath, attended parish churches as a body, and forced the clergy to preach to them from a specific text. On at least one of these occasions, some four thousand Blackburn Chartists attended the Reverend J. W. Whittaker's church and demanded that he preach from James 5 (Harold U. Faulkner, *Chartism and the Churches: A Study in Democracy* [New York: Columbia Univ. Press, 1916], 37).

18. *Herald*, 7 Sept. 1849.

19. *Mechanic*, 4 Jan. 1845; (New York) *WMA* , 11 Jan. 1845. The NEWA officially endorsed the cooperative idea in September 1845, resolving "that protective charity and concert of action in the purchase of the necessaries of life are the only means to the end to obtain that union which will end in their amelioration." The first Division of the WMPU was formed in Boston the following month. During the next two years, the movement spread throughout the region, and in January 1848 the group changed its name to the "New England Protective Union." A factional dispute in 1853, however, inaugurated a slow decline. By the late 1850s, the NEPU concentrated on developing cooperatives among the trades alone and lost its original identity as a working-class movement. Although some cooperative stores survived into the 1860s and 1870s, most had become the property of the storekeepers. See *Harbinger*, 27 Sept. 1845; MBSL, *Eighth Annual Report* (1877), 59–85; Foner, *History of the Labor Movement* 1:181–83; Edwin Charles Rozwenc, *Cooperatives Come to America: The History of the Protective Union Store Movement, 1845–1867* (orig. ed., 1941; repr. ed., 1975, Porcupine Press); Guarneri, *Utopian Alternative*.

20. In his effort to distinguish utopian reformers from those with "a more realistic approach to the industrial problem," Ware mistakenly portrayed the Associationists as opponents of cooperation. "In their earlier enthusiasm," he wrote, "the Associationists would have nothing to do with cooperative stores." Only later were they won over "to a more realistic point of view," he contended, as "they eventually claimed the cooperative movement as part of their own." In fact, the Associationist vision was at the core of the early cooperative movement in New England. One of the committeemen in the Boston Mechanics' and Laborers' Association was John Allen, president of the Lowell Union of Associationists in 1846 and later editor of the Associationist organ, the *Harbinger*. As George Henry Evans reported at the time, the committee's original plan, which called for a scheme of "society ownership, occupation, and use," was for "a sort of Fourier

Association" (Ware, *Industrial Worker,* 163–64; *Harbinger,* 29 Aug. 1846; [New York] *WMA,* 11 Jan. 1845; *Mechanic,* 4 Jan. 1845). See, too, Guarneri, *Utopian Alternative,* 309ff, who argues that working-class Associationists were critical in the formation of the WMPU (calling cooperation the "most direct and radical form" of "working class Fourierism," 313).

21. *Voice,* 17 Dec. 1847.

22. MBSL, *Eighth Annual Report* (1877), 62.

23. Ibid., 77.

24. The first stirrings came in 1847 with a strike among Cincinnati iron-molders; the failure of that strike led to the incorporation of a Journeymen Moulders' Union Foundry and plans to build an entire city of cooperatives ("Home City"), with factories and workshops owned cooperatively and individual homes built with worker dividends (Ross, *Workers on the Edge,* 160–61). The most dramatic events in the "Uprising" took place in New York City (Wilentz, *Chants Democratic,* chap. 10).

25. A response to a threatened wage reduction, the founding of the BPU sparked a national unionization effort among American printers.

26. Even before the release of their public circular in September 1849, the tailors had begun to look to the establishment of a cooperative enterprise. For, although the strike enjoyed substantial community support, the large wholesalers held firm. In early September, they established the Boston Tailors' Associative Union, which drew up plans for a store for the manufacture and sale of clothing. Reflecting the strikers' complaints about the prevailing conditions of work, the clothing was to be produced in "large, lofty, well-ventilated workshops" operating on the ten-hour day (*Herald,* 13 Sept. 1849). The store opened in December and apparently operated throughout the 1850s (ibid., 27 Dec. 1849; *Chronotype,* 15 Sept. 1849; *Post,* 7 Sept. 1849; *Pilot,* 22 Sept. 1849; MBSL, *Eighth Annual Report,* 85–86; Ware, *Industrial Worker,* 195). Seamstresses, cabinetmakers, and bookbinders also established cooperatives during this upsurge.

27. The rising sentiment for producer cooperatives emerged within the WMPU in 1848, but the precise connections between this sentiment and the developments among Boston trade unionists discussed here is unclear (Guarneri, *Utopian Alternative,* 314).

28. Including the involvement of the Associationists (ibid., 316–17).

29. See (Boston) *Protective Union,* (*PU*), 1, 8 Dec. 1849, 2, 10; 9, 16, 23 Feb., 87, 92, 101, 124; 18 May, 185, 190; 27 July, 244, 266–67; 10 Aug, 284; 14, 28 Sept., 321, 337, 341; 19 Oct. 1850, 365. Also, "Out of Sorts," *Bee,* 6 Dec. 1848; reprints from *Pathfinder,* ibid., 8 Dec. 1848; 20 Apr. 1849; "An Old Trade Unionist," *Herald,* 7 Dec. 1848; 26 Jan., 9 Nov., 24 Dec. 1849. For millennial references, see *PU,* ("Emanuel of Labor") S. H. Lloyd, 18 May 1850, 185; ("Workingmen's Jubilee") "Ever-Hope," 15 Dec. 1849, 19; ("New Jerusalem") Lloyd, "The Toiling Hand," 14 Sept. 1850, 321; ("Good Time Coming") editorial, 21 Sept. 1850, 332; Ever-Hope, "Workingmen's Hotel," 9 Mar. 1850, 119; resolutions of printers' meeting at Faneuil Hall, *Herald,* 26 Nov. 1849. For "Christianity grown practical," *PU,* 10 Aug. 1850, 284; for "power of the beast," see "Mechanic," ibid., 9 Feb. 1850, 85. For a composite, see the reports of the BPU's traveling lecturer in ibid., Sept., 5, 19, 26 Oct. 1850, 316, 348, 350, 365, 372.

30. Their weekly meetings were at the offices of the Boston Union of Associationists.

31. Ibid., 1 June, 1850. Also, 18, 25 May, 188, 196; 15 June, 220; 13 July, 252; 14 June, 324; 19 Oct. 1850, 361.

32. See discussion in intro.

33. The ten-hour movement of the early 1850s is described in Ware's *Industrial Worker,* chap. 10. Though he correctly described this activity as a "political" movement that sought the passage of legislation, with apparently little organizational base in the towns, he overstated his case for a radical departure from the 1840s, missing the participation of these men, as well as the ideological continuity described here. Young and Cluer were still engaged in the 1880s (*Quarterly Reports of Directory of the Knights of Labor Assemblies of District No. 30* [Boston, 1886]; McNeill, *Labor Movement,* 105).

34. "Hours of Labor."

35. The association claimed to have settled fifty textile families in Iowa and Missouri. Its cooperatives (Philadelphia Carpet Hall Manufacturing Association and Delaware County Carpet Manufacturing Association in Darby) employed four hundred; the militia was drawn from the workingmen in these cooperatives. They claimed their reading room was visited by "thousands" (Philip Scranton, *Proprietary Capitalism: The Textile Manufacture at Philadelphia, 1800–1885* [New York: Cambridge Univ. Press, 1983], 209; *Jubilee*, Sept., Dec. 1852, 70–71; June, Sept. 1853; May, Aug. 1854; Jan., Sept. 1855, 142–43). The *Jubilee* appeared over a period of three years from 1852 to 1855. On claims about circulation, see ibid., Dec. 1852, 133; Sept. 1855, 142. Compare the association's circulation claims to the New York *WMA* of the early 1830s which, Philip Foner asserts, "probably did not total more than a few hundred copies" (*History of Labor Movement* 1:133n).

36. Wallace, *Rockdale*, 454. Among their leaders were Gen. John Sidney Jones, a longtime and fairly prominent political and business figure in the Philadelphia area, and his wife Fannie Lee Townsend of Rhode Island, the Christian labor reformer who had offered the anticlerical resolution at an early meeting of the Industrial Congress (see chap. 7). Veterans of the Dorrite effort to broaden the suffrage in Rhode Island in the early 1840s, they were active in the Industrial Congresses of the early 1850s. Townsend had experienced a religious conversion just after her first marriage, to Solomon Townsend, Jr., the son of a Providence merchant, and joined the First Baptist Church there, becoming, according to the *Jubilee*, a "pillar" of that congregation (*Jubilee*, Sept. 1855, 113–14). (This was the very same church from which Luther had been expelled.) By her Pioneer days, she had left the church and was a fierce opponent of the contemporary church. Jones regularly attended an Episcopal chapel near his home in Philadelphia and was much more sanguine than his wife that the church could reform itself. Both, though, were most profoundly influenced by the late 1840s rebellion within Hicksite Quakerism known as the "Progressive Friends," of which Jones and Townsend formed the radical fringe. Also called the "Congregational Friends" and the "Friends of Human Progress," the movement began in the late 1840s and spread from Pennsylvania through New York into the Midwest. A species of come-outerism that adopted camp meetings, this religious movement emphasized a return to simplicity over ritual, works over doctrine, and private judgment over discipline, and advocated a range of reforms, including temperance, education, peace, abolitionism, free land, and labor reform. Among their numbers in the 1850s were the sons of Wilmington Working Man Benjamin Webb. See Albert J. Wahl, "Pennsylvania Yearly Meeting of Progressive Friends," *Pennsylvania History* 25 (Apr. 1958): 122–36; *Jubilee*, Oct. 1852. On Jones, a descendant of Pennsylvania Quakers, see A. Atherton Leach Collection (PHS), 91; Philadelphia City Directories (1840–55); *Jubilee*, Dec. 1852; Oct. 1853; Sept. 1855, 110–11. On Townsend (nee Drew), see ibid., Sept. 1855, 109–14.

37. Ibid., Sept. 1852.

38. Ibid., Feb. 1853, 189–90.

39. Ibid., Sept. 1855, 124.

40. Ibid., Oct. 1853. On the belief that the contemporary church was infidel, see, e.g., ibid., Sept. 1852.

41. "A Friend to Justice," ibid., May 1853, 289.

42. "Churchianity," ibid., Aug. 1852.

43. This was, of course, Gutman's central point in "Protestantism and the American Labor Movement."

Tables

Table 4.1. Fall River ten-hour petitioners, nativity, 1842–45

			Identified as:	
Year	Total	Identified	Native	Foreign
1842	81	45 (56%)	41 (91%)	4 (9%)
1843	117	59 (50%)	54 (92%)	5 (8%)
1845	488	259 (53%)	235 (91%)	24 (9%)

NOTE: Percentages in these tables are rounded off and sometimes total more or less than 100%. Repeat signatures were counted each time they appeared.

SOURCES: *Names*—Massachusetts Archives, Nos. 1077/5, 1215a/10, 1587/7, John F. Kennedy Library, Boston. *Nativity*—U.S. *Seventh Census* (1850), Massachusetts and Rhode Island.

Table 4.2. Fall River church membership

Church	General membership 1841	Labor leaders 1830s–1840s	Ten-hour petitioners 1842–45
Baptist	615	15	76
Christian	426	5	52
Congregationalist	324	3	20
Methodist	225	5	34
Quaker	134	1	4
Episcopalian	64[a]	1	10
Unitarian	30[b]	5	14
Universalist[c]	27[d]	0	13
Swedenborgian	3[e]	1	1
Catholic	110[f]	1[g]	16
Free Will Baptist[h]	—	—	—
Millerite[i]	—	—	—
Presbyterian[j]	0	0	3
Total	1,958	37	243
(Nonmembers)		(21)	(360)[k]
% church members		64%	40%[l]

NOTE: Though denominated "members," these figures occasionally include individuals for whom there is evidence of direct involvement in church life (e.g., pew ownership) but no evidence of church membership (e.g., by profession of faith).

[a] The minister of this congregation reported that although there were 64 communicants in his church, the average attendance "seldom exceeded" 125 (*Journal of the Proceedings of the Convention of the Episcopal Diocese in Massachusetts* [Boston, 1841]). [b] Represents the number of communicants. The number of families connected to the church, according to Orin Fowler, was 95 (*Historical Sketch of Fall River*, [Fall River: Benjamin Earl, 1844], 55). [c] Although no records of this church exist, town valuations sometimes listed household heads with shares in the "Berean Temple Association," the name of the local Universalist Society. [d] Denotes membership; the number of families was 35 (*Historical Sketch*, 56). [e] Represents the three families connected to the Church of New Jerusalem in Bridgewater, Mass. (ibid.). [f] Denotes families (ibid.). [g] The baptismal records of St. Mary's Cathedral list "sponsor" and "parent." The marriage records include both the partners and "witnesses." [h] Met in private homes in 1842–43; organized in March 1844 (no records). [i] Meetings, 1842–44 (no records). [j] Organized in 1846; meetings earlier. [k] Forty-two joined later. [l] Of those for whom a precise date of admission could be determined, 122 (54%) joined before 1840; 70 (31%) joined between 1840 and 1843; 32 (14%) joined between 1844 and 1846. Seventy-nine (35%) were revival converts—27 were admitted in 1836, 25 in 1840, 12 in 1842, and 15 in 1843.

SOURCES: *General membership—A Brief History of the First Baptist Church, of Fall River, with the Declaration of Faith, the Church Covenant, and a List of Members* (Fall River, 1872); Fowler, *Historical Sketch*, 54–56; "Minutes of the General Association of Massachusetts" (Boston, 1842); *Journal of the Proceedings of the Convention of the Episcopal Diocese in Massachusetts* (Boston, 1841). *Labor leaders (names)*—see chap. 4, nn. 12–15; *(church membership)*—*A Brief History of the First Baptist Church;* "Membership Book 1, 1829–53," First Christian Church of Fall River, FRHS; "Pew Deeds, 1844–49," Second Christian Church, FRHS; "Membership Book," North Christian

Table 4.2 321

Church, in possession of Albert W. Canedy, Fall River; "Record Book No. 1, 1827–37," "Account Book, 1827–38," "Book A," "Book B, Board of Stewards and Leaders of the First Methodist Church in Fall River, May 13, 1844," First Methodist Episcopal Church of Fall River, United Methodist Church, Fall River; "Record Book No. 1, 1851–54," "Record Book No. 2, 1853–64," Second Methodist Episcopal Church, United Methodist Church, Fall River; "Unitarian Membership Rolls," in possession of the Reverend Bruno J. Visco, Fall River; *The Confession of Faith, and Covenant, of the First Congregational Church, Fall River; with Brief Proof Texts, together with a Catalogue of its Members* (Fall River, 1864); "Parochial Register of the Church of the Ascension, 1841–43," Church of the Ascension, Fall River; "Monthly Meetings of the Society of Friends, Fall River, Massachusetts . . . 1845–62," Church of the Latter Day Saints, Salt Lake City; *Fifteenth Anniversary of the Society of the New Jerusalem at Bridgewater, Massachusetts, May 29, 1883* (Boston, 1883); "Baptismal Records," vol. 1 (1838–49), vol. 2 (1849–60), "Marriage Records," vol. 1 (1838–63), St. Mary's Cathedral, Fall River. *Ten-hour petitioners*—table 4.1, sources; labor leaders, above. *Universalists*—"Tax Valuations for the Town of Fall River, 1840–45," FRHS. *Presbyterians*—table 4.1, sources; "Members Roll No. 1, Record of the Associate Reformed Presbyterian Church, Fall River, Massachusetts, organized June 30, 1846," United Presbyterian Church, Fall River; *The 100th Anniversary of the United Presbyterian Church in Fall River, Massachusetts, 1846–1946* (Fall River, 1946), 3.

Table 4.3. Fall River ten-hour petitioners, church membership by occupation, 1842–45

Church	Occupation							
	Farmer	Retailer	Professional	Clerk	Artisan	Factory worker	Laborer	Other
Baptist	2	6	1	1	14	38	6	2[a]
Christian	8	2	0	1	9	23	2	2[b]
Methodist	1	6	1	2	4	12	3	0
Congregational	0	5	0	1	4	2	2	0
Quaker	0	1	0	0	2	1	0	0
Episcopalian	1	0	0	0	1	3	1	0
Unitarian	0	5	1	1	4	4	0	0
Universalist	0	2	1	1	1	3	0	0
Swedenborgian	0	0	0	0	1	0	0	0
Presbyterian	1	0	0	0	0	2	0	0
Catholic	0	0	0	0	1	6	6	0
Subtotal	13	27	4	6	41	94	20	4
Nonmembers	11	19	2	5	50	65	21	12[c]
Total	24	46[d]	6[e]	11	91	159[f]	41	16
% of total church membership (=394)	6%	12%	2%	3%	23%	40%	10%	4%

NOTE: The absence of city directories for the 1840s requires reading these numbers with caution.

[a] Sailor, marble manufacturer. [b] Sailor, constable. [c] Includes constable (2), teamster (4), sailor (6). [d] Includes those identified as: grocer, bookseller, trader, innkeeper, merchant, ice dealer, victualler, druggist, auctioneer, undertaker, butcher, baker, shoe dealer. [e] Includes clergy, lawyer, physician. [f] In Fall River, unskilled mill hands were not designated "operatives" in the 1850 census, as they were in other Massachusetts industrial towns. The job classifications specifically related to factory work were the more skilled positions: spinner, calico printer, nailor, and so on. Accounting for only 504 workers in the census, these categories did not constitute the total mill work force: the number of *males* employed in Fall River's textile and iron mills exceeded 1,600 by 1845 (Palfrey, *Statistics*, 275–77). It is likely that quite a few of the more than 1,200 "laborers" listed in the census were actually ordinary mill "operatives"; I have identified 67 "laborers" as employees of local mills (representing 42% of the 159 factory workers listed here). It appears from the extant mill records of the period that some farmers and artisans worked part-time for the mill owners as well.

SOURCES: See tables 4.1, 4.2, sources. Occupations—*Fall River Directory* (Fall River: R. & J. Adams, 1853); "Time Book, 1825–29," Annawan Manufacturing, Fall River Iron Works Collection, Baker Library, Harvard Univ., Cambridge, Mass.; "Labor Book, 1835–39," Annawan Manufacturing, FRHS; "Time Books, 1840–47," Fall River Iron Works, Fall River Iron Works Collection, Baker; "Payroll Records," 1829–39, 1841–43, 1845–47, Fall River Iron Works, FRHS; "Records of the

Table 4.4   323

Table 4.4. Fitchburg occupations, general work force and Fitchburg Workingmen's Association

Occupation	Work force 1835–36		Work force 1846–47		FWA 1844–45[a]	
Manufacturer	21	(4%)	28	(3%)	0	
Farmer	206[b]	(39%)	225	(23%)	10	(12%)
Retailer[c]	34	(6%)	80	(8%)	4	(5%)
Professional[d]	14	(3%)	30	(3%)	3	(4%)
Clerk[e]	1	(0%)	19	(2%)	5	(6%)
Artisan[f]	140	(26%)	265	(27%)	36[g]	(42%)
Factory worker[h]	45	(8%)	112	(11%)	10[i]	(12%)
Laborer[j]	70	(13%)	221	(22%)	13[k]	(15%)
Other[l]	2	(0%)	8	(1%)	4[m]	(5%)
Total	533	(99%)	988	(100%)	85	(101%)

[a] Since most of the data for the FWA were derived from the 1846–47 directory and the U.S. *Seventh Census* (1850), this picture of the association is biased toward its more stable members. Given the greater persistence one might expect of groups such as merchants, professionals, and farmers, it is likely that the numbers of mill workers and laborers have been understated here. This problem applies almost exclusively to the rank-and-file, as nearly the entire leadership were identified by occupation.

It was impossible to identify the occupations of most FWA women, who made up 11% of the membership. The 1850 census lists occupational data for household head only. Five of the fifteen women in the association do appear there, but the occupation of only one is listed. "Records of the First Methodist Episcopal Church" revealed that two were domestics and one was a factory worker; I was unable to find any information for the remaining seven. The presence of the two domestics suggests that Kirkpatrick is mistaken in identifying all of the women as factory workers (*City and the River*, 1:166). She was clearly following Ebenezer Bailey, whose short history of the FWA in the 1890s had concluded, "it is probable that most of the females [in the organization] worked in the mills" (Bailey, "An Early Workingmen's Association," 247). Still, there is no evidence that they were middle-class reformers or wives of male activists. Most likely, the FWA women performed some kind of unskilled labor in Fitchburg.   [b] Fifteen are listed as farmers *and* artisans and are included in both categories here.   [c] Includes trader, dealer, seller, hotelkeeper, barkeeper, restaurant keeper, druggist, barber, stage proprietor, butcher, baker, miller, grain dealer, tailor with shop, "merchant tailor," contractor.   [d] Includes lawyer, physician, minister, teacher, student.   [e] Includes store clerk, cashier, bookkeeper.   [f] Includes car builder, hat presser, bridge builder, pumpmaker, daguerreotype artist, railroad engineer.   [g] Includes five masters (one master mariner) and thirty-one journeymen (one journeyman baker).   [h] Includes millwright, wheelwright, reedmaker, machinist, iron founder, turner, dyer, foundry worker, scythe maker, papermaker, engineer, operative.   [i] Includes three skilled, seven operative.   [j] Includes ostler, teamster, stableman, stage driver, watchman, nurseryman.   [k] Includes domestics.   [l] Includes public official, railroad conductor, agent, overseer, railroad president, bank president.   [m] Teamsters, mariners.

SOURCES: *Occupations—Fitchburg Directory and Registry for the Year, 1835–36* (Fitchburg: William S. Wilder, 1836); *Brown's Almanac: Pocket Memorandum and Account Book, 1847, with Fitchburg Business Directory for the Year, 1846–47* (Fitchburg: S. & C. Shepley, 1847). The 1835–36 directory was the first of its kind in Fitchburg; another listing was compiled in 1845–46, but it did not list occupations. Note that the number of factory workers is drastically understated here, as the directories did not list children and women (a few widows were included but in only one case was an occupation provided). The 1845 Massachusetts census recorded 267 employees working in Fitchburg's textile, paper, and scythe mills alone. Compiled from Palfrey, *Statistics*, 100–102. *FWA—Fitchburg Business Directory . . . 1846–47;* U.S. *Seventh Census* (1850); "Records of the First Methodist Episcopal Church of Fitchburg," Faith United Parish, Fitchburg; "Valuations of the Town of Fitchburg, 1844," Fitchburg Town Hall. *FWA names*—"FWA Record Book."

Table 4.5. Fitchburg population growth, 1790–1850

Year	Population	Change
1790	1,151	
1800	1,390	239 (21%)
1810	1,566	176 (13%)
1820	1,736	170 (11%)
1830	2,169	433 (25%)
1840	2,604	435 (20%)
1845	3,883	1,279 (49%)
1850	5,120	1,237 (32%)

SOURCES: George A. Hitchcock, "From Hamlet to City," *FHS Proceedings* (1914), 5:261–69; *Sentinel,* 12 Sept. 1845.

Table 4.6 325

Table 4.6. Fitchburg church membership

Church	General membership 1844	FWA 1844–45
Calvinistic Congregational	367[a]	9[b] (19%)
First Parish (Unitarian)	203[c]	6[d] (13%)
Trinitarian (Third Congregational)	47[e]	6[f] (13%)
Baptist	244[g]	7[h] (15%)
Methodist	166[i]	19[j] (40%)
Universalist	50[k]	1[l] (2%)
Freewill Baptist[m]	—	—
Millerite[m]	—	—
Total	1,077	48[n]

[a] Membership as of 1 Jan. 1845. [b] Six joined before 1842–43 and 3 joined in the 1842–43 revival. [c] Number of polls, 1844. [d] Six joined before 1842–43. [e] Membership at date of formation, Apr. 1843. [f] Four joined before 1842–43 and 2 joined after 1843. [g] Membership in Dec. 1844. [h] Three joined before 1842–43, 3 joined in the 1842–43 revival, and 1 joined after 1843. [i] Membership in Dec. 1844. [j] Two joined before 1842–43, 15 joined in the 1842–43 revival, and 4 joined after 1843; by 1844–45, two had left to join the Baptists. [k] It is unclear when the one FWA Universalist, C. N. Pratt, joined the church. [l] Estimate based on a retrospective list of 150 members in 1871; 31 names from this roster appeared in the 1847 directory. [m] No records. [n] Represents 42% of total FWA membership.

NOTE: See table 4.4, sources.

SOURCES: *General membership*—Hitchcock, *A History of the Calvinistic Congregational Church and Society, Fitchburg, Massachusetts* (Fitchburg, 1902), appendix (includes list of members and year of entry, 1823–1902); "Minutes of the General Association of Massachusetts" (Boston, 1845); "Valuation of the First Parish Church of Fitchburg, 1844, 1845"; *The Principles and Rules, with the Articles of Faith and Covenant, of the Trinitarian Church, Fitchburg; with a List of the Officers and Members* (Fitchburg: W. J. Merriam, 1843); "Registry of Deeds of the Third Congregational Society in Fitchburg, Book I, 1844–55," FHS; "Records of the First Baptist Church of Fitchburg," FHS; "Records of the First Methodist Episcopal Church of Fitchburg," Faith United Parish, Fitchburg; *History of the First Universalist Society of Fitchburg, Massachusetts, organized October 9, 1844* (Fitchburg, 1894) [includes list of deceased members who joined before 1871].

Table 4.7. Fitchburg church membership by occupation

Church	Occupation								
	Manufacturer	Farmer	Retailer	Professional	Clerk	Artisan	Factory worker	Laborer	Other
Calvinistic[a] (=116)	2	59	7	3	2	28	8	6	1[b]
Parish[c] (=183)	8	61[d]	17	7	4	45	17	21	3[e]
Parish[f] (=152)	14	33	36	11	3	35	7	10	3[g]
Trinitarian[h] (=18)	1	7	3	0	0	6	1	0	0
Baptist[i] (=52)	3	13	7	0	0	14	10	4	1[j]
Methodist[k] (=62)	0	9[l]	1	0	0	24	17	9	2[m]
Universalist[n] (=34)	0	8	6	0	0	10	3	5	2[o]
Total (=617)	28	190	77	21	9	162	63	55	12

[a] Calvinistic Congregational; compiled from church membership rolls (1823–45) and directories (1835–36, 1846–47). [b] Master of almshouse. [c] Compiled from church valuation (1835) and directory (1846–47). [d] Includes four farmer-artisans. [e] Public official, bank president, railroad president. [f] First Parish (Unitarian); compiled from church valuation (1847) and directory (1846–47). [g] Overseer, agent, railroad conductor. [h] Trinitarian (Third Congregational); compiled from original members (1843) and directory (1846–47). [i] Compiled from church membership rolls (1833–45) and directories (1835–36, 1846–47). [j] One is listed as farmer and carpenter and is counted twice here, as farmer and artisan. [k] Compiled from church membership rolls (1831–45) and directories (1835–36, 1846–47). [l] Overseer. [m] Deputy sheriff, agent. [n] Compiled from church membership list (pre-1871) and directory (1846–47). [o] "Railroad man," "Botany Physician office."

Sources: See tables 4.4, 4.6.

Table 4.8. Fitchburg Workingmen's Association, church membership by occupation

Church	Farmer	Retailer	Professional	Occupation — Clerk	Artisan	Factory worker	Laborer
Calvinistic[a]	1	3	1	1	2	0	0
Parish[b]	1	0	0	1	2	0	1[c]
Trinitarian[d]	0	1	1	0	4	0	0
Baptist	1	0	0	1[e]	4	2	0
Methodist	1	0	0	1	4	3	6
Total	4	4	2	4	16	5	7

[a]Calvinistic Congregational. [b]First Parish (Unitarian). [c]Though listed as a farmer in 1835 and in the 1850 census, this individual is listed as a laborer in the 1847 directory. [d]Trinitarian (Third Congregational). [e]Formerly a Methodist.

SOURCES: See tables 4.4, 4.6.

Table 4.9. Boston labor leaders, church membership, 1830–60

Church	1830s[a]	1840s Reformers[b]	1840s Unionists[c]	1850s Reformers[d]	1850s Unionists[e]	Total
Members						
Baptist	8	2	0	2	6	18
Methodist	1	1	1	0	2	5
Congregational	6	3	3	0	6	18
Unitarian	5	3	1	3	1	13
Universalist	0	0	1	1	0	2
Episcopalian	3	1	1	1	11	17
Catholic	3	1	6	0	32	42
Swedenborgian	1	0	0	0	1	2
Total	27	11	13	7	59	117
Others						
Nonmembers	153	47	34	23	144	401
Joined later	33	4	0	0	6	43
Members and others						
Total	213	62	47	30	209	561
% members	13%	18%	28%	23%	28%	21%

[a] Includes delegates and officers of the New England Association of Farmers, Mechanics and Other Working Men, the BTU, and various city unions. [b] Includes delegates and officers of the NEWA and the Workingmen's Protective Union. [c] Includes officers and committeemen of the Journeymen Printers' Union and the Journeymen Tailors' Society. [d] Includes delegates to ten-hour conventions and members of the Workingmen's Protective Union. [e] Includes officers and committeemen of 30 trade unions.

Table 4.9   329

SOURCES: *Names*—(Boston) *Working-man's Advocate,* 4 Dec. 1830; *NEA,* 23 Feb., 22 Mar., 5, 19 Apr., 21, 28 June, 5, 26 July, 11 Oct. 1832; 2 Aug., 26 Sept., 3, 10, 17 Oct., 9 Nov. 1833; 30 Aug. 1834; *Reformer,* 3 Nov. 1834; *Post,* 6, 15 Mar., 7, 8 July 1834; 17 Apr., 6, 7 May, 28 July, 1 Aug. 1835; 7, 17, 23 Sept. 1849; *Transcript,* 27 July 1835; *ICR,* 4, 11 July, 8, 22 Aug., 26 Dec. 1835; 12 Apr. 1836; (Fall River) *Patriot,* 21 May, 1 Oct. 1840; *Voice,* 12 June, 10 July, 7, 14, 21 Nov. 1845; 16 Jan. 1846; 29 Oct., 10, 17 Dec. 1847; 17 Mar., 28 May 1848; (Boston) *New Era,* 27 July 1848; (New York) *WMA,* 7, 14, 21 Sept., 19 Oct. 1844; 11 Jan. 1845; (Boston) *New England Mechanic,* 8 Mar. 1845; (Boston) *Investigator,* 20 Nov. 1844; *Mechanic,* 4 Jan. 1845; *Third Grand Rally; Harbinger,* 27 May 1848; *South Boston Gazette,* 25 Mar., 28 Oct. 1848; 24 Aug., 14 Sept., 10 Aug. 1850; 18 Oct., 1 Nov. 1851; 2, 6, 9 Oct. 1852; 30 Apr., 18 May, 14 Nov. 1853; *Chronotype,* 20 May, 9 Dec. 1848; 29 Sept. 1849; *Herald,* 12 Apr., 2 Oct., 21 Dec. 1848; 19, 23, 28, 30 July, 3, 6, 7, 8, 11, 14, 15, 16, 22 Aug., 7, 11 Sept., 22 Dec. 1849; 10 June, 11 Oct. 1850; 16 June, 22 Nov. 1851; 28 Jan., 5, 9 Feb., 27, 30 Sept., 1, 6 Oct., 15 Nov., 13, 16, 17, 18, 21 Dec. 1852; 31 Mar., 1, 4, 5, 8, 12, 13, 15, 18, 19, 21, 22, 26, 28, 30 Apr., 4, 14, 17 May, 1, 3, 4, 5 June, 4 July, 29 Sept. 1853; 1, 7, 13, 25, 28 Mar., 1, 3 Apr., 1 May, 8, 10 June, 4 Aug., 11 Dec. 1854; 8 Jan., 26 Mar., 18 Oct., 29 Oct. 1855; 14 Mar., 16 June, 15 Sept. 1856; 21 June 1858; (Boston) *Pilot,* 30 June 1849; 3 July 1858; (Boston) *Irish-American,* 31 July, 4 Sept. 1858; (Fall River) *News,* 6 Oct. 1853. *Church membership*—"Register of the Baldwin Place (Baptist) Church," Andover Newton Library, Newton, Mass.; *A Concise History of the Baldwin Place Baptist Church, Together with the Articles of Faith and Practice* (Boston, 1854); *Articles of Faith and Covenant of the Bowdoin Square Baptist Church, With a List of the Members* (Boston, 1849); *Manual of the Central Square Baptist Church, Boston* (Boston, 1870); "Membership Book" (1807–64), Charles Street Baptist Church, Andover Newton Library; *A Brief History of the First Baptist Church in Boston, With a List of the Present Members* (Boston, 1839); "Records of the Harvard Street Baptist Church, Commencing January 1846, No. 2," Andover Newton Library; *The History of the South Baptist Church, Boston, With the Articles of Faith, Covenant, and List of Members, 1865* (Boston, 1865); Rowe Street (Baptist) Church, *A Brief History . . . with the Declaration of Faith, Church Covenant, List of Members, Etc.* (Boston, 1872); "Record Book No. 1 of the Shawmut Avenue Baptist Church, March 3, 1856, to May 24, 1877," Andover Newton Library; *A History of the Union Baptist Church, Boston* (Boston, 1857); "Index to Baptismal Records" (1823–53), Holy Cross Church, Boston Archdiocese Archives, Boston; "Index to Baptismal Records" (1836–49, 1850–58), St. Mary's Church, Boston Archdiocese Archives; *Articles of Bowdoin Street Church;* "List of Original Members," Church of Unity (Congregationalist), Congregational Library, Boston; *Church Manual of the East Street Orthodox Congregational Church in South Boston* (Boston, 1860); *The Confession of Faith and Covenant of the Edwards Congregational Church, in Boston, With a List of the Members, May, 1850* (Boston, 1850); *Articles of Faith and Covenant of the Eliot Street Church, Roxbury, Massachusetts* (Boston, 1836); *Names of Members of the First Church (Congregational),* (Cambridge, 1861); *Articles of Faith and Covenant of the First Church (Congregational), Charlestown* (Boston, 1842); *Articles of Faith and Covenant of the First Church (Congregational), Charlestown* (Boston, 1856); *Manual of the First Evangelical Congregational Church in Cambridgeport* (Boston, 1857); *Brief History of the First Free Congregational Church* (Boston, 1840); *First Religious Society in Roxbury: An Act of Incorporation* (Boston, 1871); *Origins and Formation of the Franklin Street Church, in Boston* (Boston, 1836); *Form of Administration . . . and a List of the Members of Garden Street Church, Boston* (Boston, 1842); *Articles of Faith and Covenant of the Hanover Street Church* (Boston, 1826); *Manual for the Use of the Members of the Church of Christ in Lyden Chapel* (Boston, 1846); *Articles of Faith and Covenant of the Mariners' Church* (Boston, 1854); *Condensed History and Manual of Maverick Congregational Church* (Boston, 1894); *The Confession of Faith and Covenant of the Mt. Vernon Congregational Church* (Boston, 1857); *The Confession of Faith and Form of Covenant, of the Old South Church* (Boston, 1855); *The Articles of Faith, and the Covenant, of Park Street Church* (Boston, 1859); *Alphabetical List of Members,* Phillips Church (Boston, 1872); *Articles of Faith and Covenant of the Pine Street Church* (Boston, 1833); *Articles of Salem Street Church; Covenant and Declaration of Faith, of the Second Church of Christ in Dorchester* (Boston,

TABLE 4.9

1828); *Articles of Faith and Covenant of the Shawmut Congregational Church* (Boston, 1857); *Confessional of Faith . . . of Union Church* (Boston, 1852); *Manual of Vine Street Church, Roxbury* (Boston, 1861); West Church, "Admissions to Communion" (1818–53), *New England Historical and Genealogical Register,* 94:38–47, 155–63, 290–92; *Articles of Faith and Covenant of the Winthrop Church* (Boston, 1834); "Index to Marriage Records," Christ Church, Diocesan Library, Boston; *A Sketch of the History of the Parish of the Advent* (Boston, 1894); "Records of the Church of the Messiah," Diocesan Library; *Constitutions of the Male and Female Parochial and Missionary Association of Grace Church* (Boston, 1838); "Records of Grace Church," 2 vols., Diocesan Library; "Records of St. John's Church," Diocesan Library; "Records of St. Mark's Church," Diocesan Library; "Records of St. Mary's Church," Diocesan Library; "Records of St. Matthew's Church," Diocesan Library; "Records of St. Paul's Church," Diocesan Library; "Records of St. Stephen's Chapel," Diocesan Library; *Trinity Church* (Boston, 1884); "Membership Records" (1860–73), Eighth Methodist Episcopal Church, Boston University Theology Library; Bromfield Street Church, *Directory of 1885* (Boston, 1885); "Record Book" (1838–54), "Record Book" (1851–76), Bromfield Street Church, Theology Library; "Record Book" (1837–62), Fifth Methodist Episcopal Church, Theology Library; "Record Book" (1831–48), "Record Book" (1844–48), First Methodist Episcopal Church, Theology Library; "Record Books" (1820–54, 1820–40, 1854–67), High Street Methodist Episcopal Church, Theology Library; "Membership Records" (1837–98, 1847–83), Monument Square Methodist Episcopal Church, Theology Library; *History of the North Russell Street Methodist Episcopal Church* (Boston, 1861); "Membership Records" (1850–1911), Saratoga Street Methodist Episcopal Church, Theology Library; "Membership Records" (1845–1909), Sixth Methodist Episcopal Church, Theology Library; "Pew Records" (1857–74), Third Methodist Church, Theology Library; "Membership Records" (1838–64), Winthrop Street Methodist Episcopal Church, Theology Library; *Sketch of the History of the Boston Society; The Manifesto Church: Records of the Church in Brattle Square* (Boston, 1902); *Act of Incorporation and By-Laws of the Bulfinch Street Society (Boston, 1841);* "Record Book" (1836–39), Pitt Street Unitarian Church, Andover-Harvard Library, Cambridge, Mass.; "Record Book," Church of the Disciples, Andover-Harvard Library; "Subscribers" (1842), "Pew Holders" (1810–60), Federal Street Church, Massachusetts Historical Society (MHS); "Records of the First Church in Boston, 1630–1868," in *Publications of the Colonial Society of Massachusetts,* Vol. XL Collections, Richard Pierce, ed. (Boston, 1961), 473–97; *Hollis Street Church from Mather Mayles to Thomas Starr King, 1732–1861* (Boston, 1877); "Pew Owners" (1827–50), King's Chapel, MHS; "Membership Book," New North Church, Boston Public Library (BPL), Rare Books Department; "Baptisms," "Pew Deeds," New South Church, BPL, Rare Books; South Congregational Church, *Memorials of the History . . . of the South Congregational Church* (Boston, 1878); *Historical Sketch of the Twelfth Congregational Society* (Boston, 1863); "Records of the Twenty-Eighth Congregational Society," MHS; Twenty-Eighth Congregational Society, *The Parker Fraternity* (Boston, 1864); *The Confession of Faith . . . of the Fifth Universalist Society* (Boston, 1837); "Pew Appraisals and Lists of Owners" (1837–39), First Universalist Church, Andover-Harvard Library; First Universalist Society in Charlestown, *Articles of Faith . . . in the Year of Our Lord, 1803* (Charlestown, 1844); "Record Book" (1852–61), Fourth Universalist Church, Andover-Harvard Library; *The Compact . . . of the Second Universalist Church* (Boston, 1849).

Table 5.1 331

Table 5.1. Wilmington Working Men, nativity, 1829–31

Group	Delaware		Pennsylvania		Other	
	Wilmington	Other	Philadelphia	Other	U.S.	Europe
AWPNCC[a] (=50)	6	5	1	3	1	1
WMP[b] (=50[c])	4	7	0	3	2	0
Subtotal	10	12	1	6	3	1
Total	22		7		4	

[a] Officers, chairmen of meetings, secretaries, committeemen, and "hosts" of meetings. Of last (4 in all), at least one was also a committeeman. [b] Candidates on Working Men's Tickets, officers of meetings (2), "hosts" of meetings (1). [c] Three were also members of the AWPNCC.

SOURCES: *Names—MFP*, 14 Nov. 1829; *DFP*, 17 Apr., 8, 29 May, 17, 24, July, 21 Aug., 11, 25 Sept., 9 Oct. 1830; 2 Apr., 20 Aug., 10, 17 Sept., 1 Oct. 1831. *Nativity—U.S. Seventh Census* (1850), Delaware.

Table 5.2. Wilmington Working Men, church affiliation

Group/ denomination	Type of affiliation			Total
	Member	Member II[a]	Affiliated[b]	
AWPNCC (=50)	19 (38%)	7 (14%)	7[c] (14%)	33 (66%)
Quakers	10	0	1	11
Methodists	2	6	0	8
Presbyterians	4	1	2	7
Episcopalians	2	0	1	3
Baptists	1	0	1	2
WMP (=50)	26 (52%)	9 (18%)	1[d] (2%)	36 (72%)
Quakers	12	2	0	14
Methodists	4	5	0	9
Presbyterians	4	1	0	5
Episcopalians	5	1	0	6
Baptists	1	0	0	1

[a] Evidence of earlier or later membership, or listed with no date. [b] Married by minister; Sabbath school subscriber; buried in church cemetery; from religious family. [c] Two could not be identified by denomination. [d] Not identified by denomination.

NOTE: See table 5.1, sources.

SOURCES: *Church membership*—Conrad, *History of Delaware;* idem, "Old Delaware Clock-Makers," *Papers of the Historical Society of Delaware* 3 (Wilmington: DHS, 1897–98); Scharf, *History of Delaware;* Lincoln, *Wilmington, Delaware;* Francis A. Cooch, *Little Known History of Newark, Delaware and Its Environs* (Newark: Press of Kells, 1936); Zebley, *Churches of Delaware;* "Every Evening," *History of Wilmington;* Theophilus K. Jones, *Recollections of Wilmington: From 1845 to 1860* (Wilmington: DHS, 1909); Jeanette Eckman Biographical Boxes, DHS; Genealogy File, Hagley Museum and Library, Wilmington; "Brandywine Manufacturers Sunday School (BMSS) Records," Hagley; "Friends List"; "Wilmington Friends Meeting Records," DSA; Benjamin Ferris, "A Sketch of the Proceedings" (intro. by Martin A. Klaver), *Delaware History* 13 (Apr. 1968): 67–80; "Kelso Methodist Records," DHS; "Asbury Methodist Church Records," DHS; "Asbury Membership Records" (1815–1917), DSA; "Cecil Circuit Register" (1848–69), Christiana Methodist Episcopal Church, DSA; "New Castle Methodist Episcopal Church Records," DSA; "Union Methodist Episcopal Church Records" (1816–1937), DSA; "Newark Union Meeting House Trustee Minutes" (1845–1939), DSA; "Brandywine Methodist Episcopal Church Records," DSA; "First Presbyterian Church Records" (1838–1920), microfilm, DHS; "Central Presbyterian Church Records" (1855–1920), microfilm, DHS; "Red Clay Creek Presbyterian Church Records" (1827–1971), microfilm, DHS; "White Clay Creek Presbyterian Church Records," DSA; "St. James Protestant Episcopal Church Sabbath School Class Book" (1827–39), DHS; "Hanover Presbyterian Church Records" (1772–1915), DSA; "Holy Trinity (Old Swede's) Church Records" (1800–60), bound photostats, DHS; "Welsh Tract Baptist Church Trustee Minutes" (1809–77), DSA.

Table 6.1. Rochester activists and others, occupations, 1829–49

Group	Occupation								
	Manufacturer	Farmer	Retailer	Professional	Clerk	Artisan	Factory worker	Laborer	Other
Mutual Association 1829 (=101)	1	3	20	1	1	68	2	0	5[a]
Shylock Association 1829 (=29)	0	0	6	1	0	8	0	0	14[b]
Friends[c] 1831 (= 7)	0	0	2	1	0	2	0	0	2[b]
WMBERS[d] 1841–43 (=16)	0	1	3	1	2	9	0	0	0
WMC[e] 1843–44 (=56)	0	1	2	0	0	48	0	3	2[f]
Hours[g] 1846–48 (= 8)	1	0	0	0	0	7	0	0	0
MMPA[h] 1848–49 (=15)	2	0	1	0	0	12	0	0	0

[a] Boatmen (2), constables (2), teamster.   [b] Merchants, bankers.   [c] Friends of Liberal Principles and Equal Rights.   [d] Working Men's Benevolent and Equal Rights Society: officers of meetings, committees on resolutions.   [e] Workingmen's Club ("The Democratic Working Men's Equal Rights Anti-Duebill Club"): candidates, ward committees on vigilance.   [f] Teamster, gardener.   [g] Officers and committee members of meeting to celebrate English Ten Hour Law (1847): officers, committee members, and speakers at meetings for shorter-hours legislation (1848).   [h] Mechanics Mutual Protection Association: officers and participants (addresses, toasts) at MMPA Festival; Rochester officials of national organization.

Sources: Names—"Minutes and Proceedings of the Mutual Association"; Craftsman, 24 Feb. 1829; 19, 26 Jan. 1831; "Proceedings of Friends"; RDA, 1 July, 18 Aug., 1841; 15, 22 Mar., 5 Apr. 1842; 23, 26 Mar., 13 June 1843; 5, 10 Oct. 1844; 5 July 1847; 18 Sept., 26 Oct., 2, 3, 4, 9 Nov. 1848; 1 Jan 1849; RDD, 4, 18 July, 4 Oct. 1843; 20 Aug. 1849. Occupations—Rochester directories, 1827, 1834, 1838, 1841, 1844, 1845–46, 1847–48, 1849–50, 1851–52, 1853–54.

Table 6.2. Rochester labor advocates, church affiliation, 1834–49

Group	Member	Affiliated	Joined later	Total
Carpenters, 1833–35[a] (=95)	21 (22%)	0	12[b] (13%)	33 (35%)
RTA, 1839–40[c] (=23)	9 (39%)	2[d] (9%)	3[e] (13%)	14 (61%)
Clerks, 1841–44[f] (=145)	41 (28%)	6[g] (4%)	20[h] (14%)	67 (46%)
WMBERS (=15)	3 (20%)	3[i] (20%)	4[j] (27%)	10 (67%)
Pro-WMBERS (=11)	4 (36%)	0	3[k] (27%)	7 (63%)
Subtotal, WMBERS (=26)	7 (27%)	3 (12%)	7 (27%)	17 (66%)
WMC (=89)	18 (20%)	16[l] (18%)	5[m] (6%)	39 (44%)
Hours (=17)	6 (35%)	3[n] (18%)	1[o] (6%)	9 (59%)
RTA II, 1848[p] (=7)	3 (43%)	3[q] (43%)	0	6 (86%)
MMPA (=25)	6 (24%)	8[r] (32%)	3[s] (12%)	17 (68%)
Total (=427)	111 (26%)	41 (10%)	51 (12%)	203 (48%)

NOTE: Though 98% of those identified here were directly involved in labor protest (activists), I have used the more inclusive term "advocate" because of the inclusion of WMBERS supporters (i.e., pro-WMBERS). A few here were involved in more than one organization or movement (13 of 414). Their affiliations are recorded each time they appear; although this calculation slightly inflates the aggregates, the table thus provides a more accurate sense of the number and percentage of church-affiliated advocates at any one point in time.

[a] Officers of JCJS meetings, 1833–34; JCJS petition, 1834; JCJS officers and committeemen, 1835. [b] Eight appear in extant church records from 1836 to 1846. Two were stewards in the First Methodist Church (1836, 1837); another was a Methodist trustee (1843). On Universalists Isaac Hellins and Schuyler Moses, see chap. 6, nn. 79, 83. Two appear in the records of the Presbyterian Church (1839, 1840); another is listed as a Unitarian pew owner in 1843 when the church was organized; two married in the church (1835, 1840); two were buried in the church (1840, 1874). [c] Rochester Typographical Association: founders' committee, constitutional officers, publishers and editors of the association's newspaper, the *Working-Man's Advocate* (1839–40). [d] Married by reverend (1837); baptized child in the church (1840). [e] Unitarian records, early 1840s (2); married by minister (1844). [f] Shorter-hours petitioners. [g] Two members of the

Table 6.2 335

evangelical Moral Reform Society; delegate to the Sabbath Convention (1842); married by clergymen (3). [h] Twelve married later by ministers (1843 [2], 1844 [2], 1845, 1846 [2]), 1847, 1848, 1849 [2], 1850). Seven appear later in church records from the 1840s and early 1850s. One was buried in the Free Will Baptist Church in 1845. [i] Two married by reverends. Another, Justin B. Jones, went to the quarterly meeting of the Methodist Church (June 1841) asking for a reconsideration of his dismissal for neglect of church duties (denied). But, evidence of his lifelong devotion to the faith can be gleaned from a poem he penned in 1853, "To My Mother on Her Sixty-Eighth Birthday." To this member of the Methodist Episcopal Church in Woodbridge, Connecticut, he wrote, " 'Twas my mother first pointed to Heaven the way,/And my tongue could but lisp when she taught me to pray" (*UA*, 15 June 1858). [j] Unitarian pew holder (1843); Baptist member (1843); baptized child in Catholic Church (1848); funeral at the Grace (Episcopal) Church (1855). [k] Unitarian subscriber (1842); Sabbath school librarian, Second Baptist Church (1842–46); buried, the Brick Presbyterian (1842). [l] Eleven baptized or buried children in the church; three married by reverends; member of tract society; Justin Jones (see note i). [m] Donated money to Unitarians (1846); Methodist leader (1851); attended Methodist meeting (years unknown); married by a minister (1845); baptized child in the church (1846). [n] Marriage and baptisms; a witness to a marriage. George S. Cooper (editor of the *National Reformer*), though critical of the state of religion of his day, insisted on his devotion to religion: "Men will wrangle for religion; write for it; fight for it; die for it; anything but—live for it" (quoted in *UA*, obit., 15 Feb. 1884, in "Peck's SB," 1:3). [o] Married by reverend (1850). [p] Committeemen, officers of reformulated Typographical Association. [q] Married by clergymen. [r] Two married by reverends; four were witnesses, married, baptized children, and/or were buried in the church; associated with the Sabbath school of the Bethel Free (Presbyterian) Church; member of the evangelical Moral Reform Society (1836). [s] Two owned Unitarian pews in 1853; Charles G. Cooper (see note n).

NOTE: Documentation for the Tengwall Scrapbooks is indicated below in this format: T-1 [book] SB, 54 [page].

SOURCES: *Names*—table 6.1; *RDA*, 9 Apr. 1833; 1 Oct. 1841; *RDD*, 17, 19 Apr. 1834; 17 Jan., 6, 25 Mar., 12 May 1835; 12 Dec. 1848; *WMA* 19, 23 Oct., 18 Dec. 1839; 30 Jan., 17, 26 Feb. 1840; 5 Oct. 1844; *RR*, 30 Nov., 28 Dec. 1848. In Rochester, available church records were not as complete as elsewhere, but I did benefit from an extensive biographical card file at the RPL (Ready Reference File, Biographical Section, Local History Division), which allowed me to trace a number of individuals in local newspaper obituaries, scrapbooks, and so on. These sources are listed under the heading *individuals*, below. *Church membership*—"Meeting Minutes" (1839, 1842), "List of Members" (1851), First Baptist Church, Rochester; "Original Members of the Second Baptist Church," First Baptist Church, Rochester; "Minutes of the New York Monroe (Baptist) Association," URL; "Trustee Records" (1847–72), First Baptist Church, Rochester; "Records of the Freewill Baptist Church, East Penfield, Monroe County, N.Y." (typescript, RPL); "Register of Marriages" (1843–97), vol. 1, "Register of Baptisms" (1843–67), vol. 1, St. Mary's Catholic Church, Rochester; "Baptismal Records" (from 1832), St. Patrick's Catholic Church, St. Anthony of Padua Church, Rochester; "Records of the Congregational Church of Parma and Greece," vol. 2, RPL; "Records of the St. Luke's Episcopal (SLE) Church" (1820–38), SLE Church, Rochester; "Records of the St. Paul's Episcopal (SPE) Church" (1831–39), SPE Church, Rochester; "Episcopalian Church Records" (1820–51), 2 parts, Rochester Genealogical Society, 1982; "Trustees' Book" (1820–81), First Methodist Church, "Records of the Quarterly Conference" (1821–48), First Methodist Church, East Society (ES) (1836–60), "Steward's Book" (1832–47), ES, First Methodist Church, Asbury-First United Methodist Church, Rochester; "Records of the Society of Friends (Quakers), Monroe County, N.Y." (c. 1740–1920), Cornell Univ. Library; John Cox, Jr., and Percy E. Clapp, "Quakers in Rochester and Monroe County," RHSP 14 (1936): 97–112; *Catalogue of the Members of the First Presbyterian Church in Rochester, from its organization, August 22, 1815* (Rochester, 1829); *A*

1840); *A Catalogue of the Members of the First Presbyterian Church, in Rochester, June 1850* (Rochester, 1850); "Annual Statistics" (1825–95), "Trustee Records" (1826–1973), "Sabbath School" (2 vols., 1827–43, 1843–55), "Session Minutes" (1831–40, 1838–55), Second (Brick) Presbyterian Church, 1825–95, PHS, Philadelphia; *A Catalogue of the Members of the Third Presbyterian Church in Rochester, from its Organization, February 28, 1827, to January 2, 1832* (Rochester: Observer Press, 1832); "Trustee Minutes" (1844–57), "Sabbath School Minutes" (1836–40, 1840, 1841–42, 1842–43, 1843–44), Bethel Free Church, PHS; "Membership Records" (1836–1906), "Baptisms" (1832–1906), Bethel Sabbath School, PHS; "Session Minutes" (1838–46), with register of names (1828–62), Fourth Presbyterian Church, PHS; University of Rochester (UR) Register—Unitarians; "Subscription Book" (1840), "Subscribers" (1842), "Deeds" (1843), "Records of the Treasurers" (1841–67), "Treasurers' Accounts" (1842–48), "A. B. Leases," "Records of the Unitarian Church of Rochester, N.Y.," RPL; "Records of the Sabbath School of the First Universalist Society of Rochester" (1839–52), Box V, First Universalist Society, Rochester; Raymond H. Arnot, "A Seventy-Five Years Record of the First Universalist Church of Rochester, New York" (typescript), 1933, RPL; "Records of the County Clerk of Rochester," RPL; *History of the First Universalist Church of Rochester, New York* (n.p., n.d.), RPL. *Individuals*—John Alling: "Barton Obituary Book" (B1OB), RPL, 105–6; Henry Barnard: biography, OCL, 185; Lucius Bell: *RDA,* 17 Sept. 1847; A. Bingham: ibid., 12 Nov. 1841; G. M. Bixby: *RDD,* 8 May 1852; William H. Bloss: obit., *UA,* 20 Apr. 1863; Devoy, *History of the City of Rochester,* 173–74; T-11 SB (all SBs at RPL), 54; (Rochester) *Post-Express,* 23 Sept. 1893, in "Peck's SB," 48; SB, T-11, 54; SB, T-4, 190; Martin Briggs: W. H. McIntosh, *History of Monroe County, New York* (Philadelphia: Everts, Ensign, and Everts, 1877), 308; obit., *UA,* 24 Dec., 1883; Amos Bronson: *RDD,* 18 Feb. 1853; William W. Bruff: obit., *UA* 17 Feb. 1888; B1OB, 155; Elisha W. Bryan: ibid., 171; Charles Josiah Buck: *RDD,* 7 Jan. 1847; George C. Buell: *Monroe County Biographical Record* (S. J. Clarke, 1902), 191–92; *Memorial Encyclopedia of New York* (1916), 3:300; *RGLA,* 9 Mar. 1839; William W. Cady: *RDD,* 6 Sept. 1848; Zebulon T. Case: ibid., 19 Oct. 1849; E. Chaffe: ibid., 21 June 1845; Joel Chaffee: obit., *RDA,* 14 Feb. 1840; F. Chapman: *RDD,* 15 Mar. 1849; George G. Clarkson: McIntosh, *History of Monroe County,* 150; "Peck's SB," 2:48; Patrick Connor: obit., *UA,* 29 July 1890; George G. Cooper: *NR,* 7 Dec. 1848, cited in "Peck's SB," 1:3; F. Cowdery: *RGLA,* 27 May 1843; J. Cox: ibid., 25 Nov. 1843; E. Crandle: *RDD,* 25 Dec. 1845; C. C. Cummings: ibid., 28 Dec. 1853; Joseph Curtis: B1OB, 87; John Dart: T-1 SB, 45; Silas T. Dean: *RGLA,* 10 Dec. 1836; Dellon M. Dewey: T-1 SB, 236; obit., *UA,* 20 June 1862; Robert Eliott: *RDAT,* 12 Mar. 1830; James Elwood: *RDA,* 1 Oct. 1841; GLA, 28 Oct. 1843; Moses R. Fassett: obit., *RDA,* 1 Jan. 1849; *UA,* 28 Oct. 1890; obit., ibid., 28 Oct. 1890; Jacob Fredenburgh: *RGLA,* 18 Nov. 1837; Henry C. Frink: *RDD,* 10 Mar. 1836; obit., 18 Aug. 1845; George T. Frost: *RGLA,* 2 Apr. 1838; B2OB, 116; T-1 SB, 58; James Gardner: *RDD,* 18 May 1848; O. D. Gardner: ibid., 5 Nov. 1844; E. H. Gaylord: *RR,* 27 Sept. 1849; Hosea Gibson: *RDD,* 26 Feb. 1849; Frederick E. Goodrich: obit., *UA,* 9 May 1877; T. B. Grant: *RDD,* 8 Jan. 1846; *History of the Genesee Country* (S. J. Clark, 1925), 3:330–33; Daniel Graves: W. H. Samson Notebooks (SN), 8:58–59, RPL; *UA,* 14 Feb. 1859; Kelsey, *Lives and Reminiscences,* 43–44; William Hamilton: *RDD,* 10 Sept. 1850; J. G. Hanford: *RT,* 13 Mar. 1821; Thomas Hanvy: *RGLA,* 8 Sept. 1838; A. L. Genealogy, RPL; Autobiographical Letter Folder, RPL; Timothy C. Haskell: obit., *RDA,* 24 Jan. 1840; obit., *RDD,* 24 Jan. 1840; obit., *RR,* 28 Jan. 1840; T. Hawks: *RDA,* 6 Oct. 1847; William M. Hayes: *RGLA,* 28 Jan. 1837; *RO,* 15 Feb. 1828; N. A. Herrick: *RR,* 23 July 1844; Frank Bottsford Hine: *RDD,* 15 Jan. 1848; W. T. Holman: ibid., 14 Mar. 1845; C. Hudson: *RDA,* 11 Feb. 1846; Justin B. Jones: *UA,* 15 June 1858; A. Karnes: *RGLA,* 23 Dec. 1843; Ira Allen Libby: *RDA,* 30 Mar. 1850; John F. Lovecraft: obit., *Rochester Intelligencer (RI),* 17 Oct. 1836; *UA,* 16 Apr. 1877; Joseph Lovecraft: *RDA,* 30 Mar. 1850; William Lovecraft: *RDD,* 7 Feb. 1835; obit., *UA,* 8 Nov. 1879; Charles C. Lunt: *RGLA,* 5 Mar. 1842; H. D. McArthur: obit., *RDA,* 17 Dec. 1845; D. McDonald: *RGLA,* 18 Apr. 1840; James McLaughlin: ibid., 6 Feb. 1841; Henry Martin: ibid., 1 Oct. 1842; Peter Martin: *RDD,* 2 Mar. 1849; *Monroe County Biographical Records,* 387; A. G. Matlock: *RR,* 18 Aug. 1846; John Everts Morey: *RDD,* 3 June 1846; T-1 SB, 115; B1OB 196–97; George Morgan: *RDA,* 12

Table 6.2   337

1846; John Everts Morey: *RDD*, 3 June 1846; T-1 SB, 115; B1OB 196–97; George Morgan: *RDA*, 12 Jan. 1849; Schuyler Moses: BC; Peck, *Semi-Centennial History of Rochester*, 661–63; T-1, 335; B1OB, 1:180; obit., *DC*, 31 Dec. 1888; ibid., 14 Mar. 1889; B1OB, 180; George Myers: *RDD*, 24 May 1844; Jacob H. Osgoodby: obit., *UA*, 2 Aug. 1883; John Palmer: *RDD*, 24 May 1847; E. P. Pennyman: *RDA* 20 Aug. 1839; Galusha Phillips: ibid., 4 Oct. 1848; Daniel W. Powers: Newton M. Mann, *First Unitarian Congregational Society of Rochester, New York* (1881), 512–15; Farrington Price: *RR*, 4, 9 Nov., 7 Dec. 1848; *RDA*, 1 Jan. 1849; C. S. Randall: *RDD*, 5 Dec. 1849; Edward Ray: *RDA*, 29 Dec. 1848; Samuel M. Raymond: obit., *UA*, 8 Apr. 1857; Lewis Rice: obit., *UA*, 8 Apr. 1876; B1OB, 46; J. F. Rothgangel: *RDD*, 7 Mar. 1845; William N. Sage: Mrs. George W. Fisher SB, 101; Amos Sawyer: *RGLA*, 1 June 1839; Schutt: obit., *UA*, 9 Feb. 1881; W. B. Seeley: ibid., 1 June 1838; Elliot B. Shepardson: obit., *UA*, 28 June 1864; William W. Shephard: *RGLA*, 25 Oct. 1834; N. A. Sherman: *RDA*, 25 Dec. 1841; Carlos Smith: *RR*, 19 Nov. 1844; G. M. Smith: *RDD*, 1 May 1848; Henry Franklin Smith: *UA*, 1 Dec. 1870; Daniel C. Stocking, Jr.; obit., ibid., 23 Apr. 1868; P. Teare: *RR*, 23 Feb. 1847; Willis Tuttle: Scranton, OCL, sketch (BC), 189; *RO*, 27 Feb. 1829; OCL, 189; William Varney: *RDD*, 16 Oct. 1850; James Vick: *RGLA*, 9 July 1842; Edward Voke: obit., *UA*, 2 Apr. 1874; H. P. Wade, *RGLA* 12 Nov. 1842; Nelson Weed: *RR*, 12 Mar. 1844; E. B. Wheeler: *RGLA*, 10 Aug. 1839; S. L. Wight: *RDA*, 23 Jan. 1839; Lafayette Wilder: *RDD*, 16 Sept. 1845; Charles H. Williams: *RDA*, 8 Nov. 1848; B1OB, 186; Devoy, *History of the City of Rochester*, 155–56; C. T. Wilson: *RDA*, 2 July 1852; H. H. Winants: ibid., 2 Mar. 1846; George W. Winn: ibid., 23 Dec. 1848; Samuel Finley Witherspoon: *RDA*, 24 Mar. 1842.

Table 6.3. Rochester labor leaders, church affiliation, selected groups, 1833–43

Group	Type of affiliation			Total
	Member	Affiliated	Joined later	
Carpenters[a] (=10)	3 (30%)	0	3 (30%)	6 (60%)
RTA (=23)	9 (39%)	2 (9%)	3 (13%)	14 (61%)
WMBERS (=11)	4 (36%)	1[c] (9%)	2[d] (18%)	7 (63%)

[a] Committeemen and officers of the JCJS and its meetings, 1833–35. [b] Two were Methodist leaders; the third was a Brick Presbyterian. [c] Justin B. Jones. See table 6.2., n. i. [d] One, involved in 1842, is recorded in church records in 1843. The other was buried in the church in 1855.

SOURCES: See tables 6.1, 6.2.

Table 6.4. Rochester labor advocates, length of residence, 1810–50

Group	Period of residence							
	1810–1815	1816–1820	1821–1825	1826–1830	1831–1835	1836–1840	1841–1845	1846–1850
Carpenters	0	2	2	1	1	0	0	0
RTA	0	0	1	0	2	1	0	0
Clerks	1	2	3	7	2	3	0	0
WMBERS	0	1	1	0	0	0	0	0
WMC	0	2	3	1	2	4	0	0
Hours	0	1	0	0	1	0	0	0
RTA II	0	0	0	0	1	0	1	0
MMPA	0	0	0	0	0	0	1	1
Total	1	8	10	9	9	8	2	1

NOTE: Because biographical material indicating length of residence was uncommonly found for those in town a short period of time, this table is heavily biased toward long-term residents.

SOURCES: See tables 6.1, 6.2.

Table 6.5. Rochester labor advocates, nativity, 1829–49

Birthplace	Group									
	MA[a]	Carp.[b]	RTA	Clerks	WMBERS	WMC	Hours	RTA II	MMPA	Total
New York	17	8	3	24	4	11	4	3	4	78
Massachusetts	0	1	1	4	2	0	1	0	0	9
Connecticut	5	3	0	3	0	3	0	0	0	14
Vermont	1	2	1	2	2	1	1	0	0	10
New Hampshire	2	1	0	1	1	0	1	0	0	6
New Jersey	1	1	0	0	0	1	0	0	0	3
Pennsylvania	0	1	0	0	1	0	0	0	0	1
Maryland	0	0	0	0	0	0	0	0	0	1
Ohio	0	0	0	1	0	0	0	0	0	1
Canada	0	0	0	0	1	1	0	0	1	3
Europe[c]	4	3	1	3	1	12	2	0	5	31
Total	30	20	6	38	12	29	9	3	10	157

NOTE: This table is biased toward persisters because biographical data is scarce for short-term residents, particularly for the earlier activists; most of the nativity data come from the 1850 census schedules.

[a]Mutual Association.   [b]Carpenters.   [c]Includes English, Irish, Scottish, and German.

SOURCES: See tables 6.1, 6.2; U.S. *Seventh Census* (1850), New York.

Table 6.6. Rochester labor advocates, denominational affiliation

Group	Denomination (number of church leaders in parentheses)						
	Presbyterian	Methodist	Baptist	Episcopalian	Universalist	Unitarian	Catholic
Carpenters	9 (0)	10 (8)	3 (0)	1 (0)	3 (1)	1 (0)	1 (1)
RTA	2 (0)	3 (1)	3 (1)	1 (0)	0 (0)	2 (1)	0 (0)
Clerks	21 (0)	1 (0)	13 (2)	10 (1)	0 (0)	3 (0)	1 (0)
WMBERS	3 (1)	1 (0)	0 (0)	1 (0)	0 (0)	1 (0)	1 (0)
WMC	7 (1)	6 (3)	4 (0)	2 (0)	3 (1)	1 (0)	9 (0)
Hours	2 (0)	0 (0)	0 (0)	3 (1)	2 (1)	1 (0)	0 (0)
RTA II	1 (0)	1 (1)	2 (0)	0 (0)	2 (1)	1 (0)	0 (0)
MMPA	3 (1)	0 (0)	2 (1)	5 (0)	1 (1)	2 (0)	0 (0)
Total	48 (3)	22 (13)	27 (4)	23 (2)	9 (4)	11 (1)	12 (1)

NOTE: Totals here are slightly less than in table 6.2, because denominational affiliation could not always be determined.

SOURCES: See tables 6.1, 6.2.

Index

Abell, Levi, 89
Abington, Massachusetts, 65
abuse of power, 173
Adams, Mary, 28–29
Adams, Robert, 76
"Address to the Working Men of Massachu-
setts" (NEA), 173, 178
agrarianism, 181
Albany, New York. See *Mechanics' Mirror*
Allegheny City, Pennsylvania, 63, 67
Allegheny County, Pennsylvania, 202
Allen, John, 134, 163, 166, 178, 191
Alling, John, 125
Almy, Thomas, 212
Alrichs, Jacob, 93, 108
American Federation of Labor, 221
American Protestantism: as Bible-based, 20;
characteristics of American, 9; dissenting
tradition in, 24, 138; as principal source of
beliefs/values, 18. *See also specific
denomination*
American Revolution, 151, 158–68, 208, 211,
213
American Sunday School Union, 101–2
Amesbury, Massachusetts, 129
Association of Industry (Fall River), 75, 137,
181, 182, 193–94, 215
Association of Mechanics and Workingmen
(Fall River), 75
Association of Working People of New Castle
County (AWPNCC), 72, 93, 95, 96, 97,
98–99, 100, 108
Association of Working Women and Men
(Philadelphia), 31
Associationism, 65, 192–93, 217–19
avarice: as cause of social evils, 217; and
Christian vengeance, 209; and clergy's

views of labor question, 139–40, 143, 147;
and decline of moral community, 185–86;
of employers, 139; of labor class, 186; and
quest for harmony, 184, 198; as responsible
for social conditions, 139–40; in Rochester,
120; universality of, 139–40; of workers,
139. *See also* greed
Averill, A. M., 136
AWPNCC. *See* Association of Working People
of New Castle County

Bagley, Sarah: and infidelity of organized religion, 51–52, 55–56, 60, 65; and labor's
quest for support of clergy, 133; personal/
professional background of, 51–52; on redemption, 201; as a role model, 220–21;
sources of inspiration for, 158, 166
Bailey, Ebenezer, 81–82, 86
Bailey, Goldsmith, 81–82
Baker, William, 106
Baltimore, Maryland, 157–58
Bancroft, George, 39
Baptists: in Amesbury, 129; in Buffalo, 128;
and churches as meetingplaces, 128, 129,
130; and clergy's support for labor, 136,
137; in Fall River, 76–78, 130, 136, 137; in
Fitchburg, 83, 84, 86, 165; as labor activists
in the church, 71; and labor's quest for
support of clergy, 134; in Lowell, 134; re-
vivals of, 77; in Rochester, 118, 121, 122; in
Saco, Maine, 129. *See also* Freewill Baptists
Beach, William H., 121
Bellamy, Joseph, 10
benevolence, 24, 140
Berean (Quaker periodical), 105, 106
Bible: as anti-religious, 117; as authority for